Dana Facaros & Michael Pauls

LOMBARDY
& THE ITALIAN LAKES

'Linger on a lakeshore terrace in the
evening, over a saffron risotto and
a glass of Bardolino or Franciacorta,
as landscapes that inspired the
backgrounds of Leonardo's greatest
paintings dissolve and the scents of
jasmine and night flowers fill the air.'

CADOGANguides

1 View of Bellagio, Lake Como
2 Dusk, Lake Maggiore

2

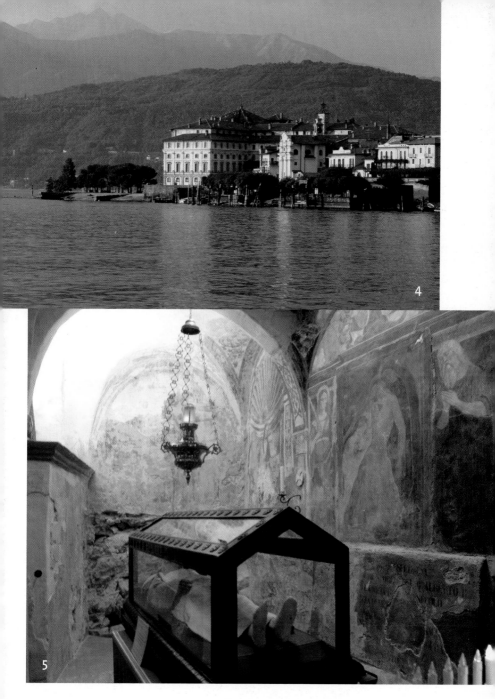

3 Villa Carlotta, Lake Como
4 Isola Madre, Lake Maggiore
5 S. Caterina del Sasso interior,
   Lake Maggiore

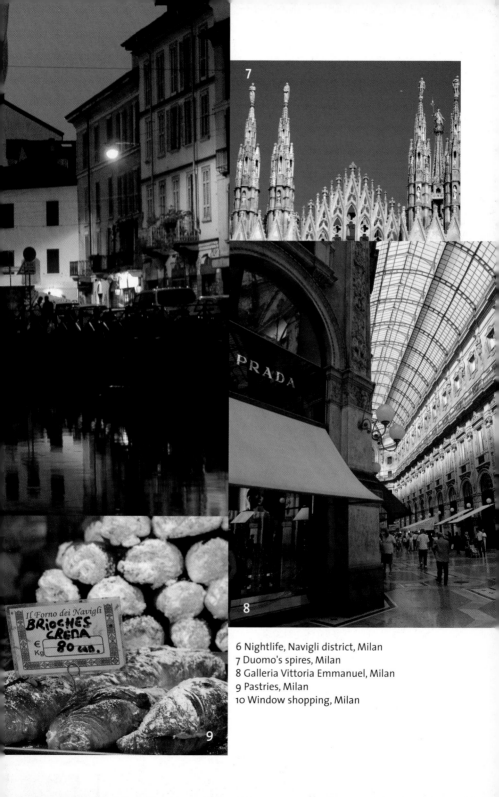

Il Forno dei Navigli
BRIOCHES
CREMA
€ 80 cad.
Kg

6 Nightlife, Navigli district, Milan
7 Duomo's spires, Milan
8 Galleria Vittoria Emmanuel, Milan
9 Pastries, Milan
10 Window shopping, Milan

11 S. Ambrogio, Milan
12 Interior, S. Maria Grazie, Milan
13 Mantua
14 Mantua

15

15 Arca di Sant'Agostino, Pavia
16 Ticino river, Pavia

17 Certosa, Pavia
18 Certosa interior, Pavia
19 Duomo, Pavia
20 Historic centre, Pavia

19

21 Vigevano

22 Vigevano

About the authors

Dana Facaros and **Michael Pauls** lived in Italy for three years, but have now moved to southwest France. They have written over 40 guides for Cadogan.

About the updater

Gabriella Cursoli is a keen and curiosity-filled traveller. Her background in history and the arts supports and nourishes her interest in different places, people and cultures. After almost six years spent in London, she has now moved to Milan, where she works as an editor, updater and translator.

Contents

Cadogan Guides
2nd Floor, 233 High Holborn,
London WC1V 7DN
info@cadoganguides.co.uk
www.cadoganguides.com

The Globe Pequot Press
246 Goose Lane, PO Box 480, Guilford,
Connecticut 06437–0480

Copyright © Dana Facaros and Michael Pauls
1994, 1997, 1999, 2001, 2003, 2006

Cover photographs: © John Lawrence/The Image
Bank; © Kicca Tommasi
Photo essay: © Kicca Tommasi
Maps © Cadogan Guides, drawn by
Maidenhead Cartographic Services Ltd

Managing Editor: Natalie Pomier
Editor: Matthew Tanner
Editorial Assistant: Nicola Jessop
Art Direction: Sarah Rianhard-Gardner
Proofreading: Joss Waterfall
Indexing: Isobel McLean

Printed in Italy by Legoprint
A catalogue record for this book is available
from the British Library
ISBN 10: 1-86011-322-2
ISBN 13: 978-1-86011-322-2

The author and publishers have made every effort to ensure the accuracy of the information in this book at the time of going to press. However, they cannot accept any responsibility for any loss, injury or inconvenience resulting from the use of information contained in this guide.

Please help us to keep this guide up to date. We have done our best to ensure that the information in this guide is correct at the time of going to press. But places and facilities are constantly changing, and standards and prices in hotels and restaurants fluctuate. We would be delighted to receive any comments concerning existing entries or omissions. Authors of the best letters will receive a copy of the Cadogan Guide of their choice.

Introduction

A Guide to the Guide

The Italian Lakes and the old art towns of Lombardy invite all kinds of indulgences. Linger on a lakeshore terrace in the evening, over a saffron risotto and a glass of Bardolino or Franciacorta, as landscapes that inspired the backgrounds of Leonardo's greatest paintings dissolve and the scents of jasmine and night flowers fill the air. Golden lights come to life along the shore as if fastening a fairy necklace around the water; little islands seem to hover in the twilight over the glassy surface before melting into the total silhouette of night.

Throughout history, the millions of frostbitten travellers, pilgrims, conquering armies, future popes and pushy emperors who lumbered over the treacherous passes of the Alps would be stopped in their tracks by a vision as powerful, terrible and beautiful as an epiphany: at their feet, wedged into the flanks of the snowcapped mountains, lay the Garden of Eden itself. Elegant, long lakes were its centrepiece, warmed by a glowing sun that had nothing in common with that old cheese in the sky they knew back home; on their chiselled shores lemons, figs, roses, pomegranates and palms grew in luxuriant abundance. And beyond these magical Mediterranean fjords, the fertile Lombard plain spread its charms back to the edge of the horizon, dangling some of the richest art cities of Italy like diamonds across its bosom.

The finished product, the Lombardy and Italian Lakes we see today, is the result of primordial blasts of ice. In the last glacial period huge masses of ice rolled down from the Alps, ironing flat the Lombard plain. On the way they gouged out deep welts in the rock, far deeper than the level of the Adriatic sea, sculpting (there's no other word for it) some of the most sublime lakes anywhere.

Lombardy's character was similarly formed by violence. Countless gangsters coveted this earthly paradise (not the least of whom were the Lombards themselves, who liked the odd swig of mead from the skulls of their enemies). Many invaders settled down to stay and turned their energy to farming and especially to trade, the natural occupation for people living at the crossroads between Italy, France, Switzerland and Austria, and the Tyrrhenian and Adriatic seas.

Early in the Middle Ages, mercantile Lombardy invented the idea of the *comune*, a kind of independent city-state, the antithesis of feudalism. The *comuni*'s new outlook on the world, freedom of action, wealth, and their increasingly sophisticated ruling families who were keen on embellishing their palaces and cities with art, were leading factors in ushering in the Renaissance, which left some of its greatest treasures behind in Milan, Mantua, Bergamo, Como and Brescia.

Lombardy has been making some big noises recently, adding more than its share to the contradictions and confusions besetting modern Italy. And for better or worse, Milan is the place controversial Italian prime minister Silvio Berlusconi likes to call home.

Pilgrims of old, descending from the Alps into this Garden of Eden, trod softly so as not to disturb God's angel with the fiery sword. Nowadays you can rest assured that he's run off to join the circus. And though lakeside holidays dwindled after the last war (when having a suntan evolved into a symbol of leisure instead of manual labour, and heading to the seashore in the summer months became obligatory), the Italian Lakes were simply too lovely to stay out of fashion for long. Today a new

Chapter Divisions

SWITZERLAND

TRENTINO-ALTO ADIGE

VENETO

PIEMONTE

VALLEY D'AOSTA

EMILIA-ROMAGNA

LOMBARDY

10 LAKES ORTA & MAGGIORE

11 LAKES LUGANO & COMO

12 THE VALCHIAVENNA & VATTELINA

13 THE EAST: BERGAMO TO LAKE GARDA

08 MILAN

09 THE LOMBARD PLAIN

Valtellina

Val Camonica

Parco Nazionale dello Stelvio

Alpi Orobie

Bormio
Sondrio
Domodossola
Locarno
Verbania
Stresa
Lugano
Varese
Como
Lecco
Bergamo
Monza
Saronno
MILAN
Pavia
Vigevano
Alessandria
Crema
Soncino
Cremona
Sabbioneta
Mantua
Brescia
Desenzano del Garda
Sirmione
Limone sul Garda
Malcesine
Riva del Garda
Verona
Vicenza

Lake Orta
Lake Maggiore
Lake Lugano
Lake Como
Lago di Garda
Lake Iseo
Franciacorta

Ticino
Adda

Malpensa (International Airport)

TURIN (TORINO)

40 km
20 miles

N

generation is busily rediscovering what their grandparents took for granted; where once visitors had to make do with small boats or leisurely steamers, the Italians have now ringed the lakes with finely engineered roads, perhaps even making them too accessible. For as is to be expected, prices have risen with demand, and between July and September (the latter is generally considered the best month for the lakes) rest and relaxation may seem a Victorian relic, unless you book into one of the grander villa hotels. Calmer havens, however, continue to exist on the smaller, less developed lakes of Iseo and Orta, the east shores of Lakes Maggiore and Como, and in the mountain valleys to the north.

A Guide to the Guide

The guide starts with chapters on the **History** and **Art and Architecture** of Lombardy and the Italian Lakes, followed by **Topics**, a chapter of essays on subjects relating to the area. The **Food and Drink** chapter provides an Italian menu guide as well as details of Lombard specialities and Italian eating and drinking customs. **Travel** and **Practical A–Z** contain everything you need to know in order to plan your visit, including a list of tour operators and airlines.

The gazetteer part of the guide covers the sights of Lombardy and the Italian Lakes, region by region: **Milan** (bustling, fashionable city of finance), the **Lombard Plain** (with the art cities of Pavia, Cremona and Mantua), **Lakes Orta and Maggiore** (the western-most lakes), **Lakes Lugano and Como** (including the Swiss parts of Lake Lugano), the **Valchiavenna and Valtellina** (the northern mountainous area bordering Switzerland), and **The East: Bergamo to Lake Garda** (including Lake Iseo and Brescia). The back of the book contains a **Glossary** of architectural, artistic and historical terms, a **Language** section, a **Chronology** and finally an **Index**.

History

02

3000–100 BC: Quarrelsome Celts, Imperialistic Romans

The first known inhabitants of Lombardy, from about 3000 BC, left us something to remember them by: the thousands of mysterious symbols incised on the rocks of the Val Camonica north of Lake Iseo. In a remarkable example of cultural continuity, these inscriptions were made well into Roman times while various peoples passed across the stage, notably the quiet folks who lived in Bronze Age villages built on piles over the water at Lakes Orta, Varese and Ledro.

By 400 BC, when most of the peninsula was inhabited by the 'Italics' – a collection of distinct Indo-European tribes with similar languages – northwest Italy stood apart. Most of the area north of the Po was occupied by various Celtic and related Ligurian tribes. A century later, when the Romans arrived, they thought of this region as not Italy at all. Their name for it was **Cisalpine Gaul**, 'Gaul this side of the Alps'. The two peoples were bound to come into conflict, and whenever there was war they usually found themselves on opposite sides. The Celts, skilled warriors who made whacking good swords and gave the Romans their word for 'chariot', often got the best of it, notably in 390 BC when they occupied Rome itself. Only the famous cackling of the geese, warning the Romans of a night attack on their last citadel within the city, saved Rome from complete extinction. From then on though, the tide turned and even the chariots couldn't keep out the legions a hundred years later, in a general Italian conflagration called the **Third Samnite War**, which pitted the Romans against the Samnites, Northern Etruscans and Celts. The Romans beat everyone once and for all and annexed most of Italy by 283 BC. As in Italy, to solidify their hold the Romans founded colonies throughout Cisalpine Gaul and populated them with army veterans; these included Mediolanum (Milan), Brixia (Brescia), Como and Cremona.

Being a less developed area, Cisalpine Gaul suffered less from Roman misrule than other parts of Italy. There was little wealth to tax, and little for rapacious Roman governors to steal. The region also managed to avoid most of the endless civil wars, famines and oppression that accompanied the death throes of the Roman Republic elsewhere. It did endure a last surprise raid by two Celtic tribes, the Cimbri and Teutones, who crossed over the Riviera and the Alps in a two-pronged attack in 102 BC. **Gaius Marius**, a capable though illiterate Roman general, defeated them decisively, using his popularity to seize power in Rome soon after.

100 BC–AD 476: The Height and Depths of Empire

In the Pax Romana of Augustus and his successors, the northern regions evolved from wild border territories to settled, prosperous provinces full of thriving new towns. The lakes became a favourite holiday destination for Rome's elite. Trade flourished along new roads like the Via Postumia to Cremona, and Mantua gave birth to Virgil just in time to put Rome's faith in its divine destiny into words. But after over two centuries at the glorious noonday of its history, in the 3rd century AD the Roman empire began to have troubles from without as well as within: a severe, long-term economic decline coinciding with a shift in military balance to the favour of the barbarians on the frontiers. **Diocletian** (284–305) completely revamped the structure of the state, converting it into a vast bureaucratic machine geared solely to meeting the needs of its army; he also initiated the division of the empire into western and eastern halves, for reasons of military and administrative necessity. The western emperors after Diocletian usually kept their court at army headquarters in Mediolanum, a convenient place to keep an eye on both the Rhine and Danube frontiers. Through most of the 4th century, this city was the western empire's *de facto* capital, while Rome itself decayed into a marble-veneered backwater.

Times were hard all over the west and, although northern Italy was relatively less hard-hit than other regions, cities decayed and trade disappeared, while debt and an inability to meet high taxes pushed thousands into serfdom or slavery. The confused politics of the time were dominated by **Constantine I** (*c.* 280–37), who ruled both halves of the empire and adroitly moved to increase his political support by the Edict of Milan (313), declaring Christianity the religion of the empire. Later in the century, Milan became an important centre of the new faith under its great bishop **St Ambrose**.

The inevitable disasters began in 406, when the Visigoths, Franks, Vandals, Alans and Suevi overran Gaul and Spain. Italy's turn came in 408, when Western Emperor Honorius had his brilliant general Stilicho (who was himself a Vandal) murdered. A Visigothic invasion followed; Alaric sacked Rome in 410; and in Milan St Augustine, probably echoing the thoughts of most Romans, wrote that it seemed the end of the world must be near. Italy should have been so lucky; judgement was postponed long enough for Attila the Hun to pass through in 451.

So completely had things changed, it was scarcely possible to tell the Romans from the barbarians. By the 470s the real ruler in Italy was a Gothic general named **Odoacer**, who led a half-Romanized Germanic army and probably thought of himself as the genuine heir of the Caesars. In 476 he decided to dispense with the lingering charade of the Western Empire. The last emperor, **Romulus Augustulus**, was retired to Naples, and Odoacer had himself crowned king at Italy's new Gothic capital, Pavia.

476–753: Fairly Good Goths and Really Nasty Lombards

At the beginning, the new Gothic-Latin state showed some promise; certainly the average man was no worse off than he had been under the last emperors. In 493 Odoacer was replaced (and murdered) by a rival Ostrogoth, **Theodoric**, nominally working on behalf of the Eastern Emperor at Constantinople. Theodoric proved a strong and able, though somewhat paranoid, ruler; his court witnessed a minor rebirth of Latin letters, most famously in the great Christian philosopher Boethius, while trade revived and cities were repaired. A disaster as serious as those of the 5th century began in 536 with the invasion of Italy by the Eastern Empire, part of the relentlessly expansionist policy of Emperor **Justinian**. The historical irony was profound: in the birthplace of the Roman Empire, Roman troops now came not as liberators, but as foreign, largely Greek-speaking conquerors. Justinian's brilliant generals Belisarius and Narses ultimately prevailed over the Goths in a series of terrible wars that lasted until 563, but the damage to an already stricken society was incalculable.

Italy's total exhaustion was exposed only five years later with the invasion of the **Lombards**, a Germanic people who worked hard to maintain the title of Barbarian; while other, more courageous tribes moved in to take what they could of the empire, the Lombards had ranged on the frontiers like mean, stray curs. Most writers, ancient and modern, mistakenly attribute the Lombards' name to their long beards; in fact, these redoubtable nomads scared the daylights out of the Italians not with beards but with their long *bardi*, or poleaxes.

Narses himself first invited the Lombards in, as mercenaries to help him overcome the Goths. Quickly understanding their opportunity, they returned with the entire horde in 568. By 571 they were across the Apennines; Pavia, one of the old Gothic capitals and the key to northern Italy, fell after a long siege in 572. The horde's progress provided history with unedifying spectacles from the very start: King Alboin, who unified the Lombard tribes and made the invasion possible, met his bloody end at the hands of his queen, Rosmunda – whom he drove to murder by forcing her to drink from her father's skull.

The Lombards certainly hadn't come to do the Italians any favours, and considered the entire population their slaves; in practice, they were usually content to sit back and collect exorbitant tributes. Themselves Arian Christians, they enjoyed oppressing both the orthodox and pagans. Throughout the 6th century their conquest continued apace. The popes, occasionally allied with the Lombards against Byzantium, became a force during this period, especially after the papacy of the clever, determined **Gregory the Great** (590–604), who in 603 managed to convert the Lombard queen **Theodolinda** and her people to orthodox Christianity. By then things had stabilized. Northern Italy was the Lombard kingdom proper, centred at Pavia and Monza, while semi-independent Lombard duchies controlled much of the peninsula.

In Pavia, a long succession of Lombard kings made little account of themselves. However, under the doughty warrior **King Liutprand** (712–44), Byzantine weakness made the Lombards exert themselves to try to unify Italy. Liutprand won most of his battles but gained few territorial additions. A greater threat was his ruthless successor **Aistulf**, who by 753 conquered almost all of the lands held by the Byzantines including their capital, Ravenna. If the Lombards' final solution was to be averted, the popes had to find help from outside. The logical people to ask were the **Franks**.

753–1000: The Threshold of the Middle Ages

At the time, the popes had something to offer in return. The powerful **Mayors of the Palace of the Frankish Kingdom** longed to supplant the Merovingian dynasty and assume the throne for themselves, but needed the appearance of legitimacy that only the mystic pageantry of the papacy could provide. At the beginning of Aistulf's campaigns, Pope Zacharias had foreseen the danger and gave his blessing to the change of dynasties in 750. To complete the deal, the new King Pepin sent his army over the Alps in 753 and 756 to foil Aistulf's designs.

By 773 the conflict remained the same, though with a different cast of characters. The Lombard king was Desiderius, the Frankish king his cordially hostile son-in-law **Charlemagne**, who also invaded Italy twice, in 775 and 776. Unlike his father, though,

Charlemagne meant to settle Italy once and for all. His army captured Pavia, and after deposing his father-in-law, he took the Iron Crown of Italy for himself.

The new partnership between pope and king failed to bring the stability both parties had hoped for. With Charlemagne busy elsewhere, local lordlings across the peninsula scrapped continually for slight advantage. Charlemagne returned in 799 to sort them out, and in return got what must be the most momentous Christmas present in history. On Christmas Eve, while he was praying in St Peter's, Pope Leo III crept up behind him and deftly set an imperial crown on the surprised king's head. The revival of the dream of a united Christian empire changed the political face of Italy forever, beginning the contorted *pas de deux* of pope and emperor that was to be the mainspring of Italian history throughout the Middle Ages.

Charlemagne's empire quickly disintegrated after his death, divided among squabbling descendants, and Italy reverted to anarchy. Altogether, the 9th century was a rotten time, with Italy caught between Arab raiders and the endless wars of petty nobles and battling bishops. To north Italians, the post-Carolingian era is the age of the *reucci*, the 'little kings', a profusion of puny rulers angling to advance their own interests. After 888, when the Carolingian line became extinct, ten little Frankish kings of Italy succeeded to the throne at Pavia, each with less power than the last. Their most frequent antagonists were the Lombard **Dukes of Spoleto**, though occasionally foreign interlopers like Arnolf of Carinthia (893) or Hugh of Provence (932) brought armies over the Alps to try their luck. Worse trouble for everyone came with the arrival of the barbarian **Magyars**, who overran the north and sacked Pavia in 924.

The 10th century proved somewhat better. Even in the worst times, Italy's cities never entirely disappeared. Maritime powers like Venice and Pisa led the way, but even inland cities like Milan were developing a new economic importance. From the 900s many were looking to their own resources, defending their interests against the Church and nobles alike. A big break for the cities came in 961 when **Adelheid**, the beautiful widow of one of the *reucci*, Lothar, refused to wed his successor, Berengar II, Marquis of Ivrea. Berengar had hoped to bring some discipline to Italy, and began by imprisoning the recalcitrant Adelheid in a tower by Lake Como. With the aid of a monk she made a daring escape to Canossa and the protection of the Count of Tuscany, who called in for reinforcements from the king of Germany, **Otto the Great**. Otto came over the Alps, got the girl, deposed Berengar and was crowned Holy Roman Emperor in Rome the following year. Not that any of the Italians were happy to see him, but the strong government of Otto and his successors beat down the great nobles, divided their lands and allowed the growing cities to expand their power and influence.

1000–1220: The Rise of the *Comune*

On the eve of the new millennium business was very good in the towns, and the political prospects even brighter. The first mention of a truly independent *comune* (a free city state; the best translation might be 'commonwealth') was in Milan, where in 1024 the first popular assembly (*parlamento*) met to decide which side the city would take in the imperial wars. And when that was done, Milan's archbishop

Heribert invited the German Frankish king Conrad to be crowned in Milan, founding a new line of Italian kings.

During this period the papacy had declined greatly, a political football kicked between the emperors and the Roman nobles. In the 1050s a monk named **Hildebrand** (later Gregory VII) worked to reassert Church power, beginning a conflict with the emperors over investiture – whether the church or secular powers would name church officials. Fifty years of intermittent war followed, including the famous 'penance in the snow' of Emperor Henry IV in Canossa (1077). The result was a big revival for the papacy, but more importantly the cities of Lombardy and the north used the opportunity to increase their influence, and in some cases achieve outright independence, razing the nobles' castles and forcing them to move inside the town.

While all this was happening, the First Crusade (1097–1130) occupied the headlines, partially a result of the new papal militancy begun by Gregory VII. For Italy the affair meant nothing but profit. Trade was booming everywhere, and the accumulation of money helped the Italians to create modern Europe's first banking system. It also financed the continued independence of the *comuni*, who began to discover there simply wasn't enough Italy to hold them all. Cremona had its dust-ups with Crema, Bergamo with Brescia, while Milan, the biggest bully of them all, took on Pavia, Cremona, Como and Lodi with one hand tied behind its back.

By the 12th century, far in advance of most of Europe, Italy enjoyed prosperity unknown since Roman times. The classical past had never been forgotten: free *comuni* in the north called their elected leaders 'consuls', and artists and architects turned ancient Roman styles into the Romanesque. Even names were changing, an interesting sign of the growing national consciousness; suddenly the public records show a marked shift from Germanic to classical and biblical surnames: fewer Ugos, Othos and Astolfos, more Giuseppes, Giovannis, Giulios and Flavios.

Emperors and popes were still embroiled in the north. Frederick I – **Barbarossa** – of the Hohenstaufen or Swabian dynasty, was strong enough back home in Germany, and he made it his special interest to reassert imperial power in Italy. In 1154, he crossed the Alps for the first of five times, settling local disputes against Milan and Tortona in favour of his allies Pavia, Como and Lodi. As soon as he was back over the Alps, Milan set about undoing all his works, punishing the cities that had supported him. Back came Frederick in 1158 to starve Milan into submission and set up imperial governors (*podestà*) in each *comune*; and, when Milan still proved defiant, he destroyed it utterly in 1161. And back over the Alps he went once more, confident that he had taught Lombardy a lesson.

What he had taught northern Italians was that the liberties of their *comuni* were in grave danger. A united opposition, called the **Lombard League**, included by 1167 every major city between Venice and Asti and Bologna (except Pavia), with spiritual backing in the person of Frederick's enemy Pope Alexander III. Twice the Lombard League beat the furious emperor back over the mountains, and when Frederick crossed the Alps for the fifth time in 1174 he was checked at Alessandria in Piedmont and forced by the league to raise his siege; then, in 1176, while his forces were in Legnano preparing to attack Milan, the Milanese militia surprised and decimated his army, forcing Frederick to flee alone to Venice to make terms with Pope Alexander. The truce he signed with the League became the **Peace of Constance**, which might as well have been called the Peace of Pigheads: all that the *comuni* asked was the right to look after their own interests and fight each other whenever they pleased.

1220–1508: Guelphs and Ghibellines, and the Renaissance

Frederick's grandson **Frederick II** was not only emperor but also King of Sicily, thus giving him a strong power base in Italy itself. The second Frederick's career dominated Italian politics for 30 years (1220–50). With his brilliant court, his half-Muslim army, his dancing girls, eunuchs and elephants, he provided Europe with a spectacle the like of which it had never seen. The popes excommunicated him at least twice. Now the battle had become serious. All Italy divided into factions: the **Guelphs**, under the leadership of the popes, supported religious orthodoxy, the liberty of the *comuni* and the interests of their emerging wealthy merchant class. The **Ghibellines** stood for the emperor, statist economic control and (sometimes) religious and intellectual tolerance. Frederick's campaigns and diplomacy in the north met with very limited success, and his death in 1250 left the outcome much in doubt.

His son Manfred, not emperor but merely King of Sicily, took up the battle with better luck. In 1261, however, Pope Urban IV set an ultimately disastrous precedent by inviting in Charles of Anjou, the ambitious brother of the King of France. As champion of the Guelphs, Charles defeated Manfred (1266), murdered the last of the Hohenstaufens, Conradin (1268), and held unchallenged sway over Italy until 1282. By then, however, the terms 'Guelph' and 'Ghibelline' had ceased to have much meaning; men and cities changed sides as they found expedient, and the old parties began to seem like the black and white squares on a chessboard.

Some real changes did occur out of all this sound and fury. As elsewhere around the peninsula, some cities were falling under the rule of military *signori* whose descendants would be styling themselves dukes, like the Visconti of Milan and the Gonzaga of Mantua. Everywhere the freedom of the *comuni* was in jeopardy; after so much useless strife, the temptation to submit to a strong leader often proved overwhelming. And yet at the same time money flowed as never before; cities built new cathedrals and created incredible skylines of tower-fortresses, dotting the country with medieval Manhattans.

This paradoxical Italy continued through the 15th century, with a golden age of culture and an opulent economy side by side with continuous war and turmoil. With no threats over the border, the myriad Italian states menaced each other joyfully without outside interference. War became a sort of game, conducted on behalf of cities by *condottieri*, leading paid mercenaries who were never allowed to enter the cities themselves. The arrangement suited everyone well. The soldiers had lovely horses and armour, and no real desire to do each other serious harm. The cities were making too much money to really want to wreck the system anyway.

By far the biggest event of the 14th century was the **Black Death** of 1347–8, in which Italy lost a third of its population. The shock brought a rude halt to what had been 400 years of almost continuous growth and prosperity, though its effects did not prove a permanent setback. In fact, the plague's grim joke was that it actually made life better for most of the Italians who survived; working people in the cities, no longer overcrowded, found their rents lower and their labour worth more, while in the country farmers were able to increase their profits by only tilling the best land.

In the north, the great power was the signorial state of Milan. Under the Visconti Milan had become rich and powerful, basing its success on the manufactures of the city (arms and textiles) and the bountiful, progressively managed agriculture of southern Lombardy. Its greatest glory came under **Gian Galeazzo Visconti** (1351–1402), who bought a ducal title from the emperor and came close to conquering all of north Italy before his untimely death, upon which the Venetians were able to snatch up tasty titbits on the fringe like Brescia and Bergamo.

And what of the Renaissance? No word has ever caused more mischief for the understanding of history and culture – as if Italy had been Sleeping Beauty, waiting for some Prince Charming to come and awaken it from a thousand-year nap. On the contrary, Italy even in the 1200s was richer, more technologically advanced and far more artistically creative than it had ever been in the days of the Caesars. The new art and scholarship that began in Florence in the 1400s and spread across the nation grew from a solid foundation of medieval accomplishment. The gilded Italy of the 15th century felt complacently secure in its long-established cultural and economic pre-eminence. The long spell of freedom from outside interference lulled the nation into believing that its political disunity could continue safely forever; except perhaps for the sanguinely realistic Florentine Nicolò Macchiavelli, no one realized that Italy was in fact a plum waiting to be picked.

1508–1796: Three Grim Centuries of Foreign Rule

The Italians brought the trouble down on themselves, when Duke Lodovico of Milan invited the French king **Charles VIII** to cross the Alps and assert his claim to the throne of Milan's enemy, Naples. Charles did just that, and the failure of the combined Italian states to stop him (at the inconclusive Battle of Fornovo, 1494) showed just how helpless Italy was at the hands of new nation-states like France or Spain. When the Spaniards saw how easy it was, they too marched in, and restored Naples to its Spanish king the following year. Before long the German emperor and even the Swiss, who briefly took control of Milan, entered this new market for Italian real estate. The popes did as much as anyone to keep the pot boiling. Alexander VI and his son **Cesare Borgia** carried the war across central Italy in an attempt to found a new state for the Borgia family, and Julius II's madcap policy led him to egg on the Swiss, French and Spaniards in turn, before finally crying, 'Out with the barbarians!' when it was already too late.

By 1516, with the French ruling Milan and the Spanish in control of the south, it seemed as if a settlement would be possible. The worst possible luck for Italy, however, came with the accession of the insatiable megalomaniac **Charles V** to the throne of Spain; in 1519 he emptied the Spanish treasury to buy himself the crown of the Holy Roman Empire, making him the most powerful ruler in Europe since Charlemagne. Charles wanted Milan as a base for communications between his

Spanish, German and Flemish possessions, and the wars began anew, bloodier than anything Italy had seen for centuries, climaxing with the defeat of the French at Pavia in 1525 and the sack of Rome by an out-of-control imperial army in 1527. The French invaded once more in 1529, and were defeated, this time at Naples by the treachery of their Genoese allies. All Italy save only Venice was now at the mercy of Charles and the Spaniards.

The final peace negotiated at Château-Cambrésis left Spanish viceroys in Milan and Naples, and pliant dukes and counts toeing the Spanish line almost everywhere else. The broader context of the time was the bitter struggles of the Reformation and Counter-Reformation. In Italy, the Spaniards found a perfect ally in the papacy; together they put an end to the last surviving liberties of the cities, while snuffing out the intellectual life of the Renaissance with the help of the Inquisition and the Jesuits.

Nearly the only place where anything creative came out of this new order was Lombardy. In Milan that incorruptible Galahad of the Counter-Reformation, Archbishop **Charles Borromeo** (1538–84), came out of the Council of Trent determined to make his diocese a working model of Tridentine reforms. One of the most influential characters in Italian religious history, he relentlessly went about creating an actively pastoral, zealous clergy, giving the most prominent teaching jobs to Jesuits and cleansing Lombardy of heresy and corruption. By re-establishing the cult of Milan's patron, St Ambrose, he developed a sense of Lombard regional feeling; with his nephew and successor **Federico Borromeo** he promoted sorely needed cultural and welfare institutions, instilling in the Lombard élite an industrious Catholic paternalism still noted in the region today.

Despite political oppression, the 16th century was a generally prosperous period for most of Italy, embellished with an afterglow of late-Renaissance architecture and art. After 1600, though, nearly everything started to go wrong for the Italians. The textiles and banking of the north, long the engines of prosperity, both withered in the face of foreign competition. The old mercantile economies built in the Middle Ages were failing, and the wealthy began to invest their money in land instead of risking it in business or finance.

Italy in this period hardly has any history at all; as Spain slouched into decadence, most of Lombardy dozed on as part of the Duchy of Milan, ruled by a Spanish viceroy. In 1713, towards the end of the War of the Spanish Succession, the Habsburgs of Austria came into control of the Duchy, and the tiny Duchy of Mantua. The Austrians improved conditions somewhat. Especially during the reigns of **Maria Theresa** (1765–90) and her son **Joseph II** (1765–90), two of the most likeable Enlightenment despots, Lombardy and the other Austrian possessions underwent major economic reforms – a head start that helped Milan to its industrial prominence today.

1796–1860: From Napoleon to Italian Unification

Napoleon, that greatest of Italian generals, arrived in 1796 on behalf of the French revolutionary Directorate, sweeping away the Austrians and setting up republics in Lombardy (the 'Cisalpine Republic') and elsewhere. Italy woke up with a start from its

Baroque slumbers, and local patriots gaily joined the French cause. In 1799, however, while Napoleon was off in Egypt, the advance through Italy by an Austro-Russian army, aided by Nelson's fleet, restored the status quo. In 1800 Napoleon returned in a campaign that saw the great victory at Marengo, giving him the opportunity to reorganize Italian affairs once more, and to crown himself King of Italy in Milan's cathedral, the Duomo. Napoleonic rule lasted only until 1814, but in that time important public works were begun and laws, education and everything else reformed after the French model; Church properties were expropriated and medieval relics everywhere put to rest. The French, however, soon wore out their welcome through high taxes, oppression and the systematic looting of Italy's artistic heritage. When the Austrians came to chase the French out in 1814, no-one was sad to see them go.

Though the postwar **Congress of Vienna** put the Italian clock back to 1796, the Napoleonic experience had given Italians a taste of the opportunities offered by the modern world, as well as a sense of national feeling that had been suppressed for centuries. Almost immediately, revolutionary agitators and secret societies sprang up all over Italy. Sentiment for Italian unification and liberal reform was greatest in the north, and in the decades of the national revival, the **Risorgimento**, Lombardy in particular would contribute more than its share.

In March 1848, a revolution in Vienna gave Italians under Austrian rule their chance to act. Milan's famous **Cinque Giornate** revolt began with a boycott of the Austrian tobacco monopoly. Some troops, conspicuously smoking cigars in public, caused fighting to break out in the streets. In five incredible days the populace of Milan rose up and chased out the Austrian garrison (led by Marshal Radetzky, he of the famous march tune). Events began to move rapidly. On 22 March revolution spread to Venice, and soon afterwards Piedmont's King Carlo Alberto declared war on Austria and his army crossed the Ticino into Lombardy. The Piedmontese won early victories, including one important one at Goito, on 30 May, but under the timid leadership of the king they failed to follow them up, and the Austrians were back in control by the end of July. The other Italian revolts, in Rome and Venice, were not put down until 1849.

Despite failure on a grand scale, the Italians knew they would get another chance. Unification, most likely under the House of Savoy that ruled Piedmont, was inevitable. In 1859, with the support of Napoleon III and France, the Piedmontese tried again and would have been successful had the French not double-crossed them and signed an armistice with Austria in the middle of the war; as a result, though, Piedmont gained Lombardy and Tuscany. That left the climactic event of unification to be performed by the revolutionary adventurer **Giuseppe Garibaldi**. When Garibaldi sailed to Sicily with 1,000 volunteers in May 1860, nearly half his men were from Lombardy. Their unexpected success in toppling the Kingdom of Naples launched the Piedmontese on an invasion from the north, and Italian unity was achieved.

1860–1987: Lombardy Takes Off

While life under the corrupt and bumbling governments of the new Italian kingdom wasn't perfect, it was a major improvement over the Austrians. The integration of the northern industrial towns into a unified Italian economy gave trade a big boost, and Milan in particular saw its industry expand dramatically. Along with that came the beginnings of the socialist movement, stronger at first in Lombardy than anywhere else; the first socialist party, the **Partito Operaio Italiano**, was founded in Milan in 1882. Strikes and riots were common in the depression of the nineties; over a hundred people were killed in one clash in 1896. Nevertheless, a rapidly increasing prosperity was drawing the northern cities into the European mainstream. The decades before the First World War, a contented time for many Italians, came to be known by the slightly derogatory term *Italietta*, the 'little Italy' of bourgeois happiness, sweet Puccini operas, the first motor cars, blooming 'Liberty'-style architecture, and Sunday afternoons at the beach.

After the war, Milan saw the birth of another movement, Fascism. **Mussolini** founded his newspaper there, the *Popolo d'Italia*, and organized bands of *squadre*, toughs who terrorized unions and leftist parties. The upper classes got on well enough with the Fascists, especially during the boom of the 1920s, when big Milanese firms like Montecatini-Edison and Pirelli came into prominence. In the Second World War the industrial cities suffered heavily from Allied bombings after the capture of Sicily in July 1943. After the government signed an armistice with the Allies in September, the German army moved in massively to take control of the north. They established a puppet government, the Italian Social Republic, at the resort of Salò on Lake Garda, and re-installed Mussolini, though he was now little more than a figurehead.

The war dragged on for another year and a half, as the Germans made good use of Italy's difficult terrain to slow the Allied advance. Meanwhile Italy finally gave itself something to be proud of: a determined, resourceful Resistance that established free zones in many areas of Lombardy and other regions, and harassed the Germans with sabotage and strikes. The *partigiani* caught Mussolini in April 1945, while he was trying to escape to Switzerland. After shooting him and his mistress, they hung him by the toes from the roof of a petrol station in Milan where the Germans had shot a number of civilians a week before.

With a heavy dose of Marshall Plan aid and some intelligent government planning, Milan (and Turin) led the way for the 'economic miracle' of the 1950s. Meaningful politics almost ceased to exist, as the nation was run in a constantly renegotiated deal between the Christian Democrats and smaller parties, but Lombard industry surged ahead, creating around Milan a remarkably diverse economy of over 60,000 concerns, from multinational giants like Olivetti to the small, creative, often family-run firms that are the model of what has been called 'Italian capitalism'.

Milan's most glamorous industry, fashion, is a fairly recent addition; it only began to move to the city from Florence in around 1968, owing to the lack of a good airport there. Italy's best fashion designers such as Armani, Prada and Gucci are now based in the city. The climax of the boom came in 1987, when it was announced that Italy had surpassed Britain to become the world's fifth largest economy; '*Il Sorpasso*', as Italians called it, was a great source of national pride – even though it was later discovered that government economists had fiddled the figures.

1987–the Present: Lombardy and Milan Today

With some 9 million people, Lombardy is the most populous region of Italy, and also the richest by far; it produces a quarter of the gross national product and a third of Italy's exports. The average income is twice that of the south, and higher than any region of Britain or France. Even after the recent recession, Lombardy isn't doing badly; on Milan's frantic stock market the number of shares traded in a day occasionally exceeds New York's. Along with prosperity has come a number of serious worries: a big increase in corruption and crime, unchained suburban sprawl and pollution, in the air and in Europe's filthiest river, the Po. Some 250,000 immigrants from southern Italy and Sicily have moved to Milan since the war, and the inability of many of them to adapt and get ahead, largely thanks to the bigotry of the Lombards, fuels a host of intractable social problems.

The Milanese believe their city is the real capital of Italy – because it pays the bills. But, following its old traditions, the city has remained traditionally indifferent to politics and stolidly unproductive in the arts. Milan can offer fashion and industrial design – both of course highly profitable. It is the nation's publishing centre, and probably its art centre, with more galleries than anywhere else. Endlessly creative in business, it has so far had little else to offer the world.

In politics, however, the indifference may be gone forever. The lid blew off Italy's cosily rotten political system and its Byzantine web of bribery and kickbacks in 1992 in Milan. **Antonio di Pietro** was a poor boy from the most obscure region of Italy, the Molise. He worked in electronics while studying law at night in Milan, and became a judge in the early 1980s. The electronics background gave him a thorough knowledge of computers and what they could do, and he used them skilfully to pile up and collate evidence and connections between cases. He first made a name for himself in 1987, breaking open bribe scandals in the vehicle licence bureau and city bus company. In 1992 a divorced woman wrote him a letter complaining of how her ex-husband, an official in a city old age hospice, was driving around in a new Alfa and wearing silk suits while claiming he couldn't afford her alimony. That man was the now famous Mario Chiesa, a hapless grafter and Socialist party hack who had been skimming off L100,000 (approx €50) from undertakers for every corpse they took out of the place. He was had, and he squealed, revealing a wealth of interesting information about similar shady deals all over Milan.

One thing led to another – to put it mildly. Even di Pietro was amazed at how information on one racket tied in inevitably with others, each one bigger than the last. The affair, now known around the world as *Tangentopoli*, or 'Bribe City', resulted in hundreds of leading politicians and business magnates being convicted in the subsequent *Mani Pulite* ('clean hands') investigation. One of the country's most respected business leaders, Raul Gardini, committed suicide in his cell. The Christian Democrat and Socialist parties were utterly annihilated and the face of Italy's politics changed forever. Even di Pietro, after being chosen as the most popular man in Italy and serving briefly as minister of public works in the Prodi government in 1996, was put under investigation, a warning to judges who tread on powerful toes. *Tangentopoli* could make a good film – no doubt somebody's already working on the screenplay.

Today, unfortunately for the Milanese, everyone knows where Bribe City really is. All along, it seems, the two extremities of the nation have had their separate and distinct ways of doing business – the Sicilians' was just a little more colourful. For every proud, honest citizen of the city of silk suits and Alfas, the events of the 1990s must have been a profound revelation. Paradoxically, the tremendous drama of indictments, trials and retaliations, north and south, may become the greatest impetus towards a true Italian unity since Giuseppe Garibaldi. Italians have only to look at what is happening to realize that they're all in the same boat, that Palermo and Milan aren't so different after all.

Other spoons have been busily stirring the pot. Even before *Tangentopoli*, a new Lombard League, the **Lega Lombarda**, led by the noisy yet enigmatic **Umberto Bossi** (the only Italian political figure to dress badly since the time of King Aistulf), made its breakthrough in the 1990 elections, and became the leading party of the region in 1992. On most issues the Lega's position can change by the hour, but its basic tenet of federalism, to cut out the voracious politicians and bureaucrats in Rome and allow the wealthy north to keep more of its profits for itself, has understandably struck a deep chord in the Lombard soul. Other 'Leagues' have emerged and prospered in other northern regions, uniting in 1994 as the **Lega Nord**. In September 1996 Bossi attracted a lot of media attention by declaring the north (as far south as Umbria and the Marches) the independent Republic of Padania, accompanied by a triumphant three-day rally and march down the Po to Venice. If nothing else, the threat of an independent Padania has moved the idea of federalism, perhaps on the Spanish model, up a notch on the Italian political agenda.

That leaves Milan's other gift to Italian politics, **Silvio Berlusconi** (*see* **Topics**, p.32), in some ways the essence of Milan distilled into a single individual. A self-made man, Berlusconi's empire includes half of Italy's television audience, a third of its magazine readership, books, newspapers, a department-store chain and a TV-created political party, **Forza Italia**. Before *Tangentopoli*, no journalist or author ever dared to mention some of things about Italy that everyone knew – say, the close alliance between the Christian Democrats and the Mafia. Today, some courageous Italian prosecutors are looking very closely into how Berlusconi came by all his prizes, or into his membership in P2, a shadowy clique of politicians, industrialists and security chiefs which created or manipulated most of the terrorist groups of the 1960s and '70s.

Berlusconi's Forza Italia exploded on the scene by winning the elections in 1994, only to rule in an uncomfortable and ultimately untenable coalition with the Lega Nord and Fini's Alianza Nazionale, the spruced-up successor to the old Fascist MSI. Berlusconi put on a not entirely convincing and occasionally shrill show as Prime Minister for a season; succeeded in 1996 by Prodi's centre-left Olive Tree Coalition, which managed to stay in the driver's seat longer than anyone predicted. The Italians, who place more hope in Europe than in their national leaders, bit the bullet and supported Prodi's stringent economic measures, allowing them to squeak into Euroland in January 1999. Prodi had little time to bask in the glory: the same strict measures led to the Communists withdrawing their support of his government in late 1998 and giving it to left wing darling Massimo D'Alema of the DS (Democratici di Sinistra) party, forming Italy's 60th government since the Second World War. The D'Alema government did not last long either (until April 2000), and was replaced by yet another coalition of the left, headed by former minister Giuliano Amato.

Economic discontent gave the May 2001 elections resoundingly to Berlusconi's Forza Italia, which got 30 per cent of the vote to become Italy's dominant political party, in a coalition Berlusconi calls the *Case della Libertà* ('Houses of Freedom'). In reality, it is a triumvirate with post-Facist Fini and xenophobe Bossi. Without any meaningful opposition in parliament or in the media, Berlusconi seems on track to create what Nobel-prize winner Dario Fo has called a 'new Fascism', based on his control of much of Italy's media.

Berlusconi continues on despite constant scrutiny into his often controversial business dealings, even in the face of political ally and former Italian premier Giulio Andreotti's recent legal troubles when he was found guilty and later acquitted of conspiracy to murder a journalist. The new boss has gone on the offensive, waging a war of intimidation against what he calls Italy's 'Jacobin' magistrates, whom he claims are out to ruin his political career. In his coalition's 17 months in power, false accounting has been decriminalized (a charge that Berlusconi faced on three counts), and a law was passed enabling defendants to freeze trials while claims of a judge's 'bias' were examined (just in time to help a Berlusconi lawyer accused of bribing judges). Going further on the offensive, the Forza Italia party has also proposed a law that would jail judges for handing down 'incorrect sentences'; and most recently, the government has announced a *'condono fiscale'* – a tax amnesty, which means tax evaders can now simply pay a small fine to 're-enter' the legal world.

Yet it seems not even Berlusconi can escape the grip of Italy's true puppeteers of Italian politics; fresh allegations of Mafia links are gaining ground. After being arrested in 2002, top Cosa Nostra *mafioso* and former agricultural sciences teacher Antonino Giuffre, known as *Manuzza* ('the Hand'), claims that Berlusconi's close friend and Forza Italia senator Marcello Dell'Utri promised the Mafia's legal problems would be resolved within 10 years in exchange for the organization's electoral support (in the last election, Sicily returned all its 61 seats to Forza Italia – an unprecedented result). Berlusconi, as expected, has dismissed these and other tales of Mafia ties as 'monstrous slurs'. However, when speaking of the Cosa Nostra's role in Italy's political affairs, Giuffre summed it up in his recent court deposition: 'It's very simple: we are the fish and politics is the water'.

At the latest regional administrative elections (held in April 2005) Forza Italia and the right-wing coalition parties supporting Berlusconi were heavily defeated in almost all of the Italian regions apart from Lombardy and the Veneto. Middle-left parties celebrated a new triumph and have now been waiting for the next elections (to be held in April 2006), in the hope that the result will bring a new government, headed by a left-wing leader (Romano Prodi, the former European Parliament President, being one of the favourites).

In the meantime, Berlusconi is still leading the country, where, at the time of writing, the provision of measures against terrorism represents the main concern.

Art and Architecture

Like the rest of Italy, Lombardy is packed to the gills with notable works of art and architecture, and it's hard to find even the smallest village without a robust Romanesque chapel, curlicued Baroque *palazzina*, or mysterious time-darkened painting by a follower of Leonardo or Caravaggio. Because the 'art cities' of this region flourished at different periods, there is no one dominant 'golden age' comparable to the Renaissance in Tuscany or Venice, or the Baroque in Rome. On the other hand, you'll find examples of art of all periods, and of nearly every school. For what the Lombards didn't make, they had the money to buy, so their churches and galleries are endowed with many masterpieces.

Prehistoric and Roman

The most remarkable works from the Neolithic period up to the Iron Age are the thousands of graffiti rock incisions left by the Camuni tribes in isolated Alpine valleys north of Lake Iseo, especially in the national park of the **Valle Camonica** (others are in the Upper Valtellina at **Teglio** and **Grósio**). Remains of Neolithic and Bronze Age pile-dwelling communities have survived on an islet in **Lake Varese** and by **Lake Ledro**. Apart from the odd menhir and pot, the Ligurians and Celts have left few traces, and even the arches and amphitheatres erected by their Roman conquerors have almost disappeared as the towns and colonies grew into modern cities. **Brescia**'s forum has come down remarkably intact, and there are the sizeable remains of Roman villas on Lake Garda, at **Desenzano** and **Sirmione**; also *see* Milan's archaeological museum.

Early Middle Ages (5th–10th Centuries)

Although the brilliant mosaics such as those in Ravenna, Venice and Rome – the delight of this period in Italy – are rare here (*see* the chapels in Sant'Ambrogio and San Lorenzo Maggiore, both in **Milan**), the work of the native population under its Lombard rulers was certainly not without talent. See the treasury of 6th-century Lombard Queen Theodolinda in **Monza**; the 5th-century baptistry at **Lomello**; the Carolingian-era stuccoes and treasure in San Salvatore, **Brescia**); other Lombard stucco reliefs in San Pietro al Monte, above **Civate**; the 8th-century frescoes at **Castelséprio**; and those from the 10th-century San Vincenzo at Galliano, near **Cantù**.

The key work of the age, one that would become the great prototype of the Lombard Romanesque, Sant'Ambrogio in **Milan**, dates from the 880s, a design respected in its last rebuilding in the 1080s. The chief ingredients are all there: the broad, triangular façade, the decorative rows of blind arches, sometimes called 'Lombard arcading'; the passages under exterior porticoes; and a rib-vaulted interior, with the presbytery raised over the crypt, and aisles delimited by arches (in some churches supporting internal galleries).

Romanesque and Gothic (11th–14th Centuries)

In many ways the Romanesque was the most vigorous phase in Italian art history, when the power of the artist was almost that of a magician. Lombardy shone in particular; even many of Tuscany's finest Romanesque churches were built and decorated by roving schools of builders and sculptors (the Maestri Comaschi and

Maestri Campionesi) from Lakes Como and Lugano. Prime examples of Lombard Romanesque, based on Milan's Sant'Ambrogio, are the cathedrals of **Cremona**, **Crema**, **Lodi** and **Monza**, Sant'Abbondio in **Como** (which also has an exceptionally pure Romanesque town hall or Broletto), Santa Maria Maggiore in **Lomello**, the church at **Agliate**, and San Michele and San Pietro in Ciel d'Oro in **Pavia**. Sometimes, however, architects built in the round, as in the old cathedral in **Brescia**, the Rotunda di San Lorenzo in **Mantua** and San Tomé at **Almenno San Bartolomeo**. Gabled porches supported by crusty lions (usually having a human for lunch) or hunch-backed telamones were a common fixture, even into the 14th century (Santa Maria Maggiore, **Bergamo**).

With such a strong local building tradition, it may not be surprising that Gothic ideas imported from France never made much of an impression and caught on only briefly – but long enough to reach a singular climax and size in the spire-forested Duomo, the cathedral of **Milan**. The transition that came soon after, from pointy, vertical Gothic to the more rounded, classically proportioned Renaissance, reads like a textbook in **Como**'s Duomo, built half in one style, and half in the other.

Renaissance (15th–16th Centuries)

The fresh perspectives, technical advances and discovery of the individual that epitomize the Renaissance were born in *quattrocento* Florence and spread to the rest of Italy at varying speeds. Wealthy Lombardy played a major role, although perhaps most notably in its capacity to patronize and appreciate talent. Outdoor frescoes – one of the most charming features of the region – were within the realm not only of the nobility but of merchants and bankers. Celebrated patrons of indoor art include Cardinal Branda Castiglioni, who hired the Florentine Masolino (1383–c. 1447) to paint the charming frescoes in **Castiglione Olona**. The Duke of Milan, Lodovico il Moro, sponsored the Milanese sojourns of **Leonardo da Vinci**. Leonardo's smoky shading (*sfumato*) so dazzled the local painters that the next generation or two lay heavily under his spell. Most talented of his many followers (Boltraffio, Giampietrino, Cesare da Sesto, Andrea Solario, Salaino and Marco d'Oggiono) was **Bernardino Luini** (d. 1532), whose masterpiece is the fresco cycle in Santa Maria degli Angioli in **Lugano** (other great works are in Milan's church of San Maurizio and Brera Gallery, and in **Saronno**'s Santuario della Madonna dei Miracoli). Even sculptors were inspired by Leonardo, among them **Cristoforo Solari** (1439–1525), whose tombs of Lodovico il Moro and Beatrice d'Este are among the many treasures at the **Certosa di Pavia**.

The perfect symmetry and geometrical proportions of Renaissance architecture were introduced into **Milan** in the 1450s by Francesco Sforza, who hired **Filarete** to design the city's revolutionary Ospedale Maggiore, modelled on Brunelleschi's Ospedale degli Innocenti in Florence. Lodovico il Moro brought architect **Donato Bramante** of Urbino (1444–1514) to Milan, where he designed the amazing, illusionistic 3ft-deep apse of Santa Maria presso San Satiro, the great tribune of Santa Maria delle Grazie and the cloisters of Sant'Ambrogio before going on to Rome. Most Tuscan of all, however, is the Cappella Portinari in Sant'Eustorgio, built for an agent of the Medici bank, perhaps by the Florentine Michelozzo.

Elsewhere in Lombardy, **Mantua**, thanks to its sophisticated, free-spending Gonzaga dukes, became one of Italy's most influential art cities of the Renaissance. Their court painter was **Andrea Mantegna** (c. 1431–1506), the leading northern Italian artist of the day, along with his brother-in-law Giovanni Bellini; Mantegna produced, among other works, the frescoes of the *Camera degli Sposi* (1474). He studied the ancients with an intensity only rivalled by Florentine theorist and architect **Leon Battista Alberti** (1404–72), who designed two Mantuan churches, notably **Sant'Andrea**, in an imaginative reuse of the forms of Vitruvius. Ideal cities, designed from scratch according to Renaissance theories of humanism, were a popular concept, but Vespasiano Gonzaga was one of few to ever actually build one, **Sabbioneta**.

Uncomfortable next to such classicizing idealism is the Mannerist masterpiece of Raphael's star pupil, **Giulio Romano** (d. 1546): Federico Gonzaga II's Mantuan pleasure palace, the **Palazzo Te** (1527–34). Its beginning coincided with the 1527 Sack of Rome, an event that shook Italians to the core; some of the artists who witnessed it (like Rosso Fiorentino) went mad. Giulio Romano, a native of Rome, was safe in Mantua, but in the Palazzo Te one can sense reverberations of the calamity: the limits of art and architecture become ambiguous; delight and illusion mingle with oppression; violent contrasts between light and dark echo the starkly defined good and evil of the Counter-Reformation.

Elsewhere in Lombardy, the region's traditional art of sculpture reached its epitome in the Renaissance in the person of **Giovanni Antonio Amadeo** of Pavia (d. 1522), best known for the extraordinary ornate façade of the **Certosa di Pavia** and for the design of the Colleoni Chapel in **Bergamo**. Even more prolific than Amadeo was his follower **Bergognone** (d. 1530s), sculptor and painter, whose calm, undramatic style is often enhanced by lovely landscape backgrounds (especially in the *Incoronata* in **Lodi**).

Brescia became a minor centre of Renaissance painting, beginning with **Vincenzo Foppa** (c. 1427–1515), one of the leaders of the Lombard Renaissance, a school marked by a sombre tonality and atmosphere; Foppa was especially known for his monumental style (works in **Bergamo**'s Accademia Carrara and **Milan**'s Sant'Eustorgio). Later, when Brescia came under Venetian rule, its artists also turned east: Alessandro Bonvincino, better known as **Moretto da Brescia** (d. 1554), was more influenced by Titian, and painted the first-known full-length Italian portrait (1526; works in **Brescia** are the Duomo Vecchio and the Galleria Tosio-Martinengo). His Bergamasque pupil, **Giovanni Battista Moroni** (c. 1525–78), painted many run-of-the-mill religious works, but also penetrating portraits of the first calibre (in **Bergamo**'s Accademia Carrara) as did Lorenzo Lotto of Venice (c. 1480–1556) who spent many years in the city (Accademia Carrara and Santo Spirito in **Bergamo**). A third painter of this period was **Girolamo Romanino** (c. 1484–1562), whose works combine the richness of Titian with the flatter Lombard style (Santa Maria delle Neve in **Pisogne** and **Cremona** cathedral). The rather naïve but sincere works of the prolific **Giovan Pietro Da Cemmo**, a *Quattrocento* painter from Brescia's Valle Camonica, turn up in many a country parish and in the monastery of Sant'Agostino in **Crema**.

Besides the followers of Leonardo and assorted Brescian masters, Lombardy did produce two extraordinary native geniuses: Arcimboldo and Caravaggio. **Giuseppe Arcimboldo** (c. 1527–93) of Milan painted portraits made up entirely of seafood, vegetables or flowers which anticipate the surrealists and the collages of *objets trouvés*. Arcimboldo became the court painter to the Habsburgs in Prague and has left one of his works in **Milan**, in the Castello Sforzesco. More immediately influential, not only in Italy but throughout 17th-century Europe, was **Michelangelo Merisi da Caravaggio** (c. 1571–1610) who, despite a headlong trajectory through life (perhaps the first true bohemian – anarchic, rebellious and homosexual, he murdered a man over a tennis game, was thrown out of Malta by the Knights, and was almost killed in Naples before dying on a Tuscan beach), managed to leave behind paintings of dramatic power. His use of light, of foreshortening, and of simple country people as models in major religious subjects were often copied but never equalled. Most of his paintings are in Rome, where he moved in 1590, with some works in **Milan** (in the Ambrosiana and Brera Gallery).

Baroque (17th–18th Centuries)

Architecturally, in these centuries the real show in north Italy took place in Piedmont, notably in the revolutionary works of Juvarra and Guarini. In **Milan** these two centuries were far more austere, in part thanks to St Charles Borromeo, who wrote a book of guidelines for Counter-Reformation architects. **Fabio Mangone** (d. 1629) epitomized this new austerity (the façade of the Ambrosiana, Santa Maria Podone); the more interesting **Lorenzo Binago** (d. 1629) designed Sant'Alessandro, with its innovative combination of two domed areas. Most important of all Baroque architects in Milan was **Francesco Maria Ricchino** (d. 1658), whose San Giuseppe follows Binago's Sant'Alessandro with its two Greek crosses. He created a style of crossings and domes that enjoyed tremendous success (other works include the Palazzo di Brera and the Collegio Elvetico, now the Archivo di Stato, the first concave palace façade of the Baroque style).

Milan's best painters of the age all worked in the early 1600s – the mystic though somewhat cloying Giovanni Battista Crespi (called **Cerano**, c. 1575–1632) and the fresco master of Lombardy's sanctuaries, Pier Francesco Mazzucchelli, called **Morazzone** (d. 1626), whose works are at **Varese**). These two, along with the less interesting Giulio Cesare Procaccini, teamed up to paint the Brera Gallery's unusual 'three masters' painting of *SS. Rufina and Seconda*. A fourth painter, Antonio d'Enrico, **Il Tanzio** (d. 1635), was inspired by Caravaggio, with results that range from the bland to the uncannily meticulous.

After 1630, when Milan and its artists were devastated by plague, **Bergamo** was left holding the paintbrush of Lombard art, in the portraits of **Carlo Ceresa** (d. 1679) and **Evaristo Baschenis** (1617–77), whose precise still-life paintings of musical instruments are among the finest of a rather un-Italian genre. From **Brescia** came **Giacomo Ceruti** (active in the 1730s–50s), whose sombre pictures of idiots, beggars and other social outcasts are as carefully obsessive. In sculpture, **Antonio Fantoni** (1659–1734), from a big family of woodcarvers in Rovetta, stands out with his scrolly, elegantly decorative rococo altarpieces and pulpits (works in Santa Maria Maggiore, **Bergamo**, and in the Valle Seriana, especially **Alzano Lombardo**).

Two late Baroque painters marched to a different drummer: **Alessandro Magnasco** (1667–1749) of Genoa, who worked mainly in Milan and produced with quick, nervous brushstrokes weird, almost surreal canvases haunted by wraiths of light (Civic Museum, **Crema**) and **Giuseppe Bazzani** (1690–1769) of Mantua, who used similar quick brushstrokes to create the unreal and strange.

Neoclassicism and Romanticism (Late 18th–19th Centuries)

Baroque proved to be a hard act to follow, and in these centuries Italian art and architecture almost ceased to exist. Three centuries of stifling oppression had taken their toll on the national imagination, and for the first time Italy not only ceased to be a leader in art but failed even to a make a significant contribution. The period did, however, sprinkle the shores of the lakes with superb private villas: one, the **Villa Carlotta**, on the banks of Lake Como, is a triumph of neoclassicism with statues by the master of the age, **Antonio Canova**, and his meticulous follower **Thorvaldsen**. Also of note is the 19th-century glassed arcade of the Galleria Vittorio Emanuele II in **Milan**. Despite this artistic lull, the romantic-era Lombard artists, the *Scapigliati* ('Wild-haired Ones'), were well-received; their works are in **Milan**'s Galleria d'Arte Moderna.

20th Century

Italian Art Nouveau, or Liberty-style, left its mark in the grand hotels of the Italian Lakes and the residential area around Corso Venezia in **Milan**, and reached an apotheosis in the spa of **San Pellegrino Terme**. But Liberty's pretty, bourgeois charm and the whole patrimony of Italian art only infuriated the young **Futurists**, who produced manifestos and paintings which attempted to speed Italy into modern times; their works are in **Milan**'s Brera Gallery. This same urge to race out of the past also created modern Italy's most coherent and consistent sense of design. Fascist architecture may be charmingly Art Deco, or warped and disconcerting (**Brescia**'s Piazza della Vittoria, **Bergamo**'s Piazza Matteotti and around, or its domestic variety, D'Annunzio's villa in **Gardone Riviera**). A remarkable exception are the visionary works of Giuseppe Terragni (Casa Terragni, **Como**).

However uneven the Fascist contribution, modern Italian architects have yet to match it, hardly ever rising above saleable and boring modernism (Milan's 1959 **Pirelli Building** by Gio Ponti and Pier Luigi Nervi is the pick of the bunch, and has recently been restored after being damaged by a small aircraft that flew into it in 2002). The aforementioned museums in Milan have collections of contemporary art – the bronzes of **Mariano Marini** in the Galleria d'Arte Moderna in **Milan** deserves special mention. But most artistic talent these days is sublimated into film, or the *shibboleth* of Italian design – clothes, sports cars, furniture – and even these consumer beauties are more often packaging than content. As if to emphasize this point, Milan's smaller modern art galleries, though growing in number, tend to walk hand-in-hand with the city's ever-present fashion industry, often providing little more than an extension of the fashion catwalk.

Topics

04

The Caffè of Italian Enlightenment

Java had little to do with it, but *Il Caffè* had the same effect as an espresso on sleepy 18th-century Lombardy – a quick jolt of wakeful energy. This was, in fact, the name of Italy's first real newspaper. It was published for only two years in the 1760s, by brothers Pietro and Alessandro Verri and a small circle of young Milanese aristocrats who called themselves the *Accademia dei Pugni*, or 'the Fists'.

The opinions it published derived from England and the philosophers and encyclopedists of France. They wrote of the need for economic, humanitarian and judicial reforms, not once challenging the authority of the absolute monarchy of the Austrian Habsburgs in Lombardy, or even suggesting anything as radical as Italian unity. But at a time when Italy was still languishing in the enforced ignorance of the Church and foreign rulers, this newspaper, such as it was, was revolutionary for merely encouraging people to think.

When *Il Caffè* was published, only a few thousand lay Italians were literate enough to read it. But they were the elite of the system, and it was their opinions that the Verri brothers hoped to influence in their editorials. Also, conditions in Milan, if nowhere else in Italy, were ripe for change. Lombardy's sovereign, Maria Theresa of Austria, was a benevolent, enlightened despot prepared to tolerate a certain amount of local autonomy and opinion; while Milan was starting to wake up, on the verge of its great capitalist destiny, the rest of Italy snored away, festering under papal and Spanish Bourbon rule.

The most important fruit of the Fists' endeavours came from the youngest member of the Academy, a plump stay-at-home mamma's boy named Cesare Beccaria. Pietro Verri saw potential in this muffin that no one else could fathom and assigned him the task of writing a pamphlet on the group's opinions on justice – not a pleasant subject: torture was the most common way of extracting a confession and in Milan alone someone was executed nearly every day. There was even a strict hierarchy of death: nobles got a quick decapitation with a sharp axe and cardinals had the right to be strangled with a gold and purple cord, while the lower classes could expect to have their tongues and ears chopped off, their eyes put out and their flesh burned with hot irons before being allowed to die.

No one suspected Beccaria of any talent whatsoever, and all were astonished when he roused himself to produce the brilliant, succinct *Dei Delitti e delle Pene* (*Of Crimes and Punishments*), published in 1764 in Livorno, out of the reach of local censors. Although the Church hastily consigned the work to its index of prohibited books, it can be fairly said that no other work on jurisprudence had such an immediate effect on the day-to-day lives of everyday men and women. Beccaria's eloquent logic against torture and the death penalty, his insistence on equality before the law and for justice to be both accountable and public, moved Voltaire to write in his commentary on the work that Beccaria had eliminated 'the last remnants of barbarism'. The absolute monarchs of the day (with the notable exception of Louis XVI) moved at once to follow Beccaria's precepts, at least in part: Maria Theresa in Austria, Charles III in Spain, Catherine the Great in Russia, Frederick the Great of Prussia, Ferdinand I in

Naples and most of all Peter Leopold in Tuscany, who went the furthest of all by completely abolishing torture and capital punishment. Beccaria wrote of the 'greatest happiness shared by the greatest number', a phrase adopted by Jeremy Bentham and Thomas Jefferson, who used Beccaria's ideas of equal justice for all as a starting point in framing the American constitution.

Guelphs, Ghibellines and Old Red Beard

The origins of the conflict between Guelphs and Ghibellines are lost in the mists of legend. One medieval writer blamed two brothers of Pistoia named Guelph and Gibel, one of whom murdered the other and began the seemingly endless factional troubles that to many seemed a God-sent plague, meant to punish the proud and wealthy Italians for their sins. Medieval Italy may in fact have been guilty of every sort of jealousy, greed and wrath, but most historians trace the beginnings of the party conflict to two great German houses, *Welf* and *Waiblingen* (Edmund Spenser, looking on amusedly from England, fancifully suggested the names were the origins of our 'Elfs' and 'Goblins').

Trouble was brewing even before the conflict was given a name. The atmosphere of contentious city states, each with its own internal struggles between nobles, merchants and commons, crystallized rapidly into parties. In the beginning, at least, they stood for something. The Guelphs, largely a creation of the newly wealthy bourgeois, were all for free trade and the rights of free cities; the Ghibellines from the start were the party of the German emperors, nominal overlords of Italy who had been trying to assert their control ever since the days of Charlemagne. Naturally, the Guelphs found their protector in the emperors' bitter temporal rivals, the popes.

Nothing unifies like a common enemy, though, and in 12th-century Lombardy the battle lines between Guelphs and Ghibellines broke down in the face of a terror sown by the biggest Goblin of them all, Emperor Frederick Barbarossa (1152–90). Barbarossa understood his election as a mission to restore the lost dignity of the Roman Empire. He even got the Bologna University masters of jurisprudence to proclaim that, according to ancient Roman law, only the emperor had power over the appointment of magistrates, taxes, ports and such.

To maintain the fond fiction that he was the heir of the Caesars required that Barbarossa possess Italy (*see* also **History**, p.38). His sheer ruthlessness in attempting to do so in seven different forays over the Alps was enough to make him one of Hitler's heroes: to subdue Crema, he captured a number of children and bound them to the front of his siege engine to act as a human shield; their parents could hear their pathetic cries. But the Cremaschi hated Barbarossa so much that they fought determinedly on, and after a six-month siege he razed their city to the ground – his usual technique in dealing with independent-minded city states. The original *Lega Lombarda*, or Lombard League, united against him and finally crushed the big thug at Legnano. (This victory over northern tyranny found an echo in the 19th-century struggles of the Risorgimento and in Verdi's rambunctious opera of 1848, *La Battaglia* *di Legnano.* Verdi's personality, and many of his operas, made him a rallying point for partisans of Italian unity. Crowds at the Scala in the 1850s would shout 'VERDI! VERDI!' whenever there were any Austrians around to hear it, and the composer probably didn't mind that the real message, as everyone knew, was 'Vittorio Emanuele, Re D'Italia!')

Ironically, Barbarossa himself was at that same time a symbol for those Germans who wanted their own national unity. The Germans will tell you that Barbarossa wasn't such a bad fellow after all, that the Italians simply invented most of the horror stories, as Italians are wont to do. In later legend – severely embroidered by Romantic poets – the old emperor slept under a mountain called the Kyffhäuser, like King Arthur; sitting around a table with his knights, his red beard growing through the table as he slept, he would wake up once every hundred years and the raven perched on the back of his throne would tell him whether Germany was yet united – only then could Barbarossa finally rest in peace.

After Legnano, Barbarossa was forced to make peace with his arch enemy, Pope Alexander III, kneeling to pay him homage in the atrium of San Marco (the Venetians triumphantly installed a stone to mark the exact spot). The pope brokered the Peace of Constance of 1183, in which the *comuni* maintained their sovereign rights while recognizing the overall authority of the emperor. Perhaps this was some small consolation to Barbarossa, who shortly afterwards departed for the Crusades, only to fall off his horse crossing a shallow river in Turkey and drown in six inches of water.

The Best Fiddles in the World

The modern violin, developed in Cremona in the 16th century in the workshops of Guarneri, Stradivarius and the two Amatis, was the perfect instrument to usher in the opulent pageant of Baroque style. Its rich, sonorous tone, its capacity for thrilling emotions and drama, equalled rarely even by the human voice, was enough to make the typical Baroque dome's population of saints and angels pause on their soaring flight to heaven to let a tear fall for the earth they were leaving behind.

The sensuous shape of the violin and the very complexity of its manufacture are as Baroque as its sound. Stradivarius and company used the finest wood from the Dolomites and from the dense groves that covered the Lombard plain. The main body of the violin was made from maple and spruce, the neck and other bits from poplar, pear and willow. The fluted edges and scrolls and the beautiful curves come straight from the vocabulary of Cremona's Baroque architecture.

Shaped and preserved with an alchemist's varnish, the violins made by the 16th- and 17th-century masters have mellowed and aged over the years like bottles of the finest Sauternes, to develop a quality of sound so powerful, rich and luscious that the violins themselves seem to have a soul. The priceless examples displayed in Cremona's Palazzo del Comune are taken out at least once a week and given a bit of exercise, a caress over the old strings, because there is something alive in them.

The year after Andrea Amati fathered the first violin prototype (1566), Cremona gave birth to Claudio Monteverdi. Growing up amid the rich music flowing from the violinmakers' shops must have had a seminal influence on his career. As a pioneer composer of opera and *maestro di cappella* of St Mark's in Venice, his sumptuous polyphonic music for four to six choirs got him in trouble with the Church, which complained that no one could make out a word of the sacred texts. But that's Baroque for you – the beauty and feeling is the meaning. And perhaps it's not surprising, in our strange modern Baroque world, that an organization called the *Associazione Cremonese Liutai Artigiani Professionisti* is attempting to revive the intricate, painstaking craftsmanship that made Cremona's violins the happiest of all instruments of passion.

Romans of the Lakes

Pliny the Elder (Gaius Plinius Secundus), born in Como in AD 23, was a man with an endless capacity for collecting facts, gossip and hearsay. The result can be read in his greatest work, the 37 books of the *Historia Naturalis*, the world's first encyclo-pedia, which he himself proudly claimed contained '20,000 matters worthy of consideration'. Though above all a scholar and a natural scientist, Pliny died with his boots on – he was the admiral of the fleet in Campania when Vesuvius erupted in AD 70; as he went closer to inspect the phenomenon he was suffocated in the fumes.

There's hardly a subject Pliny failed to expound on in his master work – geography, botany, agriculture, mineralogy, zoology and medicine are all there, much of it taken from lost Greek works. What can be traced back to an original source shows that what he read was often ill-digested, and that he failed to apply much critical judgement; the truth is, much of the *Historia Naturalis* is pure poppycock – like the accounts of blue men in India who hopped around on a single foot, or others who fed only on the scent of flowers – although that hardly stopped it from being one of the most plagiarized works of all time.

Less known, perhaps, is the influence wielded in the Renaissance by Pliny's entries on art and artefacts (again from Greek sources – the Romans themselves were far too practical to theorize about such things). In the 15th and 16th centuries, most artists were of humble origin, and got about as much respect as the local baker. In Pliny (translated into Italian in 1473) they found justifications for their obsession with mathematics, for painting nude figures and for their search for ever more accurate illusions of reality. Best of all to their minds were Pliny's anecdotes on the honour and respect given by the ancient Greeks to artists. One of their favourites was the story of how Alexander the Great gave his mistress Campaspe to Apelles, when he noticed that the artist had fallen for her while painting her in the nude.

If the Greeks that the Elder Pliny studied so intensely were great classicists in their shunning of all excess and in their search for beauty in simple, everyday things, the Romans always preferred realism (their finest achievements in sculpture were portrait busts showing all the warts and wrinkles, exactly the opposite of the idealizing Greeks). Long doses of ugly realism, however, are hard to bear and lead almost inevitably to an escape into the imagination, into romance. Although today we tend to lump all Greek and Roman literature together as 'classics', the greatest Roman writers in the golden age of Augustus were, as the very name suggests, the first Romantics, from Virgil (born in Mantua in AD 70) down to Petronius.

Perhaps the immeasurable, excessive beauty of Lake Como and Lake Garda had something to do with the fact that two other important Roman romantics grew up on their shore. Pliny's own nephew, Pliny the Younger (born in AD 61 in Como), was a famous lawyer and consul whose *Letters* are an invaluable source for his times. But he also wrote of his quiet villas on the lake, to evoke the magic of the scenery – not something the Romans had ever paid much attention to, except when working out where to build the next aqueduct.

To Garda, however, goes the honour of hosting the most highly strung Romantic of them all, the poet Catullus, born in AD 87 in Verona, although he spent most of his time at the family villa at Sirmione – the delicious descriptions by the Younger Pliny of fishing out of his bedroom window resulted in a veritable craze among the first century's smart set to build their own holiday homes there. Catullus' burning, tortured poems for his mistress Lesbia deserve a chapter of their own in the literature of love; she is a grand married woman of the world living on the Palatine Hill, who is gradually won by the young poet's passionate verses. But she soon tires of him and takes new lovers by the score; in despair Catullus flees to Sirmione, only to be summoned back to Rome a decade later by the ageing Lesbia for one last bitter fling. He finds her holding reckless orgies, and about to go on trial for having murdered her husband. In his final poem, shortly before his early and perfectly romantic death from consumption and unrequited love, he leaves a picture of his old flame worthy of a final scene in a Puccini opera:

> Caelius, Lesbia – she, our Lesbia – Oh, that
> only Lesbia, whom Catullus only
> loved as never himself and all his dearest,
> now on highways and byways seeks her lovers,
> strips all Rome's noble great-souled sons of their money.
>   translated by Edith Hamilton

The Immortal Fool

The first recorded mention of Arlecchino, or Harlequin, came when the part was played by a celebrated actor named Tristano Martinelli in 1601 – the year that also saw the début of *Hamlet*. Theatre as we know it was blooming all over Europe in those times: Shakespeare and Marlowe, Calderón and Lope de Vega in Spain, the predecessors of Molière in France. All of these learned their craft from late-Renaissance Italy, where the *commedia dell'arte* had created a fashion that spread across the continent. The great companies, such as the Gelosi, the Confidenti and the Accesi toured the capitals, while others shared out the provinces. Groups of ten or twelve actors, run as cooperatives, they could do comedies, tragedies or pastorals to their own texts, and provide music, dance, magic and juggling between acts.

The audiences liked the comedies best, with a set of masked stock characters, playing off scenes between the *magnificos*, the great lords, and the *zanni*, or servants, who provided the slapstick, half-improvised comic relief. To spring the plot there would be a pair of lovers or *innamorati* – unmasked, to remind us that only those who are in love are really alive.

It had nothing to do with 'art'. *Arte* means a guild; it merely emphasized that these companies involved professional players. The term was invented in 1745 by Goldoni (who wrote one of the last plays of the genre, *Arlecchino, servitore di due padroni*); in the 1500s the companies were often referred to as the *commedia mercenaria* – they would hit town, set up a stage on trestles and start their show within the hour. Cultured Italians of the day often deplored the way the 'mercenary' shows were driving out serious drama, traditionally written by scholarly amateurs in the princely courts. In the repressive climate of the day, caught between the Inquisition and the Spanish bosses, a culture of ideas survived only in free Venice. Theatre retreated into humorous popular entertainment, but even then the Italians found a way to say what was on their minds. A new stock character appeared, the menacing but slow-witted 'Capitano', who always spoke with a Spanish accent, and Italians learned from the French how to use Arlecchino to satirize the hated Emperor Charles V himself – playing on the French pronunciation of the names *harlequin* and *Charles Quint*.

Arlecchino may have been born in Oneta, a village north of Bergamo (*see* p.251), but he carries a proud lineage that goes back to the ancient Greeks and Romans. From his character and appearance, historians of the theatre trace him back to the antique *planipedes*, comic mimes with shaved heads (everyone knew Arlecchino wore his silly nightcap to cover his baldness). Other scholars note his relationship to the 'tricksters' of German and Scandinavian mythology, and it has even been claimed that his costume of patches is that of a Sufi dervish. No doubt he had a brilliant career all through the Middle Ages, though it was probably only in the 1500s that he took the form of the Arlecchino we know. At that time, young rustics from the Bergamasque valleys would go to Venice, Milan and other cities to get work as *facchini*, porters. They all seemed to be named Johnny – *Zanni* in dialect, which became the common term for any of the clownish roles in the plays (and it's the origin of our word 'zany').

The name 'Arlecchino' seems actually to have been a French contribution. At the court of Henri III, a certain Italian actor who played the role became a protégé of a Monsieur de Harlay, and people started calling him 'little Harlay', or Harlequin. The character developed into a stock role, the most beloved of all the *commedia dell'arte* clown masks: simple-minded and easily frightened, yet an incorrigible prankster, a fellow as unstable as his motley dress. His foil was usually another servant, the Neapolitan Puricinella, or Puncinella – Punch – more serious and sometimes boastful, but still just as much of a buffoon. Try to imagine them together on stage, and you'll get something that looks very much like Stan Laurel and Oliver Hardy. No doubt these two have always gone through the world together, and we can hope they always will.

How to Make Your Own Political Party, Italian-style

First, take a former ocean-line crooner-turned-property developer with a boundless ego ('There is no one on the international scene who can presume to measure up to me. My greatness is unquestionable, my humanity, my history; others can only dream of such.') and combine it with the greatest fortune in Italy (€14.5 billion, the 29th richest pot in the world). Add to this heady mix a near monopoly on the country's media – ownership of three national private TV channels, as well as Italy's biggest advertising, insurance, publishing and film production and distribution companies; a brother who owns a major daily newspaper, a wife who owns another. Then stir in one of Europe's most de-politicized countries, where often less than half the electorate vote and half admit in polls that they are disgusted, angered or just bored with politics. Get your media consultants to come up with a spiel to sell the product (i.e. yourself), and link it up fuzzily to something that *does* fire the passion of your audience – football – complete with the battle cry of the national team, *Forza Italia!* ('Go Italy!'). Hypnotize and vaguely promise everybody lower taxes and more jobs in an onslaught of soft touch ads, while creating the cult figure of 'Berlusconi, talented son of a Milanese bank clerk who made good, and by extension, who can make good for Italy too'. At the same time, blanket the airwaves with demogogy and insults towards the opposition on a level unheard of in any other European country.

Run like a business rather than a traditional political party, Forza Italia has no platform, no local groups, no congresses. Its members, who pay a large sum to join, have no power: all activities of the party are determined by Berlusconi's marketing department which views politics, marketing and advertising as all the same. Local and regional Forza Italia candidates need no political experience; many, in fact, are head-hunted, corporate style, and judged by their sales ability. If they fit the image (Silvio doesn't like beards and glasses) and pass the background check, they are asked to swear party loyalty and don the regimented uniform of blue blazers and brown shoes. A marketing team then goes out and determines what are the local issues and the local 'look', and tailors the candidate to fit. Those who distribute the most Forza Italia literature and win the most votes earn incentives – from free AC Milan football tickets to a day at Berlusconi's villa in Calaviere, outside of Milan.

Once in office, denounce anyone who questions unadulterated free enterprise (Margaret Thatcher is Berlusconi's hero) or your own business practices as a 'communist'. To ensure further control, take over other minister's portfolios; then legislate away what remains of laws against tax evasion, conflict of interest, false accounting and bribery, all of which have been charges levelled at you by the courts. Finally, apply stringent censorship rules to any of the country's remaining independent media, and gloss over racist statements as being misunderstood out of context (despite your party's coalition with the xenophobic Northern League). Now sit back while the rest of Europe (who seem to simply hope you'll self-destruct) wonders anxiously who will be the next self-styled 'hero' to create and market his own Berlusconi-style political party. *See also* **History**, p.17.

Food and Drink

05

There are those who eat to live and those who live to eat, and then there are the Italians, for whom food has an almost religious significance, unfathomably linked with love, *La Mamma* and tradition. In this singular country, where millions of otherwise sane people spend many of their waking hours worrying about their digestion, standards both at home and in the restaurants are understandably high. Few Italians are gluttons, but all are experts on what's what in the kitchen; to serve a meal that is not properly prepared is tantamount to an insult.

Restaurant Generalities

People who haven't visited Italy for years and have fond memories of eating full meals for under a pound will be amazed at how much prices have risen; though in some respects eating out in Italy is still a bargain, especially when you figure out how much all that wine would have cost you at home. In many places you'll often find restaurants offering a *menu turistico* – full, set meals of usually meagre inspiration for €13–18. More imaginative chefs often offer a *menu degustazione* – a set-price gourmet meal that allows you to taste their daily specialities and seasonal dishes. Both of these are cheaper than if you had ordered the same food à la carte. In Italy the various terms for types of restaurants – *ristorante, trattoria,* or *osteria* – have been confused. A *trattoria* or *osteria* can be just as elaborate as a restaurant, though rarely is a *ristorante* as informal as a traditional *trattoria*. Unfortunately, the old habit of posting menus and prices in the windows is not as common as it once was and it can be difficult to judge variety or cost. Invariably the least expensive type of restaurant is the *vino e cucina*, simple places serving simple cuisine for simple everyday prices.

Breakfast (*colazione*) in Italy is no lingering affair, but an early-morning wake-up shot to the brain: a *cappuccino* (espresso with hot foamy milk, often sprinkled with chocolate – and incidentally, first thing in the morning is the only time of day at which any self-respecting Italian will touch the stuff), a *caffè latte* (white coffee) or a *caffè lungo* (espresso with hot water), accompanied by a croissant-type roll, called a *cornetto* or *brioche*, or a fancy pastry. This repast can be consumed in any bar and repeated during the morning as often as necessary. Breakfast in Italian hotels seldom represents very good value, although American-style buffets are becoming increasingly popular.

Lunch (*pranzo*), generally served around 1pm, is the most important meal of the day for the Italians (except for many office workers in Milan and other cities who get by on a rapid snack or a one-course meal). This consists of, at the bare minimum, a first course (*primo piatto* – any kind of pasta dish, broth or soup, or rice dish or pizza), a second course (*secondo piatto* – a meat dish, accompanied by a *contorno* or side dish, usually a vegetable, salad, or potatoes), followed by fruit or dessert and coffee. You can, however, begin with the *antipasti* – the appetizers Italians do so brilliantly, ranging from warm seafood delicacies to raw ham (*prosciutto crudo*), salami in a hundred varieties, lovely vegetables, savoury toasts, olives, pâté and many, many more. There are restaurants that specialize in *antipasti*, and they usually don't take it amiss if you decide to forget the pasta and meat and just nibble on these scrumptious hors-d'œuvres (though in the end it will probably cost more than a full meal). Most Italians accompany their meal with wine and mineral water – *acqua minerale*, with or without bubbles (*con* or *senza gas*), which supposedly aids digestion – concluding their meals with a *digestivo* liqueur. *Cena*, or **supper**, is usually eaten around 8pm. This is much the same as *pranzo* although lighter, without the pasta (the Italians believe it lies too heavily on the stomach at night): a pizza, eggs or a fish dish and salad are common. In restaurants, however, they offer all the courses, so if you eat a light lunch you can still go for the works in the evening.

There are several alternatives to sit-down meals. The 'hot table' (*tavola calda*) is a stand-up buffet where you can choose a simple prepared dish or a whole meal, depending on your appetite. The food in these can be impressive; many offer only a few hot dishes, pizza and sandwiches, though in every fair-sized town there will be at least one *tavola calda* with seats where you can contrive a complete dinner outside the usual hours. Little shops that sell pizza by the slice or weight are common in resorts and city centres. At any grocer's (*alimentari*) or market (*mercato*) you can buy the materials for countryside or hotel room picnics; some places in the smaller towns will make the sandwiches for you. For really elegant picnics, have a *tavola calda* pack up something nice. And if everywhere else is closed, there's always the railway station – bars will at least have sandwiches and drinks, and perhaps some surprisingly good snacks you've never heard of before. Some of the station bars also prepare *cestini di viaggio*, full-course meals in a basket to help you through long train trips. Common snacks you'll encounter include *panini* of *prosciutto*, cheese and tomatoes, or other meats; *tramezzini*, little sandwiches of plain, square white bread that are always much better than they look; and pizza, of course.

Lombard Specialities

Food

The Lombards like their food and they like it to be fairly substantial; they tend to use butter instead of olive oil, and there's a great fondness for cheese and frying in bread-crumbs. Some Lombard dishes, like the *cotoletta alla milanese*, are devoured with relish across Italy, while others are so quirky (the sweet tortellini of Crema, for instance) that you can only find them in one place. Favourite ***antipasti*** include meats (*salami di Milano, carpaccio, prosciutto* and *bresaola* – dried salt beef served with lemon, oil and *rucola*), *carciofi alla milanese* (artichokes with butter and cheese), mozzarella fried in breadcrumbs, *peperonata* (red pimentos, onions and tomatoes cooked in butter and olive oil).

First and often second courses are often based on **polenta** (yellow cornmeal, a bit like American cornmush), boiled until thick and served with butter and cheese, or cut in slices, or shaped and fried, baked or grilled. Lombard classics are *polenta e osei* (polenta slices topped with roast birds), *polenta alla Lodigiana* (round slices of polenta fried in breadcrumbs), *polenta pasticciata* (baked with cheese, meat and mushroom

Italian Menu Vocabulary

Antipasti

These before-meal treats can include almost anything; the following are among the most common.

antipasto misto mixed antipasto
bruschetta garlic toast (sometimes with tomatoes)
carciofi (sott'olio) artichokes (in oil)
frutti di mare seafood
funghi (trifolati) mushrooms (with anchovies, garlic and lemon)
gamberi ai fagioli prawns (shrimps) with white beans
mozzarella (in carrozza) cow/buffalo cheese (fried with bread in batter)
olive olives
prosciutto (con melone) raw ham (with melon)
salami cured pork
salsicce sausages

Minestre (Soups) and Pasta

agnolotti ravioli with meat
cacciucco spiced fish soup
cannelloni meat/cheese rolled in pasta tubes
cappelletti small ravioli, often in broth
crespelle crêpes
fettuccine long strips of pasta
frittata omelette
gnocchi potato dumplings
lasagne sheets of pasta baked with meat and cheese sauce
minestra di verdura thick vegetable soup
minestrone soup with meat, vegetables and pasta
orecchiette ear-shaped pasta, served with turnip greens
panzerotti ravioli with mozzarella, anchovies and egg
pappardelle alla lepre pasta with hare sauce
pasta e fagioli soup with beans, bacon, and tomatoes
pastina in brodo tiny pasta in broth

penne all'arrabbiata quill-shaped pasta with tomatoes and hot peppers
polenta cake or pudding of corn semolina
risotto (alla Milanese) Italian rice (with stock, saffron and wine)
spaghetti all'Amatriciana with spicy pork, tomato, onion and chilli sauce
spaghetti alla Bolognese with ground meat, ham, mushrooms etc.
spaghetti alla carbonara with bacon, eggs and black pepper
spaghetti al pomodoro with tomato sauce
spaghetti al sugo/ragú with meat sauce
spaghetti alle vongole with clam sauce
stracciatella broth with eggs and cheese
tagliatelle flat egg noodles
tortellini pasta caps filled with
  al pomodoro meat, cheese or vegetables with tomato sauce
  con panna with cream
  in brodo in broth
vermicelli very thin spaghetti

Carne (Meat)

abbacchio milk-fed lamb
agnello lamb
animelle sweetbreads
anatra duck
arista pork loin
arrosto misto mixed roast meats
bistecca alla fiorentina Florentine beef steak
bocconcini veal mixed with ham and cheese and fried
bollito misto stew of boiled meats
braciola hop
brasato di manzo braised beef with veg
bresaola dried raw meat
capretto kid
capriolo roe-buck
carne di castrato/suino mutton/pork
carpaccio thinly sliced raw beef
cassoeula pork stew with cabbage
cervello (al burro nero) brains (in black butter sauce)

sauces) and Lake Iseo's famous baked polenta with tench. As Europe's major producer of rice, Lombardy is also famous for its *risotti*, which are typically served as a first course. Look for traditional saffron-tinted *risotto alla milanese*, *risotto alla Monzese* (with sausage meat, tomato and Marsala) and Mantuan *risotto alla pilota*, with butter and onions; or more seasonal concoctions with porcini mushrooms or asparagus, or even fruit and raisins in some *cucina nuova* restaurants. Lombardy's **pasta**

cervo venison
cinghiale boar
coniglio rabbit
cotoletta veal cutlet
  alla Milanese fried in breadcrumbs
  alla Bolognese with ham and cheese
fagiano pheasant
faraona guinea fowl
  alla creta in earthenware pot
fegato alla veneziana liver with filling
lepre (in salmi) hare (marinated in wine)
lombo di maiale pork loin
lumache snails
maiale (al latte) pork (cooked in milk)
manzo beef
osso buco braised veal knuckle
pancetta rolled pork
pernice partridge
petto di pollo boned chicken breast
  alla fiorentina fried in butter
  alla bolognese with ham and cheese
  alla sorpresa stuffed and deep fried
piccione pigeon
pizzaiola beef steak in tomato and oregano
pollo chicken
  alla cacciatora with tomatoes and
  mushrooms, cooked in wine
  alla diavola grilled
  alla Marengo fried with tomatoes, garlic
  and wine
polpette meatballs
quaglie quails
rane frogs
rognoni kidneys
saltimbocca veal scallop with prosciutto and
  sage, cooked in wine and butter
scaloppine thin slices of veal sautéed in butter
spezzatino pieces of beef/veal, usually stewed
spiedino meat on a skewer/stick
stufato beef and vegetables braised in wine
tacchino turkey
trippa tripe
uccelletti small birds on a skewer
vitello veal

Pesce (Fish)

acciughe or *alici* anchovies
anguilla eel
aragosta lobster
aringa herring
baccalà dried salt cod
bonito small tuna
branzino sea bass
calamari squid
cape sante scallops
cefalo grey mullet
coda di rospo angler fish
cozze mussels
datteri di mare razor (or date) mussels
dentice dentex (perch-like fish)
dorato gilt head
fritto misto mixed fried delicacies,
  mainly fish
gamberetto shrimp
gamberi (di fiume) prawns (crayfish)
granchio crab
insalata di mare seafood salad
lampreda lamprey
merluzzo cod
nasello hake
orata bream
ostriche oysters
pesce spada swordfish
polipi/polpi octopus
pesce azzurro various small fish
pesce di San Pietro John Dory
rombo turbot
sarde sardines
seppie cuttlefish
sgombro mackerel
sogliola sole
squadro monkfish
stoccafisso wind-dried cod
tonno tuna
triglia red mullet (rouget)
trota trout
trota salmonata salmon trout
vongole small clams
zuppa di pesce mixed fish in sauce or stew

specialities may be served with gorgonzola, or stuffed with pumpkin and cheese, meat, fish, or spinach in melted butter and sage. If served *alla mantovana* the sauce will include meat, pounded walnuts, white wine and cream. Another local pasta speciality is *pizzoccheri* (buckwheat noodles from the Valtellina, served with butter and cheese).

Contorni (Side Dishes, Vegetables)

asparagi asparagus
  alla fiorentina with fried eggs
broccoli broccoli
carciofi (alla giudea) artichokes (deep fried)
cardi cardoons/thistles
carote carrots
cavolfiore cauliflower
cavolo cabbage
ceci chickpeas
cetriolo cucumber
cipolla onion
fagioli white beans
fagiolini French (green) beans
fave broad beans
finocchio fennel
funghi (porcini) mushrooms (boletus)
insalata (mista/verde) salad (mixed/green)
lattuga lettuce
lenticchie lentils
melanzane aubergine/eggplant
patate (fritte) potatoes (fried)
peperoncini hot chilli peppers
peperoni sweet peppers
peperonata stewed peppers, onions, etc.
  (similar to ratatouille)
piselli (al prosciutto) peas (with ham)
pomodoro(i) tomato(es)
porri leeks
radicchio red chicory
radice radish
rapa turnip
rucola rocket
sedano celery
spinaci spinach
verdure greens
zucca pumpkin
zucchini courgettes

Formaggio (Cheese)

bel paese soft white cow's cheese
cacio/caciocavallo pale yellow, sharp cheese
caprino goat's cheese
fontina rich cow's milk cheese

groviera mild cheese (gruyère)
gorgonzola soft blue cheese
parmigiano parmesan cheese
pecorino sharp sheep's cheese
provolone sharp, tangy; *dolce* is less strong
stracchino soft white cheese

Frutta (Fruit, Nuts)

albicocche apricots
ananas pineapple
arance oranges
banane bananas
cachi persimmon
ciliegie cherries
cocomero watermelon
datteri dates
fichi figs
fragole (con panna) strawberries (with cream)
lamponi raspberries
limone lemon
macedonia di frutta fruit salad
mandarino tangerine
mandorle almonds
melagrana pomegranate
mele apples
mirtilli bilberries
more blackberries
nespola medlar fruit
nocciole hazelnuts
noci walnuts
pera pear
pesca peach
pesca noce nectarine
pinoli pine nuts
pompelmo grapefruit
prugna/susina prune/plum
uva grapes

Dolci (Desserts)

amaretti macaroons
cannoli crisp pastry tubes filled with ricotta,
  cream, chocolate or fruit
coppa gelato assorted ice cream
crème caramel caramel-topped custard

A wide variety of **fish**, fresh or sun-dried, comes from the Lakes, especially trout, pike, perch, tench, chub, whitefish, barbel, bleak, eel, allice shad and, in Lake Garda, the prized *carpione*, a kind of plankton-feeding carp that lends its name to a common preparation, *in carpione* (fried and marinated with herbs). Chefs in the better restaurants do magical things with them. Admirers of slippery dishes like eels, frogs or snails will find happiness in the lowlands of the Po. Donkey meat appears with

crostata fruit flan

gelato (produzione propria) ice cream (home-made)

granita flavoured ice, often lemon or coffee

monte bianco chestnut pudding with cream

panettone sponge cake with candied fruit and raisins

panforte dense cake of chocolate, almonds and preserved fruit

saint-honoré meringue cake

semifreddo refrigerated cake

sorbetto sorbet/sherbet

spumone a soft ice cream

tiramisù layers of sponge, mascarpone, coffee and chocolate

torrone nougat

torta cake, tart

torta millefoglie layered pastry and custard cream

zabaglione eggs and Marsala wine, whipped until frothy and served hot

zuppa inglese trifle

Bevande (Beverages)

acqua minerale mineral water
  con/senza gas with/without fizz

aranciata orange soda

birra (alla spina) (draught) beer

caffè (freddo) (iced) coffee

cioccolata chocolate

gassosa lemon-flavoured soda

latte (intero/scremato) (whole/skimmed) milk

limonata lemon soda

succo di frutta fruit juice

tè tea

vino wine
  rosso red
  bianco white
  rosato rosé

Miscellaneous Cooking Terms

aceto (balsamico) (balsamic) vinegar

affumicato smoked

aglio garlic

alla brace on embers

bicchiere glass

burro butter

cacciagione game

conto bill

costoletta/cotoletta chop

coltello knife

cucchiaio spoon

filetto fillet

forchetta fork

forno oven

fritto fried

ghiaccio ice

griglia grill

in bianco without tomato

magro lean meat/pasta without meat

marmellata jam

menta mint

miele honey

mostarda candied mustard sauce

olio oil

pane bread

pane tostato toasted bread

panini sandwiches (in roll)

panna cream

pepe pepper

piatto plate

prezzemolo parsley

ripieno stuffed

rosmarino rosemary

sale salt

salmè wine marinade

salsa sauce

salvia sage

senape mustard

tartufi truffles

tavola table

tazza cup

tovagliolo napkin

tramezzini finger sandwiches

umido cooked in sauce

uovo egg

zucchero sugar

alarming frequency on menus from Lake Orta to Mantua; even King Kong would balk before *stu'a'd'asnin cünt la pulenta* (stewed donkey with polenta). But don't despair – other **meat courses** include classics such as *ossobuco alla milanese* (veal knuckle braised with white wine and tomatoes, properly served with *risotto*), *cotoletta alla milanese* (breaded cutlet – the Lombard wiener schnitzel), duckling (excellent in *Nedar*, with macaroni), *fritto misto* (veal slices, calves' liver, artichokes and zucchini, fried in breadcrumbs), *busseca* (tripe stew, with eggs, cheese and cream), *fritto alla lombarda* (rabbit pieces fried in breadcrumbs) and the hearty regional pork and cabbage stew, *cazzoela* or *cassuoela* (two of 25 different spellings).

Gorgonzola, Marscarpone, Bel Paese and *grana padano* (like parmesan) are the region's most famous **cheeses**, and *Bitto*, made of goat's and sheep's milk in the Valtellina, is worth a try. Polenta sneaks its way into **desserts**, but *torta di tagliatelle* (a cake with egg pasta and almonds) is perhaps more appealing. Each province has its own highly individual sweets, although the Milanese cake *panettone*, a light fruit cake with raisins and candied fruit, has become a Christmas tradition all over the country.

Wine

Italy is a place where everyday wine is cheaper than cola or milk, and where nearly every family owns vineyards or has relatives who supply their daily needs – which are not great. Despite living in one of the world's largest wine-growing countries, Italians imbibe relatively little; shockingly, teetotallers number in the millions.

To accompany its infinite variety of regional dishes, Italy produces an equally bewildering array of regional wines, many of which are rarely exported and best drunk young. Unless you're dining at a restaurant with an exceptional cellar, do as the Italians do and order a carafe of the local wine (*vino locale* or *vino della casa*). It's inexpensive, and you won't often go wrong. Most wines are named after the grape and the district they come from. If the label says **DOC** (*Denominazione di Origine Controllata*) it means that the wine comes from a specially defined area and was made according to a certain method. Lombardy produces many commendable wines which are comparable with the more illustrious vintages of Piedmont and Tuscany, although its residents often snobbily prefer to drink wine from other regions, leaving the enterprising Swiss (many of whom own local vineyards) to snap up the most interesting vintages and whistle them over the border.

Lombardy's noblest wines come from the **Valtellina**, where the vines grow on steep walled terraces, and cables are used to transfer the harvested grapes to the valleys below (*see* p.228). Delicious light sparkling wines, fresh white wines and mellow reds hail from the **Franciacorta** region, and are often found in restaurant carafes around the Lakes. Southwest Lombardy's Po valley produces a large quantity of wine, in a huge zone known as DOC **Oltrepò Pavese**, much sold through cooperatives; the three potent reds with funny names, Buttafuoco, Barbacarlo and Sangue di Giuda, go down especially well. **Lake Garda** is surrounded by vineyards, from the well-known Bardolino and Bianco di Custoza to the elegant dry white Lugano.

Italians are fond of post-prandial digestives – the famous Stock or Vecchia Romagna **brandies** are always good. *Grappa* (*acquavite*) is usually tougher, and often drunk in black coffee (a *caffè corretto*). **Fernet Branca**, **Cynar** and **Averna** are other popular aperitif/digestives, as are liqueurs like **Strega**, the witch potion from Benevento, as well as apricot-flavoured **Amaretto**, lemon-flavoured **Limoncello**, cherry **Maraschino** from Sorrento, aniseed **Sambuca**, and locally brewed elixirs, Braulio or San Giacomo.

Travel

Getting There

By Air from the UK and Ireland

International flights to Milan (the gateway to Lombardy) use **Malpensa Airport**, 50km northwest of the city; domestic and European flights use **Linate Airport**, 7km east, or **Orio al Serio** Airport, Bergamo, 50km northeast. Flights are often diverted to Malpensa in winter due to fog. Between late October and early March, try to book a flight that will arrive 10am–3pm; this is when the fog lifts.

Direct scheduled flights to Milan are operated by Alitalia, Lufthansa, easyJet, Ryanair and British Airways. Besides London, you can also fly from Birmingham, Bristol, Southampton, Liverpool, Newcastle or Manchester. Alternatively, BA has one direct flight a day to Verona – which will bring you much closer to Lake Garda.

The advantages of paying a **scheduled** fare is that few restrictions are imposed on when you travel or how long you stay. Promotional perks, such as rental cars and tours, may also be included. On the more expensive '**flexible fares**', children travel for greatly reduced prices (10% for the under-twos on an adult's lap; 33% discount for children aged 2–11). Bona fide **students** with ID also receive handsome discounts. Special fares booked in advance, however (APEX and so on), may save you as much as 50% of the cost.

Typical economy fares to Milan on British Airways, KLM or Alitalia are currently around £110–£150 return (not including taxes) in high season. Ticket changes involve high penalties.

The direct flights from **Ireland** to Italy are from Dublin to Milan with Aer Lingus, with connections for Cork and Galway on certain

Airline Carriers

UK and Ireland
Aer Lingus, UK, t 0845 084 4444; Ireland, t 0818 365 000, www.aerlingus.com.
Alitalia, London, t 0870 544 8259; Dublin, t (01) 677 5171, www.alitalia.com.
bmibaby, t 0870 264 2229, www.bmibaby.com.
British Airways, t 0870 850 9850, www.ba.com.
British Midland, t 0870 60 70 555, www.flybmi.com.
easyJet, t 0870 607 6543, www.easyjet.com.
KLM Direct, t 0870 507 4074, www.klm.com.
Lufthansa, t 0845 7737 747, www.lufthansa.com.
Ryanair, UK t 0906 270 5656; Ireland t 1530 787 787, www.ryanair.com.

USA and Canada
Air Canada, t 888 247 2262, www.aircanada.ca.
Alitalia, USA, t 800 223 5730, www.alitaliausa.com; Canada, t 800 361 8336, www.alitalia.ca.
American Airlines, t 800 433 7300, www.aa.com.
British Airways, t 800 AIRWAYS, t 416 250 0880, www.ba.com.
Continental, t 800 231 0856, www.continental.com.
Delta, t 800 241 4141, www.delta.com.
Northwest Airlines, t 800 447 4747, www.nwa.com.
United Airlines, t 800 UNITED, www.ual.com.

Discounts and Students

Besides saving 25% on regular flights, young people under 26 have the choice of flying on special discount charters.

UK and Ireland
Budget Travel, 134 Lower Baggot Street, Dublin 2, t (01) 631 1075, www.budgettravel.ie.
Europe Student Travel, 6 Campden Street, London W8, t (020) 7727 7647. They cater for non-students as well.
Italflights, 125 High Holborn, London WC1V 6QA, t (020) 7405 6771, www.sardinia-holidays.co.uk.
LAI, 185 King's Cross Road, London, WC1X 9DB, t (020) 7837 8492, www.laitravel.co.uk.
MagicTravel Group, King's Place, 12–42 Wood St, Kingston-upon-Thames, KT1 1JF, t 0870 027 0480, www.magictravelgroup.co.uk. Italian travel specialists which incorporate Italy Sky Shuttle, Magic of Italy and Italian Escapades.

days (£200, not including taxes); or Alitalia. Both fly at least once daily, less often out of season. Alternatively, travel to London and fly from there. The cheapest Dublin to London fares are often found with Ryanair, flying several times a day to Stansted or Luton, though Aer Lingus and British Midland take you direct to Heathrow for around £75. Both British Airways and British Midland operate direct flights from Belfast to Heathrow.

Cheap Flights, Discounts and Special Deals

London is a great centre for discounted flights; both Alitalia and BA often have competitive fares, and **easyJet** often have flights from Stansted to Milan Linate from £40. **bmibaby** flies from the East Midlands or Cardiff to Milan (Bergamo) from £20 one way, **Ryanair** flies from London Stansted and Luton airports to Bergamo from £10 (without taxes) one way.

Classified sections of weekend newspapers also advertise discounted fares (in London, get *Time Out* or other listings magazines, and the *Evening Standard*, or the newspapers such as *TNT* or *Trailfinder* from outside tube stations). Peak seasons are Easter and summer, when there are generally a couple of flights a day from London (book well ahead).

The major specialist agencies are **Italy Sky Shuttle**, **Italflights** and **LAI**. Rock-bottom fares are often subject to restrictions, and departure or arrival times may be inconvenient or uncertain.

By Air from the USA and Canada

American Airlines, British Airways, Continental, Delta, Northwest Airlines, United Airlines and Air Canada all have direct flights to Rome or Milan from a number of cities,

STA, t 0870 160 0599, 6 Wrights Lane, W8 6TA, London, *www.statravel.co.uk*. With several UK branches.
Trailfinders, 215 Kensington High Street, London W8 6BD, t (020) 7937 1234, *www.trailfinders.com*. Branches in many UK cities.
United Travel, Stillorgan Bowl, Stillorgan, Ireland, t (01) 283 2555, *www.unitedtravel.ie*.

Websites
www.expedia.co.uk
www.lastminute.com
www.majortravel.co.uk
www.opodo.co.uk
www.skydeals.co.uk
www.sky-tours.co.uk
www.thomascook.co.uk
www.travellersweb.ws
www.travelocity.com
www.travelselect.com

USA and Canada
Airhitch, t (212) 864 2000, *www.airhitch.org*. Last-minute seating.
Council Travel, 205 E. 42nd Street, New York, NY 10017, t 800 2COUNCIL, *www.counciltravel.com*. Specialists in student and charter flights; several US branches. Can also provide Eurail and Britrail passes.

Last Minute Travel Club, 41–1154 Chemong Road, Peterborough, Ontario, K9H 7J6, Canada, t 877 970 3500, *www.lastminuteclub.com*.
Now Voyager Travel, 315 W49th St, New York, NY 10019, t 800 781 4040, *www.nowvoyagertravel.com*. For courier flights.
STA, 10 Downing Street, New York, NY 10014, t (212) 627 3111, *www.statravel.com*; ASUC Building, 2nd Floor, University of California, Berkeley, CA 94720, t (510) 642 3000. With branches at other US universities.
TFI Tours, 34 West 32nd Street, NY, NY 10001, t (212) 736 1140, t 800 745 8000, *www.tfitours.com*.
Travel Cuts, 187 College St, Toronto, Ontario M5T 1P7, t 866 246 9762, *www.travelcuts.com*. Canada's largest student travel specialists.

Websites
www.air-fare.com
www.expedia.com
www.flights.com
www.orbitz.com
www.priceline.com
www.travellersweb.ws
www.travelocity.com
www.smarterliving.com

including New York, Boston, Miami, Chicago, Los Angeles, Toronto or Montreal, but Alitalia has the most options. Summer round-trip fares from New York to Italy cost around US$1,300; from Montreal or Toronto about CAN$1,500–2,000.

A reasonably economical alternative is to take a flight to London or some other European city and change there. APEX or SuperAPEX deals are also better value than scheduled fares, though you may prefer to pay extra for security, flexibility and convenience on such a long journey (9–15 hours' flying time). Beware the restrictions imposed on special fares, and plan well in advance. Low-season flights (Nov–March) tend to be cheaper than peak-season ones, and mid-week fares are usually lower than at weekends.

As in Britain, cheap deals are often advertised in the travel sections of major US and Canadian newspapers.

By Train

Lombardy is easy to access by rail from the UK. The journey is usually accomplished in two stages, with a change at Paris. First take the **Eurostar** from London Waterloo to Paris Gare du Nord (3hrs). From Paris you can either travel by day to Milan on a fast TGV (7hrs), which leaves from the Gare de Lyon; or you can travel overnight (in a couchette) on a slower train (10½hrs) from the Gare de Bercy. Allow one hour to cross Paris (by *métro*). High season tickets from London to Milan start at about £216 return on the TGV route, and £195 return for the overnight route; in other words, travelling by train from the UK is scarcely cheaper than flying, unless you are able to take advantage of student or youth fares (about £150 for those under 26). Discounts are available for families and young children. Interail (UK) or Eurail (USA/Canada) passes give unlimited travel for all ages throughout Europe for one or two months. If you are just planning to see Italy, these passes may not be worthwhile (*see* 'Getting Around', p.47, for details on specific Italian rail passes). A month's full Interail pass costs £355, or £249 for the under-26s; for France and Italy only it costs £265, or £189 for the under-26s. Contact **Rail Europe**, 178 Piccadilly, London W1V 0BA,

t 0870 837 1341, *www.raileurope.co.uk*, or in the US, **Rail Europe**, 44 S. Broadway, White Plains, NY 10601, t (877) 257 2887; in Canada, t 800 361 RAIL, *www.raileurope.com*.

Cheap youth fares are also available, but you should organize these before you leave home. For timetables see **Italian Railways**, *www.trenitalia.com*. To purchase Italian rail passes before you leave home contact **Rail Choice**, UK t (020) 7939 9915, *www.railchoice.co.uk*. Rail Choice often have further discounts for students and under-26s using Eurostar.

CIT offices, which act as agents for Italian State Railways, offer various deals; contact them in the **UK** at The Atrium, London Road, Crawley, West Sussex, t 0870 909 7555, *www.citalia.co.uk*; in the **USA** at 10th floor, 15 West 44th St, New York, NY 10173, t 800 CIT TOUR, *www.cit-tours.com*; in **Canada** at 7007 Islington Avenue, Suite 205, Woodbridge, Ontorio, t (905) 264 1158, *www.cittours-canada.com*.

In **Italy**, a good bet for discounted train tickets, flights etc. is **CTS**, at Corso P. Ticinese 83, Milan, t 02 837 2674, *www.cts.it*.

A convenient pocket-sized **timetable**, detailing all the main and secondary Italian railway lines, is now available in the UK for a small cost. Contact the Italian State Tourist Board (ENIT), 1 Princes Street, London W1B 2AY, t (020) 7408 1254, or Italwings Travel Services, 162–8 Regent St, London W1R 5TB, t (020) 7287 2117. If you wait until you arrive in Italy, however, you can pick up the Northern Italy timetable at any station.

By Coach

Eurolines, 52 Grosvenor Gardens, London SW1, t 08705 808080 or t 08705 143 219, *www.nationalexpress.com,* is Europe's main international **coach** operator, with representatives in Italy and many other countries; tickets are booked through National Express. Regular services run to many northern Italian cities (on Wed or Sat), including Milan, where they will generally arrive at the Piazza Castello. The journey is long (20–24 hours), with a small saving in price compared with air fares, or even rail travel. However, if it isn't pitch-dark, you'll catch a fleeting glimpse of Mont Blanc and Turin on the way.

By Car

To bring a UK-registered car into Italy, you need a vehicle registration document, full driving licence and insurance papers. Non-EU citizens should have an international driving licence with an Italian translation incorporated. Your vehicle should display a nationality plate indicating its country of registration. From the UK, it's about 24 hours' driving time even if you stick to fast toll roads.

Eurotunnel trains, **t** 08705 353 535, *www. eurotunnel.com*, shuttle cars and their passengers through the Channel Tunnel from Folkestone to Calais on a simple drive-on-drive-off system (journey time 35mins). In off-peak months it may be possible to turn up without a reservation and take the next available service. Eurotunnel runs 24 hours a day, year round, with a service at least once an hour through the night. Standard return fares range from £170 to £350, but special offers can bring them as low as £99.

There are several options if you take your car over by sea. Prices range from £51 return for a foot passenger to £450 and upwards return for a vehicle with two passengers in high season, but cheaper APEX fares are available if you book in advance. **Brittany Ferries**, **t** 08703 665 333, *www.brittany-ferries.co.uk*, sail Poole–Cherbourg, Portsmouth–Caen and St-Malo, and Plymouth–Roscoff. **Hoverspeed Fast Ferries**, **t** 0870 240 870, *www.hover speed.com*, sail Dover–Calais (1hr). **P&O**, **t** 0870 600 0600, *www.poferries.com*, sail Dover–Calais, and Portsmouth–Le Havre.

Once on the Continent, the most scenic and hassle-free route is via the Alps, avoiding crowded Riviera roads in summer, but if you take a route through Switzerland expect to pay for the privilege (£14 or SF30 for motorway use). In winter, the passes may be closed and you will have to stick to those expensive tunnels (one-way tolls range from about €16 for a small car). You can avoid some of the driving by putting your car on a train and travelling with it overnight on a sleeper, but only as far as Nice. The service starts from Calais in the summer, and from Paris in the winter. Prices start at £250 one way, so this is scarcely a cheap option. For further information, contact **French Motorail**, **t** 08702 415 415, *www.frenchmotorail.com*.

Entry Formalities

Passports and Visas

EU nationals with a valid passport can enter and stay in Italy as long as they like. Citizens of the USA, Canada, Australia and New Zealand need only a valid passport to stay up to three months in Italy; this can be extended by obtaining a special visa in advance from an Italian embassy or consulate (*see* p.54).

By law you should register with the police within eight days of your arrival in Italy. In practice this is done automatically for most visitors when they check in at their first hotel. Don't be alarmed if the owner of your self-catering property proposes to 'denounce' you to the police – it's just a formality.

Customs

Since July 1999, duty-free goods have been unavailable on journeys within the European Union but prices haven't necessarily gone up, as shops at airports do not always choose to pass on the cost of the duty. It does mean that if you are travelling within the EU there is virtually no limit on how much you can buy, as long as it is for your own use. Guidelines are issued and, if they are exceeded, you may be asked to prove you are going to consume it all.

Non-EU citizens visiting the EU can buy duty-free on their way home, but face restrictions on how much they can take back. If they have been away for more than 48 hours, North Americans over the age of 21 can take 1 litre of alcohol, 200 cigarettes and 100 cigars home with them. They can take $400 worth of goods duty-free, and pay 10% tax on the next $1,000 worth of goods. After that, the tax is worked out on an item-by-item basis.

For more information, contact **US Customs**: PO Box 7407, Washington, DC 20044, **t** (202) 927 6724, *www.customs.ustreas.gov* and request the free booklet, *Know Before You Go*.

> ## Motoring Organizations
> **AA**, **t** (0870) 600 0371 (UK), *www.theaa.com*.
> **RAC**, **t** (0800) 550055 (50p per minute), *www.rac.co.uk*, in the UK.
> **AAA**, **t** (800) 222 4357/(212) 757 2000, *www.aaa.com*, in the USA.

Tour Operators and Special Interest Holidays

UK operators offer holidays in the Italian Lakes area, including many tours of gardens and villas, and painting courses. City and opera visits to Milan can also be arranged. Not all those operators listed below are necesssarily ABTA-bonded; check before booking.

In the UK

Abercrombie & Kent, Sloane Square House, Holbein Place, London SW1W 8NS, t 0845 070 0610, *www.abercrombiekent.co.uk*. Milan in all seasons; gardens of the Veneto and Lombardy.

ACE Study Tours, Babraham, Cambridge CB2 4AP, t (01223) 835 055, *www.study-tours.org*. Italian lakes, villas and gardens.

Brompton Travel, Brompton House, 64 Richmond Road, Kingston-upon-Thames, KT2 5EH, t (020) 8839 83672, *www.brompton travel.co.uk*. Tailor-made and opera tours.

Cosmos, Wren Court, 17 London Rd, Bromley, Kent BR1 1DE, t 0870 443 5285, *www.cosmos holidays.co.uk*. Lakes guided tours.

Cresta Holidays, Tabley Court, Victoria St, Altringham, Cheshire WA14 1EZ, t 0870 238 7711, *www.crestaholidays.co.uk*. Milan city tours; Como.

Eclipse Direct, First Choice House, Peel Cross Road, Salford, Manchester, M5 2AN, t 0870 243 4300, *www.eclipsedirect.co.uk*.

Italiatour, 71 Lower Road, Kenley, Surrey, CR8 5NH, t 0870 733 3000, *www.italiatour.co.uk*. Milan opera and football package tours.

JMB, 3 Powick Mills, Old Road, Worcester WR2 4BU, t (01905) 422 282, *www.jmb-travel. co.uk*. Opera tours.

Kirker, 4 Waterloo Court, 10 Theed Street, London SE1 8ST, t 0870 112 3333, *www. kirkerholidays.com*. Milan city breaks.

Magic Travel Group, King's Place, 12–42 Wood St, Kingston-upon-Thames, KT1 1JY, t 0800 980 3378, *www.magictravelgroup.com*.

Martin Randall Travel, Voysey House, Barley Mow Passage, London W4 4GFH, t (020) 8742 3355, *www.martinrandall.com*. Duchy of Milan and opera tours (guest lecturers).

Page & Moy, 136–140 London Rd, Leicester LE2 1EN, t 0870 906 3518, *www.page -moy.co.uk*. Gardens.

Prospect Music & Art, 36 Manchester St, London W1U 7LH, t (020) 7486 5704, *www.prospecttours.com*. Opera, villas and gardens.

Saga, The Saga Building, Middelburg Sq, Folkestone, Kent CT20 1AZ, t (01303) 771 111, *www.saga.co.uk*. Offers trips devoted to the majesty of the lakes.

Shearings, Miry Lane, Wigan, Lancashire WN3 4AG, t (01942) 824 824, *www.shearings holidays.com*. Provide accompanied tours of the lakes.

Travel for the Arts, 12–15 Hanger Green, London W5 3EL, t (020) 8604 2242, *www. travelforthearts.co.uk*. Custom-made Milan opera holidays.

Venice Simplon-Orient Express, Sea Containers House, 20 Upper Ground, London SE1 9PF, t (020) 7928 6000, *www. orient-express.com*.

Wallace Arnold, Lowfields Road, Leeds, LS12 6DH, t (0113) 263 4234, *www.wallacearnold. com*. Coach tours of the lakes.

In the USA

Abercrombie & Kent, 1520 Kensington Rd, Suite 212, Oak Brook, IL 60532, t 800 554 7016, *www.abercrombiekent.com*.

CIT Tours, *www.cit-tours.com*, 10th floor, 15 West 44th St, New York, NY 10036, t 0800 CIT-TOUR; in Canada, 7007 Islington Avenue, Suite 205, Woodbridge, Ontario, t (905) 264 0158, *www.cittours-canada.com*.

Dailey-Thorp Travel, 475 Park Avenue S., New York, NY 10016, t (307) 673 1555, *www. daileythorp.com*. Milan opera.

Maupintour, 10650 W. Charleston Bvd, Summerline, NV 89135, t 800 255 4266, *www.maupintour.com*.

Trafalgar Tours, t 8665 444 434, *www. trafalgartours.com*.

Travel Concepts, Suite 101, 8245 Cordova Rd, Cordova TN 38016, t 8901 261 2600. Wine and food.

For camping and self-catering specialists *see* pp.63–4.

Getting Around

Italy has an excellent network of airports, railways, highways and byways, and you'll find getting around fairly easy – until one union or another takes it into its head to go on strike (to be fair, they rarely do it during high season). Certainly learn to recognize the word in Italian: *sciopero* (*sho-per-o*). There's always a day or two's notice, and strikes usually last only a day. Keep your ears out and watch for notices posted in the stations.

By Boat

All the major lakes are crisscrossed by a complex network of *battelli* (boats) and *aliscafi* (hydrofoils), some of which are regular ferries, others cruise or excursion boats either available for hire or operating to set schedules. All services are seasonal, and are massively reduced during the winter. Passes allowing unlimited travel on any particular lake are available. Some services transcend frontiers and pass into Swiss waters. Ask for timetables at tourist offices, or if you're in Milan call in at the *Gestione Navigazione Laghi*, Via L Ariosto 21, t 02 467 6101, t 800 551801 (toll-free from Italy), *www.navlaghi.it*. Individual companies are listed by each lake.

By Train

FS Informa (train info), 7am–9pm, t 89 2021, www.trenitalia.it.

Italy's national railway, the **FS** (*Ferrovie dello Stato*), the most serendipitous national line in Europe, is well run, inexpensive and often a pleasure to ride. (Note that Lombardy also has several private rail lines, which, unlike the FS, won't accept Interail or Eurail passes.) Possible FS unpleasantnesses you may encounter, besides a strike, are delays, crowding (especially at weekends and in the summer), and crime on overnight trains, where someone rifles your bags while you sleep. It is wise to reserve a seat in advance, for a small fee, at the *prenotazione* counter. On the upper-echelon trains, **reservations** are mandatory and can be made up to the last minute. For standard trains, reservations close three hours before departure; at Rome and Milan stations, reservations for standard trains and wagon-lits close four hours before departure. Do check when you buy your ticket in advance that the date is correct: tickets are valid for two months from the day of purchase, unless specified otherwise. Tickets need to be punched before getting on the train (machines are on the platforms and in the station halls). They are valid 6 hours after this for journeys up to 200km, 24 hours for longer trips (48 in case of intermediate stops, provided they are punched again); and return tickets must be punched before each journey. A number on your reservation slip will indicate which car your seat is in – find it before you board rather than after. The same goes for sleepers and couchettes on overnight trains, which must also be reserved in advance.

Tickets may be purchased not only in the stations, but at many travel agents in the city centres. Fares are determined by the kilometres travelled. The system is computerized and runs smoothly, at least until you try to get a reimbursement for an unused ticket (not worth the trouble). Ask which platform (*binario*) your train arrives at; the big boards posted in the stations are not always correct. If you get on a train without a ticket you can buy one from the conductor, but you will have to pay a 20% penalty. You can also pay a conductor if you want to move up to first class or get a couchette. Try to avoid travel on Friday evenings, when the major lines out of the big cities are packed.

There is a fairly straightforward **hierarchy of trains**. At the bottom of the pyramid is the humble *locale* (euphemistically known sometimes as an *accelerato*) which often stops even where there's no station in sight – it can be excruciatingly slow. When you're checking the schedules, beware of what may look like the first train to your destination – if it's a *locale*, it will be the last to arrive. A *diretto* stops far less, an *expresso* just at the main towns. *Intercity* trains whoosh between the big cities and rarely deign to stop. *Eurocity* trains link Italian cities with major European centres. Both of these services require you to pay a supplement some 30% more than a regular fare. Reservations are free but must be made at least five hours before the trip, and on some trains there are only first-class coaches. The real lords of the rails are the *ETR 450 Pendolino* trains (also known as Eurostar), kilometre-eaters that will speed you to your destination as fast as trains can go (in Italy). For these there is a more costly supplement and, on some only, first-class luxury cars.

The FS offers several **passes**. One, which you should ideally arrange at a CIT or Italian rail agent office (*see* p.44) before arriving in Italy, is the 'Trenitalia Pass', which is valid from 4 to 10 (consecutive or non-consecutive) days within a two-month period. It can be bought at major Italian stations or requested in travel agencies abroad. There are three types of pass: 'Basic' is for adults and can be either for first or second class travel. A youth pass is available for 12-26 year olds, travelling in second class, while small groups (2–5 people) travelling in either first or second class can buy a 'Saver' card. Prices are fairly reasonable. At the time of writing an 8-day second-class ticket for an adult is €264. A 10-day youth ticket is €235.

Remember that you'll need an 'Italian Eurostar Upgrading', if you take Eurostar, which always allows you to reserve a seat (compulsory on Eurostar). You will need other supplements if you book a couchette or bed in overnight trains, and further tickets and fares if you catch Artesia trains.

Other options include the 'Rail Plus Card', which offers a discount of 25% on inter-national and national tickets of the main European rail companies, when combined with an international ticket. This card is valid for one year; costs are €45 for adults and €20 for young people up to the age of 26 years, or for seniors over 60.

European Community citizens can obtain an 'Inter Rail Pass'. These are available from travel agents and railway stations. Italy is located in zone G along with Slovenia, Greece and Turkey. Once you've paid a price equal to 50% of the ticket between your homeland and your final destination country, you are entitled to free unlimited internal travel in the zone you are visiting. Inter Rail passes range from £145 for 16 days unlimited travel in one zone to £285 for a global pass lasting a month. Alternative versions are available for people aged over 26. Further details can be obtained at *www.interrailnet.com*.

Non-European residents might like to consider the 'Eurail Pass', which allows un-limited rail travel around Europe from 4 to 15 days within a two-month period.

Other discounts, available only once you're in Italy, are 15% on same-day return tickets and 3-day returns, and discounts for families of 3–5 people travelling together. Senior citizens (over 60) can also get the yearly *Carta D'argento* ('silver card'), entitling them to a 15% reduction on first or second-class fares. A *Carta Verde* gives the 10% reductions to under 26s, with reductions at Gardaland and youth hostels. *See also* 'Getting There: By Train', p.44.

A *Carto Blu* is ideal for disabled persons. It costs €5 and allows a free ticket for disabled individuals and a full-price one for a companion. The card is valid for five years.

Refreshments on routes of any great distance are provided by bar cars or trolleys; you can usually get sandwiches and coffee from vendors along the tracks at intermediary stops. Station bars often have a good variety of takeaway travellers' fare; consider at least investing in a plastic bottle of mineral water, since there's no drinking water on the trains.

Besides trains and bars, Italy's stations offer **other facilities**. All have a *deposito bagagli*, where you can leave your bags for hours or days for a small fee. The larger ones have porters (who charge per piece) and luggage trolleys; major stations have an *albergo diurno* ('Day Hotel', where you take a shower, get a shave and have a haircut), information offices, currency exchanges open at weekends (but not at the best rates), hotel-finding and reservation services, kiosks with foreign papers, and restaurants. You can also arrange to have a rental car awaiting you at your destination – Avis, Hertz, Europcar and Maggiore are Italy's most widespread firms.

The FS is an honest crap shoot; you may find a train uncomfortably full (in which case stand by the doors or upgrade to first class) or unexpectedly be treated to a dose of genuine Italian charm. If there's a choice, opt for one of the older cars, grey outside but fitted with upholstered seats, Art Deco lamps and old framed pictures. You may just have a beautiful 1920s compartment all to yourself for the night – great if you're travelling with your beloved – and be serenaded on the platform.

By Coach and Bus

Inter-city coach travel is sometimes quicker than train travel, but a bit more expensive. The Italians aren't dumb; you will find regular coach connections only where there is no train to offer competition. **Coaches** almost always depart from the vicinity of the train station, and tickets usually need to be purchased before you get on. In many regions they are the only means of public transport and are well used, with frequent schedules. If you can't get a ticket before the coach leaves, get on anyway and pretend you can't speak a word of Italian; the worst that can happen is that someone will make you pay for a ticket. The base for all **country bus** lines will be the provincial capitals.

City buses are the traveller's friend. Most northern cities label routes well; all charge flat fees, though the price depends on the town. Milan currently charges €1 both for the underground and for train/bus tickets (the latter are valid for 75mins after punching). Bus tickets must always be purchased before you get on, either at a tobacconist's, a newspaper kiosk, in bars or from ticket machines near the main stops. Once you get on, you must 'obliterate' your ticket in the machines in the front or back of the bus. Controllers stage random checks to make sure you've punched your ticket, although many passengers take a chance and travel without a ticket.

By Car

A car is the best and most convenient way to get to the more remote parts of Lombardy, but quite unnecessary in Milan, where public transport is extremely efficient and parking is hell on wheels. Other large towns, like Bergamo, can also be a headache.

Third-party insurance is a minimum requirement in Italy. Obtain a Green Card from your insurer, which gives proof you are covered. Also get a **European Accident Statement** form, in case you are unlucky enough to have an accident. Always insist on a full translation of any statement you are asked to sign.

Breakdown assistance insurance is a sensible investment (e.g. AA's Five Star or RAC's Eurocover Motoring Assistance). Don't give the local police any excuse to fine you on the spot for minor infringements like worn tyres or burnt-out sidelights. A **red triangular hazard sign** is obligatory; also recommended are a spare set of bulbs, a first-aid kit and a fire extinguisher. Note that spare parts may be tricky to find for non-Italian cars.

Petrol (*benzina*; unleaded is *benzina senza piombo*, and diesel *gasolio*) is very expensive, about €1.20 a litre. Many petrol stations close for lunch in the afternoon, and few stay open late at night, though you may find a 'self-service' machine which takes nice, smooth €5 notes. **Motorway** (*autostrada*) tolls are also quite high (though the rest-stops and petrol stations along the motorways stay open 24 hours). Other roads – *superstrade* on down through the Italian grading system – are free of charge. **Speed limits** (generally ignored) are 130kph on motorways (110kph for cars under 1100cc or motorcycles), 110kph on main highways, 90kph on secondary roads and 50kph in built-up areas. Speeding fines can be very high and include penalties for jumping red lights.

Italians are famously anarchic behind the wheel, though perhaps a smidgeon less so in the Lombardy region than further south. Warnings, signals, and general rules of the road are frequently ignored; a two-lane carriageway becomes an impromptu three-lane road at a moment's notice. The only way to beat the locals is to join them. Bear in mind the ancient maxim that those who hesitate are lost. All drivers, from boy racers to elderly nuns, tempt Providence by overtaking at the most dangerous of bends, and no matter how fast you are hammering along the *autostrada*, plenty of other drivers, headlights a-flashing, will fly past at supersonic rates. North Americans used to gentler road manners may find the Italian interpretation of the highway code especially stressful.

If you are undeterred by these caveats, you may actually enjoy driving in Italy, at least away from the congested tourist centres. Signposting is generally good and roads are usually well maintained. Some of the roads are feats of engineering that the Romans themselves would have admired – bravura projects suspended on cliffs, crossing valleys on vast stilts, winding up hairpins. Milan is a major motorway junction, but take care on the A4 (Milan–Turin), which is very busy and an accident blackspot.

Buy a good road map (the Italian Touring Club series is excellent). The **Automobile Club of Italy** (ACI), *www.aci.it*, is helpful for foreign motorists. They offer a free breakdown service, and can be reached from anywhere by dialling **t 803 116** (toll free from Italy) – also use this number if you have to find the nearest service station. If you need major repairs, the ACI can make sure the prices charged are according to their guidelines.

Hiring a Car

Hiring a car or camper van (*autonoleggio*) is simple but not particularly cheap. There are both large international firms through which you can reserve a car in advance, and local agencies, which often have lower prices. Air or rail travellers should check out possible discount packages. Most companies will require a deposit amounting to the estimated cost of the hire. VAT of 19% is applied, so make sure you take this into account when checking prices. Most companies have a minimum age limit of 21 (23 in some cases). A credit card makes life easier, and you will need to produce your licence and a passport. Current rates are around €125 a day for a medium-sized car with unlimited mileage and collision damage waiver, including tax (hire for three days or longer is somewhat less pro rata). Most major rental companies have offices at Milan's airports or the Stazione Centrale. If you need a car for longer than three weeks, leasing may be a more economic alternative. The National Tourist Office has a list of firms in Italy that hire caravans (trailers) or camper vans. Non-residents are not allowed to buy cars in Italy.

By Taxi

Taxis are fairly expensive, so don't take too many of them if you're on a tight budget. The average meter starts at €3 Mon–Sat till 9pm, €5.10 Sun till 9pm; €6.10 daily 9pm–6am, and adds about €1 per kilometre (Milan fares). There are extra charges for luggage (not in Milan) and trips to the airport, and rates go up after 9pm (additional €3, Milan fares) and on Sundays and holidays (€2.10, Milan fares). Extra charges are added automatically (the extra fee flashes on the meter). Taxis usually don't stop if hailed on the streets; head for a taxi-rank (marked with a yellow line on the road). Radio-taxi services operate in Milan.

Hitchhiking

It is illegal to hitch on the *autostrade*, though you may pick up a lift near one of the toll booths. For the best chances of getting a lift travel light, look respectable and take your shades off. Hold a sign indicating your destination if you can. Never hitch at points which may cause an accident or obstruction; Italian traffic conditions are bad enough already. Risks for women are lower in northern Italy than in the more macho south, but it is not advisable to hitch alone. Two or more men may encounter some reluctance.

By Motorcycle or Bicycle

The means of transport of choice for many Italians, motorbikes, mopeds and Vespas can be a delightful way to see the country. You should only consider it, however, if you've ridden them before – Italy's hills and alarming traffic make it no place to learn. You must be at least 14 for a *motorino* (scooter) and 16 for anything more powerful. Helmets are compulsory. Costs for a *motorino* range from about €10 to €17.50 per day, scooters cost somewhat more – up to €25.

Italians are keen cyclists as well, racing drivers up the steepest hills; if you're not training for the Tour de France, consider the region's topography well before planning a cycling tour, especially in the hot summer months. You can hire a bike in most Italian towns. Prices are about €5–€10 per day, which may make buying one worthwhile if you plan to spend much time in the saddle, either in a bike shop or through the classified ad papers put out in nearly every city and region. Alternatively, if you bring your own bike, do check the airlines to see what their policies are on transporting them. Bikes can be transported by train in Italy, either with you or within a couple of days; ask at the baggage office (*ufficio bagagli*).

Practical A–Z

07

Children

Children are still the royalty of Italy, and are pampered, often obscenely spoiled, probably more fashionably dressed than you are, and never allowed to get dirty. In spite of it all, most of them manage to be well-mannered little charmers. If you're bringing your own *bambini* to Italy they'll receive a warm welcome. Many hotels offer advantageous rates for children and have play areas, and many larger cities have permanent **Luna Parks** or funfairs. Child-orientated entertainment is concentrated in the east: Lake Garda's **Gardaland** (similar to Disneyland), the **Parco Minitalia** at Capriate S. Gervasio, the **Parco della Preistoria** (dinosaurs) at Rivolta d'Adda, and the **Parco Natura Viva**, near Lazise east of Lake Garda, which has another leisure park with still more dinosaurs (alas, concrete ones) and an 'autosafari' park. A pair of **water-fun parks** compete in Valeggio sul Mincio, south of Garda. On Lake Maggiore, Stresa's **Villa Pallavicino** has a children's zoo with sea lions and zebras, and children may also like the **doll museum** at Anghera and the **puppet museum** on Isola Madre. There are several places around Lake Como to watch **silk spinning**, and there is a **motorcycle museum** in Mandello sul Lario. Milan's **Natural History Museum** has stuffed rhinos and a good playground in the gardens nearby. Other good bets are **canal tours** or a trip to the top of Milan's **Duomo**. **Lake cruises** are fun for everyone, and children under 12 travel half-price. If a **circus** visits town you're in for a treat; it will either be a sparkling showcase of daredevil skill or perhaps a poignant, family-run, modern version of Fellini's *La Strada*.

Climate and When to Go

Lombardy has the most exciting weather in Italy. Here the climate of the Alps meets the Mediterranean head-on; the large lakes are shielded by the mountains from the worst of winter and they are large enough to maintain a Mediterranean microclimate at prealpine altitudes. The Po valley is another story: chilly and fog-bound in winter, and a steam basket in August.

Winter is a good time not only for skiing but for seeing Milan at its liveliest. The lakes themselves, however, may well be shrouded in mist for weeks on end. **Spring** brings warmer temperatures, blossoming trees and flowers – and few crowds apart from Easter. During the **summer** the lakes are very crowded, though the cities are more or less abandoned to tourists in August and early September. It rarely rains and outside the plains the temperatures are usually remarkably pleasant. Early **autumn**, especially September, is an ideal time for the magnificent colours, the grape harvests and blue balmy days (though rain may intrude during October and November).

Crime and the Police

Police t 113
Carabinieri t 112

Milan, Italy's second city, has even outscandalled Rome in the last few years. This won't affect you, but a fair amount of petty crime might – purse snatchings, pickpocketing, minor thievery of the white-collar kind (always check your change) and car break-ins and theft – but violent crime is rare.

Average Temperatures in °C (°F)

	Jan	April	July	Oct
Milan	1.9 (35)	13.2 (55)	24.8 (76)	13.7 (56)
Lake Como	6 (43)	13.3 (55)	23.7 (74)	9.8 (50)
Lake Maggiore	5.2 (41)	12.9 (55)	23.9 (75)	10.1 (50)
Lake Garda	4 (39)	13.2 (56)	24.5 (75)	14.7 (58)

Average Monthly Rainfall in mm (in)

	Jan	April	July	Oct
Milan	62 (2½)	82 (3)	47 (2)	75 (3)
Lake Como	74 (3)	47 (2)	12 (0.5)	20 (1)
Lake Maggiore	90 (3½)	61 (2½)	20 (1)	22 (1)
Lake Garda	31 (1)	62 (2½)	72 (3)	89 (3½)

Purse-snatchers can be discouraged if you stay on the inside of the pavement and keep a firm hold on your property. Pickpockets strike in crowded buses and gatherings; don't carry too much cash, and split it so you won't lose the lot at once. In popular tourist sights beware groups of scruffy-looking women or children with placards, apparently begging for money. They use distraction techniques to perfection, and in general the smallest and most innocent-looking child is the most skilful pickpocket. Be extra careful in train stations, don't leave valuables in hotel rooms, and always park your car in guarded lots or on well-lit streets. Purchasing small quantities of soft drugs for personal consumption is technically legal in Italy, though it is best avoided.

The *carabinieri*, quasi-military squads of black-uniformed police, deal mostly with national security. Local matters are usually in the hands of the *polizia urbana*; the nattily dressed *vigili urbani* are concerned with traffic issues and parking fines.

Disabled Travellers

Italy's provisions for disabled travellers are fairly poor, though progress is gradually being made. The Italian national tourist office or CIT (travel agency) can advise on hotels, museums with ramps, etc. If you book your rail travel through CIT you can request assistance if you are a wheelchair user. Local tourist offices are also helpful.

Alternatively, you can contact Milano per tutti, an organization dedicated to disabled people who want to visit Milan, which can provide detailed information about restaurants, hotels, museums and nightlife. Their website is at *www.milanopertutti.it* and has an English-language version. Otherwise you can contact them on **t** (02) 330 2021.

UK
Assistance Travel Service, 1 Tank Lane, Purfleet, Essex RM19 1TA, **t** (01708) 863198, *www.assistedholidays.com*. Organizes tailor-made trips for people with any disability.
Holiday Care Service, 7th Floor, Sunley House, 4 Bedford Park, Croydon, Surrey CR0 2AP, **t** 0845 124 9971, minicom: **t** 0845 124 9976,

www.holidaycare.org.uk. Information sheets on travel for those with disabilities.
RADAR (Royal Association for Disability & Rehabilitation), 12 City Forum, 250 City Rd, London EC1V 8AF, **t** (020) 7250 3222, *www.radar.org.uk*. For information and books on travelling abroad.
RNIB (Royal National Institute for the Blind), 105 Judd Street, London WC1H 9NE, **t** (020) 7388 1266, *www.rnib.org.uk*. For the blind and visually impaired.

USA
Alternative Leisure Co, **t** (718) 275 0023, *www.alctrips.com*. Organizes vacations abroad.
American Foundation for the Blind, 11 Penn Plaza, Suite 300, New York, NY 10001, **t** 800 232 5463, *www.afb.org*. For visually impaired travellers.
Mobility International USA, PO Box 10767, Eugene, OR 97440, **t** (541) 343 1284, *www.miusa.org*. Offers practical advice and information.
MossRehab ResourceNet, **t** 1 800 CALLMOSS, *www.mossresourcenet.org/travel.htm*.
SATH (Society for Accessible Travel and Hospitality), 347 Fifth Ave, Suite 610, New York 10016, **t** (212) 447 7284, *www.sath.org*.
The U.S. Department of Transportation, 400 7th Street, SW, 4107, Washington, DC, 20590, **t** (202) 366 4000 (voice), **t** 800 455 9880 (TTY), *www.dot.gov*.

Other Useful Contacts
Access Ability, *www.access-ability.co.uk*. Offers information on access and travel agencies.
ACROD (Australian Council for the Rehabilitation of the Disabled), P.O. Box 60, Curtin, ACT 2605, Australia, **t** (02) 6283 3200, *www.acrod.org.au*. Information and contact numbers for specialist travel agents.
COIN, Via Enrico Giglioli 54a, 00169 Rome, toll free from Italy **t** 800 271 027, and **COINtel**, **t/f** (06232) 69231, *www.coinsociale.it*. Assists with guided tour bookings and transport information in Italy.
Disabled Persons Assembly, PO Box 27-524, Wellington 6035, New Zealand, **t** (04) 801 9100, *www.dpa.org.nz*.
Emerging Horizons, *www.emerginghorizons.com*. On-line travel newsletter.

Eating Out

If you're uncertain about where to eat, do as you would at home – look for lots of locals. The tip is often included in the bill (*servizio compreso*); if not, it will say *servizio non compreso*, and you will have to add to the bill (*conto*) the bread and cover charge (*pane e coperto*), and a 15% service charge. When you leave a restaurant you will be given a receipt (*scontrino* or *ricevuta fiscale*), which according to Italian law you must take with you out of the door and carry for at least 60 metres!

Since January 2005, smoking is not allowed in restaurants and indoor public venues except for reserved spaces, usually called 'Sala Fumatori' (smoking rooms).

Embassies and Consulates

Italian Consulates Abroad

Australia and New Zealand: Level 45, 'The Gateway', 1 Macquarie Place, Sydney NSW 2000, t (02) 6273 3333, *www.ambitalia.org.au*.

Canada: 136, Beverly Street, Toronto, Ontario M5T 1Y5, t (416) 977 1566, *www.toronto.italconsulate.org*; 3489 Drummond Street, Montreal, Quebec H3G 1X6, t (514) 849 8351, *www.italconsul.montreal.qc.ca*.

Ireland: 63–5 Northumberland Road, Dublin, t (01) 660 1744.

UK: 38 Eaton Place, London SW1X 8AN, t (020) 7235 9371; (embassy), 14 Three Kings' Yard, London W1Y 2EH, t (020) 7312 2200, *www.embitaly.org.uk*; 32 Melville St, Edinburgh EH3 7HA, t (0131) 226 3631; Rodwell Tower, 111 Piccadilly, Manchester M1 2HY, t (0161) 236 9024, *www.italianconsulate.co.uk*.

USA: 690 Park Ave, New York, NY 10021, t (212) 737 9100, *www.italconsulnyc.org*; 12400 Wilshire Blvd, Suite 300, Los Angeles CA 90025, t (310) 820 0622, *www.sedi.esteri.it/losangeles*.

Restaurant Price Categories

For a three-course meal with wine, per person:

very expensive over €45
expensive €30–45
moderate €20–30
inexpensive up to €20

Consulates and Embassies in Italy

Australia: Via Borgogna 2, Milan, t 02 777 041, *www.australian-embassy.it*.

Ireland: Piazza San Pietro in Gessate 2, Milan, t 02 5518 7569.

Canada: Via V. Pisani 19, Milan, t 02 67581, *www.canada.it*.

UK: Via San Paolo 7, Milan, t 02 723 001, *www.britain.it*.

USA: Via P.Amedeo 2/10, Milan, t 02 290 351, *www.usembassy.it*.

Festivals

Festivals in Italy are often more show than spirit, but there are several exceptions to this rule. Some are great costume affairs dating back to the Middle Ages or Renaissance; others recall ancient pre-Christian religious practices. Many festivals are devoted to the favourite national pastime – food. Check with local tourist offices for precise dates: many are liable to slide into the nearest weekend. For a Calendar of Events, *see* pp.55–6.

Gay and Lesbian

ARCIGay, Via Bezzecca 3, Milan, t 02 5412 2225, *www.arcigay.it*, and **ARCILesbica** Corso Garibaldi 91, t 02 2901 4027, *www.arcilesbica.it*. Provide advice and information for gay and lesbian visitors. There's further information on *www.gay.it/guida*, with listings of gay-friendly bars, clubs, festivals and magazines.

Health and Emergencies

Fire t 115

Ambulance (or emergencies) **t 118**

Non-emergencies can be treated at a *pronto soccorso* (casualty/first aid department) at any hospital clinic (*ambulatorio*), or at a local health unit (*unita sanitaria locale* – ASL). Airports and main railway stations also have **first-aid** posts. Most Italian doctors speak at least rudimentary English, but if you can't find one contact your consulate. Standards of health care in Milan and Lombardy in general are high. If you have to pay for any health treatment, make sure you get a receipt to claim for reimbursement later.

Calendar of Events

January

Jan–July Opera and ballet at La Scala, **Milan**

5 Pesa Vegia (old weight) festival in **Bellano** (Lake Como); mixes the three kings story with local opposition to Napoleon's introduction of the metric system

6 Three Kings Procession, **Milan**

End of Oct–mid-May Musical afternoons (*I pomeriggi musicali*), **Milan**

17 Sant'Antonio fair, with folklore and human chess game, **Mantua**; *I sarmenti ed i falò* at **Volongo** (Cremona): in a gigantic fire all the 'runners' picked up by the young people are 'burnt'. Meanwhile, the women of the town prepare the local speciality *'torta dura'* (hard cake), flavoured with mint

19 San Bassiano fair, with free tripe, **Lodi**

Last Thurs of Jan Bonfire of the Giubiana, **Cantù** (Como), with fireworks

31 San Giulio, boat procession, **Lake Orta**

February

Carnivals at **Schignano** (Como) with a parade of *bei* or elegant figures and *brutt* (ragged ones), ending with a bonfire; **Bagolino** (Brescia); **Milan** (processions, floats, children's events). **San Giovanni Bianco** (Bergamo), home town of the harlequin, with a bonfire of the famous mask; **Clusone** and **Crema** have cars and masks parades. **Bormio** has a good one, too, with masks

Ash Wednesday Bigolada celebrations at **Castel d'Ario**, (Mantua): communal feasting on spaghetti with anchovies in main piazza

8–13 San Bello at **Berbenno** (Sondrio), folk festival in honour of Fra' Benigno, a handsome local friar

Lent, first Sun Traditional carnival with floats and food, **Grosio** (Sondrio). Middle of Lent; to exorcize winter, **Bergamo** has the bonfire of the *Vecia*, the old woman (Piazza Pontida)

15 Fair for San Faustino, **Brescia's** patron saint

March

Autumn Fashion collections, **Milan**; spring rites 'calling up the plants', **Aprica**

Mid-March Sant'Ambrogio carnival, **Milan**

Easter Parade of floats, **Bormio**

March–April Concerts at San Maurizio church in Monastero Maggiore, **Milan**

April–May

Early April, a national exhibition of camellias in **Verbania**, Lake Maggiore

7 Re-enactment of the Oath of the Lombard League (historical costumes and pageantry, **Pontida** (Bergamo)

End April–first week May Ortafiori flower festival, **Orta San Giulio**

April–May Jazz festival Città di Milano, **Milan**

May Piano competition, **Bergamo** and **Brescia**. Palio del Carroccio (medieval parade and horse race), for the 1176 defeat of Barbarossa by the Lombard League, **Legnano** (Milan)

Second Sun Asparagus festival, **Cilavegna** (Pavia)

Corpus Domimi Processions with decorated streets, **Premana** (Como) and **Grosio** (Sondrio)

June

Throughout June Festival Cusiano di Musica Antica, **Orta San Giulio**

First Sun Navigli Festival, **Milan**; historical pageant and flag-tossing to commemorate imprisonment of François I, **Pizzighettone**

6 Festa of San Gerardo, **Monza** (feast of patron saint who once rescued the sick during a flood by turning his cloak into a raft)

23–24 300-year-old festival with illuminations in snail shells on Comacina, boat procession, and folk music, **Ossuccio** (Como)

Last Sun San Pietro, with fish, wine, and dancing, **Limone sul Garda**

June-Nov Canto delle Pietre: medieval music festival in **Como** and province

You can insure yourself for almost any possible mishap including cancelled flights, postponed departure, stolen or lost baggage and health. Check your current policies to see if they cover you while abroad, and under what circumstances, and judge whether you need a special **travellers' insurance** policy (check student cards and credit cards to see if they entitle you to some medical cover abroad). Travel agencies as well as insurance companies sell traveller's insurance; they are, however, not cheap.

Citizens of EU countries and Australia are entitled to reciprocal health care in

July

2 Festa della Madonna della Foppa, **Gerosa** (Bergamo), marks an apparition of the Virgin

Early July Piazza di Spagna fair; concerts, fireworks and donkey races in **Casalmaggiore** (Cremona); Feast of the Big Noses; prizes for the biggest and strangest nose, **Gromo** (Bergamo); Fiera di San Bernardo (first weekend), religious procession, alpine market, music and folklore, **(Macugnaga)**

16 Contrada del Brodo, 3-day festival at **Gallarate** (Varese)

29–30 Melon festival, **Casteldidone** (Cremona)

Last Sat–Sun Pizzoccheri festival, woodland feasting on grey noodles, **Teglio** (Sondrio)

August

Throughout Aug Vacanze a Milano, theatre and music in **Milan**

Second Sun Osei fair, hunting dogs, decoys, and nightingale imitations, at **Almenno San Salvatore** (Bergamo)

14–15 Ferragosto holiday, with exhibition of the *madonnari*, pavement artists, **Mantua**

15–20 Passeggiando fra i Vecchi Mestieri, one-day festival to rediscover old crafts, **Santa Maria Maggiore** (Val Vigezzo)

16 Feast of gnocchi and small salami, **Pognana Lario** (Como)

Last week San Vito, with big fireworks, at **Omegna** (Lake Orta)

End Aug–mid-Sept Settimane Musicali, musical weeks at **Stresa** on Lake Maggiore

September

Italian Grand Prix, **Monza**; World Pumpkin Weigh-off, **Sale Marasino**, Lake Iseo

End Aug–first half Palio Baradello, **Como**, for the victory of Barbarossa against Milan: parade and competitions between the boroughs of Como and surrounding towns

First Sun Duck festival, with food, games and music, **Desenzano del Garda**

First weekend International gathering of chimney sweeps, **Santa Maria Maggiore** (Val Vigezzo). Corso Fiorito, mid-Sept, parade of flower carriages, classical concerts and fireworks on the lake, **Verbania** (Lake Maggiore)

Second Sun Centomiglia yacht race, **Gargnano**, Lake Garda; horse *palio* with Renaissance costumes at **Isola Dovarese** (Cremona); feast of the Missoltino, feast of sun-dried fish, **Mezzegra** (Como); polenta feasting and the 'Big Pot of Italy' (whoever eats the most sausages), **Corno Giovine** (Milan) Oct

Third Sun Crotti festival at **Chiavenna** second week in Sept (Sondrio) with songs, food and wine. Il Grappolo d'Oro, grape harvest festival, **Chiuro** (Sondrio); bean feast, dancing and handicrafts, **Gaverina Terme** (Bergamo)

Second half of Sept: Mushroom Festival in Quistello (Mantua)

October

Throughout Oct Spring fashion collections, **Milan**; big food fair, **Morbegno** (Sondrio) second week

Sept–Oct Organ concerts at San Maurizio in Monastero Maggiore, **Milan**

First Sun Festa della Madonna del Rosario, **Montodine** (Cremona), with illuminated procession of boats down the River Serio and fireworks; duck and macaroni feasting at **San Benedetto Po** (Mantua)

Third Sun Feast of chicory, **Soncino** (Cremona)

December

7 La Scala opera season opens; Feast of Sant'Ambrogio and 'O Bei O Bei' antique market, **Milan**

Christmas Eve Torchlight procession of the shepherds at **Canneto dell'Oglio** (Mantua); underwater Christmas crib at **Laveno** (Varese) until Epiphany; living crib with music and costumes, **Triangia** (Sondrio)

Nov–beginning of April Stagione di Prosa, theatrical performances, **Brescia**

Italy's National Health Service and a 90% discount on prescriptions. If you live in Britain, bring your European Health Insurance Card (EHIC) with you – the replacement for the E111 – which entitles you to reduced-cost, sometimes free, medical treatment should you need it while in a European Economic Area (EEA) country or Switzerland. The EHIC does not cover all medical expenses (e.g. no repatriation costs and no private treatment) and you may want to take out separate travel insurance for full cover. Note that there are no reciprocal agreements between Italy and New Zealand, Canada or the USA.

Dispensing **chemists** (*farmacia*) are generally open 8.30–1 and 4–8. Pharmacists are trained to give advice for minor ills. Most large cities will have a *farmacia* that stays open 24 hours (in **Milan** it's at the Stazione Centrale); others take turns to stay open (the address rota is posted in the window). Prescriptions can be hard to match; bring any drugs you need regularly.

Maps

The maps in this guide are for orientation only; to explore in any detail invest in a good, up-to-date regional map before you arrive. For an excellent range of maps in the UK, try **Stanford's**, 12–14 Long Acre, London WC2 9LP, **t** (020) 7836 1321; in Bristol at 29 Corn Street, BS1 1HT, **t** (0117) 929 9966; and in Manchester at 39 Spring Gardens, M2 2BG, **t** (0161) 831 0250, *www.stanfords.co.uk*. There's also the **Travel Bookshop**, 13 Blenheim Crescent, London W11, **t** (020) 7229 5260; and **Daunt Books**, 83 Marylebone High Street, London W1, **t** (020) 7224 2295. In the USA, try **The Complete Traveller**, 199 Madison Avenue, New York, NY 10016, **t** (212) 685 9007.

Excellent maps are produced by the **Touring Club Italiano**, **Michelin** and the **Istituto Geografico de Agostini**. Tourist offices can often supply area maps and town plans; those around the lakes often provide good walking maps and trail guides put out by the **Club Alpino Italiano**.

Media

Books are expensive in Italy, and outside the cities **English-language books** are usually limited to paperback bestsellers at the larger newsstands. National **newspapers** include the centrist daily *La Repubblica*, the Milan-based *Il Corriere della Sera*, and Turin-based *La Stampa*. *Corriere* also edits an English-language supplement to the *Herald Tribune* called *Italy Daily*. Major English-language newspapers and magazines can be found in the cities and resort areas.

The daily, rose-pink *Gazzetta dello Sport* has all the latest shenanigans from Italy's football clubs, plus back pages on minor sports.

For **TV news** in English, most hotel rooms should offer either CNN or BBC World.

Money

The single European currency is now a part of everyday life in Italy. All non-cash transactions are in euros (€), and euro notes are used alongside eight denominations of coin, ranging from 1 cent to 2 euros (100 cents in each euro). At the time of writing, the euro is worth approximately £0.69, US$.20 and CAN$1.40.

It is a good idea to order euros from your home bank to have on hand when you arrive in Italy, the land of strikes, unforeseen delays and quirky banking hours, though take care how you carry it.

Obtaining money in Italy is often frustrating, involving much queueing and form-filling. The major banks and exchange bureaux licensed by the Bank of Italy give the best exchange rates. Hotels, private exchanges in resorts and FS-run exchanges at railway stations usually have less advantageous rates, but are open outside normal banking hours. There are several weekend exchange offices in Milan: **Banca Ponti**, Piazza del Duomo 19 (*open Sat 8.30–1*); **Punto Duomo**, Via Orefici 2 (*open daily 9–9*); and **Money Shop**, Piazza Duomo 17 and Via Dante 16 (*open daily 9–8*), and exchange offices at both airports and the Stazione Centrale.

Besides traveller's cheques, most banks will give you cash on a recognized credit card or Eurocheque with a Eurocheque card (taking little or no commission), and ATMs at nearly every bank spout cash if you have a PIN number. Read the instructions carefully or the machine may devour your card. MasterCard is much less widely accepted in Italy. Large hotels, resort restaurants, shops, car hire firms and petrol stations will generally accept plastic as well; always check the signs on the door.

Toll-free numbers for lost or stolen credit cards and traveller's cheques include **American Express**, **t** 800 864 046 (lost cards), **t** 800 521313 (traveller's cheques); **Eurocard**, **t** 800 821 001; **Cartasì Visa**, **t** 800 819014; **Diners Club International**, **t** 800 64064;

Mastercard Eurocard Cartasì, **t** 800 68086 (also for traveller's cheques).

The American Express office in Milan is located at: Via Brera 3, **t** 02 7200 3693 (*open Mon–Thurs 9–5.30, Fri till 5*).

National Holidays

Most museums, as well as banks and shops, are closed on the following national holidays:

1 January, New Year's Day
6 January, Feast of the Epiphany
Easter Monday
25 April, Liberation Day
1 May, Labour Day
2 June Republic Day
15 August, Assumption, known as *Ferragosto*, the peak of the Italian holiday season
1 November, All Saints' Day
7 December, the feast day of Saint Ambrose (*Sant'Ambrogio*); the closest the Milanese have to a civic holiday
8 December, Immaculate Conception
25 December, Christmas Day
26 December, Santo Stefano, St Stephen's Day

Opening Hours

Italy (except bars and restaurants) closes down at 1pm until 3 or 4pm to eat and digest the main meal of the day. Afternoon hours are 4–7, often 5–8 in the hot summer months. Most of Milan closes down completely during August, when locals flee from the polluted frying pan to the hills, lakes or coast.

Banks: Banking hours vary, but core times in Milan and Lombardy are more or less Monday to Friday from 8.30am to 1pm and 3 to 4pm, closed weekends and on local and national holidays (*see* above). Outside normal hours, you will usually be able to find a travel office or hotel or even a machine in a wall to change money for a small commission.

Shops: Shops are usually open Mon–Sat 9.30–1 and 3.30–7.30. In Milan, shopping capital of Italy (if not the universe), hours are longer. A few supermarkets and department stores stay open throughout the day.

Churches: Italy's churches have always been a prime target for art thieves and as a consequence are usually locked when there

isn't a sacristan or caretaker. All churches, except for the really important cathedrals and basilicas, close in the afternoon at the same hours as the shops, and the little ones tend to stay closed. Always have a pocketful of coins for the light machines, or whatever work of art you came to inspect will remain shrouded in ecclesiastical gloom. Don't visit during services, and don't come to see paintings and statues in churches in the week preceding Easter – you will probably find them covered with mourning shrouds.

Museums and galleries: Many of Italy's museums are magnificent, many are run with shameful neglect, and many have been closed for years for 'restoration', with slim prospects of reopening in the foreseeable future. With two works of art per inhabitant, Italy has a hard time financing the preservation of its national heritage; it's as well to enquire at the tourist office to find out exactly what is open and what is 'temporarily' closed before setting off on a wild-goose chase.

In general, Sunday afternoons and Mondays are dead periods for the sightseer – you may want to make them your travelling days. Places without specified opening hours can usually be visited on request but it is best to go before 1pm. **Entrance charges** to Lombardy's star museums are quite steep but others are fairly low, and some sights are completely free. For museums and galleries the average is €5–6, for churches, cathedrals, castles, palaces, villas and their gardens the price is cheaper. Prices that substantially exceed these amounts will be marked *adm exp*. EU citizens under 18 and over 65 get free admission to state museums, at least in theory.

Packing

It's hard to overdress in Italy – it's not that the Italians are very formal; they simply like to dress up. The few places with dress codes are casinos and a few smart restaurants, as well as major churches and basilicas (no shorts, sleeveless shirts or strappy sundresses – women should always tuck a light scarf in a bag to throw over their shoulders).

Bring any prescription medicine you need, an extra pair of glasses or contact lenses if you wear them, a pocket knife and corkscrew (for picnics), a torch/flashlight for dark frescoed churches, caves and crypts, and a travel alarm (for those early trains). If you're a light sleeper, you may want to invest in earplugs. Your electric appliances will work in Italy if you adapt and convert them to run on 220 AC, with two round prongs on the plug.

Photography

Films and **developing** are much more expensive than they are in either the UK or the USA. You are not allowed to take pictures in most museums and in some churches. Lombardy's light is less dazzling than in the vivid south, and clarity may be affected by Milanese air pollution or local mists, but allow for extra brightness reflected off the water if you're by the Lakes. Most cities now offer one-hour processing if you're in a hurry.

Post Offices

Dealing with *la posta italiana* has always been a risky, frustrating, time-consuming affair. One of the scandals that mesmerized Italy in recent years involved the minister of the post office, who disposed of tons of backlog mail by tossing it in the Tiber. When the news broke, he was replaced – the new minister, having learned his lesson, burned all the mail the post office was incapable of delivering. Not surprisingly, fed-up Italians view the invention of the Internet as a gift from the Madonna. First-class mail (*posta prioritaria*), recently introduced and guaranteeing national delivery within 24 to 72 hours, has partly improved their mood.

Post offices, *www.poste.it*, are usually open Monday to Friday 8.30–1.50 and Saturday 8.30–12.30, or until 7.30pm (Mon–Fri) and 5.30pm (Sat) in the central and rail station offices of a big city. To have your mail sent *posta restante* (general delivery), have it addressed to the central post office (*Fermo Posta)* and allow three to four weeks for it to arrive. Make sure your surname is clearly written in block capitals. To pick up your mail you must present your passport and pay a nominal charge. Stamps (*francobolli*) may be purchased in post offices or at tobacconists.

Prices fluctuate and the rates for letters and postcards can vary according to the whim of the government ministry, the speed you want it delivered and the weight. You can also have money telegraphed to you through the post office; if all goes well, this can happen in a mere three days, but expect a fair proportion of it to go into commission.

Shopping

'Made in Italy' has become a byword for style and quality, for everything from fashion and leather to kitchenware and sports cars. This is especially true in glossy Milan, Italy's epicentre of innovative style and fashion (*see* p.69). Surprisingly, big-city competition keeps prices lower than in most Italian cities and much lower than you'll find in posh resort boutiques.

Demand a certificate of authenticity for antiques – reproductions can be very good. To get your antique or modern art purchases home, apply to the export department of the Italian Ministry of Education and pay an export tax; your seller should know the details. Be sure to save receipts for Customs.

Sports and Activities

Beaches

Most beaches around the lakes are shingly strips – useful platforms for sunbathing or landing boats, but little more. Many of them shelve steeply and the water is never very warm. Some shores suffer from pollution and bathing may not be as healthy as you think; Garda, one of Europe's cleanest lakes, is a great exception, with the longest beaches.

Casinos

A curious outpost in the centre of Lake Lugano, surrounded by the Swiss canton of Ticino, Campione d'Italia's *raison d'être* is a prosperous casino where the Swiss get a chance to throw caution and any spare cash at the croupiers. Other nationalities with money to burn are also welcome (take your passport and a jacket and tie).

Fishing

Lombardy's rivers are renowned for good fishing; to try your luck you need to purchase a year's membership card from the *Federazione Italiana della Pesca Sportiva*, which has an office in every province; they will inform you about local conditions and restrictions. Local offices also sell weekly and even daily cards. Bait and equipment are readily available.

Football

Soccer (*calcio*) is a national obsession. For many Italians its importance far outweighs tedious issues like the state of the nation or any momentous international event. The sport was introduced by the English but a similar game, like a cross between football and rugby, has existed in Italy since the Renaissance. Italian teams are known for their defensive teamwork; rivalries are intense, scandals rife, racism an occasional problem, yet crowd violence is minimal. *Serie A* is the equivalent of the premier division, with 18 teams; Milan's teams, **Inter** and **AC Milan**, are at the top of the tree (*see* p.73 for buying match tickets).

Golf

Lombardy has beautiful courses, particularly near Lake Como; check the site *www.golf lombardia.it*. Most take guests and hire equipment, including: **Bergamo** (27 holes), 24030 Almenno S. Bartolomeo, **t** 035 640 028; **Carimate** (18 holes), 22060 Carimate, **t** 031 790 226; **La Pinetina** (18 holes), 22070 Appiano Gentile, **t** 031 933 202; **Menaggio e Cadenabbia** (18 holes), 22010 Grandola e Uniti, **t** 034 432 103; **Milan** (27 holes), 20052 Parco di Monza, **t** 039 303 081; **Molinetto** (18 holes), 20063 Cernusco sul Naviglio, **t** 02 9210 5128; **Monticello** (36 holes), 22070 Cassina Rizzardi, **t** 031 928 055; **Varese** (18 holes), 21020 Luvinate, **t** 033 222 9302; **Villa d'Este** (18 holes), 22030 Montorfano, **t** 031 200 200.

Hiking and Mountaineering

These sports become steadily more popular among native Italians every year, and Lombardy now has a good system of marked trails and Alpine refuges run by the **Club Alpino Italiano** (CAI), (*see* p.64, 'Alpine Refuges'), located in every province (even the flat ones), where they organize excursions into the hills). Walking in the Alps is generally practicable between May and October, after most of the snow has melted; all the necessary gear – boots, packs, tents – is available in Italy but for more money than you'd pay at home. The CAI can put you in touch with Alpine guides or climbing groups if you're up to some real adventure, or write to the Italian national tourist board for a list of operators offering mountaineering holidays.

Some alpine resorts offer *Settimane Verdi* (Green Weeks) – accommodation and activity packages for summer visitors similar to skiers' White Weeks. Trails around Lakes Como and Iseo are particularly interesting. Another area to head for is the **Parco Nazionale dello Stelvio e della Val Malanca**. For arduous climbing, the northern province of Valtellina is best.

Motor-racing

Monza hosts the Italian Grand Prix every September. The **Formula 1 track**, built in 1922, is 15km out of town, reached along Viale Monza from Piazzale Loreto, **t** 039 24821, *www.monzanet.it*.

Skiing and Winter Sports

Lombardy's most famous ski resort, **Bormio**, at the entrance to Italy's largest national park, has hosted world events in recent years and doubles as a summer resort and spa. The Valtellina, Ossola and Bergamasque valleys have other skiing facilities; Monte Baldo on Lake Garda's east side and the Grigna range near Lecco also have well-equipped resorts.

Facilities in Italy now compare with other European skiing areas, but are usually less expensive. Prices are highest during Christmas and New Year holidays, in February and at Easter. Most resorts offer *Settimane Bianche* (White Weeks), economical off-season packages. Sports such as ice-skating and bobsleighing are available at larger resorts.

Watersports

Riva on Lake Garda is the main watersport resort, with sailing, diving and windsurfing schools. Try Bouwmeester Windsurfing Centre by the Hotel Pier, **t** 0464 551 730, *www.wind surfmb.it*. Nearby, Torbole is another popular windsurfing spot. Contact Conca D'Oro Windsurfing Centre, **t** 0464 548 192, *www.windsurfconca.com*. Lake Como has well-equipped sailing and **windsurfing** schools. **Waterskiing** is possible on all major lakes. Fraglia della Vela, **t** 0464 552 460, *www.fraglia velariva.com*, in Riva, can provide plenty of information about **sailing** on Lake Garda. Horca Myseria, Via Pelitti 1, 20126 Milan, **t** 02 255 2585, *www.horcamyseria.it*, organizes sailing courses. For further information, contact the **Italian State Tourist Office**.

Telephones

Public phones in Italy take either coins (increasingly rare) or phone cards (*schede telefoniche*), available in roughly €2, €5 or €10 amounts at tobacconists or newsstands; stock up for a long international call or look for a metered *telefoni a scatti* (often in bars).

In cities there are phones in the offices of Telecom Italia – head to galleria Vittorio Emanuele II for the city centre office in Milan (*open daily 8am–9.30pm*), although places offering cheap international calls are mushrooming to serve the ever-growing population of immigrants. Try to avoid phoning from hotels, which often add 25% to the bill. Telephone numbers in Italy change with alarming regularity. Many places have public fax machines, but the speed of transmission makes costs high.

Direct calls abroad may be made by dialling the international prefix (for the UK 0044, Ireland 00353, USA and Canada 001, Australia 0061, New Zealand 0064). If you're **calling Italy from abroad**, dial the country code (39), then the full number, including the initial zero. From the UK and Ireland call 00 39; from the USA and Canada 011 39; from Australia 0011 39; from New Zealand 00 44 39. Dial **t** 176 for international information, **t** 170 for a collect call.

Time

Italy is one hour ahead of Greenwich Mean Time. From the last weekend of March to the end of September, Italian Summer Time (daylight-saving time) is in effect.

Toilets

Although Italy's public conveniences have had a poor reputation in the past, frequent travellers have noted a steady improvement over the years in the cleanliness of public toilets. Ask for the *toilette* or *gabinetto*; in stations and smarter bars and cafés there are washroom attendants who expect a couple of euros for keeping the place decent. Don't confuse the Italian plurals: *signori* (gents), *signore* (ladies).

Tourist Information and the Internet

Tourist offices, known variously as EPT, APT, IAT or AAST, or more modestly as *Pro Locos* (for lunatics), usually stick to shop hours, although in summer they often stay open on Saturday afternoons or even Sundays. They can provide hotel lists (most will call around and make bookings on the spot), town plans and information on local sights and transport; sometimes, however, a friendly travel agency may prove more helpful. English is spoken nearly everywhere. The Italian National Tourist Office (ENIT) can help before you leave home; in some countries, tourist information is also available from the offices of Alitalia or CIT (Italy's State Tourist Board), *www.enit.it*.

Canada: 17 Bloor St East, Suite 907, S. Tower, Toronto, OT M4W 3R8, **t** (416) 925 4882.
UK: 1 Princes Street, London W1B 2AY, **t** (020) 7408 1254 or **t** 0800 0048 2542 toll-free from UK and Ireland, *www.italian touristboard.co.uk*.
USA: 630 Fifth Avenue, Suite 1565, New York, NY 10111, **t** (212) 245 4822; 12400 Wilshire Bvd, Suite 550, LA, CA 90025, **t** (310) 820 1898, *www.italiantourism.com*.

It can be useful to look at the **Internet** before your trip. The Italians are no slouches in cyberspace; in fact, the Italian slice of the web can be as gaudy as Italian television these days.

Among the directories, Lycos and MSN are probably the best places to look, with an index of sites in a few score of Italian towns; Google and Infoseek (under 'Travel: Destinations') are also helpful. Several sites in these listings offer tips on accommodation and hotel reservations in Milan and elsewhere. When trying to say 'www' in Italian, do not attempt to say the word *doppia-vu* three times – the Italians simply say *vu-vu-vu-punto.*

From the top museums to the top sport's clubs, Milan's many attractions are especially well covered on the web; Inter (*www.inter.it*) and AC Milan (*www.acmilan.com*) both keep up pages for their fans, as does La Scala opera theatre: *www.teatroallascala.it* (the theatre's website includes the facility to purchase tickets). An excellent English language site covering Milan is *www.ciaomilano.it* – a virtual offspring of the Key to Milan guide which includes up-to-date info on what's on. Also worth a look is: *www.cityvox.com*, a highly recommended website for Milan listings, and *www.milandaily.com*, an excellent English-language site for headlines, sports and entertainment news on Milan.

Good general sites on Lombardy include *www.lombardiadautore.regione.lombardia.it*, the region's general tourism site; and *www.itwg.com*, the Italian tourist web guide, which has a a database on hotels and facilities for online booking. Also check out the website of FAI, *www.dimorestoriche.com*, the private Italian association which looks after some of the country's historical villas.

Almost all of the provincial APT tourist offices and many rural offices maintain sites. Lake Garda's *www.gardainforma.com* and *www.gardalake.com* are both particularly helpful. Other interesting local sites are detailed in the text.

Where to Stay

All accommodation in Italy is classified by the Provincial Tourist Boards. Price control however, has been deregulated since 1992, leaving hotels to set their own rates, which means that in some places prices have rocketed. After a period of rapid and erratic price fluctuation, tariffs are at last settling down again to more predictable levels. In general, the quality of furnishings and facilities has improved in all categories in recent years. But you can still find plenty of older hotels and *pensioni* whose often charming eccentricities of character and architecture may frequently be at odds with modern standards of comfort. Milan has the

most expensive and heavily booked hotels in Italy, and a major trade fair could put all your travel plans in jeopardy.

Hotels and Guesthouses

Italian *alberghi* come in all shapes and sizes. They are rated from one to five stars, depending strictly on the facilities they offer. The star ratings are some indication of price level, but for tax reasons not all hotels choose to advertise themselves at the rating to which they are entitled, so you may find a two-star hotel just as comfortable as, or more so than, a four-star one. Conversely, you may find that a hotel offers few stars in hopes of attracting budget-conscious travellers, but charges just as much as a higher-rated neighbour. *Pensioni* are generally more modest establishments, though nowadays the distinction between these and hotels is becoming blurred. *Locande* used to be an even more basic form of hostelry, but these days the term may denote somewhere chic.

Price lists must, by law, be posted on the door of every room, along with meal prices and extra charges (such as air conditioning, or even a shower in cheap places). Many hotels display two or three different rates, depending on the season. Low-season rates may be about a third lower than peak-season tariffs. Resort hotels tend to close down altogether for several months a year. During high season you should always book ahead to be sure of a room (a phone or Internet reservation is less frustrating to organize than one by post). If

---

Hotel Price Categories

Prices are for double rooms with bath/shower.

In Milan
luxury over €300
very expensive €200–300
expensive €120–200
moderate €80–120
inexpensive up to €80

Elsewhere in the Region
luxury over €230
very expensive €150–230
expensive €100–150
moderate €60–100
inexpensive up to €60

Self-catering Operators

One of the most enjoyable and best-value ways of visiting Italy is to opt for self-catering accommodation. Centralized booking agencies exist in many countries as well as Italy, sometimes offering discounted air or ferry fares and fly-drive schemes. Watch for the small ads, or see the list below.

In the UK

Auto Plan, Auto Plan House, Stowe Court, Stowe St, Lichfield, Staffs WS13 6AQ, **t** (01543) 257 777, *www.autoplanhols.co.uk*.

Interhome, 383 Richmond Rd, Twickenham, Middx TW1 2EF, **t** (020) 8891 1294, *www.interhome.co.uk*.

Lakes and Mountains Holidays, The Red House, Garstons Close, Titchfield, Fareham PO14 4EW, **t** (01329) 844 405, *www.lakes-mountains.co.uk*.

The Apartment Service, 5–6 Francis Grove, Wimbledon, London SW19 4DT, **t** (020) 8944 1444, *www.apartmentservice.com*. For apartments in Milan; free 96-page colour guide.

The Italian Connection, 1st Floor Suite, 252–4 Pentonville Rd, London N1 9JY, **t** (020) 7520 0470, *www.italian-connection.co.uk*. Reliable company offering hotel and self-catering holidays.

In the USA

At Home Abroad Inc, 405 E. 56th Street, Suite 6 H, New York, NY 10022 2466, **t** (212) 421 9165, *www.athomeabroadinc.com*. To live with a host or host family; suitable for teenagers or students travelling abroad for the first time.

Global Home Network, 501 N. Fairfax Drive, Arlington, VA 22203, **t** (703) 387 3600, **t** 800 278 73388, *www.globalhomenetwork.com*. For apartments and hotels.

Rentals in Italy, 700 E. Main St, Ventura, CA 93001, **t** 800 726 6702 (toll-free), *www.rentvillas.com*.

---

you have paid a deposit your booking is valid under Italian law, but don't expect it to be refunded if you have to cancel. Tourist offices publish annual lists of hotels and pensions with current rates and will usually ring around if you show up without a place to sleep. Major railway stations also have accommodation booking desks.

If you arrive without a reservation, begin looking or phoning round for accommodation early in the day. If possible, inspect the room (and bathroom facilities) before you book, and check the tariff carefully. You will be asked for your passport for registration purposes. Italian hoteliers may legally alter their rates twice during the year, so printed tariffs or lists (and therefore prices quoted in this book) may be out of date. Hoteliers who wilfully overcharge should be reported to the local tourist office.

Prices listed in this guide are for double rooms with bath/shower; you can expect to pay about two-thirds of the rate for single occupancy, though in high season you may be charged the full double rate in a popular resort. Extra beds are usually charged at about a third more than the room rate. Rooms without private bathrooms generally charge 20–30% less, and most offer discounts for children sharing parents' rooms, or children's meals. If you want a double bed, specify a *camera matrimoniale*. Breakfast is usually optional in hotels but obligatory in *pensioni*. In high season you may be expected to take half-board in resorts if the hotel has a restaurant, and one-night stays may be refused.

Youth Hostels

Youth hostels (*ostelli per la gioventù*), are few and far between. However, you'll find them in **Milan**, **Menaggio**, **Como** and also **Bergamo**, **Lovere** (Bergomo), **Modesimo** (Sondrio), and **Riva del Garda**; they are pleasant and sometimes located in historic buildings. The *Associazione Italiana Alberghi per la Gioventù* (Italian Youth Hostel Association, or **AIG**) is affiliated to the International Youth Hostel Federation, Via Cavour 44, 00184 Roma, **t** 06 487 1152, *www.ostellionline.org* (for a full list of hostels). An international membership card will enable you to stay in any of them (cards can be purchased on the spot in many hostels – €17 per person or €18 per family with at least one minor child. It expires after 14 months). Rates are usually €13–18. Discounts are available for senior citizens and for young people aged up to 26. Some family rooms are also available. You generally have to check in after 5pm and pay for your room before 9am. Hostels usually close for most of the daytime and many operate a curfew. During the spring, noisy school parties cram hostels for field trips. In the summer it's advisable to book ahead. Contact the hostels directly.

Camping

Most of the official sites in Lombardy are near the lakes, though you can camp somewhere near most of the principal tourist centres (Milan's camp site is some way out of the city). Camping is popular with holiday-making families in August, when you can expect to find many sites at bursting point. Unofficial camping is generally frowned on. Camper vans (and facilities for them) are increasingly popular.

You can obtain a list of local sites from any regional tourist office. To obtain a camping carnet and to book ahead, write to the Federazione Italiana Campeggiatori, Via Vittorio Emanuele 11, 50041 Calenzano, Firenze, **t** 055 882 391, *www.federcampeggio.it* (ask for their list of camp sites as well as the booking form – their website is in Italian only). An interesting site to consult for camping in Italy is also *www.camping.it*. The Touring Club Italiano (**TCI**) publishes a comprehensive annual guide to camp sites and tourist villages throughout Italy. Write to TCI, Corso Italia 10, Milan, **t** 02 852 6304, *www.touring.it* (part of the services are for members only).

UK operators offering camping or caravan (trailer) holidays in the lakes include:
Caravan & Camping Service, 69 Westbourne Grove, London W2 4UJ, **t** (020) 7792 1944.
Caravan Club, East Grinstead House, East Grinstead, West Sussex RJ19 1UA, **t** (01342) 326 944, *www.caravanclub.co.uk*.
Eurocamp, Hertford Manor, Greenbank Lane, Northwich, Cheshire CW8 1HW, **t** 0870 901 9410, *www.eurocamp.co.uk*.
Select Sites Reservations, Travel House, 34 Brecon Rd, Abergavenny, Gwent NP7 5UG, **t** (01873) 859 876, *www.select-site.com*.

Agriturismo

For a breath of rural seclusion, Italians head for a spell on a working **farm**, in accommodation (usually self-catering) that often approximates to the French *gîte*. Often, however, the real pull of the place is the restaurant in which you can sample some home-grown produce (olives, wine, etc.). Outdoor activities may also be on tap (riding, fishing, cycling, and so forth). An apartment or cottage is usually rented by the week.

Agriturismo is very popular around the Italian Lakes. Local tourist offices will have information for their areas; otherwise contact:
Agriturist Lombardia, Viale Isonzo 27, Milan, **t** 02 5830 2022, *www.agriturist.it*.
Assotour Lombardia, Viale Murillo 12, **t** 02 463 460.
Terranostra Lombardia, Via Tommaso Salvini 1, **t** 02 7602 5840, *www.terranostra.it*.
Turismo Verde, Piazzo Caiazzo 3, Milan, **t** 02 670 5544, *www.turismoverde.it*.

Some good Internet sites include *www.agritour.net*, *www.agriturismo.it* and *www.turismoverdelombardia.it*.

Alpine Refuges

The Italian Alpine Club operates refuges (*rifugi*) on the main mountain trails (some accessible only by funiculars or cable cars). These may be predictably spartan or surprisingly comfortable. Many have restaurants. For an up-to-date list write to the **Club Alpino Italiano**, Via Silvio Pellico 6, **t** 02 8646 3516, **t** 02 3651 5702 (info on activities), *www.caimilano.it*. Charges average €17–21 per person per night, including breakfast. Most are open only from July to September, but those used by skiers are about 20% more expensive from December to April. Book ahead for August. Book ahead also if you're taking some of the most popular trails in summer (especially in the Stelvio National Park or around the lakes).

Milan

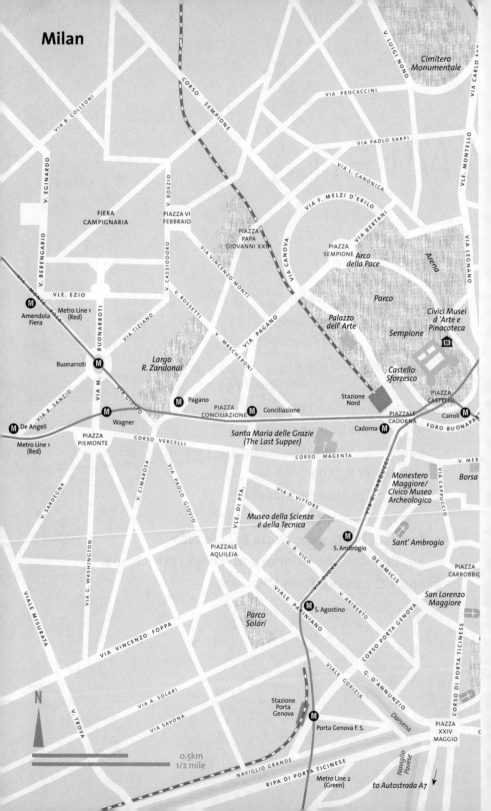

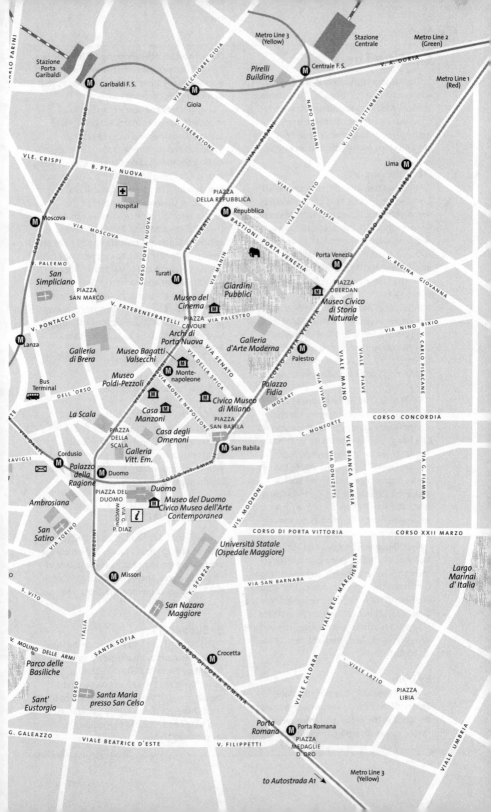

Getting There

The transport hub of northern Italy, Milan is well served by a full range of international services. Milan's expanding **metro** network is, as well as one of the quickest means of getting from A to B, a very useful orientation aid, and stops are listed in the text below.

From the Airport

Milan has two main airports, **Linate**, 8km from the centre, **t** 02 7485 2200, *www.sea-aeroportimilano.it*, and the larger **Malpensa**, 50km to the west, **t** 02 7485 2200, *www.sea-aeroportimilano.it*, both of which receive national and international flights. As a rule, intercontinental flights use Malpensa while Linate handles most of the European and domestic traffic. Charter flights often use a third airport, **Orio al Serio**, near Bergamo, **t** 035 326 323, *www.orioaeroporto.it*. STAM buses, **t** 035 318 472, link it to Milan's Stazione Centrale (*departures correspond to flight timetables; €6.70*). For information about **flights**, ring **t** 02 7485 2200 or visit the website (*see above*).

STAM buses run between Linate and Stazione Centrale (*€2.50; every 30mins, 5.40am–9pm; journey time approx 20mins*). **City bus 73** also runs to Linate from Piazza San Babila (*€1; metro line 1; every 10mins, 5.30am–2am*). The quickest way to the city centre from Malpensa is by rail shuttle **Malpensa Express**, **t** 02 27763, to Cadorna North Railway Station (*€9 or free for Alitalia passengers; metro Cadorna, every 30mins, 5am–11pm; journey time 40mins*).

Air Pullman bus shuttles, **t** 02 5858 3185, link Malpensa to the Stazione Centrale (*€5.50; takes 1 hour; every 20mins, 4.15am–midnight*). Every hour there is a bus service that stops at the Fiera di Trade Fair upon request. There is a direct Air Pullman connection from Linate to Malpensa (*€9; hourly, 6am–8pm, journey time approx 75mins*). Taxis from Malpensa to Milan cost a fortune.

By Train

Milan's splendiferous main **Stazione Centrale** (conected to metro lines no.2 and 3), designed in the 1930s with the travelling Fascist satrap in mind, dominates the Piazza Duca d'Aosta northeast of the centre. Centrale, **t** 89 20218 (*open 7am–11pm*), *www.trenitalia.it*, handles nearly all international trains, as well as most of the domestic routes .

Useful **trams** and **buses** from Centrale include tram no.1 to Piazza Scala and Nord Station (Codorne), and no.33 to Stazione Garibaldi and the Cimitero Monumentale; bus no.60 goes to Piazza del Duomo and bus no.65 runs down Corso Buenos Aires, Corso Venezia and through the centre to Corso Italia.

Stazione Garibaldi (*metro no.2*) is the terminus for car-train services, as well as trains for Pavia, Monza, Varese, Como and Bergamo. **Stazione Lambrate** (*metro no.2*), on the east side of the city, has connections to Genoa, Bergamo and towards the Simplon Pass. **Stazione Cadorna** (*metro Cadorna*) is the main station of Lombardy's regional Milan Nord railway, **t** 02 20222 (*open 24hrs*), *www.ferrovienord.it*, with connections to Como, Varese, Saronno, Erba and Laveno (Lake Maggiore).

Left Luggage at Centrale, **t** 02 6371 2212. *Open 4am–1.30am*.
Lost and Found, t 02 6371 2667.

By Coach

Inter-city coaches arrive in the Piazza Castello (*metro Cairoli*), where several companies have their offices. Contact the tourist office (*see p.69*) for information on destinations, schedules and prices.

Getting Around

Milan is not a difficult place to find your way around. Though the city looks like a bloated amoeba on the map, Milan marks its age in rings, like a tree, and most of its sights are in the highly walkable innermost ring, the Cerchia dei Navigli.

By Bus and Tram

The buses, trams and trolleys run by the **Milan transport authority** (ATM), toll free from Italy **t** 800 808181, *www.atm-mi.it*, are convenient and their routes well marked, though most of the cheerful old caboose-like trams have now been sold to San Francisco, and have been replaced by modern, streamlined trams.

Purchase **tickets** (€1, or carnets of 10 tickets, €9.20) in advance at tobacco shops, news-stands, metro stations or at the coin-gobbling machines at the main stops, and stamp them in the machines on board. A ticket is valid for 75 minutes' travel anywhere on the network above ground, regardless of how many trans-fers you make. Tickets cannot be used twice on the metro. Remember to stamp your ticket once on board a bus or tram.

Most bus routes run from about 6am to midnight, after which time special **night bus** routes operate with reasonable frequency.

If you plan to be riding around a fair bit, buy a one-day pass (€3), or two-day pass (€5.50), valid for all buses, trams and the metro. A useful bus, no.94 from the Piazza Cavour, makes the circuit of the former canal and is convenient for the Castello Sforzesco, Santa Maria delle Grazie or Sant'Ambrogio.

The ATM also publishes a useful **map** (€2) showing all the bus routes and metro stops, the *Pionta dei trasporti pubblici*, available at the tourist office and the Stazione Centrale.

By Metro

The Metropolitana Milanese, begun in the 1960s, is sleek and well run, and a boon for the bewildered tourist. There are three lines, the **Red** (no.1), **Green** (no.2) and **Yellow** (no.3). The Metro is open from 6am to midnight daily, and tickets are the same as those used for the buses or trams.

By Taxi

Milanese taxis are white and their drivers are generally honest and reliable. It is not possible to flag a free cab down; you must call to book or go to a stand. They can be found waiting at ranks in the Piazza del Duomo, by the Stazione Centrale, and in several other central piazzas. To **book a taxi**, ring **t** 02 8383, **t** 02 6767 or **t** 02 5251. On entering the taxi you pay a charge of €3. Note that taxi drivers may charge extra for suitcases if you allow them to put them in the boot. They also have an aversion to coins, believing them to be worth less than bills.

By Car

Driving in Milan requires chutzpah, luck and good navigation skills. One-way streets are the rule, signs are confusing, parking impossible, and bringing a vehicle into the city centre 8am–8pm is not only foolhardy but illegal unless you have a foreign number plate.

If you must bring a car into the centre, look for ATM **car parks** on the outskirts, or dump your car in one of the large car parks at the termini of the metro lines. Parking is permitted in the areas marked by a blue line, provided you display a 'Sostamilano' scratch card on the dashboard. You can buy this card at tobacconists, bars or news kiosks. Yellow lines are for residents only, with a special parking permit. The *Sostamilano* card (€1.50 *per hour until 8pm*) allows you to park in the blue areas for up to 2 consecutive hours. Cost is €7.50 cumulatively for 8pm–12pm.

Ask at the tourist office for details of the 'Welcome Milano' card which includes a daily public transport pass as well as a number of other 'perks', such as a boat trip on the Naviglio and tickets for a live classical concert. It costs €8.

Tourist Information

Piazza del Duomo on Via Guglielmo Marconi 1, **t** 02 7252 4301/2/3, *www.milano infotourist.com*. *Open Mon–Fri 8.30–7; Sat 9–1 and 2–6; Sun 9–1 and 2–5.*

Stazione Centrale: *Open Mon–Sat 9am–6.30pm, Sun 9–12.30 and 1.30–5.*

Galleria Vittorio Emmanuele II: Piazza della Scala, **t** 02 869 0734. *Open Mon–Sat 8am–7pm, Sun 9–12.30 and 1.30–6.*

Milan Hoteliers Association: Corso Buenos Aires 77, **t** 02 674 8031, *www.traveleurope.it*. Free hotel reservation service.

Milano Hotels Central Booking: **t** 02 805 4242, *www.hotelbooking.com*. Hotel reservations.

Shopping

Milan is Italy's best shopping city, especially for clothes and designer goods. Most shops are closed all day Sunday and Monday morn-ings (except during the Christmas period), and in August. Food stores tend to close on Monday afternoons. The big **sales** begin in the second week of January. There are also sales around the middle of July.

The Quadrilatero d'Oro

Many of the big names in fashion have their boutique 'headquarters' in what is known as the Quadrilatero d'Oro, defined by Via Monte Napoleone, Via della Spiga, Via Sant'Andrea and Via Borgospesso (*metro Monte Napoleone*). Nearly all the shops here have branch offices elsewhere in Milan and in other cities. You may just find the latest of the latest designs on Monte Napoleone, but be assured they'll soon show up elsewhere, expensive enough but without the high snob surcharges.

The jewellers were actually here first, in the 1930s; since then, an address on Via Monte Napoleone has meant status and quality. Have a look in the windows at **Buccellati** (No.4), considered by many as the best jewellery designer in Italy, featuring exquisitely delicate gold work and jewels, each piece individually crafted. Other classics, all on Monte Napoleone, are **Faraone** (No.7a), **Martignetti** (No.10), **Cartier** (corner Via del Gesù), **Damiani** (No.16), **Cusi** (No.21a) and **Calderoni**, the city's oldest (No.23); for **Bulgari** head for Via della Spiga (No.6); for antique jewellery try **Romani Adami**, Via Bagutta 3.

Milan's artsy displays of clothing and accessories are a window-shopper's paradise. **Missoni**'s ravishing knits for women and men are at Via Sant'Andrea, corner of Via Bagutta; **Valentino** and his classics are at Via Montemapileone 20; **Armani** is at Via Durini 23–25. **Armani's Megastore**, Via A. Manzoni 31, has three floors dedicated to the maestro's new home collection as well as his Emporio lines. A sushi bar and Mediterranean café and restaurant are added pleasures (*see* 'Eating Out', p.77).

For more trendy shopping, just around the corner is the ethno-chic showroom of **Giuliana Cella**, in Via Borgonuovo 12, with exclusive wools and refined embroidery; **Laura Biagiotti** is at Via Borgospesso 19; **Versace** display their innovations at Monte Napoleone 11.

Via della Spiga is chock-a-block with top designers: **Byblos**, **Krizia**, **Luciano Soprani** and **Dolce e Gabbana** are all there. Via Monte Napoleone also has its share: **Alberta Ferretti**, **Roccobarocco**, **Prada**, **Ungaro** and **Versace**.

On Via Sant'Andrea are **Chanel**, **Prada** (again, and Via della Spiga as well), **Helmut Lang**, **Fendi**, **Ferré**, **Trussardi**, as well as Milan's bad boy of fashion, **Moschino**, also at Via Durini 14. For second-hand designer fashions, try **Mercatino Michela**, Via della Spiga 33 and Corso Venezia 8.

Italian leather is known in most parts of the world simply through the name **Gucci**, at Monte Napoleone 5; you can also have a look at **Bottega Veneta**, Via della Spiga 5; **Nazareno Gabrielli**, Monte Napoleone 23; **Ferragamo**, Via Monte Napoleone 3 and corner Via Borgospesso; **Fendi**, Via Sant'Andrea 16; and **Fratelli Rossetti**, Via Monte Napoleone, corner Via Matteotti; and **Pollini**, in Corso Vittorio Emanuele II 30, for designer shoes.

Lorenzi, Monte Napoleone 9, is the city's most refined pipe and male accessories shop, with a remarkable shaving museum, and **D Magazine**, Monte Napoleone 26, has Gigli and Armani, up to 50% off. **Il Salumaio**, at No.12, has an infinite array of nearly every gourmet item imaginable and has recently set up a restaurant (*expensive*). **Rosy**, Via Manzoni 42, is the place to go for elegant and very sensual designer underwear for designer bottoms.

Don't miss **Cova**, Via Monte Napoleone 8, for elegant confectionery dating back to 1817 amid crystal surroundings. Try the *sachertorte* and, at Christmas, the *Pan di Toni*, Antonio Cova's original *panettone*.

City Centre

Besides the great **Galleria Vittorio Emanuele II**, several minor galleries branch off the Corso Vittorio Emanuele II, each a shopping arcade lined with good quality reasonably-priced shops.

In Piazza del Duomo a monument almost as well known as the cathedral itself is Milan's biggest and oldest department store, **La Rinascente**; it's also the only one to have been christened by Gabriele D'Annunzio. La Rinascente has six floors of merchandise, with especially good clothing and domestic sections, offering a wide array of kitchen gear dear to the heart of an Italian cook. The cafeteria on the top floor has great views over the cathedral.

Other shops in the centre include: **Guenzati**, Piazza Cordusio 2 (*metro Duomo*), which will make a velvet-lover's heart flutter (they also do made-to order); **Diffusione Tessile**, Galleria San Carlo 6, specializes in MaxMara clothes;

and **Al Guanto Perfetto**, Via Mazzini 18, which is Milan's best-known glove shop for over a hundred years.

Near the Duomo, Via Spadari is a food shopper's heaven; at No. 9, stop at **Peck**, the home of Milanese gastronomy, where you can queue for a wide choice of Italian and foreign delicatessen. Peck has also extended the original **Casa del Formaggio** on nearby Via Speronari (where the best cheeses, from the most exotic to the most everyday, have been sold since 1894), and **Bottega del Maiale** (cheese and pork shops) to include delicacies (from caviar to escargots and exotic fruits), a wine cellar with over 40,000 labels, and an exclusive restaurant (*very expensive, see* p.76). **Peck Rosticceria**, with a *tavola calda* where you can have lunch, has opened in nearby Via Cesare Cantù, and there is a **Peck Bottega del Vino**, a wine bar, in Via Victor Hugo.

Rizzoli, Galleria Vittorio Emanuele 79, is one of the city's best-stocked bookshops (with many English titles), owned by the family that founded the *Corriere della Sera*, Milan's newspaper. In the Galleria del Corso, **Messaggerie Musicali** is one of the best in town for musical scores and recordings.

Fnac, Via Torino, on the corner with Via della Palla, has a good selection of music, and films as does **Ricordi Mediastore**, Galleria Vittorio Emanuele, another Milanese music megastore (sells tickets for events).

The shops on busy Via Torino offer some of Milan's more affordable wares, especially in clothes and footwear.

Elsewhere in Milan

Brera offers some of Milan's most original shops and boutiques, as well as old standbys like **Surplus**, Corso di Porta Ticimese 103, which has a marvellous array of second-hand garments, and the big **COIN** department store, Piazza 5 Giornate 1/a, a good bet for reasonably priced fashions.

On Corso Buenos Aires (*metro Lima*), one of Milan's longest and densest shopping thoroughfares, you can find the unusual **Le Mani d'Oro**, Via Gaffurio 5 (near Piazzale Loreto), which specializes in *trompe l'œil* objects and decorations. **Sadler Wine & Food**, on Via Conchetta in the Navigli area is a famous and well-stocked deli.

Another shopping street with excellent merchandise and reasonable prices is Via Paolo Sarpi (*metro Moscova*), formerly the city's Chinatown. To the south, Corso di Porta Ticinese and Corsa Porta Romana offer several quirkier, smaller designer shops; try **Dibiemme Fashion,** on Corso di Porta Romana 121, set back from the street, but a label gold mine.

Several outlets are also sprouting up outside the city centre, with designer labels at up to 70% off: **Dolce & Gabbana Industria**, Via Goldoniro (*metro San Babila*), is a bit of a trek, but worth it, and **Il Salvagente**, on Via Fratelli Bronzetti 26 (*tram 27*) stocks surplus exclusive labels.

For an excellent selection of English books, try **The English Bookshop**, Via Mascheroni 12 (*metro Conciliazione*), or **The American Bookstore**, Via Camperio 16, in the historical centre (*metro Cairoli*).

For beautiful art editions **Franco Maria Ricci**, Via Durini 19, is another bookshop to visit (only own publications). **Feltrinelli**, another classic Italian bookshop in Via Ugo Foscolo 3 (*metro Duomo*), has foreign language magazines.

Worth a visit is the **Mondadori Multicenter**, Via Marghera 29 (*metro De Angeli*), a mega-store with large stocks of software, hardware, a digital piazza on the ground floor with latest-generation software, hardware, games, e-books and portable phones, as well as an on-line travel agent and ticket booking. There are over 60,000 'traditional books' on the first floor, an auditorium and Internet café on the top floor and a terrace.

If you're interested in the latest designs in furniture, Milan has a major concentration of showrooms and stores near the centre: well worth a look are **Artemide**, Corso Monforte 19; **Flos**, Corso Monforte 7; **Fontana Arte**, Via Santa Margherita 4, for designer lamps; **De Padova**, Corso Venezia 14; **Dilmos**, Piazza San Marco 1; **Cassini**, Via Durini 18, for designer sofas and chairs; and **Alias**, Via Vicenzo Monti 2.

Children

For **books and toys**, try Imaginarium, Largo Augusto 10 (*metro Duomo*), or for alternative toys from natural materials, check out La Citta 'del Sole, Via Orefici 13 (*metro

Duomo). For nature-related traditional toys; **Albero della Vita**, Via Maiocchi 14, off Via Stoppani (*metro Porta Venezia*), has a good selection of books for children as well as DVDs and computer games. Libreria dei Ragazzi, Via Tadino 53 (*metro Lima*), is the first bookshop in the city to specialize in children's books.

For **children's clothes**, try La Luna e, Via F Ferruccio 16 (*metro Buonarroti*), a small boutique, or Meroni Si', Via Madonnina 10 (*metro Lanza*), for designer children's gear.

Markets

The tourist office publishes a complete list of markets. Most are open mornings 9–1, but nearly all markets close in Aug:

Fiera di Senigallia, in Viale Gabriele D'Annunzio, along the banks of the Darsena (*metro Porta Genova*). *Open Saturday 7.30–5.*

San Donato market, south of Milan (*metro San Donato*). *Open Sunday mornings.*

Mercato del Sabato, Viale Papiniano (*metro Sant'Agostino*). For clothes; sometimes features cast-offs from the fashion shows. *Open Tues mornings and Sat all day 7.30–5.*

Mercatone dell'Antiquariato, along the Naviglio Grande (*metro Porta Genova*). For antiques (very popular). *Open every last Sunday of the month (exc July).*

Mercato Antiquariato di Brera. Via Fiori Chiari (*metro Lanza*). Also good for antiques. *Open third Saturday of each month.*

Postcard, stamp and coin market, Corduso Arcade in Piazza Duomo (*metro Duomo*). *Open Sunday mornings.*

Plant, flower and pet market, Piazzetta Reale or Piazzetta Mercanti (*metro Duomo*). *Open Sunday mornings Mar–June and Sept–Dec.*

Mercato della Darsena, along the banks of the Darsena (*metro Porta Genova*). An excellent food market. *Open daily.*

Mercato di Piazza Wagner (*metro Wagner*). A lovely, old covered food market. *Open Tues–Sat and Mon morning.*

Late Shopping

Autogrill Duomo, Piazza Duomo, **t** 02 8633 1922. A small market. *Open 6.30pm–12am.*

Supercentrale shopping centre, Stazione Centrale. *Open daily, supermarket until 12am, shops until 9pm.*

Sports and Activities

A dip in one of Milan's public swimming pools can make a hot day of sightseeing far more tolerable:

Parco Solari, Via Montevideo 20 (*metro Sant'Agostino*), **t** 02 469 5278. Floor-to-roof windows overlooking the park. *Closed Aug.*

Lido di Milano, Piazzale Lotto 15 (*metro Lotto*), **t** 02 3926 6100. Two outdoor pools and water slides (*see* p.73).

Piscina Cozzi, Viale Tunisia 35 (*metro Repubblica*), **t** 02 659 9703. An Olympic-size pool with a Fascist-era exterior.

Idropark Fila, Viale dell'Idroscalo 1, east of Milan (*bus no.73 from San Babila*), **t** 02 756 0393. Built around an artificial lake designed as a 'runway' for seaplanes in the 1920s, this is a lovely complex of three pools known as 'Milan's Riviera'. The **Luna Park** at Idroscalo also has water slides and rides.

Other aquatic park include:

Aquatica, Via G. Airaghi 61 (*tram 24*), **t** 02 4820 0134; *www.parcoaquatica.com*. With slides, pools and waterjets. *Closed Aug.*

Play Planet, Via Veglia 59, **t** 02 668 8838, *www.playplanet.it*, and Via Copernico 9 in Trerrano Sul Nariaglio, **t** 02 4840 9408; (*metro Zara*). A recreation centre with slides, pools and games.

The best **golf** course in the Milan area is the **Golf Club Milano**, **t** 039 030 081, *www.golf clubmilano.it*, in the Parco di Monza in Monza, north of the city (*see* p.106).

A popular **bicycle excursion** from Milan is to pedal along the Naviglio Grande canal from the Darsena to the Ticino river (around 40km), passing by way of Cassinetta di Lugagnano, home of one of Italy's top restaurants (*see* p.75). Like the Venetians, with their villas along the Brenta canal, the 18th-century Milanese built sumptuous summer houses along the Naviglio. Only one, the 15th-century frescoed **Villa Gaia** in Robecco, is open to visitors, **t** 02 947 0424 (call ahead). Bicycles can be rented at AWS, Via Ponte Seveso 33, **t** 02 6707 2145 (*metro Sondrio*). For more information on cycling, ring **Ciclobby**, Via Cesariano 11 (*metro Moscova*), **t** 02 331 3664 (*open Tues–Fri 5–7pm*). For boating tours of the canals try: **Amici dei Navigli Tours**, Via Marconi 1 (*metro Duomo*), **t** 02 6702 0280.

Milan's two first-division **football** clubs, **AC Milan** (*www.acmilan.com*) and **Inter** (*www.inter.it*), play on alternate Sundays during the Sept–May season at the San Siro stadium, Via Piccolomini 5 (*metro Lotto*). San Siro Stadium has a **football museum** which offers guided stadium tours, t 02 404 2432 (*open daily 10–5, exc match days; adm exp*).

Tickets for matches are available at the stadium, or from Milan Point, Via P. Verri 8, t 02 780398. For Inter matches, you can also buy tickets at branches of Banca Popolare di Milano; for AC games from branches of the Banca Cariplo.

American football (the 'Rhinos') and **rugby** are semi-professional and can often be seen at the Giurati sports centre.

Milan has a good **basketball** team, which plays in the Olimpia Milano stadium on Via Caltanissetta (*bus no.54 or 61*). Tickets can be bought at Banca Commerciale Italiana.

Milan's two **race tracks**, the Ippodromo and the Trottatoio (trotters), are both near San Siro.

The following sports centres also offer many indoor and outdoor activities:

Centro Sportivo Saini, Via Corelli 136 (*bus 38*), t 02 756 1280. A completely equipped sports complex. *No membership is necessary.*

Filaforum Milanofiori, Via Di Vittorio 6, Assago (*metro Famagosta; 7km from city centre*), t 02 4570 0466, *www.filaforum.it*. For bowling, basketball, roller-skating, squash and swimming.

Lido di Milano, Piazzale Lotto 15, t 02 3927 91 (*metro Lotto*). For tennis and football as well as swimming and windsurfing.

Other child-based activities include the following:

Acquario Civico, Parco Sempione, Via Gerolamo Gadio, t 02 584 861, *www.acquariocivico.mi.it* (*metro Lanza*). Closed for a major renovation but due to open towards the end of 2006.

Planetarium, Corso Venezia 57 (*metro Porta Venezia*), t 02 8846 3340 (call 9am–12), *www.comune.milano.it/planetario*. A place for children to sit and wonder at the stars. *Open Mon–Fri 9–12.30 and 2–5.30. Closed Jul–Aug.*

Teatro delle Marionette, Via degli Olivetani 3 (*metro Sant'Ambrogio*), t 02 469 4440. A puppet theatre performing Italian variations on the Punch and Judy theme.

Where to Stay

Milan has basically two types of accommodation: smart hotels for expense accounts, and seedy dives for new arrivals from the provinces. This bodes ill for the pleasure traveller, who has the choice of paying a lot of money for an up-to-date modern room with little atmosphere, or paying less for a place where one may not feel very comfortable (or, worse, very safe). Reserve in advance, because exceptions to the rule are snapped up fast – Hotel Associations (*see* p.69) provide a free hotel reservation service. Bear in mind also that in August much of Milan closes down, so that at this time it can be surprisingly easy to find a hotel. On the other hand, during the trade fairs (especially the big fashion shows in March and the autumn, and the April Fair) you may find no room at the inn.

Luxury

*****Excelsior Gallia**, Piazza Duca d'Aosta 9, ✉ 20124 (*metro Centrale*), t 02 67851, Opened in 1932, this prestigious hotel's guests have included Toscanini and Gorbachev. The hotel has spacious, elegant, air-conditioned rooms with satellite TV. The Health Centre offers Turkish baths and beauty treatments. Restaurant.

*****Four Seasons**, Via Gesù 8, ✉ 20121 (*metro Montenapoleone*), t 02 77088, *www.fourseasons. com*. A beautiful hotel in a 15th-century monastery. The church is the lobby and most of the spacious rooms overlook the cloister; enormous bathrooms, and plush sofas around the blazing fire in the winter. Private garage.

*****Grand Hotel et de Milan**, Via Manzoni 29, ✉ 20121 (*metro Montenapoleone*), t 02 723 141, *www.grandhoteletdemilan.it*. Open since 1863, and a favourite with Verdi, Hemingway and Nureyev, this hotel is now the fashion headquarters of supermodels. Rooms are individually furnished with antiques; the atmosphere is grand and gracious. *Wheelchair accessible.*

*****Principe di Savoia**, Piazza della Repubblica 17, ✉ 20124 (*metro Repubblica*), t 02 62301, *www.hotelprincipedisavoia.com*. Elegant and prestigious, this hotel was built in 1927 and has been visited by the Duke of

Windsor, Aristotle Onassis and Maria Callas. The presidential suite is considered by *Architectural Digest* to be one of the world's most beautiful retreats. There is an airport bus, a divine restaurant (**La Galleria**, *see* below) and a private garage. *Wheelchair accessible.*

Very Expensive

★★★**Antica Locanda Dei Mercanti**, Via San Tomaso 6, ✉ 20121 (*metro Duomo*), **t** 02 805 4080, *www.locanda.it*. In a pedestrian side street, this is a charming, discreet yet very centrally situated inn. Classically furnished rooms have fine white fabrics; the top floor rooms have canopy beds and individual roof terraces. Note: there is no sign outside; ring the buzzer. *Wheelchair accessible.*

★★★**Ariosto**, Via Ariosto 22, ✉ 20145 (*metro Conciliazione*), **t** 02 481 7844, *www.brera hotels.com/ariosto*. An early 20th-century mansion with character and a lovely court-yard, overlooked by the nicer rooms. Internet access, and weekend and children's rates.

★★★★**Hotel Ambasciatori**, Galleria del Corso 3, off Piazza Beccaria (*metro San Babila or Duomo*), **t** 02 7602 0241, *www.ambasciatori hotel.it*. Luxuriate here in beautifully refurbished period surroundings.

★★★★**Manin**, Via Manin 7, ✉ 20121 (*metro Turati*), **t** 02 659 6511, *www.hotelmanin.com*. Faces the Giardini Pubblici; reception is friendly and the rooms are quiet, modern and comfortable; nice private garden.

★★★★**Sheraton Diana Majestic**, Viale Piave 42, ✉ 20129 (*metro Porta Venezia*), **t** 02 20581, *www.dianamajestic.hotelsinmilan.it*. A fashionable, Liberty-style hotel built at the turn of the last century, with charming rooms, views over a garden and a lovely breakfast buffet.

★★★**Ariston**, Largo Carrobbio 2, ✉ 20123 (*south end of Via Torino; tram 2, 5 or 14*), **t** 02 7200 0556, *www.brerahotels.com/ariston*. An environmentalist's dream, with 100% cotton futons, hydro-massage water-saving showers, recycled everything and ion-emitting machines in every room (with a no-smoking floor and bicycles). Internet access and weekend/children's rates.

★★★★**Cavour**, Via Fatebenefratelli 21, ✉ 20121 (*metro Montenapoleone*), **t** 02 620 001,

www.hotelcavour.it. An elegantly furnished hotel. Note the public halls, the spiral steps and the collection of drawings of costumes at La Scala Theatre by Gio Ponti.

★★★★**De La Ville**, Via Hoepli 6, ✉ 20121 (*metro Duomo*), **t** 02 879 1341, *www.delavillemi-lano.com*. Modern, with antique furnishings and courteous service, comfortable lounges, bar and excellent restaurant; great weekend rates. *Wheelchair accessible.*

★★★**Gala**, Viale Zara 89, ✉ 20159 (*metro Zara*), **t** 02 6680 0891. Set in a quiet garden, a fine moderate-size hotel with wrought iron beds.

★★★**Giulio Cesare**, Via Rovello 10, ✉ 20121 (*metro Cairoli*), **t** 02 7200 3915, *www. giuliocesarehotel.it*. On a quiet street; has air conditioning.

★★★★**Hotel Spadari**, Via Spadari 11 (*metro Duomo*), **t** 02 7200 2371, *www.spadari hotel.com*. Modern Italian swank in one of Milan's true designer hotels.

★★★**Manzoni**, Via Santo Spirito 20, ✉ 20121 (*metro Montenapoleone*), **t** 02 7600 5700. A pleasant hotel on a quiet street near the city centre, with a private garage, sound-proofed rooms, and bright bathrooms. *Book in advance.*

★★★**Soperga**, Via Soperga 24, ✉ 20127 (*metro Centrale*), **t** 02 669 0541, *www.hotelsoperga milano.it*. Recently renovated, this hotel is central and comfortable, with soundproofed rooms and big breakfasts.

Expensive

★★★★**Hotel Regency**, Via Giovanni Arimondi 12 (*tram 12*), **t** 02 3921 6021, *www.regency-milano.com*. A must for Italian Art Nouveau fans, with rhapsodic floral wallpaper and vases.

★★★★★**Pierre Milano**, Via de Amicis 32 (*tram 2*), **t** 02 7200 0581, *www.hotelpierremilano.it*. Friendly hotel with well-designed rooms, along with all the amenities. *Wheelchair accessible.*

★★**Antica Locanda Solferino**, Via Castelfidardo 2, ✉ 20121 (*metro Moscova*), **t** 02 657 0129, *www.anticalocanda solferino.it*. An atmospheric 19th-century inn. All of the rooms have been individually decorated. The bathrooms are clean if some-what spartan. Breakfast is brought to your room. *Book well in advance.*

★★London, Via Rovello 3, ✉ 20121 (*metro Cairoli*), **t** 02 7202 0166, *www.albergo-hotel-london-milano.it*. On a quiet street near the castle; air conditioning, satellite TV.

★Valley, Via Soperga 19, ✉ 20127 (*metro Centrale*), **t** 02 669 2777, *www.hotelvalley.it*. Good budget hotel with comfortable rooms. Two of the cheaper rooms have communal baths.

Moderate

★★★★Hotel Regina, Via Cesare Correnti 13 (*metro Sant'Ambrogio*), **t** 02 5810 6913, *www.hotelregina.it*. Stylish, yet well-priced hotel. *Wheelchair accessible*.

★★★Hotel Promessi Sposi, Piazza Oberdan 12 (*metro Porta Venezia*), **t** 02 2951 3661, *www.hotelpromessisposi.com*. A romantic hotel with all amenities.

★★★Hotel Vittoria, Via Pietro Calvi 32 (*tram 27, bus 60*), **t** 02 545 6520, *www.hotelvittoria milano.it*. A small, friendly and romantic hotel with comfortable rooms.

★★Casa Mia, Viale Vittorio Veneto 30, ✉ 20124 (*metro Repubblica*), **t** 02 657 5249, *www .casamiahotel.it*. An excellent value hotel just north of the Giardini Pubblici, with all amenities, including air conditioning in some rooms.

★Atena, Viale Piave 5, ✉ 20129 (*metro Porta Venezia*), **t** 02 7602 3880, *www.hotel atena.com*. Small and safe; bathrooms down the hall. *Wheelchair accessible*.

Inexpensive

★Albergo Commercio, Via Mercato 1, entrance on Via Erbe (*metro Lanza*), **t** 02 8646 3880. Clean, good value hotel. *Book ahead*.

★Hotel Ullrich, Corso Italia 6 (*metro Missori*), **t** 02 8645 9156. More of a *pensione* with the family touch; a pleasant place on the 6th floor of an old *palazzo*.

La Cordata (Casa Scout), Via Burigozzo 11 (*metro Missori*), **t** 02 5831 4675, *www.lacor data.it*. Private hostel with kitchen facilities. *Book in advance*.

Ostello Piero Rotta, Via Salmoiraghi 1 (*near San Siro stadium, metro QT8*), **t** 02 3926 7095, *milano@ostellionline.org*. Milan's modern youth hostel. An IYHF card is required, though one can be bought on the spot. *Closed 23 Dec–13 Jan, max stay 3 days*.

Eating Out

In moneyed Milan you'll find some of Italy's finest restaurants and the widest range of international cuisine. On the downside, an average meal will cost you considerably more than it would almost anywhere else in Italy. The best places to find a selection of cheaper restaurants are in the Brera, Ticinese and Navigli districts. Presume, unless otherwise stated, that all are closed in August.

Saffron is Milan's fetish spice, and appears in most dishes *alla milanese*. The origins of its use go back to a Belgian stained-glass maker, working on the Duomo in 1574, who was called 'Saffron' by his fellows because he always sprinkled a bit of the stuff in his mixes to make the glass colours richer. The other glass-workers joked that he loved saffron so much that he would soon be adding it to his food. During the wedding of Saffron's daughter, his apprentice had the chef put saffron in the rice as a prank; everyone was astonished at the yellow concoction, but it was delicious, and the Milanese have been making their saffron *risotto alla milanese* ever since.

Very Expensive

Il luogo di Aimo e Nadia, Via Montecuccoli 6 (*metro Bande Nere*), **t** 02 416 886, *www. aimoenadia.com*. Aimio and his wife Nadia have earned themselves an unparalleled reputation for high quality Lombard and national cuisine, made from stringently selected fresh, local ingredients. *Closed Sat eve, and Sun. Book ahead*.

Antica Osteria del Ponte, Piazza G.Negri in Cassinetta di Lugagnano (30km from Milan), **t** 02 942 0034, *www.anticaosteriadelponte.it*. A holy temple of Italian cuisine which shouldn't be missed by serious gourmets. Intimate and elegant decor. *Closed Sun, Mon, 3 weeks between Dec and Jan*.

Don Lisander, Via Manzoni 12 (*metro Duomo*), **t** 02 7602 0130. A creative menu offering international dishes. *Closed Sun*.

La Galleria, Piazza della Repubblica 17 (*metro Repubblica*), **t** 02 62301, *www.hotel principedisavoia.it*. The Hotel Principe di Savoia's restaurant serves excellent gourmet Paduan food in luxurious surrounds: marble, crystal and *trompe l'œil*.

La Scaletta, Piazzale Stazione Porta Genova 3 (*metro Porta Genova*), **t** 02 5810 0290. The culinary workshop of Italy's *nuova cucina* sorceress, Pina Bellini, who does exquisite things with pasta and risotto, fish and rabbit, all beautifully presented. Excellent desserts and wines finish off a truly memorable meal. *Closed Sun, and Mon lunch; reservations advised.*

Gianni e Dorina, Via Pepe 38 (*metro Garibaldi; tram 3,4; bus 41, 51*), **t** 02 606 340. Not far from the tracks of Stazione Garibaldi, this delightful restaurant offers local and national specialities. There is a wide selection of bread and oils. The owner is a professional wine taster and the quality of the wines are a testament to his expertise. *Closed Sat and Sun lunch.*

Nobu, Via Pisoni 1 (*metro Montenapoleone*), **t** 02 7231 8645. Part of the Armani flagship store; sushi downstairs and a chic New York-style restaurant upstairs, with great wines. *Closed Mon, Sat at lunch, Sun, 2 weeks between Dec and Jan.*

Peck, Via Victor Hugo 4 (*metro Duomo*), **t** 02 876 774, *www.peck.it*. This delicatessen and shop (*see* p.71) also has a good quality modern cellar restaurant. Their *risotto alla milanese* is hard to beat. *Closed Sun, 3 weeks between Jan and Feb, and 3 weeks in Aug.*

Ran, Via Bordoni 8 (*metro Gioia*), **t** 02 669 6997, *www.ristoranteran.it*. If you need a break from Italian cuisine, try this elegant sushi bar. *Closed Mon, Sat and Sun lunch. Reservation advisable.*

Sadler Osteria di Porta Cicca, Via Troilo 14, off Via Conchetta (*tram 3 or 15*), **t** 02 5810 4451, *www.sadler.it*. A moveable feast of new combinations and ingredients, all served up in a small, refined setting. *Closed Sun, first 2 weeks of Jan and Aug. Reservation required.*

Savini, Galleria Vittorio Emanuele II, **t** 02 7200 3433, *www.savini.thi.it.* (*metro Duomo*). A bastion of Milanese tradition (since 1867), with Lombard classics at the pinnacle of perfection – especially the *secondi*. *Closed Sun, first week of Jan and 3 weeks in Aug. Reservation advisable.*

Sogo im Brera, Via Fiori Oscuri (*metro Montenapoleone*), **t** 02 8646 5367. A stylish and expensive sushi bar, with a creative touch. *Closed Sun.*

Expensive

13 Giugno, Via Carlo Goldoni 44 (*metro Porta Venezia*), **t** 02 719 654. Sicilian seafood recipes in a 1930s ambience and a piano bar, plus a pleasant garden in summer. *Booking advisable. Closed Sun and first week of Dec, 3 weeks in Aug.*

Al Porto, Piazzale General Cantore (*metro Porta Genova*), **t** 02 8940 7425. A fish restaurant located in a 19th-century toll house with a beautiful winter garden. *Closed Sun and Mon lunch.*

Al Vecchio Porco, Via Messina 8 (*tram 12 or 14 or bus 94*), **t** 02 313 862, *www.alvecchio porco.it*. A trendy pizzeria serving such delights as pizza with ricotta, tomatoes and olives, or the *del Porco* (sausage, gorgonzola and egg). *Closed for lunch and on Sun.*

Antica Trattoria della Pesa, Viale Pasubio 10, close to Porta Comasina (*metro Garibaldi*), **t** 02 655 5741. This *trattoria* dates back to 1880 and has fed generations of Milanese publishers and journalists, as well as Maria Callas and Visconti. *Closed Sun.*

Aurora, Via Savona 23 (*in the Navigli, metro Porta Genova*), **t** 02 8940 4978. Lovely *belle époque* dining rooms and equally lovely Piedmontese cuisine, with an emphasis on mushrooms and truffles, and a bewildering array of cheeses. Save some room for the superb *tarte tatin. Closed Mon.*

Bice, Via Borgospesso 12 (*metro Montenapoleone*), **t** 02 7600 2572, *www.bice milano.it*. Sophisticated, traditional cuisine and impeccable service; the favourite restaurant with Milan's VIPs. *Closed Sun.*

Centro Ittico, Via Martiri Oscuri 19 (*metro Loreto*), **t** 02 614 3774, *www.rawfishcafe.it*. Fish comes directly from the market counter to your plate. *Closed Sun and Mon lunch.*

Hong Kong, Via Schiaparelli 5 (*metro Centrale*), **t** 02 670 1992. This secluded place combines Chinese *haute cuisine* with elegant and refined decor. One of the best Chinese restaurants in Milan. *Closed Mon.*

Il Giardino dei Segreti, Via P. Sottocorno 17 (*tram 9, 20 or 23*), **t** 02 7600 8376, *www. ilgiardinodeisegreti.it*. One half 'Hanging Gardens of Babylon', the other half airy and simple, with tasty delicacies and traditional, wholesome fare. *Closed Sun and Mon at lunch. Booking advisable.*

La Terrazza, Via Ozanam 1 (*metro Lima*), t 02 204 8433. On the 6th floor of the Hotel Galles Milano; offers *al fresco* traditional dining with a view over the Duomo's spires. *Closed Mon eve.*

La Volpe e l'Uva, Via Senato 45 (*metro Montenapoleone*), t 02 7602 2167. Owned by two imaginative sisters – great cooking in intimate surroundings. *Closed Sun and Mon, and Wed and Sat eves.*

Piccolo Sogno, Via Stoppani 5 (*metro Porta Venezia*), t 02 2024 1210. Traditional and regional cuisine prepared to perfection. *Closed Sat lunch and Sun, plus first 10 days of Jan and 3 weeks in Aug. Booking advisable.*

Quattrocento, Via Campazzino 14 (*tram 79*), t 02 895 1777. A converted 15th-century monastery, transformed into a very stylish and popular, wood-filled, minimalist Zen shrine with delicious nouveau cuisine also fish recipes Unusual first-course flavours. *Closed Mon. Booking essential.*

Vini e Cucina, Via Tadino off Via Castaldi. (*metro Repubblica*), t 02 2951 9840, *www. alistair.it.* An internationally acclaimed New York-style restaurant specializing in seafood dishes. *Closed Sat lunch and Mon.*

Moderate

Al Pont de Ferr, Via Ripa Ticinese 55 (*metro Porta Genova*), t 02 8940 6277. Try the smoked salami, and dishes such as pigeon with mushrooms and polenta. Arrive early to avoid the queues. *Closed Sun, 3 weeks in Aug.*

Armani Caffè, Via Croce Rossa 2 (*metro Montenapoleone*), t 02 7231 8680. Mediterranean dishes served in designer surroundings. Note vegetarian and fish dishes. *Closed Sat eves and Sun.*

Endo, Via Fabio Filzi 8 (*metro Loreto*), t 02 6698 6117. Milan's oldest Japanese restaurant. Good-value lunch menu. *Closed Mon.*

Pizza Big, Viale Brianza 30 (*metro Loreto*), t 02 284 6548. Another name in Milanese pizza lore. *Closed Sun.*

Innocenti Evasioni, Via Bindellina 1, in the San Siro area (*tram 14*), t 02 3300 1882, *www. innocentievasioni.com.* Offers an escape from the city, with country-style rooms overlooking a garden. Eclectic, ever-changing dishes. *Closed Sun, Mon, first week of Jan and 2 weeks in Aug.*

Al Muleto, Corso XXII Marzo 57 (*metro Porta Vittoria*), t 02 7012 6814. Owned and run for over 30 years by the Papaluca family, this spacious restaurant is arranged over two floors and specializes in fish and seafood. The wine list is excellent. *Closed Wed.*

Kota Radja, Piazzale Baracca 6 (*metro Conciliazone*), t 02 468 850. Chinese restaurants in Italy have somehow adapted to local cuisine, so be prepared for less familiar but possibly tastier dishes than at home. *Closed Mon.*

Compagnia Generale dei Viaggiatori, Naviganti e Sognatori, Via Cuccagna 4 (*metro Porta Romana*), t 02 551 6154. For a cosmopolitan mix, try this Japanese restaurant managed by Italians and Brazilians in an old *cascina* (country house); the result is convincing. *Closed lunchtime, Sun and Mon.*

La Felicità, Via Rovello 3 (*metro Cairoli*), t 02 865 235. Another Chinese restaurant in the city centre; a romantic, cheaper meal.

Latteria San Marco, Via San Marco 24 (*metro Moscova*), t 02 659 7653. Favoured by media types, this busy inn maintains its family-run status: father in the kitchen, mother and two daughters serving. Excellent desserts. *Closed Sat and Sun. Cash only. No booking possible, arrive early (only 10 tables).*

Officina 12, Alzaia Naviglio Grande 12 (*metro Porta Genova*), t 02 8942 2261, *www. officina12.it.* In an enormous hi-tech loft – traditional pizzeria meets urban regeneration. Also American bar, open till 2am. *Closed Mon.*

Osteria delle Vigne, Ripa di Porta Ticinese 61 (*metro Porta Genova*), t 02 857 5617. A chilled out, good value, friendly restaurant; the pick of many in this buzzing district. *Closed Sun and Mon, 2 weeks in Dec, Aug.*

Ponte Rosso, Via Ripa di Porta Ticinese 23 (*metro Porta Genova*), t 02 837 3132. Soak in a romantic old-world bistro atmosphere, where excellent cuisine mixes traditional dishes from Italy specialities. *Closed Sun and Wed eve, Aug. Booking advisable.*

Nameless, Via Montebianco 2/a (*metro Lotto*), t 02 481 4677, *www.ristorantenameless.it.* This newly-opened restaurant excels at creative and experimental cuisine fused with traditional Italian recipes. *Closed Sun. Reservations advisable.*

San Fermo, Via S. Fermo della Battaglia 1 (*metro Moscova or Turati*), **t** 02 2900 0901. Business Milan's secret: light, tasty lunches and affordable full dinners; often busy, but service is fast and efficient. *Closed Sun.*

Trattoria Tipica Pugliese, Via Tadino 5 (*metro Lima or Porta Venezia*), **t** 02 2952 2574. You can eat cheaply here by just filling your dish of antipasti from a selection of 40 specialities from Apulia (the heel of Italy). Friendly atmosphere and service. *Closed Sun.*

Tomoyoshi, Via Sacco 4 (*metro De Angeli*), **t** 02 466 330. A Japanese sushi bar with cold dishes only. Fixed menu at lunch time, *à la carte* is more expensive. Takeaway also available. *Closed Mon.*

Trattoria all'Antica, Via Montevideo 4, in the Ticinese area (*metro Sant'Agostino*), **t** 02 8372 849. Abundant Lombard fare prepared simply, but with the freshest ingredients. *Closed Sat lunch and Sun, Aug.*

Trattoria Milanese, Via Santa Marta 11 (*metro Duomo*), **t** 02 8645 1991. A family-run *trattoria* which offers true Milanese dishes in a sober, yet homely ambience. *Closed Tues and 2 weeks between Dec–Jan, Aug.*

Trattoria Toscana, Corso Porta Ticinese 58 (*tram 3, 20*), **t** 02 8940 6292. A jolly place, with music in the garden, and dishes like gnocchi filled with ricotta and swordfish with thyme. *Open until 2am (kitchen closes at 1); closed lunchtimes, and Sun.*

Tre Pini, Via Tullio Morgagni 19 (*bus 42, 43*), **t** 02 6680 5413. Hidden behind a monument- al pine in the Maggiolina, this is one of the best places to go for roasted meat and fish. Cooking takes place in a chimney that burns olive wood in the middle of the conservatory in winter, and in the garden pergola in summer. *Closed Sat, Aug. Booking advisable.*

Inexpensive

Highly recommended are self-service chains Brek and Pastarito (pasta dishes only, so large that one portion often feeds two people).

Da Rino Vecchia Napoli, Via Chavez 4 (*between Stazione Centrale and Parco Lambro, metro Pasteur*), **t** 02 261 9056. Prize-winning pizzas, with a vast selection to choose from. One of the best pizzas in Milan. *Closed Sun lunch and Mon. Booking advisable.*

Govinda, Via Valpetrosa 3/5 (*metro Duomo*) **t** 02 862 417. Very good vegetarian and macrobiotic food as well as Indian dishes and a takeaway. *Closed Sun, Mon lunch.*

Osteria Conchetta, Via Conchetta 8 (*tram 3 or 15*), **t** 02 832 3389. Popular with actors, this friendly restaurant offers a tempting blend of Milanese and traditional Italian recipies. Delicious wines. *Closed lunch times and Tues.*

Joya, Via P. Castaldi 18 (*metro Porta Venezia*), **t** 02 2952 2124. Considered one of the best vegetarian restaurants in Italy (*inexpensive at lunch time, expensive–moderate in the evening*). *Closed Sat lunch and Sun and 3 weeks in Aug. Booking advisable.*

Osteria del Treno, Via S. Gregorio 46 (*metro Porta Venezia*), **t** 02 6700 479. At lunchtime, this atmospheric former railway workers' club has an excellent, good value self-service counter. The wonderful sit-down dinners are moderately priced. *Closed Sat and Aug.*

Tagiura, Via Tagiura 5, in the San Siro area (*bus 50, 90, 91*), **t** 02 4895 0613. At this affordable and friendly family-run *osteria* you can have a good full meal, or just a piece of cake or a dish of salami. Fish on Fridays, home-made pasta every day, different daily traditional dishes; unparalled *testaroli al pesto. Open daily for lunch, and Thurs and Fri eves; closed Sun and Aug. Booking necessary at dinner.*

Ristorante San Tomaso, Via San Tomaso 5 (*metro Cairoli*), **t** 02 874 510. A popular choice at lunchtime with Milanese workers who come here to make the most of its self-service buffet (*moderately priced in the evening*). *Closed Sat lunch and Sun.*

La Rosa Nera, Via Solferino 12 (*metro Lanza or Turati*), **t** 02 659 8972, *www.larosanera.net.* Not far from the Pinacoteca of Brera, La Rosa Nera offers a range of seasonal Tuscan specialities along with some good fish recipes. Try the home-made tagliatelle with seafood and courgettes or the Costata alla Fiorentina. *Closed Wed.*

Trattoria del Nuovo Macello, Via C. Lombroso (*tram 27*), **t** 02 5990 2122, *www.trattoriadel nuovomacello.it.* A compelling range of creative, good-value cuisine is on offer at this eternal of the Milan gastro scene. *Closed Sat at lunch and Sun, 2 weeks Dec–Feb, Aug. Cash only.*

Happy Hour, Brunch and *Panini*

Milan has adopted the Anglo-Saxon habit of brunch and happy hours, athough the latter, the *aperitivo*, is an old Milanese tradition. Another Milanese tradition is the *panino* (sandwich), a quick tasty snack at any time of day.

10 Corso Como Caffè, Corso Como 10 (*metro Garibaldi*), Mediterranean sushi, truffle omelettes and other delicacies for a classy minimal brunch or late-night cocktails. Since 2004 it is possible to eat at lunch for €25 (fixed menu). Good place for an aperitif too. *Closed Mon lunch.*

L'Acerba, Via Orti 4 (*metro Porta Romana*). Daily brunch in an old carriage garage. Excellent choice of cakes, also has a restaurant. Fun for an aperitif. *Closed Mon.*

Al Panino, in Viale Crispi 5 (*metro Garibaldi or Moscova*). The latest sandwich shop to open; there are 80 types to choose from, as well as warm *focaccias*, cold dishes and fries. *Closed Mon.*

Art & Soul Café, Piazza XXIV Aprile 10 (*metro Garibaldi*). New Age vegetarian brunches are served here inside the Smeraldo theatre. Cultural events featuring music, art, poetry. *Closed Wed.*

Atomic Bar, Via F. Casati 24 (*metro Repubblica*), *www.atomicbar.it*. Avant-garde disco bar, popular for after-concert parties. Alternative punk, rock. Daily happy hour (*6–8*), with DJs after 10pm. *Closed Tues.*

Bar Basso, Via Plinio 39, Città Studi area (*metro Lima*), *www.barbasso.com*. The place to go for happy hour: over 500 cocktails and home-made ice creams, in a venue with a 19th-century *salotto* and a country-style section. Try 'Mangue Beri': ice cream with spirits. *Closed Tues.*

Bar della Crocetta, Corso di Porta Romana 67 (*metro Crocetta*). After the theatre, go for a *Panino Augusto*. *Closed Aug.*

Bar Quadronno, Via Quadronno 34 (*metro Crocetta*). The oldest sandwich maker, which opened in 1966. Attended by a loyal though not young clientele. A large choice of *paninis*. *Closed Mon and till 2am daily.*

Berlin Café, Via G. Mora 9 (*metro Porta Genova*). Sunday brunches in a historical bar of Teutonic inspiration. Try the *panini* or *bruschette*. Happy hour 6.30–9. *Closed on Sun.*

Blues Canal, Via Casale 7, in the Navigli (*metro Porta Genova*). Has an American/Irish Sunday brunch (*12–4*) with live classical music. Top live jazz in the evenings too. Spot Louis Armstrong's trumpet among those hanging on the walls. Happy hour 6.30–9. *Closed Mon.*

Caffè Cova, Via Monte Napoleone 8, *www.panettone.it* (*metro Montenapoleone*). A Milanese institution famous for its pastries, open since 1837. Also restaurant with Milanese cuisine. *Closed Sun.*

Coquetel, Via Vetere 14, *www.coquetel.it* (*tram 2, 3 or 8*). Popular bar with hundreds of cocktails. Happy hours 7–9.

Caffè Sant'Ambroeus, Corso Matteotti 7 (*metro Montenapoleone*). Founded in 1936, this bar, with its wonderful period decor, is a favourite with Milanese. Try *cioulatimo ambrofiotto*, a special chocolate. *Closed Mon.*

Le Biciclette, Via Torti, corner Conca del Naviglio, *www.lebiciclette.com* (*tram 2 or 14*). This trendy café is housed in an old bicycle shed. On Sunday it serves one of the best brunches in Milan (*12.30–4.30*). There is also a restaurant with a monthly menu.

Martinique Café, Via P. da Cannobio 37 (*metro Missori*). Standing bar with jazz and soul, and over 100 distilled labels. Happy hour (*6–9*) comes with sushi. *Closed Mon.*

Panino del Conte, Via Brioletto, corner Via dei Bossi 7 (*metro Duomo*). Noble sandwiches in Brera, where you can try the famous *Piadina del Conte* and warm focaccia. *Closed Sun.*

Panino Giusto is a chain with shops in the Navigli, Garibaldi and the city centre areas. The nicest and oldest ones are in Piazza Beccaria 4 (*metro Duomo*) and in Piazzale XXIV Maggio (*metro Porta Genova*).

Radetsky, Corso Garibaldi 105 (*metro Moscova*). Trendy bar on the corner; home-made cakes of all kinds and over 200 cocktails. Brunches (*daily 10–3*) and aperitivos, popular among city managers.

Speakeasy, Via Castelfidardo 7 (*metro Moscova*). This atmospheric 1930s US-style bar is in front of the historical Ponte delle Gabelle. It has a popular Sunday brunch (*12–4*), daily happy hour (*7–9*), a vast selection of US dailies and also Mexican food. *Closed Mon.*

Entertainment and Nightlife

Check listings in the daily *Corriere della Sera* and *La Repubblica*'s Wednesday *Tutto Milano* magazine. For clubs with live music check under the heading '*Ritrovi*'. Other sources include the free *Milano Mese* and *Hello Milan*, available at the main tourist office.

Tickets are sold at **Ricordi**, in the Galleria Vittorio Emanuele II; **La Biglietteria**, Via Molino delle Armi 3; **Box Ticket**, Largo Cairoli; and in a kiosk in Stazione Cadorna.

Film

Anteo, Via Milazzo 9 (*metro Moscova*), t 02 659 7732, *www.anteospaziocinema.com*. Regularly shows films in English – make sure it says *versione originale. Closed Aug.*

Opera and Classical Music

Auditorium di Milano, Largo G. Mahler, Navigli district (*tram 3 or 15*), t 02 8338 9201, *www.auditoriumdimilano.org*. Concerts by the Symphonic Conservatory Giuseppe Verdi, plus jazz, choral and chamber music.

Giuseppe Verdi Conservatorio, Via del Conservatorio 12 (*metro San Babila*), t 02 762 1101, *www.conservatorio.it*. Classical music. *Closed July–mid-Sept.*

La Scala, Piazza della Scala (*metro Duomo*): For many people, an evening at La Scala is in itself the reason for visiting Milan. Book tickets on t 02 860 775 (24 hours; bookings can be made approx two months in advance), or *www.teatroallascala.org*. You can only order two tickets at a time (stalls and gallery), although you can make consecutive reservations. The CIT office, in the Galleria Vittorio Emanuele II, t 02 863 701, has a certain number of tickets to sell to foreign tourists who make hotel reservations through them. Finding a good seat at short notice is all but impossible; try the box office an hour or so before the performance starts to see what's available. La Scala theatre and opera company – and Milan's orchestra, **Orchestra Filarmonica** – also perform here. The ticket office is at Piazza Diaz 6 (*metro Duomo*), t 02 7202 3671, *www.filarmonica.it*. The season runs 7 Dec–mid-July and mid-Sept–mid-Nov.

Theatre

Piccolo Teatro (also known as Teatro Gress), Via Rovello 2, near Via Dante (*metro Cordusio*), t 02 7233 3222, *www.piccoloteatro.org*. Milan is also the home of Italy's best theatre company. Founded after the Second World War and run for years by brilliant director Giorgio Strehler, the Piccolo has a repertory ranging from *commedia dell'arte* to the avant-garde. The Piccolo Teatro now divides its performances between the historical venue of Via Rovello, **Teatro Giorgio Strehler**, Largo Greppi and **Teatro Studio**, Via Rivolo 6. Organization and booking is centralized.

Teatro Nazionale, Piazza Piemonte 12 (*metro Wagner*), t 02 4800 7700, *www.teatro nazionale.com*. For plays and musicals.

Jazz

Blues House, Via S. Uguzzone 26 (*metro Precotto*), off Viale Monza, in Sesto San Giovanni, northeast of the city, t 02 2700 3621, *www.blueshouse.it*. Plays blues exclusively. *Closed Tues.*

Gimmis, Via Cellini 2 (*metro San Babila*), t 02 5518 8069. Exclusive piano bar favoured by Italian media celebs and theatre types.

Grilloparlante, Alzaia Naviglio Grande 36 (*metro Porta Genova*), t 02 8940 9321. Alternates jazz with blues by amateurs and professionals. Also has a restaurant with Mediterranean cuisine. *Closed Tues.*

Le Trottoir alla Darsena, Piazza XXIV Maggio 1 (*metro Porta Genova*), t 02 837 8166, *www.letrottoir.it*. Andrea Pinketts, the new owner of Le Trottoir, is a crime novel writer. Offers a blend of good food and entertainment. Well worth a visit.

Scimmie, Via Ascanio Sforza 49 (*metro Porta Genova*), t 02 8940 2874, *www.scimmie.it*. Diverse but high-quality jazz offerings. There is also a restaurant (*moderate–inexpensive*).

Sakhalin, Via Pezzotti 52 (*metro Famagosta*), t 02 8950 3509. The range of live music on offer here covers most musical genres. *Closed Mon.*

Zythum, Via Rutilia 16, t 02 569 1616, *www.zythum.it* (*metro Porta Romana*). A brewery-cum-fusion restaurant with a sushi corner. The warehouse hosts live music and events. *Closed Mon.*

Gelaterie

Antica Gelateria del Corso, Galleria del Corso 4 (*metro Duomo*). Three floors of saccharine paradise, including delicious ice creams, sandwiches, pastries, salads and cocktails; Sat and Sun brunch (12–4).

Cremeria Buonarroti, Via Buonarroti 9 (*metro Buonarroti or Wagner*), *www. cremeriabuonarroti.it*. *Crème de la crème* – literally, especially the strawberries bathed in Gianduja chocolate. Try full-cream parfaits with 'gianduia' chocolate. *Closed Mon.*

Ecologica, Corso di Porta Ticinese 40 (*tram 3 or 20*). Totally natural ingredients go into these ice cream treats. 30 different flavours with natural ingredients. *Closed Wed.*

Cafés and Bars

Casablanca, Corso Como 14 (*metro Garibaldi*), t 02 626 0186, *www.casablancacafe.it*. Trendy cocktail bar-restaurant. Live music evenings alternate with DJs; summer dancing in the garden. *Closed Mon.*

Club Diana, Viale Piave 42 (*metro Porta Venezia*), t 02 20581. One of Milan's fashionable *aperitivo* destinations, set in an illuminated hotel garden. *Closed Sat–Sun.*

Frescobar, Via Bramante 9 (*metro Moscova*), t 02 349 4576. An informal and elegant bar with an eclectic decor. *Closed Mon.*

Jamaica, Via Brera 32 (*metro Lanza*), t 02 876 723, *www.jamaicabar.it*. Old rendezvous of artists in the 1920s and 1930s, once the meeting place of the *Scapigliati* painters.

Julep's, Via Torricelli 21, in the Navigli area (*tram 15*), t 02 8940 9029, *www.juleps milano.com*. For fajitas and New York-style cuisine, with jazz music and a big counter for you to eat at. *Closed Mon.*

L'Exploit, Via Pioppette 3 (*tram 3*), t 02 8940 8675, *www.exploitmilano.com*. A popular *aperitivo* hang-out, set against the ancient Roman columns of the basilica of San Lorenzo. *Closed Mon.*

La Bodeguita del Medio, Via Col di Lana (*tram 9 or 15*), t 02 8940 0560. A popular cigar bar, with Cuban music, food and a lively atmosphere. *Closed Sun.*

Light, Via Maroncelli 8 (*metro Garibaldi*), t 02 6269 0631, *www.lightlounge.it*. The definitive late lounge, in mellow surrounds.

Magenta, Via Carducci 13 (*tram 19 or 24*), t 02 805 3808. A historical Art Nouveau bar and beer house. *Open daily.*

Moscatelli, Corso Garibaldi 93 (*metro Moscova*) t 02 655 4602. Milan's oldest *bottiglieria* (wine bar). *Closed Sun.*

Pogue's Mahones, Via Salmini 1 (*metro Porta Romana*), t 02 5830 9726, *www.pogue.it*. Lively pub with live Irish bands.

Roialto, Via Piero della Francesca 55 (*bus 57 or 94*), t 02 3493 6616. Friendly, cool bar in a former garage.

Shambala, Via Ripamonti 337 (*metro Porta Romana*), t 02 552 0194. Atmospheric resto-bar that serves fusion cuisine inspired by Southeast Asia. *Closed Sun.*

Xe Mauri, Via Confalonieri 5 (*metro Garibaldi*), t 02 6085 6028. A laguna-bar, ideal for early evening drinks. *Closed Sun and Aug.*

Clubs and Discos

Generally, clubs open every day until 3am (often extended at weekends). Two venues are currently hot: **Hollywood**, Corso Como 15 (*metro Garibaldi; closed Mon*), and **Shocking**, Via Bastioni di Porta Nuova 12 (*metro Repubblica; closed Sun and Mon*).

Plastic, Viale Umbria 120 (*metro Porta Romana*) *www.thisisplastic.com*. Eclectic clientele, drag-queen shows and fussy doormen; Thursday is gay night. *Closed Mon–Wed and July–Aug.*

C-Side, Via Castelbarco 11 (*metro Porta Genova*). Alternates disco and live concerts. *Wed eve free for students. Closed Mon–Tues.*

Tropicana Club Latino, Viale Bligny 52 (*metro Porta Romana*), *www.tropicanaclub latino.com*. For Latin American dancing. *Closed Sun, Mon and Wed.*

Alcatraz, Via Valtellina 25 (*tram 3,4,1, metro Zara*) t 02 6901 6352, *www.alcatraz milano.com*. Three separate dance floors playing a mix of 1980s and 1990s music.

Gay and Lesbian Clubs and Discos

Nuova Idea, Via De Castilla 30 (*metro Garibaldi*) *www.lanuovaidea.com*. Milan's foremost gay club. *Closed Mon–Wed.*

Sottomarino Giallo, Via Donatello 2 (*metro Loreto*) *www.sottomarinogiallo.it*. Gay hotspot with disco music, most nights are for women only. *Closed Mon.*

Most tourists don't come to Italy looking for slick and feverishly busy Milan, and most of those who find themselves here take in only the obligatory sights – Leonardo's *Last Supper*, La Scala, the Duomo, and the Brera Art Gallery – before rushing off to shop. And most Italians (apart from the 4 million Milanese, that is) have little that's good to say about their second city: all the Milanese do is work, all they care about is money, they are just as corrupt as everyone else, and they defiantly refuse to indulge even in the myth of *la dolce vita*.

Yet the Italians who deride Milan are mostly envious, and the tourists who whip through it in a day are mostly ignorant of what this great city has to offer. Milan is certainly atypical, devoid of the usual Italian daydreams and living-museum mustiness. Like Naples it lives for the present, and as one of Europe's major financial centres and a capital of fashion, Milan dresses in a well-tailored, thoroughly cosmopolitan three-piece suit. The skills of its workers, above all in the luxury clothing trades, have been known for centuries – as evoked in the English word 'millinery'.

And yet, as the Milanese are the first to admit, Milan has made its way in the world not so much by native talent as through the ability to attract and make use of those from other places, from St Ambrose and Leonardo da Vinci to its most celebrated designer of the moment. It has produced no great music of its own, but La Scala opera house is the world's most prestigious places to sing; it has produced very few artists of its own but has amassed enough treasures to fill four superb galleries. Milan is the Italian melting pot, Italy's picture window on the modern world, where the young and ambitious gravitate to see their talents rewarded. Here history seems to weigh less; here willowy Japanese models slink down the pavement with natty young gents whose parents immigrated from Calabria. Roiling, moiling, toiling, constantly evolving, Milan is *sui generis*; in Milanese dialect they have said simply, long before Gertrude Stein's 'a rose is a rose', *Milan l'e Milan*, Milan is Milan.

History

Milan was born cosmopolitan. Although located far from any sea or river, in the midst of the fertile but vulnerable Lombard plain it occupies the natural junction of trade routes through the Alpine passes, from the Tyrrhenian and Adriatic ports and from the River Po. This commercially strategic position has also put Milan square in the path of every conqueror tramping through Italy.

Mediolanum, as it was called for its first millennium and a half, first became prominent in the twilight of Rome when, as the headquarters of the Mobile Army and the seat of the court and government of the West, it became the de facto capital of the empire; Diocletian preferred it to Rome, and his successors spent much of their time here. The official Christianization of the empire began here in 313, when Constantine the Great established religious toleration with his **Edict of Milan**.

The Rise of the *Comune*

During the barbarian invasions of the next few centuries *Mediolanum* was shortened to *Mailand*, the prized Land of May, for so it seemed to the frostbitten Goths and Lombards who came to take it for their own. In the early 11th century Milan evolved into one of Italy's first *comuni* under the leadership of another great bishop, **Heribert**, who organized a *parlamento* of citizens and a citizen militia. The new *comune*, Guelph in defiance of imperial pretensions, at once began subjugating the surrounding country and especially its Ghibelline rivals Pavia, Lodi, and Como. To inspire the militia, Heribert also invented that unique Italian war totem, the *carroccio*, a huge ox-drawn cart that bore the city's banner, altar and bells into battle.

It was Lodi's complaint about Milan's bullying to Holy Roman Emperor **Frederick Barbarossa** that first brought old Red Beard to Italy in 1154. It was to prove a momentous battle of wills and arms between the emperor and Milan. Barbarossa sacked Milan in 1158; the *Ambrosiani* promised to behave but attacked his German garrison as soon as the emperor was back safely over the Alps. Undaunted, Barbarossa returned again and for two years laid waste to the countryside around Milan, then grimly besieged the defiant city. When it surrendered he was merciless, demanding the surrender of the *carroccio*, forcing the citizens to kiss his feet with ropes around their necks, and inviting Milan's bitterest enemies, Lodi and Como, to raze the city to the ground, sparing only the churches of Sant'Ambrogio and San Lorenzo.

But this total humiliation of Milan, meant as an imperial lesson to Italy's other *comuni*, had the opposite effect; it galvanized them to form the **Lombard League** against the foreign oppressor (only Pavia hated Milan too much to join). Barbarossa,

St Ambrose (Sant'Ambrogio)

No sooner had Christianity received the imperial stamp of approval than it split into two hostile camps: the orthodox, early-Catholic traditionalists and the followers of the Egyptian bishop Arius. Arians denied that Christ was of the same substance as God; the sect was widespread among the peoples on the fringes of the Roman Empire. An early bishop of Milan was an Arian and persecutor of the orthodox, and a schism seemed inevitable when he died. When the young consular governor Ambrose spoke to calm the crowd during the election of the new bishop, a child's voice suddenly piped up: 'Ambrose Bishop!' The cry was taken up, and Ambrose, who hadn't even been baptized, suddenly found himself thrust into a new job.

According to legend, when Ambrose was an infant in Rome, bees had flown into his mouth, attracted by the honey of his tongue. Ambrose's eloquence as bishop (374–97) is given much of the credit for preserving the unity of the Church; when the widow of Emperor Valentine desired to raise her son as an Arian, demanding a Milanese basilica for Arian worship, Ambrose and his supporters held the church through a nine-day siege, converting the empress's soldiers in the process. His most famous convert was St Augustine, and he also set what was to become the standard in relations between Church and Empire when he refused to allow Emperor Theodosius to enter church until he had done penance for ordering a civilian massacre in Thessalonika.

Ambrose left such an imprint on Milan that to this day genuine Milanese are called *Ambrosiani*. Their church, which was practically independent from Rome until the 11th century, still celebrates Mass according to the Ambrosian rite and holds its own carnival of Sant'Ambrogio in March.

on his next trip over the Alps, found the *comuni* united against him, and in 1176 he was soundly defeated by the Lombard League at Legnano. Now the tables had turned and the empire itself was in danger of total revolt. To preserve it, Barbarossa had to do a little foot-kissing himself in Venice, the privileged toe in this case belonging to Pope Alexander III, whom Barbarossa had exiled from Rome in order to set up another pope more malleable to his schemes. To placate the Lombard *comuni* the **Treaty of Constance** was signed after a six-year truce in 1183, in which the signatories of the Lombard League received all that they desired: their municipal autonomy and the privilege of making war – on each other. The more magnanimous idea of a united Italy was still centuries away.

The Age of the Big Bosses

If Milan was precocious in developing government by the *comune*, it was also one of the first cities to give it up. Unlike their counterparts in Florence, Milan's manufacturers were varied in their trades and limited themselves to small workshops, failing to form the companies of politically powerful merchants and trade associations that were the power base of a medieval Italian republic. The first family to fill Milan's vacuum at the top were the **Torriani** (*della Torre*), feudal lords who became the city's *signori* in 1247, only to lose their position to the **Visconti** in 1277.

The Visconti, created dukes in 1395, made Milan the strongest state in all Italy, and marriages into the French and English royal houses brought the family into European affairs as well (they fêted a certain Geoffrey Chaucer, in town to find a princess for a Plantagenet). Most ambitious of all the Visconti was **Gian Galeazzo** (1351–1402), married first to the daughter of the king of France and then to the daughter of his powerful and malevolent uncle Bernabò, whom Gian Galeazzo neatly packed off to prison, before conquering northern Italy, the Veneto, Romagna and Umbria. His army was ready to march on Florence when he suddenly died of plague. In his cruelty, ruthlessness and superstitious dependence on astrology, and in his love of art and letters (he founded the Certosa of Pavia, began the Duomo, held a court second to none in its lavishness, and supported the University of Pavia) Gian Galeazzo was one of the first 'archetypal' Renaissance princes. The Florentines and the Venetians took advantage of his demise to carry bits of his empire and, while his sons, the obscene **Giovanni Maria** (who delighted in feeding his enemies to the dogs) and the gruesome, paranoid **Filippo Maria**, did what they could to regain their father's conquests, Milan's influence was eventually reduced to Lombardy, which its leaders ran as a centralized state.

Filippo Maria left no male heirs, but a daughter named Bianca, whom he betrothed to his best *condottiere*, **Francesco Sforza** (1401–66). After Filippo Maria's death the Milanese declared the Golden Ambrosian Republic, which crumbled without much support after three years, when Francesco Sforza returned peacefully to accept the dukedom. One of Milan's best rulers, Sforza continued the scientific development of Lombard agriculture and navigable canals and hydraulic schemes, and kept the peace through a friendly alliance with the Medici. His son, Galeazzo Maria, was assassinated, but not before fathering Caterina Sforza, the great Renaissance virago, and an infant son, Gian Galeazzo II.

Lodovico il Moro

It was, however, Francesco Sforza's second son, **Lodovico il Moro** (1451–1508), who took power and became Milan's most cultivated ruler, helped by his wife, the delightful **Beatrice d'Este**, who ran one of Italy's most sparkling courts until her early death in childbirth. Lodovico was a great patron of the arts, commissioning from Leonardo's *The Last Supper*, engineering schemes and magnificent theatrical pageants. But Lodovico also bears the blame for one of the greatest political blunders in Italian history, when his quarrel with Naples grew so touchy that he invited Charles VIII of France to come and claim the Kingdom of Naples for himself. Charles took him up on it and marched unhindered down Italy. Lodovico soon realized his mistake, and joined the last-minute league of Italian states that united to trap and destroy the French at Fornovo. They succeeded, partially, but the damage was done: the French invasion had shown the Italian states, beautiful, rich, in full flower of the Renaissance, to be disunited and vulnerable. Charles VIII's son, **Louis XII**, took advantage of a claim on Milan through a Visconti grandmother and captured the city, and Lodovico with it. The Duke of Milan died a prisoner in a Loire château, an unhappy Prospero, covering the walls of his dungeon with bizarre graffiti that perplexes visitors to this day. After more fights between French and Spanish, Milan ended up a strategic province of Charles V's empire, ruled by a Spanish viceroy.

In 1712 the city came under the **Habsburgs** of Austria and with the rest of Lombardy profited from the enlightened reforms of **Maria Theresa**, who did much to improve agriculture, rationalize taxes and increase education; her rule saw the creation of La Scala, the Brera Academy and most of central neoclassical Milan. After centuries of hibernation the Ambrosiani were stirring again, and when Napoleon arrived the city welcomed him fervently. With a huge festival Milan became the capital of Napoleon's 'Cisalpine Republic', linked to Paris via the new Simplon Highway.

The Powerhouse of United Italy

After Napoleon's defeat in 1814, the Austrians returned, but Milan was an important centre of Italian nationalist sentiment during the Risorgimento and rebelled against the repressive Habsburg regime in 1848. The city's greatest contribution during this period, however, was the novelist **Manzoni**, whose masterpiece *I Promessi Sposi* caused a nationwide sensation and sense of unity in a peninsula that had been politically divided since the fall of Rome (*see* p.215).

After joining the new **Kingdom of Italy**, Milan rapidly took its place as the country's economic and industrial dynamo, attracting thousands of workers from the poorer sections of Italy. Many of these workers joined the new Italian Socialist Party, which was strongest in the regions of Lombardy and Emilia-Romagna. In Milan, too, **Mussolini** founded the Fascist Party and launched its first campaign in 1919. The city was bombed heavily in air raids during the **Second World War**. In May 1945, Milan's well-organized partisan forces liberated it from the Germans before the Allies arrived, and when Mussolini's corpse was hung up on a meat hook in the Piazzale Loreto the Milanese turned out to make sure that the duke of delusion was truly dead before beginning to rebuild their battered city on more solid ground.

Milan was, again, the centre of Italy's postwar economic miracle when it began to take off in the late 1950s, drawing in still more thousands of migrants from the south. Despite economic ups and downs and a few hiccups, the city's wealth has continued to grow by near-mathematical progression ever since. In the early 1990s, however, the whole structure came crashing down. For it was in Milan that the first allegations of the large-scale taking of *tangenti* (bribes) came to light, initially involving the Socialists and their ineffable boss, Bettino Craxi, though the mud later spread to cover all the established parties. Craxi and his cronies have disappeared from the political map (Craxi disappeared from Italy altogether, and spent his last years holed up in Tunisia). Power in Milan is now held by a right-wing government, after being disputed between a left/green alliance and Umberto Bossi's Lega Nord, though Italian prime minister Silvio Berlusconi, who calls Milan home, also has a strong political influence.

Piazza del Duomo

Duomo

Via Arcivescovado 1, www.duomomilano.com. Open daily 9–7; adm free; baptistry Santo Stefano free, baptistry (San Giovanni) €1.50, tickets at the bookshop, closed 1–3pm; treasury and crypt adm €1. Cathedral roof, open daily Nov–Feb 9–5, Mar–Oct 9–6; adm €4 by foot or €6 by lift; metro Duomo.

In the exact centre of Milan towers its famous **Duomo**, a monument of such imposing proportions (the third largest in the world after St Peter's and Seville) that on clear days it is as visible from the distant Alps as the Alps are visible from its dome. Bristling with 135 spires, defended by 2,244 marble saints and one cheeky sinner (Napoleon, who crowned himself King of Italy here in 1805), guarded by 95 leering gargoyles, energized by sunlight pouring through the largest stained-glass windows in Christendom, Milan Cathedral is a remarkable bulwark of the faith. And yet for all its monstrous size, for all the hubbub of its busy piazza, traversed daily by tens of thousands of Milanese and tourists, the Duomo is utterly ethereal, a rose-white vision of pinnacles and tracery woven by angels. In Vittorio de Sica's *Miracle in Milan* (1950) it serves its natural role as a stairway (or rather launching pad) to heaven for the broomstick-riding heroes. Gian Galeazzo Visconti began the Duomo in 1386 as a votive offering to the Mother of God, hoping that she would favour him with an heir. His prayers for a son were answered in the form of Giovanni Maria, a loathsome degenerate assassinated soon after he attained power; as the Ambrosiani have wryly noted, the Mother of God got the better of the deal.

The Cathedral Interior

The remarkable dimensions of the interior challenge the eye to take in what seems like infinity captured under a canopy. Its tremendous volume is defined into five aisles by 52 pillars of titanic dimensions, unusually crowned by rings of niches and statues, and is dazzlingly lit by acres of stained glass, embellished with flamboyant Gothic

The Making of a Cathedral

Gian Galeazzo Visconti was the Man Who Would Be King – King of Italy, or whatever fraction of it he could snatch. A well-nigh psychotic ambition drove the frantic career of this paradigm of Renaissance princes, and such an ambition required a fitting symbol. Milan was to have a new cathedral, the biggest in Italy, dedicated to the greater glory of God, Milan and the Visconti. The demolition of a huge part of the city centre made a space ready for it by 1386, when building began.

All Gian Galeazzo's schemes and aggressions came to nothing, as the little empire he built disintegrated after his death, but Milan did get its cathedral as a kind of consolation prize. From the beginning, the Duke called in all the most skilled builders of the day who were available. Their names are recorded: men such as Bonino da Campione and Matteo da Campione, two of the Campionese masters, and also a number of foreigners – Gamodia of Gmünd, Walter Monich and Peter Monich from Germany, and a Parisian known as Mignot. In the court of the Duke, they argued over the sacred geometry appropriate to the task, over the relative merits of beginning the work *ad triangulum* or *ad quadratum*, that is, whether the plans and the measures should be based on the proportions of the equilateral triangle or the square. The latter, the more common form, was decided on. After that, over the years to come, they would work out all the details, every vault, column, buttress and pinnacle, from the same set of proportions. Equally important to medieval builders was the mystical accord of the numbers, the transcendant harmonies required in a house of God – which the Milanese were willing to adapt for the effects they desired, much to the disappointment of the experts brought in from Germany and France to pronounce on whether or not the Duomo would stand (most said no). The last expert, the Frenchman Mignot, predicted calamity and left in a snoot, writing 'Art is nothing without science', to which the Milanese replied, 'Science without art is nothing.'

The building would be a major drain on Gian Galeazzo's budget – almost as expensive as his endless wars. A normal, modest cathedral would have been a sufficiently difficult project. To get the Candoglia marble they wanted, for example, the master builders had to build roads and even canals to bring the stone down from the

tracery; the oldest windows, from the 15th century, are along the naves at the crossing. All other decorations seem rather small (the better to emphasize the vast size) but you may want to seek out in the right transept Leone Leoni's fine Mannerist tomb of the Marquess di Marignano, Gian Giacomo de' Medici – Il Medeghino, the pirate of Lake Como – erected by his brother Pope Pius IV. Fine bronze statues of Peace and Military Virtue sit on either side of a statue of the hero, portrayed with sword on hand, ready to go to war again. A relief of the Adoration of the Magi on top is the only nod towards religion, and its placement covers up part of the window. His sarcophagus was originally here as well, until his nephew, St Charles Borromeo, removed it in accordance with the edict from the Council of Trent that 'receptacles and vain trophies' be removed from church interiors and buried under the floor.

In the same transept you'll find one of the most peculiar of the cathedral's thousands of statues: that of San Bartolomeo holding his own skin, with an inscription assuring

quarries north of Lake Maggiore. The duke's passion for decoration made it even more difficult; he demanded angelic hosts of statuary – over 2,000 on the exterior and 700 more inside. As many as 300 sculptors found employment at one time in the cathedral workshops. These too came from all over Europe; names like Pietro di Francia and Fritz di Norimberga on the pay lists are a reminder of the Christian, pan-European universality of the age. Men might speak different tongues, but for all the language of faith and art were the same.

How did Milan and the duke pay for all this? The records mention a big campaign by local church authorities to sell religious indulgences, while the state contributed sums from a steep increase in fines in the courts. It wouldn't have been enough. The financing would have been a formidably complex matter, no doubt partially arranged by loans from the Lombard and Tuscan bankers, but no one can say exactly how deeply the Duke dug into his own pockets, how much he coaxed or squeezed out of the other great families, how much the pope, Milan's ally, threw in and how much was wrung out of the poor. New technology helped to lower the costs, especially the machines invented by a Master Giovanni da Zellino for hoisting stone more easily – it's often forgotten how the late Middle Ages was a time of dizzying technological progress, creating advances in everything from navigation to farming to the first mechanical clocks. For all the complexity, the duke and his builders knew what they were about; the cathedral was substantially complete by 1399.

However, by the time they got to the façade, the Gothic style had become unfashionable. This bewildered front went through several overhauls of Renaissance and Baroque, then back to Gothic, with the end result, completed in 1809 under Napoleon, resembling a shotgun wedding of Isabelline Gothic with Christopher Wren. In the 1880s there were plans to tear it down and start again, but no one had the heart, and the Milanese have become used to it. Walk around, though, to the glorious Gothic apse, with its three huge windows (1389) to see what its original builders were about. The subjects of the bas-reliefs on the bronze doors are a Milanese history lesson: the Edict of Constantine, the Life of St Ambrose, the city's quarrels with Barbarossa and the history of the cathedral itself.

us that it was made by Marco Agrate and not by Praxiteles, just in case we couldn't tell the difference. Other treasures include the beautiful walnut choir stalls, carved between 1572 and 1620, and the 12th-century bronze Trivulzio Candelabrum by Nicola da Verdun, as well as medieval ivory, gold and silverwork in the Treasury, located below the main altar by the crypt, where the mastermind of the Counter-Reformation, St Charles Borromeo (1538–84), lies in state. He was lucky that he didn't die in the cathedral as well; when he returned to Milan as resident archbishop at the end of the Council of Trent he infuriated many members of Milan's then cosy clergy by making them toe the line of the new reforms to set a good example to other bishops. One dissident of many shot him during mass, but he was saved by the heavy brocade of his vestments. Throughout the Duomo you can see the alchemical symbol adopted as the Visconti crest, now the symbol of Milan: a twisting serpent in the act of swallowing a man. The story goes that in 1100, in the Second Crusade, the battling bishop Ottone Visconti (the founder of the family fortunes) fought a giant Saracen, and when he slew him he took the device from his shield.

Near the cathedral entrance a door leads down to the 4th-century remains of the Baptistry of San Giovanni delle Fonti, excavated in the 1960s, containing the octagonal baptismal font where St Ambrose baptized St Augustine, as well as remains of the Roman road and other churches demolished to make way from the Duomo. For a splendid view of Milan, take a walk through the enchanted forest of spires and statues on the **cathedral roof**. The 15th-century dome by Amadeo of Pavia, topped by the main spire with the gilt statue of *La Madonnina* (who at 12ft really isn't as diminutive as she seems 354ft from the ground), offers the best view of all – on a clear morning, all the way to the Matterhorn.

Museo del Duomo and Palazzo Reale

Piazza del Duomo 14, t 02 7202 2656, www.duomomilano.com. Open daily 10–1.15 and 3–6; adm.

On the south side of the cathedral, the Palazzo Reale was for centuries the head-quarters of Milan's rulers, from the Visconti down to the Austrian governors, who had the place redone in their favourite neoclassical style. In one wing, the **Museo del Duomo** contains art and artefacts made for the cathedral over the past six centuries, including some of the original stained glass and fine 14th-century French and German statues, gargoyles, tapestries and a Tintoretto. Other rooms document the cathedral's construction, including a magnificent 16th-century wooden model, façade designs from the 1886 competition and castings from the bronze doors.

The main core of the Palazzo Reale used to accommodate the Civico Museo dell'Arte Contemporanea (CIMAC). Though there are tentative plans to see the Palazzo Reale host all the city's contemporary art in the future, the museum is now closed for major restructuring, its collections divided between the Civica Galleria d'Arte Moderna (*see* p.92) and the Esposizione Permanente delle Belle Arti (*see* p.93). Behind the palace, on Via Palazzo Reale, be sure to note the beautiful 14th-century apse and octagonal campanile of the royal palace's church of **San Gottardo** (*Via Pecorari 2, t 02 8646 4500; open daily 8–12 and 2–4*), which also contains the reconstructed funerary monument of Azzone Visconi by Giovanni di Balduccio as well as part of a fresco of the Crucifixion by the school of Giotto. The porticoes around the Piazza del Duomo are occupied by some of the city's oldest bars. In the centre of the square, old Vittorio Emanuele II on his horse looks ready to charge into action.

North of the Duomo

Piazza della Scala and Around

The Piazza della Scala is the address of one of the world's great opera houses, the neoclassical **La Scala** (*see* p.80 for ticket and performance details). Its name is derived from the church of Santa Maria alla Scala, which formerly stood on the site.

Inaugurated in 1778, with Salieri's *Europa Riconosciuta*, La Scala saw the premieres of most of the 19th-century classics of Italian opera. When bombs smashed it in 1943, it was rebuilt as it was in three years, reopening under the baton of its great conductor Arturo Toscanini. Since its reopening in 1946, La Scala has never closed, except for a major €49-million refurbishment in 2004.

Le Scala is also home to the **Museo Teatrale alla Scala** (*Largo Glininghelli 1, Piazza Scala; open 9–12.30 and 1.30–5.30; adm*), which has an excellent collection of opera memorabilia (especially on Verdi) including scores, letters, portraits and photos of legendary stars, and set designs; there's even an archaeological section related to ancient Greek and Roman drama, and a great collection of costumes.

Nearby is the **Galleria Vittorio Emanuele II**, an elegant glass-roofed arcade linking Piazza Duomo and Piazza della Scala. It was designed by Giuseppe Mengoni, who tragically slipped and fell from the roof the day before its inauguration in 1878. For nine years at least, until Naples built its Galleria Umberto, it was the largest in the world. Here are more elegant bars and some of the city's finest shops. In the centre, under a marvellous 157ft glass dome, is a mosaic figure of Taurus; the Milanese believe it's good luck to step on the bull's testicles. The Galleria has seen a number of historical events, including a parade of elephants on their way to play the part in a production of *Aida* at La Scala.

Next to La Scala, the church of **San Giuseppe** (*t 02 805 2120; open Mon–Sat 7–6.30, Sun 9–12.30*) was a great architectural landmark in its day, and if it looks like hundreds of other churches in Italy, it proves the old adage that imitation is the sincerest form of flattery. Begun in 1607, it was the first independent project of Milan's most innovative Baroque architect Francesco Maria Ricchino, before his patron Cardinal Federico Borromeo sent him to Rome to finish his training. When he returned, this was the result: a church designed on the basis of two simple Greek crosses with very abbreviated arms. The dome rises over the congregation on arches, but here, Ricchino added a high arch between the congregation and sanctuary to fuse the two spaces in a new and exciting way that would be endlessly repeated by later Baroque architects, who loved its rich possibilities for scenographic effects.

San Giuseppe's façade, designed at the same time as the church but not added until 1630, was another innovation. Previous Italian façades had been merely decorative, hardly related to the structure of the church itself. Here Ricchino strove for integration: the façade, designed as a pair of aedicules (compositions of a pediment over paired columns), one set inside the other, reflects the proportions and decorative style of the interior, and draws the eye to the other visible parts of the exterior rather than just the immediate 'show front'. The impression of unity is so immediate that Ricchino's aedicule façade became the favourite in the Baroque style – so common, in fact, that most people walk past this once cutting-edge church without a second glance. Originally a convent was attached to it, but it was demolished to allow La Scala to build a deeper stage.

An unloved 19th-century statue of Leonardo stands in the middle of the Piazza della Scala, while opposite the theatre the imposing **Palazzo Marino** (*Piazza della Scala 2; courtyard only open to the public*) is a fine 16th-century building hiding behind a

19th-century façade; now the Palazzo Municipale, it has one of the city's loveliest courtyards. A few steps away, on Via Catena, the unusual 1565 **Casa degli Omenoni** (*closed to the public*) was built by sculptor Leone Leoni for his retirement. He made his house into a tribute to his hero, the philosopher-emperor Marcus Aurelius; the six large and uncomfortable-looking telamones he sculpted for the façade probably represent members of the barbarian tribes subdued by the emperor. Around the corner of cobblestoned Piazza Belgioioso, at Via Morone 1 (*metro Montenapoleone or Duomo*), the handsome old home of Alessandro Manzoni (1785–1873) is now a shrine, the **Museo Manzoniano** (*t 02 8646 0403, www.museidelcentro.mi.it; open Tues–Fri 9–12 and 2–4; adm free*), filled with items relating to the Milanese novelist's life and work, including illustrations from *I Promessi Sposi* and an autographed portrait of his friend Goethe. For more on the man, *see* p.215.

Museo Poldi-Pezzoli

In front of La Scala runs one of Milan's busiest and most fashionable boulevards, the **Via Manzoni**. Verdi lived for years and died in a room in the Grand Hotel (No.29); at No.10 is the lovely 17th-century palace of Gian Giacomo Poldi-Pezzoli, who rearranged his home to fit his fabulous art collection, then willed it to the public in 1879. Repaired after bomb damage in the war, the **Museo Poldi-Pezzoli** (*Via Manzoni 10, metro Montenapoleone or Duomo, t 02 796 334, www.museopoldipezzoli.it; open Tues–Sun 10–6; adm*), houses an exquisite collection of 15th- to 18th-century paintings, including one of Italy's best-known portraits, the 15th-century *Portrait of a Young Woman* by Antonio Pollaiuolo, depicting an ideal Renaissance beauty. She shares the most elegant room of the palace, the **Salone Dorato**, with the other jewels of the museum: Mantegna's Byzantinish *Madonna*, Giovanni Bellini's *Pietà*, Piero della Francesca's *San Nicolò* and, from a few centuries later, Francesco Guardi's *Grey Lagoon* (*c.*1790), a beautiful, dreamlike, visionary work. Other outstanding paintings include Vitale da Bologna's *Madonna*, a polyptych by Cristoforo Moretti and works by Botticelli, Luini, Foppa, Turà, Tiepolo, Crivelli, Lotto, Cranach (including portraits of Luther and wife) and a crucifix by Raphael. The collection is also rich in decorative arts: Islamic metalwork and rugs – note the magnificent Persian carpet (1532) depicting a hunting scene in the Salone Dorato – medieval and Renaissance armour, Renaissance bronzes, Flemish tapestries, Murano glass and more.

Quadrilatero d'Oro

Just up Via Manzoni is the entrance to Milan's high-fashion vortex, the **Quadrilatero d'Oro**, concentrated in the palace-lined Via Monte Napoleone and elegant Via della Spiga. Even if you're not in the market for astronomically priced clothes by Italy's top designers, these exclusive lanes make for good window-shopping and perhaps even better people-watching. It's hard to remember that up until the 1970s Florence was the centre of the Italian garment industry. When Milan took over this status – it has the airports Florence lacks – it added the essential ingredients of business savvy and packaging to the Italians' innate sense of style, to create a high-fashion empire rivalling Paris, London and New York.

There are two museums in the sumptuous 18th-century Palazzo Morando Bolognini, on Via S. Andrea 6, between 'Montenapo' and Via della Spiga: the **Civico Museo di Milano** (*metro Montenapoleone, t 02 7600 6245, www.museidelcentro.mi.it; open Tues–Sun 2–5.30; adm free*) and the **Civico Museo di Storia Contemporanea** (*metro Montenapoleone, t 02 7600 6245, www.museidelcentro.mi.it; open Tues–Sun 10–6 only for exhibitions; adm free*), the first displays a good selection of paintings of old Milan, the second is devoted to Italian history between the years 1914 and 1945. A third museum, the **Museo Bagatti Valsecchi** (*Via Santo Spirito 10, metro Montenapoleone, t 02 7600 6132, www.museobagattivalsecchi.org; open Tues–Sun 1–5.45; adm*) was the life's work of two brothers, Fausto and Giuseppe Bagatti Valsecchi, who built a neo-Renaissance palace to integrate the period fireplaces, ceilings and friezes that they had collected, carefully disguising 19th-century conveniences such as the bathtub. Some of the city's top designers have made their own unique creations, which are inspired by the museum's displays. A selection of these are on sale in the shop in the lobby.

Near the intersection of Via della Spiga and Via Manzoni, the **Archi di Porta Nuova**, the huge stone arches of a gate, are a rare survival of the city walls of 1171. If you look around the inside of the arches you can see some of the old Roman tombstones used to build the wall, and a Gothic tabernacle has statues of the saints.

The Giardini Pubblici

From Piazza Cavour, Via Palestro curves between the two sections of Milan's Public Gardens. The romantic **Giardini di Villa Reale** (*metro Palestro*) were laid out in 1790 for the Belgiojoso family by Leopoldo Pollak, who later built the Villa Reale, Napoleon's residence while in the Cisalpine Republic. The neoclassical villa is now the **Civica Galleria d'Arte Moderna** (*t 02 7600 2819; open Tues–Sun 9–11, Thurs until 10, at the time of writing only ground floor and first floor are open to visitors; adm free*), which includes the ground floor **Vismara collection** of paintings (works by Picasso, Matisse, Modigliani, de Pisis, Tosi, Morandi and Renoir) and the Marino Marini sculpture collection. Marini (d. 1980), generally acknowledged as the top Italian sculptor of the 20th century, spent most of his career in Milan. The gallery's first floor hosts a collection of 17th-century Italian art, which includes the famous painting of *The Fourth State* by Pelizza da Volpedo. Also on display are the fine paintings of the self-consciously romantic *Scapigliati* 'the Wild-Haired Ones' of Milan.

The **Padiglione d'Arte Contemporanea** (PAC) (*next to Villa Reale on Via Palestro, t 02 7600 9085, www.comune.milano.it/pac; open Tues–Sun 9.30–5.30; adm*) houses a good collection of contemporary art. Built after the Second World War, it was considered one of the major architectural buildings of 1950s Milan. The gallery was substantially renovated following a terrorist attack in 1993.

The **Giardini Pubblici** proper, a shady Arcadia between Via Palestro and the Corso Venezia, was laid out in 1782; artificial rocks compensate for Milan's flat terrain. A good place to take children, with its zoo, swans, pedal cars and playgrounds, it is also the site of Italy's premier **Natural History Museum** (*t 02 8846 3280; open Tues–Fri 9–6, Sat–Sun 9.30–6.30 (free entrance from 5pm, from 2pm on Fri)*), near the Corso Venezia.

Look out for the Canadian cryptosaurus, the Colossal European lobster, the Madagascan aye-aye and the 40-kilo topaz. The gardens also contain the **Museo del Cinema** (*Viale Manin 2, t 02 655 4977; open Fri–Sun 3–6; adm*), located in the late 17th-century Palazzo Dugnani, with a small collection on early animation techniques, posters, cameras and so on.

Close to the Giardini Pubblici in a classy palace of the 1800s, the **Esposizione Permanente delle Belle Arti**, Fine Arts Society and Permanent Exhibition (*Via Turati 34, metro Turati, t 02 659 9803; open Tues–Fri 10–1 and 2.30–6.30; Sat, Sun and holidays 10–6.30; adm*) temporarily displays 100 sculptures and paintings of the 20th century from the Civico Museo dell'Arte Contemporanea, as well as 40 contemporary works of the **Jucker collection**, with paintings by Picasso, Klee, Kandinsky, Boccioni, and Modigliani.

Corso Venezia itself is lined with neoclassical and Liberty-style palaces – most remarkably, the 1903 **Palazzo Castiglione** at No.47 and the neoclassical **Palazzo Serbelloni**, Milan's press club, on the corner of Via Senato. The district just west of the Corso Venezia was the city's most fashionable in the 1920s, and there are a smattering of rewarding buildings: the **Casa Galimberti** with a colourful ceramic façade at Via Malpighi 3, off the Piazza Oberdan; the good Art Deco foyer at Via Cappuccini 8; the eccentric houses on Via Mozart (especially No.11); and the romantic 1920s **Palazzo Fidia** at Via Melegari 2.

Northwest of the Giardini Pubblici, the Piazza della Repubblica has many of the city's hotels; the Mesopotamian-scale **Stazione Centrale** (1931), blocking the end of Via Vittor Pisani, is the largest train station in Italy. Designed in 1906, it was built between 1925 and 1931. The five metal roofs extending over the tracks are an impressive 236ft (72m) across and 118ft (36m) high. The nearby skyscraper, the **Pirelli Building**, known as *Pirellone* (big Pirelli), is one that the Milanese are especially proud of, built in 1959 by Gio Ponti, while Pier Luigi Nervi designed the concrete structure. It's now the seat of Lombardy's regional government, and you can see most of the city from its terrace (*call ahead, t 02 67651*). In April 2002, a small, private plane flew into the top of the Pirelli building, damaging several floors; a subsequent investigation interpreted the incident as an act of suicide.

Further to the northwest, at Via Petteri 56, the Palazzo Martinitt houses the **Museo del Giocattolo e del Bambino** (*metro Lambrate, t 02 2641 1585, www.museodel giocattolo.it; open Tues–Sun 9.30–12.30 and 3–6; adm*) with a beautiful display of toys dating back to 1700.

Brera and its National Gallery

Another street alongside La Scala, Via G. Verdi, leads into the **Brera**. The district has been ambitiously compared to Montmartre in Paris, or to London's Portobello Road, but although hip and arty to a degree, it fails to quite measure up. Yet, in a city that was heavily bombed in the Second World War, Brera's cobbled and narrow streets were left relatively unscathed, retaining an appealing old-world artiness that the Milanese have enthusiastically cashed in on. This is best seen in the atmospheric **Via Fiori Chiari** ('Street of Light-coloured Flowers'), which offers a very Milanese impression of *la dolce vita*, with its chic boutiques, small art galleries, and trendy bars and restaurants. The quarter's banner street, cobbled **Via Brera**, once poor and arty, is now lined with achingly exclusive bars and shops. But once a month, for those who would rather have a taste of what life used to be like in the district, it hosts a slightly more down-to-earth, though still pricey, antiques market on the third saturday of each month (*see* 'Shopping', p.69).

At the corner of Via Brera and Via Fiori Oscuri ('Street of the Dark Flowers') is the elegant courtyard of the **Galleria Nazionale di Brera** (*metro Lanza or Montenapoleone, t 02 722 631; open Tues–Sun 8.30–7.30, may close at 6pm in winter; adm*), one of the world's finest hoards of art, especially of 14th–18th century Northern Italian painting. The collection was compiled by Napoleon, whose bronze statue, draped in a toga, greets visitors as they enter; a believer in centralized art as well as centralized govern-ment, he had northern Italy's churches and monasteries stripped of their treasures to form a Louvre-like collection for Milan, the capital of his Cisalpine Republic. The museum first opened in 1809; after Waterloo, Milan had become rather used to its role as the capital of Northern Italy and the paintings stayed put. A private collection, the **Donazione Jesi**, has been added since and there are plans to expand into the 18th-century Palazzo Citterio at Via Brera 12–14. Ongoing improvements and restorations since 1988 may lead to certain sections being closed.

Perhaps the best known of the Brera's scores of masterpieces is Raphael's *Marriage of the Virgin*, a Renaissance landmark for its evocation of an ideal, rarefied world, where even the disappointed suitor snapping his rod on his knee performs the bitter ritual in a graceful dance step, all acted out before a perfect but eerily vacant temple in the background. In the same room hangs Piero della Francesca's last painting, the *Pala di Urbino*, featuring among its holy personages Federico da Monfeltro, Duke of Urbino, with his famous nose. The Venetian masters are well represented: Carpaccio, Veronese, Titian, Tintoretto, Jacopo Bellini and the Vivarini, but especially Giovanni Bellini, with several of his loveliest Madonnas and the great *Pietà*, as well as a joint effort with his brother Gentile of *St Mark Preaching in Alexandria*. The *Flagellation* by Luca Signorelli of Cortona is his first documented work (it's signed *Opus luce cortonesis* on the building in the background).

There are luminous works by Carlo Crivelli (the golden, gorgeously dressed *Madonna della Candelletta*, in an arch of Crivelli's trademark fruit and cucumbers) and Cima da Conegliano; Paris Bordone's *Venetian Couple*. There are several paintings by Mantegna, including his remarkable study in foreshortening, the *Cristo Morto*; Mantegna's subdued colouring was an inspiration for Bramante. Other famous works include *Christ at the Column* by Bramante, transferred to canvas); Caravaggio's striking *Supper at Emmaus*; the *Pala Sforzesca* by a 15th-century Lombard artist, depicting Lodovico il Moro and his family; a polyptych by Gentile da Fabriano; and fine works by the Ferrarese masters da Cossa and Ercole de' Roberti. Outstanding among the non-Italians are Rembrandt's *Portrait of his Sister*, El Greco's *St Francis* and Van Dyck's *Portrait of the Princess of Orange*.

When the Great Masters become indigestible, take a breather in the new 20th-century wing of the gallery, populated mainly by futurists like Severini, Balla and

Boccioni, who believed that to achieve speed was to achieve success, and the meta-physical followers of De Chirico, who seem to believe just the opposite.

Brera's other principal monument is **San Simpliciano** (*Piazza San Simpliciano 7, just off Corso Garibaldi, metro Lanza, t 02 862 274; open daily 7–12 and 3–7*). Perhaps founded by St Ambrose, it retains its essential palaeo-Christian form in a 12th-century wrapping, with an octagonal drum. The apse has a beautiful fresco of the *Coronation of the Virgin* (1515) by Bergognone, and the larger of the two cloisters, from the mid-16th century, is especially charming with its twin columns.

Castello Sforzesco

Marking the western limits of the Brera, the **Castello Sforzesco** (*metro Cairoli*) is one of Milan's best-known landmarks. It was originally a fortress. The Visconti made it their base, though it was razed to the ground by the Ambrosian Republic in 1447. Rebuilt three years later under Francesco Sforza, it was again rebuilt after air raids in the Second World War; this time, water cisterns were disguised in its stout towers.

Today the castle houses the city's excellent collections, the **Civici Musei d'Arte e Pinacoteca del Castello** (*t 02 8846 3703; open Tues–Sun 9–5.30; adm*). The entrance, by way of a tower rebuilt on a design by Filarete (1452) and the huge Piazza d'Armi, is through the lovely Renaissance Corte Ducale and the principal residence of the Sforza. There are intriguing fragments of Milanese history: the equestrian tomb of Bernabò Visconti and a beautiful 14th-century monument of the Rusca family, reliefs of Milan's triumph over Barbarossa, and the city's gonfalon. Leonardo designed the ilex decorations of the **Sala delle Asse**, and the next room, the **Sala dei Ducali**, contains a superb relief by Duccio from Rimini's Tempio Malatestiano. The Sala degli Scarlioni contains the two finest sculptures in the museum, the *Effigy of Gaston de Foix* (1525) by Bambaia and Michelangelo's unfinished *Rondanini Pietà*, a haunting work that the aged sculptor worked at off and on during his last nine years, repudi-ating all of his early ideals of physical beauty in favour of such blunt, expressionistic figures; the difference between this and his *Pietà* in St Peter's couldn't be greater.

Upstairs, most notable among the fine collection of Renaissance furnishings and decorative arts are the 15th-century Castello Roccabianca frescoes illustrating the popular medieval tale of Patient Griselda. The **Pinacoteca** contains a tender *Madonna with Child* by Giovanni Bellini, his brother-in-law Mantegna's more austere, classical *Madonna* in the Pala Trivulzio, and the lovely *Madonna dell'Umiltà* by Filippo Lippi. Lombards, not surprisingly, predominate: Foppa, Solario, Magnasco (who spent most of his life in Milan), Bergognone (especially the serene *Virgin with SS. Sebastian and Gerolamo*) and Bramantino, with an eerie *Noli me tangere*. There's a room of Leonardo's followers, and then the *Primavera*, by Milanese Giuseppe Arcimboldo (1527–93), who was no one's follower at all, but the first surrealist – the *Primavera* is a woman's face made up entirely of flowers. From 18th-century Venice, Francesco Guardi's *Storm* looks ahead to another school: Impressionism.

The castle's third court, the beautiful **Cortile della Rocchetta**, was designed by the Florentines Bramante and Filarete, both of whom worked for several years for Francesco Sforza. The basement of the courtyard is filled with an extensive Egyptian collection of funerary artefacts and the prehistoric collection of items found in Lombardy's Iron Age settlements, most notably the 6th-century BC bronzes from the tomb of the warrior of Sesto Calende. The first floor houses the **Museum of Musical Instruments**, with a beautiful collection of 641 string and wind instruments and a spinet that was played by Mozart. The **Sala della Balla**, where the Sforza family played ball, now contains the *Tapestries of the Months* designed by Bramantino.

Parco Sempione and Cimitero Monumentale

Behind the Castello stretches the Parco Sempione, Milan's largest park, where you can find De Chirico's **Metaphysical Fountain**; the 1930s **Palazzo dell'Arte**, used for exhibitions, especially the **Milan Triennial** of modern architecture and design; the **Arena**, designed in 1806 after Roman models, where 19th-century dilettantes staged mock naval battles; and an imposing triumphal arch, the **Arco della Pace**, marking the terminus of Napoleon's highway (Corso Sempione) to the Simplon Pass. At Corso Sempione 36 the **Casa Rustici** (1931), designed by Giuseppe Terragni of Como on the proportions of the Golden Rule, is often considered Milan's finest modern building.

Also in the park is the panoramic steel **Branca Tower** (*open Wed 10.30–12.30 and 4–6.30; Fri 2.30–6; Sat 10.30–1 and 4–6.30; Sun 10.30–2 and 2.30–7; adm*). It was designed by Gio Ponti and erected in 1933 in the record time of two and a half months, in time for the Triennale. Reopened to the public after closing in 1972 for safety reasons, the tower no longer has a café at the top, but the views are still lovely.

Further out, the **Cimitero Monumentale** (*tram 14; open Tues–Sun 8.30–5.30*) is the last rendezvous of Milan's well-to-do burghers. Their lavish monuments – Liberty-style temples and pseudo-ancient columns and obelisks – are just slightly less flamboyant than those of the Genoese, the Italian champs for post-mortem splendour. The cemetery keeper has guides to the tombs – Manzoni, Toscanini and Albert Einstein's father are among the best-known names. The memorial to the 800 Milanese who perished in German concentration camps is very moving.

West of the Duomo

Santa Maria delle Grazie and *The Last Supper*

Metro Cadorna, then Via Boccaccio and left on Via Caradosso. Open: Church, Mon–Fri 7–12 and 3–7; Sat–Sun 7.15–12.15 and 3.30–9; Cenacolo, Tues–Sun 8.15–7; adm exp. Booking compulsory on t 02 8942 1146 or www.cenacolovinciano.org. Only 15 visitors are admitted at a time.

Milan's greatest painting, Leonardo da Vinci's *Last Supper*, or the *Cenacolo* (*see* box, opposite), is in the refectory of the convent of **Santa Maria delle Grazie**. Before entering, get into the proper Renaissance mood by first walking around the 15th-century church and cloister. Built by Guiniforte Solari, with later revisions by Bramante under Lodovico il Moro, it is perhaps the most beautiful Renaissance church in Lombardy. Its exterior is articulated with fine brickwork and terracotta that respects the local delight in a bit of fancy stuff – Bramante would never do anything as lavish again. His greatest contribution, however, is the majestic tribune, added in 1492, inspired by Brunelleschi in Florence but with an eye towards the imposing style of the ancient Romans, which in the next decade Bramante would take back to Rome itself. Nearly every element in the tribune is based on the circle, from the decorative motifs to the play of geometric forms, to the great cupola that crowns it all. Bramante also designed the choir, the sacristy and the elegant little cloister, all simple, geometric and pure.

Monastero Maggiore and the Archaeology Museum

From Santa Maria delle Grazie, the Corso Magenta leads back towards the centre. At the corner of Via Luini stands the Monastero Maggiore. The monastery's pretty 16th-century church of **San Maurizio** (*metro Cadorna; open daily 9–12 and 2–5*) contains frescoes by Bernardino Luini, one of Leonardo's most accomplished followers. The former Benedictine convent houses the city's Etruscan, Greek and Roman collections in the **Civico Museo Archeologico** (*entrance at Corso Magenta 15; open Tues–Sun 9–5.30; adm. Free entrance on Fri after 2pm*). As important as Milan was in the late

The Last Supper

Leonardo painted three of his masterpieces in Milan: the two versions of the mystery-laden *Virgin of the Rocks* and *The Last Supper*. The former two are in London and the Louvre; the latter would have been in Paris too, had the French been able to figure out a way to remove the wall.

Ever since the 14th century, it had been the fashion in Italy to paint a *Cenacolo* or scene of the Last Supper on the walls of monastic refectories, and as the Dominicans at Santa Maria were special favourites of Lodovico il Moro, he sent them his favourite artist to make their *Cenacolo* the last word on the subject. When Leonardo unveiled his *Last Supper* (1494–98), made even more famous in recent years by the success of Dan Brown's Da Vinci Code, it was immediately acclaimed as the greatest work of the greatest living artist, a masterful psychological study, an instant caught in time, the apostles' gestures of disbelief and dismay captured almost photographically by one of the greatest students of human nature. According to Vasari, Leonardo left the portrait of Christ purposely unfinished, believing himself unworthy to paint divinity; Judas, the isolated traitor, also posed a problem, but the artist was eventually able to catch the expression of a man caught guiltily unawares but still nefariously determined and unrepentant.

Unfortunately for posterity, damp was a problem even as Leonardo worked on the fresco and the ever-experimental genius was not content to use established fresco technique (where the paint is applied quickly to wet plaster) but painted with tempera on glue and plaster as if on wood, enabling him to return over and over to achieve the subtlety of tone and depth he desired. Leonardo knew even as he painted his masterpiece that it wouldn't last, but the fact only stimulated his restless mind, which was fascinated with the unfinished and the transitory. Almost immediately the moisture in the walls began its deadly work of flaking off particles of paint.

Roman Empire (there's a model of the city inside), relatively little has survived the frequent razings and rebuildings: the 3rd-century tower in the garden, Roman altars, sarcophagi, stelae, glass, ceramics, bronzes and mosaics. Other sections are Greek, Etruscan, Indian, Gothic and Lombard. Opposite the church of **San Maurizio**, Francesco Maria Ricchini's **Palazzo Litta** (1648) has a roccoco facade by Bartolomeo Bolli, added a hundred years later, and a lovely courtyard surrounded by twinned columns.

Sant'Ambrogio

Located just off San Vittore and Via Carducci (*metro Sant'Ambrogio*), the stern towers of the 12th-century gate, the **Pusterla di Sant'Ambrogio**, bristle with the armour, antique weapons and torture instruments of the **Museo della Criminologia e Armi Antiche** (*open daily 10–1 and 3–7; adm*). The Pusterla guards the last resting place of Milan's patron saint and the city's holy of holies, the beautiful church of **Sant'Ambrogio** (*t 02 8645 0895; open Mon–Sat 10–12 and 2.30–6, Sun 3–5*). Founded by Ambrose in 379, it was enlarged and rebuilt several times (most notably by Archbishop Anspert in the 870s, when it became the prototype of the Lombard Romanesque basilica). Its current appearance dates from the 1080s.

Although it was considered a 'lost work' by the 17th century, various restorers have tried their hand at this most challenging task. In the Second World War the refectory was massively damaged by a bomb, and *The Last Supper* was only preserved thanks to piles of mattresses and other precautionary measures. In 1953, master restorer Mauro Pelliccioli covered what remained of the work with a rock-hard protective shield of clear glue. In 1977, the Ministry of Arts decided to let Italy's communications company Olivetti pay €3.5 million to make *The Last Supper* a showcase restoration project. The leader of the project, Pinin Brambilla, was given the job of chipping off Pelliccioli's protective coating, cleansing the work of its previous restorations and repaintings, then stabilizing the wall to prevent further damage, and finally painting in the gaps. In May 1999, Brambilla's work was displayed to howls of fury by art critics around the world.

Italians for the most part are proud of the restoration, though one of the harshest critics, James Beck from the Department of Art History at Columbia University, has argued that: 'This woman has simply produced a new Brambilla. What you have is a modern repainting of a work that was poorly conserved. It doesn't even have an echo of the past.' Brambilla (who was quoted as saying she communed daily with Leonardo's ghost while working on the project) notoriously even went where the living Leonardo feared to tread and put some finishing touches on Christ's face.

A number of permanent exhibitions have been set up to highlight Leonardo's presence in Milan as an artist, a scientist and a citizen. The **Museo d'Arte e Scienza** (*Via Quintino Sella 4, metro Cairoli or Lanza*) offers a three-hour tour of the city following in Leonardo's steps. Dubbed 'Ecce Leonardo', the tour takes in the Museo d'Arte e Scienza, Castello Sforzesco, Santa Maria delle Grazie and Museo della Scienza e della Tecnica. Call **t** 02 72022 488 for reservations and info or visit *www.leonardoda vincimilano.com* for further information.

The church is entered through a porticoed atrium, which in 1140 replaced the original Carolingian paved court or *parvis*. It sets off the simple, triangular façade with its rounded arches and towers; the one to the right, the Monks' Campanile, was built in the 9th century, while the more artistic Canons' Campanile on the left was finished in 1144. The bronze doors, in their decorated portals, date from the 10th century. In its day the finely proportioned if shadowy interior was revolutionary for its newfangled rib vaulting; rows of arches divide the aisles, supporting the women's gallery or Matroneum. On the left, look for the 10th-century bronze serpent and the richly sculpted pulpit, a vigorous masterpiece carved in 1080, set on an enormous late Roman sarcophagus. The apse is adorned with 10th–11th-century mosaics of the Redeemer and saints, while the sanctuary contains two ancient treasures: the 9th-century *Ciborium* on columns, and a magnificent gold, silver, enamel and gem-studded altarpiece (835), both signed by a certain '*Wolvinus magister phaber*'. In the crypt below moulder the bones of Saints Ambrose, Gervasio and Protasio. At the end of the south aisle the 4th-century *Sacello di San Vittore in Ciel d'Oro* ('in the sky of gold') contains brilliant 5th-century mosaics in its cupola and a presumed authentic portrait of St Ambrose.

After working on Santa Maria delle Grazie, Bramante spent two years on Sant' Ambrogio, contributing the unusual Portico della Canonica and the two cloisters, now incorporated into the adjacent Università Cattolica; these display Bramante's new interest in the ancient orders of architecture, an interest he was to develop fully when he moved to Rome.

Museum of Science and Technology

From Sant'Ambrogio, Via San Vittore leads to the Olivetan convent of San Vittore, repaired after the War to house the **Leonardo da Vinci Museo Nazionale della Scienza e Tecnica** (*t 02 485 551, www.museoscienza.org; open Tues–Sun 9.30–5, weekends until 6.30; adm*). Most of this vast and diverse collection, still arranged in its original 1950s format, is mysterious for the uninitiated, and if you're not keen about smelting and the evolution of batteries you may want to head straight for the Leonardo da Vinci Gallery, lined with pretty wooden models and explanations of his machines and inventions.

In 1481 Leonardo wrote to Lodovico il Moro, applying for a job in his court. He had been recommended to the duke as musician and player of the lyre (he played a beautiful lyre that he had made himself, of silver, in the shape of a horse's head); of all things, in his letter of introduction Leonardo boasts of his other talents as a military engineer, as a designer of war machines and fortifications, a canal builder, an arranger and festival decorator, a sculptor, a caster of bronzes, and mentions only at the end of the letter that he could paint too, if required. In fact, exactly what he did and for whom seemed to matter little. 'I work for anyone who pays me,' he said, and to prove it directly after his Milan period he worked with the nefarious Cesare Borgia. For Leonardo, at any rate, the results of his genius weren't half as important as the quest. In Milan he filled notebook after notebook (many are on display in the Ambrosiana) with studies of nature, weather and anatomy and ideas for inventions in the applied sciences. His most practical work in canal-building Milan, however, was in hydraulic engineering. He painted occasionally; besides the *Virgin of the Rocks* and the *Last Supper*, he did a range of portraits including one of Sforza's mistress, Cecilia Gallerani, called the *Lady with an Ermine* (in Cracow). Although the effortless master of the most beautiful painting technique of his time, Leonardo was chiefly interested in solving problems in composition and, once solved, he often left the painting unfinished out of boredom. Though he seemed to disdain painting, more than any other painter he was responsible for the intellectualizing of what had hitherto been regarded as a mere craft. This culminated in the Renaissance evolution towards the use of mathematics in art, the study of the nude form and the taste for illusion that had motivated the great artists of ancient Greece – as explained by the Elder Pliny, whose works had been rediscovered and published in Italian in 1473.

Leonardo's Horse

'Of the horse I shall say nothing, because I know the times,' wrote Leonardo in 1497, expressing his regret at not being able to complete the largest equine statue ever conceived. The statue was commissioned by the Duke of Sforza to honour his father Francesco. During the 17 years that followed the initial request, the artist worked on *The Last Supper* and a series of portraits of Italian nobles, and his talent for engineering produced a city plan for Milan, new weapons designs and a defence system for the castle. And if that wasn't enough, the Duke expected Leonardo to create stage sets, manage gala parties and compose rhymes and puzzles for the ladies of the court. Finally, a 24ft clay model of the horse was erected in a vineyard near the castle. But after the French seized Milan in September 1499, their archers used it for target practice, reducing it to a mound of clay. Legend has it that Leonardo never ceased mourning over his lost horse. Many of the working sketches, along with a revolutionary method to cast the statue in bronze, were detailed in Leonardo's notebooks. These were lost for centuries, though one set of notebooks, known as the Windsor Collection, came into the possession of the British royal family; another was discovered in Madrid's Biblioteca Nacional in 1966, the now famous *Codex Madrid II*. Then in 1977 a retired airline pilot, artist and art collector from Pennsylvania, Charles Dent, wrote an article in *National Geographic* proposing that Leonardo and Italy should have a horse as a gesture of appreciation from the American people for all that the Renaissance has meant to culture. He initiated the Leonardo's Horse Foundation; the romantic legend with its combination of creative genius and human frailty cast its spell over Dent, who died in 1994, before the project was completed.

Five hundred years after Leonardo's clay model was destroyed, the 24ft horse reappeared in Milan cast in bronze by US sculptor Nina Akamu. The horse, which weighs 12 tons, is engineered to withstand windshear and earthquakes. The Comune of Milan placed the horse in its natural setting, in the grounds of the city's Ippodromo del Galoppo racecourse, in the San Siro area (*metro Lotto; open 9–6.30*). Just one month after its inauguration in September 1999, a second cast appeared in Grand Rapids, Michigan: once the spell is broken, the horse can gallop anywhere.

Other rooms include musical instruments and displays on optics, radios, computers, clocks and astronomy; downstairs you can push buttons and make waterwheels turn. Another building is devoted to trains, and another to ships and naval history.

Milan's Financial District

For centuries, the area between Sant'Ambrogio and the Duomo has been the head-quarters of Milan's merchant guilds, bankers, and financiers, concentrated in the bank-filled **Piazza Cordusio**, Via degli Affari and Via Mercanti, just off Piazza del Duomo (*metro Cordusio or Duomo*). Milan's imposing **Borsa** in Piazza Affari was founded by Napoleon's viceroy Eugène de Beauharnais and is now the most important stock exchange in Italy. The current imposing Palazzo della Borsa dates from 1931, and sits smack on the ruins of *Mediolanum*'s ancient theatre; bits remain in the cellars and in the lower parts of the buildings along Via Vittore al Teatro. On Via Mercanti, the **Palazzo della Ragione** (1233), the old Hall of Justice, was given an extra floor with oval windows by Maria Theresa.

On the side facing Piazza Mercanti, look for a beautiful early 13th-century equestrian relief; while facing Via Mercanti don't miss the bas-relief of a sow partly clad in wool, discovered when the foundations for the *palazzo* were dug. According to legend, a tribe of Gauls under their chief Belloveso defeated the local Etruscans in the 6th century BC and wanted to settle in the area. An oracle told them to found their town on the spot where they found a sow half-covered in wool, and to name it after her. The sow was eventually discovered, and when the Romans conquered the Gauls, they translated the Celtic name of the town into the Latin *Mediolanum*, 'half-woolly'.

The Ambrosiana

Still in the financial district, in Piazza Pio XI (off Via Spadari and Via Cantù), the Ambrosiana is Milan's most enduring legacy of its leading family, the Borromei. Cardinal Federico Borromeo (cousin of Charles) founded one of Italy's greatest libraries here in 1609, containing 30,000 rare manuscripts, including ancient Middle Eastern texts collected to further the cardinal's efforts to produce a translation of the Bible; a 5th-century illustrated *Iliad*; Leonardo da Vinci's famous *Codex Atlanticus*, with thousands of his drawings; early editions of *The Divine Comedy*; and much, much more (*the library is open for study or special exhibits; ring for times,* **t** *02 806 921*).

The Cardinal's art collection or **Pinacoteca** (*open Tues–Sun 10–5.30; adm exp*) is housed in the same building. The gallery is essentially a monument to one man's taste – which showed a marked preference for the Dutch and the peculiar, and ranges from the truly sublime to some of the funniest paintings ever to grace a gallery. Here are Botticelli's lovely *Tondo*, and his *Madonna del Baldacchino* nonchalantly watering lilies with her milk; a respectable *Madonna* by Pinturicchio; paintings by Bergognone (including the altar from Pavia's San Pietro in Ciel d'Oro), a lovely portable altar by Geertgen tot Sint Jans, and the dramatic *Transito della Vergine* by Baldassarre Estense. Further along, an *Adoration of the Magi* by the Master of Santo Sangue is perhaps the only one where Baby Jesus seems thrilled at receiving the very first Christmas presents. A small room, illuminated by a pre-Raphaelitish stained-glass window of

Dante by Giuseppe Bertini (1865), contains the glove Napoleon wore at Waterloo, a 17th-century bronze of *Diana the Huntress* so ornate that even the stag wears earrings, and entertaining paintings by the Cardinal's friend Jan Brueghel the Younger, who delighted in detail and wasn't above putting a pussycat in Daniel's den of lions.

These are followed by more masterpieces: a Page, perhaps by Giorgione, Luini's *Holy Family with St Anne* (from a cartoon by Leonardo), Leonardo's *Portrait of a Musician*, a portrait of Beatrice d'Este attributed to Leonardo's follower Ambrogio da Predis, and then Bramantino's *Madonna in Trono fra Santi*, a scene balanced by a dead man on the left and an enormous dead frog on the right. Challenging this for absurdity is the nearby *Female Allegory* by 17th-century Giovanni Serodine, in which the lady, apparently disgruntled with her lute, astrolabe and books, is squirting herself in the nose.

The magnificent cartoon for Raphael's *School of Athens* in the Vatican is as interesting as the fresco itself; here too is a copy of Leonardo's *Last Supper*, painted by order of the Cardinal, who sought to preserve what he considered a lost work (the copy itself has recently been restored). A 16th-century *Washing of Feet* from Ferrara has one Apostle blithely clipping his toenails. Another room contains pages of drawings from Leonardo's *Codex Atlanticus*. The first Italian still life, Caravaggio's *Fruit Basket*, is also the most dramatic; it shares the space with more fond items like Alessandro Magnasco's *The Crow's Singing Lesson*. Further on is Titian's *Adoration of the Magi*, painted for Henri II of France and still in its original frame.

San Satiro

Via Torino (metro Duomo), t 02 874 683. Open Mon–Fri 7.30–11.30 and 3.30–6.30, Sat–Sun 9.30–11 and 3.30–7.

A bland 19th-century façade conceals one of the most remarkable Renaissance churches in Italy – officially Santa Maria presso San Satiro. It was rebuilt by Bramante in 1476, his first project in Milan. Faced with a lack of space in the abbreviated, T-shaped interior, Bramante created a perfect illusion of a deep choir extending back by three bays under a coffered vault, in a space only a few feet long. Bramante also designed the beautiful little octagonal Baptistry off the right aisle, with terracottas by Agosto De Fondutis; to the left, San Satiro's 9th-century Cappella della Pietà is one of the finest examples of Carolingian architecture in north Italy, though it was touched up in the Renaissance, with decorations and a *Pietà* by De Fondutis. San Satiro's equally antique **campanile** is visible on Via Falcone.

South of the Duomo: Porta Romana

This corner of Milan, the main traffic outlet towards the *autostrada* to the south, can be busy. Trams 4 and 24 will take you to **San Nazaro Maggiore** on Corso Porta Romana, a church that has undergone several rebuildings since its 4th-century dedication by St Ambrose; it was last restored in the Romanesque style. The most original feature of San Nazaro is the hexagonal *Cappella Trivulzio* by Bramantino (1512–47), built to contain the tomb of the *condottiere* Giangiacomo Trivulzio, who wrote his own epitaph in Latin: 'He who never knew rest now rests: Silence'. Trivulzio did have a busy career: a native Milanese who disliked Lodovico Sforza enough to lead Louis XII's attack on Milan in 1499, he became the city's French governor, then went on to lead the League of Cambrai armies in thumping the Venetians at Agnadello (1509).

Just behind San Nazaro, in Via Festa del Perdono, the **Ospedale Maggiore**, or **Ca' Granda**, was commissioned by Francesco Sforza in 1456. He asked Filarete (who wrote an architectural treatise on the ideal city called *Sforzinda* in honour of his patron) to design one building to incorporate all the little hospitals spread across Milan. The result, now the centrepiece of the Università degli Studi, is a beautiful early Renaissance work with ornate brickwork and terracotta and the first cross-shaped wards; inside are over 900 portraits of hospital benefactors since 1602. North of the Ca' Grande is the **Santa Maria della Passione** (*Via Bellini 2, metro San Babila*, **t** *02 7602 1370; open 7–12 and 3–6.15*), which was begun as a Greek cross in 1482, with a fine octagonal dome added in 1530. The Laternesi monks who worshipped here converted it into a Latin cross and in 1729 gave it its Baroque façade. In the fine Renaissance interior are a number of important paintings by Baroque painter Daniele Crespi (mostly under the dome) including his best, *St Charles Borromeo at Supper* (1628), as well as a *Deposition* by Luini in the right transept and a *Redeemer and the Apostles* by Bergognone, who also painted the pretty frescoes in the 15th century sacristy.

On Corso Italia, another main artery south, **Santa Maria presso San Celso** (1490–1563) offers a fine example of the Lombard love of ornament, with its handsome, lively façade by Alessi. Within, beyond an attractive atrium, the interior is paved with an exceptional marble floor and decorated with High Renaissance paintings by Paris Bordone, Bergognone and Moretto. On the day of their marriage, Milanese brides and grooms traditionally stop by to pray in the chapel of the Madonna. The adjacent 10th-century church of **San Celso** has a charming interior restored in the 19th century and a good original portal.

South Milan: The Ticinese and Navigli Districts

Southwest of the city centre, Via Torino leads into the artsy quarter named for the Ticino river, traversed by the main thoroughfare, Corso di Porta Ticinese (*tram 3 from Via Torino*). In the Ticinese you can find pieces of Roman *Mediolanum*, which had its forum in modern **Piazza Carrobbio**. There's a bit of the Roman circus on Via Circo, off Via Lanzone, and the **Colonne di San Lorenzo**, on the Corso: 16 Corinthian columns, now a favourite teenager hangout but originally part of a temple or bath, were transported here in the 4th century to construct a portico in front of the **Basilica di San Lorenzo Maggiore** (*Corso di Porta Ticinese 39, tram 3, 15 or 20,* **t** *02 8940 4129; open daily 7.30–6.45*), the oldest surviving church in Milan; it acquired its octagonal form, encircled by an ambulatory and crowned with a dome, in the 4th century, predating the church it resembles most, San Vitale in Ravenna. Carefully spared by Barbarossa in the sack of Milan in 1164 it has since suffered severe fires, and in the 16th century when it was near total collapse it was rebuilt, conserving as much of the old structure as possible. Luckily, the beautiful **Cappella di Sant'Aquilino** (*adm*) has come down intact, with 4th- or 5th-century mosaics of Christ and his disciples and an early Christian sarcophagus. Below are blocks from a Roman building from the 2nd century.

A green walkway, the Parco delle Basiliche, links San Lorenzo to the **Basilica di Sant'Eustorgio** (*Piazza Sant'Eustorgio, tram 3, 15 or 20, t 02 5810 1583; open 7.45–12 and 3–6.30*), one of the most important medieval churches in Milan. It was rebuilt in 1278 along the lines of Sant'Ambrogio, with a lofty campanile (1309). The chapels, added in the 15th century, are finely decorated with early Renaissance art; in the first chapel on the right look for a tryptych by Bergognone. The transept has a chapel dedicated to the Magi, where a large Roman sarcophagus held the relics of the Three Kings until Frederick Barbarossa hauled them off to Cologne.

The highlight of the church, however, is the pure Tuscan Renaissance: **Cappella Portinari** (1468), built for Pigello Portinari, an agent of the Medici bank in Milan (*t 02 8940 2671; open Tues–Sun 10–6; adm*). Attributed to Michelozzo and often compared with Brunelleschi's Pazzi Chapel in Florence in its elegant cubic simplicity and proportions, the chapel is crowned by a lovely dome, adorned with stucco reliefs of angels. This jewel is dedicated to the Inquisitor St Peter Martyr (who was axed in the head on the shores of Lake Como in 1252), whose life of intolerance was superbly frescoed on the walls by Vincente Foppa – he never did anything finer. Foppa's remains are buried in the magnificent marble Arca di San Pietro Martire (1339) by the Pisan Giovanni di Balduccio. Balduccio also added the relief of saints on the nearby 14th-century **Porta Ticinese**, built in the Spanish walls.

The colourful **Navigli** district (*metro Porta Genova, tram 2 or 14*) is named for its medieval navigable canals, the Naviglio Grande (linking Milan to the river Ticino, Lake Maggiore and the Candoglio marble quarries) and Naviglio Pavese (to Pavia) that meet to form the docks, or Darsena, near Porta Ticinese. Up until the 1950s Milan, through these canals, handled more tonnage than seaports like Brindisi and, like any good port, the Navigli was then a funky working-class district of warehouses, workshops, sailors' bars and public housing blocks. Although some of this lingers, the Navigli is now a relaxed, fashionably bohemian zone, where many of the city's artists work, the restaurants are cheaper and you can hear jazz in the night.

Short Excursions from Milan

South of Milan

Southeast of the city centre lies the **Abbey of Chiaravalle** (*on Via Sant'Arialdo 102 in Chiaravalle Milanese, metro Corvetto, bus 77, t 02 5740 3404; open Tues–Sun 9.15–11.30 and 3–5.30. Guided tours: winter 11, 2.30, 4; summer 11, 3, 4.30; adm by donation*). Founded in 1135 by the Cistercians, the abbey has all but gone the way of all worldly things except for its French Gothic church, the cemetery and ruins of the Gothic cloister. It has a beautiful tall bell tower and in the nave, something rather unusual for Lombardy – 17th-century Flemish frescoes. There are also a few by the school of Giotto and in the right transept, a Madonna by Luini.

Certosa di Garegnano, also to the south, though further west (*Via Garegnano 28, tram 14, t 02 3800 6301; open 3–5*), was founded in the 14th century; the Charterhouse has left only its church behind, which was redone in the late 16th century. On the walls of the nave are frescoes on the history of the Cistercians, by Daniele Crespi (1629) – his masterpiece, painted the year before he died at age 31.

Monza

Only a hop and a skip from Milan, Monza seems to be unfairly slighted by most visitors to Lombardy. Monza attracts throngs in early September when it hosts the Italian Grand Prix; otherwise you may have its venerable monuments to yourself. Back in the late 6th century Monza was the darling of the Lombard Queen Theodolinda, who founded its first cathedral after her conversion from Arianism by Pope Gregory the Great. Rebuilt in the 13th century, the **Duomo** on Via Napoleone bears a lovely green and white striped marble façade by the great Matteo da Campione (1396). The massive campanile dates from 1606, when the interior was given its Baroque facelift. To the left of the presbytery, **Theodolinda's chapel** has charming 1444 frescoes by the Zavattari brothers depicting the life of the queen who left Monza its most famous relic, preserved in the high altar: the gem-encrusted **Iron Crown of Italy** (*Duomo, t 039 389 420; open Tues–Sun 8–12 and 3–6.30; museum open Tues–Sat 9–11.30 and 3–5.30, Sun and hols 10.30–12 and 3–5.30; adm*). The story goes that when his mother Helena unearthed the True Cross in Jerusalem, Emperor Constantine had one of its iron nails embedded in his crown. It became a tradition in the Middle Ages for every newly elected emperor to stop in Monza or Pavia to be crowned King of Italy

Getting There

Monza is 15 minutes by **train** from Milan's Garibaldi Station, or 20 minutes by ATM **bus** from the same place.

Less frequent trains depart also from Stazione Centrale. CTNM buses link Monza and Saronno.

Tourist Information

Monza: Palazzo Comunale, Piazza Carducci (*closed Sat pm and Sun*), t 039 323 222, *promonza@monza.net*.

Festivals

Monza Più, *1st week of Sept.* A series of events in the city's piazzas during the Grand Prix, including market stands and shows.

San Giovanni Battista festival, *end of June.* The celebration of the local patron; includes concerts and fireworks in the Villa Reale park.

Market Days

Central Via Bergamo: Antique market. *Every 2nd Sun of the month.*

In the Duomo's Piazza: Organic market. *Every fourth Sun of the month.*

Where to Stay and Eat

Monza ✉ 20052

★★★★Hotel de la Ville, Viale R. Margherita 15, t 039 382 581, *www.hoteldelaville.com* (*luxury*). Overlooking the park, a cosy place with a garden and the town's finest food in its Derby Grill restaurant: try *spaghetti alla crudaiola. Closed Sat and Sun lunch, and Aug.*

★★★Della Regione, Via Elvezia 4, t 039 387 205, *www.hoteldellaregione.it* (*very expensive –expensive*). Hotel with restaurant.

★★Antica Trattoria Dell'Uva, Piazza Carrobiolo 2, t 039 323 825 (*moderate*). For somewhere less pricy. The restaurant seves good, local cuisine.

before heading on to Rome to receive the Crown of Empire from the pope – a tradition Napoleon briefly revived when he had himself crowned in Milan's Duomo in 1805. The cathedral's **museum** (*same hours; combined adm available*) contains Theodolinda's treasure: a processional cross given to her by Gregory the Great, the 5th-century ivory diptych of Stilicho, her crown and the famous silver hen and seven chicks symbolizing Lombardy and its provinces, as well as a precious Syriac cross belonging to her son Agilgulfo (it's not hard to see why Lombard names soon fell out of fashion) and Gian Galeazzo Visconti's goblet.

Just north of the Duomo, the 13th-century Palazzo Comunale or **Arengario** is the city's finest secular building. From here, Via C. Alberto leads north to the beautiful 800-hectare **Parco di Monza** (*t 039 030 081, www.parcodimonza.org; open 7–7, till 8.30 in the summer*). One of greater Milan's 'lungs', it is home to a horse-racing course, the 1922 Autodromo, site of the Italian Grand Prix and the 27-hole Golf Club Milano, as well as other recreational facilities. Until 1806 the park was the grounds of the neoclassical **Villa Reale** (*t 039 322 003; open for visits by appointment through the tourist office, which organizes groups of minimum 20 people; adm*), built by Archduke Ferdinand of Austria and the favourite residence of Napoleon's viceroy Eugène de Beauharnais. The single sombre note is struck behind the 18th-century residence – an expiatory chapel built by Vittorio Emanuele III that marks the spot where his father Umberto was assassinated by an anarchist in 1900.

North of Monza near Carate, **Agliate** has one of the earliest of many Romanesque churches modelled on Milan's Sant'Ambrogio, the 9th–10th-century basilica of **San Pietro**: inside, rough 5th-century columns define the three naves, while the presbytery (with remains of original frescoes) is raised over the choir and apses. The proximity of a baptistry to the south forms what would soon become the archetypal Lombard temple complex; it too conserves its 10th-century frescoes and its original font.

Alfa Romeos and Saronno

Northwest of Milan, on the road and rail line to Varese, **Arese** has been the home town of Lombardy's car industry since 1910 (the *Associazione Lombarda Fabbrica Automobilistiche*, or Alfa Romeo), when a group of Lombard magnates bought up the French Darracq manufacturer. Alfa, in turn, has been bought up by Fiat, but in Arese you can visit the six floors of the 'family album', the **Museo Storico dell'Alfa Romeo** (*www.museoalfaromeo.it; open Mon–Fri 9–12.30 and 2–4.30, reserve ticket 2 weeks in advance, closed Aug and Christmas holidays; adm free*).

Further along towards Varese, **Saronno** is synonymous with *amaretto*, either in the cocktail glass or in the biscuits, but students of Lombard Renaissance art will recognize it at once for its **Santuario della Madonna dei Miracoli**, built by Giovanni Antonio Amadeo in 1498. The façade with its trumpeting angels was added in the next century by Pellegrini, while highlights in the rich interior include the dome's startling, innovative fresco, the *Concert of Angels* by Gaudenzio Ferrari (1534) and Bernadino Luini's beautiful frescoes in the chapel of the Madonna (1531).

The Lombard Plain

09

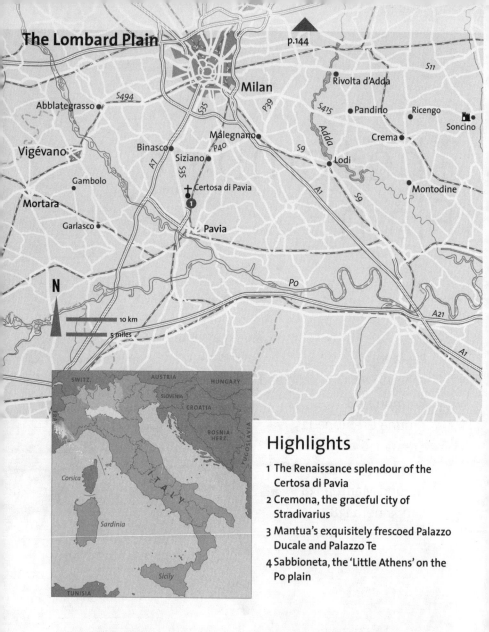

The Lombard Plain

p.144

Milan

Rivolta d'Adda
Pandino
Ricengo
Soncino
Crema
Montodine
Lodi

Abblategrasso
S494
S11
S415
S9
Adda
A1
S9

Vigévano
Binasco
Malegnano
P40
Siziano
P39
S35
A7

Gambolo
Certosa di Pavia
①

Mortara

Garlasco
Pavia

N
10 km
5 miles

Po
A21
A1

SWITZ. AUSTRIA HUNGARY
SLOVENIA
CROATIA
BOSNIA-HERZ.
YUGOSLAVIA
Corsica
ITALY
Sardinia
Sicily
TUNISIA

Highlights

1 The Renaissance splendour of the Certosa di Pavia
2 Cremona, the graceful city of Stradivarius
3 Mantua's exquisitely frescoed Palazzo Ducale and Palazzo Te
4 Sabbioneta, the 'Little Athens' on the Po plain

The three small capitals of the Lombard plain are among Italy's most rewarding art cities, each maintaining its individual character: Pavia, the capital of the ancient Lombards and the region's oldest centre of learning, embellished with fine Romanesque churches and its famous Renaissance Certosa; Cremona, the graceful city where the raw medieval fiddle was reincarnated as the lyrical violin; and Mantua, the dream shadow capital of the wealthy Gonzaga dukes and Isabella d'Este.

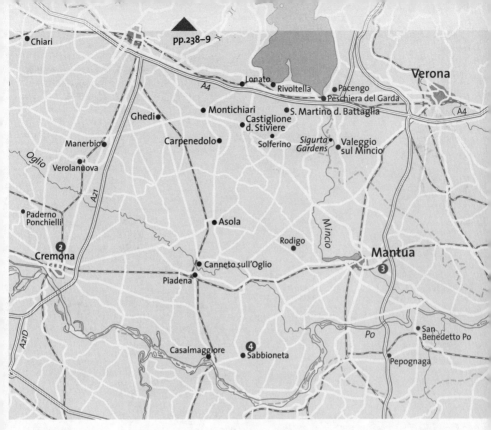

pp.238–9

Pavia

Pavia is a distinctly serious, no-monkey-business town. It is one of those rare cities that had its golden age in the three-digit years before the millennium, that misty half-legendary time that historians have shrugged off as the Dark Ages. But these were bright days for Pavia, when it served as capital of the Goths and saw Odoacer proclaimed King of Italy after defeating Romulus Augustulus, the last Roman Emperor in the West. In the 6th century the heretical Lombards led by King Alboin captured Pavia from the Goths and formed a state the equal of Byzantine Ravenna and Rome, making Pavia the capital of their *Regnum Italicum*, a position the city maintained into the 11th century; Charlemagne came here to be crowned (774), as did the first King of Italy, Berenguer (888), and Emperor Frederick Barbarossa (1155).

At the turn of the millennium the precursor of Pavia's modern university, the *Studio*, was founded, and among its first students of law was the first Norman Archbishop of Canterbury, Lanfranc, born in Pavia in 1005. Pavia was a Ghibelline *comune*, the 'city of a hundred towers' and a rival of Milan, to whom it lost its independence in 1359. It was favoured by the Visconti, especially by Gian Galeazzo, who built the castle housing his art collection and founded the striking Certosa di Pavia. It, with many other churches in the city, bears the mark of Pavia's great, half-demented sculptor-architect of the High Renaissance, Giovanni Antonio Amadeo.

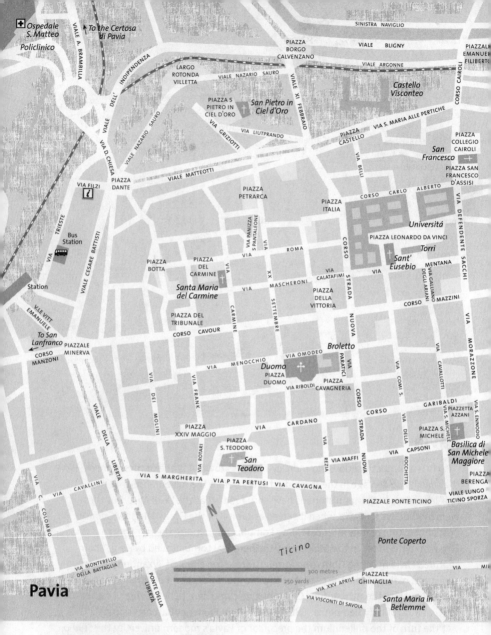

The Duomo and San Michele

Through traffic has been banished from Pavia's core, which retains its street plan from the days when it was the Roman city of *Ticinum*; the *cardus* (Corso Cavour) and the *decumanus* (Corso Strada Nuova) intersect by the town hall or **Broletto**, begun in the 12th century. The adjacent **Duomo** (*t 03 822 2156; open 7.30–12 and 3–7*), a front-running candidate for the ugliest church in all Italy, was begun in 1488, and owes its imposing design to Amadeo, Leonardo da Vinci, Bramante and a dozen others

Getting There

Pavia is quite close to Milan's **airports** (Linate 58km, Malpensa 85km). The direct **coach** service by SGEA, **t** 0382 375 405/513 506, *www.sgea.it*, runs approximately every 2 hours from Linate; same to and from Malpensa. Tickets cost €9 from Linate, €14 from Malpensa. Both stop at the Certosa di Pavia.

There are **buses** roughly every 30 minutes between Milan and Pavia, and this is also the best way to travel if you wish to stop off and visit the Certosa, some 8km north of Pavia (info **t** 02 8954 6132, *www.infopoint.it*). Buses arrive in and depart from Via Trieste, in the brand-new station-cum-shopping centre. Frequent **trains** link Pavia to Milan (30mins) and Genoa (1½ hours), and there are less frequent services to Cremona and Mantua, Alessandria and Vercelli, and Piacenza. The train station is a 10-minute walk from the centre, at the end of Corso Cavour and Viale Vittorio Emanuele II (*www.trenitalia.it*).

By **car**, Pavia can be reached very quickly from Milan by the A7 *autostrada*, or in a more leisurely fashion by the SS35, which has the advantage of passing by the Certosa.

Tourist Information

APT Pavia: Via Filzi 2, **t** 0382 22156, *www.comune.pr.it*. Near the station.

Churches are generally open daily, but closed 12–3pm. Ring **t** 0382 530 820 for more information. For **wine**, ask the tourist office for the list of the wine consortia of the Oltrepò area. A historical cellar is **Il Montù**, Via Marconi 10, in Montù Beccaria village, **t** 0385 262 252, *www.ilmontu.com*.

Markets

Pavia: Piazza della Vittoria. Antiques market. *1st Sun of the month (all year except Jan and Aug)*.

Castel Belgioioso: In the castle court, 8km outside Pavia in the direction of Cremona. An annual 10-day antiques market begins at the beginning of April (*open Mon–Fri 3–8, Thurs till 11pm; adm*). Ring **t** 0382 970 525.

Where to Stay

Pavia ✉ 27100

Most visit Pavia as a day trip from Milan, but light sleepers or the budget-minded could take in Milan as a day trip from Pavia.

Very Expensive–Expensive

★★★★**Castello di San Gaudenzio**, Via Mulino 1, San Gaudenzio, Cervesina, 30mins' drive from Pavia, **t** 0383 3331, *www.castellosangaudenzio.com*. This 14th-century castle is set in the middle of a century-old Italian-designed park with statues. The central, oldest part contains the beautifully decorated Sala Cavour and Sala delle Cariatidi, and three charming suites, including one (the most expensive) on two floors in the tower. Accommodation is normally provided in the neighbouring modern building, which has all comforts.

★★★★**Moderno**, Viale Vittorio Emanuele II 41, near the railway station, **t** 0382 303 401, *www.hotelmoderno.it*. The most comfortable hotel in town.

Moderate

★★★**Ariston**, Via A. Scopoli 10/d, **t** 0382 34334, *www.aristonpavia.it*. Centrally located and with a slightly more old-fashioned touch;

(definite proof that too many cooks spoil the broth). Its strange appearance, like that of corrugated cardboard (its façade was to be covered by polychrome marble), led to an understandable lack of interest in ever finishing it. The last two apses in the transept were added only in 1930, while the vast cupola that dominates the city skyline was added in the 1880s.

Next to the cathedral is the rubble of what was once the singularly unattractive 12th-century **Torre Civica**, the collapse of which in 1989 prompted serious attention to its rather more famous Pisan relation.

air conditioning, private bathroom, television and phone in each room.

***De La Ville**, Via al Ticino 44, Bereguardo, 8km from the city centre, **t** 0382 928 100, *www.hotel-delaville.com*. A good choice for families and people who love the country-side. In the Ticino park, within walking distance of Italy's only surviving pontoon bridge, with mountain bikes, tennis, solarium, a playground for children and a good restaurant.

***Excelsior**, Piazzale Stazione 25, **t** 0382 28596, *www.excelsiorpavia.com*. Conveniently located for the centre.

Aurora, Via Vittorio Emanuele II 25, **t 0382 21248. Another hotel located near the station. All the rooms are clean and comfort-able and all are equipped with showers, phone, TV and air conditioning.

Inexpensive

Locanda della Stazione (ring the bell), Viale Vittorio Emanuele II 14, **t** 0382 29231. A good budget option in a private house. Communal bathrooms, but the homely rooms are spacious, clean and decorated with old-style furniture. It is advisable to let them know when you are coming to make sure that someone will be there to let you in.

Agriturismo

For a break from the city, Pavia is well served by *agriturismi*, which offers a range of farm-houses that can provide food and hospitality. Ask the tourist office for an updated list or consider the following options:

Azienda Agrituristica Torrazzetta, Torrazzetta hamlet, Borgo Priolo, near Casteggio, 25km from Pavia), **t** 0383 871 041, *www. torrazzetta.it* (*moderate–inexpensive*). Combines modern service with country

hospitality in the Oltrepò wine-producing area, offering rooms with own bath and suites. It has a good selection of organically grown local products to buy or to eat at the restaurant, and its own wine. *Closed Mon*.

Castello di Stefanago, in the hamlet of La Boatta, near Borgo Priolo, **t** 0383 875 227/413, *www.castellodistefanago.it*. You can stay in the suites of the castle atop the hill (*expensive–moderate*), where legend has it that a troubled love affair similar to that of Romeo and Juliet took place, or you can stay in the Cascina La Boatta near the castle (*inexpensive*). There are horse-riding facilities and a good restaurant. *Open Mar–Oct*.

Oasi delle Cicogne, Tenuta Broccone, Robbio, **t** 0384 672 673 (*moderate*). In the Lomellina area. Set in the middle of a stork nesting area, and you can go fishing in a nearby lake. Six rooms available.

Eating Out

Pavia is well endowed with good restaurants. Specialities include frogs, salami from Varzi and *zuppa pavese* (a raw egg on toast drowned in hot broth); good local wines to try are from the Oltrepò Pavese region, one of Lombardy's best. Cortese is a fresh dry white, Bonarda a meaty, dry red, Pinot a fruity white.

Very Expensive

Al Cassinino, Via Cassinino 1, outside the city on the Giovi highway, **t** 0382 422 097. Pavia's temple of fine cuisine. Sitting on the Naviglio, the restaurant is done out in the style of a medieval inn, complete with rare antiques. Dishes are whatever the market provides – try pheasant breast with apples or *risotto alla Certosino*. *Closed Wed, and Christmas. Booking compulsory*.

From the Duomo, the Strada Nuova continues south down to the river and the pretty **Covered Bridge**, which has replaced the original Renaissance model damaged during the last war. On the opposite shore of the river lies **Borgo Ticino**, the borough of the *bursan*, inhabitants of the borgo and of Sabaudian origin, who claim to be the true people of Pavia. If you walk along the river you'll see the height of the last flood marked on the walls of the houses. You can also visit the Late-Romanesque church of **Santa Maria in Betlem**; the area is full of typical *osterias* which serve traditional food.

Locanda Vecchia Pavia al Mulino, Via al Monumento 5, t 0382 925 894, www.vecchia paviaalmulino.it. In the restored 16th-century mill of the Certosa, this restaurant mixes tradition and style, with refined dishes such as stuffed courgette flowers on Taleggio cheese, and truffle fondue. *Closed Mon, and Wed lunch, and 3 weeks in Jan, 2 weeks in Aug. Booking advisable.*

Expensive

Antica Osteria del Previ, Via Milazzo 65, t 0382 26203. An old-fashioned place serving home-made salami, risotto with frog or radicchio and speck, and for *secondi*, river-fish and snails. Also a good selection of meats, as well as stews and roasts. *Closed Sun, 10 days Jan, Aug. Booking advisable.*

Bardelli, Viale Lungoticino Visconti 2, t 0382 27441, www.bardellipv.it. A stylish restaurant in a Liberty-style villa set in its own grounds along the river shore. Serves traditional Lombard dishes with a creative touch. *Closed Sun and 1 week in Aug.*

La Zelata, Zelata di Bereguardo, in Parco di Ticino, t 0382 928 178, la.zelata@comunic.it. Not far from Bereguardo, this family-run restaurant has been serving delightful traditional Lombard dishes for the last 20 years. After the meal take some time to go heron-watching: this is the biggest nesting area in the Ticino Park. *Closed Sun, and Mon lunch, all Aug.*

Moderate–Inexpensive

Osteria del Naviglio, Via Alzaia 39b, t 0382 460 392. Situated along the Naviglio after it bends behind the Castello Visconti, this unassuming establishment is, in spite of its appearance, a gourmet wine bar and restaurant run by the former chef of Locanda Vecchia Pavia al Mulino, and a young *sommelier* with a special taste for desserts. There is a vast selection of Italian and foreign wines to be tasted, with delicacies such as a *sformato* (a kind of hearty mousse) of potato and porcini or seasonal vegetables, or *pappardelle* with duck. Desserts are also excellent – try the sorbets or hazelnut *semifreddo*. The restaurant offers a moderately priced *menu degustazione*, or you can dine cheaply at the wine bar. *Open until late; closed Mon, Sat, Sun at lunch, hols.*

Osteria della Madonna del Peo, Via Cardano 63, corner Via dei Liguri, t 0382 302 833, leo1961@libero.it. In the city centre, located in a homely vaulted inn. Serves typical Lombard dishes, such as *risotti*, roasted and braised meats, or stuffed guinea-fowl, which require lengthy cooking. Cheap menu at lunch time; good selection of Oltrepò wines. *Closed Sun. Booking advisable.*

Trattoria Ca' Bella, Via Ca' Bella 2, Borgo Ticino, t 0382 25241. A noisy, family-run place that's jam-packed at lunch. Try the four-cheese gnocchi and ravioli with walnut sauce. Try also *Fusilli la Bella* if you like hot dishes. *Closed Wed.*

Entertainment

Teatro Fraschini: Corso Strada Nuova 138, Pavia, t 0382 371 202, www.teatro fraschini.it. Tickets: t 0382 371 214. A nice Baroque theatre that dates back to 1700, designed by Antonio Galli Bibiena, who had already designed the theatres of Bologna and Mantua. The theatre, now restored to its original splendour, opens its season of opera, ballet and classical music on the day of the city's patron saint, San Siro, on 9 December.

From Strada Nuova, Via Maffi leads to the small brick 12th-century **San Teodoro**, notable for its early 16th-century fresco of Pavia when it still had a forest of a hundred towers and the original covered bridge. East of the Strada, Via Capsoni leads in a couple of blocks to Pavia's most important church, the Romanesque **Basilica di San Michele Maggiore**, founded in 661 but rebuilt in the 12th century after its destruction by lightning. Unlike the other churches of Pavia, San Michele is made of sandstone, mellowed into a fine golden hue, though the weather has been less kind to the intricate friezes that cross its front like comic strips, depicting a complete 'apocalyptic vision' with its medieval bestiary, monsters and human figures involved in the never-ending fight between Good and Evil. Mermaids are especially prominent – one impassively holds up her forked tail, a Romanesque conceit nearly as popular as the two lions by the main door. Such mermaids, displaying the entrance to the womb, with birds or dragons whispering in their ears, come straight from medieval mysticism, perhaps as a symbol of the cosmic process: the sirens, representing desire, become the intermediaries by which nature's energy and inspiration (here represented by the birds) are conducted into the conscious world.

The solemn interior, where Frederick Barbarossa was crowned with the Iron Crown of Italy, contains more fine carvings on the capitals of the columns; the most curious, the fourth on the left, portrays the 'Death of the Righteous'. Along the top runs a Byzantine-style women's gallery, while the chapel to the right of the main altar contains the church's most valuable treasure, a 7th-century silver crucifix.

The University and Castello Visconteo

The great yellow neoclassical quadrangles of the **University of Pavia**, also called the Paduan Oxford and famous for law and medicine, occupy much of the northeast quadrant of the ancient street plan. The ancient Studio was officially made a university in 1361. St Charles Borromeo, a former student, founded a college here (still supported by the Borromei in Milan) in 1561 to allow young talented yet poor men to enter university, while Pope Pius V founded another, the Collegio Ghislieri, in 1569. In the 18th century Maria Theresa worked hard to bring the university back to life after scholarship had hit the skids and financed the construction of the main buildings. The university's history is celebrated in the **Museo Per La Storia Dell' Università** (*Strada Nuova 65, t 0382 23724; open Mon 3.30–5 and Fri 9.30–12, phone to visit during other times*). Three of Pavia's medieval skyscrapers or **Torri** survive in the middle of the university, in the Piazza Leonardo da Vinci; the roof in the Piazza shelters what is believed to be the crypt of the demolished 12th-century **Sant'Eusebio** church, which was originally a 7th-century Aryan cathedral; nearby you can meet some of the university's 27,000 students (many of whom commute from Milan) at the Bar Bordoni, on Via Mentana. In the Piazza San Francesco d'Assisi, northeast of the main university, the 1228 **San Francesco d'Assisi** was one of the first churches in Italy dedicated to the saint; it has an unusual façade, adorned with lozenge patterns and a triple-mullioned window.

At the top of Strada Nuova looms the mighty **Castello Visconteo**, built between 1360 and 1365 by the Campionese masters for Gian Galeazzo II but partially destroyed in the Battle of Pavia on 24 February 1525, when Emperor Charles V captured Francis I of France, who succinctly described the outcome in a letter to his mother: 'Madame, all is lost save honour'. Three sides of the castle and its beautifully arcaded courtyard with terracotta decorations managed to survive, and now house Pavia's **Musei Civici** (*t 0382 33853, museicivici@comune.pv.it; open Tues–Sun 10–6, until 1.30 in July–Aug and Dec–Jan; adm*). The archaeological and medieval sections contain finds from Roman and Gaulish Pavia, as well as robust Lombard and medieval carvings salvaged from now-vanished churches, and colourful 12th-century mosaics. One room contains an impressive wooden model of the cathedral, built by the architect Fugazza in the early 16th century. The picture gallery on the first floor contains works by Giovanni Bellini, Correggio, Foppa, Van der Goes and others.

San Pietro in Ciel d'Oro

Behind the castle, Via Griziotti (off Viale Matteotti) leads to Pavia's second great Romanesque temple, **San Pietro in Ciel d'Oro** ('St Peter in the Golden Sky'), built in 1132 and named for its once-glorious gilded ceiling, mentioned by Dante in Canto X of the *Paradiso*. The single door in the façade is strangely off-centre; within, the main altar is one of the greatest works of the Campionese masters, the **Arca di Sant'Agostino**, a magnificent 14th-century monument built to shelter the bones of St Augustine which, according to legend, were retrieved in the 8th century from Carthage by the Lombard King Luitprand, staunch ally of Pope Gregory II, against the iconoclasts of Byzantium. Luitprand himself is buried in a humble tomb to the right, and in the crypt lies another Dark Age celebrity, the philosopher Boethius, slain by Emperor Theodoric of Ravenna in 524.

There are two other notable churches in Pavia. In the centre of town (towards the Piazza Petrarca) **Santa Maria del Carmine** (1390s) is an excellent example of Lombard Gothic, with a fine façade and rose window and, inside, a beautifully sculptured lavabo by Amadeo. Outside the centre, to the west (Corso Cavour to Corso Manzoni and Via della Riviera) it's a fifteen-minute walk to the rather plain, vertical, 13th-century **San Lanfranco**, notable for its lovely memorial, the Arca di San Lanfranco. Sculpted by Amadeo in 1498, this was his last work (though Archbishop Lanfranc was actually buried in Canterbury); the same artist helped design the church's pretty cloister. To the east, down Viale Gremona, is the 12th-century **San Lazzaro** church.

The Certosa di Pavia

Off the SS35 road from Milan–Pavia, along the Naviglio Pavese; www.certosa dipavia.com. Open Oct–Mar Tues–Sun 9–11.30 and 2.30–4.30 (until 5 Sun and hols); April 9–11.30 and 2.30–5.30; May–Sept 9–11.30 and 2.30–6; guided visits by monks; you must arrive half an hour before closing time; adm.

The pinnacle of Renaissance architecture in Lombardy, and according to Jacob Burckhardt 'the greatest decorative masterpiece in all of Italy', the Certosa or Charterhouse of Pavia was built over a period of 200 years. Gian Galeazzo Visconti laid the cornerstone in 1396, with visions of the crown of Italy dancing in his head and the desire to build a splendid pantheon for his hoped-for royal self and his heirs. It is also claimed he was following the wishes made by his second wife, Caterina Visconti, in her will. Although many architects and artists worked on the project (beginning with the Campionese masters of Milan cathedral), it bears the greatest imprint of Giovanni Antonio Amadeo, who with his successor Bergognone worked on its sculptural programme for 30 years and contributed the design of the lavish façade.

Napoleon disbanded the monastery, but in 1968 a small group of Cistercians reoccupied the Certosa. The monks of today live the same style of contemplative life as the old Carthusians, maintaining vows of silence. A couple, however, are released to take visitors around the complex. If you arrive by the Milan–Pavia bus, the Certosa is a 1½km walk from the nearest stop, a beckoning vision at the end of the straight, shaded land, surrounded by well-tended fields and rows of poplars that were once part of the vast game park of the Castello Visconteo in Pavia.

Once through the main gate and **vestibule** adorned with frescoes by Luini, a large grassy court opens up, lined with buildings that served as lodgings for visitors and stores for the monks. At the far side rises the sumptuous, detailed façade of the **church**, a marvel of polychromatic marbles, medallions, bas-reliefs, statues, and windows covered with marble embroidery from the chisel of Amadeo, who died before the upper, less elaborate level was begun.

The interior plan is Gothic but the decoration is Renaissance, with later Baroque additions. Outstanding works of art include Bergognone's five statues of saints in the chapel of Sant'Ambrogio (sixth on the left); the tombs of Lodovico il Moro and his young bride Beatrice d'Este, a masterpiece by Cristoforo Solari; the beautiful inlaid stalls of the choir, with the main altar in marble and lapis lazuli; and the tomb of Gian Galeazzo Visconti, all works of the 1490s and surrounded by fine frescoes. The old sacristy contains a magnificent early *cinquecento* ivory altarpiece by the Florentine Baldassarre degli Embriachi, with 94 figures and 66 bas-reliefs.

From the church, the tour continues into the **Little Cloister**, with delicate terracotta decorations (including a beautiful ornamental washbasin) and a dream-like view of the church and its cupola, a rising crescendo of arcades. A lovely doorway by Amadeo leads back into the church. The **Great Cloister** with its long arcades is surrounded by the 24 house-like cells of the monks – each contains a chapel and study/dining room, a bedroom upstairs and a walled garden in the rear. The frescoed **Refectory** contains a pulpit for the monks who read aloud during otherwise silent suppers.

Around Pavia: Lomello and Vigevano

West of Pavia and the Certosa lies the little-known Lomellina, a rice-growing and frog-farming district, irrigated by 14th-century canals dug by order of the Visconti. The feudal seat, **Lomello**, retains some fine early medieval buildings, most notably a lovely little 5th-century polygonal **Baptistry** near the main church, the 11th-century **Basilica di Santa Maria Maggiore**, built in the 9th century and one of the first architectural examples of a cross-vaulted ceiling.

Also in the Lomellina is the old silk town of **Vigevano** (better known these days for its high-fashion footwear manufacturers), the site of another vast castle of the Visconti and Sforza clans; it was the birthplace of Lodovico il Moro, and for the past few years has been undergoing a lengthy restoration process. Below it lies the majestic rectangular **Piazza Ducale**, designed in 1492 by Bramante (with help from Leonardo) as Lombardy's answer to Venice's Piazza San Marco. Bramante is also

attributed the design of the **tower** (t 0381 690370; open Tues–Fri 11–12 and 3–4,
Sat–Sun 10–12.30 and 2.30–6; adm). Originally a grand stairway connected the piazza
to one of the castle towers, though now the three sides are adorned with slender
arcades, while on the fourth stands the magnificent concave baroque façade of the
cathedral, designed by a Spanish bishop, Juan Caramuel de Labkowitz.

Inside there's a good collection of 16th-century paintings and a 15th-century
Lombard polyptych on the life of St Thomas of Canterbury, and an especially rich
treasury (t 0381 690 370; open Sept–July Sun and hols 3–6, or upon request. Closed Aug
and Christmas time; adm) containing illuminated codices, Flemish tapestries and
golden reliquaries.

There is a **Shoe Museum** on the ground floor of the 19th-century **Crespi Palace**
(Corso Cavour 82, t 0381 690 370; open Tues–Fri 10–12.30 and 3–6.30, Sat–Sun 10–12.30
and 2.30–6.30; adm), which is stacked with weird and wonderful footwear.

In the centre of Lomellina, **Mortara** is known as the Italian capital of the goose (oca).
A unique salame d'oca, whose recipe is protected by a local consortium, is produced
here, while goose kidney is used for a gourmet mortadella, as well as pâtés. There is
also a special festival dedicated to the goose, the Sagra dell'Oca, comprising a palio
(race) of the seven village contradas (boroughs) at the end of September. You can buy
goose at **Corte dell'Oca**, Via Sforza 27.

Apart from geese, Mortara has three churches worth a visit: the Gothic basilica of
San Lorenzo, built between 1375 and 1380 (with a wooden crib dating to the
15th century) and **Santa Croce**, dating from 1080 and rebuilt in 1596 on a design by
Pellegrino Tibaldi, both with interesting local paintings; and the **Abbey of Sant'Albino**,
southeast of the city centre on the site of the epic victory of Charlemagne over
Lombard King Desiderio in 773. The abbey, founded in the 5th century and rebuilt in
the 15th, still has its Romanesque apse and bell tower, 1,400 frescoes and the
century-old graffiti of passing pilgrims. In fact, the church and the abbey once
represented a crucial stage in the itinerary of the pilgrims travelling from Canterbury
to Rome, along the Via Francigena.

Cremona

Cremona is famous for four things that have added to the sum total of human happiness: its Romanesque cathedral complex, Claudio Monteverdi, nougat, and violins. It has been the capital of the last-mentioned industry since 1566, when Andrea Amati invented the modern violin from the old medieval fiddle. It quickly became fashionable, and demand across Europe initiated a golden age of

Getting There and Around

Closest **airports** include Milan's Linate and Malpensa, and Bergamo's Orio al Serio. Cremona's **railway** station, t 0372 407 911, *www.trenitalia.it*, is delightful, with frequent train services from Milan *(1hr 15mins; regional trains may be slower)*, Pavia, Mantua, Brescia and Piacenza, as well as three times a day from Bergamo. The station lies north of the centre, at the end of Via Palestro. Buses arrive at and depart from the **bus station** in Via Dante, next to the train station. Leave your **car** in the Via Villa Glori car park, t 0372 28243, in exchange for free use of a **bicycle**. **Boating** on the Po is possible at Portour, Via Roncobasso 8, t 368 741 3636 or 0372 231 529.

Tourist Information

IAT Cremona: Piazza del Comune 5, t 0372 23233, *www.aptcremona.it*. Has a booklet with several town intineraries. *Open daily 9–12.30 and 3–6.*

Festivals
Festival of Stringed Instruments, *every third October (next in 2006), www. entetriennale.com.*

Markets
Cremona: Piazza Stradivari. Antiques market – to buy a **violin** or visit a workshop, ask for their free list of *Botteghe Liutarie. Open every 3rd Sun of each month exc July and Aug.*

Shopping

Cremona is well known for its nougat: famous local producers include **Sperlari**, Via Sperlari 25, also renowned for its red candies, and **Vergani**, Corso Matteotti 112. Historic patisserie **Lanfranchi** (Via Solferino 30) has traditional cakes including the *Pan Cremona*, a light and delicious concoction made with almonds, honey and chocolate. Another gourmet stop is **Salumeria Iotta**, Corso Garibaldi 96, where you can buy local salami and vanilla-flavoured *cotechino* (pork leg), as well as cheeses and *marubini* (ravioli filled with bread, parmesan cheese and egg).

Sports and Activities

Cremona is at the intersection of the rivers Adda and Po; Portour (t 368 741 3636 or 0372 21529) organizes one-day **boat trips** on the latter with combined **cycling tours** in the countryside. **Bikes** can be hired at the car park of Via di Villa Glori, and the tourist office has a map of cycling tours along the river Po. There are **horse-riding** itineraries in the area of Isola Dovarese. Horses can be hired at the Azienda Agricola Ceradello, Pizzighetetone, t 0372 727 161, or Circolo Ippico Country Boys, Pessina Cremonese, t 0372 87014. For **golf**, Il Torrazzo, Via Castelleone 101, t 0372 471 563, *golf.torrazzo@libero.it*, has 9 holes.

The city also has guided visits to paintings and sculpture normally kept in local hospitals and charities (*May–July and Sept–Dec*); ring t 0372 421 011 for more information.

Where to Stay

Cremona ✉ 26100
★★★★**Continental**, Piazza della Libertà 26, t 0372 434 141, *www.hotelcontinental cremona.it* (*expensive*). Modern, comfortable, friendly and central, this hotel sets the mood with its display of Cremona-made fiddles. Parking is available in the garage. There is a restaurant too.

fiddle-making, when Andrea's son Nicolò Amati and his pupils Stradivarius and Giuseppe Guarneri made the best violins ever.

Walking around Cremona you can easily pick out the elegant curves and scrolls on the brick and terracotta palaces which inspired the instrument's Baroque form, while the sweetness of the violin's tone seems to have something of the city's culinary specialities in it: not only nougat but *mostarda di Cremona* – candied cherries, apricots, melons and so on in a sweet or piquant mustard sauce, served with boiled meats.

★★★**Astoria**, Via Bordigallo 19, **t** 0372 461 616 (*moderate*). A very pleasant hotel situated in a quiet street close to the Duomo. The rooms are tidy and comfortable. Cheaper rooms have en suite bathroom but communal showers.

★★★**Duomo**, Via Gonfalonieri 13, **t** 0372 35242 (*inexpensive*). Situated on a pedestrianized street facing the cathedral; has a very nice restaurant with a reasonably priced set menu and a pizzeria.

★★★**La Locanda**, Via Pallavicino 4, **t** 0372 457 834 (*inexpensive*). Just off the pedestrian area; similar in price to the Astoria, but slightly less comfortable bathrooms. Good restaurant (*see* below).

Eating Out

Ristorante Il Violino, Via Sicardo 3, **t** 0372 461 010, *www.ilviolino.it* (*expensive*). Located just behind the baptistry, this classy restaurant enjoys an enviable reputation for its regional dishes, starting with melt-in-your-mouth *antipasti*, *tortelli di zucca* and zesty *secondi* featuring meat or seafood. *Book in advance. Closed Mon eve and Tues, plus Aug.*

La Locanda, Via Pallavicino 4, **t** 0372 457 834 (*expensive–moderate*). Simple but stylish, offers regional fare. Try the guinea fowl cooked in marsala wine. *Closed Tues, 3 weeks in Aug. Booking advisable in eves.*

Osteria La Sosta, Via Sicardo 9, **t** 0372 456 656 (*expensive–moderate*). Good value, traditional dishes. Try their special *gnocchi vecchi* made with salami and butter, and based on a 500-year-old recipe. *Closed Sun eve and Mon, carnival and Aug.*

Porta Mosa, Via Santa Maria in Betlem 11, **t** 0372 411 803 (*expensive–moderate*). A tiny family-run place serving delicious traditional dishes such as tortelli stuffed with squash

and locally caught sturgeon steamed with herbs and capers. They also concoct a mean tiramisu. Try also the *bollito* boiled meat. *Closed Sun, and Aug. Booking advisable.*

Trattoria La Prima, Via Cavitelli 8, **t** 0372 411 383, *laprima@libero.it* (*moderate*). Truly local dishes and attitude: its owner, host and chef selects punters by keeping half of the tables reserved even if they aren't. If you overcome the selection process the service is very hospitable and the cooking excellent. Specialities are the home-made *primi*. *Closed Mon, and Sun eve.*

Trattoria Mellini, Via Bissolati 105, **t** 0372 30535 (*moderate*). An older, rather more traditional restaurant at the west end of town, featuring dishes to make animal-lovers foam at the mouth – casseroled donkey and baby horse, or raw baby horse with truffle. Less controversial dishes includes a kind of risotto with salami and savoy cabbage, fresh pasta with sausage and other hearty regional fare. *Closed Sun eve, Mon and Aug. Booking advisable, especially in the evening.*

Italo Cinese Ni Hao, Corso Garibaldi 85, **t** 0372 39153 (*inexpensive*). If your party can't decide between pizza, Thai or Chinese, the Hai Xia serves all three, and all are delicious – especially the Thai. *Closed Mon.*

Entertainment

Teatro Comunale Ponchielli, Corso Vittorio Emanuele 52, **t** 0372 022 011 (office) or **t** 0372 022 001 (to book), *www.teatroponchielli.it*. Tickets for the **opera** or the other **classical music** and **jazz** concerts can be bought at the theatre (*ticket office open Mon–Sat 4.30–7.30pm*), by phone or via the Internet at *www.charta.it* at a surcharge (no more than four people at a time).

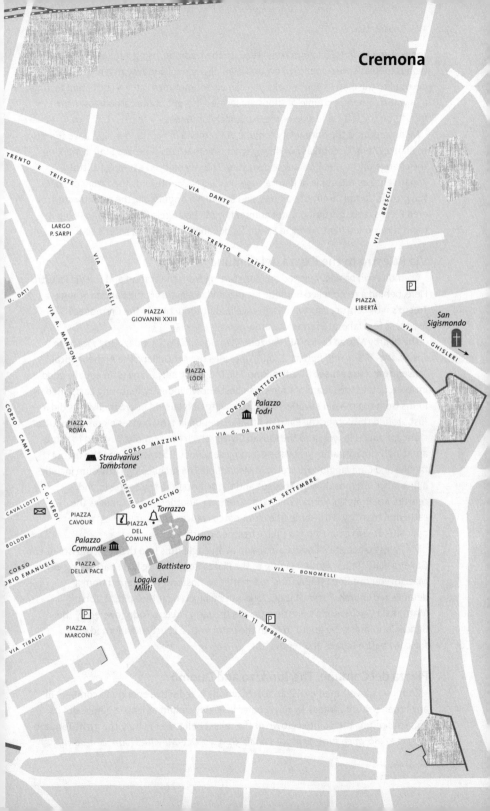

Cremona

TRENTO E TRIESTE

VIA DANTE

LARGO
P. SARPI

VIALE TRENTO E TRIESTE

VIA BRESCIA

U. DATI

VIA ASELLI

VIA A. MANZONI

PIAZZA
GIOVANNI XXIII

PIAZZA
LIBERTÀ

P

VIA A. GHISLERI

San
Sigismondo

PIAZZA
LODI

CORSO MATTEOTTI

Palazzo
Fodri

VIA G. DA CREMONA

CORSO CAMPI

PIAZZA
ROMA

CORSO MAZZINI

Stradivarius'
Tombstone

C. G. VERDI

CAVALLOTTI

BOLDORI

SOLFERINO

BOCCACCINO

VIA XX SETTEMBRE

PIAZZA
CAVOUR

i

Torrazzo

PIAZZA
DEL
COMUNE

Palazzo
Comunale

Duomo

CORSO
ORIO EMANUELE

PIAZZA
DELLA PACE

Battistero

VIA G. BONOMELLI

Loggia dei
Militi

P

PIAZZA
MARCONI

VIA 11 FEBBRAIO

P

VIA TIBALDI

Today some 50 *liutai* (violinmakers) keep up the tradition, using similar methods and woods (poplar, spruce, pear, willow and maple); a school and research institute are devoted to the craft. If you're lucky, you can also sometimes catch a craftsman testing a new instrument; a couple of shops are located in front of the cathedral's main façade, on the left-hand side of the Piazza del Comune.

Milan captured the once feisty *comune* of Cremona in 1344, and in 1441 gave the city to Bianca Maria Visconti as her dowry when she married Francesco Sforza, marking the change of the great Milanese dynasties. The city enjoyed a happy, fruitful Renaissance as the apple of Bianca's eye, producing Monteverdi, the father of opera, the prolific Campi family of painters, and Sofonisba Anguissola, the recently rediscovered Renaissance portrait painter admired by Michelangelo, Van Dyck and Philip II (who summoned her to work in Spain) for her ability to depict a sitter's soul.

Via Palestro to the Piazza del Comune

Cremona can be easily visited on foot, starting from the station and the Via Palestro. Here, behind a remodelled Baroque façade at Via Palestro 36, the **Palazzo Stanga Trecco's** 15th-century courtyard is an excellent introduction to the Cremonese fondness for elaborate terracotta ornament.

The nearby **Museo Civico 'Ala Ponzone'** (*Via Ugolani Dati 4, t 0372 407 770; open Tues–Sat 9–6, Sun and hols 10–6; adm*) includes the **Art Gallery**, the **Archeological Museum** and the **Museo Stradivariano**. The Museo Stradivariano is an equally good introduction to the cream of Cremona's best-known industry, featuring casts, models, items from the master's workshop and drawings explaining how Stradivarius did it. Just around the corner, the **Palazzo Affaitati** (begun in 1561) houses a grand theatrical staircase added in 1769 and the **Museo Civico**, which has sections devoted to some amazingly dreary paintings by the Cremonese school (Boccaccino and the Campi family) and Caravaggio's *Francesco in Meditation*. The Archaeology Museum includes a fine labyrinth mosaic with Theseus and the Minotaur in the centre (*c.* 2nd century AD) from the Roman *colonia* at Cremona; another section houses the cathedral treasury, with some fine illuminated codices and corals. The palace opposite, at Via U. Dati 7, has a pretty frescoed courtyard.

Via Palestro becomes Corso Campi, and at an angle runs into the boxy, Mussolini-era Galleria Venticinque Aprile, leading to the **Piazza Roma**, a nice little park; along Corso Mazzini you can find Stradivarius' red marble tombstone, transferred from a demolished church. Corso Mazzini forks after a block; near the split, at Corso Matteotti 17, is Cremona's prettiest palace, the 1499 **Palazzo Fodri** (owned by the Banca Cariplo; ask the guard to open the gate), with a courtyard adorned with frescoed battle scenes and terracottas.

Piazza del Comune: The Torrazzo and Duomo

Cremona's lovely medieval Piazza del Comune is seductive enough to compete in any urban beauty contest. By now you've probably caught at least a glimpse of its biggest feature, the pointed crown of the tallest bell tower in Italy, the 370ft **Torrazzo** (*t 0372 27386; open June–Sept 10–1 and 2.30–5.30; Oct–May Tues–Sun 10–1; adm*).

Only slightly shorter than Milan cathedral, the Torrazzo was built in the 1260s, has battlements as well as bells, and even tells the time thanks to a fine astronomical clock added in 1583 by Giovanni Battista Divizioli (*visits by appointment; ring tourist office*). The stout-hearted can ascend 487 steps to the top for an eye-popping view; the less ambitious can purchase a famous Cremona TTT postcard (Torrazzo, *torrone* and tits). The lower level houses a reproduction of a violinmaker's shop of Stradivarius' time, also open on request or with a guide (*same number, adm exp*).

Linked to the Torrazzo in 1525 by a double loggia, the **Portico della Bertazzola**, the **Duomo** (*t 0372 27386; open Mon–Sat 7.30–12 and 3.30–7, Sun and hols 7.30–1 and 3.30–7; wheelchair accessible, adm free*) is the highest and one of the most exuberant expressions of Lombard Romanesque, with a trademark Cremonese flourish in the graceful scrolls added to the marble front. Built by the Comacini masters after an earthquake destroyed its predecessor in 1117, the main door or **Porta Regia** remains as it was originally, flanked by two nearly toothless lion telamones and four flat prophets, and crowned by a small portico known as the Rostrum, where 13th- and 14th-century statues of the Virgin and two saints silently but eloquently hold forth above a frieze of the months by the school of Antelami.

The cathedral was begun as a basilica, but as Gothic came into fashion it was decided to add the arms of a Latin cross; the new transepts, especially the north one, are almost as splendid from the outside as the main façade. The restored interior now reveals primitive frescoes under the opulent 16th-century works by Romanino, Boccaccino and Pordenone (who painted the Crucifixion under the rose window); the right transept has some endearing sweet and simple paintings on the ceiling and Flemish tapestries. The twin pulpits have nervous, delicate reliefs attributed to Amadeo or Pietro da Rho. The choir has exquisite stalls inlaid in 1490 by G.M. Platina, with nearly all secular scenes, views of Cremona and still lifes. Also of interest is the 15th-century *Grande Croce* or 'Great Cross', created by a team of craftsmen known as the 'Fabbrica del Duomo'. A true masterpiece, the gold cross, which originally furnished the main altar, is now kept in a glass display case nearby. In the crypt with the tomb of Omobono Tucenghi (d. 1197), patron saint of tailors and the first layman to be canonized (in 1199). Note the remains of medieval mosaics as well as a painting of Jesus, the Virgin Mary and Joseph, with old Cremona and its Manhattan skyline of towers in the background.

Completing the sacred ensemble in Piazza del Comune is the octagonal **Battistero di San Giovanni** (1167) (*t 0372 27386; visits by prior arrangement; info at the Duomo's sacristy*), with another pair of lions supporting the portico and two sides of marble facing to match the cathedral. Across from the Duomo, the **Loggia dei Militi** (1292) was used as a rendezvous by the captains of the *comune*'s citizen militia; the outdoor pulpit between two of the arches is a relic of the charismatic, itinerant preachers like San Bernadino of Siena, whose sermons were so popular they had to be held outside.

Behind it, the **Palazzo del Comune** (*t 0372 22138, urp@comune.cremona.it; open Mon–Sat 9–6, Sun and hols 10–6*) was begun in 1206 as the lavish seat of the Ghibelline party and now serves as Cremona's town hall. On show are paintings salvaged from churches, a superb marble fireplace of 1502 by Giovan Gaspare Pedone in the Sala della Giunta, Baroque furniture and the **Saletta dei Violini** (*adm; tickets should be bought in advance at the bookshop on the opposite side of the courtyard*), once the chapel of the palace, now with a collection of eight violins (sometimes not all on display). The star here is Stradivarius' golden 'Cremonese 1715', which retains its original varnish – and is almost as mysterious as the embalming fluids of ancient Egypt. Another of the master's secrets was in the woods he used for his instruments; like Michelangelo seeking just the right piece of marble in the mountains of Carrara, Stradivarius would visit the forests of the Dolomites looking for perfect trees that would one day sing. Other violins include 'Charles IX of France' by Andrea Amati (1566), one of 24 violins commissioned in the 1560s by the French sovereign from the father of modern fiddles; the 'Hammerle', by Nicolò Amati (1658); Giuseppe Guarneri's 'Del Gesù', formerly owned by Pinchas Zukerman (1734); and the 1689 'Quarestani', also by Guarneri. To hear the unique sound of such rare instruments, book a listening session, held in the Saletta (*t 0372 22138; free*). Once you are in the Palazzo, take time to visit the Sala della Consulta and Sala della Giunta (if there is not a plenary session) for their original décor. The Salone dei Decurioni in the palazzo houses a splendid luxury coach, the 18th-century Corrozza Crotti, as well as a cycle of recently restored paintings on the life and miracles of Saint Omobono by Partolomeo Bersani.

Back Towards the Station

Behind the Palazzo del Comune lie Piazza Cavour and Corso Vittorio Emanuele, leading to the River Po. En route it passes one of Italy's earliest and most renowned small-town theatres, the **Teatro Ponchielli** (*see* 'Entertainment', p.119), built in 1734 and rebuilt after a fire in 1808, named for Amilcare Ponchielli who premiered several of his operas on its little stage. A street to the right of the theatre leads back to Piazza San Pietro and **San Pietro al Po**, coated with 16th-century stuccoes and frescoes by Antonio Campi. Cremona has several lofty churches with interiors that look strikingly similar to ancient Roman basilicas. One is the 14th-century church of **Sant'Agostino** (*north of the Corso Vittorio Emanuele, on Via Plasio, t 0372 22545*). Its red brick façade is adorned with fine terracotta decorations, and the centre nave is lined with statues of the virtues. There are good Renaissance frescoes in the right aisle by Bonifacio Bembo and a lovely pala of the *Madonna with Saints* (1494) by Perugino (*undergoing restoration at the time of writing*).

For something different, seek out the sinuous terracottas on the Liberty-style building nearby at Via Milazzo 16. Further up, Via Plasio joins Corso Garibaldi, site of the 11th-century church of **Sant'Agata** (*t 0372 22951; open 7.30–12 and 4–7.30*) hiding behind a neoclassical façade; the interior, a perfect Roman basilica, contains excellent frescoes by Giulio Campi of the singularly unpleasant *Martyrdom of St Agata* in the choir, a painting in the left aisle of the holy family by Lucia Anguissola, sister of the famous Sofonisba, and a medieval masterpiece, the 13th-century wooden panel painted with the life of St Agatha.

Opposite, the recently restored Gothic **Palazzo Cittanova** (1256) (*t 0372 407 263 or t 0372 464 351*), was the headquarters of the Guelph party: adjacent, note the flamboyant but phoney façade of the **Palazzo Trecchi** (*Via Trecchi 20, t 0372 460 008*).

Continuing along, the pink and white **Palazzo Raimondi** (1496) houses the Scuola Internazionale di Liuteria, where students learn to make violins (*Corso Garibaldi 178, open by appointment, t 0372 38689*), but note that visits are selected and tourists come after music schools. If you are interested in the art of fiddle-making the school's **Museo Organologico-Didattico** (*t 0372 38689, www.scuoladiliuteria.com; open Mon–Sat 9–12, closed hols and Aug; adm free*) is worth a look. Across the street stands the city's most peculiar palace, crowned with strange iron dragons. Near the station, **San Luca** (*t 0372 20262; open 6.45–11.45 and 3.30–7*) has a beautiful terracotta façade and a detached octagonal temple of 1503, a votive offering for the end of a plague.

One last church, **San Sigismondo**, is 1km east beyond the Piazzale Libertà (*Via A. Giuseppina, t 0372 431 919; bus no.2; open 8.30–12 and 3–6; no visits during Mass*). Built in 1463 by Bianca Maria Visconti to commemorate her marriage to Francesco Sforza, the interior is delicious proof that fake is better than real: rich pastel frescoes and *trompe l'œil* décors by Giulio, Antonio and Bernardino Campi, Camillo Boccaccino and Bernardino and Gervasio Gatti coat the interior. The choir stalls are by Domenico and Gabriele Capra (1590); in the cloister look for a fresco of the *Last Supper* by Tommaso Aleni (1508). Bianca's marriage also occasioned the invention of *torrone*, made of almonds, honey and egg whites – the gastronomical equivalent to the Torrazzo (and hence the name) and still made in Cremona. The regal marriage is also reconstructed in costume during the Festa del Torrone in October.

Around Cremona

Soncino and Paderno Ponchielli

Lying between the rivers Po and Oglio, the rich and strategic agricultural province of Cremona is well fortified with castles and towers that recall the glorious days when the Italian *comuni* had nothing better to do than beat each other up. The most imposing of the surviving castles, the **Rocca Sforzesca** (*open Nov–Mar Tues–Fri 10–12, Sat, Sun and hols 10–12.30 and 2.30–5.30; April–Oct Tues–Fri 10–12, Sat, Sun and hols 10–12.30 and 3–7; adm*) rears up over **Soncino**, a walled town north of Cremona on the Oglio. Built in the 12th century, it was greatly enlarged in 1473 by Galeazzo Maria Sforza as an advance base against the Venetians, who were holed up in the Brescian town of Orzinuovi directly across the river. The moat and sinister beetling towers survive intact, as well as the dungeon, which in 1259 hosted the most ferocious and hated man in Italy: Emperor Frederick II's henchman, Ezzelino da Romano. Ezzelino was severely wounded when his own army and Ghibelline allies turned on him as he crossed the Oglio on his way to surprise Milan; at the age of 65 he kept his reputation as a tough *hombre* to the end, refusing to speak or receive any medical treatment, ripping the bandages from his wounds until he died in agony. Details of other castles in the area are available from the tourist office in Soncino (*see box, p.127*).

On a more cheerful note, admire the water mill under the castle walls, and the delicious painted terracottas and frescoes (*c.* 1500) by Giulio Campi and others that cover the interior of **Santa Maria delle Grazie** (*t 0374 86883; open winter Sun 3–6,* *summer 4–7; open during the week by request only*). In the late 15th century the Sforzas invited a community of Jewish refugees to settle in Soncino, one of whom, Israel Nathan, founded a press and printed his first ornate book in Hebrew in 1483, and the first complete Old Testament in Hebrew in 1488. The site of the press is now a little **Museo della Stampa** (*open same hours as the castle*).

Between Cremona and Crema (the two Italian towns that most sound like dairy products) you'll find **Paderno Ponchielli**, birthplace of 'the Italian Tchaikovsky', Amilcare Ponchielli (1834–86). Italy has produced scores of one-opera composers, but Ponchielli can claim two that are performed with some frequency: La Gioconda and Marion Delorme; and as the teacher of Puccini and Mascagni he can claim to be grandfather to many others. His humble birthplace is now the **Museo Ponchiellano**, devoted to his life and works, with old scores and other memorabilia (*open Mon–Fri 3–7; Sat–Sun only by booking 3 days in advance; adm free; ring t 0374 367200 to book*).

Crema

It was in 1159 during Frederick Barbarossa's third war with Milan that the emperor, realizing that he lacked sufficent troops to besiege the big city, turned his German army on little Crema, Milan's staunch ally. Four hundred Milanese came to Crema's defence, but Frederick wasn't in the mood for a fair fight. He hanged all of his adult hostages from Crema and Milan outside the gates, hoping to horrify Crema into surrendering, and when that didn't work he strapped the smallest ones to his moving siege towers, so that the Cremaschi could not repulse the towers without harming their own children.

The histories tell how the parents asked their fellow citizens to kill them, to avoid witnessing their children's torture, while at the same time shouting to their children to be brave and boldly give up their lives for their country. In spite of Frederick's merciless tactics Crema held out for another six months, but at last, starving and exhausted, it surrendered on the condition that the citizens could withdraw to Milan as their town was razed to the ground.

Three hundred years later, in 1449, Francesco Sforza offered the most loyal town of Crema to Venice when the Serenissima offered to support his dukedom. It proved to be a more pleasant occupation, enduring for three centuries and endowing Crema with a tidy elegance rare in the Lombard plain. To this day it bears a white Istrian marble lion of St Mark on its gates and town hall, the latter by the pink brick **Duomo** (*t 0373 256 218; open 7–12 and 4–6*), a delightful Romanesque Gothic work built between 1284 and 1341 after Barbarossa sent the original up in flames. Its high 'wind façade' from the 1300s has windows finely decorated with curling vines, little turrets and blind arcading; next to it stands the whimsical, almost Moorish campanile of baked clay that so ravished John Addington Symonds.

Crema's narrow streets are lined by neat but secretive façades that often hide pretty courtyards and gardens. If you happen to be in Crema at the end of September–October, ask the tourist office if they are organizing special visits to private palaces

Tourist Information

Pro Loco Crema: Via dei Racchetti 8, **t** 0373
   81020, *www.prolococrema.it*. Very helpful.
   Open Tues–Fri 8.30–12.30 and 3–6, Sun 10–12.
Soncino: **t** 0374 86883, *www.proloco.soncino.it*.

Markets

Crema: in the Museo Civico. Annual antique
   books market (for the past 20 years). *June.*
Pandino: In the court of the old Visconti
   hunting lodge. Antiques market. *First Sun of
   the month except Jan, July and Aug.*

Where to Stay and Eat

Crema ✉ 26013

★★★★**Palace**, Via Cresmiero 10, **t** 0373 81487,
   www.palacehotelcrema.com (*expensive*). In
   the centre of Crema, all comforts.
★★★★**Park Hotel Residence**, Via IV
   Novembre 51, **t** 0373 86353, *www.parkhotel
   residence.it* (*expensive*). Comfortable hotel
   with a good restaurant.
★★★★**Ponte di Rialto**, Via Cadorna 7, **t** 0373
   82342, *www.pontedirialto.it* (*moderate*).
   Small but pleasant. Also has a restaurant.
   Closed Sun eves.

As for **food**, the local speciality, *tortelli
cremaschi*, is decidedly different: pasta filled
with amaretti, raisins, citron, peppermint,
nutmeg and cheese, and served in melted
butter, sage and cheese. The speciality is
celebrated in mid-August at the *Tortellata
Cremasca* (*info at the Pro Loco*).

If you are in Crema in late October–
November, you will chance upon the **Rassegna
Eno-Gastronomica**, (wine and food fair): ask
the tourist office for the list of restaurants
which participate in order to taste sumptuous
set menus at a moderate fixed price.
Mario, Via Stazione 118, **t** 0373 204 708
   (*moderate*). A good choice for local dishes.
   Closed Tues eve and Wed.
Osteria Rusignol, Via Ginnasio 4, **t** 0373 257 142
   (*moderate*). *Closed Mon.*
Da Pia, Via Podgora 2, **t** 0373 80891 (*inexpensive*). This little place has been feeding local
   workers for decades. As well as many local
   specialities, it also serves great local salami,
   tortelli, *pasta e fasoi* (pasta with beans),
   vegetable lasagne and hare with polenta.
   Closed Mon.
Pasticceria Dossena, Via Mazzini 56 (*inexpensive*). For those with a sweet tooth, this place
   offers the typical cake of the area, the
   Spongarda Dolce.

and villas. There are quite a few tidy palaces, and the uncompleted but utterly
romantic Baroque **Palazzo Terni de' Gregori** (or Bondenti), which now houses the
library and **Museo Civico** (*Via Dante, Alighieri 49, opposite the former convent of Sant'
Agostino, t 0373 257 161; open Mon 2.30–6.30, Tues–Fri 9–12 and 4–7, Sat–Sun 10–12 and
4–7; July and Aug Mon–Fri 8.30–1; adm free; guided visits available by booking*). Here
you'll find everything from medieval Lombard armour discovered in Aufoningum
(Offanengo) in 1963, Risorgimento mementoes, and scores by local composers, to two
dramatic paintings of the *Miracles of Christ* by Alessandro Magnasco with backgrounds by Clemente Spera, an expert on painting theatrical landscapes of ruins.
There are also other works by local talent, including a really gross 17th-century
Martyrdom of San Erasmo and aquafortes by Federica Galli, who lives just outside
town. Ask the curators to unlock the refectory to see the recently restored frescoes of
the *Last Supper* and *Crucifixion* (1498) by Giovan Pietro da Cemmo.

An architect from Cremona, Faustino Rodi, designed the fine neoclassical gate by
the river, the **Porta Serio**, while just north of the walls, at the end of a long tree-lined
avenue, an apparition of the Virgin is marked by the basilica of **Santa Maria della
Croce** (1490–1500) (**t** 0373 259 597; open winter 7–12 and 2.30–7, summer until 8.30), a
lovely Renaissance drum church inspired by Bramante. Encircled by three orders of
loggias and four polygonal chapels with spherical cupolas, the interior is octagonal

and contains a fine *Assumption* by Diana. Crema's Venetian period also saw the construction of fine palaces and villas, of which the 18th-century **Villa Ghisetti-Giavarina** in **Ricengo** just to the north is the most beautiful and stately, with frescoes inside (*private, not open for visits*).

West of Crema towards Milan, **Pandino** has a large 14th-century Visconti hunting lodge-cum-castle (*open summer hols 2.30–6, other times by booking; adm donations; opening hours may change, so ring ahead on t 0373 973 313, biblioteca.pandino@ libero.it and also for guided tours*), one of the best preserved of the area. The fortress now hosts the Comune offices, but its court, loggia, frescoes and two recently restored halls can be visited.

Rivolta d'Adda, 8km further on, has an 11th-century church of San Sigismondo, dwarfed by its battlemented campanile and containing some good carvings. Rivolta also offers Jurassic-era fun in its **Parco della Preistoria** (*t 0363 78184 or t 0363 370 250, www.parcodellapreistoria.it; open mid-Feb–Nov 9–7; adm*), where a zoo train chugs past 23 life-size reproductions of dinosaurs, prowling the wooded banks of the Adda.

Mantua (Mantova)

Mantua's setting hardly answers to one's great expectations of Italy, sitting in the midst of a fertile, table-flat plain on a wide thumb of land protruding into three swampy, swollen lakes formed by the River Mincio. Its climate is moody, soggy with heat in the summer and frosty under blankets of fog in the winter. The local dialect is harsh, and the Mantuans, when they feel chipper, dine on braised donkey with macaroni. Verdi made it the sombre setting of his opera *Rigoletto*. And yet, this former capital of the art-loving, fast-living Gonzaga dukes is one of the most atmospheric old cities in the country; 'a city in the form of a palace' as Castiglioni called it – dark and handsome, with few of neighbouring Cremona's sweet architectural arpeggios; poker-faced but holding in its hand a royal flush of dazzling Renaissance art.

History

Mantua gained its fame in Roman times as the beloved home town of the poet Virgil, who recounts the legend of the city's founding by the Theban soothsayer Manto, daughter of Tiresias, and her son, the hero Ocnus. Virgil was born around 70 BC, and not much else was heard from Mantua until the 11th century, when the city formed part of the vast domains of Countess Matilda of Canossa. Matilda was a great champion of the pope against the emperor; her advisor Anselmo, Bishop of Lucca, became Mantua's patron saint. Even so, Mantua soon allied itself with the opposition, beginning an unusually important and lengthy career as an independent Ghibelline *comune*, dominated first by the Bonacolsi family and then the Gonzaga.

Naturally defended on three sides by the Mincio, enriched by river tolls and enjoying the protection and favour of the emperor, Mantua became prominent as a neutral

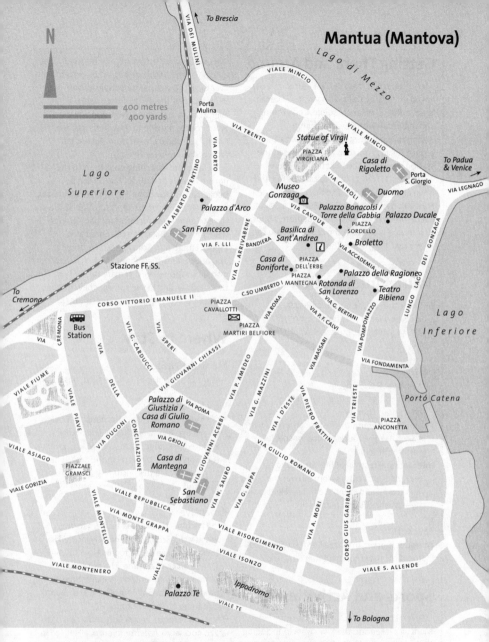

buffer state between the expansionist powers of Milan and Venice. The three centuries of Gonzaga rule, beginning in 1328, brought the city unusual peace and stability, while the refined tastes of the marquesses brought out artists of the highest calibre: Pisanello, Alberti and especially Andrea Mantegna, who was court painter from 1460 until his death in 1506.

Gianfrancesco I Gonzaga invited the great Renaissance teacher Vittorino da Feltre to open a school in the city in 1423, where his sons and courtiers, side by side with the

Getting There and Around

Mantua, 20km from Verona's airport, is linked directly by **train** with Verona, Vicenza, Firenze, Rome, Milan, Modena, and Cremona, and indirectly with Brescia (change at Piadena). The train station is at Piazza Don Leoni, **t** 89 2021. You can rent bicycles at the station, paying at the ticket office. There are also **buses**, **t** 0376 327 237, to Lake Garda and towns in the province. The bus station is near Piazza Porta Pradella in Via Mutilati e Daduti del Lavoro 4, close to Giardini Belfiore, about 10 minutes' walk from the centre. Or you can take a **taxi**, **t** 0376 368 866.

Tourist Information

APT Mantua: on the corner of Piazza dell'Erbe/Piazza Mantegna 6, **t** 0376 328 253, *www.turismo.mantova.it*. Open daily 8–7.

Festivals
Jazz festival, *April–July*.
'Music Evenings', *July and Aug*. Held throughout the city.
Pumpkin and white truffle season, *beginning of Sept*. Ask the tourist office for special gourmet itineraries.
International festival of literature, *2nd weekend Sept*. Writers from all over the world come and meet the public. Held in the city's courtyards and piazzas.

Markets
Antiques market, in Piazza Sordello. *Every 3rd Sun of the month (except Aug)*.

Sports and Activities

Several **boat** companies operate on Mantua's lakes and the River Mincio, including Motonavi Andes, Via S. Giorgio 2, **t** 0376 322 875 or **t** 0376 360 870, *www.motonaviandes.it*. It's a pleasant 1½hr trip past Gonzaga castles, a beautiful bridge designed by Nervi, water

lilies, water chestnut farms and flocks of egrets (*children €9; weekdays €76; Sun and hols over €10*). The company also sails to San Benedetto Po, the delta of the river Po and even Ferrara and Venezia (book in advance). Some routes provide a combined boat and cycling tour. Boats leave from the bridge facing St Giorgio Castle.

Evening **bird-watching boat tours** in the nature reserve of Valli del Mincio can be booked at Associazione 'Per il Parco', **t** 0376 225 724, *perilparco@yahoo.com*, although at the time of writing no foreign-language guides were provided. **Bikes** can be rented at La Rigola, Lungolago Gonzaga, **t** 0376 366 677, and at Bonfanti, Viale Piave 22B, **t** 0376 220 909 (*open Mon–Sat*). If you are taking boat tours and cycling in the summer beware that the area is also popular with mosquitoes.

Where to Stay

Mantua ✉ 46100
Mantua's few hotels tend to fill up fast.

Very Expensive
★★★★★**Villa dei Tigli**, Via Cantarana 20, Rodigo, **t** 0376 650 691, *www.hotelvilladeitigli.it*. Situated in Rodigo, 15km from Mantua, this is the only five-star hotel in the area. It has all modern facilities, including a swimming pool and a beauty and fitness centre.

Expensive
★★★★**Rechigi**, Via Calvi 30, **t** 0376 320 781, *www.rechigi.com*. Conveniently located in the historic centre; all rooms have satellite TV and air conditioning. The hotel holds permanent and temporary exhibitions of modern art. Parking is available at a charge and there are bikes for hire.
★★★★**San Lorenzo**, Piazza Concordia 14, **t** 0376 220 500, *www.hotelsanlorenzo.it*. Housed in a restored late Renaissance building in the central pedestrian zone, with views over the Piazza dell'Erbe. The hotel has comfortable rooms and a good restaurant.

children of Mantua's poorer families, were taught according to Vittorino's educational theories, which gave equal emphasis to the intellectual, the physical and the moral. His star pupil was Ludovico (1412–78), one of the most just princes of his day, who did

Moderate

★★★Bianchi Stazione, Piazza Don Leoni 24,
t 0376 326 465. Near the station. Has soberly
furnished, renovated rooms and nice bathrooms. Most of the rooms open onto a quiet
inner courtyard. From the top floor you can
see the water lilies of Lago Superiore.

★★★Broletto, Via Accademia 1, t 0376 326
784, *hotel.broletto@libero.it*. A cosy family-
run hotel in the city centre. Rooms are a bit
small but have all modern amenities
including satellite TV and air conditioning.

★★★Due Guerrieri, Piazza Sordello 52, t 0376
321 533. Housed in an older building overlooking the Palazzo Ducale. The service
and maintenance are not as good as the
location.

★★★ABC Superior, Piazza Don Leoni 25,
t 0376 322 329, *www.hotelabcmantova.it*.
Situated by the station. The renovated
rooms have all comforts including air
conditioning, and most rooms open onto an
inner courtyard. Some rooms are also very
inexpensive. Free bikes.

Inexpensive

★Maragò, Via Villanova De Bellis, just outside
the centre at Virgiliana, t 0376 370 313.
13 simple rooms, not all with bath, and
parking.

Villa-farmhouses around Mantua average
around €40 per person per night. *Remember
to book ahead.*

Corte Schiarino-Lena, Porto Mantovano,
Strode Maddalena 7–9, t 0376 398 238,
www.villaschiarino.it. Convenient for the city,
on the other side of Lago Superiore from
Mantua; rooms around a 16th-century
courtyard have been converted into
apartments. *Open May–Nov.*

Corte Bersaglio, Via L. Guerra 15, at Migliaretto,
just outside Mantua, t 0376 320 345. Has a
stable, with plenty of opportunities for a
canter in the countryside.

Corte Prada Alta, Strada San Girolamo 9, on
the cycling route to Peschiera on Lake Garda,
t 0376 391 144. Hires out bikes. *Closed Tues
and last two weeks Jan.*

Corte Feniletto, Via Francesca Est 86, 13km
from Mantua at Rodigo, t 0376 650 262.
A fully functioning farm in the midst of the
Regional Park of the Mincio. Offers boating
excursions on the river. *Open April–Oct.*

Eating Out

Mantua ✉ 46100

During the long reign of the Gonzaga the
Mantuans developed their own particular
cuisine, which other Italians regard as a little
peculiar. The notorious *stracotto di asino*
(donkey stew) heads the list, but the
Mantuans also have a predilection for adding
Lambrusco to broth and soup. The classic
Mantuan *primi* include *agnoli* stuffed with
bacon, salami, chicken livers and cheese
cooked in broth, *risotto alla pilota* (with onion,
butter and local grana cheese), *risotto con
salamelle* (with fresh salami) or *tortelli di
zucca* (little pasta caps stuffed with pumpkin,
mustard and cheese, served with melted
butter). The local freshwater fish – catfish, eel,
crayfish, pike (the delicious *luccio in salsa* is
prepared with peppers and capers) and bass –
and crispy deep-fried frog's legs are traditional
second courses. If you are shopping for food,
Mantua's porticoes are full of delis with local
specialities – a sweet local speciality to try is
the *Sbrisolona* (crumbling) cake, made of flour,
almonds and eggs. **Panificio Freddi**, Piazza
Cavallotti 7, has them all.

Mantua is also a good place to taste true,
natural **Lambrusco**, which must be drunk
young (a year or so old) to be perfectly lively
and sparkling; the test is to see if the foam
vanishes when poured into a glass. There are
three main kinds: the grand Lambrusco di
Sorbana, the mighty Lambrusco di Santa Croce
and the amiable Lambrusco di Castelvetro.

From May to Sept, Provincia di Mantova,
t 0376 204 244, *turismo@provincia.mantova.it*,
organizes **wine tastings** in Mantua's main
squares. There is also a local food and wine
route map, available at *www.mantova
stradaviniesapori.it*.

much to create Mantua according to Florentine humanist principles. Ludovico's
grandson, Gianfrancesco II, was a military commander who led the Italians against
the French at Fornovo, but is perhaps best known in history as the husband of the

Very Expensive

Aquila Nigra, Vicolo Bonacolsi 4, **t** 0376 327 180, *www.aquilanigra.it*. A lovely place with its marble and traces of frescoes, serving exquisitely prepared regional dishes and others; the pasta courses (ravioli filled with truffled duck, for instance) are a joy, and there's a wide choice of seafood as well as meat dishes. A great wine list, cheeses and delicious desserts like chestnut *torte* round off a special meal. *Closed Mon, Sun (open at lunch in April, Mar, Sept and Oct), 3 weeks in Aug. Booking advisable.*

Il Cigno – Trattoria dei Martini, Piazza d'Arco 1, **t** 0376 327 101. Overlooks an inner garden and has a menu that changes according to the season, although solidly based on local cuisine – tagliatelle with duck, lamb casseroled with herbs, or roast guinea fowl. Try also *Bigoli*, a local type of pasta. *Closed Mon, Tues and first half of Jan, Aug.*

Expensive

Ai Garibaldini, Via S. Longino 7, **t** 0376 328 263, Situated in the historic centre, in a fine old house with a shady garden for al fresco dining. The menu features many Mantuan dishes, with especially good risotto and *tortelli di zucca*, fish and meat dishes. *Closed Wed, Jan.*

San Gervasio, Vicolo San Gervasio 13, **t** 0376 323 873. Located in a superbly renovated 14th-century palace, with an excellent *menu mantovano. Closed Wed and Aug. Booking advisable.*

Moderate

Antica Osteria Fragoletta, Piazza Arche 5, **t** 0376 323 300. This former *trattoria* has been transformed in to a trendy restaurant, with a pleasant atmosphere and delicious cuisine that is appreciated as much by the local clientele as holidaymakers. Try the flavoured homemade ice cream. *Booking advised. Closed Mon, 2 weeks in Feb, 2 weeks between June–July.*

Due Cavallini, Via Salnitro 5 (near Lago Inferiore, off Corso Garibaldi), **t** 0376 322 084. The place to come if you want to bite into some donkey meat – though it has other less ethnic dishes as well. *Closed Tues, and late July–late Aug.*

Osteria al Portichetto, Via Portichetto 14, **t** 0376 360 747. Run by a former left-wing activist who has turned his hand to cooking; the results are excellent. The menu revolves around local freshwater fish, and there are lots of vegetarian options. *Closed Mon.*

L'Ochina Bianca, Via Finzi 2, **t** 0376 323 700. An ever-changing menu which might include smoked beef dressed with superb olive oil, deep-fried zucchini flowers, delicate home-made pasta and succulent meat dishes. The autumn menu offers pumpkins even as a dessert. Hosts Gilberto and Marcella are two of the founders of the 'Slow Food' association, which promotes food culture and conviviality. Also try the rice with vegetables and pumpkin flowers. *Closed Mon, and Tues lunch, Aug. Booking advisable.*

Ristorante Pavesi dal 1918, Piazza delle Erbe 13, **t** 0376 323 627. In the summer the tables fill up early here; service is friendly and they do a particularly good local cuisine. *Closed Thurs and mid-Dec–Feb.*

Taverna Santa Barbara, Piazza Santa Barbara 19, **t** 0376 329 496. A bit touristy, but you can dine outside in a quiet historical courtyard within the Palazzo Ducale walls. Good-value menu, with a cheap and hearty single-dish menu with polenta. *Closed Mon.*

Trattoria Quattrotette, Vicolo Nazione 4, **t** 0376 329 478. Away from the obvious tourist areas, this small restaurant squeezes in hordes of local clientele who relish the dishes of vegetables and salads: *melanzana grillata, carciofi alla giudia* and *peperonata*, and steaming hot bowls of pasta, and *pasticceria*. There are local seasonal specialities with daily menus. In the autumn try the crepes with pumpkins and the *sugolo*, a special vine sorbet. *Closed Sat eves, Sun.*

brilliant and cultivated Isabella d'Este, the foremost culture vulture of her day as well as an astute diplomat, handling most of Mantua's affairs of state for her not very clever husband.

The family fortunes reached their apogee under Isabella's two sons. The eldest, Federico II (1500–40), godson of Cesare Borgia, married Margherita Palaeologo, the heiress of Monferrato, acquiring that duchy for the family as well as a ducal title for the Gonzaga. He hired Raphael's assistant, the Mannerist Giulio Romano ('that rare Italian master', Shakespeare called him in *The Winter's Tale*) to design and adorn his pleasure dome, the Palazzo Te. When he died his brother, Cardinal Ercole, served as regent for his son Guglielmo, and both of these men, too, proved to be busy builders and civic improvers.

The last great Gonzaga, Vincenzo I, was a patron of Rubens, Fetti and Monteverdi, who composed the first modern opera, *L'Orfeo*, for the Mantuan court in 1607. But times got hard and in 1628 Vincenzo II sold off many of the Gonzaga's treasures to Charles I of England, including Mantegna's *Triumphs of Caesar*. It's just as well that he did; two years later Mantua suffered a near mortal blow when the Gonzaga's claims to Monferrato came into conflict with the Habsburgs, who were never ones for legal niceties and sent imperial troops to capture and sack the town. The duchy, under a cadet branch of the family, limped along until the Austrians snatched Mantua in 1707, eventually making it the southwest corner of their Quadrilateral. Until they became part of the Italian nation in 1866, the towns and the surrounding area remained part of the Austro-Hungarian Empire (except during Napoleonic rule between 1797 and 1814).

Piazza Mantegna

From the station, Corso Vittorio Emanuele and Corso Umberto I lead straight into the Renaissance heart of Mantua, where the narrow cobbled streets are lined with inviting porticoes, shielding strollers from the sun or rain. Rising up above the rest of the city in Piazza Mantegna is the great basilica of **Sant'Andrea** (*open 7.30–12 and 3–7*), designed by the great Florentine humanist Leon Battista Alberti in 1472 to house the Gonzaga's most precious holy relic: two ampoules of Christ's blood, said to have been given to St Andrew by St Longinus, the Roman centurion who pierced Christ's side with his lance. The finding of the relic is celebrated on 12th March, and the ampoules are exhibited during the Good Friday ceremonies. Ludovico Gonzaga had asked Alberti to create a truly monumental edifice to house the relic and form a fitting centrepiece for the city, and Alberti complied. In Florence Alberti had found himself constrained as an architect by his patrons' tastes, but in Mantua he was able to experiment and play with the ancient forms he loved. Sant'Andrea is based on Vitruvius's idea of an Etruscan temple, with a single barrel-vaulted nave supported by side chapels, fronted with a unique façade combining a triumphal arch and a temple. The lofty dome, designed by Juvarra, was completed in 1782. The interior is as imposing as the outside. Andrea Mantegna (d. 1506) is buried in the first chapel on the left, with a stern self-portrait in bronze. The other chapels have fine altarpieces as well, especially the second one on the left, by Lorenzo Costa.

On the east side, the unfinished flank of the basilica is lined with the porticoes and market stalls of the delightful **Piazza delle Erbe**. Sunk below the level of the modern pavement, the **Rotonda di San Lorenzo** (*open Mon–Fri 10–1 and 2–6, Sat–Sun 10–6*), modelled on the Church of the Holy Sepulchre in Jerusalem, was built by the Countess Matilda in 1082; an ambulatory supports a matroneum for the ladies and there are damaged Romanesque frescoes by the altar. Opposite the tourist office, the **Casa di Boniforte da Concorezzo** has elegant stucco decoration, almost unchanged since it was built in 1455, while the 13th-century Palazzo della Ragione has a stout clock tower topped by an odd little temple and astronomical clock, added during Ludovico's restoration of the palace in 1475. The piazza is closed by the **Broletto**, built in 1227, facing the Piazza del Broletto; note the niche holding a 13th-century statue of Virgil seated near the door. In Piazza Broletto another local hero, a racing driver, is remembered in the **Museo Tazio Nuvolari** (*www.tazionuvolari.it; open April and Oct Tues, Wed, Fri–Sun 10–1 and 3.30–6.30; Mar and Nov–Dec, Sat and Sun only; Jan Sun only; closed Feb, but can be visited by booking on t 0376 327 929; adm*). In the third weekend of September an **antique car race** takes place (*info at the museum*).

An archway leads into the grand cobbled **Piazza Sordello**, traditional seat of Mantua's bosses. On one side rise the sombre palaces of the Bonacolsi, the Gonzaga's predecessors, with their **Torre della Gabbia**, named for the iron torture cage they kept to suspend prisoners over the city (though the Mantuans claim it was only used once). At the head of the piazza stands the **Duomo** (*open 7–12 and 3–7*), with a silly 1756 façade topped by wedding-cake figures which hides a lovely interior, with five naves designed by Giulio Romano in 1545. Renaissance tapestries hang in the choir, and the enormous Trinity in the apse is by Domenico Fetti, another Roman painter who worked in Mantua in the early 17th century. The 15th-century house at No.23 has become the '**Casa di Rigoletto**' to satisfy the longings of Verdi buffs. A new museum, the **Museo Archeologico Nazionale** (*Piazza Castello, t 0376 329 223; open Tues–Sat 8.30–6.30, Sun and hols 8.30–1.30; adm free*), has a permanent exhibition on the archaeology of the Mantuan territory as well as prehistoric findings.

The Palazzo Ducale

Open Tues–Sun 8.45–7.15 (reduced tour after 6pm; ticket office closes at 6.30); to see Camera degli Sposi mid-Mar–mid-June and Sept–mid-Oct groups and individuls must book on t 0412 411897; adm.

Opposite the Bonacolsi palaces stands that of the Gonzaga, its unimpressive façade hiding one of Italy's most remarkable Renaissance abodes, both in sheer size and the magnificence of its art. The insatiable Gonzaga kept adding on until they had some 500 rooms in three main structures – the original **Corte Vecchia**, first built by the Bonacolsi in 1290, the 14th-century **Castello**, with its large towers overlooking the lake, and the **Corte Nuova**, designed by Giulio Romano. Throw in the Gonzaga's **Basilica di Santa Barbara** and you have a complex that occupies the entire northeast corner of Mantua (over 34,000 square metres). It was the focal point of Mantuan life and politics and represented Gonzaga's taste and love for the arts; the most important artists of the time were invited to court and asked to adorn the rooms using their skills. If you go in the winter, dress warmly – it's as cold as a dead duke.

Although stripped of its furnishings and most of its moveable art, the Palazzo Ducale remains imposing and seemingly endless. One of the first rooms on the tour, the former **chapel**, has a dramatic, half-ruined 14th-century fresco of the *Crucifixion*, attributed by some to Tommaso da Modena, while another contains a painting of a battle between the Gonzaga and the Bonacolsi in the Piazza Sordello, in which the Gonzaga crushed their rivals once and for all in 1328 – although the artist, Domenico Monore, painted the piazza as it appeared in 1494. Even more fascinating than this real battle is the vivid **fresco of Arthurian knights** by Pisanello, Italy's International Gothic master. Recorded as damaged in the 1480s, the fresco was believed lost until 1969, when layers of plaster were stripped away to reveal a remarkable work commissioned by Gianfrancesco Gonzaga in 1442 to commemorate his receiving from Henry VI the concession to use the heraldic SS collar of the House of Lancaster, an insignia that forms the border of Pisanello's mural, mingled with marigolds, a Gonzaga emblem. Beyond this are the remodelled **neoclassical rooms**, holding a set of Flemish tapestries from Raphael's *Acts of the Apostles* cartoons (now in the Victoria and Albert Museum, London). Woven in the early 1500s, these copies of the Vatican originals are in a much better state of preservation. Beyond, the **Sala dello Zodiaco** has vivacious 1580 frescoes by Lorenzo Costa; the **Sala del Fiume** is named for its fine views over the river; and the **Galleria degli Specchi** has mirrors and mythological frescoes and, by the door, a note from Monteverdi on the days of the musical evenings he directed there in the 1600s.

The Gonzaga were mad about horses and dogs and had one room, the **Salone degli Arcieri**, painted with *trompe l'œil* frescoes of their favourite steeds standing on upper ledges; the family used to play a kind of guessing game with them, when curtains would be drawn over the figures. Sharing the room are works by Tintoretto and a family portrait by Rubens, court painter under Vincenzo I, a picture so large that Napoleon's troops had to cut it up to carry it off. The duke's apartments hold a fine collection of classical statuary: busts of the emperors, a Hellenistic torso of Aphrodite, and the 'Apollo of Mantova', inherited from Sabbioneta after Vespasiano's death. The Sala di Troia has vivid 1536 frescoes by Giulio Romano and his pupil, Rinaldo Mantovano, while another ducal chamber has a beautiful 17th-century labyrinth painted on the ceiling, each path inscribed in gold with 'Maybe Yes, Maybe No'. From some of the rooms you can look out over the grassy Cortile della Cavallerizza, with rustic façades by Giulio Romano.

The oldest part of the palace complex, the 14th-century **Castello San Giorgio**, is reached by a low spiral ramp, built especially for the horses the Gonzaga could never bear to be without. Here, in the famous **Camera degli Sposi**, are the remarkable frescoes painted by Mantegna in 1474, who like a genie captured the essence of the Gonzaga in this small bottle of a room. Restored to their brilliant original colours, the frescoes depict the life of Ludovico Gonzaga, with his wife Barbara of Brandenburg, his children, dwarves, servants, dogs and horses, and important events – greeting his son Francesco, recently made a cardinal, and playing host to Emperor Frederick III and King Christian I of Denmark. The portraits are unflattering and solid, those of real people and not for public display, almost like a family photo album. The effect is like stumbling on the court of the Sleeping Beauty; only the younger brother, holding the new cardinal's hand, seems to suspect that he has been enchanted. Wife Barbara and her stern dwarf stare out, as if determined to draw the spectator into the eerie scene. And there is a lingering sorcery here, for these frescoes are fruit of Mantegna's fascination with the science of perspective. The beautiful backgrounds of imaginary cities and ruins reflect Mantegna's other love, classical architecture, but add an element of unreality in their realistic vividness, as do his *trompe l'œil* ceiling frescoes.

From here the tour continues to the **Casetta dei Nani**, residence of the dwarfs, tiny rooms with low ceilings and shallow stairs, although there are party-poopers who say the rooms had a pious purpose, and were meant to bring the sinning dukes to their proud knees. The last stop is the **suite of Isabella d'Este**, designed by her as a retreat after her husband's death. In these rooms Isabella held court as the Renaissance's most imperious and demanding patron, practically commanding Leonardo and Titian to paint her portrait; at one point she commissioned an allegorical canvas from Perugino so exacting that she sketched what she wanted and set spies to make sure the painter followed orders. Given an excellent classical education in her native Ferrara, she surrounded herself with humanists, astrologers, poets and scholars. Her fabulous art collection has long gone to the Louvre, but the inexplicable emblems and symbols she devised with her astrologers remain like faint ghosts from a lost world on the ceiling.

Around Town

Within walking distance of the Palazzo Ducale is the **Teatro Accademico Bibiena** (*Via Accademia 47, east of the Broletto, t 0376 327 653; open Tues–Sun 9.30–12.30 and 3–6; adm*), a gem built by Antonio Galli Bibiena, of the famous Bolognese family of theatre builders. Mozart, aged 13, performed at the inaugural concert in 1770; his father Leopold said it was the most beautiful theatre he had ever seen.

West of the Piazza Sordello, Via Cairoli leads to the city's main park, the **Piazza Virgiliana**, with a marble statue of Virgil from 1927 (in time for the poet's 2,000th birthday) and the **Museo Gonzaga** (*t 0376 320 602, www.museodiocesanomantova.it; open Mar–June and Sept–Oct Tues–Sun 9.30–12 and 2.30–5; July and Aug Thurs, Sat, Sun only; Nov–Feb Sun only; adm*), containing artefacts and treasures that once belonged to the family.

Further west, in the Piazza d'Arco, the **Palazzo d'Arco** (*t 0376 322 242, www.museo darco.it; open Nov–Feb Sat, Sun and hols 10–12.30 and 2–5; Mar–Oct Tues–Sun and hols 10–12.30 and 2.30–6; adm*) was rebuilt in 1784 over a 15th-century palace for the arty counts from Garda's north shore. It has been left more or less as it was, complete with furnishings, paintings, instruments, a superb kitchen and, in a room preserved from the original palace, fascinating frescoes of the zodiac attributed to Giovanni Maria Falconetto of Verona and painted *c.* 1515, in the period between Mantegna's death and Giulio Romano's arrival. The nearby **church of San Francesco** (1304) (*Piazza S. Francesco 5; open 7–12 and 3–7*), was rediscovered in 1944, when a bomb hit the arsenal that had disguised it for a century and a half. Now restored, it contains frescoes by Tommaso da Modena.

South of the medieval nucleus, just off main Via Principe Amedeo at Via Poma 18, the **Casa di Giulio Romano** was designed by the artist himself in 1544 while working on the Palazzo Te. He also gets credit for the quaint palace decorated with monsters nearby; the heavy **Palazzo di Giustizia** at No. 22 was built in the 1620s. Mantegna also designed his dream house, the **Casa del Mantegna**, in the same neighbourhood (*Via Acerbi 47, t 0376 360 506, www.provincia.mantova.it/casadelmantegna; open Tues–Sun 10–12.30 and 3–6; adm free; tickets for exhibitions only*). Designed as a cube built around a circular courtyard, he intended it partially as his personal museum and embellished it with classical 'Mantegnesque' decorations. Opposite stands the rather neglected **San Sebastiano** (1460), the second church in Mantua designed by Alberti, this one in the form of a Greek cross.

A Renaissance Pleasure Dome: The Palazzo Te

Viale Te, t 0376 323 266. Open Tues–Sun 9–6, Mon 1–6; adm.

At the end of Via Acerbi is Giulio Romano's masterpiece, the marvellous Palazzo Te, its name derived from *tejeto*, a local word for a drainage canal. On a former swamp, work began in 1527 when Federico II had Giulio Romano expand the stables to create a little palace for his mistress, Isabella Boschetti, of whom his mother, Isabella d'Este, disapproved. The project expanded over the decades to become a guest house suitable for the Emperor Charles V, who visited twice.

Giulio Romano had moved from Rome to Mantua in 1524 to escape prison for designing a series of pornographic prints. In his Palazzo Te, one of the very first great Mannerist buildings – which took ten years to complete – he had the same desire to shock and amaze and upset the cool classicism exemplified in Mantua by Alberti, and along the way he created one of the great Renaissance syntheses of architecture and art, combining *trompe l'œil* with a bold play between the structure of the room and the frescoes. Most of the art still has classical themes: the **Sala della Metamorfosi** is inspired by Ovid and Roman frescoes, which Giulio discovered with his master Raphael in Nero's Golden House in Rome. Gonzaga emblems fill the **Sala delle Imprese**: *putti* holding a cup, a belt, a bird catching fish, a muzzle, Mt Olympus and the salamander (a symbol of Federico's love, which is consumed, but doesn't burn); the chariot of the sun on the ceiling is a first hint of Giulio's love of wacky perspectives. The next room has more life-size Gonzaga horses up on ledges, and in the next, the **Sala di Psiche**, all glory bursts forth in the intense colours and exuberance of the scenes from The Golden Ass of Apuleius. The **Camera dei Venti** was Federico's private study, designed with the most precious materials and with a complex iconographic programme based on ancient astrological texts.

The **Loggia di Davide**, quickly thrown up for Charles V's second visit in 1532, is decorated with scenes dear to Federico's heart – he identified himself with the king, and his Isabella with Bathsheba, both of whom were relieved of their husbands in suspicious circumstances. The next room has a series of incredible antiquated stuccoes by Francesco Primaticcio, who later went on to Fontainebleau to work for François I. The climax, however, is the famous **Sala dei Giganti**, Giulio's most startling work, entirely frescoed from floor to ceiling. Above, Zeus and company rain a powerful mix of lightning, thunder, boulders and earthquakes down on the uppity Titans, creating so powerful an illusion of chaos that it seems as if the very room is about to cave in around the spectator.

Around Mantua

Mantua's western lake, **Lago Superiore**, is noted for its delicate lotus blossoms, planted in the 1930s as an experiment. They have since thrived, and turn the lake violet and pink in July and August around the city's park, the **Valletta Belfiore**. Another park, the **Bosco della Fontana** (*open Mar–Oct 9–7, Nov–Feb 9–5, daily except Tues and Fri; adm free except Sun and hols*) lies 5km to the north off the road to Brescia. Once a Gonzaga hunting reserve, with a moated little castle built as a hunting lodge in 1595 (*visits upon request only*), the Bosco's ancient, broad-leafed trees are a last relic of the ancient forest that once covered the Po plain. If you're in Mantua on 15 August be sure to visit the **Sanctuary of the Madonna delle Grazie**, on the banks of Lago Superiore at Curtatone, where there's an art competition for the *madonnari* – artists who draw pavement chalk portraits of the Madonna – among other diversions (*ring tourist offices for details*). Built as a votive offering by Francesco I after the plague of 1399, the church has a 15th-century ceiling frescoed with paintings by Lorenzo Costa Jr.

San Benedetto Po

Some 22km southeast of Mantua, San Benedetto Po grew up around the Benedictine abbey of **Polirone** (*open 8–12 and 2.30–7*), the 'Monte Cassino of the North', established in the year 1007 by the Canossa counts of Tuscany. It was especially favoured by the last of their line, the feisty Countess Matilda (d. 1115), whose alabaster sarcophagus survives in the richly appointed Basilica di San Benedetto, rebuilt in the 1540s by Giulio Romano and linked to the 12th-century church of **Santa Maria**, which preserves a fine mosaic of 1151. There are three cloisters and a refectory with frescoes by Correggio, now part of the **Musei Civici Polironiani** (*t 0376 623 036, open Mar–mid-Nov Mon 9–12.30, Tues–Fri 9–12.30 and 2.30–6.30, Sat–Sun 9–12.30 and 3–7; mid-Nov–Feb Tues–Fri by appointment only; adm*), which includes the **Museo dell'Abbazia** and the **Museo della Cultura Popolare Padana**, devoted to the traditions and culture of the surrounding countryside. Countess Matilda also built the hand-some Romanesque **San Lorenzo** near the cemetery in **Pegognaga**, 9km southwest.

Sabbioneta

Set midway between Mantua, Cremona and Parma, Sabbioneta was a rural village backwater until 1556, when its new prince, Vespasiano Gonzaga Colonna, decided to rebuild it from scratch as the capital of his little Ruritania. A member of a cadet branch of the Gonzaga family, Vespasiano had earned his title fighting and building

Tourist Information

Curtatone: Pro Loco, t 0376 369 122;
Ufficio Cultura del Comune Di Curtatone,
t 0376 358 128, *www.curtatone.it*.

At the time of writing, Sabbioneta has two
separate tourist offices, which provide
different information. A legal quarrel divides
the two, but things may change soon:

Sabbioneta: Ufficio del Turismo del
Comune, Piazza d'Armi 1, t 0375 221044,
www.comune.sabbioneta.mn.it. Controls
tours to civic monuments. Pro Loco (private),
Via Gonzaga 27, t 0375 52039. Controls tours
to ecclesiastical monuments such as
churches, the Museo d'Arte Sacra and the
Synagogue.

Pro Loco, Piazza Garibaldi 6, t 0375 40039,
www.prolococasalmaggiore.it.

Where to Stay and Eat

Sabbioneta ✉ 46018

★★★Al Duca, Via della Stamperia 18,
t 0375 52474, *al.duca@tin.it* (*moderate*).
Central hotel, with comfortable enough
rooms, en suite bathrooms and TV. Also has
a restaurant with local cuisine.

★Giulia Gonzaga, Via V. Gonzaga 65,
t 0375 528 169 (*inexpensive*). Similar if more
simple facilities for less.

Of the many restaurants, the best two are
just outside the city walls:

Dal Pescatore, Località Runate 13, 20km north
to Canneto sull'Oglio (just beyond Piadena),
t 0376 723 001, *www.dalpescatore.com* (*very
expensive*). One of Lombardy's finest and
most tranquil restaurants. The talented
female chef enchants the privileged few
(the dining room holds a maximum of 30
people) with her exquisite light cuisine
using the best and freshest of produce,
much of it picked that morning at the
Santini family farm. Mantovan favourites

like *tortelli de zucca* reach a kind of epiphany,
with the best wines and the most civilized
service. *Open Wed eve to Sun; closed 8 Aug–
3 Sept and first 3 weeks in Jan. Booking is
required. You can book on line or by telephone.*

Il Capriccio, Via Solazzi 51 (the Mantua–Parma
road), t 0375 52722, *www.ristorante
capriccio.com* (*moderate*). Serves delicious
creative dishes based on Mantuan tradition,
with a well-priced lunch menu and fish
dishes such as prawn risotto with truffles.
Closed Tues.

Parco Cappuccini, Via Santuario 30, t 0375
52005, (*moderate*). This elegant restaurant
occupies an 18th-century villa with a
veranda on the park, an inviting place to
linger over classic Mantuan cuisine. *Closed
Mon and Wed eve and last week of Dec–mid-
Jan. Booking advisable.*

Casalmaggiore ✉ 26041

The hotels in Casalmaggiore may offer more
comfort at just 3km from Sabbioneta.

★★★Bifi, Localita Rotonda, t 0375 200 938,
www.bifihotel.it (*expensive*). A modern hotel
on the Sabbioneta crossroad; has all modern
amenities and a piano bar.

★★★City, Via Cavour 54/56, t 0375 42118
(*moderate*). Offers comparable, if less
glittering, facilities at a good price.

★★★Il Leone, Piazza Quattro Martiri 2,
Pomponesco (15km away), t 0375 86077
(*moderate*). A good-value choice, situated in
a little Renaissance piazza close to the banks
of the river Po; the 16th-century building has
frescoed walls and wooden ceilings. A
flower-filled patio leads to the sunny rooms
(8 in total). Also has a swimming pool and
an excellent restaurant.

Country Club Corte Lavadera, Cogozzo di
Viadana, Via Pangona 76, t 0375 790 260,
www.countrylavadera.it (*inexpensive*). Stay
at a farmhouse complete with swimming
pool, tennis, sauna, hydromassage and a
fully equipped horse-riding centre.

fortifications for Philip II of Spain, but he never forgot his Gonzaga grounding in the
classics. His Sabbioneta would be a rational expression of humanistic ideals, with a
content and a military, civic and cultural function, a walled 'Little Athens' on the Po
plain. He gets credit as the first to consider urban planning as an act of government.
It seemed like a good idea at the time.

The Tour

Unfortunately for Sabbioneta, humanism was out of fashion even before the city was built. When its creator died without an heir, his principality reverted to Mantua and became a backwater once more, a little museum city of unfulfilled expectations with the haunting, empty air of a De Chirico painting. In the last 15 years, however, interest in Sabbioneta has been rekindled and much has been restored, and antique shops and restaurants have begun to fill some of the houses. The fascinating interiors of the principal monuments, however, can only be seen by guided tour (*Tues–Fri 10–1 and 2.30–6, Sat–Sun 10–1 and 2–7; ring ahead at the Ufficio del Turismo del Comune to book a tour in English; 1½ hours; adm*).

Vespasiano laid out Sabbioneta in polygonal star-shaped walls with two gates linked by the central axis of the main street. The street plan is rectangular, harking back to the style of an ancient Roman *castrum*, although tricks such as two off-centred main squares, irregular blocks and streets that narrow at their ends lend an illusion of greater space within the walls (although originally devised for

A New Renaissance City

The idea of building a whole new city in the lifetime of a single man had already been made possible by technological advances on the construction site. Many of these techniques first came into being during the construction of Brunelleschi's dome over Florence Cathedral; one thing Brunelleschi did was abolish the medieval 'mechanical' system, composed of skilled workers working under master masons, in favour of a 'liberal' system in which there was only one planner and his manual labourers. Equally fundamental was the evolution of the city from the Middle Ages, when it was an organic body founded on a community of interest between the merchants and craftsmen who lived in it, to the 15th and 16th centuries, when it lost its liberties and became nothing more than the seat of a higher power, a *signore* or a king – a reflection of his greater glory. Public buildings became increasingly grand, and open spaces were arranged as a stage for the ceremonies of church and state. Architects and artists were inspired by Leon Battista Alberti's monumental *De re aedificatoria* (1452), which drew on Vitruvius in its aim to orchestrate the humanist recreation of the ancient city and its monuments. For the first time since antiquity, changes in a city's structure and plan were brought about from above by an absolute prince and his architects.

Architectural treatises of the time are filled with geometrical designs of ideal cities, usually set in massive defensive works around polygonal walls, often star-shaped, the better to deflect bullets and cannonballs. According to Alberti, single buildings must always be conceived in their urban context, the whole plan of which must follow the rule of perspective, proportion and symmetry – leading to the fanciful urban backgrounds of many Renaissance paintings. Vespasiano Gonzaga was one of the few readers of Alberti ever actually to build his city and apply his ideals. One of these was a great tolerance and respect for ancient learning, something that attracted many Jewish settlers. The press the Foà family established in Sabbioneta between 1551 and 1590 was famous for the excellence of its Hebrew editions.

defensive purposes). In the larger square, **Piazza Castello**, Vespasiano constructed his castle (demolished in the 18th century) and erected a column topped with a statue of Sabbioneta's patroness, the goddess of wisdom, Athena, a classical Greek work that his father Rodomonte is said to have picked up in the infamous Sack of Rome. Along one side of the Piazza Castello runs a long brick atrium to Vespasiano's pleasure palace, a mini-version of the Palazzo Te in Mantua called the **Palazzo e Giardino**. Its elegant marbled façade, its original windows and doors and gardens are long gone, but the rich frescoes and stuccoes by the school of Giulio Romano and Bernardino Campi remain fairly intact: grotesques, mythologies, urban perspectives (one was apparently used for the stage of the Teatro all'Antica), imitation arbours that once led out to real garden arbours, monochrome Caesars, beautifully detailed animals, Roman circuses, landscapes in the Room of Mirrors, and a room dedicated to myths and Gonzaga *imprese*: uprooted branches, muzzles, dogs looking backwards and a burning temple, a reference to the Sack of Rome.

The Palazzo del Giardino was linked to the castle by way of the **Galleria degli Antichi**, a long frescoed corridor or ambulacrum, the height of architectural fashion in Renaissance France and Italy; Sabbioneta's, at 317ft, is the third longest after the Vatican's Map Gallery and Florence's Galleria degli Uffizi. The portico underneath allowed enjoyment of the gardens in inclement weather, while Vespasiano used the upper gallery to display his extensive collection of classical art (now in Mantua's Palazzo Ducale). *Trompe l'œil* perspectives on either end of the gallery make it seem even longer, while allegorical figures frescoed over the 26 windows represent virtues, sciences and seasons; they are attributed to Pietro Martire Pesenti, a master of the subtle art of painting *contrapposto* figures and architectural backgrounds that seemingly change their position, depending on the angle from which they are viewed.

The next stop on the tour, the **Teatro all'Antica** (1588), was designed by Vicenzo Scamozzi, Palladio's greatest pupil, inspired by Palladio's famous Teatro Olimpico in Vicenza and Sebastiano Serlio's *L'Idea dell'Architettura Universale* (1538), one of Vespasiano's chief sources for building his ideal city. Sabbioneta's theatre was abandoned at Vespasiano's demise; the roof crashed down on the stage and destroyed the permanent imaginary city set, and it was used as a cinema until the 1960s. What survived all these vicissitudes has been restored, including frescoes showing scenes of Rome and, around the orchestra *trompe l'œil* boxes, of chatting spectators and musicians in 16th-century costumes watching the performance. Note the man with the scissors near the stage: a barber-surgeon, he was immortalized for trepanning Vespasiano to relieve the painful pressure on his brain. The hole in his skull was successfully reopened four times; the fifth time killed the prince at the age of 60.

Sabbioneta's second piazza contains the **Palazzo Ducale**, the first building erected by Vespasiano. Although much damaged, changed and ham-handedly restored over the centuries, it has kept its simple stately façade with five arches. A number of frescoed rooms with intricately carved Venetian ceilings have survived; one – the Sala d'Oro – is completely covered with gold leaf. The large Room of the Eagles contains four wooden equestrian statues of Vespasiano and his direct ancestors, made in

Venice; originally there were ten, but only four horsemen survived intact from a fire in the 19th century. Vespasiano's private study is decorated with stucco reliefs of his more illustrious ancestors. The Sala degli Elefanti has a rare portrayal of elephants in a triumphal march, and two frescoes, of Genoa and Constantinople, surviving of the original ten paintings of port towns. The palace shares the square with the pink and white marble checked church of the **Assumption**, begun in 1578, its interior given a delightful rococo treatment in the 18th century. The artistic fireworks are in the Bibiena chapel, with its fretwork double dome with a blue sky background and a reliquary cabinet full of wax martyrs.

Continue to the octagonal church of the **Incoronata** (1586) with its impressive *trompe l'œil* dome from 1769 (Vespasiano originally intended it to be gilded) and Vespasiano's tomb in rare and antique marbles, with a bronze statue of the prince in Roman garb by Michelangelo's student Leone Leoni (1588). Vespasiano's hand is held out, as if to mould his city; the statue was originally intended for the Piazza Ducale. In 1988 the tomb was excavated, revealing not only the prince's trepanned skull but his collar of the Order of the Golden Fleece, now in the Museo dell'Arte Sacra.

The small **Museo dell'Arte Sacra** (*t 0375 220 299; open Wed–Thurs 3.30–6.30, Fri 9.30–12.30, Sat–Sun and hols 9.30–12.30 and 2.30–7.30; adm*) contains some sleepy religious paintings, brass band instruments and the Collar of the Golden Fleece, awarded to Vespasiano in 1585 by Philip II. This is an exceedingly rare authenticated example of the highest honour of Spanish knighthood and has become the prototype by which all others are judged. Near here the **Synagogue** (*t 0375 52039; open Tues–Fri 9.30–12 and 2.30–5, Sat–Sun and hols 9.30–12.30 and 2.30–6.30; adm*), rebuilt in the 1820s and still consecrated, has displays tracing the history of Judaism in the region.

If you stroll down Sabbioneta's main street, **Via Gonzaga**, you will see in the windows adjoining the Bar–Restaurant Ducale at No.24 a lavish private collection of antique dolls. If you have some spare time pop into Dal Conte, under the porticoes of Piazza Ducale, an antiques bazaar which stretches across the three storeys of Conte Michelangelo Moretti's house. You will find everything from antique furniture to small objects, including old slicing machines, coffee pots and an old marble toilet that is a prized possession of the count.

Two kilometres from the city walls on the way to Mantua is the church of **Villa Pasquali**, Sant'Antonio Abate (*t 0375 220 259*), designed by Antonio Galli Bibiena, built between 1760 and 1781. The external decoration and tower remained unfinished due to lack of funds, but the Baroque interior has original fret brickwork linings in the dome and two bowl-shaped sections of the apse. In the countryside of Casalmaggiore, 3km from Sabbioneta on the way to Cremona, the simple but imposing **Santuario della Madonna della Fontana** was built around a miraculous spring in medieval times. The painter Parmigianino, who is said to have spent his last days in a nearby *cascina* before dying of plague, is buried there.

Lakes Orta and Maggiore

10

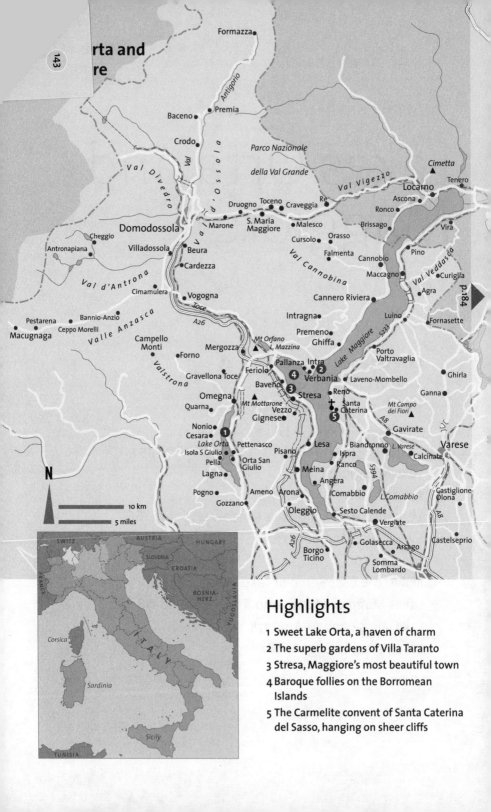

Highlights

1 Sweet Lake Orta, a haven of charm
2 The superb gardens of Villa Taranto
3 Stresa, Maggiore's most beautiful town
4 Baroque follies on the Borromean Islands
5 The Carmelite convent of Santa Caterina del Sasso, hanging on sheer cliffs

The westernmost lakes, Orta and Maggiore, evoke a soft, dreamy image of romance and beauty, a Latin Brigadoon of counts, dowagers, poets and opera composers strolling through gardens, sketching landscapes, and perhaps indulging in a round of whist on the villa veranda in the evening. The backgrounds to their fond pleasures are scenes woven of poetry: of mountains tumbling steeply into ribbons of blue and islands floating enticingly just offshore; of mellowed villas under the palms, with perfect gardens tended for hundreds of years; of spring's excess, when the lakes become drunken with colour, as a thousand varieties of azalea, rhododendron and camellia spill over the banks, blooming even at the foot of the starlit Alps.

This chapter also takes in the alpine valleys of the Ossola north of Orta and Varese, increasingly a bedroom suburb of Milan, but one with a few surprises up its sleeve.

Lake Orta and Domodossola

Lake Orta (the *Lacus Cusius* of the Romans), the westernmost lake and the only one totally in the confines of Piedmont, is relatively pint-sized, stretching a mere 13km at its longest point. But what it lacks in volume it compensates for with an exceptional dose of charm: a lake 'made to the measurements of man', according to Honoré de Balzac, which can be encompassed by a glance, surrounded by hills made soft with greenery, a haven from the excesses of tourism that sometimes scar the major lakes. Nietzsche, not a man to fall in love, did so on its soft green shores. He didn't get the girl, but the world got *Thus Spake Zarathustra*.

The waters of Lake Orta are enchanted in the moonlight, and in the centre they hold a magical isle, illuminated on summer nights to glow like a golden fairy castle in the dark. On a more mundane level, Orta's villages produce bathroom taps, saxophones, coffee pots and some of its finest chefs; so many come from Armeno that the second Sunday each November it holds an annual reunion of cooks and waiters.

Orta San Giulio, its Island and its Sacro Monte

Blithely set on its own garden peninsula, the lake's 'capital' Orta San Giulio is a perfectly fetching little town. Lanes too narrow for cars (leave yours in the car park along the main road, by the Villa Crespi) all lead into handsome lakeside **Piazza Motta**, a cosy rendezvous nicknamed the *salotto* or drawing room, with the bijou 1582 **Palazzotto**, decorated with faded frescoes, as a centrepiece. A lovely 40- to 60-minute walk (Movero/Lungolago) starts at the bottom of Via Motta, follows the shoreline around the promontory and allows a glimpse at the patrician villas through their gardens. It ends at the Via Panoramica (close to the tourist office).

Isola San Giulio was inhabited by serpents and monsters until AD 390 when Julius (Giulio), a Christian preacher from Aegina, showed up and calmly asked to be rowed to the island. The local fishermen, fearing that he would anger the dragons, refused; Giulio, undeterred, spread his cloak on the waters and surfed across. He sent the dragons packing, then built the precursor to the island's basilica by yoking a team of

Getting There and Around

The main lake resorts, Orta San Giulio, Pettenasco and Omegna, are easily reached from Turin or Milan, by **car** via the A26, on **trains** (t 892 021) heading north to Domodossola and the Simplon Pass. Orta is also easy to reach from Lake Maggiore: **buses** run from Stresa to Orta, from Arona to Orta (via Borgomanero) and from Verbania to Omegna.

Navigazione Lago d'Orta, t 0322 844 862, provides a **boat service** at least twice a day between the ports of Oria, Omegna, Punta di Crabbia, Pettenasco, L'Approdo, Orta, Isola San Giulio, Pella, San Filiberto and Lagna. The company also offers a **midnight cruise** from Orta, Pella and Pettenasco on Saturday in August and Sunday to and from Omegna for the San Vito festival.

There is also a little boat service to Isola San Giulio from Orta; (t 333 6050 288, moto scafiorta@email.it; leaves Piazza Motta every 15–20mins; €3). You can also cross over to the isle at any time on **taxi-boats**, at approximately the same price, provided you can group together about 10 people.

Tourist Information

Orta San Giulio: Via Panoramica, t 0322 905 614 ; inforta@distrettolaghi.it and on Via Bossi 11, t 0322 911 972.

Festivals

Ortafiori, the flower festival, April or May. Allows visitors to view the superb gardens of the Villa Motta.

Open Day, September. The flower season winds up, and allows visitors to visit private villas' parks and courtyards.

Markets

Orta San Giulio: in the Palazzotto, t 0322 911 372. Bric-a-brac (temporarily suspended at time of writting; ring for info). 1st Sat of month.

Shopping

For **antiques** and **jewellery**, try the Galleria Bertola, Contrada dei Monti 2, Orta San Giulio.

Where to Stay and Eat

Orta San Giulio ✉ 28016

★★★★**Villa Crespi**, Via G. Fava 8–10, t 0322 911 902, www.lagodortahotels.com (luxury). This is Lake Orta's most luxurious hotel, in a garden at the top of the town: a Moorish folly built in 1880 by Lombard cotton magnate Benigno Crespi and now painstakingly restored and furnished with period pieces. All rooms each have romantic canopied beds, marble baths and Jacuzzis. The elegant dining room (very expensive) is equalled by the ravishing dishes prepared by top chef Antonino Cannavacciuolo, whose sophisticated dishes mix Mediterranean and alpine flavours: maccaroni with lobster ragout, cherry tomatoes and light pesto sauce or pigeon breast stuffed with foie gras and wrapped in the savoy labrage. The wine list has over 500 labels. Closed Tues in winter, Wed lunch Jan and Feb.

wolves to his ox cart – a feat good enough to make him the patron of builders, who gather here on his feast day, 31 January.

Around the year 1,000, the **Basilica** (t 0322 90324; open daily 9.30–12.15 and 2–6.45; until 5.45 in winter; closed Mon until 11) was rebuilt for the first time. The chief relic of this rebuilding, the startling black marble **pulpit**, shows Giulio in high relief, wearily leaning on the hilt of his sword after chasing the dragons, along with symbols of the Evangelists – the Lion of St Mark looks like a sphinx grinning over a slice of pizza al taglio – while a griffon and crocodile duke it out in the corner. There are some good 15th-century frescoes by Gaudenzio Ferrari and his school (note especially the Story of San Giulio in the left aisle) and a marble sarcophagus belonging to the Lombard Duke Meinulphus, who had betrayed the island to the Franks and was beheaded by King

****San Rocco**, Via Gippini 11, **t** 0322 911 977, *www.hotelsanrocco.it* (*very expensive*). Located in a former 17th-century monastery, traces of which remain in the structure. Modern refurbished rooms, a pretty garden and a heated outdoor pool right on the water. In August it hosts a series of jazz and classical music concerts. Private garage. Good restaurant with local dishes.

***La Bussola**, Via Panoramica 24, **t** 0322 911 913, *www.orta.net/bussola/* (*very expensive–expensive*). Set back on a quiet hill, 16 rooms and a magnificent panorama over the lake; there's a pretty garden with a swimming pool and a good restaurant. *Closed Nov.*

***Orta**, Piazza Motta, **t** 0322 90253, *www.hotelorta.it* (*very expensive–expensive*). Brimming over with old-fashioned Italian character, and run by the same family for over a century, with big rooms and bathrooms and a charming dining terrace directly on the lake.

***La Contrada dei Monti**, Via Contrada dei Monti 10, **t** 0322 905 114, *www.orta.net/lacontradadeimonti/* (*expensive–moderate*). The same family that owns the Leon d'Oro (*below*), has just opened this charming hotel in Orta's centre. Rooms and bathrooms are all individually furnished and overlook quiet inner courtyards or the enchanting side streets of the historic centre.

***Leon d'Oro**, Piazza Motta, **t** 0322 911 991, *www.orta.net/leondoro/* (*expensive–moderate*). In 1882, Nietzsche and Lou Salomé spent their love-troubled week here and to this day the lake terrace and bar are especially amenable to such breaks from

philosophy. Rooms, recently remodelled, are small but immaculate, and there is an à la carte restaurant.

***Santa Caterina**, Via Marconi 10, **t** 0322 915 865, *www.orta.net/s.caterina/* (*moderate*). Near Sacro Monte, this is a peaceful hotel on the green hills overlooking the town. The owner also has apartments to let on a weekly basis (reduced rates for 2 weeks, higher for 2–3 nights) and also owns Hotel Olina (*see below*).

Olina, Via Olina 40, **t** 0322 905 656, *www.orta.net/olina/* (*moderate*). Very pleasant rooms, some with whirlpool shower, and an elegant restaurant, *www.orta.net/ristoolina/*, offering specialities such as home-made pasta, lake fish and meat cooked on a earthenware pot. *Closed Wed (only in low season). Booking advisable.*

Taverna Antico Agnello, Via Olina 18, **t** 0322 20259, *agnello.orta@tiscalinet.it* (*expensive*). A charming and cosy restaurant in a 17th-century house, with fish from the lake and more unusual fare such as venison *cotoletta* with juniper; also a good selection of cheeses, sliced hams and salami of the neighbouring regions, delicious *torte di verdura*, home-made pasta, *confiture* and desserts and a good wine list. There are a few rooms (*moderate–inexpensive*). *Closed Tues (except Aug), mid-Dec–mid-Feb. Book in advance (and if ordering risotto).*

Venus, Piazza Motta, **t** 0322 90256, *mistvenus@libero.it* (*moderate*). Always jam-packed for lunch due to its position in Piazza Motta's *salotto*, but standards have dropped and prices risen.

Agilulf; his decapitated skeleton was duly found inside in 1697. The vertebrae belonging to one of Giulio's dragons are no longer visible in the sacristry, but you can see what's left of the saint in a glass casket and some fragments of his 4th-century church. The monastery of San Giulio occupies most of the island, although there are a few private houses on its silent lanes, a shop or two and a little bar-restaurant; have a drink at sunset on the restaurant terrace for the beautiful view over to the opposite shore. The isle's elegant Villa Tallone hosts the Festival Cusiano in June each year, when groups in costume play ancient music, and a piano festival in September.

Orta is framed by sacred places; a road winds up the promontory behind town to the large car park under its holy acropolis or **Sacro Monte**. Orta's Sacro Monte (**t** 0322 911 960, *www.sacromonteorta.it; park is always open but chapels open 9–6.30*

Sacri Monti, or Little Theatres for the Soul

Orta, as mentioned above, is in the confines of Piedmont, a region with a special devotion to such Sacri Monti – hilltop devotional itineraries invented in the late 15th century by a Franciscan friar, Bernardino Caimi of Varallo (in the next valley to the west), after his pilgrimage to Jerusalem. Back in Varallo, Bernardino wanted to symbolically recreate his route through the Holy Land. His desire inspired the painter Gaudenzio Ferrari who, calling upon the Franciscan tradition of Christmas cribs and medieval passion plays, designed a series of tiny chapels, each containing life-size statues representing a biblical scene, with the background frescoed in – the precursor of the 3D dioramas in natural history museums.

With the Counter-Reformation and its desire to make the faith more tangible, immediate and emotive, the idea of the Sacro Monte spread beyond Varallo, encouraged in particular by Counter-Reformation Grand Vizier Charles Borromeo (*see* p.164), although his enthusiasm was tempered by the insistence that the Church maintain strict control over every aspect of the work, to keep even the slightest tinge of heresy from infecting the desired response to each scene; Varallo's Sacro Monte, created in more innocent days, had to be completely reworked. Charles Borromeo also saw the Sacri Monti as a chance to promote the cults of Mary, the Rosary and the saints – the very aspects of Catholicism most beleaguered by the Protestants.

in summer, 9–4.30 in winter), begun in 1591 and dedicated to Italy's patron St Francis, is one of the very best. Twenty-one numbered slate-roofed chapels in a wooded grove spiral to the top of the hill; in each, life-sized statues in 17th-century costume enact an important event in Francis' life – 376 figures and 900 frescoes in all, contributed by various artists over the next two centuries. What sets Orta's Sacro Monte apart from the others is its delicious setting, with very distracting views over Isola San Giulio. By the 18th century, people began to come up on Sundays with picnics, and now there's a very pleasant bar and restaurant to make relaxing even easier. While here, spare a thought for poor, shy, awkward Nietzsche who, beguiled by the nightingales of Sacro Monte, fell hopelessly head over heels for Lou Salomé, his Russian travelling companion and poet. He boldly advanced; she, surprised, retreated. He never tried love again.

Around Lake Orta

It doesn't take long to drive around the 'grey pearl in a green casket' as Balzac called Lake Orta, and there's certainly no hurry. On the way you can delve into non-figurative art and learn about saxophones and bathroom taps.

Pettenasco to Omegna

Near Orta, the little hamlet of Legro hosts a series of 24 murals painted by European contemporary artists and dedicated to films shot on the lake. On the lake north of Orta, **Pettenasco** is a quiet little resort, a perfect place to meditate: in the past couple of years it has hosted hatha yoga courses out of Berkeley, California. Villas and vantage points are scattered in the hills above, along with Ameno, the town of cooks, with a fine Romanesque church. Ameno is the centre node of a network of mountain lanes and trails, including the road up to the top of Mottarone (*see* p.163), as well as to the Santuario Bocciola in Vacciago di Ameno, with lovely views over Orta. The painter Antonio Calderara (1903–78) lived in a 17th-century villa in Vacciago, surrounding himself with avant-garde paintings from the 1950s and '60s by 133 artists from all over the world, which he left as a museum, the **Collezione Calderara** (*t 0322 998 192, www.fondazionecalderara.it; open mid-May–mid-Oct Tues–Sun 10–12 and 3–6; guided tours available*). But his own paintings are the most memorable – still-life landscapes that capture the spirit of Lake Orta far better than any photograph.

Nearby, there are two walking paths marked with *viae crucis tabernacula* rising up to Monte Mesma (1,890ft), surmounted by the enchanting **Convento Monte Mesma** (*t 0322 998 108, www.sacromonteorta.it; open summer Tues, Thurs, Sun 3–5; winter Sun 3–4.30; adm free, not open during Mass*), dating back to 1600 and including a rather large library. The two walking paths depart from Bolzano Novarese and Lortallo and cross a woody natural reserve area. Alternatively, you can drive up from Ameno, above Vacciago, or walk, ride a mountain bike or a horse on a different, wilder route along the Agogna river.

At the southern point of Orta, **Gozzano** is overlooked by the 82ft (25m) high **Torre di Buccione** (*t 0322 911 960 for info; access to the top is closed at present due to danger of*

Tourist Information

Pettenasco: Piazza Unità d'Italia 3, **t** 0323 89593, *pettenasco@distrettolaghi.it*.
Omegna: Piazza XXIV Aprile 17, **t** 0323 61930, or **t** 0323 867 235 (*both summer only*), *omegna@distrettolaghi.it*.

Festivals
San Vito festival, *last week of Aug*. Omegna's festival dedicated to the local patron saint, San Vito. Includes a market, evening concerts of Italian pop stars and culminates in a religious procession and blessing of the lake (Saturday), antique car and motorcycle racing and huge fireworks over the lake (Sunday). Book hotels well in advance. *www.sanvito-omegna.it*.

Sports and Activities

For **waterskiing**, contact Sci Nautico Cusio, **t** 0323 61365 or Sci Nautico Omegna, **t** 0323 866 150. For **sailing** contact Circolo Vela Orta, at Imolo hamlet, **t** 0322 905 672. Some hotels in Pettenasco (Approdo and Giardinetto)

have waterskiing equipment and **canoes** to rent out. You can bathe and swim in Orta's waters, but the only **beaches** suitable for children are Lido di Buccione (Gozzano), where there is also a diving board, and in Omegna and Pella.

Where to Stay and Eat

Pettenasco ✉ 28028
****L'Approdo**, Corso Roma 80, **t** 0323 89345, *www.lagodortahotels.com* (*luxury–expensive*). Run by the same family as the Giardinetto (*see* below); very family-friendly, with a big garden on the lake for kids to play and all mod cons such as heated outdoor swimming pool, tennis courts, sauna, private mooring and boats.
***Giardinetto**, Via Provinciale 1, **t** 0323 89118, *www.lagodortahotels.com* (*very expensive–expensive*). On Lake Orta, a friendly family hotel now owned by the Charme and Relax chain, with views of the Isola San Giulio. There are reduced rates for children, a swimming pool, private beach, and water sports facilities and an excellent restaurant

falling rocks), first built in the 4th century and rebuilt by the Lombards in the Dark Ages. Its bells were loud enough to warn all the communities on the lake in times of trouble. You can reach it by walking for 15 minutes through a chestnut wood, now turned into a nature reserve, from the main road linking Gozzano to Misiano. From the top there is a panorama of Lake Orta and Monte Rosa on clear days. Gozzano's **Villa Junker** has another fine garden and there are two tiny beaches under the main road.

A bit up from Gozzano, on Orta's west shore, the church of the **Madonna di Luzzara** has 15th- and 16th-century frescoes. While here, consider how often you've ever pondered over your toothbrush on the secret inner workings of your bathroom tap, then find out the truth in **San Maurizio d'Opaglio**, where the **Museo del Rubinetto** (**t** *0323 89622; open mid-July–Sept Fri–Sun 10.30–12.30 and 2.30–5.30 otherwise ring for appointment; adm free;*) is devoted to nothing else. Behind San Maurizio, a rocky outcrop supports the 18th-century **Santuario della Madonna del Sasso** (**t** *0322 981 177*), affording a grand view over the lake and the hamlets of Pella and Alzo.

On the northern tip of the lake, **Omegna** (Roman *Vomenia*) is the biggest town on the lake, where people make pots and pans, coffee pots and household appliances. Local industries include those of a famous kitchenware and industrial designers Alessi and Bialetti (the creator of Italian 'd.o.c.' coffeepot, Moka Bialetti), and Lagostina pressure cookers, to name but a few. A special museum, **Forum Omegna**, (**t** *0323 866 141, www.forumomegna.org; open Tues–Sat 10.30–12.30 and 3–6.30, Sun 3–6.30*) is

(*expensive*) serving locally cured meats, perch fillets on fresh salad, and guinea fowl pasta. The terrace has a lake view. Apartments are for rent in a green annexe behind the hotel, with free access to all facilities. *Open Easter–3rd week Oct.*

Osteria Madonna della Neve, Pratolungo, **t** *0323 89214, www.madonnadellaneve.net* (*inexpensive*). Family-run guesthouse above a *trattoria* a mile above the lake; all rooms have bathrooms. *Closed Wed and Jan.*

Pella ✉ 28010

Rosa Blu, Via Pietro Durio 106, **t *0322 969 282, www.larosabluhotel.it* (*moderate–inexpensive*). Simple, old-fashioned and sweet. Ideal if you want to stay at the quieter end of Lake Orta.

Omegna and Around ✉ 28026

Vittoria, Via Zanoia 37, **t *0323 62237, www.albergo-vittoria.it* (*moderate*). Family-run; ten tidy rooms, all with bath and TV, and a reasonably priced restaurant.

Belvedere, Quarna Sopra, **t *0323 826 198* (*moderate–inexpensive*). 7km up a winding road from Omegna, this hotel has simple

rooms but lives up to its name with enchanting bird's-eye views over Orta; also a garden and solarium.

Da Libero, Fornero, **t** *0323 87123* (*moderate*). A favourite rendezvous for its authentic, well-prepared trout, polenta, rice dishes and more, served on a lovely terrace in the summer. Rice dishes with champagne or mushrooms are the specialities. Book in advance. *Closed Tues and Jan.*

Ponte Bria, Via Ponte, Bria, in the middle of the woods, a few kilometres from Omegna near the hamlet of Cireggio di Omegna, **t** *0323 863 732* (*moderate*). The restaurant has the advantage of a children's playground and a little artificial lake for trout fishing. Specialities include home-made *crespelle*, ravioli and gnocchi, grilled trout directly from the lake and grilled venison. *Closed Mon out of season, Nov–Mar.*

*Leone, Via IV Novembre 1, in Forno hamlet, **t** *0323 885 112, www.albergodelleone.it* (*inexpensive*). Family run, peaceful and cosy. The restaurant serves typical local dishes such as young goat with polenta and home-made salami. Try the special *torta del pane* cake. *Closed Wed and Nov–April; cash only.*

devoted to them, on a former industrial site in Parco Rodari, just behind the city centre, with a shop where you can buy a good selection of locally produced items. Omegna's centre is pleasant enough, where the pretty Piazza del Municipio gives on to a bridge spanning the river that drains Orta, the **Nigoglia** – the only river in Italy to flow towards the Alps. The locals, who take some pride in being contrary themselves, like to say 'The Nigoglia flows up and we make the rules.'

From Omegna, a road curls up in ringlets through chestnut forests to the two hamlets called Quarna. **Quarna Sotto** (the lower one) has been manufacturing wind instruments for over 150 years; you can learn how they used to make clarinets, bassoons, oboes, saxophones, flutes and brass horns in the **Museo Etnografico e dello Strumento Musicale a Fiato** (*Via Roma 5, t 0323 826 123; open mid-June–mid-Sept Tues–Sun 10–12 and 3–6, or ring the custodian to book a visit; adm*). Downstairs, three traditional farmhouse rooms have been reconstructed and filled with local crafts and costumes. This museum is now part of a so-called circuit of 'eco-museums' aimed at introducing people to local culture and handicrafts; **Ecomuseo Cusius** (*t 0323 89622, ecomuseo@lagodorta.net; ring for various opening hours; most museums closed in winter*), comprising Museo del Rubinetto, Forum of Omegna, Museo dell' Ombrello e del Parasole di Gignese (umbrellas) in the hills halfway to Lake Maggiore (*see* p.164), **Museo della Tornitura del Legno** (wood turning) in Pettenasco (*open Jul–Sept Tues–Sun 10–12 and 2–6; adm free*), and **Museo dell' Arte Sacra** (sacred art) in Forno, Valstrona (*closed for restoration; ring Ecomuseo for details*). The circuit also includes visits to country houses (Il Glicine, Agrano di Omegna, Centonara), where you can learn about organic cultivation, local plants, rocks and even insects, and how to work hemp. The upper hamlet, **Quarna Sopra**, has spectacular views over Lake Orta and hosts a summer music festival (from classical to jazz and ethnic) in July and August.

A second valley radiating from Omegna, the **Valstrona**, is less intensely spectacular and the road very narrow and steep, but **Forno** is a fine little place where dogs can sleep in the middle of the street. In the festivities you may meet women wearing traditional costumes, or you can shop for locally made wooden utensils from cutlery to toys. If you happen to be in the area at the right time (*every three years on 8 September; next one 2006*) make a detour to **Luzzogno**, as you may chance upon the procession to the Sanctuary of Madonna della Colletta (15th-century frescoes and paintings of the Swiss School of the 1400s), unwinding under a cover of linen sheets at candlelight. The last hamlet in the valley, **Campello Monti**, is another Sunday-afternoon destination, where you can walk off too many tortellini.

Lake Orta to Domodossola: The Ossola Valleys

Unspoiled, and mostly unnoticed by visitors whizzing down the motorway to more Mediterranean delights, the Ossola valleys cut deep into the Alps, following the course of the River Toce and its tributaries on their way to Lake Orta. There are seven of them, and seven alpine valleys stretching north towards Switzerland surrounded by snowcapped peaks, sculpted by moody rivers and waterfalls, their wide green spaces protected by three national parks. Napoleon drove the first road through here, from the Simplon Pass to Milan, but even the improved communications couldn't help the Fascists and Nazis when the inhabitants booted them out and formed an independent republic that lasted 40 days. Nowadays the valleys are visited for their forests, rustic hospitality and alpine lakelets so blue they hurt.

Lake Mergozzo and the Valle Anzasca

North of Omega and Lake Orta, the road passes into the shadow of the mighty granite dome of Mount Orfano, which the locals are slowly whittling away to make flowerpots. Orfano in its turn guards an orphan lake, the small but deep **Lago Mergozzo**, which formed an arm of Lake Maggiore until the 9th century, when sediment from the Toce plugged it, a loss compensated for by the fact that Mergozzo is now one of the cleanest lakes in Europe – and remains so, since motorboats are banned. Between the mountain and lake, the hamlet of **Montorfano** has a striking Romanesque church in the shape of a Latin cross, with a 5th-century baptismal font. The lake's attractive main town, also called **Mergozzo**, has been a quiet place ever

Getting There and Around

Domodossola and the other towns along the Toce can be reached by **train** or **bus** from Milan (125km), Lake Maggiore or Lake Orta; the other mountain valleys of the Ossola are served by bus from Domodossola. For Macugnaga, take the train to Piedimulera or Domodossola and the connecting Comazzi bus, t 0324 240 333, www.comazzibus.com, which also runs a summer (July–Aug) service (Tues–Sun) from Varese via Lake Maggiore (Laveno/Intra). There is also a weekend service (July–Aug) from Pavia to Macugnaga through Novara and Lake Orta run by Fontaneto coaches, t 0321 391 601, www.safduemila.com.

Tourist Information

Macugnaga: Piazza Municipio, t 0324 65119, www.macugnaga-online.it. Open high season Mon–Sun 9–6, low season Mon–Sun 10.30–12.30 and 2–4, closed on Wed.

Festivals

Autani dei Sette Fratelli, 3rd week of July. The age-old procession with Latin chants and beautiful traditional songs invoking protection for crops and animals, in Cheggio. It runs for 25km along the Val d'Antrona, and starting from the Montescheno, continues from the first crack of dawn until dusk.

Sports and Activities

Opportunities for winter sports abound. Apart from **skiing** (downhill, cross-country or snowboarding) by yourself or as part of a class (there are two ski schools, one in Pecetto, near the ski lift to Passo Moro, t 0324 65217, and one in Macugnaga centre, c/o the Hotel Flora), or **ice skating** in the neighbouring hamlet Pecetto, Macugnaga offers other mountain sports such as **heli-ski** (off-piste descent of Monte Rosa to Swiss resorts), **paragliding** (from Monte Moro) and **ice waterfall-climbing**. Ski touring and **excursions** are organized by the alpine club CAI, by the tourist office, t 0324 65775, or by individual guides, t 0324 65170.

Where to Stay and Eat

Mergozzo ✉ 28802
★★★Due Palme, Via Pallanza 1, t 0323 80112, www.hotelduepalme.it (very expensive– expensive). Maintains a faded charm, and has a pretty front terrace lorded over by a whistling parrot; the gnocchi all'Ossalana with pumpkin and chestnuts in the restaurant (moderate) are equally noteworthy. Private beach. A hotel under the same ownership has opened in the town centre (no lake view, but quiet rooms).

since it lost its role as a transit centre with the construction of the Simplon road and tunnel. It has a 12th-century church made of Orfano granite, **San Giovanni** (*ring* **t** *0323 80347 or* **t** *0323 80593 for the key*). The **Museo Archeologico** (**t** *0323 80291; open winter Sat 4–6, Sun 3–7; summer Tues–Sun 5–8*) is said to contain local pre-Roman and Roman artefacts. A pleasant 10-minute walk named the Sentiero Azzurro (blue path) joins Montorfano and Mergozzo along the lake's west shore. The next town up the valley, **Candoglia**, is synonymous with the quarry, which for six centuries has been worked for the pink and white marble that built the Duomo in Milan.

The first valley splitting off to the west, the enchanting **Valle Anzasca**, leads straight towards the tremendous east face of Monte Rosa. Among the woods and vineyards, look for **Cimamulera**, where one of the oldest horse chestnut trees in Italy grows next to the church (the old mule path from here to Piedimulera is especially lovely). The slate roofs of tiny Colombetti huddle under a lofty cliff; **Bannio-Anzino**, the 'capital' of the valley, has a 1st-century BC Gallo-Roman necropolis and in its parish church a 6ft-tall, 16th-century bronze Christ from Flanders. At **Ceppo Morelli** the vertiginous bridge over the Anza traditionally divides the valley's Latin population from the

---

La Quartina, Via Pallanza 20, **t** 0323 80118, *www.laquartina.com* (*very expensive–expensive*). A warm little family-run hotel with a solarium and restaurant, slightly spoilt by the overcrowded public beach it shares with the neighbouring camp site. Rooms 1 and 3 have their own terraces overlooking the lake.

Piccolo Lago, Via Filippo Turati 87, Verbania Fondotoce, **t** 0323 586 792, *www.piccolo lago.it* (*expensive*). Managed by two young and talented brothers, Carlo and Marco Sacco. Chef Marco creatively combines local ingredients with exotic flavours: dishes include delicate wild salmon smoked by a traditional process using locally grown juniper; or the lake fish with a fondue of local cheese. Carlo, the *sommelier*, solicitously guides you through the 600-plus wine and spirit list. The spacious restaurant overlooks the lake, has large windows, a central chimney and an open grill used during the winter. All the hotel's modern rooms have satellite TV and lake views with individual terraces. There is a lake garden, private beach and an outdoor pool. *Closed Mon (not in summer), mid-Dec–mid-Jan.*

Macugnaga ✉ 28876

★★★Zumstein, Via Monte Rosa 63, **t** 0324 65118, *http://zumstein.macugnaga.it*, (*very expensive–expensive*). The largest and most

luxurious choice, with attractive rooms near the centre of Staffa and private parking. *Closed May, Oct and Nov.*

★★★Hotel Flora, Piazza Municipio 1, **t** 0324 65037, *www.albergoflora.com* (*expensive*). A friendly hotel on the main square, with pleasant, comfortable rooms including hydromassage bath in some. The pub-restaurant offers tasty, quick and abundant snacks until late, thanks to mother Ninì of Chez Felice (*see below*).

★★Chez Felice, Via alle Ville 14, **t** 0324 65229, (*moderate*). The name is misleading as the sublime chef, charming host and energetic manager is Ninì, while 'papa' Felice is the *patrone*. The restaurant fills three rooms on the ground floor of an unassuming villa, charmingly decorated with Ninì's collection of old copper and wooden pots to make risotto, milk and cheese. Chez Felice is the best restaurant in the valley, a haven of mountain *nuova cucina*, where you can sample salmon mousse with herbs, warm artichokes with a sauce of anchovies and capers, risotto with almonds, cheese and herb soufflé and many other delights; for afters, if you've got the room, there's a magnificent array of local cheeses and exquisite desserts. Reserve if you're not staying at the hotel. *Closed Thurs and Oct.* There are also basic rooms upstairs (*inexpensive*) with small baths.

Walser – German-speaking Swiss settlers from the Valais who settled many of these valleys in the 13th century. Beyond Ceppo the road plunges through a gorge to the old Walser mining town of **Pestarena**; until recently the Valle Anzasca had Italy's largest gold deposits, extracted from galleries that extended for 40km.

The various hamlets that comprise **Macugnaga**, the Valle Anzasca's popular mountain resort, seem tiny under the tremendous 'cathedral of stone and ice', **Monte Rosa** (15,305ft/4,665m). Macugnaga's Walser culture and traditions are recalled in the **Museo Casa Walser** in the hamlet of Borca (*open June–1st week of Sept, Sat and Sun 3.30–5.30; July–Aug daily 3.30–5.30; Christmas period daily, same time; for visits at other times call Anna Bettineschi on t 0324 65230; adm*); another museum, the **Museo della Miniera d'ocodella Guia** (*open June–mid-Sept 9–11.30 and 2–5.30; Christmas period daily; other periods open by request; adm; for info call Riccardo Bossone, t 0324 65570*) is dedicated to gold-mining. There is also a guided visit of 1½km of the 18th-century 11km-long gold mine. Dress warmly, as the temperature drops dramatically once inside. Macugnaga has some 40km of ski runs and two cross-country tracks; a dozen ski lifts; a chair lift that operates in the summer as well to the magnificent **Belvedere** which has views over the Macugnaga glacier, and a *funivia* to the **Passo Monte Moro** (9,410ft/2,888m), used by skiers in both the winter and spring seasons. From Macugnaga fearless alpinists attempt the steep, Himalayan-like east flank of Monte Rosa, one of the most dangerous ascents in the Alps; walkers can make a three-day trek over the mountains to Gressoney-St-Jacques in the Valle d'Aosta (trail map essential) or do a circular hike (one week) passing the Swiss resorts of Zermatt and Grachen back to Macugnaga (experienced walkers only, and guides essential).

North of the Valle Anzasca, the pretty, wooded **Val d'Antrona** is famed for its trout fishing and old-fashioned ways: the older women still wear traditional costumes and make Venetian lace. The valley begins at **Villadossola**, from where you can catch a bus to **Antronapiana**, a pleasant village lost in the trees near the lovely lakelet of Antrona, created when a landslide buried half of Antronapiana in 1642. The north branch of the valley winds up to **Cheggio**, a wee resort with refuges, restaurants and another lake.

Domodossola and the Upper Ossola Valleys

The capital of the Valle d'Ossola, Domodossola was a Roman settlement, and is perhaps best known in Italy these days as the largest town in the republic beginning with the letter D. After his victory at Marengo, Napoleon, to make French meddling in Italy easier, built the first transalpine highway from Geneva to Domodossola through the Simplon Pass (Passo del Sempione), a major engineering feat completed in 1805. Exactly 100 years later the even more remarkable Simplon rail tunnel was completed – at the time the longest in the world at 19.8km.

Domodossola

Domodossola has a compact, car-swamped historic centre called the **Motta**. In the heart of the Motta is the pretty **Piazza Mercato**, lined with 15th-century porticoes.

A few steps away, the old church of **SS. Gervasio e Protasio** was rebuilt in the 18th century, but conserving a Baroque porch and a curious Romanesque architrave carved with the *Dream of Constantine*, informing the emperor that he would conquer under the sign of the cross.

Domodossola's two museums, recently reopened, contain an eclectic mix of exhibits. Opposite SS. Gervasio e Protasio, the town's finest Renaissance building, the Palazzo Silva contains the **Museo Civico**, with Etruscan and Roman finds from the 3rd century AD necropolis in the Val Cannobina, Egyptian mummy bits and costumes (*t 0324 249001; open by appointment only, some guided visits in the summer; adm*). On the other end of Piazza Mercato, the Palazzo San Francesco contains the **Museo G. G. Galletti**, part of the Museo Civico, (*visits upon request, as above*). This incorporates a medieval church and holds something for every taste, from paintings to natural history exhibits, the construction of the Simplon tunnel and the flight of Peruvian Jorge Chavez, the first man to fly over the Alps (on 29 September 1910), only to die in a crash near Domodossola (he also has a monument in Piazza Liberazione). In 1944 the adjacent **Palazzo di Città** was the seat of the Repubblica Partigiana dell'Ossola for 40 days in one of the most significant acts of the Italian resistance.

From the centre, Via Mattarella leads up to the site of a ruined castle, where two Capuchin friars founded a **Sacro Monte** (*t 0324 241 976, www.sacromonte domodossola.it; open daily till dusk*) in 1656, with 15 Baroque chapels dedicated to the Via Crucis. Unfortunately the first and best one exploded in 1830, when it was used to store powder – this shouldn't happen again now that the Sacro Monte is part of a special reserve. Domodossola has its own ski station 10km away called **Domobianca** (*www.domobianca.it*), or you can relax at the hot mineral springs at **Bognanco** just up the next valley to the west (*t 0324 234 127; open May–Oct*).

The Val Vigezzo

Just east of Domodossola begins the Val Vigezzo, a romantic beauty of woodlands, rolling hills and velvet pastures which has produced enough minor artists to earn the name 'the Valley of Painters'. One of the most charming features of the villages is the exterior frescoes they left behind. Locals say that the valley's ever-changing natural colours are a unique source of inspiration. The Val Vigezzo had a knack for producing useful emigrants; one artist, Giuseppe Borgnis, ended up painting country homes in Buckinghamshire, where he died in 1761. In the 18th century two immigrants to Germany formulated and sold the first *acqua di colonia*, or cologne. Another family, the Mattei, who emigrated from **Druogno** to Holland in 1600, accidentally invented snuff when they bought a storm-wrecked cargo vessel and found that the casks of rum had soaked into the bales of tobacco; at first despondent, they later discovered that the rum had imparted a wonderful fragrance to the tobacco and sold it as a novelty that soon became the rage. There is also a story about a young chimney sweep who saved the King of France: while cleaning a chimney of the Louvre he happened to overhear by chance some traitors conspiring against baby king Louis XIII and promptly warned the regent Maria de' Medici. Since that time chimney sweeps, who used to be banned from trading in France, became industrious and rich. A more romantic version of the legend tells that the chimneys that revealed the treason were in Versailles and that the reward was different: the chimney sweeps became the court's jewellers, and remained so long enough to make a funerary cap for King Louis XIV, now kept in Craveggia's main church together with other treasures. The Val Vigezzo even gave birth to the inventor of modern central heating, Pietro De Zanna, who originated from Zornasco but emigrated to Vienna, where he died.

Getting There and Around

The narrow-gauge electric **railway**, La Vigezzina-Centovalli, makes the 1½-hour picturesque journey between Domodossola and Locarno on Lake Maggiore through the Val Vigezzo and through winding Swiss valleys, serving all the villages on the way. Special circular **tours** are offered (*June–Sept daily except Wed*), from Domodossola by train to Stresa, from Stresa to Locarno by boat, and then back to Domodossola by train. The train company also organizes combined itineraries on foot or by bike on the way, or detours by cable car to Madonna del Sasso in Locarno. Or travel on historical 1920s carriages; look from line nos. 5 (Domodossola to Locarno) and 7 (Locarno to Domodossola). **Domodossola station** is at Via Mizzoccola 9, **t** 0324 242 055. Visit *www.centovalli.ch* for further information.

Buses to the valleys depart from the FS station, Piazza Matteotti in Domodossola: **t** 0324 242 533 for trains; **t** 0324 240 333, *www.comazzibus.com,* for buses.

Tourist Information

Domodossola: Piazza Matteotti, at the train station, **t** 0324 248 265. If you want to get on line you can visit **Caffè Giordani**, Piazza Volontari della Libertà and **ABC**, Corso Moneta, both in Domodossola.

Santa Maria Maggiore: Piazza Risorgimento 28, **t** 0324 95091, *www.vallevigezzo.vb.it. Open Mon–Sat 8.30–12.30 and 3–6, Sun and hols 8.30–12.30.*

Parco Nazionale della Val Grande, **t** 0323 557 960, *www.parcovalgrande.it.*

Festivals

Chimney-sweep Gathering and Competition, *September.* In Santa Maria.

Market Day

Domodossola: Piazza Mercato. A market has been here for the past thousand years. *Sat.*

Sports and Activities

For **trekking**, ask at the tourist office, or contact the alpine association, CAI, **t** 0324 34737, about guided nature trails, mountaineering and climbing. There is also **horse riding**, contact the Club Lo Sperone, **t** 0324 94055, or Azienda Agrituristica Pian delle Lutte, **t** 0324 94488; and **paragliding**, through Club Volo Libero Barbagianni, with landings on Santa Maria Maggiore's plain, **t** 0324 94444. In winter there is a 15km **cross-country** track running between Santa Maria Maggiore, Druogno and Malesco and downhill **skiing** (19km in Piana del Vigezzo, Druogno).

Where to Stay and Eat

Domodossola ✉ 28845

★★★Corona, Via Marconi 8, **t** 0324 242 114, *www.coronahotel.net (expensive)*. The most stylish hotel in town has very comfortable rooms and a garage. Ask for the top-floor rooms at the back to enjoy the views over the old city centre and to the Sacro Monte beyond. The restaurant has local and international dishes.

★★★Motel Europa, Via Siberia 12, 4km south on the N33, **t** 0324 481 032 *(moderate)*. Comfortable enough; all rooms have private bathrooms and TV.

Trattoria Piemonte da Sciolla, Piazza Convenzione 5, **t** 0324 242 633 *(expensive)*. Situated in the centre and highly recommended for its regional dishes such as polenta with milk and poppyseeds, *cüchela* (made with potatoes and flat beans, slowly cooked in an oven), and its home-made

Druogno, now down to 1,000 inhabitants, has pretty frescoed chapels scattered through its picturesque dry stone hamlets, crowned with stone roofs called *piode*. **Santa Maria Maggiore**, the Val Vigezzo's main town, is built around a little park and the 18th-century church, with a lovely *piode* roof; once Santa Maria had enough souls to fill its grand rococo interior, before they emigrated to become dockers in Livorno (the older people still speak with a slight Tuscan accent). Others became chimney

desserts. *Closed Wed and late Aug–mid-Sept and 2 weeks in Jan.* They also have a few clean, basic rooms (*inexpensive*).

Trattoria Moncalvese, Corso Dissegna 54, **t** 0324 243 691 (*moderate*). Close to the station; serves local specialities. *Closed Tues.*

Druogno ✉ 28853

***Boschetto, Via Pasquaro 18, **t** 0324 93554, *www.albergoboschetto.com* (*expensive–moderate*). By the ski slopes (where you can practise summer skiing on grass) and with a kids' playground, this family-run hotel is more isolated. The rooms have been renovated; those at the back have beautiful views over the mountains.

***Stella Alpina, Via Domodossola 13, **t** 0324 93593, *www.stellaalpinahotel.com* (*moderate*). The most comfortable hotel in the village, but a bit close to the road.

Santa Maria Maggiore ✉ 28857

***Miramonti, Piazzale Diaz 3, **t** 0324 95013, (*expensive–moderate*). You can sleep and eat in style up near the station here, at the bigger hotel building, or, preferably, at the cosy chalet. with flowers flowing over the balconies. Dine in candlelight at the hotel restaurant (*moderate*) with finely prepared and served local dishes, including the traditional cake *pane e latte* (stale bread, milk, raisins), and indulge yourself afterwards with the local *digestivo* S. Giacomo, poured from tall narrow bottles. *Closed Nov. Booking avisable.*

***Delle Alpi, Via Luigi Cadorna 1, opposite the entrance of the pedestrian centre, **t** 0324 94290 (*moderate*). Another family-run hotel with a nice front terrace.

La Jazza, Via la Jazza 4, just before the entrance to Santa Maria Maggiore, **t 0324 94471, *www.hoteljazza.com* (*moderate–inexpensive*). Has a garden and a few cheaper rooms without bath.

Da Branin, Piazza Risorgimento 3, in front of the church, **t** 0324 94933 (*moderate*). Serves local dishes, fish and home-made cakes in a sober and elegant dining room. *Closed Wed Nov–mid-Dec.*

Locarno, Piazza Risorgimento 6-9, next to the church, **t** 0324 95088 (*inexpensive* for pizza, *moderate* for restaurant). Serves simple fare at lunchtime and good pizzas in the evening. *Closed Mon and Nov.*

Worth a detour at lunchtime are the refuges above Santa Maria Maggiore:

Il Camoscio, outside the hamlet of Arvina (Craveggia), **t** 0324 98604 or **t** 3386 934 875 (*inexpensive*). Packed with Lombards spending their holiday in the valley and driving up to taste the unparalled polenta and local *affettati*, and to enjoy the views from the terrace. About 7km up from the valley bottom. *Open daily in summer, weekends and festivities in winter.*

Rifugio Del Moro, Arvogno, **t** 0324 98450 (*inexpensive*). Renowned for its *minestra negra*, a potato and vegetable soup cooked with black beans for six hours. *Open daily in summer, weekends and festivities in winter.*

Malesco ✉ 28854

***Alpino, Via al Piano 61, Zornasco, **t** 0324 95118, *www.hotelalpino.org* (*expensive–moderate*). Moderate-sized, with a pool and comfortable rooms. It will shortly be opening a pub and a gym for hotel and non-resident guests.

*Lo Scoiattolo, Piazza Brindicci Bonzani 7, Villette, **t** 0324 97009, *trecom@libero.it* (*moderate–inexpensive*). Situated in an old building overlooking the main square and the church in nearby Villette, a charming village full of meridians. Rooms are basic and bathrooms are communal, but nos. 9 and 12 have views to compensate. The young host Anna also runs the bar and restaurant downstairs (*inexpensive*).

sweeps, a hard trade honoured in the little **Museo dello Spazzacamino** (*t 0324 95091; open July–mid-Sept daily 10–12 and 4–6; adm; contact the tourist office for other hours*) in the park. The **Scuola di Belle Arti**, dedicated to local painters Carlo Fornara and Enrico Cavalli, hosts exhibits and runs summer painting courses. The tourist office has a map of walks and ski facilities including challenging treks through the **Parco Nazionale della Val Grande**, one of the wildest places in Italy, stretching down to Lake Mergozzo; one of the entrances is at Scardi south of Santa Maria. The park's information centre advises against venturing out into the wilderness without a guide. Buses from Santa Maria go north up to **Toceno**, with pretty views and a Roman necropolis, and to **Craveggia**, birthplace of Giuseppe Borgnis, who left the valley's finest frescoes in the church.

Continuing up the Val Vigezzo, **Malesco** is a picturesque, higgledy-piggledy old village, where you can turn off on a road that will keep you in second gear most of the way before winding down the Val Cannobina (*see* p.169) to Lake Maggiore. Further up the Val Vigezzo, **Re**, the last Italian *comune* before Switzerland, once had a church with a crude painting of the Madonna on the wall. In 1494 the village idiot threw a stone at it, striking the Virgin on the forehead, which immediately began to bleed profusely. The bleeding Madonna still has thousands of devotees: a ghastly neo-Gothic Byzantine **Santuario della Madonna del Sangue** (*t 0324 97016*) was built in 1922, over the previous (and still existing) chapel, but it attracts enough pilgrims and is filled with sincere, home-made *ex votos*.

North of Domodossola

The **Val Divedro**, along the Simplon road, is as austere as the Val Vigezzo is gentle. Inhabited since the cows came home in the Mesolithic era (7000 BC) it teems with legends of dragons and elves. But nature is the main attraction, especially the **Alpe Veglia**, a high alpine basin set amid little lakes – including the Lago delle Streghe, named for the witches who haunt it. Buses from Domodossola also plunge north towards the San Giacomo Pass, through the spectacular scenery of the **Valli Antigorio e Formazza**, valleys along the river Toce settled by the Walser in the 13th century. Their charming, scattered villages are planted with vines and figs, and the valley's spa, **Crodo**, is famous in Italy for bottling a soft drink called Crodino, as well as iron-laced mineral water. Further north, **Baceno**'s parish church, **San Gaudenzio** (11th–16th century) is the best in the Valle d'Ossola; it has a fine front portal with sirens and a cartwheel window, 16th-century Swiss stained glass and a carved wooden altarpiece.

In **Premia** you can visit the **Orridi**, steep gorges sliced by the River Toce over the millennia. You can reach an evocatively empty old Walser settlement, **Salecchio**, by foot from Antillone; **Formazza**, further up, is a pretty, still lived-in Walser community, with sturdy wooden houses. At the end of the road is one of the most breathtaking waterfalls in all the Alps, the thundering 985ft (143m) veil of mist, the **Cascata del Toce** (*t 0324 63059; open June–Sept Tues and Thurs 11–1, Sun 9–6; 10 Aug–20 Aug daily 9–6*). At other times, like all of Italy's best waterfalls, its bounding, splashing energy spins hydroelectric turbines.

Lake Maggiore

Have you not read in books how men when they
see even divine visions are terrified?
So as I looked at Lake Major in its halo
I also was afraid ...
　　　Hilaire Belloc, *The Path to Rome*

Italy's second-largest lake after Garda, Lago Maggiore winds majestically for 65km between Piedmont and Lombardy, its northern corner lost in the snow-capped Swiss Alps. The Romans called it *Lacus Verbanus*, for the verbena that still grows luxuriantly on its shores: like Como and Garda, Maggiore is large enough to create its own warm, Mediterranean microclimate. The three jewel-like Borromean islands in its central Golfo Borromeo set the lake apart from the others, however. They still belong to the Borromei of Milan, who also possess fishing rights over the entire lake – as they have since the 1500s. The west shore of the lake, especially the triad of Stresa, Baveno and Verbania, are the most scenic places to aim for, with the best and most varied accommodation and festivals (*Easter and July–Sept are high season, booking advised*).

Arona to Baveno

If you're approaching from the south, Lake Maggiore doesn't exactly make a striking first impression, dissolving into formless and reedy lagoons until you reach **Arona**, a rail junction and sprawling market town. There are, however, views from Arona's lake promenade across to the Borromeo castle at Angera, and in the pretty cobbled Piazza del Popolo the 15th-century **Casa del Podestà** is distinguished with a portico of pointed arches. The old upper part of Arona has two worthwhile churches: Renaissance **Santa Maria**, where the Borromeo family chapel contains a lovely 1511 polyptych by Gaudenzio Ferrari, and **SS. Martiri**, with 16th-century stained-glass windows, a painting by Bergognone and another by the Venetian Palma Giovane.

A medieval fief of the Visconti, Arona passed to the Borromei in 1439. A few walls remain of their **Castle of Arona**, 2km up on top of the town; it was the birthplace of Charles Borromeo (1538–84), an event commemorated by his cousin and successor Cardinal Federico Borromeo with a church, three chapels of an unfinished Sacro Monte and **San Carlone**, a 115ft copper and bronze jug-eared colossus set in the act of blessing the lake (*t 0322 249 669; open mid-Mar–Oct 8.30–12.30 and 2–6.30; Oct–Nov till 5; Nov–Feb Sat–Sun and hols 9–12.30 and 2–5*).

From Arona to Stresa

Two roads link Arona to Stresa: the panoramic upper road through the villages of the **Colle Vergante** and the main route hugging the lake shore. This lower road passes a number of villas before reaching **Meina**, the medieval Màdina when it was the property of the Benedictines of Pavia. Meina is the base for visiting **Ghevio** and **Silvera**, charming villages immersed in the green of the hills of Vergante, and **Massino**

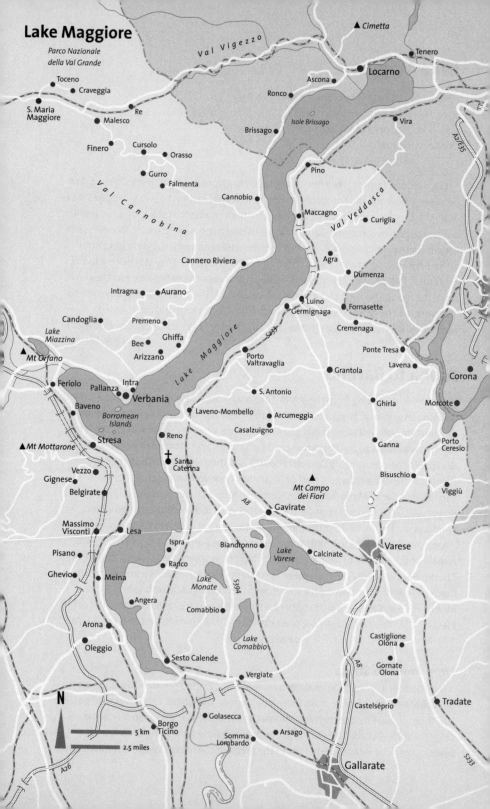

Getting There and Around

Trains from Milan's Stazione Centrale to Domodossola stop at Arona and Stresa; others from Milan's Porta Garibaldi station go to Luino. A third option is the regional railway from Milano-Nord, which passes by way of Varese to Laveno. Trains from Turin and Novara go to Arona and Stresa; Stresa is also linked by train to Orta four times a day.

From Lake Orta, **buses** run from Omegna to Verbania (*every 20mins*). Buses connecting the two lakes also run from Stresa and Arona stations, while others serve all the villages along the west shore.

Navigazione Lago Maggiore, **t** 0322 233 200, *www.navigazionelaghi.it*, runs **steamers** to all corners of the lake, with the most frequent services in the central lake area, between Stresa, Baveno, Verbania, Pallanza, Laveno and the islands; **hydrofoils** buzz between the main Italian ports and Locarno (Switzerland). Frequent services by steamer or hydrofoil from Stresa, Baveno and Pallanza sail to the Borromean Isles – a ticket for the furthest, Isola Madre, entitles you to visit all.

Car ferries run year round between Intra and Laveno.

Tourist Information

Check out the website *www.lagomaggiore. net* as a source of information on the region.
Arona: Piazzale Duca d'Aosta, **t** 0322 243 601.
Stresa: Via Canonica 3, **t** 0323 30150, and Piazza Marconi 16, **t** 0323 31308, *www.stresa.it*.

Baveno, Piazza Dante Alighieri 14, **t** 0323 924 632, *www.comune.baveno.vb.it*.

Festivals

Settimane Musicali di Stresa, *last week July– Sept*. Orchestras from around the world descend on Stresa. For information, ring **t** 0323 01095, or *www.settimanemusicali.net*.
Festival Giordano e il Suo Tempo, *1st to 3rd week of July*. A music festival dedicated to composer Umberto Giordano and his contemporaries, with concerts in the park at Teatro, Tenda, Parco di Villa Fedora.

Sports and Activities

The area is ideal for **trekking** as it has a national Park (Val Grande) and three regional ones (Ticino, Lagoni di Mecurago, and the Fondotoce area) as well as a special natural reserve (the Sacred Mountain of Trinità di Ghiffa). Ask the local tourist offices for trekking itineraries or contact the Baveno Alpine Club, Via Domo 2, **t** 0323 922 214 (*open Fri eve 9–12pm*). Trekking Team, **t** 0323 30399, in Stresa, offers **mountain bike hire**, guided excursions, **canyoning** and **bungee-jumping**.

There are three **golf courses**: Alpino, **t** 0323 20642, *www.golfalpino.it*, one of Italy's oldest, 9 holes, in Vezzo; Des Iles Borromees, **t** 0323 929 285, *www.golfdesilesborromees.it*, in a beautiful alpine setting, 18 holes, **t** 0323 929 285, *www.golfpiandisole.it*, in Brovello Campugnino; and Piandisole, **t** 0323 587 100 at the entry of the Val Grande Park, 9 holes.

It is also possible to hire **bikes** on the Mottarone, **t** 0323 30399.

Visconti, with its 13th-century castle and church. The lake road continues to **Lesa**, with the best-preserved Romanesque church on Maggiore, **S. Sebastiano** (1035); Alessandro Manzoni, better known for his links to Lecco on Lake Como (*see* p.215), spent his holidays here, in the Palazzo Stampa (now a bank). The lake really opens up at **Belgirate**, another small resort, with a pretty square, the 15th-century frescoed church of **Santa Marta** and the Villa Carlotta, a favourite retreat of Italy's intellectuals in the 19th century (now a hotel).

Stresa, the 'Pearl of Verbano'

Beautifully positioned on the lake overlooking the Borromeo islands, under the majestic peak of Mottarone, Stresa is Maggiore's most beautiful town, bursting with

Where to Stay and Eat

Arona ✉ 28041

Taverna del Pittore, Piazza del Popolo 39,
t 0322 243 366 (*very expensive*). One of Lake
Maggiore's finest restaurants. Enjoy lovely
views from the lake terrace while feasting
on seafood *lasagnette* with saffron, fragrant
ravioli with mushrooms, and exceptional
desserts. *Closed Mon and mid-Dec–Jan.*

Vecchia Arona, Lungolago Marconi 17,
t 0322 242 469 (*expensive*). For half as much,
eat a delicious menu based on the market
and the day's catch, with a lunch time menu.
Closed Fri, two weeks June, two weeks Nov.

Stresa ✉ 28838

★★★★★Des Iles Borromées, Corso Umberto I 67,
t 0323 938 938, *www.borromees.it* (*luxury*).
Opened in 1861; stylish in both its
aristocratic *belle époque* furnishings and its
mod cons. Overlooking the islands, and a
lovely flower-decked, palm-shaded garden,
the hotel has a pool, beach, tennis courts,
gym and a *Centro Benessere* where doctors
are on hand to give you a check-up,
exercises, improve your diet and de-stress
you with personalized treatments. There's
even a heli-pad. Minimum 3 days' stay for
rooms, 7 days for suites.

★★★★Regina Palace, Corso Umberto I 29,
t 0323 936 936, *www.regina-palace.it*
(*luxury*). A lovely, bow-shaped Liberty-style
palace, tranquil in its large park. The hotel
conserves its original decor and furniture in
the halls, while rooms are decorated in style.
It has a heated pool, tennis courts, sauna,
Turkish bath, gym, restaurant, beach, and
splendid views.

★★★★Milan au Lac, Piazza Marconi 9,
t 0323 31190, *www.milansperanza.it*
(*luxury–very expensive*). Another lake-front
hotel; has good-size rooms, many with
balconies and, of course, wonderful views. If
sent to sister hotel **Speranza** (*same price,
more modern*) next door, try and ask for a
top-floor lake-front room for a stunning
view or room no.606 for a larger terrace.
Tennis courts, pool and a garage in the back.
Open Mar–Oct.

★★★Du Parc, Via Gignous 1, t 0323 30335,
www.duparc.it (*expensive*). A charming
family-run hotel in a period private villa set
in its own grounds below the railway tracks
and just 300 yards from the lakeside. *Open
Mar–Oct.*

★★★Italie & Suisse, Piazza Marconi,
t 0323 30540, *www.italiesuisse.com*
(*expensive–moderate*). A good choice, near
the steamer landing.

★★★Primavera, Via Cavour 39, t 0323 31286,
hotelprimavera@stresa.it (*expensive–
moderate*). A friendly, stylish hotel with
pretty balconies.

★Elena, Piazza Cadorna 15, t 0323 31043,
www.hotelelena.com (*expensive–moderate*).
A good budget option, with a garage and 14
big modern rooms, most with balconies, and
satellite TV.

★Fiorentino, Via Anna Maria Bolongaro 9,
t 0323 30254 (*moderate*). For less, there's this
simple, central and family-run place, recently
renovated, with a nice restaurant (local and
international cuisine) in a homely dining
room or a courtyard outside.

flowers and sprinkled with fine old villas. A holiday resort since the last century,
famous for its lush gardens and mild climate, it soared in popularity after the
construction of the Simplon Tunnel in 1906; Hemingway used its **Grand Hôtel des Iles
Borromées** as Frederick Henry's refuge from war in *A Farewell to Arms*. The little
triangular **Piazza Cadorna** in the centre, shaded by age-old plane trees, is Stresa's
social centre, its number of habitués swollen by participants in international
congresses and music lovers attending the **Settimane Musicali di Stresa** (*see*
'Festivals', p.161). Two of Stresa's lakeside villas are open to the public: **Villa Pallavicino**
(1850) and its colourful gardens, where saucy parrots rule the roost, along with a small
collection of other animals (**t** 800 248039, *www.parcozoopallavicino.it*; *open
mid-Mar–Oct 9–6; adm*) and the **Villa Ducale** (1771), once the property of Catholic

★★La Locanda, Via Leopardi 19, close to the Mottarone cable car, just a short walk along the lake from Stresa's centre, t 0323 31176 (*moderate*). A quiet family-run hotel and an excellent budget option: all 14 rooms are comfortable, with their own bathrooms, and most of them have their own balcony, although with no lake view. It also has a nice restaurant.

Piemontese, Via Mazzini 25, t 0323 30235 (*very expensive*). Find a table in the garden to tuck into the divine spaghetti with melted onions, basil and pecorino and the excellent fish dishes. *Closed Mon, Dec–Jan and on Sun eves between Oct–Mar.*

The Irish Bar, Via P. Margherita 9, t 0323 31054. An Stresa institution for the past 28 years, run by the hospitable Zawettas.

Red Baron Pub, at the top of Via Roma 63, t 0323 30232. Situated below the railway tracks, a lively English-run place serving draught beer, great sandwiches and imaginative salads.

Baveno ✉ 28831

★★★★Grand Hotel Dino, Via Garibaldi 20, t 0323 922 201 (*luxury*). This modern hotel right on the water is the lake's biggest, with 360 rooms and a conference centre. Offers a long list of extras, including a private beach. Special offers in summer (July).

★★★Hotel Beau Rivage, Viale della Vittoria 36, t 0323 924 534 (*expensive*). On the lake-front road in Baveno's centre is this family-run hotel with private parking facilities, a nice back garden and old-style furniture and atmosphere on the ground floor. Rooms are neat and are all being renovated. Especially recommended among the lake-front rooms

are the top floor suites (*very expensive*): new, air-conditioned, quieter and with a nice terrace. *Closed late Oct–mid-Mar.*

★★★Villa Azalea, Via Domo 6, t 0323 924 300, www.villaazalea.com (*expensive–moderate*). Situated at the back of the church in Baveno's historical centre; this has been renovated by its new owners. Rooms are modern, with all comforts, but don't have much character.

★★★Carillon, Via Nazionale del Sempione 2, Feriolo, t 0323 28115, www.hotelcarillon.it (*expensive–moderate*). On the north edge of town; right on the beach with private mooring and parking. Nice rooms are all lake-front with a balcony; no restaurant, but the same family runs the **Serenella** restaurant, 700m from the hotel, (*see below*). *Closed out of season.*

★★★Al Campanile, Via Monte Grappa 16, t 0323 922 377 (*moderate*). In the centre, a pretty old villa in a lush garden, which has a nice restaurant (*moderate*) on the shady garden terrace with local dishes changing seasonally. *Closed Wed out of season.*

★★Serenella, Via 42 Martiri 5, Feriolo, t 0323 28112 (*moderate*). Serves delicious home-made pasta and risottos, and has a good selection of fresh lake fish or meat; has a summer garden. A few rooms are also available. *Closed Wed, Jan and Feb.*

★★Elvezia, Via Monte Grappa 15, t 0323 924 106, www.elveziahotel.com (*moderate*). The charming Monica and Marco run this bright hotel up by the church, with a little garden and a place to park. Please note that the restaurant is 700m from the hotel. *Open April–Oct.*

philosopher Antonio Rosmini (d. 1855); besides the gardens, there's a small museum on Rosmini's life and works (t 0323 30091; open 9–12 and 3–6; donation requested).

From Stresa you can ascend **Monte Mottarone** (4,920ft/1,500m), via the cable car, beginning at Piazzale Lido in Carciano di Stresa (t 0323 30295, www.stresa-mottarone.it; open 9.30–12.30 and 1.30–5.50 (last descent); every 20mins; round trip €13 adult, €7.50 aged 4–12). The views are famous, on a clear day taking in not only all seven major Italian lakes, but also glacier-crested peaks from Monviso (far west) and Monte Rosa over to the eastern ranges of Ortles and Adamello, as well as much of the Lombard plain. If you drive, walk or take the bus from Stresa, you can also stop and play golf at **Vezzo**; or visit the Alpine rock gardens of the **Giardino Alpinia** (t 0323 31308; open April–mid-Oct Tues–Sat 9–6), with more than 500 species of plants and

The World's Biggest Saint

Charles Borromeo, son of Count Gilbert Borromeo and a Medici mum, was the most influential churchman of his day, appointed 'Cardinal Nephew and Archbishop of Milan' at the age of 22 by his maternal uncle, Pope Pius IV. In Rome he was a powerful voice calling for disciplinary reform within the Church, and he instigated the Council of Trent, that decade-long Counter-Reformation strategy session in which he played a major role. There was one legendary point in Trent when the cardinals wanted to ban all church music, which by the 16th century had degenerated to the point of singing lewd love ballads to accompany the *Te Deum*. Charles and his committee, however, decided to let the musicians have one more chance, and asked Palestrina to compose three suitable Masses that reflected the dignity of the words of the service (and Charles reputedly told the composer that the cardinals expected him to fail). To their surprise, and to the everlasting benefit of Western culture, Palestrina succeeded, and sacred music was saved.

After the death of his uncle-pope, Charles went to live in his diocese of Milan, the first archbishop to do so in 80 years. Following the codex of the Council of Trent to the letter (that's the book under the arm of the San Carlone statue), he at once began reforming the once-cosy clergy to set the example for other bishops. The Milanese weren't exactly thrilled: Charles escaped an assassination attempt in the cathedral, when the bullet bounced off his brocade vestments. He was a bitter enemy of original thought and not someone you would want to have over for dinner; if New York has a Statue of Liberty, Arona has a Statue of Tyranny. For a queer sensation walk up the steps through his hollow viscera (access for people aged 8+ only, due to its steep steps): his head can hold six people, who can peer out of his eyes, each a foot and a half wide. The plastic doodahs in the souvenir shop below are a trip in themselves.

flowers; or visit **Gignese**, where the **Museo dell'Ombrello** (*Via Golf Panorama 2, t 0323 208 064, www.gignese.it/museo; open April–Sept, Tues–Sun 10–12 and 3–6; adm*) recalls the history and making of umbrellas and parasols, a traditional industry in the Colle Vergante. Once you reach the confines of the **Parco del Mottarone** and the Strada Panoramica La Borromea, you'll have to pay the toll (*€4.50 for cars, €2.50 for motorcycles*).

Baveno

Known for its quarries (source of the pink stone in Milan's Galleria Vittorio Emanuele and the Basilica of St Paul's in Rome, while the black and white was used for the Columbus monument in New York's Columbus Circle), Baveno first made the society pages in 1879, when Queen Victoria spent a summer at the Villa Clara, now Castello Branca; Wagner spent a holiday here, and Umberto Giordano composed his opera *Fedora* – the only one that features bicycles on stage – in his Villa Fedora. In the centre of Baveno, the 11th-century church of **Santi Gervasio e Protasio** has retained its original plain square façade (note the Roman inscriptions on the ancient blocks reused in the front) even though the interior was redone in the 18th century; the charming little octagonal baptistry adjacent dates from the 5th century. A pretty road leads up **Monte Camoscio**, behind Baveno.

The Borromean Islands

Lake Maggiore became a private fief of the Borromei in the 1470s, and to this day they own some of the finest bits, including the sumptuous gardens and villas of the Borromean Islands. The three main islands have restaurants, albeit satisfactory ones, if you want to make a day of it.

The closest island to Stresa, **Isola Bella** (*t 0323 30556; open end Mar–end Oct daily 9–5.30; adm exp*) was a scattering of barren rocks until the 17th century, when Count Carlo III Borromeo decided to make it a garden in the form of a ship for his wife Isabella (hence the name Isola Bella). Architect Angelo Crivelli was put in charge of designing this pretty present, and arranged it in ten terraces to form a pyramid-shaped 'poop deck', to create the kind of architectural perspectives beloved by Baroque theatre. The project was continued by Vitaliano VI Borromeo (d. 1670), who added the palace and grottoes but left it unfinished at his death. The Borromei completed the **palace** according to the original plans between 1948 and 1959 and left it a fine collection of art, with works by Annibale Carracci, Luca Giordano, Pannini, Zuccarelli, Cerano, Giambattista Tiepolo and a certain Pietro Mulier, or 'Il Tempesta' (d. 1701), who in spite of his stormy nickname was a long-time guest of the family. The room in which Napoleon slept in August 1797 is done up in the Directory style in his honour, while the music room, with its antique instruments, hosted the 1935 Stresa Conference, where Italy, Britain and France tried to decide what to do in the face of Hitler's rearmament – a sad sequel to the hopeful pact signed at Locarno ten years earlier – and ended up doing nothing, because France and Britain refused to recognize Mussolini's conquest of Ethiopia. A stair leads down to the six artificial grottoes right on the lake, covered all over with shells and pebbles – the effect is curiously confectionery-like – while the Tapestry Gallery has six 16th-century Flemish tapestries featuring the favourite Borromeo family emblem, the unicorn, who also holds pride of place in the gardens. Stendhal wrote that the panorama from the top

Getting There

There is a frequent boat service that runs from Stresa, Baveno, Pallanza and Laveno to the islands. Alternatively, you may prefer to hire a boat and row there under your own steam (ask at any of the tourist offices on the mainland).

Tourist Information

Isola Bella: t 0323 30556. *Offers guided tours daily; open mid-Mar–end Oct daily 9–5.30; adm.*
Isola Madre: t 0323 31261. *Open mid-Mar–end Oct daily 9–5.30; adm. For further info visit www.borromeoturismo.it.*

Where to Stay

Borromean Islands ✉ 28838
★★★**Verbano**, Isola dei Pescatori, t 0323 30408, (*very expensive*). A chance to see the island after most have left, with a restaurant, where romantic views compensate for average food. *Closed Jan–Feb.*
Ristorante Belvedere, Via di Mezzo, Isola Pescatori, t 0323 32292 (*inexpensive*). On the opposite side of the isle. *Open mid-Mar–beginning of Nov. Closed Nov–mid-Mar.*
Delfino, on Isola Bella, t 0323 30473, and **La Piratera**, on Isola Madre, t 0323 31171 (*both moderate*). Expect more of the views than the food at these island restaurants. *Closed Nov–Feb.*

is 'equal to the Bay of Naples, and speaks even more directly to the heart. It seems to me that these islands waken the emotions even more than St Peter's...'

The Borromei opened the delightful, larger **Isola Madre**, (*t 0323 31261; open end Mar–Oct 9–5.30, adm exp, joint adm with Isola Bella; (see box, p.164)*); to the public in 1978. Here they planted a colourful and luxuriant botanical garden, dominated by Europe's largest Kashmir cypress; its camellias begin to bloom in January (be sure to pick up the free guide to the plants). On its best days few places are more conducive to a state of perfect languor, at least until one of the isle's bold pheasants, peacocks or parrots tries to stare you out. The 16th-century villa has a collection of 18th- and 19th-century puppet theatres, marionettes, portraits and furnishings.

The third island, **Isola dei Pescatori**, is home to an almost too quaint and picturesque fishing village, and another private islet called **San Giovanni** is just off the shore at Pallanza, with a villa once owned by Toscanini.

Verbania and Maggiore's Northwest Shore

In 1994 the shore of Lake Maggiore, feeling rather neglected by the distant provincial capital Novara, became a province of its own, named for its capital, Verbania.

Verbania: Pallanza and Intra

From Baveno the shore road circles over to the north side of the Borromean bay, with fine views of the islands all the way to **Pallanza**, a resort with a famously mild winter climate. In 1939 Pallanza was united with the neighbouring towns of Suna and Intra and christened Verbania as part of Mussolini's campaign to revive old Roman names. Each town, however, retains its own identity. Pallanza, the prettiest, has several man-made attractions, especially the Renaissance **Madonna di Campagna** on the edge of town, up Viale Azari. Inspired by Bramante, the church has a curious gazebo-like arcaded drum and a Romanesque campanile, inherited from its predecessor; the lavishly decorated interior includes good 15th-century frescoes by Gerolamo Lanino (*St Bernardo*). In the centre of Pallanza the 16th-century Palazzo Dugnani houses the **Museo del Paesaggio** (*Via Ruga 44, t 0323 556 621; open April–Oct, Tues–Sun 10–12 and 3.30–6.30; adm*) with a collection of 19th- and 20th-century landscapes of Lake Maggiore and the vicinity: realistic and documentary; romantic and Impressionistic; plus landscapes with a social conscience, as in *The Diggers* (1890) by Arnaldo Ferraguti. Other rooms contain plaster casts and sculptures by Giulio Branca from Cannobio, Paolo Troubetzkoy, born in Intra of noble Russian parents (d. 1938), and Arturo Martini (d. 1947). There is also a special section dedicated to religious artefacts with over 5,000 *ex votos*, in **Palazzo Biumi Innocenti**, Salita Biumi (*same opening times as Museo del Paesaggio but open all year; adm*).

The glory of greater Verbania is the **Villa Taranto** (*t 0323 556 667, www.villataranto.it; open end Mar–Oct 8.30–6.30, until 5 in Oct; adm*), built on the Castagnola promontory between Pallanza and Intra by a certain Count Orsetti in 1875. In 1931 the derelict villa was purchased by a Scots captain, Neil McEacharn, who had one of the world's

Tourist Information

Pallanza: Corso Zanitello 8, **t** 0323 503 249, *www.verbania-turismo.it*. There are also two seasonal tourist office stands at the steamer landings at Intra and Pallanza.

Pallanza Proloco, Piazza IV, **t** 0323 504 448.

Ghiffa Pro Loco, Via Belvedere, **t** 0323 59428, *www.comune.ghiffa.vb.it*.

Cannero Riviera Pro Loco, Via Roma 37, **t** 0323 788 943, *www.cannero.it*.

Cannobio Pro Loco, Viale Vittorio Veneto 4, **t** 0323 71212, *www.cannobio.net*.

Markets

Verbania: Large market. *Sat.*

Cannobio: Bustling market on the lake front. *Sun.*

Where to Stay and Eat

Verbania-Pallanza ✉ 28922

****Majestic, Via Vittorio Veneto 32, **t** 0323 504 305, *www.grandhotelmajestic.it* (*very expensive*). Right on the lake, a comfortable grand old hotel endowed with a good restaurant and plenty of amenities – indoor pool, tennis, park and private beach. Suites nos. 4 and 6 are beautifully positioned with a corner terrace overlooking the lake and the private Isolino San Giovanni, another property of the Borromei family. A new state-of-the-art spa opened in summer 2005. *Open April–Oct.*

***Intra, Corso Mameli 133, Intra, **t** 0323 581 393 (*expensive*). Lake-front hotel in the city centre. A good choice for the price with a panoramic roof restaurant.

***Pace, Via Cietti 1, **t** 0323 557 207, *www.hotel pace.it* (*expensive–moderate*). Offers excellent value, with modern rooms and old-style writing desks.

*Meublé Villa Tilde, Via Vittorio Veneto 63, **t** 0323 503 805 (*moderate*). An old lake-front villa. Enjoys a quiet and lovely position.

***Belvedere, Viale Magnolie 6, **t** 0323 503 202, *www.hotels-belvedere-pallanza.com* (*moderate*). A good hotel for the price range, located near the steamer landing, although the rooms are a bit impersonal and some of them need refurbishing. *Open seasonally.*

Ostello Internazionale Villa Congreve, Viale Rose 7, **t** 0323 501 648 (*inexpensive*). Pallanza's nice youth hostel is in a villa up on the road to the botanical gardens of Villa Taranto. An AIG (Italian Youth Hotel Association) card is compulsory for booking. *Open mid-Mar–Oct.*

Milano, Corso Zanitello 2, **t** 0323 556 816 (*very expensive*). The best place to eat in Pallanza and located in a fine old lake-front villa, with dining out on the terrace for a very romantic evening. *Closed Tues, Mon eves, and Jan–mid-Feb.*

Osteria dell'Angolo, Piazza Garibaldi 35, **t** 0323 556 362 (*expensive*). Also on the lake front, with lovely food – *crespelle* (little crepes) stuffed with *scamorza* cheese, and various risottos (the latter needs to be booked in advance). *Closed Mon and Wed, Nov, Dec. Booking advisable.*

Boccon di Vino, Via Troubetzkoy 86, **t** 0323 504 039 (*moderate*). A family-run place near the *imbarcadero* at Suna with good-value food and wine. Try the home-made pasta or roast and casseroled meats. *Closed Sun, lunch times and Aug.*

Osteria del Castello, Piazza Castello 9, **t** 0323 516 579. A sociable meeting and drinking place to start (or indeed to end) the evening in Intra. *Closed Sun in winter.*

La Tavernetta, Via San Vittore 22, Intra, **t** 0323 402 635. Pub with a nice vaulted room and inner patio. *Closed Tues and Nov.*

Ghiffa ✉ 28823

***Ghiffa, Corso Belvedere 88, **t** 0323 59285, *www.hotelghiffa.com* (*very expensive*). On Ghiffa's main road, on the lake, this hotel is run by Mr Cattaneo and his French wife, and mantains the charm of its aristocratic past in the sunny dining room with huge windows overlooking the lake and the big staircase. Rooms are modern, except room 114, which has been renovated in style. Ask for a lake-front room with terrace, but be prepared to pay a little extra. Nice garden, swimming pool and private beach. The restaurant serves local specialities and has a set-price menu.

*Park Paradiso, Via G. Marconi 20, **t** 0323 59548 (*very expensive–expensive*). A grand old hotel also situated above Ghiffa. Set in a lush terraced garden with beautiful views of the lake, it has plenty of faded 19th-century character in the public areas, but not in the rooms. The dining room still has its original Liberty decor and furniture. Partially covered pool. No credit cards. *Closed Nov–Feb.*

**Castello di Frino, Via Cristoforo Colombo 8, Frino, t 0323 59181, *www.castellodifrino.com* (*expensive–moderate*). A 15th-century hotel situated above Ghiffa with 14 rooms in the main building and some cheaper rooms in an annexe in the garden; with a pool and tennis courts. Although the hotel still has aristocratic charm, it lacks proper maintenance and needs restoration.

Cannero Riviera ✉ 28821

****Cannero, Lungolago 2, t 0323 788 046, *www.hotelcannero.com* (*very expensive*). Balconies overlooking the lake, a swimming pool, better than average food in the restaurant, and a garage. The hotel is building a lakeside annexe which looks promising, with three-sided views of the lake, beautiful small suites and a ground-floor multilingual library. Free boats and bikes for the guests; motorboats for hire. Minimum stay three days. *Open mid-Mar–Nov.*

*Miralago, Via Dante 41, t 0323 788 282 (*moderate–inexpensive*). Much simpler, with views; the bathrooms and showers are down the hall. *Open Mar–Nov.*

Ca' Bianca, Via Casali Ca'Bianca, north of Cannero, t 0323 788 038 (*moderate*). A fine place to linger over a plate of pasta, meat or fish or a Sunday lunch, as it has a nice garden terrace overlooking the ruins of the castle and the islet.

Europa, is nearby on the Lungolago, Viale delle Magnolie 51, t 0323 788 292 (*moderate*). Get there early for a table right on the water. *Closed Thurs out of season.*

*Sano Banano, Via Marconi 30, t 0323 788 184 (*inexpensive*). For a young ambience, try this city centre place. Traditional fare at the *trattoria*, or a beer at the boat-shaped counter. It has double rooms (recently renovated) at a modest price.

Cannobio ✉ 28822

***Pironi, Via Marconi 35, t 0323 70624, *www.pironihotel.it* (*expensive*). This unusual hotel occupies a frescoed 15th-century palace in the historic centre shaped like the Flatiron building in New York. The rooms are all different in shape and are individually furnished, all have *frigo* bars, and a handful of the top-floor ones enjoy a lake view. You can book room 12 for a romantic frescoed balcony all to yourself. *Open mid-Mar–beginning of Nov.*

***Il Portico, Piazza Santuario 2, t 0323 70598 (*expensive–moderate*). Situated under the porticoes by the lake; this is another classy if more staid choice. The hotel has an annexe in a 17th-century villa behind the main building. The rooms all have modern bathrooms and decor in style – there is no lake view but they overlook a quiet courtyard and the city's bell tower. *Open Mar–Oct.*

**Antica Stallera, Via Paolo Zaccheo 9, t 0323 71595, *www.anticastallera.com* (*expensive–moderate*). The renovated rooms are nice and comfortable though the main halls have lost some of their character. The hotel, in the city centre, remains quiet, with a nice, if pricey, restaurant in the courtyard. near the lake. Dogs require an extra daily fee. Two of the rooms are suitable for wheelchair users.

Del Lago, Via Nazionale 2, Carmine, t 0323 70595, *www.enotecalago.com* (*expensive*). One of the area's best restaurants. Try the risotto with saffron, zucchini and mussels, turbot with caviar, or duck breast with honey-roasted sesame seeds. *Closed Tues and Wed lunch, and Nov–Mar. Booking strongly advised.*

Lo Scalo, Piazza Vittorio Emanuele III 32, t 0323 71480 (*expensive*). Has a pretty porticoed terrace on the lake, and serves traditional Piedmontese recipes, along with more original dishes such as black lasagna stuffed with scallops, pesto and French green beans, or rabbit cooked in Vernaccia and chestnut honey on a little *tarte* of potatoes and foie gras. Over 250 wines to choose from and a good selection of *grappas*. Four-course dinner menu at lunch time. *Closed Mon, Tues lunch time out of season, and Jan–mid-Feb, 2 weeks in Nov.*

Osteria La Streccia, Vicolo Merzagora 5, t 0323 70575 (*moderate*). Has good-value menus. *Closed Thurs and 2 weeks in Jan, 10 days in July.*

greenest thumbs and pockets deep enough to afford to import exotic plants from the tropics to the tune of some 20,000 varieties, planted over 20 hectares. The aquatic plants, including giant Amazonian water lilies and lotus blossoms, the spring tulips and the autumn colour are exceptional, as are some of the rarer species – the handkerchief tree, bottle bush and copper-coloured Japanese maple. MacEacharn left his masterpiece to the Italian state; the villa is occasionally used by the Italian prime minister for special conferences. The tourist office organizes guided tours to the park of **Villa San Remigi** , which includes a visit to the bombonnière Romanesque church (*t 0323 503 249; open weekend mornings, May–June, by reservation; adm*). You may visit other private villas' parks in the 'Open Gardens' week in September (*contact the tourist office for details*).

Intra is Verbania's industrial and business quarter, with a ferry across to Laveno; on the wall of the Casa di Comune note the almost unbelievable flood mark (3 Oct 1860). Buses from near the ferry landing serve the quiet, woodsy holiday towns in the hinterland: **Arizzano**, **Bèe** and most importantly **Premeno**, a mountain resort overlooking Maggiore and the Alps, with skiing in the winter and a beautiful golf course. In 1950 some 4th-century AD Roman tombs were discovered by Premeno's **Oratorio di San Salvatore**. The bus continues up to **Pian Cavallo** (4,102ft/1,250m), with views almost as good as those from Mottarone.

Back on the lake, north of Intra, **Ghiffa** is pleasant and quiet, with a waterside promenade. Uncover the history of felt hats in the old Panizza & Co. hat factory, Italy's most renowned brand after Borsalino, now the **Museo del Cappello** (*Corso Belvedere 279, t 0323 59209, call to visit in other periods; open April–Oct Sat–Sun 3.30–5.30*). The museum's collection displays hats dating back to the Renaissance period as well as Panizza's farm tools and machinery. Up in Ghiffa's suburb of Ronco lies the **Sacro Monte SS. Trinità**, another late 17th-century Counter-Reformation devotional trip (*see* p.147) although here only three chapels were ever finished, dedicated to the Coronation of the Virgin, St John the Baptist and Abraham. Further north, **Cannero Riviera** is a quiet resort with a mild climate, set amid glossy green citrus groves. It faces two intensely picturesque islets, former strongholds of the five brothers Mazzarditi, fierce pirates defeated in 1414 by Filippo Maria Visconti. He razed the castles, and on their ruins Lodovico Borromeo built another tower and castle (1521). They seem to rise straight out of the water; in the twilight mists they could easily be the enchanted towers of the Lady of the Lake.

Cannobio and the Val Cannobina

Cannobio is an ancient town with steep, medieval streets, and a monument honouring local genius, Giovanni Branca (d. 1645), inventor of the steam turbine. Cannobio's churches adhere to the Milanese Ambrosian Rite, revived by Charles Borromeo in an effort to promote local pride. Much of this local religious fervour is concentrated by the lake in the Bramante-inspired **Santuario della Pietà**, built to house a miraculous painting on parchment of the *Dead Christ with the Virgin and St John* ; the altarpiece by Gaudenzio Ferrari of *Christ Meeting the Three Marys on the Road to Calvary* is one of his finest.

Buses from Cannobio plunge up the wild, sparsely populated **Val Cannobina**, which rises up to meet the Val Vigezzo and Domodossola. Just 2km from Cannobio you can hire a boat to visit the dramatic **Orrido di Sant'Anna**, a deep, narrow gorge carved by the Cannobio river and waterfall. Further up the valley lies a cluster of wee hamlets of stone houses, known collectively as **Cavaglio-Spoccia**, where the valley's first road, the Via Borromeo, crosses old mossy bridges. **Falmenta**, a tiny village on the other side of the valley, has among its quaint black stone houses a 1565 parish church with a rare wooden altarpiece, crowded with small figures, from the 1300s. The next village, **Gurro**, has retained its medieval centre and keeps alive its folk traditions, with a little **Museo Comunale** of local customs and produce (*Piazza della Chinese*, *t* 0323 76100; *open 9–12 and 2–6; adm*). **Orasso** has a 13th-century Visitazione church, and another finely carved wooden altarpiece in the 15th-century parish church, San Materno.

Swiss Lake Maggiore

The northern tip of the Big Lake is in the Italian-speaking Swiss Canton Ticino, where it is highly prized as the national suntrap.

Brissago and its Islands

Switzerland begins just north of Cannobio and the first place of any importance is bustling **Brissago**, a town that has rolled its own since 1846. The cigar factory is open for tours; among the other sights is a remarkable 600-year-old **cypress** growing next to the church of SS. Pietro e Paolo, and a beautiful Tuscan-Lombard church, the **Madonna di Ponte** (mid-1500s), with a porticoed dome, which was inspired by the designs of Bramantino. From **Porto Ronco** (the lowest town in Switzerland, a mere 643ft/196m above sea level) boats sail to the **Isole Brissago** (*t* 091 791 4361, *www. isolebrissago.ch*). The little one, Santa Apollinaire, has the ruins of a Romanesque church, while larger San Pancrazio is covered with a splendid exotic garden, the **Parco Botanico del Cantone Ticino** (*open Mar–Oct 9–6; adm*), with 1,500 species of flora mostly from the southern hemisphere, created in 1883 by the Baroness Antoinette de Saint-Léger. The island's villa has a museum of African ethnography. For striking lake and mountain views you can continue along the shore: aim for **Ronco sopra Ascona**, 'the Balcony of Lake Maggiore'.

Ascona and the Mountain of Truth

On its sunny bay, **Ascona** rivals Stresa as Lake Maggiore's culture queen, counting the likes of Thomas Mann, Jung, Freud, Gropius, Klee and Kandinsky among its sojourners. Before the artists and literati it was favoured by the pope: Gregory XIII and Charles Borromeo founded a **Collegio Pontificio** here in 1584, in a fine building designed by Pelligrino Tibaldi (now a private school); the adjacent, older church, **Santa Maria della Misericordia**, has frescoes, a lovely painted casement ceiling and a polyptych of the *Madonna della Quercia* (1519) sent from Viterbo by the pope.

The tourist office occupies the Baroque **Casa Serodine** (1620), belonging to the Serodine family of painters. One, Giovanni Battista, contributed the elaborate stucco decorations, while the most famous, Giovanni Serodine, a pupil of Caravaggio, painted three canvases in **Santi Pietro e Paolo**. The **Museo Comunale d'Arte Moderna** (*Via Borgo 34,* **t** *091 780 5100; open Mar–Dec Tues–Sat 10–12 and 3–6, Sun 4–6; adm*), located in a late 16th-century palace, has frequent exhibits and a permanent collection of works by artists connected with Ascona (especially by the Russian Marianne von Werefkin, who died here, destitute) and others by Richter, Nicholson, Arp and Jawlensky to name a few.

In the late 19th century a group of artists, free thinkers, poets, anarchists, modern dancers, naturists and spiritualists, disillusioned with modern industrial society and longing to return to nature, founded a utopian vegetarian nudist commune on the promontory above Ascona that they called Monte Verità, 'the Mountain of Truth'. You can learn all about them and their 'air-light' wooden architecture in the **Percorso Museale del Monte Verità** (**t** *091 785 4040, www.monteverita.org; open April–June, Sept and Oct Tues–Sun 2.30–6; July–Aug Tues–Sun 3–7; adm*), which includes the Casa Anatta (1902), 'Switzerland's most original wooden house'; the Casa Selma, a typical residence for members, inhabited until the 1940s; and, on the site of the original solarium, a round pavilion built in 1986 to house a vast circular *Chiaro Mondo dei Beati* (1923), the 'bright world of the blessed', a vision of the ideal world painted by member Elisar von Kupffer.

Locarno

Cross the River Maggio from Ascona and you're in Locarno, the town of camellias. Once part of the Lombard duchy of Angera, and ruled by the Visconti until 1513, the town earned its international cachet in 1925 with the Treaty of Locarno, that noble attempt to create a lasting peace in Europe by fixing borders, lightening the harsh terms imposed on Germany by the Treaty of Versailles and admitting Germany into the League of Nations. Since the end of the war the treaty failed to prevent, Locarno has devoted itself to pleasure: open-air concerts and an international film festival (*see* box, p.172) take place in the city's big heart, the porticoed **Piazza Grande**; from here Largo Zorzi passes the **Casino-Kursaal** (**t** *091 756 3030, www.casinolocarno.ch; daily noon till 3am, Fri and Sat till 4am*) en route to the lake. The lake promenade, or Giardini di Muralto, is lined with beautiful rare trees, so many that the tourist office distributes a map to let you identify them as you stroll along.

Just up from Piazza Grande, the **Castello Visconteo** (*Piazza Castello 2,* **t** *091 756 3170; open April–Oct Tues–Fri 10–12 and 2–5, Sat–Sun 10–5; adm*) has well-preserved ceilings and frescoes from the 15th century. The castle houses the **Museo Civico e Archeologico**, with a collection of ancient Roman glass, ceramics from *Magna Graecia* and some good early medieval reliefs; on the second floor exhibits relate to the 1925 treaty. Admission includes the adjacent 16th-century palace, the ornately stuccoed **Casorella**, with a fine loggia and court and an enormous 18th-century *Judgement of*

Getting There and Around

Locarno is linked to Domodossola by the scenic narrow-gauge Vigezzina **train**, t 4193 336 564 (*see* p.156), while all the port towns are served by the Italian Navigazione di Lago Maggiore, t 004191 751 6140 (local), *www. navigazionelaghi.it* and the clean and never smelly Swiss FART buses, t 004191 756 04003. For Swiss rail journeys, go to *www.sbb.ch*.

Tourist Information

Ascona: Casa Serodine, t 004191 791 0090, *www.ascona.ch*. The Ascona tourist office organizes guided cultural itineraries of the city from March to November. *Open Mar–Oct Mon–Fri 9–6, Sat 10–4; Nov–Mar Mon–Fri 9–12 and 1–5.30.*

Locarno: Largo Zorzi 1, t 004191 751 0333, *www.locarno.ch*. You can also contact **Ente Turistico Lago Maggiore**, Via Luini 3, t 004191 791 0091, *www.maggiore.ch*.

Other useful sites: *www.ticino-tourism.ch*, for general info on the Ticino area and *www. ticino-gastronomico.ch* for restaurants.

Festivals

Camellia Festival, *end of March*. Brissago.
Leoncavallo Festival of Classical Music, *May*. Brissago.
New Orleans Jazz Music Festival, *late June–early July*. Ascona, *www.jazzascona.ch*.
Ticino Musica, *July*. Classical music master-classes, in Ascona and Locarno.
International Film Festival, *beginning of August*. Locarno, *www.pardo.it*.

Laughter Festival, *end of September*. Locarno, *www.festivaldellarisata.ch*.
Settimane Musicali di Ascona, *end Aug–mid-Oct*. Classical music festival, Ascona.

Sports and Activities

The **Museo Comico**, (*open Mar–Nov 5pm–12pm on performance days; other days on request; adm*) in Verscio, 5km from Locarno, Centovalli direction, t 004191 796 2544, *www.teatro dimtri.ch*, is dedicated to comic art and was created by Clown Dimitri in cooperation with Harald Szeemann. There are **golf courses** in Ascona (Golf Club Patriziale, t 004191 791 2132, *www.golf.ascona.ch*), Locarno (Locarno Driving Range, t 004191 752 3353, *www.golflocarno.ch*), and a new one in Losone Gerre, t 004191 785 1090, *www.golflosone.ch*). There is **rowing** at Club Canottieri in Locarno, t 0041 751 2997; **parachuting** or **paragliding**, Club Parapendio, Locarno, t 004191 791 4412; **archery**, Arcieri Club, Locarno, t 004191 751 2502; and several centres for **sailing** in Ascona, Brissago and Locarno. For **canoeing** and **bungee jumping** contact FART, in Locarno, t 004191 756 0400. The tourist information has itineraries for bike tours. **Bikes** can be rented at the main railway stations and from bike shops.

Where to Stay and Eat

Ascona ✉ CH6612, t (004191–)
★★★★Castello del Sole, Via Muraccio 142, t 791 0202, *www.castellodelsole.com* (*luxury*). Situated outside the city centre on the delta

Paris by local painter Giuseppe Orelli. Jean Arp donated many of his own works and those of his friends to the **Pinacoteca Comunale Casa Rusca** (*Piazza S. Antonio*, t 004191 756 3185; *open Tues–Sun 10–12 and 2–5; adm*), site of frequent summer exhibitions. Near the train station for Basle in Locarno Muralto, the frescoed crypt of the 11th-century **San Vittore** has survived successive remodellings; look for the 15th-century relief of St Victor on horseback incorporated in the campanile.

From Locarno a rope railway ascends 1,200ft (366m) to the **Santuario della Madonna del Sasso**, founded in 1497 after an apparition of the Virgin; walking up from town, however, allows you to visit the frescoed chapels of yet another 17th-century Sacro Monte. The sunflower-yellow sanctuary itself has the big art, however: a beautiful 14th-century *Pietà*, a *Flight into Egypt* by Bramantino and a *Removal of the*

of the river Maggia, amid vineyards and orchards, this splendid Relais & Châteaux hotel has all modern amenities including a swimming pool, fitness and beauty centre with solarium, sauna, tennis courts, a putting green for golf, and a private beach on Lake Maggiore. Special fitness, golf, and painting all-inclusive weeks. In the courtyard its restaurant, the **Locanda Barbarossa**, serves delicious food, including produce and poultry fresh from the farm. *Open mid-Mar–Oct.*

★★★Tamaro, Piazza G. Motta 35, **t** 791 0282, *www.hotel-tamaro.ch* (*luxury*). A charming choice on the lake in the city centre; family hospitality, good taste and attention to detail in a traditional inn. Nice restaurant in the cloister, with special children's menu or Cajun dishes during the jazz festival, music and reading room, lake-front rooms with balconies and quiet rooms overlooking a flowery inner court.

★★★★Castello Seeschloss, **t** 791 0161, *www.castello-seeschloss.ch* (*luxury–very expensive; prices go up for lake-front rooms and rooms in the tower*). One of the crenellated, vine-covered towers of the 13th-century Castle Ghiriglioni is now a hotel; central, with a lakeside garden with tall palms, pool and wine bar.

Monte Verità Hotel (Restaurant), **t** 791 4939, *www.monteverita.org* (*expensive*). One of the first modernist buildings in Switzerland and situated in the middle of the park, this restaurant reeks with atmosphere and has fine view from its veranda; the food is good too. *Closed Sun out of season.*

Locarno ☒ CH6601, **t** (004191–)

★★★★Reber au Lac, Viale Verbano 55, **t** 735 8700, *www.hotel-reber.ch* (*luxury*). A very comfortable, traditional hotel in the Locarno Nuralto area which welcomes children; private beach, swimming pool, tennis and an excellent restaurant and grill room. It offers special weekly arrangements both in high and low seasons. *Closed Nov–Mar.*

★★★★Grand Hotel, Via Sempione 17, **t** 743 0282, *www.grand-hotel-locarno.ch* (*very expensive*). A lovely turn-of-the-last-century hotel, with a pool, tennis, pretty garden and every other amenity. The signatories of the Treaty of Locarno stayed here. Special weekly rates. *Closed mid-Nov–mid-Mar.*

★★★Dell'Angelo, Piazza Grande, **t** 751 8175, *www.hotel-dell-angelo.ch* (*moderate*). Comfortable renovated rooms and pretty views from the roof terrace, and a decent restaurant pizzeria.

Ostello Giaciglio, Via Rusca 7, Garni Sempione area, **t** 751 3064 (*inexpensive*). Spartan rooms for 4, 6, and 8 people, and communal bathroom.

Centenario, Lungolago Motta 17, **t** 743 8222 (*very expensive*). One of Switzerland's top gourmet shrines. Chef Gerard Perriard buys the finest ingredients from across Europe and works culinary magic on everything he touches: Irish salmon marinated in red pepper, lobster and *gazpacho*, for instance. Sublime cheese trolley, desserts and wine; there is a more affordable menu, or celebrate with the pricier option. *Book a few days in advance. Closed Sun and Mon, 3 weeks in Feb, 3 weeks in July.*

Body of Christ, by local painter Antonio Ciseri. The recently renovated cable car and chairlift of Orselina-Cardada-Cimetta (**t** *41 91 735 3030, www.cardada.ch*), is in operation to carry you up to **Cimetta** (5,600ft/1,707m) for a fabulous view of the lake and Alps.

Continue east around Lake Maggiore for **Tenero**, a small resort (it has lovely camp sites, right on the lake) that claims the mildest climate in Switzerland and makes a decent Merlot wine from its surrounding vineyards; one small *cantine*, the Fratelli Matasci, runs a little wine museum. South of Tenero the **Bolle di Magadino**, or River Ticino delta, is a favourite stopover for migratory birds; it forms part of the **Riviera del Gambarogno**, dotted with fishing villages down to the Italian frontier.

Down the East Shore of Lake Maggiore

Recrossing the frontier into Italy at Maccagno and continuing down Maggiore's eastern, or Lombard, shore, cliffs hem in the lake and towns are fewer and more peaceful; the monastery of Santa Caterina del Sasso and Borromeo castle of Angera are the highlights.

Maccagno to Laveno-Mombello

Maccagno is a quiet haven, with only a crenellated tower to recall its glory days when it was the capital of an independent county, created in 962 by Emperor Otto I as a gift for the Mandelli brothers, who helped him in his war against King Berenguer II

Tourist Information

Maccagno: Via Garibaldi 1, **t** 0332 562 009, *www.prolocomaccagno.it*.
Luino IAT: Via Piero Chiara, **t** 0332 530 019, *www.comune.luino.va.it*. For Luino train station, ring **t** 0332 530 135.
Laveno-Mombello: Piazza Italia 2, **t** 0332 666 666, *www.laveno-online.it* or *www.prolocolavenomombello.com*. For local info on shopping, tourism, services, events.

Markets

Luino: holds one of Europe's biggest markets, selling anything from food to clothes. *Wed.*

Sports and Activities

The Palio Remiero (end of June, July), a **rowing** race between the city's boroughs, is the focal point for a weekend of events. If you are in Laveno Mobello around Christmas try not to miss the 20-year-old Christmas Eve tradition of placing the **nativity** crib at the bottom of the city-centre lake. The huge statues made of Vicentine rock remain there, lit underwater, until the end of the festivities.

There are four **golf** courses in the area: Bogogno, 36 holes (**t** 0322 863 794/5, *www.golfbogogno.com*), designed by US architect Robert Von Hagge, in Bogogno, with views over Monte Rosa; Castelconturbia, 27 holes (**t** 0322 832 093, *www.castelconturbia.it*), in Agrate Conturbia is considered one of the most beautiful in Europe as it is surrounded by century-old woods and mountains; Dei Laghi, 18 holes (**t** 0332 978 101, *www.golf*

deilaghi.it), in Travedona Monate, one of the most interesting new golf courses to come on the Italian scene; Varese, 18 holes (**t** 0332 229 302, *www.golfclubvarese.it*), in Luvinate, with a splendid clubhouse located in a 12th-century Benedictine monastery. For **sailing**: Centro Vela, Cerro di Laveno, **t** 0332 626 462, courses and rental; Club Velico Est Verbano, **t** 0332 667 588, or Top Vela, **t** 0332 666 625, *www.top vela.org*, both for courses, in Laveno Mombello; for **windsurfing** rental and courses, try Scuola Mistral-Surf Mistral, in Pino Lago Maggiore, Darsena hamlet, **t** 0332 566 492, or Tronzano Fun Centre, **t** 0332 566 331, in Tronzano Lago Maggiore, both north of Luino. Icaroo 2000, **t** 0332 626 212, *www.icaro2000.com*, in Laveno, offers **paragliding** from Sasso del Ferro and **bike** or **mountain bike** rental as well as downhill itineraries and guided tours.

Where to Stay and Eat

Maccagno ✉ 21010

Al Pozzo, on the mountain road leading up to Lake Delio, Piazza Solera 2, Campagnano, **t** 0332 560 145 (*inexpensive*). Simple but enchanting, with spectacular views and a basic but good value menu.

Luino ✉ 21016

★★★★Camin, Viale Dante 35, **t** 0332 530 118, *www.caminhotelluino.com* (*luxury–very expensive, depending on season*). In a late 19th-century Lombard villa with its own garden. Old-fashioned big rooms, plush fittings, hydro-massage baths and twin basins in marble. Private parking. *Closed Jan.*

of Italy. The counts and their descendants remained staunchly faithful to the emperor and in return were given the right to mint their own coins; in 1542 Charles V gave them permission to hold a market on Wednesday (held to this day in nearby Luino). As time went by, however, competition with the big lords of the lake, the Borromei, made the county too expensive to maintain, and in 1692 the Mandellis finally gave in and sold it to their rivals. Maccagno is the base for visiting the wild, woody **Val Veddasca**, with venerable alpine villages accessible only on foot: **Curiglia** is a good one to aim for. Another road from Maccagno leads up to little **Lake Delio**, a pretty retreat; legend has it that a village was swallowed up by its waters after its miserly inhabitants refused hospitality to a stranger, and that on stormy nights you can hear the bells of its submerged campanile.

*Camin Hotel Colmegna, Via A. Palazzi 1, in the nearby hamlet of Colmegna, t 0332 510 855, *www.camin-hotels.com* (*expensive–moderate*). Sister hotel to the Camin. Cheaper with simple rooms and decor, younger in atmosphere and with little apartments for families. Situated on the lake front, it has a beautiful terraced garden overlooking the lake and a nice outdoor restaurant. *Closed Dec–mid-Mar.*

***Ancora, Piazza Libertà 7, t 0332 530 451, *www.hotelancoraluino.com* (*moderate*). A bit basic, but on the lake front with fine views.

*Del Pesce, Via del Porto 16, t 0332 532 379 (*inexpensive*). Doesn't look like much from the outside, but has comfortable rooms and a good restaurant.

**Elvezia, near the station, Via XXV Aprile 107, t 0332 531 219 (*inexpensive*). Good-value, neat, clean and convenient.

***Internazionale, Piazza Marconi, t 0332 530 193, *www.hotelinternazionaleluino.com* (*inexpensive*). Modern interior, with fully equipped and good-size rooms, and parking facilities. Opposite the station.

Laveno-Mombello ✉ 21014

***Il Porticciolo, Via Fortino 40, t 0332 667 257, *www.ilporticciolo.com* (*expensive*). Right on the water with the ten nicest rooms in town along with the best restaurant (*very expensive*), serving a delicious risotto with scampi and watercress and plenty of lake fish, accompanied by an excellent wine list. *Closed Tues, Wed lunch, and last two weeks between Jan and Feb. Open Tues eves in July–Aug.*

**Funivia, at the top of the cable car in Poggio S. Elsa, t 0332 610 303 (*inexpensive*). A 2-hour walk from the town, with spectacular views of Lake Maggiore (for those wishing to build up an appetite for lunch in the restaurant). *Open in winter at weekends only.*

Ranco ✉ 21020

****Il Sole, Piazza Venezia 5, t 0331 976 507, *www.ilsolediranco.it* (*very expensive*). A superb retreat from the cares of the world; a lovely old inn surrounded by gardens with a charming terrace and one of the finest restaurants on the lake. Ask for room no.20 to see the lake through the branches of a lush magnolia. The exquisitely and imaginatively prepared lake fish and crayfish are worth the journey; they're complemented by a magnificent 1,200-label wine list and beautifully served delicate desserts. Five generations of the Brovelli family have run the inn since it opened in 1850. To celebrate its 150 years, special family recipes have been unearthed and an exclusive wine produced. Father Carlo Brovelli, former motor racer turned chef after an accident, is helped by his son Davide, a fine *patissier*. *Closed Mon lunch, and Tues in April–Oct; Mon and Tues in Nov–Mar; also closed end of Nov–mid-Feb. Booking advisable.*

***Conca Azzurra, Via Alberto 53, t 0331 976 526, *www.concaazzurra.it* (*expensive–moderate*). Ranco's other hotel enjoys a beautiful position on the lake overlooking the Alps, with a pool, a beach, tennis courts and a renowned restaurant with lake view. *Closed Jan–Feb.*

Five kilometres south, where the River Tresa drains into Lake Maggiore from Lake Lugano, is the most important town on the Lombard shore, **Luino**, a pleasant town with plane trees along the lake. Luino is the presumed birthplace of Leonardo da Vinci's chief follower Bernadino Luini, who left a fresco up at the cemetery church, the **Oratorio di Santi Pietro e Paolo**. In 1848 Garibaldi was staying in an inn in Luino, ill with malaria, when a force of 1,500 Austrians surprised him. Without even taking the time to dress, Garibaldi sprang out of bed and, holding up his drawers, took command of his troops and forced the Austrians to retreat. The mountain villages above Luino, such as **Dumenza** and **Agra**, are as unspoiled as they come; the latter enjoys a mighty view over Maggiore. On the shore to the south is a rocky pinnacle called **Sass Galet**, which looks like a praying nun, although it's supposed to be a chicken.

Laveno-Mombello, the ferry terminus from Intra, was known until 1980 for its ceramics, and the good old days of plates (i.e. 1895–1960) are remembered in the **Museo Internazionale Design Ceremico** (*Via Lungolago Perabo 5, in Cerro, t 0332 666 530; open Sept–Jun Tues–Thurs 2.30–5.30, Fri–Sun 10–12 and 2.30–5.30; July–Aug Tues–Thurs 3.30–6.30, Fri–Sun 10–12 and 3.30–6.30; adm*). A dramatic cable car ride from Laveno and a twenty-minute walk will take you to the top of the **Sasso di Ferro**, the 'Rock of Iron' just behind town, for fine panoramas over the middle of Maggiore. From Laveno it's 8km inland to **Casalzuigno**, where the 16th-century **Villa della Porta-Bozzolo** has rococo frescoes inside and a fine Italian Baroque garden (*t 0332 624 136; open Oct–mid-Dec Tues–Sun 10–1 and 2–5; Feb–Sept Tues–Sun 10–1 and 2–6; garden open 10–5, until 6 in summer; adm*). Just beyond Casalzuigno, a winding road cuts up the wooded flank of Monte Nudo for **Arcumeggia**, an ancient hamlet where the stone houses are piled one atop the other and where, after the First World War, the locals decided to turn their home into a work of art by inviting famous Italian artists of the day to fresco the old stone walls, creating a curious outdoor 1950s time capsule. An easy path from Arcumeggia leads to **Sant'Antonio**, with splendid views over the lake.

Santa Caterina del Sasso

Hanging – literally – on the sheer cliffs of the Sasso Ballaro between Cerro and Reno is the deserted Carmelite convent of **Santa Caterina del Sasso** (*t 0332 647 172, www.provincia.va.it/santacaterina; open April–Oct daily 8.30–12 and 2.30–6; Nov–Feb, Sat, Sun and hols 9–12 and 2–5; Christmas hols and Mar daily 9–12 and 2–5*). Visible only from the lake, it is visited by boats between April and September; if you're driving, follow the signs from the shore road and walk down from the car park.

According to legend, in the 12th century a wealthy merchant and usurer named Alberto Besozzi was sailing on the lake when his boat sank. In deadly peril, he prayed to St Catherine of Alexandria, who saved him from the waves and cast him upon this rock-bound shore. Impressed, Alberto repented of his usury and lived as a hermit in a cave, becoming famous for his piety. When his prayers brought an end to a local plague, he asked that as an *ex voto* the people construct a church to St Catherine. Over the centuries, a convent was added next to the cave of 'Beato Alberto' and it became a popular pilgrimage destination, especially after a huge boulder fell on the roof only to be miraculously wedged just above the altar, directly over the head of the priest saying Mass. The boulder finally crashed through in 1910 without harming anyone, because nobody was there; the convent had been suppressed in 1770 by Joseph II of Austria. In 1986, a 15-year long restoration of Santa Caterina was completed, revealing medieval fresco fragments (note the one in the Sala Capitolare of armed men from the 13th century). Don't miss the 16th-century fresco of the *Danse Macabre*, high up in the loggia of the Gothic convent.

South of Santa Caterina, the surprisingly suburban bungalow estates of **Ispra** and **Ranco** house the employees of EURATOM, a 'peaceful' European atomic study centre. For lower technology, follow the signs in Ranco for the **Museo Europeo dei Trasporti** (*t 0331 975 198, www.museo-ogliari.it; open April–Sept Tues–Sun 10–12 and 3–6; Oct–Mar Tues–Sun 10–12 and 2–4*), the fruit of the passion of a lawyer named Francesco Ogliari (and author of a 66-volume *History of Transportation*), who created the museum with the motto of 'Two Centuries in Two Hours'. Among the trains, buses, ski lifts and metros note the Ferrovia Eolica (1858), a quirky wind-propelled railway line that ran for a few years out of Sesto Calende. The costumed mannequins going for rides add a certain flair; there's even a wax priest in a chapel, with some food for thought over the door: 'The world of transport exists by the measure of time. Here time has no measure. Eternity redeems time.'

Angera and its Castle

Angera, just south, lies in the shadow of the **Rocca di Angera** (*t 0331 931 300; open mid-Mar–Oct 9–5.30; adm*), a castle that commands the entire south half of the lake. Built in the 11th century by the Della Torre, it passed to the Visconti in 1314, then was ceded by Milan to the Borromei in 1449. Don't miss their 17th-century wine press right by the castle entrance, so huge that only San Carlone, standing across the lake in Arona, could possibly work it. Since 1988 the occupants have been on a smaller scale: Lilliputians made of porcelain, wood, celluloid and plastic, all members of the **Museo della Bambola** or Doll Museum (*t 0331 931 300; open end of Mar–Oct 10.30–12.30 and 4–6; adm*), one of the best collections in Europe. Barbie and Ken's ancestors from the 17th century are beautifully displayed, along with their often staggeringly detailed little households and accessories; there are even nun and priest dolls for children who want to grow up to be saints. The cumulative effect of gazing at so many smiling human simulacra is surreal; expect to end up as glassy-eyed as the dolls. Other rooms contain children's clothes from the last three centuries.

There's more, including 15th-century frescoes from the Borromeo palace in Milan, or at least the bits that survived the bombs in 1943: the ghostly *Pomegranate pickers* by Giovanni da Vaprio, peacocks and Aesop's fables by Michelino da Besozzo, Borromeo family portraits and mythologies, and an *Atalanta e Ippomene* by Guido Reni. Archaeological finds litter the courtyard, includings bits of a Mithraeum discovered in 1917 in a cave under the castle. Best of all is the vast **Sala della Giustizia**, which the proud Visconti had frescoed with astrological fancies and scenes of battling bishop Ottone Visconti's victory over the Della Torre in 1277. If you don't mind the creaky old wooden steps and signs disclaiming all responsibility for your safety, you can continue up the tower for commanding views over the lake and the castle's vineyards.

Lake Maggiore to Lake Lugano: The Varesotto

The triangle formed by Lakes Maggiore, Lugano and the Swiss border is called the Varesotto, not exactly a destination you'll see in a Thomas Cook poster. Obscure, yes, but dull, no: besides ten small and hygienic lakes and the Campo dei Fiori natural park, the Varesotto is richly endowed with frescoes dating from the 8th century, including exquisite works by Tuscan charmer, Masolino, in Castiglione Olona. If you're driving, take a good map: the road sign network is a masterpiece of obfuscation.

Lake Varese and Around

Varese and the Campo dei Fiori

Varese, city of gardens, city of shoes and increasingly bedroom suburb of Milan, spills over a plateau between Lake Maggiore and the Olana river. Although it was founded by the Celts it has managed to avoid history for most of its career. Maria Theresa gave it briefly to the Duke of Modena, Francesco III d'Este (1765–80), whose main contribution was to build himself a vast spread in the centre of town, the **Palazzo Estense**, now the Municipio; its gaudiest room, the Salone Estense, can only be visited upon written request or, more easily, with a guide. The duke's park, modelled on the Schönbrunn gardens in Vienna, and the adjacent English garden of the eclectic **Villa Mirabello** are now a city park; the Villa Mirabello houses the **Musei Civici** (*Piazza della Motta 4, t 0332 281 590; open Tues–Sun 9.30–12.30 and 2–5; Sat–Sun until 5.30; adm*), with a hodgepodge of paintings, local archaeology and the butterfly collection of the great tenor Tamagno.

The central square in Varese, Piazza Monte Grappa, received a stern Mussolini facelift; stylish, perhaps, but not exactly cosy. Just beyond it, Varese's landmark, the garlic-domed 17th-century **Campanile del Bernascone**, rings the chimes for the **Basilica di San Vittore** (*t 0332 236 019, www.basvit.it*), an ancient foundation rebuilt by Pellegrino Tibaldi with a neoclassical façade pasted on; inside the most important paintings (recently restored) are by Il Morazzone. The austere 12th-century **Baptistry** contains some original frescoes.

City bus C (*every 20mins*) goes up to the base of Varese's Sacro Monte (*t 0332 830 613*), with 14 chapels filled with frescoes and stuccoes on the Mystery of the Rosary. You can reach the top by taking the renovated funicular from Stazione Vellone (*open Sat–Sun and hols 7.05–8.05*). On foot it's a 2km walk up beginning at the Prima Cappella; the most artistic one, the seventh (*The Flagellation*), was frescoed by Il Morazzone. The devotional tour climaxes at **Santuario di Santa Maria del Monte**, founded in the 5th century by St Ambrose. Rebuilt in 1473 and later lavishly baroqued, it houses a ballistically ornate marble altar, a much revered 14th-century 'Black Virgin' attributed to St Luke, and *trecento* frescoes in the crypt. Varese's Sacro Monte sculptures are so expressive that experts think Lombard mountain theatre originated from the sacred monument, the static chapels representing an *in itinere* meditation on Christ's death, just as in a religious festival, and the statues representing the

Getting There and Around

Varese, the main town between the lakes, is served by the FS and Milano-Nord **trains** from Milan – the stations in Varese are next to each other. **Buses** from Varese go to Castiglione (only four runs per day), and Lake Varese, while Arsago, and Castelseprio are, according to the tourist office, the most badly served areas. **t** 892 024, *www.tunitalia.it*.

Tourist Information

Varese: Piazza Della Libertà 1, **t** 0332 252 412, *www.turismo.provincia.va.it*.
Varese lat, Carrobbio 2, **t** 0332 283 604.
Castiglione Olona: Piazza Garibaldi, **t** 0331 858 048, *www.castiglioneolona.it* (Prol Loco, Via Roma 25, **t** 0331 850 084).

Where to Stay and Eat

Varese ✉ 21100
★★★★**Palace Grand Hotel**, Via Manara 11, Colle Campigli, **t** 0332 327 100, *www.palacevarese.it* (*luxury*). Stay in style in an Art Nouveau hotel, beautifully positioned above the city.
★★★★**Villa Castiglioni**, Via Castiglioni 1, Induno Olona (8km north), **t** 0332 200 201, *www. hotelvillacastiglioni.it* (*very expensive*). An elegant early 19th-century villa. As you stroll the shady park, swim, play tennis, or doze in one of the canopy beds, you can easily forget that this is a hotel until you come to pay the bill.
★★★★**Locanda dei Mai Intees**, Via Riva 2, Azzate, near Malpensa, **t** 0332 457 223,

www.mai-intees.com (*very expensive*). This charming restaurant and hotel occupy a 15th-century house. The chef offers selected seasonal 'Italian' dishes. *Booking advisable. Closed lunch time.*
★★★★**Colonne**, Via Fincarà 37, in Sacro Monte, **t** 0332 224 633, *www.hotelcolonne.com* (*expensive*). In an enviable position, with a superb view of Varesotto and Campo dei Fiori from its ample terraces and solarium.
★★★**Varese Lago Meublé**, Via Macchi 61, **t** 0332 310 022, *www.hotelvareselago.com* (*expensive*). Along the river shore and set in its own grounds; offers amenities such as a gym and sauna.
★★★**Bologna**, Via Broggi 7, **t** 0332 232 100, *www.albergobologna.it* (*moderate*). Central, with an excellent restaurant.
Albero Bianco, Cassano Valcuvia, Via Dante 569, **t** 0332 995 684 (*moderate*). A 19th-century *cascina* where you can look after animals, practise archery or boules as well as take decoration and cookery courses.
Al Cavallino Bianco, Via per Ferrera 50, Cassano Valcuvia, **t** 0332 995 508, *www.alcavallino.it* (*moderate*). For a farmhouse stay, this is a stud farm with 40 horses.
Lago Maggiore, Via Carrobio 19, **t** 0332 231 183 (*expensive*). One of Varese's best restaurants; the cheeseboard alone may revolutionize your ideas about Italian cooking. *Closed Sun and Mon lunch, and July. Booking advised.*
La Cantina del Borgo Osteria degli Artisti, Via Roma 32, in Castiglione Olona, **t** 0331 859 021 (*expensive–moderate*). In the city centre. Live concerts and cabaret at the weekends. A nice place to eat local *brasati*, *risotti* and polenta. *Closed Mon and Sat at lunch.*

actors, who seem to move as soon as you turn your head. The nearby **Museo Baroffio Dall'Aglio**, or Museo del Santuario (**t** *0331 777 472, www.museobaroffio.it; open April–Sept Thurs, Sat, Sun 9.30–12.30 and 3–6.30; ring for winter hours; booking advised; adm*) houses works of art donated to the sanctuary, and the **Museo Pogliaghi** (*closed for restoration*) has Egyptian, Greek and Roman antiquities, and works by the villa's former owner Ludovico Pogliaghi, including a plaster cast of his Milan cathedral door.

From the sanctuary, continue 5km up to the karst massif of the **Parco Naturale di Campo dei Fiori** (4,050ft/1,234m) (**t** *0332 435 386*), for lovely views over the lakes and mountains. Near the grand abandoned Liberty-style **Albergo Campo dei Fiori** (1912) stone steps lead up to the Monte Tre Croci, the 'Balcony of Lombardy', with views as far as Monte Rosa.

Lake Varese

Just under Varese lies its lake, an 8.5km-long sheet of water set in its low rolling hills, the big, gentle, sleepy head of the Varesotto's 'minor lakes'. There's a Renaissance vision of it just outside the centre of Varese, along the road to Gavirate, in the **Castello di Masnago** (*t 0332 220 256; open Tues–Sat 10.30–6.30, Sun 10.30–12.30 and 2.30–6.30; adm*), where in 1938 two sets of 15th-century secular frescoes were discovered under the whitewash: an elegant courtly scene by the lake and, upstairs, female vices and virtues, including Vanity, preening her elaborate muffin of hair. Recently restored, the museum also holds a *pinacoteca* with modern and contemporary art. Lake Varese's main settlement, **Gavirate**, is famous for its hand-carved pipes, and has a collection from around the world in its **Museo della Pipa** (*Via del Chiostro 1–5, t 0332 743 334, by appointment only*). Collector, pipe restorer and designer Alberto Paronelli will guide you in person through his 30,000-piece collection of pipes and his lavish library of over 3,000 titles. The first floor recreates an 18th-century French pipe laboratory. For carvings of a different nature go to Voltorre (just south of Gavirate), where the 11th-century Cluniac monastery of **San Michele** (now a cultural centre) has a cloister (*t 0332 743 914, www.fabbrica-arte.com; open Tues–Sun 10–12 and 2–5, April–Oct Tues–Sun 10–5*), with beautifully sculpted capitals, attributed to the Comacino master Lanfranco – it also hosts temporary exhibitions. The campanile has one of the oldest bells in Italy, and sounds like it too.

Catch the little boat from **Biandronno** on Lake Varese's west shore for **Isolino Virginia**, a wee wooded islet inhabited three millennia ago by people who built their homes on pile dwellings just offshore. The islet's **Museo Preistorico di Villa Ponti** (*t 0332 281 590, villa.mirabello@comune.varese.it; open April–Oct, Sat and Sun 2–6, or by appointment*) chronicles the settlement, which endured into Roman times. Isolino Virginia is a good spot for a picnic, or you can lunch in the little island restaurant. To the southwest the lake dissolves into marshlands, not as much fun for humans as for waterfowl; the same holds true for the reed beds in Lake Varese's twin baby sisters to the west, **Lago di Monate** and **Lago di Comabbio**.

Also of interest is the mid 18th-century neoclassical **Villa Menafoglio Litta Panza** (*Piazza Litta 1, Biumo, t 0332 239 669, www.varesegallery.com/villapanza; open Tues–Sun 10–6, last entrance at 5pm; adm exp*), set in its own French-style park of 330 hectares, dotted with fountains. It contains a collection of American contemporary art (1980s–90s) of over 100 works hung in the villa's apartments, and a collection of African and Pre-colombian art and furniture of the 19th century, collected by the villa's last owner Giuseppe Panza, as well as a valuable collection of Renaissance furniture dating back to previous owner Litta. Noteworthy are the neoclassical *salone* with monochrome works by David Simpson and the patrician *cappella* with the fresco of the *Immacolata* by Pietro Magatti. A separate exhibit in the *rustici* (former stables) includes minimal and environmental works especially created for the villa in the 1960s–70s by US artists Dan Flavin, James Turrel, Maria Nordman and Robert Irwin. Italian architect Gae Aulenti designed the services area (bar, bookshop, ticket office) and the setting of the former horse stables. On weekends a shuttle connects the villa to Varese's Ippodromo; on weekdays parking is allowed at the villa.

Arsago Seprio to Castiglione Olona

South of the lakelets and Lake Maggiore, the River Ticino divides Piedmont from Lombardy. This area is now a Natural Park, although you may not immediately notice it around Milan's Malpensa airport and industrial centres such as **Somma Lombardo**. Somma was defended by the large **Castello Visconti** (*Piazza Sempione 2, t 0331 256 337, www.castelloviscontidisanvito.it; open April–mid-Oct, Sat, Sun, hols 10–11.30 and 2.30–6.30; guided visits*); rebuilt in the 1400s, it expanded into a residence over the centuries. Much of its family furnishings are intact, along with monumental fireplaces, a canopied royal bed with a Visconti viper on top and a huge collection of barber's dishes. The enormous spreading cedar in the garden is as old as the castle.

North of Somma, a cemetery in **Golasecca** gave its name to the local Iron Age culture (9th–6th century BC); in the same vicinity, you can visit the cromlechs of the **Necropoli del Monsurino**, some of the oldest monumental tombs in Italy (find the Golasecca Centro Orizzonte/Parco Ticino, and follow the path from there). Celtic, Roman and Lombard finds from the area are housed in the **Museo Archeologico Romano e Longobardo** (*open Sat 3–6, Sun 10–12 and 3–6 or by request; adm free*) in **Arsago Seprio**, 2km east of Somma Lombardo. The Lombards were responsible for Arsago's 9th-century gem of a church, the **Basilica di San Vittore**, with a lovely façade, and a 9th-century campanile that has bells looped on top and aisles of Roman columns. In the 11th century, a hexagonal **baptistry** was added, crowned with a round drum dressed in blind arches; the serene interior has traces of the original frescoes.

Lake Varese to Lugano

Castiglione Olona

The little Renaissance nugget of **Castiglione Olona**, southeast of the lake 8km from Varese, is known as an islet of Tuscany in Lombardy, but it's an islet wrapped in a huge lake of suburban sprawl, with nary a sign to point the way; locate the ghastly new church and take the steep winding road down to the bottom of the valley to find the **Borgo** – the Castiglione Olona you want. It owes its *quattrocento* Tuscan charm to Cardinal Branda Castiglioni (1350–1443), who brought Masolino da Pancale, Lorenzo di Pietro (Il Vecchietta) and other artists to do up Castiglione, and incidentally introduced the first glimpse of new humanism into Lombardy.

The Borgo, the Cardinal's 'ideal citadel', is essentially unchanged since the 15th century. In central Piazza Garibaldi, the **Chiesa di Villa** was inspired by Brunelleschi, its exterior decoration limited to framing bands of grey and two giant statues on either side of the door, of St Christopher and St Anthony Abbot. Inside, nearly all the art dates from the 1400s: the *Annunciation*, the tomb of Guido Castiglioni by the school of Amadeo, and the four terracotta *Doctors of the Church*. Opposite, the cardinal's **Palazzo Branda Castiglioni** is now a museum (*t 0331 858 301; open April–Sept Tues–Sat 9–12 and 3–6; Sun and hols 10.30–12.30 and 3–6 except for Oct–Mar Sun 3–6 only; adm*). The cardinal's bedroom has charming frescoes of children playing under the fruit trees by an unknown Lombard painter, while below are various emblems and sayings. Il Vecchietta frescoed the palace chapel (1437); in the study, Masolino painted a scene of Veszprem, Hungary, as described by the cardinal from memory.

Ancient plane trees line the steep Via Cardinal Branda that leads up to the Gothic **Collegiata** (*t 0331 850 280; open Oct–Mar, Tues–Sun 10–12 and 2.30–5; April–Sept, Tues–Sun 10–12 and 3–7; adm*), built in 1421 over the Castiglioni castle (the gate still survives). The brick church contains beautiful frescoes, especially Masolino's *Life of the Virgin* in the vault, while Il Vecchietta painted the *Life of St Stephen* and Paolo Schiavo frescoed the *Life of St Lawrence*. The *Crucifixion* in the apse is attributed to yet another Tuscan master, Neri di Bicci. In 1435 Masolino frescoed the entire **Baptistry**, a work commonly considered his life's masterpiece, the culmination of his evocatively lyrical and refined style. Castiglione Olona holds the **Fiera del Cardinale**, an antiques and bric-a-brac market, every first Sunday of the month in the city centre.

The Olona valleys hold a pair of other surprises 700 years older than Castiglione. The **Monastero di Torba**, set in the woods just off the road in **Gornate Olona** (*t 0331 820 301; open Feb–Sept 10–1 and 2–6; Oct–Dec 10–4; adm*) was founded in the 5th century as a Lombard defence tower, but three centuries later it found a new use as a monastery. Acquired by the Fondo per l'Ambiente Italiano (FAI; the Italian National Trust), the 8th-century frescoes in the tower have been restored, along with the original crypt and tombs. The tower defended **Castelseprio** to the south, a Lombard *castrum* designed on the Roman model. Destroyed in the 13th century, ruins of the walls, churches and castle moulder under the trees 1.5 km from the centre, but the main reason to stop is little **Santa Maria Foris Portas**: its unique 8th-century frescoes in an Eastern Hellenistic style were discovered during the Second World War by a partisan hiding here (*t 0331 820 438; open Tues–Sat 8.30–7.20, Sun and hols 9.30–6.20; adm free*).

From Varese to Lugano

From Varese there are two valley routes to Lake Lugano. The prettiest, N233, cuts through the Valganna to Ponte Tresa, a route that takes in a Liberty-style brewery at Grotte, the **Birreria Liberty Poretti**; the 11th-century **Badia di San Gemolo** at Ganna, recently restored; the nearby **spring of San Gemolo**, also known as the spring of the red stones, with healing properties; and little **Lake Ghirla** beside a village of the same name. The second route, from Varese to Porto Ceresio, passes near **Bisuschio**, site of the magnificent Renaissance **Villa Cicogna Mozzoni**, on the SS244, just north of Arcisate (*t 0332 471 134, www.villacicognamozzoni.it; open April–Oct Sun and hols 9.30–12 and 2.30–7, in Aug also Mon–Sat 2.30–7; adm*). Built in 1400 as a hunting lodge, enlarged in 1500 as a permanent residence and still owned by the Counts Cicogna Mozzoni, the villa has delightful frescoes by the Campi brothers of Cremona and their school, forgotten for centuries under layers of whitewash (applied in the hope of 'sterilizing' the villa against the plague in the 1600s). The porticoes open out into a Renaissance garden of box hedges and fountains with a lofty water staircase, laid out in the 1560s by Ascanio Mozzoni. **Viggiù**, to the east, is a little resort and belvedere, and was the birthplace of early Baroque architect Martino Longhi.

Lakes Lugano and Como

11

Lakes Lugano and Como

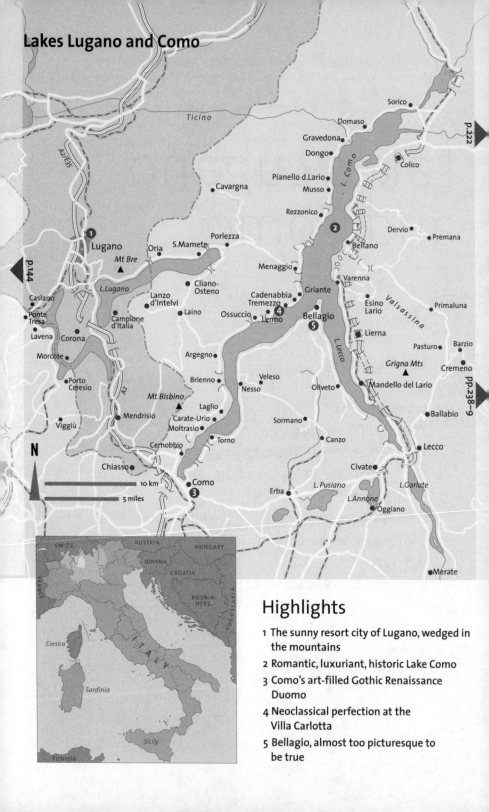

Ticino

p.222

A2/E35

p.144

Sorico

Domaso
Gravedona
Dongo
Colico
Pianello d.Lario
Musso
Dervio
Premana
Rezzonico

Cavargna

2

Bellano

1
Lugano
Mt Bre ▲

Oria
S.Mamete
Porlezza

Menaggio
Varenna

Valsassina

Cliano-
Osteno
Griante
Esino
Lario
Primaluna

L.Lugano

Lanzo
d'Intelvi
Cadenabbia
Tremezzo
4
Lierna

Caslano
Laino
Ossuccio
Lenno
5
Bellagio

Ponte
Tresa
Campione
d'Italia

Pasturo
Barzio
Cremeno

Lavena
Corona

Argegno
Grigna Mts ▲

Morcote

Brienno
Veleso
Nesso
Oliveto
Mandello del Lario

Porto
Ceresio

A2
Mt Bisbino ▲
Ballabio

Viggiù
Mendrisio
Laglio
Sormano
Carate-Urio
Moltrasio
Canzo
Lecco

Torno
Civate

Cernobbio
L.Garlate

Chiasso
3
Como
Erba
L. Pusiano
L.Annone
Oggiano

N

10 km

5 miles

Merate

pp.238-9

L. Como

L. Lecco

Highlights

1 The sunny resort city of Lugano, wedged in
   the mountains
2 Romantic, luxuriant, historic Lake Como
3 Como's art-filled Gothic Renaissance
   Duomo
4 Neoclassical perfection at the
   Villa Carlotta
5 Bellagio, almost too picturesque to
   be true

The two lakes north of Milan, Lugano and Como, are very beautiful and very accessible from the Lombard capital in less than an hour on the *autostrada*. Lake Lugano is two-thirds Swiss, which lends it a different flavour: there's more money floating around, more modern and contemporary art, more organization. Lake Como is thoroughly Italian, a prestigious retreat since Roman times; a surprising number of Lombard foundations and early Romanesque churches dot its shores and the hills of La Brianza, the region just south of its straddling legs. The dramatic Grigna mountains over the Lecco branch of the lake haunted Leonardo da Vinci, while in the 19th century the romantic villas and gardens on the west shore were a favourite haven of opera composers and their divas, on leave from rehearsals at La Scala.

Lake Lugano

Zigzagged Lake Lugano with its steep, fjorded shores is a striking sight, especially in the centre where its curious shape and narrow span closed in by mountains give it a rare intimacy and benign climate. In a few places, especially around the city of Lugano, the lake has become a victim of its own attractiveness; other shores, too steep for building, still darken the waters with emerald green and white reflections of the wooded cliffs. Lugano's extremities are Italian, but its heart has been part of the Canton Ticino ever since the Swiss snatched the province from French-occupied Milan back in 1512. Two centuries later, when Ticino had a chance to return to Italy, it stalwartly refused: as part of its punishment, the Italians insist on calling Lake Lugano by its Latin name, Ceresio. Another punishment is to have a border rimmed with petrol stations. And a crumb of Italian territory, Campione d'Italia, survives in the middle of the lake, which is just big enough to support a casino that more than welcomes Swiss francs. If you can't beat them, soak them.

Western Lake Lugano

Lugano slowly drains its rather polluted waters into Lake Maggiore through the Tresa, a river that forms the border between the Italian and Swiss halves of the village of **Ponte Tresa**. Just above all the petrol stations and the steamer landing, on the nook of a promontory, the village of **Lavena** has a pretty medieval core. If you're travelling with children, however, make for the Swiss shore, where the Alprose chocolate company in **Caslano** runs a **Chocolate Museum** on Europe's 200-year-old love affair with the brown stuff; top it off with a factory tour (*t 091 611 8856, www.alprose.ch; open Mon–Fri 9–5.30, Sat and Sun museum only 9–4.30; adm*). Nearby at Magliaso, the **Zoo al Maglio** has over a hundred animals and birds from around the world (*t 091 606 1493; open 10–5; summer 9–7; adm*). In the village of Montagnola, the **Herman Hesse Museum** (*t 091 993 3770; open Tues–Sun 10–12.30 and 2–6.30; Nov–Feb Sat and Sun only; there are readings of Hesse's works each Sun at 5, in Italian and German; adm*), opened in 1997, shows the apartment where the writer retired when he separated from his family and the First World War burst, and the Casa Rossa, where he later moved with his third wife and remained till he died. The building itself, within the Camuzzi House complex, is an interesting example of Ticinese architecture of the 19th century. The several works the author wrote there including *Siddhartha*, *Narcissus and Goldmund*, and *Steppenwolf*, as well the writer's poetry and paintings, are on display. Documentaries are shown on the top floor theatre. In the pretty village of **Morcote**, the **Parco Scherrer** (*t 091 996 2125; open daily 15 Mar–Oct 10–5, July and Aug 10–6; adm*) opens on to the lake, with exotic statues in a setting of palms, camphor, cedars, Mexican pines and other striking flora. Morcote's Romanesque **Cappella di Sant'Antonio da Padova** has interesting 13th-century frescoes (including an unusual one of dead souls squirming in a net); above, on a panoramic terrace, **Santa Maria del Sasso** has others from the Renaissance. North, near the bridge at Melide, **Carona** has a number of mansions painted with exterior frescoes and, in the church of **San Giorgio**, a rare copy of Michelangelo's *Last Judgement*, painted in 1585 by Domenico Pezzi. Copying was something of a fad in these parts (artistic copyrights obviously didn't apply once Ticino became Swiss). The church at **Capriasco** north of Lugano has an earnest copy of Leonardo's *Last Supper*, painted before 1550 by an unknown hand. It hardly measures up to the original, but it's certainly in better nick.

Lugano

Warm, palmy Lugano is an arty resort city piled between Monte Brè and Monte San Salvatore, a lovely setting that has been compared to Rio de Janeiro; in Switzerland at any rate it's as close as you can get to Paradise (its residential suburb, 10 minutes west by bus). To go with its sumptuous lake views, it has a sumptuous Renaissance gem in waterfront Piazza Luini. This is the plain church of **Santa Maria degli Angioli**, built in 1510 by the Franciscans and frescoed in 1529 with an enormous, nearly life-size *Crucifixion* by Bernardino Luini: his masterpiece, full of colour and detail. Ruskin, who wrote that Luini was 'ten times greater than Leonardo', saw it and gushed, 'Every touch he lays is ethereal; every thought he conceives is beauty and purity…'

Art from the late Gothic period and 19th and 20th centuries, including works by Renoir, Degas and Klee, is displayed in the **Museo Cantonale d'Arte**, in three 15th-century *palazzi* (*Piazza Manzoni 7, but entry is in Via Canova 10, t 091 910 4780; open Wed–Sun 10–5, Tues 2–5; adm*). On the other side of town is the **Villa Favorita** (*Via Pietro Cappelli, t 091 972 1741; temporarily closed; gardens open by request*). This was the home of Baron Heinrich von Thyssen-Bornemisza's fabulous collection of Old Masters, now on loan in Madrid and Barcelona (thanks to the Baroness, a former Miss Spain), although the villa retains the Thyssen collection of European and American modern art, with a special emphasis on the Luminists and Hudson River School. Further along the lake, along Via Cortivo (take bus 1 or 11 from Piazza Manzoni (direction Castagnola) to San Domenico and walk 5 minutes), the neoclassical Villa Heleneum is the **Museo delle Culture Extraeuropee** (*t 5886 66909; open Mar–Oct Wed–Sun 10–5; adm*), containing a fascinating collection of wooden figures and cult objects from Oceania, Africa and Asia donated by Surrealist artists Serge and Graziella Brignoni.

Getting There and Around

Lugano's **airport** in Agno, **t** 091 610 1111, is served by a Swiss info service, **t** 848 852 000 from Switzerland, and **t** 848 868 120 from Italy. It is linked up to Swiss flights from Paris, Rome, Olbia, Geneva and Zurich as well as the major Swiss airports. A shuttle service, **t** 079 221 4243 (ring in advance), connects the airport with the city. Lugano is also linked to Milano's Malpensa by a shuttlebus service via Chiasso, **t** 091 939 8878, *www.busexpress.com*. There is also **Autopostale**, **t** 004191 939 8878; or check the web site at *www.autopostale.ch*. The journey from Malpensa to Lugano takes about 45 minutes; from Milano Centrale it is about an hour and a half. From Varese, **trains** go as far as Porto Ceresio on the west end of Lugano; from Milan trains to Como continue to Lugano by way of Chiasso, while Lugano itself is linked by a local train line (the FLP, **t** 091 923 2392, *www.flpsa.ch*) to points west as far as Ponte Tresa. Porlezza, on the east end of the lake, is linked by **buses** to Como or Menaggio; buses from Lugano or Como go directly to Campione d'Italia. All lakeside towns are served by **steamers**, **t** 004191 971 5223, on the Società Navigazione Lago di Lugano line (**t** 0979 715 223, *www.lakelugano.ch*), and these run with the precision of Swiss clockwork, except when the wind's up. They also organize tours.

Tourist Information

Caslano: Ente Turistico del Malcontone, Piazza Lago, **t** 004191 606 2986, *www.malcantone.ch*. Open Mon–Fri 8–12 and 2–5.30, Sat (July–Aug) 9–12 and 2–5.
Campione d'Italia: Via Volta 3, **t** 004191 649 5051, *www.campioneitalia.com*. Open Mon–Fri 10–12 and 3–5.

Lugano: Riva Albertolli 5, **t** 004191 913 3232, *www.lugano-tourism.ch*. Open April–Oct Mon–Fri 9–7, Sat 9–5, Sun 10–3; Nov–Mar Mon–Fri 9–12 and 2–5. Offers free guided tours of the city every Mon, April–Oct, starting at 9.30am in front of S. Maria degli Augioli.
The tourist office at the airport has an **exchange service**, **t** 004191 605 1226. Open Mon–Fri 10–2 and 3–7, Sat–Sun 10–2 and 4–7. There is also a **hotel reservation service** at the train station, **t** 004191 923 5120.

Festivals

Lugano has a number of music festival concerts throughout the year:
Primavera Concertistica, *spring*. Classical music concerts.
Open air cinema, *mid-June–July*. Held in Lugano.
Ceresio Estate, *June–Sept*. Classical music.
Jazz Festival, *first half of July*.
Lugano Blues to Bop, *September*.
Concerti d'Autunno, *Oct–Dec*. Classical music.

Market Days

Lugano: Piazza Riforma, Fruit, veg and flowers. *Tues and Fri morning.*
Via Canova. Antiques. *Tues and Fri morning, and all day Sat.*
Melide: by the lake. Mostly handicrafts. *Evenings mid-July–mid-Aug.*

Sports and Activities

Water Sports

Rowing is offered at Club Canottieri Lugano, Via Foce, **t** 004191 9712 398 *www.canottierilugano.ch*; Audax, Paradiso borough, **t** 004191 9941 916; and Società Canottieri Ceresio, Gandria/Castagnola, **t** 004191 971 5777. **Diving** is at Lugano Sub Paradiso,

As ever, one of the big thrills is going up to look back down again: a funicular (*bus 1 or 11 from Lugano to the station; **t** 004191 971 3171; departures every 30mins until 6.45pm*) runs up to the summit on 3,150ft (960m) **Monte Brè**, 'Switzerland's sunniest mountain'; there's a restaurant on top and the little village of Brè to explore (**t** 800 7228, *www.montebre.ch*). Another funicular (**t** 004191 985 2828, *www.montesansalvatore.ch*; open Mar–end Oct, or later depending on weather; every 30mins, in summer till 11pm*) ascends from Lugano's suburb of Paradiso to **Monte San Salvatore** (3,000ft/914m), with more fine views over the lake and Alps, a restaurant and nature trails. For

t 004191 994 3740, and Corallo Sub, in Caslano, t 004191 606 1881. **Waterskiing** at Club Nautico Lugano, t 004191 994 1256 (the cheapest); Club Sci Nautico Ceresio, c/o Hotel Du Lac, t 079 6210 132; and Saladin Boatcenter, t 004191 923 5733. Circolo Velico Lago di Lugano offers **sailing** courses, t 004191 994 2206. You can **windsurf** at Club Nautico Lugano, t 004191 994 1256, and Caslano Surf, t 004191 606 2525. The tourist office has a list of good **beaches**.

Mountain Activities

Tourist offices have guided walks and information on fitness trails and lists of **horse-riding** centres. Contact CAS for **moutaineering** in Caslano, t 004191 606 8633, Asbest for adventure sports, t 004191 966 1144 , and Alpe Foppa t 004191 946 2303 and Pink Baron, t 004191 648 3088, for **paragliding**. Or try a **hot air balloon**: Baloon Team Lugano, t 004191 921 0672. Monte Tamaro and Monte Lema have **ski slopes**.

Other Activities

Open-air **chess** is common: in Rivetta Tell, Piazza Manzoni, Belvedere (Riva Caccia), Parco Florida (Loreto) and at the Paradiso steamer landing in Lugano. *Boules* and **hockey** (ice and field) are also popular: ask the tourist office. There is an 18-hole **golf course** in Magliaso, Golf Club Lugano, t 004191 606 1557. To hire **scooters** call Gerosa Motocicli, t 004191 923 5636 in Lugano; for **bikes** ask the local tourist offices; for **rowing boats** contact Loris Gottardo, Caslano, t 004191 606 2159 (*June–Sept*).

Where to Stay and Eat

Lugano ⊠ CH6900, t (004191–)
*****Villa Principe Leopoldo**, Via Montalbano 5, t 985 8855, www.leopold

hotel.com (*luxury*). If money's no object, this 19th-century Relais & Châteaux in a beautiful hillside park overlooking the city will keep you in the style you can become accustomed to, complete with a health centre. Gourmet Mediterranean and international cuisine at the restaurant and café.

***International au Lac**, Via Nassa 68, t 922 7541, *www.hotel-international.ch* (*very expensive*). This comfortable hotel has a pool, garden terrace and underground parking. Situated near the lake in the city centre. *Closed end Oct–first week April.*

***Continental Park**, Via Basilea 28, t 966 1112, *www.continentalpark.ch* (*expensive*). Near the railway station, in a turn-of-the-last-century inn purposefully built after the construction of the San Gottardo tunnel; offers all amenities including a palmy park with pool and Ticinese entertainment in the evening. Bike and trekking excursions are nearby. *Closed Nov–end Mar.*

Fischer's Seehotel, Sentiero di Gandria 10, t 971 5571, *fischers-hotel@bluewind.ch* (*expensive–moderate; depending on type of room. Some of the rooms only have a toilet; others have toilet and bathroom*). Simple and pleasant, and smack on the lake, far from the traffic. A nice restaurant, but beware – the kitchen closes at 8.30pm for dinner. *Closed Nov–Feb.*

*Montarina**, Via Montarina 1, t 966 7272, *www.montarina.ch* (*moderate*). Hotel and hostel which welcomes families and backpackers in a 19th-century villa set in a palm garden near the station, with pretty views over the lake and free parking. Comfortable rooms with private bathrooms at an extra fee. Also has a chicken farm, and there's a swimming pool in the garden.

even bigger views, catch the steamer down the south arm of the lake to Capolago and take the rack railway for 40 minutes up to the summit of 5,623ft (1,714m) **Monte Generoso** (t 091 6305 111, www.montegeneroso.ch; open daily). Once there, you can go mountain biking, paragliding, climbing and birdwatching. Boats from Lugano call at Gandria for visits to the **Museo Doganale Svizzero** (t 091 910 4811, www.museo-suisse.ch; open April–Oct 1.30–5.30), dedicated to Swiss customs. Learn about all the cracks and crevices they've found in cars, false passports, counterfeit goods: children like the night-vision tunnel and the 'catch-the-smuggler' computer games.

Lugano is chock-full of top-notch restaurants, but lunch at some of these temples of cuisine can be quite reasonable.

Parco Saroli, Via Stefano Franscini 8, t 923 5314 (*expensive*). This fashionable eaterie serves an excellent and unusual selection of home-made pasta dishes and seafood along with a wide choice of superb breads, cheeses and mouth-watering desserts. There is also an award-winning wine list. *Closed Sat lunch, Sun and hols.*

Antica Osteria Gerso, Piazzetta Solaro 24 at Massagno, t 966 1915 (*moderate*). An intimate, utterly simple restaurant serving a limited but discriminating menu: favourite dishes include onion soup with tangy pecorino cheese, *tortelli di zucca alle mandorle* and duck with oranges, all accompanied by a fair wine choice from the adjacent *enoteca*. *Book a day or two ahead. Closed Sun.*

Campione d'Italia ✉ CH22060, t (004191–)

There are no hotels in Campione and the enclave will remain unserved until restructuring of the traditional Grand Hotel and construction of the new casino, designed by Swiss architect Mario Botta, with an inside hotel. In the meantime you can go to the rather Swissified hotels just before the entry arch to Campione:

★★★★Lago di Lugano, in Bissone, t 649 8591, *www.hotellagodilugano.ch* (*expensive*). This is a good value choice for families with small children as it offers mini-apartments (all of which are terraced), adults' and children's pools and a pirate world playground for the kids to let off steam. There is also a 'Pinocchio club' for kids aged 6 months to 13 years running daily 10–9, and restaurant **Orchidea** where kids eat for free, as well as *boules*, chess in the garden, bicycles to rent,

windsurfing, canoeing, pedalos and a fitness centre. *Dogs admitted except July–Aug. Closed Jan–Feb.*

★★★Hotel Campione, Via Campione 62, t 640 1616, *www.hotel-campione.ch* (*moderate*). Renovated with all mod cons, including separate kids' and adults' pools, garage and a restaurant terraced overlooking the lake.

★★La Palma, Piazza Borromini, in Bissone, t 649 8406, *www.bordognaweb.com* (*moderate–inexpensive*). Family-run hotel with a restaurant that makes pizza to take away or eat in.

La Taverna, Piazzale Roma 2, t 649 4797 (*expensive*). This top-notch restaurant has a good menu, which includes some delicious truffle and mushroom dishes. *Closed Wed.*

Da Candida, Via Marco 4, t 649 7541, *www.dacandida.com* (*expensive*). A charming and stylish restaurant in a single vaulted room containing a huge chimney dating from the turn of the last century. Candida has long been a well known inn of Lugano for traditional polenta dishes, once cooked by Candida herself over the chimney's fire. The restaurant has now been turned into a romantic *bombonniere* by fine French chef Bernard Fournier and his wife Adriana, an experienced hotelier (look at the impressive list of diplomas hanging on the entrance walls) and offers an unequalled mix of French and Italian cuisine across the menu and in the wine list, although desserts are definitely French. Bernard prepares in-house his own *pâté de foie gras*, bread and pasta, and has an enviable selection of oysters direct from Brittany (strictly for months with an 'r' only). Menus change regularly. *Book in advance for dinner. Closed Mon–Tues at lunch time, 1 week in Feb, July.*

Campione d'Italia

Campione has been a little enclave ever since its Lombard owner Totone bequeathed it to the church of Sant'Ambrogio in Milan in 777, and to this day its church follows the Ambrosian rites and prolonged carnival. In the Middle Ages Campione was celebrated for its master builders, the Maestri Campionesi, symbolized by the big snail on the fief's coat of arms. The Maestri Campionesi had a hand in most of Italy's great Romanesque cathedrals – Milan's Sant'Ambrogio, Cremona, Monza (by Matteo da Campione, one of the rare masters to leave his name), Verona and Modena – and such was their reputation that when Hagia Sophia in Constantinople began to sag, the Emperor of Byzantium hired them to prop it up. Rather disappointingly, in Campione itself they left only a small sample of their handiwork: ancient San Zenone (thoroughly mutilated in the 17th century), now the town art gallery, and **San Pietro** (1326). There is also the Baroque-encased church of the **Madonna dei Ghirli** (Our Lady of the Swallows – the swallows being the masons who periodically returned home), with a lively, personalized *Last Judgement* (1400) by Lanfranco and Filippolo De Veris under the portico, and inside 13th-century frescoes and the monochrome *Labours of the Months*. The church is located near the entry of the enclave and is beautifully positioned facing the lake on top of an imposing staircase, best seen from the lake.

Although part of Italy since Napoleon passed through in 1797, Campione is best known these days as the Las Vegas of Lombardy. The **Casinò Municipale** was founded in 1917 in bizarre circumstances: Italian naval intelligence, hoping to capture the displacement plans of the imperial fleet in the Adriatic, which were locked in the safe of the Austro-Hungarian ambassador in Bern, opened a casino to draw in foreign diplomats; the games tables were operated by Italian spies and safe-crackers released from prison to serve their country. These days the profits go for public works in the province of Como and the bandits are all one-armed (*game tables open 3.30pm–3.30am; casino closed 24 and 25 Dec*). Although Campione is an Italian enclave, it belongs to Switzerland in terms of customs, economy, currency and telephone networks and you will need a passport to reach it from Italy. Beware also that you will need a special coupon (*validity one year €25*) to drive on Swiss motorways, which can be bought at the local customs. Campione is 15 minutes by ferry from Lugano.

Back in Italy: Eastern Lake Lugano

East of Lugano, the lake enters the Italian province of Como. The hamlets on the north shore all belong to the *comune* of **Valsolda**, among them pretty **San Mamete**, a steamer landing with an arcaded piazza by a lake, and picturesque **Oria**, site of Antonio Fogazzaro's famous (in Italy, at any rate) novel, *Piccolo Mondo Antico*. **Porlezza**, a pleasant if rather Swissified town on the far east end of the lake, was the Roman *Portus Retiae* (gate to the Rhaetic tribes) and the cradle of the Della Porta sculptors (including Guglielmo, Michelangelo's pupil). Buses from Porlezza cross over to Menaggio on Lake Como, passing on the way the tiny, enchanting **Lago di Piano**, a bit of Lake Lugano that got away in a landslide. A new road from here leads up to **Cavargna** (3,534ft/1,077m) in the Lepontine Alps, a region so remote it was once called 'Little Tibet'; its traditional crafts and characters (the Blacksmith, the Carpenter, the Smuggler) are recalled in the **Museo della Valle** (*t 0344 63162; open Sun 2–5, or ask at the Trattoria Butti; adm free*).

Lake Lugano to Lake Como: The Val d'Intelvi

An alternative, longer and more meandering route between the lakes runs through the Val d'Intelvi. In the Middle Ages (when it was called the Val Antelami) the valley

Tourist Information

Pro Loco Porlezza: Via Ceresio 2, **t** 0344 62196, *prolocop@hotmail.com*. Ask for the 'Walk of the Nine Bell Towers', and for directions to Cima hamlet, 2,625ft (800m) above sea level: a picturesque village perched above the lake with narrow streets and ancient walls, a nice Baroque church and a beautiful panorama from the cemetery.

Market Days

Porlezza: *Sat 8–6pm*.

Festivals

Carnival, *February*. One of Lombardy's most famous festivals, in Schignano.

Sports and Activities

The tourist office can provide maps for mountain bike itineraries. **Bikes** can be rented at Bici Club, Via Ceresio 84, Porlezza, **t** 0344 72334. There is **horse-riding** at Caraco, Azienda Agrituristica 'Ranch Prato Rotondo' **t** 0344 61154 and Il Bivacco, **t** 0338 451 0362, in Lanzo, where you can stay as well. A nice drive is to the top of Monte Sighignola (1,300ft/396m), above Lanzo d'Intelvi, with a breath-taking panorama of Lake Lugano. There is a nine-hole **golf course** at Lanzo d'Intelvi, Piano delle Noca, **t** 031 839 060, *www.golflanzo.it* (*open April–mid Nov*).

Where to Stay and Eat

San Mamete (Valsolda) ✉ 22010

★★★**Stella d'Italia**, Piazza Roma, **t** 0344 68139, *www.stelladitalia.com* (*expensive*). This charming lakeside hotel has its own lido and garden as well as a good restaurant under the pergola and waterside terraces. Inside, there's a nice library. Each room has a balcony, and you can hire the hotel's boat for outings. *Open April–mid-Oct. Restaurant closed on Wed.*

★★**Riviera**, Via Statale 127, Oria, **t** 0344 68156, *www.hotelriviera.com* (*inexpensive*). A good-value hotel on the lake, with a pretty lido and an excellent restaurant (*moderate*) with plenty of fish and a flair for flambées. Rooms are basic, but spacious and with beautiful views over the lake: ask for the top ones for a private sunny terrace. The hotel and restaurant are run by Vittorio from Valtellina and Josephine, his Londoner wife. Vittorio is happy to show you around in his motorboat. *Closed Wed.*

Porlezza ✉ 22018

★★★**Europa**, Lungolago Matteotti 19, **t** 0344 61142, *www.hoteleuropaitaly.com* (*moderate*). Slightly less attractive, in a quieter position in front of the small harbour. Family-run, with a small garden and a restaurant. *Closed Mon.*

★★★**Regina**, Lungolago Matteotti 11, **t** 0344 61228 (hotel), **t** 0344 61684 (restaurant), *www.hregina.com* (*moderate*). Refurbished rooms with all conveniences. The restaurant features good home-made pasta, excellent fish and specialities such as breast of duck with grapes. *Closed Mon.*

Il Crotto del Lago, Cima di Porlezza hamlet, Via Fontanella 3, **t** 0344 69132 (*moderate*). For outdoor dining on a terrace above the lake, offering speciality fish. *Closed Mon.*

La Siesta, Via per Osteno 12, **t** 0344 61493 (*moderate–inexpensive*). A restaurant and pizzeria with outside dining. *Closed Thurs.*

Lanzo d'Intelvi ✉ 22024

★★★★ **Belvedere**, Via Poletti 27, by the funicular station, **t** 031 840 122, *www.albergo belvedere.it* (*expensive–moderate*). Lanzo's finest for some time, with a garden and superb views. *Restaurant closed Mon.*

Al Marnich (*agriturismo*), Via per Marnico 8, in Marnico hamlet, close to Schignano, **t** 031 819 242, *www.al-marnich.it* (*inexpensive*). For food and a farmhouse stay in a country house full of old agricultural objects. Ask for a room with a fireplace for a romantic winter break. There is also trout fishing in the nearby river, plus horse-riding and trekking to neighbouring Monte Generoso and Bisbino. *Closed mid-Jan–March.*

Locanda del Dosso, Via elle Fente 6, **t** 031 840 401 (*moderate*). Set off on its own amid the trees, serving delicious trout and mushroom dishes, *fagottini di manzo intelvese* and home-made desserts. *Closed Tues.*

produced dynasties of masons and master builders – most importantly the inimitable Benedetto Antelami, 12th-century architect and sculptor of Parma's baptistry. These cousins of the Campionese masters reached the peak of their fame in the 18th century, when the courts of Naples, Spain, Austria and Russia kept them busily employed on a hundred projects.

The Val d'Intelvi follows the stream Telo, which flows into Lake Lugano at **Osteno**, west of Porlezza. You can make a boat excursion up the watery ravine and take in the marble *Madonna and Child* (1464) in the parish church, carved by Osteno native Andrea Bregno. From Osteno the road winds up to **Lanzo d'Intelvi**, the valley's most important resort, with a golf course and nearby ski runs up at Pellio and San Fedele.

The valley's builders left a number of churches in the Intelvi, many decorated with sculpture and stuccoes, another local speciality. You'll find especially good examples at **Laino** (16th-century San Lorenzo) and **Scaria** (13th-century Santi Nazaro e Celso). Scaria also has a museum dedicated to the Val Intelvi, the **Museo Diocesano d'Arte Sacra** (*Piazza Corloni 1,* **t** *031 840 143; open July and Aug daily 3–7, other times by reservation*) with works salvaged from its churches, including a Byzantine cross. Clutches of medieval houses remain at unspoiled **Ponna Superiore** and **Ponna Inferiore**, both set in some of the Intelvi's prettiest landscapes; also **Pellio Superiore**, **Castiglione d'Intelvi** (at Montronio) and **Dizzasco**. The church at **Casasco d'Intelvi** has a fresco attributed to Luini while **Pigra** has another famous viewpoint, overlooking Lake Como.

Lake Como

Sapphire Lake Como has been Italy's most popular romantic lake ever since the early days of the Roman empire, when it was called Lario and the Plinys wrote of the luxuriant beauty surrounding their villas on its shores. It was just the sort of beauty which enraptured the children of the romantic era, inspiring some of the best works of Verdi, Rossini, Bellini and Liszt, as well as enough good and bad English verse to fill several anthologies. And it is still there, the Lake Como of the Shelleys and Wordsworths, the grand villas and lush gardens, the mountains and beloved irregular shore of wooded promontories. But there are times when the lake can seem schizophrenic, its nostalgic romance and mellowed dignity challenged by demands that it serve as Milan's weekend Riviera playground. Even so, Como is large and varied enough to offer retreats where, to paraphrase Longfellow's ode to the lake, no sound of Alfa Romeo or high heel breaks the silence of the summer day.

Third largest of the Italian Lakes, 50km long but only 4.4km at its widest point, Como is one of the deepest in Europe, plunging down 1,345ft (410m) near Argegno. It forks in the middle like a pair of legs: the prettiest region of Tremezzo, Bellagio and Varenna hangs like a belt on its waist, and the mountain-bound east branch is known as the Lago di Lecco. The seven excellent golf courses on the lake are a legacy of the English, while the waters around Domaso are excellent for windsurfing. As a rule, the further you go from the city of Como, the cleaner the water, and the more likely you are to find wooden racks of fat twaite shad drying in the sun (Como's famous

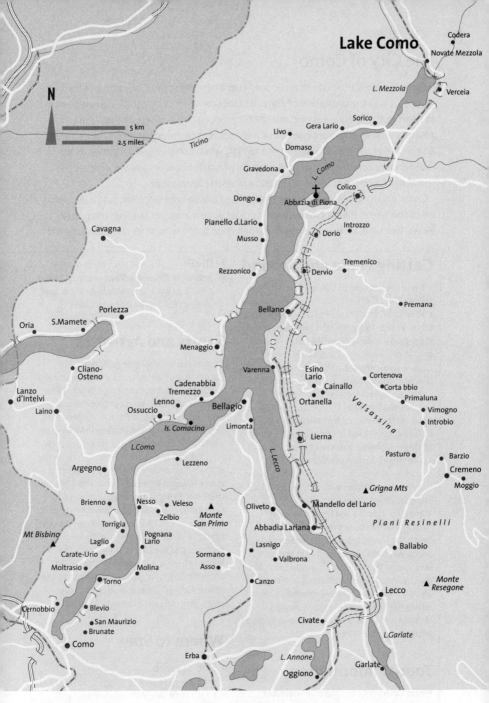

Lake Como

N

5 km
2.5 miles

Codera

Novate Mezzola

Verceia

L. Mezzola

Sorico

Gera Lario

Livo

Domaso

Ticino

Gravedona

L. Como

Colico

Dongo

Abbazia di Piona

Pianello d.Lario

Introzzo

Dorio

Musso

Tremenico

Rezzonico

Dervio

Premana

Bellano

Cavagna

Porlezza

Oria

S.Mamete

Menaggio

Esino
Lario

Cortenova

Cliano-
Osteno

Varenna

Cainallo

Corta bbio

Primaluna

Lanzo
d'Intelvi

Cadenabbia
Tremezzo

Ortanella

Valsassina

Vimogno

Laino

Lenno

Bellagio

Introbio

Ossuccio

Is. Comacina

Limonta

Lierna

Pasturo

Barzio

L.Como

Cremeno

Lezzeno

Moggio

Argegno

L. Lecco

Grigna Mts

Brienno

Nesso

Veleso

Oliveto

Mandello del Lario

Torriggia

Zelbio

*Monte
San Primo*

Abbadia Lariana

Piani Resinelli

Laglio

Pognana
Lario

Lasnigo

Ballabio

Carate-Urio

Sormano

Valbrona

Mt Bisbino

Moltrasio

Molina

Asso

*Monte
Resegone*

Torno

Canzo

Lecco

Cernobbio

Blevio

San Maurizio

Civate

L.Garlate

Brunate

Como

Erba

L. Annone

Garlate

Oggiono

missultit (or *missoltini*) are best served lightly grilled with oil and vinegar and slices of polenta). The winds change according to the time of day; the *breva* blows northwards from noon to sunset, while the *tivà* blows south during the night.

The City of Como

Como is a lively little city that has long had a bent for science, silk and architecture. In AD 23 it was the birthplace of Pliny the Elder, compiler of antiquity's greatest work of hearsay, the *Natural History,* and later it produced his nephew and heir Pliny the Younger, whose letters are one of our main sources for information on the cultured Roman life of the period. From *c.* 1050 to 1335, when Como enjoyed a period as an independent *comune,* it produced a school of master builders, known generally as the Maestri Comacini, rivals to Lugano's Maestri Campionese.

Como's historic centre, its street plan almost unchanged since Roman times, opens up to the lake at **Piazza Cavour**, with its cafés, hotels, steamer landing and pretty views. Two landmarks in the public gardens just to the west offer an introduction to

Getting There and Around

There are frequent FS **trains, t** 892 021, from Milan's Porta Garibaldi, Centrale or Cadorna stations, to Como's main San Giovanni station, **t** 034 147 888 088 (40mins). Slow trains run on the regional Milano-Nord line to the lakeside station of Como-Lago. From Como, trains to Lugano and Lecco depart from San Giovanni (change train in Mousa to Milan). **Buses** from Como run to nearly every lakeside town.

A **steamer** (the 1926 *Concordia,* July–Aug only), **motorboats** and **hydrofoils** are operated by Navigazione Lago di Como, based in Como at Via per Cernobbio 18, **t** 031 579 211, or **t** 800 551 801 (free), *www.navigazionelagli.it,* for schedules and tourist passes (1–3 days). In the summer **night cruises** with dinner and dance on board depart from Como, Bellagio, Menaggio, Varenna and Lecco. The most frequent connections are between Como, Tremezzo, Menaggio, Bellagio, Varenna and Colico, with additional services in the central lake, and at least one boat a day to Lecco. Note that hydrofoil tickets cost about half as much again as the more leisurely steamers. **Car ferries** run between Bellagio, Menaggio, Varenna and Cadenabbia. Some services stop altogether in the winter.

Tourist Information

Piazza Cavour 17, **t** 031 330 0111, *www.lake como.com, www.lagodicomo.com.* Internet access is at the Black Panther Bar, Via Garibaldi 59, **t** 031 243 005, in the centre.

Festivals
Il Canto delle Pietre: Medieval music festival in Como, Brunate and Province usually in Sept – contact the tourist office for dates

Sports and Activities

Como has a full 18-hole **golf course**, the Circolo Villa d'Este, which is a mere 4km away in Montorfano, **t** 031 200 200, *www.golfvilla deste.com.* To hire a **boat**, contact the yacht club Circolo Vela Annje Bonnje, Via Perlasca 4, **t** 031 301 419, *www.annjebonnje.it.* **Rowing** is available at Canottieri Lario, Viale Puecher 6, **t** 031 574 720, *wwwcanottierelario.it;* **canoeing** at Kayak Como, Viale Geno 14, **t** 031 341 705; **water-skiing** at Villa Olmo, **t** 335 682 9850; and there is a **diving** centre at Viale Geno 14, **t** 031 342 127. For **bikes**, go to Montagna Sport, **t** 031 240 821 and Arnaboldi, Via Regina, **t** 031 273 053. **Horses** can be hired at the Centro di Equitazione Comasco, in Grandate in the Frazione Barella, **t** 031 450 235. The tourist office has maps for **walkers** published by the Italian Alpine Club, and an exceptionally pretty trek runs from Como to Bellagio.

Where to Stay

Como ✉ 22100
****Albergo Terminus**, Lungo Lario Trieste 14, **t** 031 329 111, *www.albergoterminus.com* (*very expensive*). An elegant 1902 hotel right in the heart of town, carefully restored to mantain the original Liberty style in the

Como's more recent scientists and architects. The first, the circular **Tempio Voltiano** (*Lunger Lamio Marconi, t 031 574 705; open April–Sept, Tues–Sun 10–12 and 3–6; Oct–Mar, Tues–Sun 10–12 and 2–4; adm*), was built in 1927 to house the manuscripts, instruments and inventions of Como's electrifying native son, the self-taught physicist Alessandro Volta (1745–1827), who lent his name to volts in a hundred languages.

A bit further on, the **Monumento ai Caduti** – a First World War war memorial – was designed by the Futurist architect Antonio Sant'Elia of Como (1888–1916), who himself died in action on the Front. The monument was actually built by Giuseppe Terragni (1904–34), a native of Como province. His buildings are spread throughout Como (the 1927 Hotel Metropole Suisse in Piazza Cavour is one) and the tourist office offers a special Terragni town plan. One ends up wishing that he, like Sant'Elia, had lived a little longer.

halls, reading room and charming Bar delle Terme, with a panoramic terrace on the lake. Rooms are decorated in style and have all modern comforts. Sauna and underground garage at an extra fee.

****Barchetta Excelsior**, Piazza Cavour, t 031 3221, www.hotelbarchetta.com (*very expensive*). A grand old hotel. Many rooms have balconies overlooking the lake. The hotel offers special gourmet, shopping and golf weekends.

****Palace Hotel**, Lungo Lario Trieste 16, t 031 303 303, www.palacehotel.it (*very expensive – but 20% discount on bed & breakfast Jan–Feb*). Situated on the lake, this luxurious hotel partly occupies the former palace of the Archbishop. Its rooms are big and modern, and some have fax machines. There is a well-priced lunch menu in the hotel restaurant.

****Villa Flori**, just outside Como on the west shore, Via Cernobbio 12, t 031 33820, www.hotelvillaflori.com (*very expensive*). Classy and romantic 19th-century hotel, with Como's finest restaurant to boot. All of the rooms are stylishly decorated and have a terrace overlooking the lake. At an extra fee you can plunge into the past and spend a night in the Garibaldi Suite, part of the original one-storey villa built by Marquis Flori as a gift upon the marriage of his 18-year-old daughter Giuseppina to the Hero of the Two Worlds. It was one of the most sensational and yet shortest high society marriages of the time, as Garibaldi soon rejected his spouse when he discovered she had a shady past.

****Le Due Corti**, Piazza Vittoria 15, t 031 328 111 (*very expensive–expensive*). The place to stay in Como for character, charm and history, located in front of Porta Vittoria, main entry to the walled city centre. Converted from a monastery into a post house, it reopened in 1992 as a hotel. Rooms are arranged around the former cloister and all are individual, preserving much of their original architecture, and decorated with local fabrics, antique furniture and old prints. Concessions to modernity include air conditioning, satellite TV, minibar and Jacuzzis in some bathrooms, and a small outdoor pool in the cloister. The hotel has opened an adjoining Art Deco bar and a wine bar under the Roman bricked vaults of the basement. Good restaurant.

***Marco's**, Via Colomiola 43, t 031 303 628, www.hotelmarcos.it (*expensive*). Eleven small rooms, all with TV, phone and balcony, strategically located near the lake front, the city centre and the cable car to Brunate.

***Park Hotel**, Viale Fratelli Rosselli 20, t 031 572 615, www.parkhotelcomo.it (*moderate*). Medium-size and welcoming, but without a restaurant. Near the lake and close to S. Giovanni railway station, recently renovated. *Open Mar–Nov.*

Posta, Via Garibaldi 2, t 031 266 012, www.hotelposta.net (*moderate*). You can dream about the glories of the corporate state here at a hotel that was designed in 1930 by Terragni, although refurbishments have changed the original interiors. The restaurant's good quality set menu offers meat or fish.

The Historic Centre

From Piazza Cavour, Via Plinio leads back to Como's elegant salon, the Piazza Duomo. Unusually, the chief monuments are all attached to each other: the **Torre del Comune** to the charming white, grey and red marble striped town hall or **Broletto** (both built in 1215), one of the rare Romanesque (and not Gothic) symbols of civic might in the north; and this in turn to the magnificent **Duomo** (1396) (*t 031 265 244; open daily 8–12 and 3–7*), the whole now looking spanking new thanks to a thorough cleaning for its 700th birthday. The Duomo is Italy's most harmonious example of transitional architecture, although Gothic dominates in the façade and lovely rose window and pinnacles. The sculpture and reliefs are mainly by the Rodari family (late 15th–early 16th century) who also sculpted the lateral doors (the most ornate one, facing the Broletto, is called the Frog Door, although half the frog was chopped away by vandals).

Ostello dell'Olmo, Via Bellinzona 2, Villa Olmo Park, t 031 573 800, *ostellocomo@tin.it* (*inexpensive*). Youth hostel. *Open Mar–Nov.*

Eating Out

Sant'Anna, Via Filippo Turati 1/3 (you need a car to get here), t 031 505 266, *www.santanna1907.com* (*very expensive*). This used to be a family establishment frequented by silk toilers, featuring typical Lombard dishes. The new managment offers ever-changing seasonal menus of nouvelle cuisine. *Closed Sat at lunch, Sun, all Aug, Christmas period.*

Terrazzo Perlasca, Piazza De Gasperi 8, t 031 300 263 (*very expensive*). Como is one of those towns where the restaurants can tend to process clients with slipshod food and service, especially in summer. This is one that doesn't. It's run by four brothers, two in the kitchen and two out front. The menu changes daily and features typical dishes like *filetto di laverello* and *fettuccine e funghi*, pasta with local mushrooms, all accompanied by wonderful views over the lake. *Closed Mon and two weeks in Aug.*

Le Sette Porte, Via A. Diaz 52A, t 031 267 939 (*expensive*). In the pedestrian centre, within the walls. Italian delicacies imaginatively mixed with unusual and exotic ingredients, such as ravioli with carrots and yoghurt. Good salads and meats – try the hot *carpaccio* with vegetables and sweet cheese – and fish, served in two stylish vaulted rooms. Good wine list. *Closed Sun.*

Locanda dell'Oca Bianca, Via Canturina 251, Trecallo (5 minutes drive on the road to Cantù), t 031 525 605, *www.hotelocabianca.com* (*expensive*). Another winner, serving sit-up-and-take-note dishes out on its summer terrace, from a variety of Italian regions and some French – especially foie gras, keeping loyal to its name (*oca bianca* means white goose). *Closed Mon and Jan. Sun lunch by reservation only.*

Osteria Angolo del Silenzio, Via Lecco 25, t 031 337 2157 (*expensive, but inexpensive one-course lunch time menu on weekdays*). Just outside the city centre walls. Has home-made pasta (try the *tris*) fish and meat, local game and mushrooms in season, and a nice inner court for outdoor dining. A good cellar for aperitifs and wine tasting. *Closed Mon, Tues lunch, two weeks in Jan and two weeks in Aug.*

Villa Flori's Ristorante Raimondi, Via Canobbio 12, t 031 338 233, *www.hotelvillaflori.com* (*expensive*). For an elegant splurge, join Como society at the aforementioned hotel, where exquisite renditions of classic Italian and Lombard cuisine are served on the lakeside terrace or in the luminous dining room. *Closed Mon, Sat at lunch, Dec–mid-Feb.*

Villa Olmo Parco, Via Cantoni 1, t 031 572 321 (*moderate*). Well-prepared food and fine wines, served near the beach. *Closed Tues.*

Ristorante Teatro Sociale, near the cathedral at Via Maestri Comacini 8, t 031 264 042 (*inexpensive*). Post-theatre traditional inn, with a €15 menu including wine. Also some rooms available. *Closed Tues.*

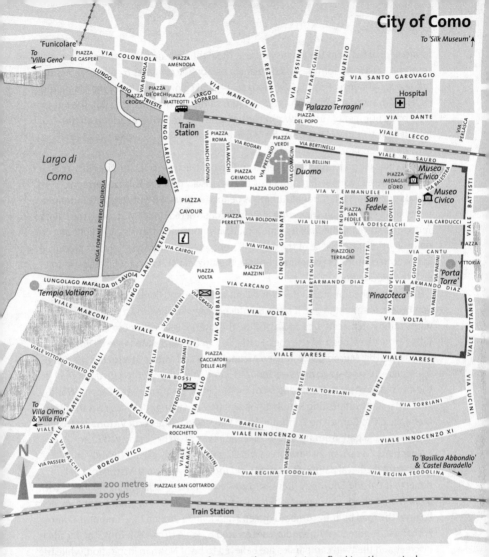

City of Como

To 'Silk Museum'

'Funicolare'
To 'Villa Geno'
PIAZZA DE GASPERI
VIA COLONIOLA
PIAZZA AMENDOLA
VIA REZZONICO
VIA PESSINA
VIA PARTIGIANI
VIA MAURIZIO
VIA SANTO GAROVAGIO

LUNGO LARIO
VIA BONGIA
PIAZZA DE'ORCHI
PIAZZA MATTEOTTI
LARGO LEOPARDI
VIA MANZONI
'Palazzo Terragni'
Hospital
PIAZZA CROGGI
PIAZZA TRIESTE

Train Station
VIA BIANCHI GIOVINI
PIAZZA ROMA
VIA RODARI
PIAZZA VERDI
VIA PRETORIO
VIA BERTINELLI
VIA BELLINI
PIAZZA DEL POPO
VIALE LECCO
VIA DANTE
VIA PERLASCA
VIALE N. SAURO

Largo di Como
DIGA FORANEA PIERO CALDIROLA
PIAZZA GRIMOLDI
PIAZZA DUOMO
VIA COMACINI
Duomo
PIAZZA MEDAGLIE D'ORD
Museo Civico
VIA BALESTRA
VIA V. EMMANUELE II
Museo Civico

PIAZZA CAVOUR
PIAZZA PERRETTA
VIA BOLDONI
VIA LUINI
San Fedele
VIA ROVELLI
VIA CARDUCCI
VIA GIOVIO
VIA INDEPENDENZA
PIAZZA SAN FEDELE
VIA ODESCALCHI
PIAZZA

VIA CAIROLI
VIA VITANI
PIAZZA MAZZINI
VIA CINQUE GIORNATE
PIAZZOLO TERRAGNI
VIA NATTA
VIA CANTU
PIAZZA VITTORIA

'Tempio Voltiano'
PIAZZA VOLTA
VIA LAMBERTENGHI
VIA CARCANO
VIA ARMANDO DIAZ
VIA ROVELLI
VIA GIOVIO
VIA PARINI
VIA ARMANDO DIAZ
'Porta Torre'

LUNGOLAGO MAFALDA DI SAVOIA
VIA RUBINI
VIA GARIBALDI
VIA GRASSI
VIA VOLTA
VIA PARINI
'Pinacoteca'
VIA CATTANEO

VIALE MARCONI
VIALE CAVALLOTTI
VIA SANT'ELIA
VIA ORIANI
VIA VOLTA
VIALE VARESE
VIALE VARESE

VIALE VITTORIO VENETO
VIA FRATELLI ROSSELLI
VIA BOSSI
PIAZZA CACCIATORI DELLE ALPI
VIA BORSIERI
VIA TORRIANI
VIA BENZI
VIA TORRIANI
VIA LUCINI

To Villa Olmo & 'Villa Flori'
VIALE MASIA
VIA RECCHIO
VIA PETROLOLO
VIA GALLIO
VIA BARELLI
VIALE INNOCENZO XI
VIA BORSIERI
VIALE INNOCENZO XI

N
VIA RISCHI
VIA PASSERI
VIA BORGO VICO
PIAZZALE ROCCHETTO
VIALE TOKAMACHI
VIA VENINI
VIA REGINA TEODOLINA
VIA REGINA TEODOLINA
To 'Basilica Abbondio' & 'Castel Baradello'

200 metres
200 yds
PIAZZALE SAN GOTTARDO
Train Station

Perhaps even more unexpected than frogs are the two statues flanking the central door, under delicate stone canopies: Pliny the Elder (on the left) and Pliny the Younger. And just what are such famous pagans doing on a cathedral? Although Pliny the Younger did write a letter to Trajan on the subject of Christians, praising their hard work and suggesting that they be left in peace, the fact is that Renaissance humanists regarded all noble figures of antiquity as honorary saints, especially if they were home boys.

Inside, the three Gothic aisles combine happily with a Renaissance choir and transept, crowned by a dome designed by the great late Baroque master Filippo Juvarra in 1744. Nine 16th-century tapestries hang along the nave, lending an air of palatial elegance to the scene; a pair of Romanesque lions situated near the entrance are survivors from the cathedral's 11th-century predecessor. But most of the art to be found here dates from the Renaissance: in the right aisle are six reliefs with scenes from the Passion by Tommaso Rodari, and a pair of fine canvases by two of Leonardo's followers, Gaudenzio Ferrari (*Flight into Egypt*) and Luini (*Adoration of the Magi*). The latter's famous *Madonna with Child* and four saints adorns the high altar. The left aisle has a number of further works by the same trio: Rodari's *Deposition* on the fourth altar, Ferrari's *Marriage of the Virgin* and Luini's *Nativity*, as well as a 13th-century sarcophagus.

For a contrast, go behind the Duomo and across the train tracks to the Piazza del Popolo, where Giuseppe Terragni's ex-Casa del Fascio, now the **Palazzo Terragni,** stands out in all its functional, luminous beauty. Built in 1931 but completely unlike the typically ponderous travertine buildings constructed under Mussolini, the Palazzo Terragni is 50 years ahead of its time, practically transparent, an essay in light and harmony, the masterpiece of the only coherent architectural style Italy has produced in the 20th century. Its present occupants, the Guardia di Finanza, will let you in to visit the ground floor.

From the cathedral, main Via Vittorio Emanuele leads to Como's old cathedral, **San Fedele**, first built in 914. It has a unique pentagonal apse and a doorway carved with chubby archaic figures and a griffon; the interior is lavishly decorated with 18th-century frescoes and stuccoes. Further up, in the Piazza Medaglie d'Oro Comasche, the **Museo Civico**, **Museo Archeologico** and **Museo Storico** (*t 031 271 343; open Tues–Sat 9.30–12.30 and 2–5, Sun 10–1; adm, children under 15 with adult free*) is the city's attic of artefacts, dating from the Neolithic era up until the Second World War, with some interesting Roman finds and frescoes along the way. From the Piazza Medaglie d'Oro Comasche, continue down Via Giovio to the **Porta Vittoria**, a striking skyscraper of a gate from 1192, its immaculate tiers of arches rising 72ft (22m).

Near here, Como's small **Pinacoteca**, Via Diaz 84, contains carved capitals and wonderful medieval paintings from the old monastery of Santa Margherita del Broletto (*t 031 269 869; open Tues–Sat 9.30–12.30 and 2–5; adm, children under 15 with adult free*). A short walk away from the Porta Vittoria, at the beginning of the Via della Regina (the road built by Lombard queen Theodolinda around Lake Como), is Como's Romanesque gem **Sant'Abbondio**, consecrated by Pope Urban II in 1095. The façade is discreet and the twin campaniles are believed to be of Norman inspiration, while the interior, with its lofty vaults and forest of columns forming five aisles, offers a kind of preview of coming great events in Italian architecture. Its clean, unadorned majesty is relieved by the rich bands of reliefs around the windows of the nave and apse, imitating the intricate patterns of damasks from the Near East. The elegant apse is decorated with 14th-century frescoes – note the knights in armour arresting Christ in Gethsemane.

If you've brought your walking shoes or car, continue 3km south up to the **Castello Baradello**, built by Emperor Barbarossa in 1158. In 1277 it became the military head-quarters of the Archbishop of Milan, Ottone Visconti, exiled by Milan's arrogant Guelph boss Napo della Torre. Napo marched out to capture the archbishop, but so carelessly disdained his opponent that he was captured instead, spending the last 19 months of his life suspended in a metal cage from its 112ft (34m) tower; you can enjoy the same view that tormented him (*t 031 592 805; open Thurs, Sat and Sun 2.30–6, other days by appointment only, but check at the tourist office*).

Around Como: Watersports, Silk and Lace

Como is framed by beaches. One is on the west end of town in Via Cantoni, by the neoclassical **Villa Olmo** (1782). The villa and garden are used for special exhibitions and concerts; the top floor preserves architectural drawings by Antonio Sant'Elia (*t 031 252 443; garden and interiors open daily 9–7 winter, 8–11pm summer; adm free*). The other lido, on the east end of town, is by the **Villa Genio**, with another park and a geyser fountain spouting high over the lake. Close by, in Piazza De Gasperi, funiculars wind up to **Brunate**, a mountain village with views across the lake and Alps as far as Monte Rosa (*t 031 303 608; every 15–30mins, in summer until midnight; combined ticket for ferry/funicular*). If you drive up to Brunate you can take in one of the quainter contemporary works of Italian piety at Garzola: the reinforced concrete **Tempio Sacrario degli Sports Nautici** (*Via per Brunate 39, t 031 305 958, funicolarecomo @libero.it; open Sun 2.30–6; groups need to book in advance*), 'a spiritual clubhouse for all who practise water sports'. Built by a speedboating parish priest, its shipshape walls and sea-crib altar are covered with seashells, and display cases are packed with water sport memorabilia. Lastly, architecture buffs can seek out the Villa Elisi in **San Maurizio** (the village next to Brunate), the only work Sant'Elia actually built in his abbreviated life.

When Como lost its independence to Milan in the 14th century, it gained a major market for its textiles. In 1510 it turned to silk in a big way and has been Italy's leading producer ever since. Although the mulberry-munching worms are no longer raised by the lake, Chinese thread is woven and dyed here to the specifications of the Milanese fashion industry. In 1990 the Silkmakers' School set up the **Silk Museum**, south of central Como (*Via Valleggio 3, entrance is in Via Castelnuovo 1, t 031 303 180, www. museosetacomo.com; open Tues–Fri 9–12 and 3–6; adm; wheelchair accessible*), to display their work; shops in town sell it by the yard, but don't expect good discounts.

If Como supplies Milan's silk, the industrious town of **Cantù**, a short hop away on the Lecco train or SPT bus, provides its handmade lace as well as some of its furniture. Cantù's landmark is the tall Romanesque campanile of its parish church, but the main point of interest, the 10th-century **Basilica di San Vincenzo** and **Battistero di San Giovanni**, is a kilometre to the east of the station in the neighbouring hamlet of Galliano (*open daily 9–11.30 and 3–5*). Isolated in the pines, the basilica is decorated with a fresco cycle painted just after the first millennium; the baptistry with its little cupola is one of the oldest in Lombardy (*contact the parish, t 031 714 126, before setting out*).

The West Shore to Cadenabbia

This stretch of Lake Como, famous for its mild climate and azalea gardens, was the aristocratic high-rent district in the 19th century. The main lake road, Via Regina, is named after the queen who laid it out: 7th-century Theodolinda of the Lombards.

Cernobbio to Argegno

Only a few minutes from Como, at the foot of green Monte Bisbino, **Cernobbio** (which sounds disconcertingly like 'Chernobyl' if you're not listening closely) dates its status as an aristocratic enclave back to 1816–17, when Queen Caroline of England held her wild parties in what is now the fabulous Hotel Villa d'Este; these days politicians book it for somewhat more discreet conferences at Italian taxpayers' expense (*see* p.201). Cernobbio has a few old lanes off its lakeside square, and superb views across the Alps from atop **Bisbino** (4,347ft/1,325m), a dizzy 17km drive up from the centre.

Moltrasio, the next resort to the north, clings to the slopes of Bisbino on either side of a deep ravine. Here the **Villa Passalacqua** has a lovely Italianate garden decorated with ceramics, while a plaque on the nearby **Villa Salterio** commemorates Vincenzo Bellini, who stayed here in 1831, in love with its tenant Giuditta Turina Cantù, while he composed his operas *La Straniera* and much of *La Sonnambula*. In **Carate-Urio**, the next resort again to the north, at the summit of a chapel-lined Via Crucis (1752), the panoramic **Santuario di Santa Marta** dates from *c.* 1000 but was much rebuilt in the 12th century (the date of its campanile); inside are charming frescoes from the 1400s.

North once more, the road passes the hamlet of **Torriggia**, where prehistoric cave bears once looked out of their lairs over the narrowest stretch of Lake Como (2,133ft/650m). The waters lick many of the houses in Brienno, further north, where the parish church claims to possess the relics of Barbarossa, 'canonized' by the Comaschi for razing hated Milan to the ground (flying in the face of the fact that the emperor drowned in six inches of water and that every German knows he sleeps under Köningsberg, ready to return in the hour of Germany's greatest need). At Argegno, north of Brienno, a monument stands to Pietro Vassena who in 1948 went to the bottom of the lake in his bathysphere – then a world depth record. Argegno enjoys a privileged position overlooking the snow-clad mountains to the north.

Isola Comacina

Up the shore from Argegno, **Sala Comacina** and **Ossuccio** have irresistibly romantic views over Como's only island, **Isola Comacina**, sheltered in the arm of the long Lavedo peninsula. This intimate nook of Como, once the independent Pieve dell'Isola Comacina, is sometimes called the *zoca de l'oli* or 'oil hollow' for the olive trees that once made it rich. First inhabited by the Romans, it prospered to the extent that Isola Comacina was nicknamed Chrysopolis, the city of gold. By the 12th century it was a fierce rival of Como, joining Milan to crush their mutual enemy in 1128. In 1190 Como, back in favour with Barbarossa, sent raiders to decimate the little island state, burning it to the ground and forbidding its inhabitants ever to return. By some twist of fate in the 19th century the island came to be owned by the King of the Belgians, who donated it as a retreat for Milanese artists; their cottages share the island with a good restaurant (*see* p.202), the 16th-century church of **San Giovanni** and the ruins of five ancient churches, including a 6th-century baptistry.

On the mainland, Sala's **Villa Beccaria** was a favourite retreat of Cesare Beccaria when the Church drove him crazy (*see* p.26); the parish church has Romanesque frescoes. Boats from Sala transport visitors to the gardens of the famous **Villa del**

Tourist Information

Cernobbio: Via Regina 33b, t 031 510 198, *cernobbio@tin.it. Open May–Oct.*
Tremezzo: Via Regina 3, t 0344 40493. *Open May–Oct.*

Festivals

St John's Day Celebration. Comacina puts on a display of fireworks, parades and hundreds of *lumaghitti* – snail shells made into tiny oil lamps and then illuminated. Contact Navigazione Lago di Como about evening island cruises, t 800 551 801, or *www. navigazioneaghi.it.*
Venerd di Villa Carlotta, *June–Sept.* Classical music concerts held in the villa, in Tremozzo, t 0344 40405, *www.villacarlotta.it.*

Sport and Activities

Boat Service at Argegno's port rents **motorboats** and **mountain bikes**, and also offers **water-skiing**, t 031 821 1955 (June–Sept). BCA Demko Kit, Via Regina 48, t 031 511 262, Cernobbio, also rents motorboats, rowing boats and paddle boats.

In the first weekend of September, Cernobbio has plenty of **summer events**: music and shows in the centre's piazzas, theatre, opera (Lario Lirica) and horse-riding competitions in the park of Villa Erba.

Where to Stay and Eat

Cernobbio ✉ 22012

*****Grand Hotel Villa d'Este, Via Regina 40, t 031 3481, *www.villadeste.it* (*luxury*). Lake Como's most glittering showcase, this was built in 1557 by Pelligrini for Cardinal Tolomeo Gallio, the son of a Como noble family who went on to become one of the most powerful men in the Vatican. Besides this villa, he had seven along the road to Rome so he never had to spend a night 'away from home'. Queen Caroline was not the only crowned head to make use of the cardinal's old digs; since 1873 it has been a hotel. Each room is individual, furnished with antiques or fine reproductions. The public rooms are regal and the food is

superb, prepared by a battalion of 40 chefs supervised by chef Luciano Parolari (at the hotel for the last 20 years), and served in the panoramic veranda (jacket and tie required in the evening) or the more informal grill. In addition, the glorious gardens are in themselves a reason to stay. Add a floating swimming pool, another indoor pool, a fine golf course, squash, tennis, sailing, sauna, Turkish bath, a sybaritic spa, nightclub and more. The hotel has a long list of regal guests and film stars, as well as fashion moguls on their visit to the capital of silk. Be warned that the rooms cost a king's ransom, and non-guests are welcome at the restaurant, but the average bill is €100. *Open Mar–mid-Nov.*
***Asnigo, Via Noseda 2, Piazza S. Stefano, t 031 510 062 (*very expensive–expensive*). A nice hotel above the city centre, built in 1914 with a beautiful terrace overlooking Cernobbio and Como. Pretty rooms, friendly service, a special service for golfers and a good restaurant with a €20 daily menu. *Closed Mon.*
*La Vignetta, Via Monte Grappa 32, t 031 334 7055, *lavignetta@tin.it* (*moderate*). An excellent value choice; clean, cosy and with a nice restaurant (*moderate–inexpensive*). Not all the rooms have bathrooms en suite. Convenient family rooms with 3–4 beds. *Restaurant closed Tues.*
Giardino, Via Regina 73 (the main road), t 031 511 154 (*moderate–inexpensive*). Restaurant and pizzeria with a nice inner court for outside dining. The hotel above (*moderate*) has standard rooms. *Closed Wed.*
**Terzo Crotto, just behind the city centre, Via Volta 21, t 031 512 304, *www.terzocrotto.it* (*inexpensive*). Set in its own green and peaceful grounds, it has nine rooms, all with bath, and an excellent family-run restaurant. *Closed Mon and Tues at lunch.*
Trattoria Gatto Nero, Via Monte Santo 69, 5mins drive up from the city centre in Rovenna hamlet, t 031 512 042 (*expensive*). Rustic restaurant with lovely lake views; it has plenty of character and little rooms and terraces full of nice furniture, objects and pictures, as well as delicious food and a good wine list. *Closed Mon and Tues lunch. Booking advised.*

Moltrasio ✉ 22010

***Posta**, Piazza San Rocco 5, on the left of the main road as you enter Moltrasio from Como, **t** 031 290 444, www.*hotel-posta.it* (*expensive–moderate*). Renovated and furnished in style, this cosy hotel and restaurant occupies a former posthouse; it serves mouthwatering trout and decent wine on the small shady terrace. Seasonal tasting menus from €25. *Closed Wed only at lunch and Jan–Feb.*

Crotto dei Platani, Via Regina 73, on the main lakeside road between Moltrasio and Ossuccio, Brienno, **t** 031 814 038, *www. crottodeiplatani.it* (*expensive*). A rustic and elegant, historic restaurant, selected by the Accademia Pliniana for convivial meals and open since 1885. You can eat excellent Larian recipes in the traditional *crotto* (cave) in winter, or on the beautiful veranda or garden above the lake in the summer. Private mooring. *Closed Tues and Wed lunch, and 3 weeks in Nov.*

Ossuccio ✉ 22018

Locanda dell'Isola Comacina, **t** 0344 55083, *www.locanda-isola-comacina.com* (*expensive*). The Isola Comacina is deserted except for this 50-year-old restaurant. For one fixed price (€54) you are picked up in a boat at Cala Comacina or Ossuccio, and regaled with a set meal of *antipasti* followed by grilled trout, fried chicken, wine and dessert. You are given a rendition of poetry while you sip your flambéed coffee, called *caffè all'uso delle canaglie in armi* (coffee for the armed blackguards – ask the host why), and then you're returned to the mainland. Boats pick you up at Ossuccio and Sala Comacina for about €5. *Open Mar–Oct, closed Tues except summer.*

Tremezzo ✉ 22019

*****Grand Hotel Tremezzo**, Via Regina 8, **t** 0344 42491, www.*grandhoteltremezzo.com* (*luxury*). Next door to Villa Carlotta; couples the generous comforts and charm of a large 19th-century hotel with all modern facilities, including tennis, a swimming pool and a sports centre. The hotel has a special connection with cinema: the 1930's film *Grand Hotel* starring Greta Garbo was shot here, and *A Month by the Lake* by John Irving

had the Grand Hotel as a background, while George Lucas stayed here during the filming of the Star Wars saga in neighbouring Villa Balbianello. A monumental staircase in the back of the hotel leads out into a park where you can stroll through the 'Iron Forest' of modern art sculptures or climb up to a breathtaking view of Bellagio, Varenna, Lecco and the Grignean mountains. The lakeside restaurant offers a five-course menu. *Open Mar–Oct.*

***Villa Marie**, Via Regina 30, **t** 0344 40427, *www.hotelvillamarie.com* (*moderate*). An intimate Victorian-style hotel with pleasant rooms and an outside pool. Overlooks the lake and a shady garden. *Open April–Oct.*

Azalea, Via Portici S. Pietro 1, on the main lakeside road close to the Grand Hotel, **t** 0344 40424 (*inexpensive*). Offers decent rooms and plenty of atmosphere, especially in the ground floor bar.

Cadenabbia ✉ 22011

In both of these hotels you may stumble on package tours in the high season:

***Bellevue**, Via Regina 1, **t** 0344 40418, *www.albergobellevue.it* (*moderate*). A large and pleasant place to stay, with sun terraces, a garden and a pool. Right on the lake and charmingly old-fashioned, but rooms have modern fittings. Inexpensive tourist menu. *Open mid-Mar–mid-Oct.*

***Britannia Excelsior**, Via Regina 13, **t** 0344 40413, *www.hotelbritanniacadenabbia.com.* (*moderate*). A cosy old hotel in Cadenabbia's piazza overlooking the lake, with lots of rooms with balconies. *Open April–Oct.*

Lenno ✉ 22016

Santo Stefano, Piazza XI Febbraio 3, **t** 0344 55434, *www.santostefano.too.it* (*moderate*). Situated on the market square; serves delicious, reasonably priced lunches and dinners. Try the *olive ascolane* – deep-fried olives stuffed with a mild fish pâté – marvellous golden ravioli stuffed with ricotta and asparagus, and ravioli with lake fish and radicchis, caramelly grilled courgettes and grilled lake fish, and wind up with apple cake or an apple and calvados sorbet. *Closed Mon, 2 weeks between Jan and Feb. Booking strongly advised.*

Balbianello (or Arconati Visconti) (*open Tues–Fri 10–1 and 2–6, Sat–Sun and hols 10–6; gardens, interiors by appointment only, call* **t** *0344 56110; the villa is only accessible by boat on weekdays, pedestrian access from Lenno at weekends and Tues; adm*) at Punta Balbianello, the very tip of the Laveno peninsula. Built by Cardinal Duini in the early 18th century over the ruins of a medieval monastery, its enchanting garden spilling down to the stone arches of its boat entrance is the distilled quintessence of Italian lake romanticism: don't miss it. The main road passes next to Ossuccio's landmark, the delightful brick and terracotta Gothic campanile on the 11th-century church of **Santa Maria Maddalena**, but you'll have to get out of the car to walk to the panoramic **Santuario della Madonna del Soccorso** (early 1500s). In the 17th century, the pious locals gave it a home-made **Sacro Monte** (*see* p.147) of 14 little chapels, each filled with earnest sculptures and frescoes.

The Tremezzina

North of Ossuccio at **Lenno** the lake opens up again to become the 'mirror of Venus' in the sheltered district of the Tremezzina, where carpets of azaleas, agaves, camellias and magnolias bloom under the towering cypresses and palms. Lenno was the site of Pliny the Younger's Villa Comedia; in one of his letters he describes how he could fish from his bedroom window. The Museo Civico in Como houses two columns of the villa found near the church **Santo Stefano**, where ruins of Pliny's baths were found under the floor. The church's crypt dates from the 11th century, as does its sturdy octagonal **Battistero San Giovanni**, a classic example of the Lombard style of its day, and restored to its original appearance. In nearby **Giulino di Mezzegra**, Mussolini and his mistress Claretta Petacci spent their last night in a room at Via Riale 4 after local partisans captured them at Donga as they attempted to flee in a German truck to Switzerland. A plaque in nearby Via XXIV Maggio marks the spot where they were executed 28 April 1945; Claretta was killed trying to shield the Duce from the bullets.

Beautiful villas are chock-a-block along the shore at **Tremezzo**, including two of the finest on Como: the early 18th-century **Villa La Quiete** with its stone balustrades at Bolvedro and, from the same period, the celebrated **Villa Carlotta** (*Via Regina 2,* **t** *0344 40405, www.villacarlotta.it; open Mar and Oct daily 9–11.30 and 2–4.30; April–Sept daily 9–6; adm exp*) on the north end of Tremezzo. Originally built in 1747 as the Villa Clerici, the villa took its name from Princess Carlotta of the Netherlands, who received it as a wedding gift from her mother upon her marriage to the Duke of Saxony-Meiningen in the 1850s. But most of what you see was the work of the former owners, the Counts Sommariva, who laid out the magnificent gardens and park, where in April and May the thousands of azaleas, camellias and rhododendrons put on a dazzling display of colour. But no matter when you come you can also take in the neoclassical interior, filled with cool, virtuoso, insufferable neoclassical statuary that the Sommarivas couldn't get enough of: a copy of Antonio Canova's *Cupid and Psyche* (one of three copies made by Canova; another is in St Petersburg), *Venus and Paris*, *Mary Magdalene* and *Palmedes* (rebuilt by Canova after someone understandably smashed it) and, in the drawing room, Icelander Bertel Thorvaldsen's marble frieze of *Alexander's Triumphant Entrance of Babylon*, commissioned by Napoleon but completed after Waterloo for the Sommarivas. After the Villa Carlotta, look for 'the leafy colonnade' of trees described by Longfellow marking the entrance to **Cadenabbia**, still served by an Anglican church built in the 19th century when the English came here in droves. Verdi composed *La Traviata* at the **Villa Margherita-Ricordi** at Maiolica and Konrad Adenauer spent his holidays at the **Villa Rosa.** Other sumptuous villas and a core of old houses fill **Griante**, a village just above Cadenabbia, and above Griante the isolated 16th-century church of **San Martino** offers an incomparable view over the Bellagio headland.

The Central Lake: Bellagio and the Larian Triangle

If time or inclination limit you to one destination on Lake Como, make it Bellagio, spectacularly set at the tip of the mountainous Triangolo Lariano that divides Como in two. From Cadenabbia the ferry crosses over to Bellagio, and buses make the journey as well, but to really see it all walk the easy two-day, 30km *Dorsale del Triangolo Lariano* trail along the ridge; pick up the free brochure at the tourist office.

Como to Bellagio

Just around Cape Geno from Como, the road winds around the mountain to **Blevio**, a collection of hamlets and villas that attracted all the prima donnas and ballerinas in the 19th century: Adelaide Ristori, Maria Taglioni and the great soprano Giuditta Pasta, who is buried in the parish church. **Torno** (ancient Roman *Turnum*) once had a population of 5,000 and rivalled Como until 1522, when the bigger town squashed it for good. Torno has some fine old houses; its church of **San Giovanni** has a marble door by the Rodaris, a wooden roof of 1469, old frescoes on the pillars and a 6th-century tombstone. The north end of town is occupied by the grounds of the 16th-century **Villa Pliniana**, rising straight from the lake. The villa must hold the local record for hosting literati, among them Byron, Ugo Foscolo, Stendhal and Bellini; Rossini composed *Tancredi* in a record six days during his stay and Shelley loved it so much that he tried to buy it. Its name comes from its peculiar intermittent 240ft waterfall, described by Pliny in his *Natural History* and in a letter of Pliny the Younger; you can only see it from the lake.

Waterfalls are almost run of the mill here: there's another one at **Molina** and yet another to the north at **Nesso**, a picturesque place, where the water splashes into the lake under a quaint stone bridge. At Nesso a road zigzags up to the **Triangolo Lariano**, that wedge of karst that makes Como do the splits. Aeons of dripping water have bored long caverns in its very intestines – one cave at **Zelbio** meanders for 9km and has yet to be explored to its end. A number of paths, best in the spring and autumn, crisscross the **Piano del Tivano** basin, where rain off the surrounding 4,000ft mountains is sucked into a natural drain called the Buco della Niccolina.

After Nesso the shore road passes through the long-drawn-out *comune* of **Lezzeno**, which has its own version of Capri's Blue Grotto, **Buco dei Carpi** (Carp Hole). The reflections are best in the afternoon. After Lezzano cliffs plummet into the lake all the

Tourist Information

Promo Bellagio: Piazza della Chiesa 14,
t 031 951 555, *www.bellagiolakecomo.com.*
Open Tues–Sun 9–12 and 3–6.
Bellagio tourist office: Piazza Mazzini,
t 031 950 204; same website as above.
Open April–Oct 9–12 and 3–6; Nov–Mar.
Closed Tues and Sun.
Internet access can be found at Gelateria
Il Sorbetto, Salita Serbelloni 34, Bellagio,
ilsorbetto@tiscalinet.it.

Sports and Activities

There are pleasant excursions to be made
from Bellagio on foot or bike; ask the tourist
office for information. **Mountain bikes** can be
rented at Arco Sport, Salita Monastero 6, **t** 031
950 959, in Bellagio; or directly in Gallasco
hamlet (Guello), 3km up from Bellagio, at
Cavalcalario Club, **t** 031 964 814, *www.bellagio-
mountains.it* for downhill mountain-biking,
plus **canyoning**, two-seat **paragliding**, **cave
exploration** (guide and equipment provided)
and **horse-riding**. Cavalcalario also organizes a
minibus service from Bellagio, **t** 339 530 8138.

Pescallo, the charming fishing village on the
other side of the promontory of Bellagio, is the
place to go **sailing**, and you can **windsurf** at
Circolo Vela, **t** 031 950 932, *www.circolodella
velapescallo.it*, which organizes summer
courses and regattas. Onno on the eastern
branch (western shore) of the lake towards
Lecco (10mins drive from Bellagio) is the place
to **windsurf** in the afternoon; Parè, further
down (15mins' drive) has a fresh breeze in the
morning and surf rental. **Water-ski** at
Bellagio's Lido, where there is the Scuola
Italiana di Sci Nautico, **t** 031 950 597, at Liquid
Park in Pescallo, **t** 335 828 1065. You can hire
canoes and **kayaks** at the Jolly Racing Club,
Sossana hamlet (Lezzeno), **t** 031 914 645,
www.jrcwakeboard.com.

Adored by Anglo-Saxon tourists, Bellagio
offers a truly Anglo-Saxon sport, **badminton**,
at Palazzetto dello Sport, Via Lazzaretto (ask
for Mr Davide Lindenblatt), **t** 031 950 492. At
the Palazzetto there is also a **rock climbing
gym**. You may hire **motorboats** with or
without a driving licence at Smanboats, in

Calvasino hamlet, near Lezzeno, **t** 031 914 621.
Cantiere Matteri, also in Calvasino, hires **old
local boats**, **t** 031 914 456. **Scooters** can be
rented at Turba Scooter, Via per Lecco 15,
t 031 661 348.

Where to Stay and Eat

Torno ✉ 22020

★★★**Villa Flora**, Via Torrazza 10, **t** 031 419 222
(*moderate*). Just the ticket for a peaceful
atmosphere, swimming pool and friendly
hosts in a beautiful hotel. Discover great
antipasti, fine cuisine and a choice list of
wines served in the restaurant overlooking
the lake. Ask for the bigger rooms in the
older part. *Open Mar–Dec.*

Lezzeno ✉ 22025

★★**Crotto del Misto**, in Crotto hamlet,
t 031 914 541, *www.crottodelmisto.com*
(*moderate, min 3 days stay*). The ideal place
for nautical sports fans – offers all-inclusive
weeks or weekends of water-skiing lessons
(4 daily). Facilities include an outdoor pool,
canoes and rowing boats, hobie cats and the
typical *gozzo* (fishing boat) for lake
excursions. With a friendly and young
atmosphere, the Crotto has an excellent
restaurant dating back to 1832, with local
dishes and a well supplied cellar. *Restaurant
closed Tues.*

Bellagio ✉ 22021

★★★★★**Grand Hotel Villa Serbelloni**, Via Roma 1,
t 031 950 216, *www.villaserbelloni.it* (*luxury*).
Romantic Bellagio has several fine hotels,
among them this magnificent, ornate one
set in a flower-filled garden at the very tip of
the headland. The frescoed public rooms are
glittering and palatial, and the sense of
opulence is greatly enhanced by the heated
pool and private beach, tennis, gym, boating
and water-skiing, and dancing in the
evening to the hotel orchestra. You can also
swim in the lake and bask on an anchored
raft. Facilities include a fully equipped spa
and an inner pool with fake rocks, waterfalls,
slides and an adventure path for children
designed by the architect of Gardaland.
Open mid-Mar–mid-Nov.

***Firenze**, Piazza Mazzini 46, **t** 031 950 342, *www.bellagio.com/florence* (*expensive*). Located in a 19th-century villa next to Bellagio's harbour, owned by the same family for over a century. Rooms are stylishly decorated and the atmospheric coffee bar has live music in the evening once a week. The terraces and many of the rooms have lake views, there's a cosy lobby with heavy beams and a Florentine fireplace, and a restaurant under an arbour by the lake. *Open April–Oct.*

***Hotel Du Lac**, Piazza Mazzini 32, **t** 031 950 320, *www.bellagiohoteldulac.com* (*expensive*). Genial and family-run, this hotel occupies a 16th-century building near the centre, with fine views from the rooftop terrace and a traditional restaurant. Ask for one of the rooms with wonderful lake views. There is also a sporting club with swimming pool, tennis courts, football and Turkish baths. *Open end Mar–end Oct,*

***Excelsior Splendide**, Lungo Lazio Manzoni 28, **t** 031 950 225 (*expensive–moderate*). A lake-front hotel with faded Liberty charm, big old rooms (most with a view, be sure to ask), a pool and its own garden. Often booked by groups. *Open mid-Mar–Oct.*

***Nuovo Hotel Metropole**, Piazza Mazzini 1, **t** 031 950 409, *www.albergometropole.it* (*expensive–moderate*). Lake views, but slightly smaller rooms and less character. *Open Mar–mid-Nov.*

****La Pergola**, Piazza del Porto in Pescallo hamlet, 10 mins' walk from Bellagio (follow the path among the vineyards), **t** 031 950 263, *www.lapergolabellagio.it* (*moderate*). Situated in a tiny fishing harbour, this is a small, charming olde-worlde place with stylish rooms, with all comforts. Its waterside restaurant (*moderate–inexpensive*) has a nice pergola above the lake. *Closed Tues out of season.*

****Silvio**, a few kilometres from the centre in Loppia, on the road to Como, Via Carcano 12, **t** 031 950 322, *www.bellagiosilvio.com* (*moderate*). An absolute must for good value accommodation, friendly service, peaceful surroundings and excellent home cooking. Rooms are comfortable, and all with lake or garden view. Fresh fish are caught daily by father and son, who often fold the nets in

the terrace in front of you while you're eating. Try the home-made pasta, the fish ravioli and the very good tiramisu, approved by the likes of Pavarotti, Robert de Niro and former Chancellor Kohl.

La Genzianella, in the forest of San Primo, **t** 031 964 734 (*inexpensive*). Hotel and restaurant with mountain dishes of the Como region such as buttery polenta *uncia* (or *oncia*) and game. *Closed Wed Sept–June.*

Barchetta, Salita Mella 13, **t** 031 951 389 (*expensive*). The best place to eat in Bellagio, where you can feast on Lombard cuisine creatively revisited by chef Armando Valli in the terrace overlooking Bellagio's narrow and deep streets. Try the foie gras and pasta dishes, rigorously home-made, or the lake delicacies. The wine list is unparalleled. *Booking advised for evenings. Closed Tues; in winter, open eves only.*

Bilacus, Salita Serbelloni 30–32, **t** 031 950 480, *ristorantebilacus@libero.it* (*moderate*). One of the nicest places to dine in the centre of Bellagio, where you sit on a romantic terrace, feasting on excellent, intense *spaghetti alle vongole*, saffrony mushroom risotto or simple grilled fish. *Closed in winter and Mon.*

Mella, Piazza San Giovanni 7, **t** 031 950 205, *ristorantemella@libero.it* (*moderate*). A pleasant half-hour walk through the Villa Melzi and beyond. The place to go for a feast of fish – starve yourself first. Order the mixed fish *antipasto*, the mixed grilled fish and a bottle of lemony Soave. *Closed Tues and Dec.*

Chalet Gabriele, Piano Rancio hamlet, **t** 031 963 624, *www.polentoteca.com* (*inexpensive*). If you are tired of lake fish, drive up the green mountains behind Bellagio. This place serves typical local cheese, *tocc*, polenta and a variety of fondues. Try also meat and salami. *Closed Tues.*

Pasticceria Bar Sport, Piazza della Chiesa (*inexpensive*). A good ice cream shop and patisserie with 'Mataloc', a typical Bellagio cake with raisins.

Rifugio Capanna Martina, in Alpe dei Picetti, above Lezzeno (15km from Bellagio and then 15mins' walk up), **t** 031 964 695 (*inexpensive*). Yet more mountain food and a beautiful lake view from the garden terrace. *Open June–Sept, Sat and Sun only in winter.*

way to **San Giovanni** on the outskirts of Bellagio, where its Baroque church has an explosively ornate 18th-century high altar by Valtellina sculptors, an *Ascension* by Gaudenzio Ferrari and an *Immaculata* by Bernini's school. San Giovanni is also the seat of the **Nautical Instruments Museum** (*Museo degli Strumenti per la Navigazione*), in Piazza Don Miotti, which contains, among other items, 18th-century cardboard telescopes, sundials of different periods, old compasses and a narrated history of 19th-century sailing (*t 031 950 309, www.bellagiomuseo.com; open Easter and May–Oct Tues–Sun 10–1; adm*).

Bellagio

Enjoying one of the most beautiful sites in all Italy, spilling over the promontory in the very centre of Lake Como, Bellagio (from the Latin *bi-lacus*, or, between the lakes) is as charming as its setting: steep, stepped lanes of handsome old houses, ornate balconies spilling over with flowers and an endlessly fascinating waterfront, where you can linger all day watching the waltz of the ferries gliding to and fro over the mountain-bound lake.

Although Bellagio was fortified and fought over by Como and Milan, its first mention in history appropriately has to do with pleasure, referring to Pliny the Younger's Villa Tragedia. The villa sat rather higher over the lake than his Villa Comedia in Lenno, and got its name not only because tragedy was considered a 'loftier' art than comedy but because in his day tragic actors wore high heels. Most scholars place Pliny's old digs in the spectacular grounds of the **Villa Serbelloni**, extending to the summit of the Punta Bellagio. The villa is now the **Study and Conference Centre of the Rockefeller Foundation** (*t 031 951 555, guided tours of the grounds run April–Oct Tues–Sun at 11 and 4; tickets are available from the Promo Bellagio tourist office up to 10mins beforehand; in season the morning tour is often solidly booked by groups; adm, children under 7 free*). Although the villa is now a private house where researchers and scholars come to study, write or take part in conferences, the park and gardens (English, Italian and Mediterannean, commissioned by Count Allessandro Serbelloni at the beginning of the 19th century) are well worth a visit for their beauty and magnificent views on the three branches of Lake Como. While up at the top of Bellagio, take in Romanesque **San Giacomo**, built by the Como masters between 1075 and 1125, near a tower from Bellagio's fortifications. The Evangelists on the pulpit are from the 11th century, and the Madonna delle Grazie in the sacristy is by Foppa.

Also open for visits is the white neoclassical **Villa Melzi** (*t 339 644 6830; open late Mar–Oct 9–6; adm, children under 6 free*). This elegant country home was built in 1808 for one of Napoleon's henchmen, the Duke of Lodi, Francesco Melzi d'Eril (1753–1816), Vice President of the First Italian Republic. Topped with a score of pointy little chimneys, the villa has immaculate lawns, banks of flowers, a rare Montezuma pine and a water lily pond, all decorated with Egyptian, Roman and Hellenistic sculpture, and a little Moorish temple where in 1837 Liszt composed his sonata dedicated to Dante and Beatrice. The best period to visit its gardens is between April and May when orchids and azaleas are in bloom.

Other Roads from Bellagio

The narrow corniche road from Bellagio to Lecco is wilder and lonelier, with stunning views over the jagged Grigne range. **Oliveto Lario**, the main *comune* here, encompasses **Limonta**, a pretty place with a tiny port which until the advent of Napoleon in 1796 was a tiny independent state. Before getting to Limonta you can make a stop in Pescallo, a typical fishing hamlet just a few miles from Bellagio, so characteristic to be called 'Little Portafino' by locals. Alternatively, for a big dose of lake and mountain scenery, take the high road from Bellagio towards the Valsassina, to Erba in Brianza (*see* p.220); there are famous views over the entire lake from the summit of **Monte San Primo** (5,630ft/1,716m, a 2-hour walk from the refuge at Guello). Cyclists pedal up to pay their respects to their patroness, the **Madonna di Ghisallo**, to whom the great Italian champions have dedicated their bikes, shirts and trophies. Further south, the hamlet of **Lasnigo** has a fine 11th-century church, **Sant' Alessandro**, with a slender bell tower and bright 16th-century frescoes by Andrea de Passeris, a local painter from Torno.

Como's Upper West Shore and the Alto Lario

The last really stylish address for villas and hotels on the west shore, Menaggio (linked by ferries to Bellagio and Varenna) was a favourite of Venice's Cardinal Roncalli (later Pope John XXIII) and Churchill, who came here to sketch. It has always been one of Como's more important trading towns, thanks to its position at the head of two valleys: the Val Menaggio, an easy route to Lake Lugano (*see* p.185) and the Val Sanagra. To the north in the Alto Lario (Upper Como) the shores are more rugged and decidedly less visited.

Menaggio to Musso

Although flowerbeds and lindens line the lake and lido, pink and ochre Menaggio's main vocation is as a base for sport. Just above town there's a lovely 18-hole golf course which also has a golf library (**t** *0344 32103, www.golfclubmenaggio.it*), and the tourist office has good detailed information in English on the many well-marked walks in the area, ranging from the expert-only Alta Via Lario to easier targets, reached from the panoramic Rifugio Menaggio atop Monte Grona (5,729ft/1,746m); from here you can make one of the finest ascents from the lake, up **Monte Bregagno** (6,910ft/2,106m).

After Menaggio, the Via Regina road plunges through tunnels en route to the waterside hamlets of **Santa Maria Rezzonico** (where the parish church has a fresco of the Battle of Lepanto) and **Rezzonico**, cradle of the family of Venetian patricians who built one of the grandest palaces on the Grand Canal and produced Pope Clement XIII. Further up, a 19th-century spinning mill in **Pianello del Lario** houses a rich collection of 160 traditional boats from Lake Como, the **Raccolta della Barca Lariana** (**t** *0344 87235; open July–Sept daily 2.30–6.30, Easter–Nov Sat–Sun; other periods on request; adm*). The old photos of the lake traffic in the last century are especially winsome; it would be fun to bring them back.

Tourist Information

Menaggio: Piazza Garibaldi, **t** 0344 32924, *www.menaggio.com*.

Dongo: IMAGO, in Piazza Paracchini near the town hall, **t** 0344 82572, *www.imagolario. com*, offers guided tours in the summer.

Festivals

Festa dei Fiori (flower festival), *beginning of May*. A seasonal event in Menaggio with flowers, folklore groups, music, and regattas.

Strasc & Besasc, *end of June*. A fair selling secondhand clothes, in Menaggio.

Market Days

Menaggio: Giardino Comunale. *Every Friday evening in July and Aug, 2nd and 4th Fri other periods*.

Sports and Activities

There is plenty of **hiking**, **trekking** and **climbing** to do around Menaggio. The hike up to Mount Gona has the best views of the Prealps and of Lake Como, Lugano and Piano. Ask the local tourist office for maps, detailed itineraries, information on shelters, etc. Before setting off you can practise rock climbing at the natural gym on the right side of the gallery which connects Menaggio to Nobiallo – ask the tourist office for information; they also have detailed itineraries for one-day trips by car or bus and a historical itinerary through Menaggio. For **water sports** in Menaggio contact Centro Lago Service, Lungo Lago Castelli, **t** 0344 32003, to hire motorboats, paddle boats or go water-skiing *(June–Sept)*. At Lido Giardino, **t** 0344 32007, you can hire **mountain bikes**. There is an 18-hole **Golf** Club Menaggio Griante on the road to Lugano, **t** 0344 320 103, *(open Mar–Nov)*.

Where to Stay and Eat

Menaggio ✉ 22017

★★★★**Grand Hotel Victoria**, Lungolago Castelli 7, **t** 0344 32003 *(very expensive)*. This upmarket hotel was built in 1806 next to the lake; during renovation its original decor was carefully preserved and complemented with creature comforts like designer bathrooms, TVs and minibars. The public rooms are elegant and there's a swimming pool in the garden. Special discount for Menaggio and Cadenabbia Club golfers, and during Nov–Feb. *Open all year*.

★★★★**Grand Hotel Menaggio**, Via IV Novembre 69, **t** 0344 30640 *www.grandhotelmenaggio. com (very expensive–expensive)*. Stands in its own grounds on the lake. Rooms are fully equipped, most with stunning views. Heated pool. *Open Mar–Oct*.

★★★**Bellavista**, Via IV Novembre 21, **t** 0344 32136, www.*hotel-bellavista.org (expensive–moderate)*. Central and right on the lake, with nice rooms. *Open Mar–Oct*.

★★**Corona**, Largo Cavour 3, **t** 0344 32006, *www.hotelgarnicorona.com (inexpensive)*. Centrally located with lake views. *Closed Nov–mid-Mar*.

Ostello La Primula, Via IV Novembre 86, **t** 0344 32356, *www.menaggiohostel.com (inexpensive)*. Menaggio's youth hostel, with a restaurant serves some of the best-value meals in the area. *Open mid-Mar–Oct*.

Vecchia Menaggio, Via al Lago 13, **t** 0344 32082 *(moderate)*. Come here for a friendly low-key restaurant which serves great pizzas and pasta at affordable prices – better than the obvious tourist havens by the lake. There are also rooms *(inexpensive)* to stay in, four of which have bathrooms en suite. *Closed Tues and Nov–mid-Dec*.

Bar and Pub Tana Mana, Via IV Novembre 80, **t** 0344 32558, *www.tanamana.it (inexpensive)*. In front of the ferry landing; offers a younger atmosphere.

Sorico ✉ 22010

Al Beccaccino, Via Boschetto 49, **t** 0344 84241 *(moderate)*. Sorico is a good place to stop for a meal of river, sea and lake fish and game, serving the full works. *Closed Tues*.

Domaso ✉ 22013

La Vespa Youth Hostel, Via delle Case Sparse 12, halfway between Menaggio and Colico, **t** 0344 97449, *ostellovespa@ lombardiacom.it (inexpensive)*. Conveniently located for visiting Lake Como, the Valtellina and Switzerland, with food. *Open April–Oct, restaurant Mon and Tues*.

Continuing up the coast, **Musso** is gathered under the Sasso di Musso, the lofty, almost inaccessible rocky abutment dominating the Via Regina, the source of the marble in Como cathedral and other buildings around the lake. Its castle was the stronghold of Lake Como's notorious pirate Gian Giacomo de' Medici, nicknamed Il Medeghino. Born during the Medici exile from Florence in 1498, he was given the castle by Francesco II Duke of Milan in 1523 for helping to remove the French from Milan and assassinating the duke's best friend for him.

Il Medeghino made it the base for a fleet of armed ships that terrorized the lake and extorted levies from towns and traders for a decade, until the same Duke Francesco II, with help from the Swiss, managed to dislodge him and demolish his citadel. As a consolation prize the old pirate (brother of Pope Pius IV and uncle of Charles Borromeo) was made Marquis of Marignano by Charles V, and in return he helped the emperor win Siena and oppress the burghers of Ghent. The site of the castle, by the little church of Santa Eufemia, was made into an eclectic Giardino di Merlo in the 1850s; abandoned, you can imagine it while you get lost in its labyrinth of paths.

Dongo, Gravedona and Sorico

To the north, Como's shapely figure spreads; the shore loses its clear definition amid reedy shallows and camp grounds full of Northern European families. Things were livelier in the Middle Ages, when the three towns of **Dongo**, **Gravedona** and **Sorico** formed the independent republic of the Tre Pievi or Three Parishes. In the 12th and 13th centuries, the Tre Pievi was a hotbed of Paternene (or Cathar) heresy, and scores of citizens were sent to the stake by the inquisitor Peter of Verona for doubting, among other things, that the pope was Christ's representative on earth. In 1252 Peter was waylaid and murdered for his trouble – earning himself an express canonization the very next year from the pope as St Peter Martyr; he's the saint who figures in so much Dominican art, standing about nonchalantly with a hatchet sticking out of his tonsure. Dongo was also the end of the road for Mussolini and his mistress, who were caught here while trying to escape to Switzerland.

Gravedona was and still is the most important town of the three. By its parish church of San Vicenzo (with an intact 5th-century crypt), the tall 12th-century grey and white striped Santa Maria del Tiglio was founded as a detached baptistry, and rebuilt reusing Palaeo-Christian carvings (the centaur pursuing a deer is Early Christian symbolism, representing the persecution of the Church); the solemn interior, lined with two lofty galleries, has damaged frescoes and a stark 13th-century crucifix over the altar. Just above Gravedona, **Santa Maria delle Grazie** (1467) contains frescoes by local painters, the De Donatis, a few invoking divine aid against the plague and the funniest one portraying the Virgin taking a swipe at the devil.

In **Peglio**, just above Gravedona, **Sant' Eusebio** (*open Sat and Sun during Mass*) is a model Counter-Reformation church, its frescoes (1611–25) the masterpiece of Como painter Giovan Mauro della Rovere, better known as the *Fiammenghino* or 'little Fleming'. He was granted asylum here after murdering a man, a fact that inspired him to take special care over the torments of hell in his *Last Judgement*. He left his own portrait (elegantly dressed, listening to the Sermon of St John), in the Cappella di San Carlo, next to the local woman he loved and their children. The fishing village Sorico, the northernmost of the three parishes, has a tower that guarded the entrance to Lake Como from the north and a church dedicated to San Mirus, a 14th-century hermit and local rain god who floated to Sorico on his cloak, inspired by a similar feat perfomed by St Giulio at Orta; *ex votos* attest to his control over precipitation.

In Roman times Lake Como encompassed shallow **Lake Mezzola**, part of which is now an important nature reserve and breeding ground for swans and other aquatic birds. On the west shore of the lake, accessible only by boat or path from Albonico, the square 10th-century **Oratorio di San Fedelino** is a minor jewel, with a fresco of Christ and the Apostles from the year 1000. Across the lake from San Fedelino, **Novate Mezzola** is the base for walks into the enchanting and unspoiled **Val Codera**, which is just as inaccessible to cars. The track up passes a granite quarry lost in the woods, as well as two tiny granite hamlets, **San Giorgio di Cola** and, beyond the chasm of the Gola della Val Ladrongo, **Codera** (2 hours), where the **Museo Storico della Val Codera** (*Piazza della Chiesa, t 342 211 572; open June–Sept daily 10–12 and 3–6; Oct–May, weekends only*) has exhibits on the valley's history and customs.

Como's East Shore: Colico to Lecco

The mountains are even more dramatic on Como's east shore, and with the exception of charming Varenna, the villas and hotels are scarcer – there's scarcely any room to build them. Northern Lake Como and the Lago di Lecco are favourite destinations for windsurfers and are rich in *agoni* (freshwater shad), one of the tastiest of freshwater fish.

The Pian di Spagna and the Abbazia di Piona

The vaguely eerie grassy marshland between the Lago di Mezzola and river Adda has been known as the Pian di Spagna ever since 1603, when the Spanish governor of Milan built a massive fort on a hillock at Fuentes Montecchio. The fort was the furthest outpost of Spain in Italy, guarding the strategic entrance to the Valtellina, the principal warpath between Milan to Austria. Today, horses and waterfowl share the wetlands with Telespazio's futuristic parabolic aerials.

South of **Colico**, Como's northernmost steamer landing, the road passes the green waters of the Lago di Piona, a basin of fossils and garnet notched into the side of Como. On the lick of land enclosing the basin, monks from Cluny took over the ruined apse of a 7th-century church in 1138 and established the **Abbazia di Piona** (*t 0341 940 331; open daily 9–12 and 2–6.30*), adding a pretty cloister of 1257 with animals and faces on some of the columns. The church, Lombard Romanesque with a crown of arches, has a single nave, where you'll find the marble lions that once guarded the porch and remains of 13th-century frescoes. It was restored by the Cistercians of Casamari (in Frosinone), whose brothers distil a potent herb liqueur called *gocce imperiali* ('imperial drops'), best taken in small doses for fire-safety reasons.

Dervio and a Detour up the Val Varrone

To the south, the lake road climbs to tiny **Corenno Plinio**, where plane trees shade the cobbles by the church of **San Tommasso di Canterbury** (1356), or Thomas Becket, a popular saint in medieval Italy (he was on the pope's side, after all). Corenno Plinio belongs to Dervio, with some of Como's widest beaches. Behind it are three ruined tombs (late 1200s and 1371) by the Maestri Campionesi, and inside are 14th-century frescoes and a 16th-century Tuscan Annunciation. Next to the church are two embattled towers of the **Castello Andreani**. Steps lead up to the old Castello district, marked by a massive stump of a tower.

From Dervio a road leads up into the Val Varrone, dotted with old settlements like **Tremenico** and **Introzzo**, where the church of **San Martino** (1583) has a pulpit carved by rococo master Antonio Fantoni and a campanile with an excellently preserved clock of 1707. At the top of the valley, **Premana** is a large ironworking village with a picturesque main street, where some older women continue to wear their traditional costumes. Premana specializes in scissors, although in the past it rather more romantically produced the iron beaks of gondolas, some of which are in the **Museo Etnografico Comunale** (*Via Roma, open April–July, Sept and Oct, Sat and Sun 3–6; Aug daily 3–6; at other times call Antonio Codega, t 0341 890 175, to book; adm*).

Tourist Information

Varenna: Piazza Venini 6, t 0341 830 367, *www.varennaitaly.com. Open Tues–Sat 10–12 and 3–5, Sun 10–12.*

Festivals

Festa del Lago, *1st Sat in July.* A festival in Varenna recalling the landing of the refugees from the Isola Comacina: folklore, costumes and plenty of polenta and fish for everyone, and fireworks above the lake in the evening.

International organ music festival and a naïve paintings exhibition, *August.* Held in Varenna.

Markets

Varenna: At the steamer landing. Antiques. *Every third Sunday of the month, May–Oct.*

Sports and Activities

Dervio is the **sailing** centre of the area. There is the Centro Vela, t 0341 850 626, *www. centroveladervio.it,* for sailing lessons all year round, the Lega Navale Italiana Santa Cecilia, t 0341 850 672, *www.leganavale.it,* for courses June–Sept, Orza Minore, t 039 850 459,

www.orzaminore.it, open weekends all year round, daily in August, which also has sailing boats for hire. Lario Vela, t 0341 810 207, a one-man company of Giorgio Momoli, offers sailing boat hire with skipper on a 45ft boat. Varenna also has its own sailing and boat centres: Centro Velico Varenna, t 0341 830 488, and Club Nautico Varenna, t 0341 830 272, both in Perledo hamlet. For **windsurfing**, Fun Surf Center, also in Dervio, t 039 990 2770 or t 338 814 8719, offers windsurfing courses and hire (daily July–Aug, weekends April–Sept) and hire of **canoes, paddle boats** and **mountain bikes**. For activities in Esino Lario, the mountainous area behind Varenna, contact the Varenna Pro Loco, and the **alpine guides**, CAI, t 0341 860 080 (*Thurs only, July–Aug 9–10pm*).

Where to Stay and Eat

Varenna ✉ 22050

****Hotel du Lac, t 0341 830 238,*www. albergodulac.com* (*very expensive*). Right on the lakeside in the quiet, medieval part of the city centre, this luxury hotel has been renovated by the new management, with fully equipped and nicely decorated rooms,

Bellano

South again, **Bellano** lies at the bottom of the steep gorge or **Orrido** of the Pioverna torrent, where a series of steps and gangways threads through the rocky chasm and its bulging walls, offering remarkable views of the thundering water just below (*t 0341 821 124, open April–Sept daily 10–12.30 and 2–11; Oct–Mar Sat–Sun 10–12.30 and 2–7; adm*). Bellano has a fine Lombard church, **Santi Nazzaro e Celso** (1348), built by the Campionese and Intelvi masters (*open most days for religious services*) with a rose window in majolica and a fine 16th-century painting of the *Madonna and Child*, inspired by Luini. From Bellano you can head up the Valsassina; only 8km up there are more watery thrills at the **Tomba di Taìno**, a cascade in a 98ft (29m) abyss, located by Cosmasira, near **Vendrogno**.

Varenna and its River of Milk

Wedged on a promontory under the mountains, picturesque Varenna has been the most important village on Como's east shore since the Middle Ages; as the ferry port for Bellagio, Cadenabbia and Menaggio, it makes a fine base for visiting the entire lake. But Varenna itself is well worth exploring: its 10th-century **Oratorio di San Giovanni**, with later frescoes inside, is one of the oldest surviving churches on the

suites and bathrooms with marvellous views. Nice terrace, pergola and own mooring. There's also a good restaurant at lake level (*expensive*). *Closed mid-Nov–mid-Feb.*

★★★**Albergo Milano**, Via XX Settembre 29, t 0341 830 298, *hotelmilano@varenna.net* (*expensive*). Enjoys an exquisite setting in the village; 8 rooms with balconies and wonderful views. The ones to request (months in advance) are nos. 1 or 2 with their large terraces, ideal for couples and incurable romantics. *Open Mar–Nov.*

★★★**Villa Cipressi**, Via IV Novembre 18, t 0341 830 113, *www.hotelvillacipressi.it* (*expensive*). Stay here if it's not booked up for an event; gorgeous garden and lake terraces, but rooms, although fully equipped, do not match the exterior's standards and style. *Closed Dec–mid-Feb.*

★★**Olivedo**, Piazza Martiri 4, near the steamer terminal, t 0341 830 115, *www.olivedo.it* (*moderate*). Run by the friendly Colombo family (the daughter speaks English). The meals, served on the terrace if the weather's nice, are excellent; old furnishing and decor provide the hotel with a warm and cosy atmosphere. Rooms are all lake-front; there are some cheaper rooms available, without en suite baths.

Vecchia Varenna, Via Scoscesa 10, t 0341 830 793, *www.vecchiavarenna.it* (*expensive*). For gastronomic joy book a table here, where the sumptuous views are matched by dishes prepared with the finest ingredients from France and Italy: the lake fish is exquisite. *Closed Mon only in winter and Jan.*

Mandello del Lario ✉ 23826

Relais Villa delle Rose, Strada Statale 125–127, t 0341 731 304 *www.villadellerose.com* (*very expensive–expensive*). A turn-of-the-last-century villa set in its own grounds among century-old cedars and roses – a lakeside park of 100 hectares – with private mooring, dock and even natural caves. The former summer resort of a noble Milanese family, the villa has had Fermi, Churchill and Adenauer among its guests. Current hosts combine top-class hospitality with the cosiness of a private home. The 6 rooms – 2 suites and 4 doubles – are stylish, comfortable and all have a lake view. The restaurant matches the classy surroundings for service and quality of food, with aromatic herbs blended in creative dishes directly from the villa's garden. It also boasts a fireplace, billiard rooms and a solarium. They also host special evenings featuring regional cuisine.

lake, while the larger, Romanesque **San Giorgio** (1313) is marked by a lofty campanile and an exterior fresco of St Christopher (giant-size, the better to bring luck to passing travellers). Inside are 14th- and 15th-century frescoes and polyptychs by Como-based artists. Varenna's proudest lakeside villas are now used as congress centres (*gardens open to the public*). The oldest, **Villa Monastero** (*t 0341 295 450; open April–Oct 9–7; adm*), was built on the site of a 13th-century convent suppressed by Charles Borromeo in 1567 for the scandalous behaviour and luxurious lifestyles of its nuns. The garden, with statues and bas-reliefs, is famed for its citrus trees. The nearby **Villa Cipressi** (*t 0361 830 113; open daily spring 9–6, summer 9–7; adm*), built between 1400 and 1800, also has a fine garden under its towering cypresses. Varenna's museum is for the birds, literally: the **Museo Ornitologico** (*currently closed*) houses 700 species that frequent Como's shores.

Varenna's other attractions are higher up, and include the partially ruined **Castello di Vezio** (*t 0341 814 011, www.castellodivezio.it; open Feb–Mar Sat–Sun 10–5; April–May daily 10–7; Jun and Sept daily 10–8; July–Aug 10–9; Oct Sat–Sun 10–6; Nov–Dec Sat–Sun 10–4; adm*), founded in the 7th century by Lombard Queen Theodolinda; you can drive or walk up (about 20mins) for the fantastic view over the Bellagio headland. Recently restored, it frequently hosts exhibitions. South of Varenna, the scenic path to the cemetery continues up to the headspring of Lake Como's most curious natural wonder, the **Fiumelatte** ('River of Milk'), Italy's shortest river, lasting only 820ft (250m) before blasting down in creamy foam into the lake. Not even Leonardo da Vinci, who delved deep into the cavern from which it flows, could discover its source, or why it abruptly begins to flow in the last days of March and just as abruptly ceases at the end of October. A stair and iron bridge allow you to get quite close to the source. From the headspring (the Sorgente) another path descends to the river's mouth in the hamlet of Fiumelatte; a third path branching off from the walk to the source leads to another lovely viewpoint over the lake, the cypress-fringed **Baluardo**.

Behind Varenna stretch the northernmost peaks of the saw-toothed Grigna massif. Only a few minutes up in Perledo, the 14th-century **Castello di Vezio** still guards the central lake. Further up, the little resort of **Esino Lario** is the site of the **Museo delle Grigne** (*open July and Aug Wed 6–7 and Fri 8.30–10 pm, Sun 10.30–12; other times book ahead on t 0341 860 111*) housing local Gallic and Roman finds, minerals and fossils. For beautiful views continue up from Esino to the plateau of **Ortanella**, a natural balcony over the lake and site of the thousand-year-old church of **San Pietro**; another road from Esino leads up to **Cainallo** and Vo di Moncòdeno, near the centre of the North Grigna range and a favourite place to begin daring walks. The main road from Esino continues up through grand scenery to Cortenova in the Valsassina.

The Lago di Lecco

South of Varenna, the shores close in around the Lago di Lecco, a brooding fjord where mountains plunge down steeply into the water, entwined in rushing streams and waterfalls and carved with shadowy abysses – landscapes that so enchanted Leonardo da Vinci when he visited Lecco to plan Milan's canals and water schemes that he used them as backgrounds in his *Virgin of the Rocks* and *The Virgin and*

St Anne. The mountains of the east shore – Resegone and the Grigna range – are wild and sharp dolomitic peaks of limestone shot through with fossils from a primordial sea – including those of Lake Como's very own dinosaur, the Lariosaurus.

For all that, the last two towns on the lake are known for their industries. **Mandello del Lario** rolls out Guzzi motorcycles, manufactured here since 1921; you can learn all about them at the **Museo del Motociclo** (*Via E. Parodi 57,* **t** *0341 709 111; free guided tours Mon–Fri at 3 and 4pm*). Further south, on a spur over the lake, the 15th-century church of **San Giorgio** has an interior like an illuminated manuscript, decorated with wall-to-wall frescoes on everything from heaven to hell. The old silk town of **Abbadia Lariana** offers demonstrations at its **Civico Museo del Setificio** (*t 0341 731 241, www.museoabbadia.it; open Sun and hols 10–12 and 2–6, weekdays upon reservation, ring ahead; guided tours,* **t** *0341 731 300; adm*) in the 1869 Monti throwing mill, with an impressive round throwing machine of 432 spools from the 1850s.

Lecco

A sombre industrial city, magnificently positioned at the foot of jagged Mount Resegone, Lecco grew up where the River Adda leaves Lake Como to continue its journey south to the Po (a typical entry in Pliny's *Natural History* records how the Adda passes pristinely through the lake without mingling its waters). After a rocky history of wars and plagues and emigration, Lecco found its feet under the Austrians, who improved transportation with the Paderno d'Adda canal – an idea first proposed by the Duke of Milan's hydraulic engineer, Leonardo da Vinci, in 1498 – and opened up the city for growth and industry (most notably in iron) by demolishing its tight girdle of walls. Feeling neglected by its old rival Como, Lecco split away and became a provincial capital in its own right in 1994, taking the east shore of the lake, the Grigna mountains and La Brianza with it.

Although Lecco's charm is mostly concentrated in its spectacular surroundings, there are a few things to see as well. When Leonardo da Vinci passed through town,

Desperately Seeking Lucia and Renzo

What most Italians want from Lecco is Manzoniana. For the city, as it will gently remind you wherever you turn, was the childhood home of Alessandro Manzoni (born in Milan 1785, died 1873) and provided the setting of his *I Promessi Sposi* (*The Betrothed*), Italy's 19th-century fictional classic. Revolutionary in its day, the *Sposi* was the first to look at Italy's history through the eyes of the common man, and it sparked pro-unification sentiments in the breast of every Italian who read it. The novel was also a sensation for its language: a new popular national Italian that everyone could understand – no small achievement in a country of a hundred dialects where the literary language had remained unchanged since Dante. Even now the perils of young Lucia and Renzo's union remain required reading for every schoolchild, a sacred cow breathlessly milked by every denizen of Italian culture – but confessedly something of a hard slog for the uninitiated.

Getting There and Around

Lecco is connected by **rail** with Milan, Como, Bergamo and Colico (Lecco rail info **t** 0341 364 130). SAL **buses** from Via Pergola 2, **t** 0341 363 148, serve towns in the provinces, and the lake.

Tourist Information

Via Nazario Sauro 6, **t** 0341 362 360, *www.aptlecco.com.*

Festivals

A series of sport and cultural events, *every Sunday in June.* In Lecco.
Classical Music Concerts, *June.* In Sant' Alessandro church, Lecco.
Carnival, *June.* Opened in Lecco by the carriage carrying King Resegone and Queen Grigna. *First Sunday:* the traditional *Pedalata Manzoniana* cycling tour, 25km around the sites described by the novelist. *Second Sunday:* the *Festa dei Colori*, with a painting competition and an antiques market. *Third and fourth Sundays:* a dedication to the mountain and then the lake, with regattas and blessing of an underwater statue.
Assault on Mt Resegone in Erna, *July.* Cycling.
Alborella Festival, *July.* Dedicated to the local fish, in the borough of Pescarenico with open-air tasting, music and dance.

Organ Concerts, *August.* Held around the local parishes throughout the Valsassina.

Markets

Lecco: in Piazza XX Settembre. Running since 1149. *Every Wed and Sat.*
Malgrate: Antiques. *First Sun of each month except Jan–Feb.*

Sports and Activities

The mountains around Lecco are renowned for **rock climbing** and **hiking**: contact the Alpine Club, Via Papa Giovanni XXIII 11, **t** 0341 363 588, *www.cai.lecco.it (open Tues and Fri 8pm–10.30pm).* There are also several winter **ski resorts** in the area: Piani di Bobbio (30km of ski slopes), Piani d'Erna and Piani delle Betulle (12km each), and Piani di Artavaggio (10km): again, the Lecco tourist office has all the relevant information. For **canoeing** and **rowing** contact Società Canottieri Lecco, Via Nullo 2, **t** 0341 364 273, *www.canottieri.lecco.it.*

Where to Stay and Eat

Lecco ✉ 22053

Lecco doesn't exactly brim over with hotels: **★★★★Il Griso**, Via Provinciale 51, situated a kilometre away at Malgrate, **t** 0341 202 040,

he liked to stand on the 11-arch **Ponte Azzone Visconti,** built over the Adda in 1336 as part of Azzone's defensive line from Lecco to Milan, and watch what he called 'the great gathering of waters' as the river, flowing from the lake, swells to form the Lago di Garlate. Once bristling with towers, the bridge isn't quite as Leonardo saw it. From the bridge, Via Azzone Visconti leads to Piazza Manzoni with its large **Monument to Manzoni**, the author sitting pensively over a base covered with scenes from the *Sposi* (*see* p.215). From here Via Roma leads to the old centre of town, Piazza XX Settembre. Its landmark, the **Torre Viscontea,** (**t** *0341 282 396; open for temporary exhibitions*) is all that survives of the towers and walls that Azzone built around Lecco; there are plans to make it into a museum of the mountains.

From Piazza XX Settembre, Via G. Bovara and Corso Matteotti lead to the **Castello** quarter of 18th-century mansions, among them the **Palazzo Belgiojoso** (*Corso Matteotti 32*, **t** *0341 481 247; open Tues–Sun 9.30–2*) with an old-fashioned natural history collection, archaeological finds and a section on Lecco's metallurgy. Literary pilgrims flock to the museum in Manzoni's boyhood home, the **Villa Manzoni** (**t** *0341 481 247; open Tues–Sun 9.30–5.30; adm*), now lost amid the urban sprawl at Via Guanella 7; from Piazza Manzoni, walk up Viale Dante . Here you can inspect the great

griso@griso.info (expensive). A moderate-sized but elegant hotel with fine views of the lake from its wide terrace, also with a sauna, a gym and billiards. The food and beautiful views compensate for the faded charm and 1970s decor of the interiors. There's a swimming pool in the garden, and one of the region's best gourmet restaurants – *menu degustazione* at €54 and €57. *Reservations essential*.

★★★**Don Abbondio**, Piazza Era 10, on the main square of the fishing village of Pescarenico, **t** 0341 366 315 (*moderate*). With charming surroundings and views over the River Adda and the fishing boats. Has simple rooms with small baths, but plenty of romantic atmosphere. Ask for rooms 2 or 12 for a little private terrace. Take some time to visit the lively neighbouring streets and art gallery, La Nassa, Piazza Era 6, for a very good selection of local contemporary art.

★★★**Moderno**, Piazza Diaz 5, **t** 0341 286 519, *hotel.moderno@promo.it (moderate)*. In town, this hotel doesn't have much character but the rooms are adequate with all mod cons.

★**Marchett**, Via per Erna 11, up the funicular at the Pian d'Erna, **t** 0341 505 019, *mono. locatellilz@tim.it (inexpensive)*. Simple rooms with views. Good restaurant with set menu (*inexpensive*).

Al Porticciolo, Via Valsecchi 5, **t** 0341 498 103, *alporticciolodilecco@acena.it (very expensive)*. Lecco's best restaurant, where you pick your fish from the tanks. The chef concentrates on bringing out the natural flavours of the seafood. *Closed Mon, Tues, Aug and early Jan, Aug open at lunch weekends only.*

Nicolin, Via Ponchielli 54, in the hamlet of Maggianico Sud, behind Pescarenico, **t** 0341 422 122 (*very expensive*). A hidden gourmet restaurant with surprises such as home-made *foie gras* treated with a marmalade of figs and *pan brioche*, or rice with watercress and *ragù* of frogs, or lamb cooked in *lardo* (bacon fat) with a pumpkin sauce. Excellent wine list. *Closed Tues & Aug.*

Trattoria Vecchia Pescarenico, Via Pescatori 8, fishing village of Pescarenico, **t** 0341 368 330, *vecchiapescarenico@libero.it (moderate)*. Serves lake fish, risotto and tagliatelli with fish too – treat yourself to the *tris*. *Closed Mon, 2nd half Aug, 1st half Jan.*

Taverna ai Poggi, Via ai Poggi 14, just outside town, on the road to the Pian d'Erni funivia, **t** 0341 497 126, *poggi@tim.it (moderate–cheap)*. Serves regional specialities such as local salami, *brigioli* with Valsassina cheese and lake fish, as well as good sandwiches and soup, at reasonable prices. You can sit outside in summer. Lunch time *menu lavoro* (working lunch) available. *Closed Mon.*

man's cradle, tobacco boxes and nightcap, although the house itself, little changed since the 18th century, forms the main attraction. The upper floor is now a gallery of 16th–20th-century paintings by local artists.

Want more? The tourist office distributes a special Manzoni brochure with an itinerary that pinpoints the various scenes and buildings from *I Promessi Sposi*, most of which (Lucia's house, Don Rodrigo's castle, the marriage church) are in **Olate**, the neighbourhood just east of Castello. Another scene from the novel took place at Padre Cristoforo's convent (now ruined) at **Pescarenico**, an old fishing village just south of the Ponte Visconti, where the fishermen still use their traditional narrow, thin-bowed boats and nets; the village's quirky, triangular campanile, erected in the 1700s, survives in better condition and has been listed as a national monument.

Just east of Lecco towers **Monte Resegone** ('Big Saw'), a jaggedy, bumpety Dolomite that got away; on weekends it becomes a major Milanese escape route, especially for rock climbers. Those not up to grappling on crusty cliffs can take the *funivia* 4,360ft (1,329m) up Resegone's flank to the woods and meadows of the **Piani d'Erna** (*leaves from Versasio, 6km from Lecco, every 30mins at weekends; take bus no. 5 from Piazza Mazzini; for info, **t** 0341 497 337*); on a clear day, the view is quite extraordinary.

Around Lecco: the Grigna Range and the Valsassina

The magnificent pale peaks of the Grigna mountains attract skiers in the winter and walkers and rock climbers in the summer. The range is divided into two distinct groups: the southern **Grigna Meridionale** (7,142ft/2,177m) may be approached from Lecco by way of **Ballabio Inferiore**, where a long and winding road leads up to the green saddle of **Piani Resinelli** and its Rifugio Porta. Here begins a spectacular trail (suitable for experienced trekkers) called the *Direttissima* which heads north to Rifugio Rosalba, passing the fantastical pinnacles over the Val Tesa.

The more massive northern group, **Grigna Settentrionale** (7,903ft/2,409m), runs between Lake Como and the **Valsassina**, the lofty valley on either side of the torrent Pioverna. The road north of Ballabio Inferiore reaches it by way of a gloomy gorge and **Colle di Balisio**, another green saddle (with access to the popular ski resorts of **Barzio**, **Cremeno** and **Moggio**) then continues up to **Pasturo**, market town of the Valsassina, famous for its soft cheeses. Further up, the valley's medieval capital **Introbio** is still defended by its stalwart medieval **Arrigoni Tower**; the environs are full of abandoned silver, lead and iron mines. Introbio looks east to the mighty **Piazzo dei Tre Signori** (8,380ft/2,554m) that once marked the border between Milan, Venice and Switzerland.

The next village in the Valsassina, **Vimogno**, has a lovely waterfall, the **Cascata del Troggia**, while **Primaluna**, further up, was the cradle of the Della Torre family, who ruled Milan from 1240 until the Visconti came along and snuffed them out. Some of the small palace-fortresses in town still bear their coat of arms; the church, **San Pietro**, has paintings in the manner of Titian and a beautiful golden 15th-century Torriani Cross, of Tuscan manufacture. Neighbouring **Cortabbio** was the first feudal court of the archbishop of Milan; here the oldest Christian tombstone in Lombardy (AD 425) was discovered. At **Cortenova** the road forks, and a hard choice it is because both routes, one to Varenna and the other to Bellano and the Val Varrone, take in spectacular mountain scenery.

Between Lecco and Como: La Brianza

South of the mountainous Triangolo Lariano, La Brianza is a gentle region of little lakes that span the legs of Lake Como like blue footprints. Its villages spun the silk that was woven into cloth in Como and Lecco, and Milanese nobles erected summer villas on their shores in the 18th and 19th centuries. Today La Brianza, close to the big-name designers in Milan, is the most important furniture-making region in all Italy.

The lake just south of Lecco, the **Lago di Garlate**, was also closely associated with the silk industry. In 1950 the Abegg silk mill, on the SS30 in the town of Garlate, was converted into the **Museo Civico della Seta**, or Silk Museum (**t** *0341 650 488; open Wed, Sat, Sun 9–12.30 and 2–5; adm*). Here you can find out more about one of the nicest things ever made by worms; exhibits include some 500 tools and machines, including 19th-century throwing-machines, capable of 10,000 revolutions a minute.

Where to Stay and Eat

Oggiono ✉ 22048

★★★Fattorie di Stendhal, Via Dante 16,
t 0341 577 589 (*moderate*). Sleep in a quiet
room in Stendhal's farmhouse, with a lovely
view over Lake Annone. There's also a good
restaurant. *Closed Fri.*

Pierino Penati, Via XXIV Maggio 36, Viganò
Brianza, 9km south of Lake Annone,
t 039 956 020, *www.pierinopenati.it* (*very
expensive*). It's well worth a special trip to
this tiny village just to sample the cuisine
at this restaurant. Delicious regional
specialities and a superb wine list
complement the chef's own innovations (try
fried ravioli with vegetables), followed by an
excellent choice of cheeses and desserts.
*Closed Sun eve and Tues–Sat lunch, Mon, Aug,
first 10 days of Jan.*

Santa Polenta, Via Dante 25, t 0341 576 166
(*moderate–inexpensive*). Also has lovely
views over Lake Annone; serves polentas of
all kinds, plus pizza. *Closed Mon.*

Erba ✉ 22036

★★★★Castello di Casiglio, Via Cantù 21,
t 031 627 288, *www.hotelcastellodicasiglio.it*
(*very expensive*). Offers a luxury stay in a
medieval castle. The 45 rooms are furnished
in style with attention to detail. The *relais*
also has a good restaurant with an open-air

grill. Often booked for weddings and
meetings. Swimming pool in the park.

La Corte, Via Mazzini 20, Lurago d'Erba,
south of Lago di Alserio, t 031 699 690 (*very
expensive*). This charming restaurant is
known for its superb regional dishes, from
the home-made breadsticks, to pâtés, to
exquisite, artistic desserts. *Closed Sun eve,
Wed, and two weeks in Aug.* It also has several
(*expensive*) rooms with bathrooms: eight
doubles and an apartment. *Closed Aug.*

La Rimessa, Via C. Ferrari 13/B, Mariano
Comense, south of Erba, t 031 749 668
www.larimessa.it (*very expensive*). Another
gourmet heaven, in an elegant 19th-century
coach house set in the grounds of the villa
of the Conti Besana. Menus change monthly
and feature traditional Italian and local
dishes and flavours, carefully mixed by
passionate chef Sergio Mauri. The speciality
is the rabbit loin cooked the '*Vecchia Brianza*'
way, in red wine, marsala, broth and
perfumed with laurel, rosemary, cloves and
nutmeg. But you can have dishes as simple
and divine as fried eggs with melted *casera*
cheese and white truffle, or gorgonzola with
a green tomato mustard, or refined fish,
meat and *antipasti* and delicious desserts.
Excellent selection of wines, with over 300
labels and plenty of half-litre bottles to
accompany individual dishes. *Closed Sun eve,
Mon, Jan, Aug.*

Civate: Churches from the First Millennium

Lake Annone, the next lake to the west, is the biggest and most striking in La
Brianza, its waters nearly split in two to the north by a long narrow promontory
and islet. Near here stands **Civate**, a major pilgrimage destination in the Dark Ages
thanks to its abbey of **San Calocero**, founded in 705 to house the relics of the Roman
martyr Calogerus and the keys of St Peter – a spare set, one hopes, or perhaps Peter
eventually descended from heaven's gate to collect them, because they're long gone.
In the 1080s the abbey led the post-Patariane reformation in Lombardy, and in the
1590s it became an Olivetan monastery until its suppression in 1803. During
restorations of the basilica in 1983, 11th-century frescoes (including a *Judgement of
Solomon*) were discovered behind the 17th-century vaulting and in the Romanesque
crypt. The beautiful cloister and abbey buildings are now a rest home for the blind.

A lovely hour and a half's walk up from Civate to Monte Cornizzolo (2,095ft/638m)
will take you to the even older **San Pietro al Monte** (*open summer Sun 9–4, winter Sun
9–12 and 2–3 or contact the Canali family at Via Monsignor Gilardi 3, t 0341 551 576*),

founded by Desiderius, the last king of the Lombards, taking its final form in the 11th century, with a pair of choirs, a door like a giant's oven and a great round gallery. The twin apses have remarkable Byzantine-style frescoes and stuccoes inspired by the Apocalypse, of the four rivers of the New Jerusalem, St Michael slaying the dragon (unusually, with plenty of help from the saints, transfixing the beast with their spears) and the Christ of the Second Coming liberating Lady Church. The high altar has a rare *baldacchino* from the 1050s, decorated with vivid reliefs of imaginary animals and a Tree of Life; the ancient crypt, unusually enough, also has beautiful if damaged stuccoes. The adjacent centrally planned **Oratorio di San Benedetto** has an unusual 12th-century painted altar.

Stendhal often took refuge at Lake Annone, retreating there whenever Milan, much as he loved it, got on his nerves; his farm in **Oggiono** on the south shore is now a hotel and restaurant. Oggiono was the home town of one of Leonardo's pupils, Marco d'Oggiono, who left a fine polyptych of *S. Maria Assunta and Saints* in the parish church of **Santa Eufemia**, which still retains its Romanesque bell tower (in spite of a cyclone in 1898) and an octagonal 11th-century baptistry, Battistero di San Giovanni (*open first Sun of each month 10.30–12 and 3–5.30 or contact t 0341 576 633*).

South of Lake Annone, the **Monte di Brianza** is one of the most unspoiled corners of the region; south of Castello stand the romantic ruins of the **Campanone della Brianza**, a tower built by Lombard Queen Theodolinda. South of Campanone the regional **Parco delle Valle del Curone** (near Missaglia and Montevecchia) offers pretty walks through chestnut and birch woods. The big attraction in these parts is **Merate**, where the gentle hills are scattered with noble Milanese villas, mostly from the 1700s: the beautiful **Villa Belgioso** has a superb garden. Two kilometres from the centre, the **Osservatorio Astronomico** (*open for guided tours the first Friday of each month, at 9.30, 10.30, 2.30 and 3.30; t 039 999 111; adm; advance booking essential for night visits*) was founded in 1927 and remains today one of the most important in Italy.

Erba and Around

The central lakes of La Brianza, Pusino, Segrino and Alserio, are less compelling although they have their interest, mostly concentrated in and around **Erba**, the most important town between Lecco and Como. Erba's environs were another favourite place for planting villas; one, in the suburb of Crevenna, holds the **Museo Civico Archeologico** (*Via Foscolo 27, t 031 615 262; open Tues 9–12, Wed and Fri 3–6*). In another suburb, Incino, **Santa Eufemia** has a magnificent 11th-century Romanesque campanile. To the west above Erba, in Paravicino, the **Buco del Piombo**, 'Lead Hole' (*t 031 629 599, www.museobucodelpiombo.it; open April–Oct Sat 2–6, Sun and hols 10–6, more frequently in Aug, ring for advance booking; adm*), is a spectacular chasm-cave with sheer 330ft (100m) walls threaded by a stream. Legend has it that the cave is connected to Lake Como; children and adults can be guided through the caves by speleologists. Outside, watch for the peregrine falcon which nestles there. Near here, Napoleon's viceroy Eugène de Beauharnais planted a double row of pine trees leading up to the pastures of the panoramic **Alpe del Vicerè**, a popular outing for picnics. From Erba a scenic road heads through the Valsassina to Bellagio (*see* p.207).

The Valchiavenna and Valtellina

12

The Valchiavenna and Valtellina

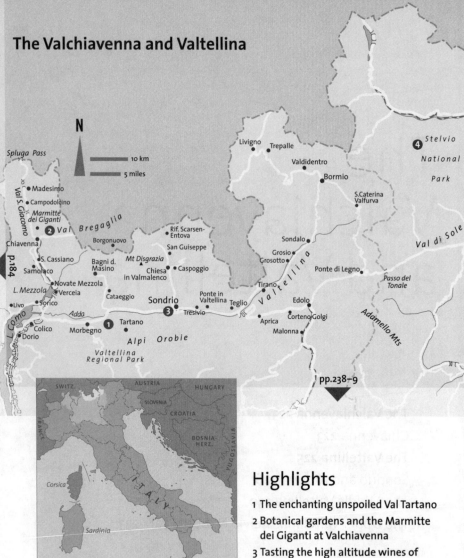

N

10 km
5 miles

Spluga Pass
Val S. Giacomo
Madesimo
Campodolcino
Marmitte dei Giganti
Chiavenna
S. Cassiano
Samolaco
Novate Mezzola
L. Mezzola
Verceia
Livo
Sorico
Colico
Dorio
Como
L. Como

Val Bregaglia
Borgonuovo
Bagni d. Masino
Mt Disgrazia
Chiesa in Valmalenco
Cataeggio
Morbegno
Tartano
Adda
Alpi Orobie
Valtellina Regional Park

Rif. Scarsen-Entova
San Guiseppe
Caspoggio
Sondrio
Tresivio
Ponte in Valtellina
Teglio

Livigno
Trepalle
Valdidentro
Bormio
S.Caterina Valfurva

Stelvio National Park

Sondalo
Grosio
Grosotto
Tirano
Ponte di Legno
Valtellina
Edolo
Corteno Golgi
Aprica
Malonna

Val di Sole
Passo del Tonale
Adamello Mts

Stelvio

p.184
pp.238–9

SWITZ.
AUSTRIA
HUNGARY
SLOVENIA
CROATIA
FRANCE
BOSNIA-HERZ.
YUGOSLAVIA
Corsica
ITALY
Sardinia
Sicily
TUNISIA

Highlights

1 The enchanting unspoiled Val Tartano
2 Botanical gardens and the Marmitte dei Giganti at Valchiavenna
3 Tasting the high altitude wines of Sondrio
4 Superb skiing and walking in Stelvio National Park

North and east of Lake Como lies the majestic mountain-bound wine-growing province of Sondrio, sandwiched between the Orobie Alps and Switzerland. It occupies a watershed in central Europe; its glacier-fed rivers flow into Como and the Mediterranean, but also into the Danube and the Black Sea and through the Rhine into the North Sea. Only four roads link Sondrio's two main valleys, the Valchiavenna and the Valtellina, with the rest of Italy. Both valleys are among the least-exploited regions in the Alps, offering plenty of opportunities to see more of the mountains and fewer of your fellow creatures.

The Valtellina has always clung to its own hard-working cultural traditions, while politically it often played the part of a football between Milan and the Swiss Grison dynasty. Milan had it in the 14th century, but when the Spanish took Milan the Valtellina, with its many Protestants, joined the Grisons. Years of war followed; in 1620 the Spanish in Milan instigated the Valtellina's Catholics to perform the 'Holy Butchery' of four hundred of their Protestant neighbours, a move that backfired in 1639 when the Grisons regained the province. The Valtellina rejoined Italy only in the Napoleonic partition of 1797.

One place where the old Valtellina has thrived is at the table, most famously in its wines (*see* p.228) but also in every course of the meal. Buckwheat is the staff of life, in the Valtellina's grey *polenta taragna*, mixed with butter and cheese, *sciatt*, buckwheat pancakes filled with cheese, and *pizzoccheri*, buckwheat tagliatelle with vegetables; there are delicious cheeses like *bitto* (cow's milk mixed with a maximum 20 per cent goat's milk, becoming stronger with age), mild *casera*, the low-fat *matûsh*, *scimudin* and Valtellina d'Alpe. Mushrooms abound, and local chestnut-fed pork, hams, salami and *bresaola*, thin slices of beef or venison cured in salt, spices and wine, and then left to dry, are excellent. Desserts are based on walnuts, chestnuts and honey; try *fiurett*, a cake flavoured with fennel seeds, *sambucco* and aniseed, or *bisciöla*, a rich chewy cake with raisins, walnuts and figs, served with cream.

The Valchiavenna

The Valchiavenna stretches from Novate Mezzola north of Lake Como to the Spluga and Maloja passes, threading through the Lepontine and Rhaetic Alps. Many of the towns here started as stations along the Roman road and prospered thanks to the thick veins of potstone in the mountains – turned on a lathe and carved into cooking pots (*laveggi*), or sculpted into decorations, especially on windows and portals.

Chiavenna

Chiavenna, the valley metropolis, is a pleasant town along the Mera river. Its distinctive natural rock cellars, the **Crotti**, maintain a steady year-round temperature of 4–8°C and have long been used for ripening local cheeses and hams; some have been converted into restaurants and wine cellars. *Crotti* are usually inherited; those who own the key to one are considered to be very lucky. Chiavenna's most important church, **San Lorenzo** (*t 0343 37152; open winter Tues–Fri 2–4, Sat 10–12 and 2–4; Sun 2–5; summer Tues–Fri 3–6, Sat 10–12 and 3–6; Sun 3–6; adm*), was begun in the 11th century and contains a treasure including a 12th-century golden gem-studded 'Pax' cover for the Gospels. Also, note in the Romanesque baptistry (*t 0343 32117; open Mar–May Sat–Sun 9–12 and 2–4; June–Sept Tues–Sun 9–12 and 2–6; Oct Sat 9–12 and 2–5*) – the octagonal font (1156) is carved from a single chunk of potstone. Above the 15th-century Palazzo Baliani you can walk up to the **Parco Botanico Archeologico Paradiso** (*open Tues–Sat 2–5; Sun 10–12 and 2–5; adm*), an ancient potstone quarry

Getting There and Around

At Colico the **railway** from Milan and Lecco forks, one line heading north to Chiavenna. **Buses** from there link up to Madesimo and other valley towns.

Tourist Information

Chiavenna: Via Vittoria Emanuele II 2, t 0343 36384, www.valchiavenna.com.
Madesimo, Via alle Scuole, t 0343 53015, www.madesimo.com.
Cooperativa Turistica Valtellina-Morbegno, t 0342 610 015.

Festivals

Sagra dei Crotti, *mid-Sept*. Annual celebration in Chiavenna of the surrounding *crotti* caves, many of which are wine cellars.

Sports and Activities

Ask the tourist office for maps of the Valchievenna, or contact the Alpine Club, t 0343 40358, or cooperative Touristico,

t 0343 33442. The Madesimo tourist office also provides information on trails, refuges and contact with the alpine guides. In Madesimo, the Centro Sportivo offers **tennis, squash, ice-skating, gym, sauna, Turkish bath,** a **rock-climbing gym,** and **mountain bike** hire. For the 4-hole **golf course**, ring Golf Club Madesimo, t 0343 53239 (*open mid-June–mid-Sept*). Contact the tourist offices about **horse-riding, archery** and where to play open-air **chess**. To see how the typical **potstone** is worked visit Roberto Lucchinetti, Via alla Chiesa 5, Prosto di Piuro hamlet, t 0343 35905.

Where to Stay and Eat

For **gourmet** travellers a local *affettato* to taste is *violino*, a special ham of *pecora*; goat, locally produced in brine with aromatic herbs and dried in the open air; local cakes *bisciola*: brown, with nuts, figs, raisins and honey, or *torta di fioretto*, with anis seeds.

Chiavenna ✉ 23022

Passerini, Via Dolzino 128, t 0343 36166 (*expensive*). A friendly, family-run restaurant

where workers once cut out stones and pots for architectural details. This also includes the Natural History section, the **Torione** (*open summer Tues, Thurs, Sat and Sun 2.30–5.30*). In the park, the **Mulino di Bottonera** (windmill) is now a museum of industrial archaeology (*open 26 Mar–5 June, Sat–Sun and hols 2.30–5.30; 11 June–11 Sept, Wed–Mon 3–6; 17 Sept–1 Nov, Sat–Sun and hols 2.30–5.30; adm*). Further up, the **Parco Marmitte dei Giganti**, the 'Giants' Kettles', is named for its remarkable round glacial potholes, the finest collection in Europe (*contact t 0343 33795 or t 0343 40358 for guided tours*). The path up to the park passes *crotti* under the horse chestnuts and charming meadows; beyond the potholes a sign directs the way to the *incisioni rupestri* – etchings in the boulders left by centuries of passers-by (but you can bet the guards don't want you to add your two cents' worth). Close by is **Pian di Spagna**, a natural reserve around Lake Mezzola, with many aquatic birds (*see* p.211).

East of Chiavenna on the St Moritz road in the Val Bregaglia, a magnificent waterfall (beautifully frozen in winter), the **Cascate dell'Acqua Fraggia**, is just above **Borgonuovo**; 2,000 leg-aching steps lead up past *crotti* to the ancient hamlet of Savogno atop the waterfall. In 1618 a landslide off Monte Conto buried the town of **Piuro**, next to Borgonuovo; you can visit the excavations of this humble 17th-century Pompeii, once an important potstone quarrying town, and finds are displayed in the church of **Sant'Abbondio** in Borgonuovo (*t 0343 33795; open end Mar–end Oct Sat and Sun only 3–5; adm*). Before it was buried, Piuro had fine mansions like the 16th-century

which offers a value lunch menu as well as à la carte. *Booking advised. Closed Mon and July, and two weeks in Jan.*

Al Cenacolo, Via Pedretti 16, t 0343 32123 (*moderate*). Serves a stylish mix of regional dishes and innovative cuisine, based on local seasonal ingredients, while Valtellina wines fill the cellar. You can eat outside on a small balcony overlooking the river in the summer. *Booking advised. Closed Tues eve, Wed and June.*

La Lanterna Verde, Villa di Chiavenna, 10km west of Chiavenna, t 0343 38588, *www. lanternaverde.com* (*very expensive*). A family-run restaurant that is one of the best places to taste regional cuisine, elevated to a gourmet level. The restaurant is well-known for trout and meat dishes. The beautifully prepared desserts include such delights as the *mousse au chocolat fondant* with a passion fruit heart in a rum sauce. If you like fish, try the 'Menu della Memoria', all based on trout flavours. The enormous wine list comprises a good selection of half bottle wines. *Booking advised. Closed Tues eves, Wed, last two weeks of Nov, and 10 days end of June.*

Madesimo ✉ 23024

★★★Cascata e Cristallo, Via Carducci 2, t 0343 53108, *www.giemmehotels.com* (*moderate*). A large hotel at the top of the list in the city centre, with a pool, and a health and fitness centre nearby. *Booking advised. Closed 10 Sept–10 Dec.*

Il Cantinone, Via De Giacomi 41, t 0343 56120, *www.cantinone.com* (*expensive–moderate*). A good place, with excellent wines and an innovative menu. *Closed May–mid-June; mid-Sept–Nov.*

Osteria Vegia, Via Cascata 7, t 0343 53335 (*moderate*). Plenty of local atmosphere: the place to go for *pizzoccheri* and other local treats for the past 280 years. The poet Carducci used to stop here during his 15 summers spent in Madesimo. *Closed on Mon. Booking advised.*

Dogana Vegia, Via Emet 19, 10mins walk from the city centre, t 0343 54082 (*moderate*). A noisy restaurant and pub full of objects and pictures hanging on the walls. Young atmosphere; food and snacks all day until late, and a nice terrace for outdoor dining in beautiful scenery. *Open all day in season. Closed on Mon. Booking required.*

Palazzo Vertemate Franchi in nearby **Prosto di Piuro** (*open April–Oct daily 10–12 and 2.30–5.30, closed on Wed (except Aug); call t 0343 37485 for guided tours; adm*), its rooms decorated throughout with beautiful carved ceilings and lush mythological frescoes by the Campi brothers of Cremona. At Santa Croce di Piuro, the church of **San Martino in Aurogo** has 11th-century frescoes.

North of Chiavenna, the **Valle San Giacomo** becomes increasingly rugged and steep, with dramatic landslides, glaciers and waterfalls. The village of **Campodolcino**, with a Roman bridge and a church with florid rococo altars, shares the 45km 'Skirama' ski slopes with Madesimo, watched over by a 44ft (13.5m) gilt statue of the **Madonna d'Europa**. **Madesimo**, further up, is a high-rise, high-altitude international summer and winter resort (skiing, cross-country skiing, ice-skating, trekking and riding) – before the 6,948ft (2,118m) **Splügen Pass** (*generally closed Dec–April*).

The Valtellina

East of Colico and Lake Como the thoroughly unpleasant, traffic-swollen SS38 enters the Valtellina, giving a false first impression: the rest of the great valley of the Adda, where villages and vineyards hang precariously on the faces of the mountains, is as pure and unadulterated and fresh as any, a great alpine playground only a couple of hours from smoggy Milan. In 1989, the Orobie Alps south of the Adda were set aside as the **Parco Regionale delle Orobie Valtellinesi** (*t 0342 211 236, www. parcorobievalt.com*), to protect, among other things, the rare local wood grouse.

Sondrio and Around

The Costiera dei Cèch

To enter the lower valley from Colico is to enter the territory of the Cèch, a people whose origin is as mysterious as their name. One interpretation is that Cèch comes

Getting There and Around

FS **trains** from Milan and Lecco serve the valley as far east as Tirano, where you can pick up the '*trenino rosso del Bernina*' for St Moritz, 70km away, **t** 0342 701 353 (in winter you can obtain a combined train ticket and ski pass for skiers). A network of **buses**, connecting with the trains, serves most of the villages and points east, and there are direct coach connections to Sondrio from Milan, as well as direct summer and winter services to Bormio and Stelvio National Park from Milan, Varese and Como.

Tourist Information

Morbegno: Piazza Bossi, **t** 0342 610 015, *www.panvaltellina.com*. Promotes tourism in the Valtellina and organizes free guided tours of the city's monuments on summer evenings.
Valtellina: Piazza Bossi 7–8, **t** 0342 601 140, *info@portedivaltellina.it*. Tourist information for the Valtellina.
Sondrio: Via Trieste, **t** 0342 512 500. Has a lot of information on walking, climbing, mountain biking, riding, and skiing.
Valli Orobiche Consortium: *www.vallidelbitto. it*. Offers tourist information for the region.

Festivals

Festa dell'Alpeggio, *end of Sept.* Join the locals in Chiesa in Valmalenco to greet the descent of the farmers from the summer alpine pasture, with local choirs, bands, and Pantagruelic meals (at fixed prices, ask the tourist office for restaurants participating). Piazza SS. Giacomo e Filippo 1, **t** 0342 451 150,

Don't miss the competition for the best decorated cow.
Bitto Cheese Festival, *3rd Sun in Sept.*

Sports and Activities

The tourist office of Chiesa Valmalenco has a list of **alpine guides** for excursions and a map of the shelters. With the newly opened Snow Eagle cableway connecting Sasso Alto and Palù, there are now 50km of **ski slopes** accessible in the area and plenty of cross-country opportunities, including circular routes in Palù, Caspoggio and Lanzada of up to 40km.

Where to Stay and Eat

Morbegno ✉ 23017
★★★**Margna**, Via Margna 36, **t** 0342 610 377, *www.margna.com* (*moderate*). In business since 1886, but completely modernized, with a nice roof terrace solarium. The stylish restaurant is particularly well looked after, with crêpes filled with *bitto* cheese, risotto with wild mushrooms, and venison cutlets in juniper. Ask about their special wine and food weekends.

Tartano ✉ 23010
★★★**La Gran Baita**, Via Castino 7, **t** 0342 645 043, *www.albergogranbaita.it* (*inexpensive*). A cosy, comfortable hotel offering rooms with bathroom, beautifully overlooking the valley. *Closed Feb and Mar.*
★★★**Vallunga**, Via Roma 12, **t** 0342 645 100 (*inexpensive*). This family-run modern little chalet has rooms with bathroom and a good restaurant; the *risotto ai funghi porcini* is excellent.

from *ciechi* (blind) as the locals were the last to convert to Christianity. Located just above and north of the Adda, the nine old vine-wrapped villages of the Costiera dei Cèch are veritable suntraps and make for pretty, not too demanding walks; there's also an 18th-century wine press and museum, the **Museum del Vino** and **Torchio di Cerido** (*open Thurs and Sun 3–5 or call* **t** *0342 611 342*). The Cèchs' busy and pleasant main town, **Morbegno**, is just over the river, where you'll find a pair of interesting churches: 14th-century **Sant'Antonio**, with a Rodari Pietà and a fresco by Gaudenzio Ferrari on the façade and another within, and **San Giovanni Battista**, frescoed in the 18th century by local rococo master Gianpaolo Ligari. Natural history predominates in

Sondrio ✉ 23100

****Della Posta, Piazza Garibaldi 19, **t** 0342 510 404, *www.hotelposta.so.it* (*expensive–moderate*). Part of the chain of historical public buildings in Italy; Garibaldi is only one of the illustrious guests to have slept here. Formerly the old stage post, this grand old family-run hotel offers big rooms with lots of charm, as well as amenities like TV, phone and minibar. It also has a cosy reading room, American bar and an excellent restaurant.

****Vittoria, Via Bernina 1, **t** 0342 533 888, *www.vittoriahotel.com* (*moderate*). With all the comforts you could expect, including no-smoking rooms and a courtesy laptop computer for Internet access from the privacy of your room.

***Campelli, Via Moia 6, Albosaggia, 5km south of Sondrio, **t** 0342 510 662, *www.campelli.it* (*moderate–inexpensive*). A family-run hotel; the cooking offers a lighter, updated version of Valtellina's somewhat rich delights. There's a nice park in the back, solarium, health farm and hotel disco. *Closed Sun and Mon at lunch and most of Aug.*

Torre della Sassella, a couple of kilometres outside Sondrio in Loc. Sassella 17, **t** 0342 218 500 (*expensive*). In a 16th-century tower, high up on a hill, this wonderful restaurant serves fine cured fish, risotto, meats and excellent wines in four elegant yet rustic dining rooms, each set on a different level. The restaurant is now managed by three young partners, who add to traditional dishes more unusual fare such as the *tagliata* of ostrich meat. Eat in the top dining room – it has less character but there's a 360-degree view of the valley. *Booking advised. Closed Wed, most of July.*

Cima 11, Via Pelosi 3, **t** 0342 515 040 (*inexpensive*). Near Piazza Campello, this is a traditional inn complete with long tables and benches, where diners feast on hearty old-style Valtellina cooking. It has lunch time set dishes, such as *tarozzi* on Tues, polenta on Wed, *pizzoccheri* on Thurs and Fri. *Closed Sun, hols, and Aug.*

Eden, Via Nazario Sauro 40, **t** 0342 214 038 (*inexpensive*). Excellent value for money for its national cuisine. *Lunchtime only. Closed Sun and 2nd and 3rd week of Aug.*

Amici Vecchie Cantine, Via Parravicini 8, **t** 0342 512 590. A wine bar serving excellent locally cured meats, cheeses and vegetables in oil. *Closed Sun.*

Chiesa in Valmalenco ✉ 23023

****Tremoggia, Via Bernina 6, **t** 0342 451 106, *www.tremoggia.it* (*expensive*). This welcoming place has its own sauna, gym and hydromassage pool. The rooms come with TVs and minibars, while the restaurant serves good, cheesy *sciatt* and beef marinated in juniper; try the *pizzoccheri*. *Closed Wed and Nov.*

***Chalet Rezia, Via Marconi 27, **t** 0342 451 271, *www.hotelrezia.it* (*moderate–inexpensive*). A nice little place with a covered swimming pool, recommended by readers. Needs some maintenance work.

La Volta, Via Milano 48, **t** 0342 454 051, (*expensive*). Serves local cuisine creatively revisited, with several menus. *Closed Wed, Thurs at lunch, May. Booking advised.*

Il Vassallo, in Vassalini hamlet No 27, **t** 0342 451 200 (*expensive*). An old stone chalet restaurant which effortlessly combines traditional and original recipes. Excellent home-made *gnocchi* and *pappardelle*. *Closed Mon.*

Valtellina in a Bottle

Valtolina, as it's called, a valley surrounded by tall and fearsome mountains, makes wines that are heady and strong...

Leonardo da Vinci, *Codex Atlanticus 214*

People have been making wine in the Valtellina since the days of the ancient Ligurians and Etruscans. They soon found that while the easy, deep, rich soil in the valley yielded a fresh light red wine – as it does to this day (DOC Valtellina) – body and alcohol content improved dramatically with altitude. The thirst for a wine that aged well led generations to build dry-stone terraces like tiny shelves in the mountains, some wide enough for only two or three rows of knotty vines, then to laboriously carry up soil in woven baskets on their backs. Their efforts in the upper valley or Valtellina Superior (which continue today – of necessity everything has to be done by hand) have been awarded DOC status since 1968.

Red, with a distinctive rich, almost pungent character, capable of ageing ten years or longer, Valtellina Superior is made from a minimum of 95 per cent *chiavennasca* (the local name for nebbiolo, the same noble grape that goes in Barolo) and aged for a minimum of two years in oak.

The DOC area is divided into four subzones, each with a different climate and growing conditions. Sassella, just west of Sondrio, is the sunniest and most inaccessible area, named for its pretty frescoed church of the Madonna di Sassella (1521); the ruby wines are elegant, made with 5 per cent rossola, for fragrance.

the **Museo Civico** in the Palazzo Gualteroni (*Via Cortivacci, t 0342 612 451; open Tues, Thurs, Sat and Sun 2.30–5.30*). The museum suggests an eight-stop walking tour of the valley (Sentiero delle Valli): if you make it within 15 days and get all the correct stamps at the refuges on the way you get a diploma! You can also visit the **Museo dell'Homo Salvadego** in Cosio just to the west: a country house, frescoed in 1464 with the hairy, club-wielding 'Wild Man' of the Alps, the local incarnation of the Green Man, the spirit of nature (*open 9–12 and 2–6; call resident caretaker, t 0342 617 028*).

From Morbegno buses make excursions towards the south into two scenic valleys, the **Valli del Bitto** (named for the local cheese) and **Valle di Albareto e Valgerola**, both of which have iron ore deposits that made them a prize for the Venetians for two centuries; the Pescegallo ski resort, comprising 15km of slopes, sits up on top. Also, there is the rural **Val Tartano**, a 'lost paradise', dotted with alpine cottages, woods and pastures, its declining population still farming as their ancestors did. The road through the valley was finished only in 1971, though many hamlets even today are accessible only by foot or mule.

A third valley running to the north, the wild granite **Val Masino**, is the beginning of the magnificent 'Sentiero Roma', the six-day path to the Valchiavenna laid out in the 1920s. It begins at the little 15th-century spa **Bagni di Masino** at 3,845ft (1,172m) (*t 0342 641 010; open May–Sept*), although other paths from Bagni can be walked in a single day, especially up to the meadows and torrents of the Piano Porcellizzo. The Val Masino also serves as the base for the ascent of **Monte Disgrazia** (39,600ft/12,070m),

Grumello, northeast of Sondrio, produces a warm, garnet, almond-scented wine. Inferno, named for the extra heat and sun the vines receive in a pocket microclimate just east of Sondrio, yields exceptionally warm, powerful wines. Valgello, 10km northeast of Sondrio (between Chiuro and Teglio), the largest subzone, produces lighter, but dry, savoury wines with a toasted almond aftertaste. Another DOC wine from the Valtellina, Sforzato (or Sfursat), is partly made from grapes left to dry on the vine, producing a rich, powerful, velvety soft wine that is perfect with strong cheeses or for sitting by the fireside after dinner on a cold winter's eve.

If you are interested in wines, it is possible to visit the cellars of some of the region's best firms: **Pellizzatti Perego** (*Via Buon Consiglio 4, t 0342 214 120, www.arpepe.com*), and **Fondazione Fojanini** (*Via Valeriana 32, t 0342 512 954, fondazione.fojanini@provinicia.so.it*), both in Sondrio. To the east in Chiuro, it is also possible to visit one of the most venerable firms, the excellent **Nino Negri** (*Via Ghibellini 3, in Chiuro, t 0342 482 521, giv@giv.it*).

Tirano also has two beautiful cellars to visit: **Corti Sertoli Salis**, in patrician Palazzo Salis in the city centre (*Via Salis 3, guided tours of the Palazzo and the cellar are offered by advance booking only, open Mon–Fri 10–12 and 3–6; Sat 10–12; ring t 0342 710 404 and ask for Signora Angela, www.sertolisalis.com*), with a sombre Baroque portal designed by Vignola, and *trompe l'œil* frescoed halls. **Triacca** is housed in a former 16th-century Dominican convent among the original horizontal terraced vineyards (*Villa di Tirano, Via Nazionale 121, in Brianzone south of Tirano – follow the signs for La Gazza-Triacca; call for an appointment, t 0342 701 352, or www.triacca.com*).

one of the highest peaks in the region, first climbed in 1862 by Leslie Stephen, father of Virginia Woolf. According to legend, Disgrazia is haunted by the huge and hairy Gigiat, a kind of monster goat – the yeti of the Valtellina. **Val di Mello**, a little branch valley to the east, is equally tempting for its crystal streams and waterfalls and granite bulwarks, reminiscent of Yosemite, cut and carved by local granite workers and scaled by rock climbers, who also like to pit themselves against the biggest monolith in Europe: the granite **Sasso Remenno**, near the village of Cataeggio.

Sondrio

The provincial capital Sondrio (from the Lombard *sonder*, then changed into the Latin *sundrium*, the land Lombard lords gave to their peasants) is a mostly modern town, built on either side of the flood-prone Torrente Mallero which devastated the city in 1987. Many of Sondrio's surviving old mansions have been put to new uses: in the 18th-century Palazzo Sassi De' Lavizzari, the new **Museo Valtellinese di Storia e Arte** (*Via M. Quadrio 27, t 0342 566 269; open summer Tues–Sat 10–12 and 3–6; winter Tues–Sat 9–12 and 3–5; adm*) has statues, gold work and frescoes salvaged from churches, and an exceptional collection of rococo drawings, etchings and oils by the 18th-century Ligari family. At the time of writing the **Collezione Fulvio Grazioli**, one of Italy's most important collections of rocks and minerals, nearly all from the Val Malenco (*see p.230*), is being kept in Palazzo Martinengo (*Via Dante, t 0342 526 269; open Tues–Thurs 5–6 (6–7 in summer), Fri–Sat 10–12 and 5–6 (6–7 in summer)*).

Palazzo Sertoli, which formerly held the collection, will open some of its rooms, including the fancy *trompe l'oeil* ballrooms, for temporary exhibitions.

Opposite the Palazzo Sertoli, Via Scarpaletti leads up into the old Sondrio, which is dominated by the oft-remodelled **Castello Masegra**, dating from 1041. On the other side of the Torrente Mallero the **Palazzo Carbonera** (1533) is Sondrio's finest, with a beautiful courtyard. But most of all, Sondrio is known for its lovely wine (*see* p.228).

North of Sondrio: The Val Malenco

The lovely Val Malenco, with its deep chestnut forests and pretty glacier lakes, is a top destination in the lower Valtellina and a paradise for rock hounds. No valley in all the Alps comes close to matching the 260 different minerals that have been found here, including the commercially mined serpentine (green marble) and potstone. **Chiesa in Valmalenco** and **Caspoggio** are the main towns and ski resorts in the valley, while the former has a small **Museo Storico Etnografico e Naturalistico della Valmalenco**, located in the former parish church of SS. Giacomo e Filippo (*www. valmalenco.it; open July–Aug Wed–Mon 5–7; Sept Sat only 5–7; Jan–Mar Sat 4.30–6.30; Christmas and Easter periods daily 4.30–6.30; groups on request, call the tourist office at the APT in Valmalenco, t 0342 451 150; adm*), containing various stone objects found in the valley from Roman times to the present day.

The high road or **Alta Via della Val Malenco** offers a seven-day trekking excursion around the rim of the valley, beginning at Torre di Santa Maria, south of Chiesa; the less ambitious can drive most of the way from San Giuseppe (north of Chiesa) up to the site of the Rifugio Scarscen-Entova for a spectacular mountain view. Another fine (and easy) excursion is up to the rugged lakes of **Campo Moro**, on the east branch of the valley; a white road will take you as far as the Rifugio Zoia (*t 0362 451 405; open June–Sept*), and from here it's an easy three-hour hike up to the glacier-blasted peaks around the Rifugio Marinelli (*t 0342 511 577; open April–May and July–Sept*).

The Middle Valtellina

East of Sondrio the SS38 rises relentlessly, but if you're not in a hurry take the scenic 'Castel road' running through the vineyards north of the highway, beginning at Tresivio and the melancholy ruins of Grumello castle.

Ponte in Valtellina to Aprica

The old patrician town of **Ponte in Valtellina** is mostly visited for its parish church of **San Maurizio** (*t 0342 482 158*), with an unusual bronze *cimborio* or lantern (1578), and frescoes by Bernardino Luini. In 1746 it was the birthplace of astronomer Giuseppe Piazzi who, as a monk in Palermo, had such a passion for observing the heavens that he inspired the Viceroy of Naples to send him to England to study astronomy, and to finance the manufacture of a lens twice the size of the one in Greenwich observatory. He brought it back to Palermo to discover Ceres, the first asteroid, on New Year's Day 1801.

Tourist Information

Aprica, Corso Roma 150, **t** 0342 746 113, www.apricaonline.com.
Tirano: Piazza Stazione, **t** 0342 706 066, infotirano@provincia.so.it.
Teglio: Piazza S. Eufemia 6, **t** 0342 782 000, www.teglioturismo.it.

Festivals

Traditional festivals, *spring*. In the Valtellina.
Jazz, Classical and Sacred Music Festivals, *summer*. Held around the Valtellina.
Sagra dei Pizzoccheri, *last weekend of July*. A festival celebrating Teglio's *pizzoccheri* (noodles with butter and vegetables) info on **t** 0342 782 000.
Woodcutters' Competition, *Aug*. Along with other harvesting and traditional activities, in Bormio.
Carnival, *winter*. A parade of traditional masks in Grosio, (**bonfire** in Tirano). A folklore group from Grosio also tours the area.

Sports and Activities

Ask the local tourist offices for maps of **bike** and **trekking** itineraries in the area as well as information on **horse-riding**, **skiing** and **climbing**. You can go **rafting** and **canoeing** with Base Valtellina Rafting, **t** 0342 212 213, and **canyoning** with the Associazione Top Canyon

Valtellina, **t** 3355 470 126, www.topcanyon.com, down Valtellina's Adda river. The Italian **rafting championship** is held in June, and runs between Chiuro and Piateda.

Where to Stay and Eat

Ponte in Valtellina ✉ 23026
Cerere, Via Guicciardi 7, **t** 0342 482 294 (*expensive–moderate*). One of the region's best restaurants, occupying a 17th-century palace, this has long set the standard of classic Valtellina cuisine with dishes like *sciatt* and *pizzoccheri*. Good wine list. *Closed Wed (not in Aug) 3 weeks in Jan, July.*

Teglio ✉ 23036
La Corna, Via della Chiesa 9, in San Giacomo di Teglio, **t** 0342 786 105 (*moderate*). A beautiful dining room with polished wooden floors and elegant round tables, creating a warm atmosphere that complements the home-made pastas, local specialities and excellent wines produced by the owners themselves. *Closed Mon and July.*

Aprica ✉ 23031
★★★De La Ville, Via Europa 16, **t** 0342 746 054, www.saintjane.it (*moderate–inexpensive*). A typical, moderate-sized establishment with a garden.

Further east, charming **Teglio** gave its name to the entire valley (from Tellina Vallis). The stumpy tower of its castle still stands guard above, while the Renaissance **Palazzo Besta** is the finest in the region (*t 0342 781 218; open May–Sept Tues–Sat 9–12 and 2–5; Oct–April Tues–Sat 8–2; also open the 1st, 3rd and 5th Sun of the month, the 2nd and 4th Mon and hols, 8–2; closed 1 May, Christmas, and 1 Jan; adm*). Built in 1539, the arcaded courtyard is embellished with fine *chiaroscuro* frescoes from the *Aeneid* and *Orlando Furioso*; inside, the Sala della Creazione has a world map dated 1549. Downstairs, the **Antiquarium Tellinum** (*same ticket*) houses the Stele di Caven, known as the Mother Goddess, an exceptional example of the prehistoric rock incisions common in these parts, which the locals once believed were made by the claws of witches. Among the old lanes in the centre, look for 11th-century **San Pietro**, with geometric decorations, a fine campanile and a Byzantine-style fresco of Christ Pantocrator in the apse; the **Oratorio dei Bianchi**, its exterior frescoed with a ruined 15th-century *danse macabre*; and the **Ca' del Boia** with blackened arcades, once the home of a particularly adept and sought-after executioner. These days Teglio takes special pride not only in its wines but in its *pizzoccheri*, narcotic grey noodles with butter and vegetables.

★★★Serenella, Via Europa 142, **t** 0342 746 066, *sangiani@novanet.it* (*inexpensive*). Older, in a typical local building. The owners have a little local monopoly which also includes the De La Ville, Hotel Cristallo, the swimming pool and the disco Charlie.

La Stua, Via Valtellina 11, **t** 0342 747 776 (*moderate*). Named for its pretty ceramic stove; the various *risotti* are superb, and the game dishes are served with imaginative flair. *Closed Wed. Booking advised.*

Baita le Lische, **t** 0342 746 401 (*inexpensive*) in San Pietro di Aprica. Will fill you up with huge portions of deliciously warm *torte* covered with melting Gruyère cheese and mouthwatering desserts – the *pannacotta* is a must. Hot snacks at lunchtime. *Closed Tues except during ski season (Dec–May).*

Tirano ✉ 23037

★★Bernina, Via Roma 24, **t** 0342 701 302, *www.albergobernina.it* (*moderate*). Opposite the *trenino rosso* station, this hotel has been run by the Cioccarelli family for over a hundred years. Most rooms have bathrooms. The restaurant, with its pretty summer terrace, offers a *menu del giorno* for €15; you can also feast here on something rare in the Alps: fish. *Closed Mon out of season, Nov and Jan.*

Casa Mia, Via Arcari 6, **t** 0342 705 300 *www.geocities.com/eccocasamia* (*inexpensive*). A

nice bed and breakfast in the old city centre, which couples the familiar hospitality of Mrs Baruffaldi and her husband with all comforts. Every room is tastefully decorated, and includes a TV.

Ai Portici, Viale Italia 87, **t** 0342 701 255, *www.aiportici.com* (*moderate–inexpensive*). The place to go for excellent local food at competitive prices, and within walking distance from the Bernina express station, the Santuario and the city centre. Local cuisine: pissocchen, polenta, meat. Serves sea fish at weekends at a moderate price. *Closed Mon except mid-May–mid-Oct, when it's open for Mon lunch.*

Grosio ✉ 23022

★★★Sassella, Via Roma 2, **t** 0342 847 272, *www.hotelsassella.it* (*moderate*). A fine old hotel and restaurant run by friendly chef and owner Jim Pini (the chef who feeds the Italian ski team), and his family, where all the rooms are big and fitted with private bath and TV. The restaurant serves a refined version of local specialities like *bresaola condita* (served with olive oil, lemon and herbs), crêpes with mushrooms and local cheese, an unparalleled *sciatt*, smoked trout and Valtellina wines. The excellent menu changes daily, and there are children's menus and thematic tastings. *Closed Mon in winter. Booking advised.*

East of Teglio, the road splits: the SS38 heads north to Tirano, while SS39 runs east to **Aprica** (3,897ft/1.118m), a winter and summer resort with a covered pool, roller rink, riding school, tennis, 40 kilometres of ski runs and three ski schools, including one for international competitors. Aprica itself it is not an attractive town, as it was built as a ski resort. However, you can unexpectedly chance upon glimpses of the past, such as women washing laundry in the street fountains. Aprica is also conveniently located to visit the protected areas of Pian di Gembro, San Antonio valleys, and the Park of the Orobie Valtellinesi. You can escape the crowds at **Corteno Golgi**, where you can hire a horse at the Centro Ippico Aprichese (*t 0342 746 208*) to explore two remote valleys, the **Val Brandet** and **Val Camovecchio**, both part of a little-known park of firs, rhododendrons, tiny lakes, wooden bridges and old stone alpine huts. Or you can continue towards Edolo and the Valle Camonica (*see* p.263).

Tirano to Sondalo

The vines begin to give way to lush apple orchards as you approach **Tirano**, a historic crossroads: mule trains from Venice and Brescia would pass up the Valle Camonica, and at Tirano either turn west to trade in the Valtellina or continue north into Switzerland and Germany. Today the town is the terminus of the FS trains from Milan, as well as the narrow-gauge **Trenino rosso del Bernina** (*info at Rhaetian Railways in Triano, t 0342 701 353, www.rdb.ch*) that plunges and twists 70km through dramatic gorges to St Moritz; in July and August special open cars make it even easier to drink in the stupendous scenery. Once the site of a major annual Swiss-Italian fair, Tirano has a fine clutch of 16th- and 17th-century buildings in its centre, but its most famous, the **Santuario della Madonna di Tirano** (1505), is a kilometre away, marking the spot where the Virgin made one of her appearances in September 1504. It became the focal point of Catholicism during the Counter-Reformation, and was exuberantly baroqued, painted and stuccoed and given an impressive wood-inlaid organ to keep the faithful dazzled when the Valtellina was quickly sliding away into the Protestant camp. Just above the basilica, the little 10th-century church of **Santa Perpetua** (*arrange to get inside with the Tirano tourist office, or call t 0342 701 181*) has rare frescoes from the same period, discovered in 1987. The **Museo Etnografico Tiranese** (*Piazza Basilica, same tel as S. Perpetua; open June–Sept Tues–Sun 10–12 and 3.30–6.30; Mon only open to groups by apppointment; Oct–May Sat 10–12 and 2.30–5.30*), located in the 18th-century Casa del Penitenziere, documents rural activity, traditional furnishings (such as the *stua*, or stove), tools and objects, some of which date back to the Bronze Age. The Stelvio road continues up to **Grosotto**, with another major church to the Madonna, the 17th-century **Santuario della Beata Vergine delle Grazie**, with an even better 18th-century organ and a painting by Michelangelo's friend Marcello Venusti.

The large old village of **Grosio**, another 2km on, was long the fief of the Visconti Venosta family, whose ruined castle sits on top of town. Just below the castle, however, is evidence that Grosio was important long before their arrival, in the curious stick-man engravings (2200–1000 BC) on the whaleback rock of its **Parco delle Incisioni Rupestri** (*t 0342 847 596, parco.grosio@provincia.so.it*). Art in Grosio took another step forward in the 16th century with the birth of Cipriano Valorsa, the 'Raphael of the Valtellina', who in Grosio frescoed **San Giorgio** and his own house, the **Casa di Cipriano Valorsa**. The early 20th-century Villa Visconti Venosta contains the **Museo Civico** (*info at the library, t 0342 847 454; open July–Sept Tues–Sun 10–12 and 2–5; Oct–June Tues–Sat 10–12 and 2–5*); among the exhibits are Venetian-inspired costumes, with bright kerchiefs and colourful, Burano-embroidered aprons that the older women in Grosio still wear. **Sondalo**, the next town, has courtly 16th-century frescoes by another local painter, Giovannino da Sondalo, in its 12th-century church of Santa Marta.

The Upper Valtellina: Stelvio National Park

The east end of Sondrio province, where the mountains kiss the sky, was an ancient county not unjustifiably called the Magnifica Terra. Today much of the Magnifica Terra is in Stelvio National Park, Italy's most majestic; it also has some of the best skiing in Europe.

Tourist Information

Bormio: Via Roma 131, **t** 0342 903 300, *infobormio@provincia.so.it.*
Livigno: Via Gesa 65, **t** 0342 996 379, *info@aptlivigno.it.*

Sports and Activities

Stelvio National Park is administered by the provinces of Sondrio, Trento and Bolzano, all of which have **park visitor's centres.** Bormio's is at Via Roma 26 (**t** *0342 910 100, www.stelviopark.it; open July–10 Sept daily 9–12 and 3–6*); they can tell you where to find the 1,500km of marked trails at all levels of ability, or the best place to watch for the park's *chamois,* the not very shy marmots and other wildlife including the ibex, reintroduced in 1968. The last bear in these mountains was bagged in 1908, but hunting is now illegal, at least in the Lombard section of the park.

Above the visitor's centre, the **Giardino Botanico Alpino Rezia** (**t** *0342 927 370; open June, Sept Tues–Sun 9–12 and 3–6; July, Aug Tues–Sun 9–12 and 2–7*) contains many of the 1,800 species of plants and flowers that grow in Stelvio. The local tourist offices have plenty of information on summer and winter sports in the area.

You can also plunge into the **Bagni Vecchi** thermal waters in beautiful surroundings, either in the panoramic Beauregard outdoor pool overlooking the valley, or under natural and artificial hydromassages, or in the sweating caves – the original Roman baths. The Bagni, **t** 0342 910 131, *www.bagnidibormio.it,* are in Valdidentro on the way to Stelvio, outside Bormio (*open all year round daily 10–8pm*). A shuttle service runs from Bormio five times a day.

Where to Stay and Eat

Bormio ✉ 23032
★★★★**Baita dei Pini,** Via Don Peccedi 15, **t** 0342 904 346, *www.baitadeipini.com* (*very expensive*). Central and pleasant with very good rooms, all with bathroom, and offering a fitness centre with Turkish bath, sauna hydromassage and a fully equipped gym. *Open all year.*
★★★★**Palace,** Via Milano 54, **t** 0342 903 131, *www.palacebormio.it* (*very expensive*). A modern and upmarket establishment that offers tennis, swimming pool and very comfortable rooms, all with bathroom and TV. *Closed May–mid-June.*

Bormio

Bormio, the seat of the Magnifica Terra, is splendidly situated in a mountain basin 4,019ft (1,225m) up. The occasional host of the World Alpine Ski Championships, Bormio keeps visitors coming year round with an indoor sports complex, ice palace, golf courses, tennis courts and a new congress centre. But along with all of its sporty infrastructure, Bormio is also a picturesque old town of narrow medieval lanes and frescoed palaces, recalling the days of prosperity when Venice's Swiss trade passed through its busy Via Roma. One rare survival is the 13th-century council chamber or **Kuerc,** from where the Magnifica Terra was administered.

The 18th-century **Palazzo De Simoni,** Via Buon Consiglio 25, now houses the **Museo Civico** (*open Jan–Easter Mon–Sat 3–7; mid-Jun–mid-Sept Tues–Sun 10–12.30 and 3–7, Fri also 9–11pm; Christmas and Easter hols daily 10–12.30 and 3–7; other periods Tues, Thurs, Sat 3.30–6.30; ring ahead on* **t** *0342 912 236 as opening times change regularly*); the Romanesque **San Vitale** is frescoed in and out, while outside the centre at Combo the **Chiesa del Santo Crocifisso** contains good 15th-century frescoes. Bormio is also known for its waters, either distilled into Braulio, an alpine herbal tonic made since 1875, or in the **Bagni di Bormio,** first mentioned by Pliny the Elder, where the water steams out of

****Rezia**, Via Milano 9, **t** 0342 904 721, *www.reziahotel.it* (*very expensive*). In the centre of Bormio, this is one of the town's cosiest hotels, furnished throughout with locally handcrafted furniture. The restaurant (*moderate*) is especially good, serving up delicious mushroom dishes in season as well as solid Valtellina homecooking. In the **Rezia Jazz Café** you can listen to live music. *Hotel closed mid-April–mid-June.*

*****Hotel Bogin Vecchi**, in Valdidentro on the way to Stelvio, just outside Bormio, **t** 0342 910 131 (*expensive–moderate*). Recently renovated turn-of-the-last-century hotel at the Bagni Vecchi thermal waters and Roman caves, with special weekend rates and access to the renowned thermal facilities (*see* 'Sports and Activities', opposite page). *Closed Dec–April.*

****Everest**, Via S. Barbara 11, **t** 0342 901 291, *everest@bormio.it* (*inexpensive*). Has flowery balconies, a little back garden and standard rooms, all with bathrooms, but no restaurant. *Closed Oct, Nov.*

Al Filò, Via Dante 6, **t** 0342 901 732, *filo@mio.it* (*expensive–moderate*). Serves Valtellinese cuisine in an old, stylishly decorated *Taulà* (old hay-loft under vaults of local stone). *Closed Tues, Mon lunch (not in July–Aug); first half of June, 2nd half of Nov.*

Kuerc, Piazza Cavour 7, **t** 0342 910 787 (*moderate*). Situated in the heart of old Bormio and named after the ancient council of Bormio, this is a good place to try local dishes in an attractive setting. *Closed Tues and 25 Sept–25 Oct. Booking advised.*

La Rasiga, Via Marconi 6, **t** 0342 901 541, *rasiga@tiscoli.it* (*moderate–inexpensive*). Restaurant located in an old sawmill across the river. *Closed Mon.*

Livigno ✉ 23030

With 97 hotels and 800 holiday flats, you'll probably find a place to sleep in Livigno.

*****Alpina**, Via Bondi 15, **t** 0342 996 007, *www.alpinahotel.it* (*moderate*). This family-run hotel is one of the best, operating for over a century, with a woodsy elegance. Its excellent restaurant is usually packed with hungry diners feasting on game and mushroom dishes, tasty local cheeses and excellent Valtellina wines. *Closed May and June.*

*****Camana Veglia**, Via Ostaria 583, **t** 0342 996 310, *www.camanaveglia.com* (*moderate*). An atmospheric B&B; occupies a historic building near the centre and also has a good restaurant serving dishes based on local ingredients. *Restaurant closed Tues; hotel closed May and first half of Dec.*

the rocks at 40°C and is good for everything from acne to vaginitis (*Bagni Vecchi*, **t** *0342 910 131, or Bormio Terme*, **t** *0342 901 325*).

Bormio is the western gateway to the **Parco Nazionale dello Stelvio** (*see* 'Sports and Activities'), Italy's largest national park. A tenth of Stelvio is permanently covered with a hundred glaciers, including one of Europe's largest, the *Ghiacciaio dei Forni*. The peaks offer good climbing especially **Grand Zebrù** (12,631ft/3,850m) and **Ortles** (12,811ft/3,905m). The park includes Europe's second-highest pass, the **Passo dello Stelvio** (9,048ft/2,758m) where you can ski all summer and continue into the South Tyrol between the months of June and October. Building the road here was such an engineering feat that its mastermind has a small museum in the pass, the **Museo Carlo Donegani** (**t** *0342 903 030 or* **t** *0342 904 534; open May–beginning of Nov Mon–Sat 9–12 and 1.30–5, Sun 9–12.30 and 1.30–5*).

Some 14km east of Bormio in the confines of the park is 'the skier's last white paradise', perhaps better known as **Santa Caterina Valfurva**. This is a typical alpine village and cradle of future ski champions (most recently Olympic gold medallist Deborah Compagnoni), who learn to ski as soon as they can toddle on the snow that lasts from early autumn to late spring.

Into Little Tibet and Livigno

From Bormio a white road winds up along the Valle di Fraele, towards the source of the River Adda, into a landscape called 'Italy's Little Tibet', as much for its quantity of snow as for its rugged mountains. Two towers, the stark 16th-century **Torri di Fraele**, guard the mule road, the old German Via Imperiale. The towers were the last garrison of the old defensive network of the valley, which allowed other castles and towers to receive signals and alerts; it proved very helpful when Frederick I – Barbarossa – was about to invade the area, and also in 1629, when the Landsknecht mercenaries were close to Italy. A more modest route diverging to the west is known as the *sentiero dei Contrabbandieri* or smugglers' path. The steep gorge of the Adda survives, although the river does not, diverted by a hydroelectric plant to feed the industries of Milan; the source of the Adda is now dammed back to form the artificial lakes of Cancano and San Giacomo di Fraele.

From Bormio the N301 follows the **Valdidentro**, another ski haven, west into the **Valle di Livigno**. Before reaching **Livigno** proper, however, you must first pass through customs – for this old paradise for smugglers has been Europe's highest duty-free zone since 1805, thanks to Napoleon, a status confirmed in 1960 by the EU. Besides being a favourite weekend destination for Bavarians who barrel down through the Drossa tunnel to replenish their tobacco or hooch supplies, Livigno preserves many of its old wooden houses or *baites* and has excellent skiing, with snow most of the year; its outer hamlet of **Trepalle** claims to be the highest settlement in Europe inhabited year-round, at 6,234–7,382ft (1,900–2,250m).

The East: Bergamo to Lake Garda

Morbegno
p.222
Alpi Orobie
Malonno
Cedegolo
Como Stella
Foppolo
San Simone
Carona
Capo di Ponte
Piazzatorre
Val Brembana
Cerveno
Val di Scalve
Nadro
Roncabello
Breno
Piazza Brembana
Bienno
p.184
Passo della Presolana
Berzo
Esine
Valcanale
Castione d. Presolana
Boario Terme
Oneta
Clusone
Rovetta
Angolo Terme
S. Giovanni Bianco
S. Pellegrino Terme
Lovere
Mt Campione
Endine Gaiano
Gandino
Zogno
Pisogne
Collio
Bovegno
Lake Endine
Almenno S. Bartolmeo
Riva di Solto
Zone
Monasterolo del Castello
Clanezzo
Val Trompia
S342
Marone
Alzano Lombardo
Pontida
Lake Iseo
Sale Marasino
Bergamo
2
Trescore Balneario
Tavernola Bergamasca
Gardone Val Trompia
Sulzano
Sarnico
Pilzone
A4
Iseo
Lumezzane
Capriate S. Gervasio
Clusane
1
Cavernago
Franciacorta
Erbusco
Passirano
Concesio
Bornato
Rodengo Saiano
Brescia
3
S11
Treviglio
Chiari
Caravaggio
P185
S11
Rivolta d'Adda
Pandino
Ghedi
Manerbio
pp.108–9
SWITZ
AUSTRIA
HUNGARY
SLOVENIA
CROATIA
FRANCE
BOSNIA-HERZ.
YUGOSLAVIA
Corsica
ITALY
Sardinia
Sicily
TUNISIA

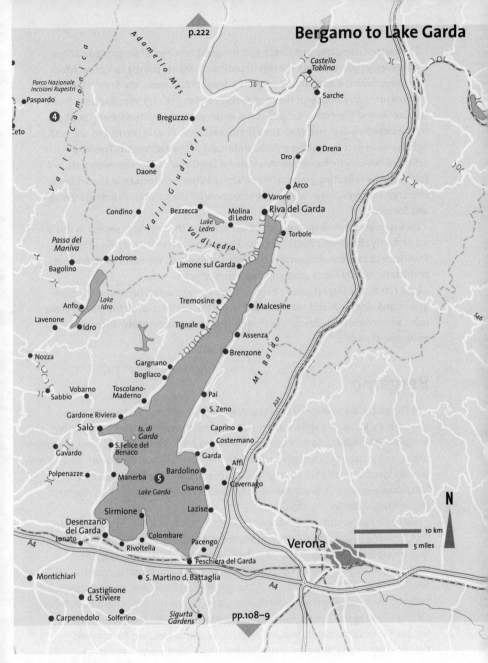

p.222

Bergamo to Lake Garda

Parco Nazionale
Incisioni Rupestri
Paspardo
Ceto
④

Adamello Mts

Castello
Toblino
Sarche

Breguzzo

Drena

Daone

Dro

Arco

Varone

Condino
Bezzecca
Molina
di Ledro
Riva del Garda

Lake
Ledro
Val di Ledro
Torbole

Passo del
Maniva
Lodrone
Limone sul Garda

Bagolino

Anfo
Lake
Idro
Tremosine
Malcesine

Lavenone
Idro
Tignale
Assenza

Nozza
Brenzone

Gargnano
Mt Baldo

Bogliaco

Vobarno
Toscolano-
Maderno
Pai

Sabbio
S. Zeno

Gardone Riviera
Caprino

Salò
Is. di
Garda
Costermano

Gavardo
S.Felice del
Benaco
Garda

Polpenazze
Affi

Manerba
Bardolino
Cavernago

⑤
Cisano

Lake Garda

Lazise

Sirmione

Desenzano
del Garda
Lonato
Colombare
Pacengo
Verona

Rivoltella
Peschiera del Garda

Montichiari
S. Martino d. Battaglia

A4

Castiglione
d. Stiviere

Carpenedolo
Solferino
Sigurta
Gardens
pp.108–9

N

10 km
5 miles

Highlights

1 The charming wine-growing region of Franciacorta
2 The urbane perfection of Bergamo's Piazza Vecchia
3 Brescia's fascinating Roman and Lombard relics
4 The prehistoric rock incisions of the Valle Camonica
5 Magnificent Lake Garda, reflecting the Dolomites

The eastern lakes, Iseo and Garda, and the great art cities of Bergamo and Brescia are markedly different from the rest of Lombardy, thanks mostly to Venice, which ruled here from the early 1400s until the advent of Napoleon, the Serenissima's *numero uno* party-pooper. If the medieval Venetians got very mixed reviews from the Greeks and their other subject states in the eastern Mediterranean, they had, by the time they acquired their *terra firma* real estate in Italy, learned to rule with a light hand, in part by making a visual statement of their dominion. This was achieved not only by fixing a marble relief of the lion of St Mark to every gate and tower, but by reflecting graceful bits of Venice in the architecture, in the art in the churches and in exceptional paintings that now fill the galleries in both Bergamo and Brescia.

Lake Iseo, between Bergamo and Brescia, is one of the best-kept secrets in this book – a perfectly charming little lake rimmed by the mellow vine-clad hills of the Franciacorta to the southeast and the Valle Camonica to the north, with fascinating prehistoric rock incisions spanning thousands of years.

Lake Garda, the largest lake in Italy, is stunning, with colourful towns and olive groves and vineyards and too many tourists in the summer; of all the lakes it is the most whole-heartedly devoted to sheer fun, with its water sports, discos and amusement parks.

Bergamo

At the end of *A Midsummer's Night Dream*, Bottom and his mechanic pals who played in 'Pyramus and Thisbe' dance a bergamask to celebrate the happy ending. Bergamo itself has the same happy, stomping magnificent spirit as its great peasant dance, a city that mixes a rugged edge with the most delicate refinement: it has given the world not only a dance but the maestro of *bel canto*, Gaetano Donizetti, the Renaissance painter of beautiful women, Palma il Vecchio, and the great master of the portrait, Gian Battista Moroni.

Piled on a promontory on the edge of the Alps, the city started out on a different foot, founded by mountain Celts who named it 'Bergheim' or hill town. To this day the Bergamasques speak a dialect that puzzles even their fellow Lombards; their language, courage and blunt up-front character are all a part of the essential *bergheimidad* that sets them apart. Although old Bergamo owes many of its grace notes to the long rule of Venice (1428–1797), it was by no means a one-way traffic of culture from Lagoon Land to hill peasants: Bergamo contributed not only artists, but the Serenissima's most brilliant and honourable *condottiere*, Bartolomeo Colleoni (1395–1475), as well as many of Venice's servants, porters and stock comic characters.

The city prospered to the extent that in the 16th century another Bergamo, Bergamo Bassa, grew up on the plain below; the two cities, high and low, contributed so many men to Garibaldi in its enthusiasm for the Risorgimento that it received the proud title 'City of the Thousand'.

Getting There and Around

Bergamo is an hour's **train** ride from Milan, and also has frequent connections to Brescia, but only a few trains a day to Cremona and Lecco; for information, call **t** 89 20 21 (toll-free number in Italy). Bergamo's **airport**, Orio al Serio, **t** 035 326323, *www.orioaeroporto.it* (moderate), has connections to Rome, Naples and Palermo as well as a host of European cities including London (Stansted and Luton), Glasgow, Newcastle, Dublin and others.

There are regular **bus** services through the Societa Autoferrovie Bergamasche, **t** 800 139 392 (toll-free number), *www.sab-autoservizi.it*, to Milan, Como, Lake Garda (via Brescia), the Bergamasque Valleys and Boario in the Val Camonica. Lecco can be reached by train. Both train and bus stations are located near Viale Papa Giovanni XXIII (Piazzale G. Marcani).

If you're **driving**, try to leave your car elsewhere. Bergamo is purgatory to navigate, hell at rush hours, and once you reach your destination you may be unable to park. You can, however, find some supervised parking; in the Città Alta, in the Piazza del Mercato del Fieno.

Tourist Information

Bergamo has two tourist offices:
Viale Vittorio Emanuele 20, t 035 210 204, *aptbg@apt.bergamo.it*. In a beautiful 19th-century villa set in its own grounds, a few hundred yards from the funicular station.
Città Alta, at Vicolo dell'Aquila Nera 2, **t** 035 242 226, *www.apt.bergamo.it*.

Internet

The **Youth Hostel** (*see* p.242) has Internet access. **Bergamonline**, in Palazzo Rezzana, by the train station, and **Willy e Elisa** in Via A. Azimonti 14, near the hospital Romano di Lombardia, **t** 0363 910 260, *www.internet cafe.to*, have Internet access.

Where to Stay

Bergamo ✉ **24100**

★★★★**Excelsior San Marco**, Piazzale della Repubblica 6, **t** 035 366 111, *www.hotelsan marco.it* (*very expensive*). The city's most comfortable hotel, situated a few minutes from the funicular, with air-conditioned, modern rooms, and an excellent restaurant, **Colonna** (*expensive, though there are set menus at moderate prices*). The hotel has a beautiful roof terrace with a 360-degree view over old and new Bergamo. From June to Sept you can dine outside on grilled meat and fish. Breakfast is served in the conservatory on the terrace, all year round. Rooms at a cheaper price available upon request.

★★★★**Best Western Hotel Cappello d'Oro**, Viale Giovanni XXIII 12, **t** 035 232 503 (*very expensive*). Well-equipped modern rooms with satellite TV, lovely bathrooms, and a very good restaurant. Beware that extra rooms rented out when the hotel is booked up may not meet the category's standards. Do check in advance.

★★★★**San Lorenzo**, Piazza L. Mascheroni 9/A, **t** 035 237 383, *www.hotelsanlorenzobg.it* (*expensive*). Conveniently located in Bergamo Alta, outside the pedestrian area; can be reached by car. All comforts including air conditioning and minibar.

★★★**San Vigilio**, Via S. Vigilio 15, **t** 035 253 179, *www.sanvigilio.it* (*expensive*). Up beyond the Città Alta – reached by the S. Vigilio cable car – this hotel was built earlier in the last century by a local bank for its employees' holidays. It has just seven rooms – five with magnificent views – and a nice olde-worlde atmosphere. Host and owner Tiziana De Franceschi is an artist with a fine touch both in her paintings (she specializes in fakes of famous painters) and in the dishes she cooks, which make the most of local produce. *Closed Tues.*

Bergamo Bassa

The heart of Bergamo's pleasant Città Bassa was laid out in the 1920s by Marcello Piacentini (1881–1960), wide and stately, lined with trees and always full of cars. Viale Giovanni XXIII goes up from the station to the elongated **Piazza Matteotti**, where a wide leafy pedestrian-refuge, the *Sentierone*, the 'Big Path', is flanked by cafés, the 18th-century **Teatro Donizetti**, with five tiers of boxes, and the church of **San**

***Il Gourmet**, Via San Vigilio 1, **t** 035 437 3004, *www.gourmet-bg.it* (*moderate*). Family-run and conveniently located within walking distance from the Città Alta and at the foot of San Vigilio cable car. Nice terrace for outdoor dining and, something very rare in Bergamo, free private parking for hotel and restaurant guests. Loyal to its name, with gourmet cuisine ranging from fish to meat and delicacies such as Iranian caviar and fresh foie gras. The restaurant (*expensive*) is popular among local sports teams (see the flags hanging from the reception wall) and has a wide selection of wines. *Closed Tues.*

Agnello d'Oro, Via Gombito 22, **t 035 249 883, *www.agnellodoro.it* (site under construction) (*moderate*). The most atmospheric hotel in the Città Alta was built in 1600, although rooms are modern, all with bathroom and TV. The excellent restaurant (*expensive–moderate*) offers regional dishes including *casoncelli, maize foiade* and rice dishes, and beef stew, sausages and quails with polenta. Outside dining in the little square in front in the summer. *Closed Mon, and Sun eve, 4 weeks Jan–Feb.*

Sole, Via B. Colleoni 1, **t 035 218 238 (*moderate*). Nearby, on the corner of the Piazza Vecchia, the Sole is homey but a shade noisier, although most rooms are in the back. Bathrooms are in all the rooms. The restaurant has a terrace to dine on in the summer and specializes in traditional cuisine, fish and especially mushroom dishes. *Closed Thurs Nov–Feb.*

San Giorgio, Via S. Giorgio 10, **t 035 212 043 (*inexpensive*). Situated near the station, this has quiet rooms in spite of its location, with private bathrooms; some rooms are without bathrooms, TVs and other comforts.

*Caironi, Via Torretta 6, a 20min walk from the station or take bus nos. 5, 7 or 8, **t** 035 243 083 (*inexpensive*). In Bergamo Bassa, this family-run, traditional locanda has a nice back garden where you can dine in summer. Rooms have communal bathrooms on each floor. The restaurant looks promising (*inexpensive*). *Closed Mon and Aug.*

Youth Hostel, Via G. Ferraris 1, **t** 035 361 724, *www.ostellodibergamo.it*. 2km from the station (take bus no.16 from the railway station). Cheaper if you have an AIG card (Italian Association of Youth Hostels), which can be bought there (*see* 'Where to Stay', p.63). Double and single rooms available.

Eating Out

Bergamo prides itself on its cooking: look for *casoncelli* (ravioli filled with tangy sausage-meat in a sauce of melted butter, bacon and sage), *polenta taragna* (with butter and cheese), risotto with wild mushrooms. Many restaurants, surprisingly, feature seafood – Bergamo is a major inland fish market. In August, however, you might find you have to resort to a picnic.

Baretto di San Vigilio, Via Castello 1, **t** 035 253 191, *www.baretto.it* (*very expensive*). Just off the exit of San Vigilio cable car, a fine restaurant with a stylish and secluded atmosphere. Fish is a speciality, but there's also mouthwatering pasta (black tagliolini with shrimps), soups (porcini soup in autumn), meat dishes – try the *maialino* (pork), cooked in the oven on an aubergine tarte – a great table of *antipasti* and a good selection of wines and cigars. *Best to reserve. Closed Mon in winter.*

Da Vittorio, Viale Papa Giovanni XXIII 5, **t** 035 213 266, *www.davittorio.com* (*very expensive*). The classic for fish, specializing in seafood prepared in a number of exquisite ways, as well as a wide variety of meat dishes, polenta, risotto and pasta. Try Branrino with olives. *Closed Wed, and three weeks in Aug.*

Bartolomeo, housing a 1516 altarpiece of the *Madonna* by the Venetian Lorenzo Lotto, who spent 15 years working around Bergamo. The north extension of Piazza Matteotti, Piazza Vittorio Veneto, was graced by Marcello Piacentini with one of the more elegant *Fasciste* bell towers anywhere. Further up Viale Vittorio Emanuele II, don't miss the Liberty-style Banca d'Italia and the Art Deco post office just behind it off Via Zelasco.

La Colombina, Via Borgo Canale 12, t 035 261
402 (*very expensive*). Near Donizetti's
birthplace; the almost perfect restaurant,
with stunning views from its dappled
terrace, and a pretty Liberty-style dining
room. Try the salad of local *taleggio* cheese
with slivers of pear, a plate of cured meats,
and the best *casoncelli* in town. *Closed Mon
and Tues, 2 weeks in Jan and 2 weeks in June.*

Marianna, by the Porta S. Alessandra in Largo
Colle Aperto 2, t 035 247 997, *www.
lamarianna.it* (*very expensive*). The place to
go for ice cream, where you can sit on the
shady terrace gorging on fig, apricot, rose
petal or peach flavours. Also a good restaurant for Tuscan cuisine. *Closed Mon in winter,
Jan, 1 week in Aug.*

Bar Donizetti, Via Gombito 17a, t 035 242 661
(*expensive*). Another nice spot, which has
tables inside the arcaded market, a wine bar
serving gourmet snacks and hot dishes.
Closed Tues, 25 Dec and 1 Jan.

Taverna dei Colleoni & dell'Angelo, Piazza
Vecchia 7, t 035 232 596 (*expensive*). A
celebrated restaurant in a historic palace,
featuring exquisite classical Italian cuisine.
Slightly cheaper menu at lunchtimes. *Closed
Mon and two weeks in Aug.*

Antica Hosteria del Vino Buono, Piazza
Mercato delle Scarpe, in Bergamo Alta, in
front of the exit of the *funivia*, t 035 247 993
(*moderate*). A hearty meal serving polenta
(try the *tris*) and local hot and cold dishes.
Closed Mon. Booking advisable.

Da Ornella, Via Gombito 15, t 035 232 736
(*moderate*). The place to come for *polenta
taragna* with rabbit, chicken and porcini
mushrooms, served in hot cast-iron
bowls (their speciality) and *casoncelli*, local
affettati and braised meats. *Closed Thurs.
Booking advisable.*

Caffè Balzer, Portici Sentierone 41, t 035 234
083, *www.balzer.it* (*inexpensive*). In Bergamo
Bassa, facing the Teatro Donizzetti, this

historical café sells pâtisserie and also
prepares business lunches.

Pasticceria Cavour, Via Gombito 7a, t 035 243
418 (*inexpensive*). Another place to stop for
those with a sweet tooth: the sweets here
are made by the pâtissier of the renowned
restaurant **Da Vittorio** (*see* opposite page).
The interior is decked out in period furniture.

San Vigilio, Via San Vigilio 34, t 035 253 188,
www.ristorantepizzeriasanvigilio.it (*inexpensive*). A bar, pizzeria and *ristorante* serving
pizzas with a view: an enchanting panorama
of the Paduan plain. A good choice at all
times, and for all purses. *Closed Wed.*

The Funicolare Bar (*inexpensive*). A popular
place for a snack, with beautiful views to be
had over Bergamo Bassa.

Agriturismo

La Peta, Via Peta 3, in Costa Serina, on the
peaks of Valle Seriana, about 15km from the
city, t 0345 97955, *lapeta@aeper.it*
(*moderate*). A charming 15th-century inn,
carefully restored. Serves local cuisine (for
non-residents also) and home-made goat's
cheeses; offers trekking, skiing, trout-fishing,
climbing and paragliding.

Cascina Grumello, Agriturismo Ardizzone, in
Via Ripago, Nese hamlet, Alzano Lombardo
(6km from Bergamo), t 035 510 060,
ardizzone@uninetcom.it (*inexpensive*). A
15th-century country house, also high in the
hills, offers horse-riding and archery.

Cascina Ombria, Via Ombria 1, in Celana
hamlet, Caprino Bergamasco, near Pontida,
about 10km from Bergamo, t 035 781 668,
www.cascinaombria.it. Above the hills in a
typical *cascina* made of stone; offers good
eating (risotto with berries is one of the
specialities), but also *casoncelli*, mixed
grilled meats on a spit with polenta, local
cheeses and a special *pannacotta* dessert.
*Restaurant open Thurs–Sat eves and Sun
lunch. Booking advised.*

The oldest part of Bergamo Bassa lies a few blocks east: **Via Pignolo**, lined with
16th-century *palazzi* built for the local cloth merchants, and their three churches,
each containing paintings by Lotto. The Renaissance **Santo Spirito** (*t 035 220 518; open
Sept–June Mon–Sat 7–11.30 and 4–6.30, Sun and hols 8–12 and 4–7; July–Aug Mon–Sat
7–11 and 5–6.30, Sun and hols 8.30–12 and 5–9*) located on the corner of Via Torquato
Tasso, was part of a monastery that was rebuilt in the 16th century to a design by

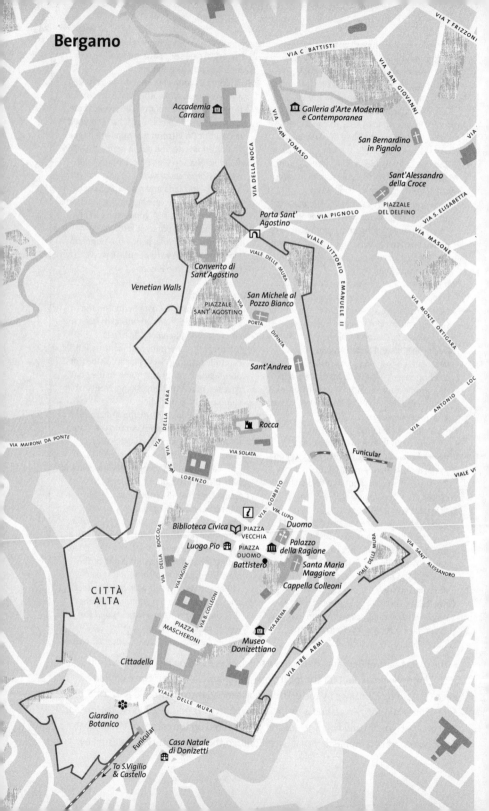

Bergamo

Accademia
Carrara

VIA C BATTISTI

Galleria d'Arte Moderna
e Contemporanea

VIA T FRIZZONI

VIA SAN GIOVANNI

VIA SAN TOMASO

VIA DELLA NOCA

San Bernardino
in Pignolo

Sant'Alessandro
della Croce

PIAZZALE
DEL DELFINO

VIA S. ELISABETTA

Porta Sant'
Agostino

VIA PIGNOLO

VIA MASONE

Convento di
Sant'Agostino

VIALE VITTORIO EMANUELE II

VIALE DELLE MURA

Venetian Walls

PIAZZALE
SANT' AGOSTINO

San Michele al
Pozzo Bianco

VIA MONTE ORTICARA

PORTA

VIA DIPINTA

Sant'Andrea

VIA ANTONIO LOC

VIA DELLA FARA

Rocca

VIA S LORENZO

Funicular

VIA MAIRONI DA PONTE

VIA SOLATA

VIALE VI

VIA GOMBITO

VM. LUPO

i

Duomo

Biblioteca Civica

PIAZZA
VECCHIA

VIA DELLE MURA

VIA SANT'ALESSANDRO

Luogo Pio

PIAZZA
DUOMO

Battistero

Palazzo
della Ragione

Santa Maria
Maggiore

VIA DELLA BOCCOLA

CITTÀ
ALTA

Cappella Colleoni

VIA VAGINE

VIA B. COLLEONI

VIA ARENA

PIAZZA
MASCHERONI

Museo
Donizettiano

Cittadella

VIA TRE ARMI

VIALE DELLE MURA

Giardino
Botanico

Funicular

Casa Natale
di Donizetti

To S.Vigilio
& Castello

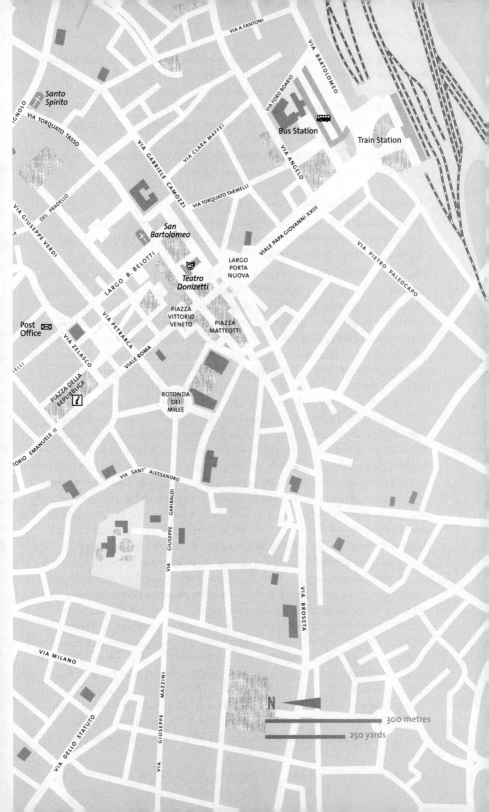

VIA A. FANTONI

VIA BARTOLOMEO

VIA FORO BOARIO

Santo
Spirito

VIA TORQUATO TASSO

VIA GABRIELE CAMOZZI

VIA CLARA MAFFEI

Bus Station

VIA ANGELO

Train Station

DEL PRADELLO

VIA TORQUATO TARMELLI

VIA GIUSEPPE VERDI

San
Bartolomeo

VIALE PAPA GIOVANNI XXIII

VIA PIETRO PALEOCAPO

LARGO B. BELOTTI

Teatro
Donizetti

LARGO
PORTA
NUOVA

Post
Office

VIA PETRARCA

PIAZZA
VITTORIO
VENETO

PIAZZA
MATTEOTTI

VIA ZELASCO

VIALE ROMA

ROTONDA
DEI
MILLE

PIAZZA DELLA REPUBBLICA

i

TORIO EMANUELE II

VIA SANT' ALESSANDRO

VIA GIUSEPPE GARIBALDI

VIA BROSETA

VIA MILANO

VIA MAZZINI

N

VIA DELLO STATUTO

VIA GIUSEPPE

300 metres

250 yards

Pietro Isabello and with paintings by Bergamo native Previtali and Bergognone; **San Bernardino in Pignolo** on the corner of Via S. Giovanni, with a superb *Pala of the Madonna and Saints* (1521) by Lotto; and near pretty Piazzetta del Delfino, **Sant'Alessandro della Croce** (Saint Alexander is the patron saint of the city), with a *Trinity* by Lotto and excellent works by Costa and Previtali, all a preview to the Accademia Carrara, just up Via S. Tomaso.

Another part of old Bergamo stretches west of Teatro Donizetti around the portico-lined Piazza Pontida; it is also the city's shopping area.

The Accademia Carrara

Piazza Carrara 82/A, t 035 399 643, www.accademiacarrara.bergamo.it. Open Tues–Sun, April–Sept 10–1 and 3–6.45; Oct–Mar 9.30–1 and 2.30–5.45; guided visits by prior booking; adm.

This is nothing less than one of the top provincial art museums in Italy, and certainly one of the oldest, founded in 1796 by Count Giacomo Carrara and housed in this neoclassical palace since 1810. It has exquisite portraits – Botticelli's haughty *Giuliano de' Medici*, Pisanello's refined *Lionello d'Este*, Gentile Bellini's *Portrait of a Man*, Lotto's *Portrait of Lucina Brembati* with a vicious weasel under her arm and a sickly moon overhead, and another strange painting of uncertain origin, believed to be of Cesare Borgia, with an uncannily desolate background. Other portraits (especially the *Young Girl*, one of the most beautiful portraits of a child ever painted) are by Bergamo's Giovan Battista Moroni (1520–78), the master to whom Titian sent the *Rectors of Venice* with the advice that only Moroni could 'make them natural'. There are beautiful *Madonnas* by the Venetians, three superlative ones by Giovanni Bellini, others by Mantegna (who couldn't do children), Fra Angelico, Landi and Crivelli (with his cucumber signature). The anti-plague Saint Sebastian is portrayed by three contemporaries from remarkably different aspects – naked and pierced with arrows before a silent city by Giovanni Bellini; well-dressed and rather sweetly contemplating an arrow, by Raphael; and sitting at a table, clad in a fur-trimmed coat, by Dürer, who also painted the eerie black and silver *Calvary*. Other paintings are by Cariani, Fra Galgario (Vittore Ghislandi), Palma Vecchio and Previtali (all from Bergamo), Bergognone, the Venetians Carpaccio, Vivarini, Titian, Veronese, Tintoretto, Tiepolo and Guardi; also Cosmè Tura, Foppa, Luini, Savoldo, Moretto, Clouet, Van Dyck and Bruegel.

Opposite, in Via S. Tommaso 53, the **Galleria d'Arte Moderna e Contemporanea** (*t 035 399 528, www.gamec.it; open Tues–Sun 10–1 and 3–7 – although hours may vary according to exhibitions; adm free*) was opened in 1991 for temporary exhibitions, mostly of 20th-century art. Follow Via della Noca up to Piazzale Sant'Agostino, where the 16th-century **Porta Sant'Agostino**, bearing the Lion of St Mark, is the main gate to the Città Alta. From just inside the gate, the Viale delle Mura circles the top of the mighty **Venetian walls**, built between 1561 and 1588; the impressive underground passage in one of the ramparts, the **Cannoniera di San Michele**, has recently been restored (*open June–Sept; contact t 035 262 565, or the Speleological Guides Group, t 035 251 233 – they organize guided tours during the week lasting 1 ½ hours; adm*).

The Città Alta: Piazza Vecchia

The view of the Città Alta, its domes and towers rising boldly on the hill against a background of mountains, is one of the most arresting urban views in Italy. City bus no.1 from the station stops at the **funicular**, built in 1887 to rise to the heart of the Città Alta, only a short walk from the beautiful **Piazza Vecchia**. Architects as diverse as Frank Lloyd Wright and Le Corbusier have heaped praise on this square, encased in a magnificent ensemble of medieval and Renaissance buildings, overlooking a low, dignified fountain with marble lions donated by the Contarini of Venice in 1780. At the lower end of the piazza, the white **Biblioteca Civica** (*t 035 399 430, www. bibliotecamai.org; open Mon, Tues, Thurs, Fri 8.30–6.30, Wed and Sat 8.30–12.30; closed Sat in July–Aug, week of Ferragosto and hols*) was begun in 1604 on a design by Palladio's student Vincenzo Scamozzi, modelled after Sansovino's famous library in Venice; one treasure inside is Donizetti's autograph score of *Lucia di Lammermoor*. Next is the 12th-century **Torre Civica** (*t 035 224 700; open May–15 Sept Mon–Thurs and Sun 10–8, Fri–Sat 10–10; mid-Sept–Oct Mon and Fri 9.30–12.30 and 2–7, Sat, Sun and hols 10–7; Nov–Feb Sat 10.30–12.30 and 2–4, Sun and hols 10.30–4; Mar–April Wed–Sat 10.30–12.30 and 2–6, Sun and hols 10.30–6; adm*), with a 15th-century clock and curfew bell that still vainly orders the Bergamasques to bed at 10pm; visitors can walk up the stairs for fine views over Bergamo. Closing the square, the 12th-century **Palazzo della Ragione** has some interesting capitals and a relief of the Lion of St Mark, added in 1800 to commemorate Bergamo's golden days under Venice.

In the 15th century, the ground floor walls of the Palazzo della Ragione were removed to allow glimpses of a second square, **Piazza Duomo**, and what appears to be a jewel box. The jewel box reveals itself as the sumptuous façade of the 1476 **Colleoni Chapel** (*t 035 210 061; open daily 9–12.30 and 2–6.30; Nov–Mar Tues–Sun until 4.30*) designed by Giovanni Antonio Amadeo, who was moonlighting while he was working on the Certosa at Pavia. Colleoni, whose coat of arms features a pair of testicles or *coglioni* (a play on his name – but there's Bergamasque humour for you), was born just around the corner. At the height of his fame as a *condottiere*, he was given complete control of Venice's armies – a unique act of trust from a republic that never trusted any individual – and when he died he received the equally unique honour of an equestrian statue in Venice (it helped that Colleoni left the Republic a fortune in exchange). Somehow there were enough ducats left over to demolish the sacristy of Santa Maria Maggiore and build a dashing tomb in its place, a project the old soldier directed from his retirement castle at Malpaga (*see* below).

The Colleoni Chapel is even more ornate and out of temper with the times than Amadeo's Certosa, a crazy quilt of medieval motifs and flourishes that spits in the face of the usual Renaissance aims of proportion and serenity. Amadeo also sculpted the tombs within, a double-decker model for Colleoni and his wife (his remains, in a silk gown and red hat, were found intact in 1969, but Mrs Colleoni was buried elsewhere). On top, a golden equestrian statue by Sixtus of Nuremburg makes the *condottiere* look like a wimp compared to Verrocchio's haughty Klaus Kinski version in Venice – neither, however, was carved from life. Another wall has the calmer tomb of Colleoni's young daughter Medea, brought here in the 19th century from another church. The fine paintings under the dome were done by G.B. Tiepolo in 1733, and on the altar there's a *Holy Family* by Goethe's constant companion in Rome, the Swiss painter Angelica Kauffmann.

Flanking the chapel are two works by Giovanni, a master from Campione: the octagonal **Baptistry** of 1340 (*open by appointment only,* **t** *035 210 223*) in white and red marble from Verona, and the colourful porch (1353) of the **Basilica of Santa Maria Maggiore**, with lions and an equestrian statue of St Alexander (**t** *035 223 327; open Nov–Feb Mon–Fri 9–12 and 2.30–4.30, Sat, Sun and hols 9–1 and 3–6; Mar–Oct Mon–Fri 9–12 and 3–6; Sat, Sun, hols 9–1 and 3–6*). Giovanni da Campione also built the basilica's second door, to the left, tucked up the steps in the corner of the transept and decorated with reliefs of the *Nativity of Mary* (1367). The basilica itself dates from 1137 and is one of the finest Romanesque churches in Lombardy, although much has been hidden by other buildings; the fine apse and drum are just about visible from the east end, blocked by the new sacristy; up the steps around back, past the campanile, is another excellent door by Giovanni and the tiny 11th-century church of Santa Croce (**t** *035 278 111*).

Once past the door, however, the palatial late 16th-century interior hits you like a gust of old lilac perfume. Sumptuous 16th-century tapestries hang from the walls: nine are scenes from the *Life of the Virgin* by Alessandro Allori, while the others are more secular – one shows a deer hunt, another the Triumph of Emperor Vespasian. Here is also Donizetti's tomb with mourning putti, and there's a florid confessional by Fantoni, but the best art is up in the chancel and choir, where Lorenzo Lotto designed a series of 33 Old Testament scenes, beautifully executed in intarsia in 1552 by Capodiferro ('Ironhead') di Lovere. Only the four along the chancel rail, *Crossing the Red Sea*, *David and Goliath*, *Judith beheading Holofernes* and *Noah's Ark*, are generally visible, and then only on Sunday or by special arrangement with the sacristan; at other times their locked wooden covers are in themselves food for thought, their subjects unfathomable allegories and abstractions, a veritable fad at the time.

Piazza Vecchia is also the address of the 6th-century **Duomo** (**t** *035 210 223; open 7.30–11.45 and 3–6.30*). The cathedral, designed by Florentine humanist Filarete in 1459, was remodelled by Carlo Fontana two hundred years later and given a pseudo late Baroque façade in 1886. Inside there's a statue of the 'Good Pope' John XXIII, born in nearby Sotto il Monte, the *Martyrdom of St John* by Tiepolo by the main altar, a boxwood bishop's throne by Fantoni, *SS. Fermo, Rustico and Procolo* by Sebastiano Ricci (all from the 1700s) and Cariani's early 16th-century *Madonna of the Turtle Doves*.

Around the Città Alta

The Visconti, who ruled Bergamo until the Venetians snatched it in 1428, built the 14th-century **Rocca** at the highest point in the Città Alta; the *torrione* (fortified tower) has been restored (**t** *035 224 700; open weekends and hols May–mid-Sept 10–8, 16 Sept–Oct 10–6; Nov–Feb 10.30–12.30 and 2–4; Mar–April 10.30–12.30 and 2–6*), while from the park you can enjoy a fine view of the northeast part of the city. Below the Rocca, Via Porta Dipinta curves around to the Porta S. Agostino (*see above*), passing two churches on the way: neoclassical **Sant'Andrea**, housing a superb altarpiece of

> ## A Bitter End for a Sweet Composer
>
> Gaetano Donizetti (1787–1848), son of the doorkeeper of Bergamo's pawnshop, composed 65 of the most lyrical operas of all time – grand old chestnuts of the *bel canto* repertoire such as *Lucia di Lammermoor*, *L'Elisir d'Amore* and *La Favorita* as well as a score of one-act pieces, down to the much-scoffed-at (by English singers anyway) *Emilia di Liverpool*. By 1843 he was the toast of Europe, when all of a sudden the syphilis he had contracted in his bachelor days manifested itself during the Paris rehearsals of his *Dom Sébastien*, when the composer, usually as affable and charming as his own music, burst forth in fits of uncontrollable anger. His creeping madness alternated with bouts of helpless despair. When the Paris sanatorium could do no more for him, he was packed off to Bergamo to die, where his friends tried to cheer his last days in the Palazzo Scotti with arias from his most famous operas; Donizetti, reduced to a vegetative state, could no longer respond. The Palazzo della Misericordia, now the town conservatory, has a few wistful sticks of furniture, his little piano, and portraits and daguerreotypes that recall happier days.

the Madonna and saints by Moretto; and Romanesque **San Michele al Pozzo Bianco** (*t 035 247 651; open daily 8–6, no visits during Mass*), rebuilt in the 1400s, its solemn interior illuminated with frescoes from the 1200s and 1500s and frescoes by Lotto. By the car park, the **Convento di Sant'Agostino** with its elegant Gothic façade was Bergamo's cultural centre in the 15th century; inside are more frescoes, from the 14th and 15th century, including some by Vicenzo Foppa.

Bartolomeo Colleoni lived at Via B. Colleoni 9–11, where he founded the **Luogo Pio** religious charity; among the frescoes there's a portrait of the *condottiere* (*call in advance to visit, t 035 217 185*). Via Colleoni continues to the west end of the Città Alta, closed off by Piazza Mascheroni and the 14th-century **Cittadella**, former residence of the Venetian captains, and now of the **Museo di Scienze Naturali E. Caffi** (*t 035 286 011; open 25 Oct–Mar Tues–Sun 9–12.30 and 2.30–5.30; April–25 Oct Tues–Fri 9–12.30 and 2.30–6, Sat–Sun 9–7; open most hols*), with stuffed animals and birds, and the **Museo Civico Archeologico** (*t 035 242 839; open Tues–Sun 9–12.30 and 2.30–6; adm free*), with finds from the Bronze Age to the Lombards. The **Giardino Botanico** nearby, at the top of the Scaletta Colle Aperto (*www.comune.bergamo.it/ortobotanico; open Oct–Mar Mon–Fri 9–12 and 2–5; April–Sept Mon–Fri 9–12 and 2–6; Sat, Sun, hols 9–7; adm free*), is planted with more than 600 species of mostly medicinal plants. Near the Cittadella, Bergamo's second funicular rises to **San Vigilio** where there's another fortress, the **Castello** (*for the keeper, t 035 236 284; open April–Sept 9–8; Mar and Oct 10–6; Nov–Feb 10–4*), with superb views over the green Parco dei Colli, dotted with old farmhouses and villas. Near the lower funicular station, picturesque Via Borgo Canale is the address of the **Casa Natale di Donizetti** (*open Sat–Sun 11–6.30, or ring t 035 399 208 at least a week in advance. Bookings can also be made Wed–Fri 9–12.30 on t 035 244 483*), where the composer was born. From the Cittadella, Via Arena leads around to the back of the cathedral, passing by way of the elegant 13th-century Palazzo della Misericordia, now the **Museo Donizettiano** (*t 035 399 269; open Oct–Mar Tues–Fri 10–1, Sat, Sun and hols 10–1 and 2.30–5; April–Sept Tues–Sun 10–1 and 2.30–5; adm free*).

Around Bergamo

The year after Bartolomeo Colleoni was appointed Captain General of Venice, he purchased the ruined **Castello di Malpaga** in Cavernago, 8km southeast of Bergamo (*t 035 840 003, www.castellomalpaga.it; open Feb–Nov Sun only, 3–6.30, or by booking for groups only; adm*), which he had purchased in 1456 and restored for his old age. His heirs added a series of frescoes by Romanino (or someone like him) commemorating a visit by Christian I of Denmark in 1474, portraying Colleoni hosting the de rigueur splendid banquets, jousts, hunts and pageants of Renaissance hospitality.

At **Trescore Balneario**, 14km east of Bergamo on the road to Lovere, the chapel of the **Villa Suardi** (*call t 035 944 777, Wed–Sat 9–12.30, to arrange a visit*) has an utterly charming fresco cycle by Lorenzo Lotto, painted in 1524 during his 15-year stint in Bergamo when he was driven from his home in Venice by the merciless 'Triumvirate' of Titian, Sansovino and the poison pen of Aretino. The subject of the frescoes is the story of St Barbara, patroness of artillerymen, architects and gravediggers. Her apocryphal life reads like a fairy-tale – her pagan father locked her in a tower, and after various adventures had her martyred for being a Christian, although he paid for his wickedness by being struck down by a bolt of lightning – and Lotto gave it just the treatment it deserved.

Southwest of Bergamo, **Caravaggio** was the birthplace of Michelangelo Merisi da Caravaggio, who left not a smear of oil paint behind, not even in the popular pilgrimage shrine of the **Santuario della Madonna del Fonte** (*Portici Santuario 10, t 0363 3571; open summer Mon–Sat 6.30–12 and 2–7, Sun 6.30am–7pm; winter Mon–Sat 6.30–12 and 2–5, Sun 6.30am–6pm*), designed in a cool Renaissance style by Pellegrino Tibaldi (1575) on the site of a 1432 apparition of the Virgin. **Treviglio**, a large, rather dull town nearby, has an exquisite 15th-century polyptych in the Gothic church of San Martino.

In **Capriate San Gervasio**, off the *autostrada* towards Milan, the **Parco Minitalia Fantasy World** (*www.fantasyworld.it; open April–5 Aug Mon–Sat 9.30–6, Sun 9.30–7.30; 6 Aug–28 Aug daily 9.30–7.30; 29 Aug–18 Sept daily 9.30–6; 19 Sept–1 Nov, Sat–Sun 9.30–6; 5 Nov–18 Dec Sat–Sun, hols 10–5; adm*) cuts Italy down to size – 1,310ft (399m) from tip to toe, with mountains, seas, cities and monuments all arranged in their proper place. Due east of Bergamo, **Sotto il Monte** was the birthplace of the beloved Pope John XXIII (1881–1963), and is an increasingly popular pilgrimage destination; there's a **Museo Papa Giovanni** (*t 035 792 956; open Tues–Sun 8.30–12.30 and 2–5.30*) near his birthplace, filled with memorabilia.

Towards the Orobie Alps: Bergamasque Valleys

North of Bergamo the two Bergamasque valleys plunge into the heart of the Orobie Alps, the wall of mountains that isolate the Valtellina further north. The western one, the Val Brembana, was the main route for Venetian caravans transporting minerals from the Valtellina; the eastern Valle Seriana is Bergamo's favourite summer retreat.

Tourist Information

San Pellegrino Terme: Viale Papa Giovanni
XXIII 18, **t** 0345 23344.
Clusone: Piazza dell'Orologio, **t** 0346 21113.
Castione della Presolana: Piazza Roma 1,
t 0346 60039.

Market Days

Clusone: *Mon.*

Where to Stay and Eat

San Pellegrino Terme ✉ 24016

****Terme, right by the baths, Via Bartomeo
Villa 26, **t** 0345 21125, *terme.hotel@san
pellegrino.it* (*moderate*). The Grand Hotel has
been closed for years, but the Terme with
its garden and pool preserves some of the
tone of bygone days. *Open late May–
mid-Oct.*

***Albergo Papa, Via de Medici 4,
t 0345 21194, *www.albergopapa.it*
(*inexpensive*). A friendly, central, family-run
hotel with a good restaurant.
Rifugio Laghi Gemelli, east of Piazza
Brembana, at the beginning of the *Sentiero
delle Orobie* hiking trail, **t** 035 662 269,
www.sentierodelleorobie.it (*inexpensive*). For
experienced hikers only. *Open daily mid-
June–mid-Sept, weekends only
May–mid-June and mid–Sept–Oct.*

Castione della Presolana ✉ 24020

****Milano, Via Silvio Pellico, at Bratto, **t** 0346
31211, *www.hotelmilano.com* (*expensive*). A
large, family-oriented complex in a park,
complete with two restaurants. *Closed Oct
and Nov, and the first 3 weeks of Dec.*
***Prealpi, Via Provinciale 54, Bratto, **t** 0346
31180, *www.hotelprealpi.it* (*inexpensive*).
Older hotel, rooms with bathroom. *Closed
mid-Sept–mid-Oct.*

The Val Brembana: Sparkling Water and the Birthplace of Harlequin

A clutch of old villages guards the entrance to the valley, where merchants once had
to pay a toll in Clanezzo, 13km from Bergamo, before continuing up to **Almenno San
Bartolomeo**. Here, isolated just off the main road, the late 11th-century church of **San
Tomè** (*open Oct–April Sun and hols only 2–4; May–Sept Sat, Sun and hols till 6; for other
visiting hours ring* **t** *035 549 3337*) is a jewel of Lombard Romanesque, built by the
Comaschi masters. Composed of three cylinders, stacked one atop the other, the interior has sturdy pillars and arches circled by a matriorum (the space set apart for
women). **Zogno**, further up the valley, is the site of the **Museo della Valle Brembana**
(*Via Mazzini 3,* **t** *0345 9147, www.museodellavalle.com; open Tues–Sun 9–12 and 2–5;
adm*). with artefacts from the valley's history. Next up the valley, **San Pellegrino Terme**
(**t** *0345 22455; open May–Nov*) is synonymous with delicious mineral water and still
makes some claim as Lombardy's most fashionable spa, especially recommended for
recuperating heart-attack patients. Hoping to attract the crowned heads of Europe,
San Pellegrino splashed out in 1907 on a fabulously ornate Grand Hotel, casino and
Palazzo del Fonte bathhouse in the most florid *stile Liberty*.

According to legend, the humorously frescoed 15th-century **Casa dell'Arlecchino**
(*ring* **t** *0345 43555 to book a visit; open daily 10–12 and 3–6*) at Oneta in **San Giovanni
Bianco** was the birthplace of Harlequin (*see* pp.30–31). The role was supposedly
invented by a *commedia dell'arte* actor named Ganassa who lived there, though more
likely it is just a reminder of the many men and women who, like Harlequin, chose to
forsake their poor hills to become servants in Venice or Bergamo. There are any
number of lovely, forgotten hamlets like Oneta in these mountains; many of them lie
in a mini-region called the Val Taleggio, on the other side of the spectacular **Torrente
Enna** gorge.

The next town north, medieval **Cornello dei Tasso**, may be down to 30 inhabitants, but it preserves as if in aspic its appearance as a relay station on the merchants' road, with an arcaded lane to protect the mule caravans. In the 13th century much of the business of expediting merchandise here was in the hands of the Tasso family, whose destiny, however, was far bigger than Cornello. One branch went on to run the post between Venice and Rome; another moved to Germany in the 1500s to organize for Emperors Maximilian I and Charles V the first European postal service. Their network of postal relay stations was still in use into the 19th century. Another branch of the family operating out of Sorrento produced the loony, melancholy Renaissance poet Torquato Tasso. As well as the muleteers' arcades, Cornello preserves the ruins of the Tasso ancestral home and frescoes in the 15th-century church.

Beyond **Piazza Brembana** the road branches out into several mountain valleys. The most important and developed resort is **Foppolo**; besides winter sports it offers an easy ascent up the **Corno Stella** (8,596ft/2,620m), with marvellous views to the north and east. Other ski resorts include **Piazzatorre** and **San Simone** near Branzi; **Carona** is a good base for summer excursions into the mountains and alpine lakes.

East of Piazza Brembana, a lovely road rises to **Roncobello**; from here your car can continue as far as the Baite di Mezzeno, the base for a bracing 3-hour walk up to the **Laghi Gemelli**. From here you can stop at the Rifugio of the same name (*see* box p.251). It is also here that experienced hikers can pick up the beautiful **Sentiero delle Orobie**, a 6-day trail that begins at Valcanale to the east in the Valle Seriana and ends in the Passo della Presolana. Another important village on the Via Mercantum, **Averara**, was the last station before the Passo San Marco into the Valtellina; its covered arcade for the caravans survives, as do buildings decorated with exterior frescoes from the 1500s.

Valle Seriana

Bergamo's eastern **Valle Seriana**, industrial in its lower half and ruggedly alpine in the north, is known for the whirling Baroque wood sculptures and carvings by the Fantoni and Caniana families. You can see one of their finest works, a fabulously ornate pulpit, every inch covered with reliefs and soaring cherubs, in the **Basilica di San Martino**, 8km from Bergamo in **Alzano Lombardo** (*Piazza Italia 8, t 035 516 579, www.museosanmartino.org; open Sun and hols 3–6 or by booking in advance; guided visits at 4; adm*); the basilica also has fine 17th-century inlaid and intarsia work, cupboards and other precious woodwork in its three sacristies.

Gandino is another town to aim for, just off the main Valle Seriana road at the bottom of its own valley. In the Middle Ages Gandino was the chief producer of a heavy, inexpensive cloth of wool and goat hair called bergamot, and the picturesque centre of town has changed little since. The 17th-century **Basilica di Santa Maria Assunta**, with its garlic-domed campanile, has confessionals and other works by the Fantoni and Caniana, and an octagonal wooden '*tempietto*' of 1500 inside the modern baptistry. The rarely opened basilica museum, (*t 035 745 425; visits by appointment only; adm*) houses portraits and relics of the old textile industry. Another church, the 15th-century **Santuario della Trinità**, contains a fresco of the *Last Judgement*.

Clusone, in the middle of the valley, is the prettiest town and capital of the Valle Seriana. In central Piazza dell' Orologio, the 11th-century **Palazzo Comunale** is covered with secular frescoes – the most joyfully decorated building in Lombardy – and bears a beautiful 16th-century astronomical clock called the **Orologio Planetario Fanzago** (*ring tourist office, t 0346 21113, for opening hours; guided tours July–Sept, Thurs*). Near the clock, the **Oratorio del Disciplini** is adorned with an eerie 1485 fresco of the *Danse Macabre* and the *Triumph of Death*, where one skeleton mows down the nobility and clergy with arrows, while another blasts them with a blunderbuss. There are more frescoes inside from the same period, especially a superb *Crucifixion*; the *Deposition* is another work by the Fantoni, who also contributed works in the late 17th-century **Santa Maria Assunta**. But it's the exterior frescoes and porticoes that lend Clusone so much of its charm; in the 1980s others were reclaimed from under the grimy stucco, including one glorious, grinning Venetian lion. Just east, **Rovetta**, the cradle of the Fantoni, remembers them in the **Casa Museo Fantoni** (*Via A. Fantoni 1, www.valser iana.bg.it; open July–Sept 3.30–5.30; ring t 0346 73523 for further times; adm*), with a special focus on the swirling, curling extroverted rococo works of Andrea.

Further up, **Castione della Presolana** is the biggest resort in the Valle Seriana, surrounded by striking dolomitic mountain scenery: the population in August goes from three thousand to thirty thousand. The pulpit in the parish church was sculpted by the Fantoni workshop. One of the biggest attractions is the lovely **Passo della Presolana** (3,691ft/1,257m) near sheer dolomite walls and Monte Pora, a ski resort, with tremendous views over Lake Iseo.

Lake Iseo, Franciacorta and the Valle Camonica

Lake Iseo (the Roman *Lacus Sebinus*) is only the fifth in size but one of the first in charm, well endowed with what it takes to get under your skin; even back in the 1750s it was the preferred resort of Italophile Lady Montagu, who disdained the English that 'herd together' by the larger lakes. The southeast shore borders on the lovely wine-growing region of Franciacorta; the lake's main source, the river Oglio, runs through the lovely Valle Camonica, the rocky palette for some of the world's most intriguing prehistoric art.

Up Lake Iseo's West Shore: Sarnico to Lovere

The west shore of Iseo is the quieter one, much of it being too steep for serious building. The road from Bergamo meets the lake at **Sarnico**, a pleasant town with a 15th-century church of **San Paolo** at the top of the city centre and a sprinkling of Liberty-style villas, most notably the two **Villas Faccanoni**, built by Milanese architect Giuseppe Sommaruga on the west end of town, along the Predore road. **Predore** itself was a fierce bone of contention between Guelphs and Ghibellines in the Middle Ages, and has a small historical museum recalling the feud in its Romanesque church. North of Predore, cliffs force the road through a tunnel and it turns sharply north for **Tavèrnola Bergamasca**, its Monte Saresano scarred by lime quarries and cement

Getting There and Around

Buses run frequently from Bergamo to the lake towns of Tavèrnola and Lovere. FS **trains** run from Bergamo to Palazzolo sul Oglio to link up to the little steam train, Ferrovia del Basso Sebino, to Sarnico, with direct connections to the lake steamers; the fare includes train, ferry and lunch, ring info 'Treno blu' **t** 030 740 2851, or *www.ferrovieturistiche.it*.

Iseo town is served by frequent buses from Brescia, and a regional railway, the FNME, runs along the entire east shore of Lake Iseo from Brescia or the FS rail junction at Rovato, between Bergamo and Brescia. From Pisogne at the north end of the lake several FNME trains a day continue up the Valle Camonica to Edolo; timetables are on the site, or at *www.ferrovienord.it*, or call (Milano Cadozue station) **t** 02 20222 (24 hours).

Steamers run by Navigazione Lago d'Iseo, Via Nazionale 16, Costa Volpino, Bergamo, **t** 035 971 483, *www.navigazionelagoiseo.it*, run between Lovere and Sarnico, calling at 15 ports and Monte Isola. Timetables are posted by the quays or on the site.

Tourist Information

OTC Clusane: OTC (private), Via Ponta 23, **t** 030 982 9142, *www.tuttomonteisola.it*.

Lovere Pro Loco: Piazza XIII Martiri, **t** 035 962 178, *turismo.lovere@apt.bergamo.it*.

Iseo IAT: Lungolago Marconi 2, **t** 030 980 209, *iat.iseo@tiscali.it*.

Sarnico Pro Loco: Via Lantieri 6, **t** 035 910 900, *proloco.sarnico@tiscalinet.it*.

Sports and Activities

Trekking paths begin at Sale Marasino – ask the local tourist office for maps. **Sportime**, Via Ronzone 35, **t** 030 982 0863, offers **paragliding** in the area. **Lido Sassabanek**, at Iseo, in Via Colombera, **t** 030 980 600, *www.sassabanek.it*, offers all **water sports** facilities and **camping**. **Bird-watching** on rowing boats and **cycling** are allowed in Torbiere del Sebino nature reserve, south of Iseo (information on tours and maps at the Iseo tourist office).

Where to Stay and Eat

Sarnico ✉ 24067

★★★★Hotel Sebino, P. Oliva Besenzoni 1, **t** 035 910 043, *www.hotelsebino.it* (*moderate*). In the town centre, with a restaurant. *Closed Mon.*

Casa Magnolia, Via Rinaldo Colombo 13, **t** 348 780 1045 (mobile), *www.casa magnolia.it* (*inexpensive*). B&B.

Al Desco del Vicolo Scaletta, Piazza XX Settembre 19, **t** 035 910 740 (*very expensive*). The best seafood in town: the fresh tagliatelle with shrimp and scampi is a treat. *Closed Mon, and Tues lunch and all Jan. All credit cards accepted.*

L'Angolo Antico, same address as below, **t** 035 913 331 (*inexpensive*). Offers a glass of wine with a *bruschetta* or a sandwich in the court below. *Closed Wed.*

Taverna Lantieri, Via Lantieri 53, **t** 035 914 477 (*inexpensive*). Pizzeria. *Closed Tues.*

Lovere ✉ 24065

★★★Albergo S. Antonio, Piazza XIII Martiri 2, **t** 035 961 523, *www.albergosantantonio.it* (*inexpensive*). This hotel, located on the main square, has modern, soundproofed rooms and a scenic 5th-floor restaurant and terrace overlooking the lake. The restaurant has inexpensive daily menus.

Sale Marasino ✉ 25057

★★★★Villa Kinzica, Via Provinciale 1, **t** 030 982 0975, *www.villakinzica.it* (*expensive*). Opened in July 1996 with every comfort, although there's a busy road just in front. Elegant, intimate, and by the lake. No restaurant but *see* Le Palafitte below. Offers guests all kinds of comforts. *Open all year.*

★★★Rotelli, Via G. Verdi 31, **t** 030 986 115, *www.hotelrotelli.it* (*inexpensive*). An excellent bargain: magnificent views, a pool, tennis and gym, and well-sized, modern rooms. *Closed Jan–Feb.*

Le Palafitte, Via C. Battisti 7, 5km south in Sulzano, **t** 030 985 145 (*expensive*). Restaurant run by the same family as the Villa Kinzica (above), with a nice lakeside terrace. *Closed Mon eve (not in the summer), and Tues.*

Iseo ✉ 25049

★★★★I Due Roccoli, 4km from Iseo (direction Polaveno), in the hills above the town in Fraz. Invino di Sotto, Via Silvio Bonomelli, **t** 030 982 2977, *www.idueroccoli.com* (*expensive*). Iseo's top choice occupies part of an old hunting lodge, set in its own large gardens. The beautifully-designed suites, rooms and bathrooms have either garden views or lake views. There's a sun terrace, pool and an intimate dining room with an open log fire, impeccable service and superb food. *Closed Oct–Mar; restaurant open to non-residents Thurs–Mon only.*

★★★★Iseolago, Via Colombera 2B, **t** 030 98891, *www.iseolagohotel.it* (*expensive*). An ideal retreat for families, close to the Lido Sassabenek sports centre south of Iseo's centre. Six rooms, one suitable for disabled people. Amenities include a fitness centre, tennis courts, swimming pool, gym and sauna, a children's playground, beach volleyball and football fields, a pizzeria, a restaurant, a little supermarket and an *enoteca*. Tennis, surfing, swimming and canoeing courses available. Nearby are the cycling paths of the Franciacorta area and the natural reserve of Le Torbiere.

★★★Ambra, Via Porto G. Rosa 2, **t** 030 980 130 (*moderate*). On the lake and near the town centre. Unexciting, modern rooms, most with bathrooms and balconies, though there's no restaurant.

★★★Albergo Rosa, Via Roma 47, **t** 030 980 053, *albergorosa@tiscalinet.it* (*inexpensive*). A neat family-run hotel on the provincial road, but better than it appears.

★★Milano, Lungolago Marconi 4, **t** 030 980 449, *www.hotelmilano.info* (*inexpensive*). A small, modest hotel, with comfortable old-fashioned rooms, many with lake views, and more pleasant than the Ambra (*see above*). On the lake, with a small restaurant with terrace and bar.

Il Volto, Via Mirolte 33, **t** 030 981 462, *ilvolto@libero.it.* (*very expensive–expensive*). Dine in an old-fashioned inn, serving a mix of Italian and French cuisine. Dishes feature lake fish (excellent with tagliolini) and also tasty meat dishes such as roast pigeon in a mustardy cream sauce. *Best to reserve. Closed Wed and Thurs lunch.*

Ginepro, on the way to Polaveno, Via Bonomelli 23, **t** 030 982 2972, *info@2rr.ir* (*expensive*). Beautiful views over the lake. *Closed Tues.*

Osteria del Vicolo, Via Pieve 4/a, **t** 030 982 1616 (*inexpensive*). A good-value restaurant run by a local doctor and his wife, with a passion for gastronomy. *Closed Tues.*

Monte Isola ✉ 25050

There are two wonderful, inexpensive places in Siviano:

★★Bellavista, Via Siviano 88, **t** 030 988 6106, *www.albergo-bellavista.it* (*inexpensive*). Cosy rooms, small and simple with outstanding views, and there's a nice little restaurant too.

★Canogola, *Via Siviano 200*, **t** 030 982 5310 (*inexpensive*). A quiet and romantic hotel in the trees by the lake. It would be wise to book in advance as it has only seven rooms (all with bathroom). Beautiful wisteria in April.

Clusane ✉ 24023

When it's time to tuck into a steaming plate of *tinca al forno* or a long list of other lake specialities, such as pike terrine, marinated bleak – *aole in carpione* – grilled sardines or a warming plate of fish stew, washed down with a fine wine from the nearby Franciacorta, you won't go wrong at the following selection of restaurants:

★★★Punta dell'Est, Via Ponta 163, Frazione Clusane, **t** 030 989 060 (*moderate–inexpensive*). A very pleasant lakeside restaurant and hotel, with a nice garden above the water. *Restaurant closed Mon.*

Al Porto, Piazza Dei Pescatori 12, **t** 030 989 014, *www.alportoclusane.it* (*expensive*). The oldest. *Closed Wed.*

Muliner, Via San Rocco 16, **t** 030 982 9206 (*moderate*). For yet more local fare under a vine pergola.

Paratico ✉ 25030

★★★Ca' Bianca, Via Mazzini 36, **t** 035 910 110 (*moderate*). All comforts.

Il Cuoco, Via Mazzini 48 ,**t** 035 914 711 (*expensive*). The place to dine in Paratico: cosy, with lake views and excellent dishes cooked by several generations of the Marini family. *Closed Tues eve, and Wed, 15 days in Aug and Jan.*

Lake Iseo, Franciacorta and the Valle Camonica

SWITZ.

Mt Disgrazia ▲

Caspoggio

So ndalo

Grosio

Grosotto

Ponte di Legno

Passo del Tonale

Tirano

Valtellina

Val di Genova

S38 Sondrio Tresivio Ponte in Valtellina Teglio

Edolo

Passo del Tonale

Aprica

S39

Adamello Mts

TRENTINO-ALTO ADIGE

Alpi Orobie

Malonno

Cedegolo

Rock engravings

Parco Nazionale

Incisioni Rupestri

Foppolo

Carona

Valbondione

Capo di Ponte

Paspardo

Cimbergo

Val di Daone

Valle Seriana

Val di Scalve

Schilpario

Cerveno

Ceto

Dezzo

Rock engravings

Breno

Nadro

Daone

Passo della Presolana

Borno

Cividate Camuno

Castione d. Presolana

Rock engravings

Esine

Bienno

Berzo

Condino

Clusone Rovetta

Angolo Terme

Darfo Boario Terme

Corni Freschi

Passo de Maniva

Valle

Valle Camonica

Lovere

Mt Campione ▲

Collio

Bagolino

Lodrone

Gandino

Endine Gaiano

Pisogne

Bovegno

Anfo

Lago d'Idro

Bianzano

L. Endine

Riva di Solto

Zone

Cislano

Lavenone

Idro

Monasterolo del Castello

Lake Iseo

Marone

Sale Marasino

Nozza

Tavernola Bergamasca

Siviano

Monte Isola

Gardone Val Trompia

Gargnano

Predore

Sulzano

Bogliaco

Sarnico

Pilzone

Lumezzane

Val Trompia

Vobarno

Toscolano-Maderno

Paratica

Iseo

Sabbio

Clusane

Provaglio

Gardone Riviera

A4 Columbaro

Franciacorta

Concesio

Is. di Garda

Lago di Garda

S42 Erbusco

Passirano

Gavardo

Salò

Bornato

Rovato

Polpenazze

Brescia

N

10 km

5 miles

works. There are some good 15th-century frescoes in the church, and a fine panorama over the lake from **Santuario di Dosso**, a kilometre up from the village. Until 1910 the road stopped at Tavèrnola, and even today the rugged scenery around **Riva di Solto** is best seen from the little lake steamers; the view of its coves, rugged rocks, ravines and formidable Adamello mountains in the distance is said to have caught the fancy of Leonardo da Vinci, who used it as the background for his *Mona Lisa*: the black marble columns of St Mark's in Venice were quarried here.

North of Riva di Solto a scenic road zigzags up to the Val Cavallina and Lake Iseo's baby sister, the long, narrow **Lago di Endine**, which because of its currents freezes in bizarre shapes and patterns each winter. There are a pair of medieval villages on its shores: **Endine Gaiano** to the north and **Monasterolo del Castello** to the south, and an exceptionally well-preserved 13th-century **Castello di Suardi** up in Bianzano.

From Endine Gaiano the main road rejoins Lake Iseo at **Lovere**. The largest town of the west shore, it has a medieval core dating from its days as a Venetian textile centre. In 1630 it shifted from cloth to steel, and to this day Lovere mixes grit with art. There are 16th-century frescoes in the restored Baroque interior of **Santa Maria in Valvendra** (*t 035 983 567; open mid-April–Oct Mon–Sat 10–12 and 4–6, Sun 4–6; Nov–mid-April daily 4–6*), a *Martyrdom of St George* by Palma il Giovane on the altar of **San Giorgio**, a church partly built into a medieval tower; and twenty rooms of fine paintings in the **Galleria dell'Accademia Tadini** in a neoclassical palace (*Via Nazionale; open late April–Oct Mon–Sat 3–4, Sun 10–12 and 3–7, open during Easter period too; adm*), including works by Tiepolo, Lorenzo Veneziano, Strozzi, Piazza, Parmigianino, Bordone, and a lovely *Madonna* by Jacopo Bellini.

Down the East Shore: Pisogne to Clusane

From Lovere, the road circles the north lake and reaches the sprawling village of **Pisogne**; you can see traces of walls and gates around its medieval core, arcaded Piazza del Mercato. The gate to the Camonica Valley, Pisogne owed its strategic position to the the manufacturing of arms. A strategic viewing-point is the so-called Bishop Tower, after locals gave the priest the authority to hang, blindfold or whip the rebels there in 1299. The main reason to stop in Pisogne, however, is north of the centre: the 15th-century church of **Santa Maria della Neve** (*open Tues–Sun 9.30–11.30 and 3–6; if the church is closed you can get the key from the Bar Romanino next door, t 0364 87032*), covered between 1532 and 1543 with frescoes of the *Passion*, and *Prophets* and *Sibyls* by Romanino. Take some time to visit Pisogne's oldest church, **Santa Maria in Silvis**, dating back to the 8th century and rebuilt in 1485. The church, whose portal is very similar to that of Santa Maria della Neve, contains frescoes by local painter Giovanni da Marone, whitewashed at the end of the 16th century by St Carlo Borromeo, possibly to cover the unusual themes such as the particularly interesting *Danse Macabre*. Brought back to light in 1933, the frescos have just been restored. South, beyond the tunnels, **Marone** overlooks the cute private Isolina di Loreto and stands at the crossroads of the little **Val Valeriana**, an ancient road, now a walking path (buy the map at Iseo's bookshop) and a fascinating detour through uncanny scenery: here glaciers deposited their debris aeons ago atop the dolomitic rock, to be eroded into striking spiky 'earth pyramids', many balancing boulders on top like something out of a Road Runner cartoon. There's a famous view of the pyramids – locally known as 'the fairies' – at **Cislano** (where the church has an exterior fresco of St George) on the way to **Zone** (2,224ft/678m), an old-fashioned village at the end of the road, where the church **San Giovanni Battista** houses an 18th-century life-size *Entombment of Christ* sculpted by Antonio Fantoni.

Back on the lake, olive groves surround **Sale Marasino**, a little resort built around a 16th-century town, one of the prettier and warmer spots on the lake; **Sulzano**, just south, is the closest point and main port for the Arcadian, car-less (but well motor-biked) island of **Monte Isola**, the largest lake island in Europe at 45km wide, a fair-sized copy of Gibraltar soaking in its own bathtub. Already inhabited during the Roman period, it was once a hunting reserve of the local nobles and Visconti; now some 200 souls live year round in its genteelly decaying hamlets. The locals, especially in **Peschiera Maraglio** where the steamer docks, still catch fish, but their talent for making nets has led to the more profitable weaving of professional tennis and basketball nets. The business has turned them into one of the highest-earning *comuni* in Italy. Stroll through the olive groves to Sensole to the west, and up to **Siviano**, the main village, and perhaps through ancient chestnut groves as far as the chapel of the **Madonna della Ceriola** – over 1,000ft (305m) above the lake (*ask the keeper for entry,* **t** *030 988 6172*).

South of Sulzano, **Iseo** is the lake's endearing, low-key and thoroughly fetching 'capital' where flowers spill out of every window and the narrow alleys have kept their medieval names. In central **Piazza Garibaldi** a statue of the hero, looking tired and philosophical, contemplates the comings and goings and the Friday market from the top of a great mossy lump; here the small **Santa Maria del Mercato** has some late medieval frescoes. The 11th-century **Pieve di Sant'Andrea** has an air of benign neglect, its façade unfinished, with a tomb of the old town boss Giacomo Oldofredi stuck on as an afterthought. The long, curved lake promenade, shaded with ancient plane trees, is the perfect place to laze on a summer's day and watch the sailboats and little steamers dart to and fro.

Clusane, west of Iseo, is crowned by an abandoned Castello di Carmagnola – it briefly belonged to the famous Venetian captain – and has a fishing fleet of white-, blue- and pink-rimmed boats called *naêcc* in the local dialect. They spend the day bagging the ingredients of *tinca al forno* (baked lake tench with polenta), a dish based on a recipe invented in 1800 and served in 20 restaurants, seating 4,000 – in a village with a population of 1,500.

The Franciacorta

The triangle formed by Lake Iseo, Brescia and the A4 is a sweet and mellow corner of old Lombardy. Originally the *corte franca*, 'free court', it was wild and poverty-stricken in the Middle Ages, then colonized and reclaimed by monastic courts, an effort encouraged by tax-free concessions. Other historians refer the 'Francia' part of the name to France and date the origin of the name to Charlemagne's stay in Rodengo, where he was trapped by the prolonged war to conquer Brescia: the French king, missing his mother country, 'brought France to him', naming the area Franciacorta and celebrating St Denis' day there. Others attribute the name to the short stay of the Angevin militia in 1265, dispersed by a popular uprising. The lack of taxes endeared the Franciacorta to the patricians of Lombardy, who built castles and villas and planted the vineyards, producing an excellent champagne-method wine, Franciacorta Spumante DOC (Ca' del Bosco makes one of the best) as well as a fragrant white wine from pinot bianco and/or chardonnay, and a ruby herbaceous red with an unusually mixed pedigree: cabernet, barbera, nebbiolo and merlot.

The initial project in the Franciacorta was the reclamation of the swamps in **Provaglio** just in from Iseo town, when monks from Cluny founded **San Pietro in Lamosa** in 1083 (*open 9–12 and 2.30–6, but book in advance during the week in low season, call Sig. Simonini on t 030 383 477*). Part of their project, an emerald bog called **Le Torbiere**, has remained defiantly wet, and after a century of peat extraction is now a protected area; in late spring it becomes an aquatic garden of pink and white water lilies, navigable by hired rowing boats. Cluny also founded the abbey of San Nicola at **Rodengo Saiano**, with three cloisters now occupied by Olivetan monks; there are frescoes by Romanino and Moretto in the church and a **Museo del Ferro** (*ring ahead t 030 610 182 for booking; Abbey open Mon–Sat 9–11.30 and 4.30–6, Sun 4–6; guided visits Sat 3–6 and Sun, hols 4–6; donations*), dedicated to iron.

The Franciacorta is filled with 16th–18th-century villas, castles and parks. There's a well preserved 14th-century castle with swallowtail battlements in **Passirano**; in nearby **Bornato** a Roman fortress was expanded in the 13th century by a faithful follower of Charles d'Anjou into the **Castello di Bornato** (*open mid-Mar–mid-Nov Sun and hols 10–12 and 2.30–6; Oct and late Nov Sun and hols till 5; adm*). Dante slept here, and over the years an Italian garden and vineyards were added; there are fine frescoed rooms from the 16th–18th centuries with Olympian gods and landscapes and the wine is good too. Bornato is surrounded by 18th-century villas, including **Villa**

Where to Stay and Eat

Colombaro ✉ 25040

★★★★**Relais Franciacorta**, Via Manzoni 29, t 030 988 4234 (hotel), t 030 982 6461 (restaurant), *www.relaisfranciacorta.it* (*very expensive*). A lovely old villa by a wine estate. The *trattoria* serves excellent meals. *Closed Mon eve and Tues.*

Erbusco ✉ 25030

★★★★★**L'Albereta**, Via Vittorio Emanuele 11, t 030 776 0550 (hotel), t 030 776 0562 (restaurant), *www.albereta.it* (*luxury*). An old renovated villa containing 39 beautifully designed rooms and suites. There's every possible attention to detail, with wall paintings by Jacques Margerin, cosy open log fires, Jacuzzis in the bathrooms and a range of amenities that includes a swimming pool, sauna, tennis, golf course and garage. The restaurant (*very expensive*) is run by one of Italy's most famous chefs, Gualtiero

Marchesi, but it has a rather patchy reputation nowadays. *Closed Mon, Wed, Sun eve, and most of Jan.*

Rovato ✉ 25038

Antica Cucina de Biagi, on the edge of the Franciacorta, Corso Bonomelli 160, t 030 772 1450 (*moderate*). Serves meaty, hearty food including pasta in duck sauce; *agnoli* filled with hare; stuffed pheasant, guinea fowl or pigeon; and Rovato's typical *manzo all'olio* and *brasato. Closed Sat lunch, Sun eves and two weeks in July. Must book.*

Ricci Curbastro, Via Adro 37, in Capriolo, in the Franciacorta region, 5km south of Iseo. t 030 736 094, *www.riccicurbastro.it* (*moderate–inexpensive*). A hospitable, comfortable farmhouse – rooms with bathrooms and kitchen en suite in an old *cascina* among the vineyards, plus a museum on farm life, a cellar to taste house wine and an exhibition of antiques in the granary. *Always open 8.30–12 and 2–7; adm.*

Rossa with its lovely garden, stair and belvedere. **Villa Lana da Terzo** in **Colombaro** has Italy's oldest cedar of Lebanon in its garden. **Erbusco** has the fine 17th-century Villa Lechi and a 13th-century church of Santa Maria, and another excellent Franciacorta vineyard that welcomes visitors, **Longhi-De Carli** (*Via Verdi 6, t 030 776 8280, www. longhidecarli.com*). **Berlucchi**, Italy's top producer of spumante, also originates from Franciacorta, at Borgognato di Franciacorta (*t 030 984 451, www.berlucchi franciacorta.com; visits should be booked for 25–30 people*). A beautiful villa hosts yet another wine producer, **Catturich** (*Azienda Agricola Catturich Ducco, Via Degli Eroi 32, at Camignone, t 030 685 0566*). Ask the Iseo tourist office (*see page 254*) for information on Franciacorta's Via dei Vini, a guided tour of the local vineyards.

North of Lake Iseo: The Valle Camonica, or History on the Rocks

From Pisogne the road and railway continue northeast of Lake Iseo into the fertile Valle Camonica. Its name is derived from a Rhaetian tribe, the Camuni, whose ancestors used the valley's smooth, glacier-seared Permian sandstone as tablets to engrave their enigmatic solar discs and labyrinths, mysterious figures and geometric designs, animals, weapons and people. What is especially remarkable is the continual span of creativity: the oldest engravings have been dated to the 9th millennium BC and the last date from 16 BC, the year the Romans conquered the valley – a period enabling scholars to trace intriguing prehistoric stylistic evolutions, from the random scratched symbols of the Palaeolithic era to the finely drawn narrative figures of the Bronze and Iron Ages. Although one can only hazard guesses at the significance these etchings had for their makers, their magic must have been extraordinary: in the valley some 180,000 examples have been discovered so far. Some are beautiful, some ungainly and peculiar, some utterly mystifying; a few fuel crackpot theories. UNESCO has shortlisted them as part of the artistic patrimony of humanity.

(Darfo) Boario Terme to Breno

Liver playing you up? Consider a cure at **Boario Terme**, 12km north of Pisogne, where the medicinal springs are protected by a pretty Liberty-style cupola, set in a lavish garden at Terme di Boario (*Viale Igea 3, t 0364 525 011, www.termediboario.it*). Boario bottles a popular mineral water, but the water's true allure rests on people visiting the springs to be soaked and sprayed and jetted with the stuff, then massaged in therapeutic mud. The first inhabitants, however, were into rocks: in the **Parco delle Luine** (*t 348 737 4467; open Tues–Sun 9–12 and 1–5; until 6 in summer*), 1.5km up from the spa, they scratched the oldest incisions yet discovered in the Valle Camonica (8000 BC) and others from the Bronze Age (*c.*1500 BC) – men on horses, with shields and weapons, and a labyrinth – while some distance apart, at Corni Freschi, they carved nine halberds like the heads of swans. Unfortunately, the rock has weathered here more than at other sites and the graffiti – there are some 10,000 drawings in all – can be hard to decipher. A favourite excursion from Boario is up the Val di Scalve to a

Tourist Information

Bienno Pro Loco: Pizzale Lorenziri 1,
t 0364 300 307.
Boario Terme: Piazza Einaudi 2, t 0364 531 609,
iat.boario@tiscali.it.
Capo di Ponte, by the highway, Via S.
Briscioli 42, t 0364 42080, *www.
comunecapo-di-ponte.bs.it*.
Edolo: Piazza Martiri della Libertà 2, t 0364
71065, *iat.edolo@tiscali.it*.
Ponte di Legno: Corso Milano 41, t 0364 91122,
iat.pontedilegno@tiscali.it

Where to Stay and Eat

The Camonica Valley is badly served for
accommodation, and Boario Terme may be the
most convenient place to stay to visit the
valley. Being a thermal resort, though, it tends
to be rather old-fashioned. Beware that most
hotels in Boario stipulate a minimum three-
day stay and full board only.

Boario Terme ✉ 25041

★★★★**Rizzi**, Via Carducci 11, t 0364 531 617,
www.albergorizzi.it (*moderate*). 100m from
the Terme. The most comfortable rooms in
town, some with soundproofing and air
conditioning. It has its own garden, with an
outside veranda and a very nice restaurant.
Open April–Oct.
★★★**Brescia**, Via Zanardelli 6, t 0364 531 409,
www.hotelbrescia.it (*moderate*). Slightly old-
fashioned, but with fully equipped rooms,
and a very stylish dining room and a
pub/disco downstairs.

★★★**Diana**, Via Manifattura 12, t 0364 531 403,
info@albergodiana.it (*inexpensive*). Opposite
the Terme. Stylish and modern: good-sized
rooms with all mod cons, large bathrooms
and wonderful mountain views, with a
restaurant and garden. Candlelit dinners in
the evening. *Closed Nov–Mar.*
★★★**Armonia**, Via Manifattura 11, t 0364 531 816
(*inexpensive*). Simple rooms, all with TV and
bath, and perhaps serving the most
generous lunches and dinners in all Italy.
★★**Ariston**, Piazzale Einaudi 9, in the station
forecourt, t 0364 535 325 (*inexpensive*). Small,
clean, good-value rooms with modern
fittings and old-fashioned hospitality. Pets
are welcome. *Closed Nov–Mar.*

Capo Cumilí Ponte ✉ 25044

★★**Cumili**, Viale della Stazione 1, t 0364 42034,
www.italiaabc.it (*inexpensive*). Small, simple
rooms offered here, with bathrooms, and
with a restaurant. *Full board only.*

Ponte di Legno ✉ 25056

★★★★**Mirella**, Via Roma 21, t 0364 900 500,
www.hotelmirella.it (*expensive–moderate*).
Sleek and modern: the top choice, with a
pool and tennis courts.
★★★**Dolomiti**, up at the Passo del Tonale,
Via Case sparse del Tonale 102, t 0364 900
251, *www.hoteldolomiti.it* (*inexpensive*). Less
glamorous but still a quite adequate choice.
Closed May.
★★**Al Maniero**, Via Roma 54, t 0364 900 041,
www.almaniero.com (*inexpensive*). Cosy
hotel with hearty local cuisine served in the
restaurant. Nice terrace too.

smaller spa, **Angolo Terme** (*Viale Terme 1, t 0364 548 244*), near pretty little sapphire
Lago Moro, then continuing into the wild and narrow **Dezzo Ravine**. You can learn to
hang-glide at the national school in **Montecampione**, to the south, or come back in
the winter to enjoy 'Europe's largest computerized snowfields.'

Heading up the Valle Camonica from Boario Terme, you can make a brief but scenic
detour east into the Vallata della Grigna, where the villages have their churches
adorned with some surprisingly good art: **Santa Maria Assunta** at **Esine** (*open 9–5,
summer until 6; ask local priest for the key, t 0364 360 522*) is a national monument,
with its *trecento* campanile and charming, brightly coloured frescoes by the valley's
own Giovan Pietro Da Cemmo (1493), who also contributed to the church of San
Lorenzo in **Berzo Inferiore**, and to the 15th-century Santa Maria Annunziata in
Bienno (*ring tourist office; open 9–4.30, Sat and Sun until 6pm*); the latter also contains

frescoes by Romanino and an altarpiece by Fiamminghino. Bienno has a pretty medieval core, and the **Fucina-Mulino Museo** (*Via Artigiani 13, ring t 0364 300 307; open Mon–Sat 9.30–11.30, Tues and Thurs also 2–3, Sat 2–4; adm free, €1 per person for large groups; book in advance at the tourist office*), **Mulino Museo** (*Via Glere, open Mon–Sat 9.30–11.30*) tracing the history of ironworking in the valley. Here, too, the rather difficult **Strada delle Tre Valli** rises through 18km of pure mountain scenery to the **Passo di Croce Domini** (6,244ft), where you can pick up roads to the Val Trompia or Lake Idro: fill up the tank before you go.

Below Bienno, **Breno** is the modern capital of the Valle Camonica, under the towers of an imposing 14th-century castle, with a spooky dungeon you can explore (*t 036 422 970; open daily 2pm–12pm mid-June–mid-Sept*). The keys are at the town hall in Piazza Ghislandi, along with the **Museo Civico Camuno** (*temporarily closed; ring t 0364 220 421*), housing an ethnographic collection and paintings from the valley. The church of **Sant'Antonio** (*always open, if closed ask info at nearby foodstore on t 0364 22412*) has a pretty Renaissance door and excellent frescoes (1535) by Romanino. Four kilometres south of Breno, **Cividate Camuno Archeologico** was the Romans' administrative centre in the valley; its small **Museo** (*Via Roma 29, t 0364 344 301; open Tues–Sun 8.30–2; adm*) remembers their passing with mosaics, tombstones and other finds. West of Cividate, **Ossimo Inferiore**'s 15th-century **Santuario dell'Annunciata** (*t 0364 45005; open Mon–Sat 7.30–4; Sun and hols 10–4; July and Aug 10–5.30; adm free*) has a pretty pair of cloisters and frescoes on the *Life of Mary* (1475) by Da Cemmo, while in upper Ossimo, a group of statue-stelae carved with the valley's first representations of carts and metal tools and weapons suggest a Bronze Age holy site.

Capo di Ponte and its National Park

In the centre of the Valle Camonica, near Capo di Ponte, are the most extensive and best-preserved prehistoric engravings: pick up a map in the tourist office (*t 0364 42080*). The most notable and accessible are in the **Parco Nazionale delle Incisioni Rupestri Preistoriche** (*t 0364 422 140; open Mar–mid-Oct Mon–Sat 8.30–7.30; mid-Oct–Feb 8.30–4.30; adm.*), where the enormous **Naquane rock** attracted artists from the Neolithic to the Etruscan periods. Over a thousand figures are etched into the rock: labyrinths, dogs, hunters and deer; enigmatic processions, armed warriors and horsemen; priests, a funeral; looms, carts, huts, even an Iron Age smithy. Certain symbols are repeated so often as to suggest a code: 'blades', slashes, and four-petalled, dotted 'Camuna roses'.

Capo di Ponte's **Centro Studi Preistorici** has a small museum, with plans of Camuni sites among other items (*t 0364 42091; open Mon–Fri 9–4; adm*), while just up beyond a car park two great lumps of sandstone, the **Massi di Cemmo**, once formed part of a much longer megalithic alignment, covered with engravings of animals and human figures, all dating from the 3rd millennium BC. A bit further up, **Archeodromo** (*t 0364 42148, www.graffitipark.it; open daily 8.30–12.30 and 1.30–5.30; July–Aug until 6; adm*), the 'Centre of Experimental Archaeology', has a reconstructed Iron Age village; above this, a path leads to the 11th-century **San Siro** (*open Mon and Fri 9–12 and 2.30–4.30, Sat 9–12, Sun 9–12 (summer only); key at the Capo di Ponte Pro Loco, t 0364 42080*), its three tall apses rising over the River Oglio. Across the river, the equally beautiful Cluniac church of **San Salvatore** (*under restoration, open 9–11 and 3–5; ring the keeper on t 0364 42389, or call the Capo di Ponte Pro Loco*) was built in the late 11th century in the Burgundian style, its monastic grounds still protected by walls.

A few kilometres south, another great concentration of engravings was discovered in 1975 in what is now the **Riserva Regionale Incisioni Rupestri Ceto-Cimbergo-Paspardo** (*t 0364 433 465; open 9–5, until 6 in summer; adm*). The main entrance is in tiny **Nadro**, where from the small museum a path leads up to Foppe di Nardo, dotted with rocks etched from Neolithic to Etruscan times: scenes of solar worship, weapons, a village, footprints and what looks like a god by praying figures. The reserve also encompasses the rocks of Campanine, just under the ruined castle and village of **Cimbergo**, where Iron Age graffiti mingles with a Latin dedication to Jove and Early Christian symbols, and Iron Age etchings in three different sites in **Paspardo**. Down on the main Valle Camonica road below Ceto is the crossroads for **Cerveno**, up in the hills to the west, where the Sacro Monte-style chapels of the **Santuario della Via Crucis-San Martino** (*t 0364 434 014; open Oct–Sept 8–11.30 and 2.30–5; June–Sept until 6*) contain 198 life-size figures from the 18th century acting out the Passion of Christ.

North of Capo di Ponte

Further up the Valle Camonica the mountain scenery becomes grander as the Adamello Dolomites (11,733ft/3,576m) loom up to the right. Beautiful excursions into the range are possible from **Cedegolo**, into the lovely **Val di Saviore** with its mountain lakes Arno and Salarno. Further north, from **Malonno**, travel a scenic road through the chestnut woods of the **Valle Malga**, with more pretty lakes and easy ascents.

Surrounded by majestic mountains, **Edolo**, where the railway ends, is a busy market town at the crossroads of the Valle Camonica and the Valtellina (*see p.225*) and the Passo di Tonale. To the west are the ski stations of the **Valle di Corteno** (Corteno Golgi, the main centre, is named for Dr Camillo Golgi, a native who won the 1906 Nobel prize in medicine) and to the north those of **Ponte di Legno**, the region's most developed ski resort. From Ponte di Legno the road rises north through Stelvio National Park to Bormio (*see p.234*). The main road continues to the **Passo del Tonale**, with more skiing: **Passo Paradiso** (8,366ft/2,550m), reached by the cableway, has skiing year round. From the Passo di Tonale the road goes east into Trentino's Val di Sole.

Brescia and Around

Brescia

Lombardy's second city, Brescia is a busy and prosperous place but somehow it's no one's favourite town, even though it has a full day's supply of fine art, architecture and historic attractions: Brescia's Roman and Lombard relics are among the best preserved in northern Italy. Perhaps it's the vaguely sinister aura of having been Italy's

Getting There and Around

Brescia is conveniently reached from three **airports**: Verona's Catullo, *www.aeroporto verona.it*, Bergamo's Orio al Serio, *www.orioaeroporto.it* and Montichiari's Gabriele D'Annunzio, halfway between Brescia and Lake Garda.

Brescia is on the main Milan–Venice **railway** line, 55mins from Milan, an hour from Verona, and less to Desenzano del Garda, the main station on Lake Garda. There are also frequent services to Bergamo (1 hour), Lecco (2 hours), to Cremona (just over an hour), and to Parma via Piadena (2 hours). For FS rail information, call **t** 892 921 (no prefix from Italy). The regional FNME railway line, **t** 02 20222, winds north along Lake Iseo's east shore and up the Valle Camonica to Edolo (2½ hours).

There is an even more extensive **bus** network with frequent links to the towns of Lakes Garda and Iseo, and less frequently to Idro; also to Turin and Milan, Padua and the Euganean Hills, Marostica, Bassano del Grappa and Belluno; to Trento via Riva and to the resorts of Pinzolo and Madonna di Campiglio in Trentino, as well as to all points within the province.

The **bus** and **railway** stations, *www. trasportibrescia.it*, are located next to each other just south of the city centre: on Viale Stazione, the railway station and the SIA bus station serving the Brescia province, **t** 840 620 001 (toll-free number); just around the corner, in Via Solferino 6, the other bus services serving all other destinations including Garda, Cremona, etc., **t** 840 620 001, toll-free number. Bus C connects them to the centre, or you can walk there in 10mins up the Corso Martiri della Libertà.

Tourist Information

Comune Tourist Office: Piazza della Loggia 6, in the Monte di Pietà Nuova, Brescia, **t** 030 297 8988, *turismo@comune.brescia.it*. Provides regional tourist information. *Open Mon–Fri 9.30–12.30 and 2–5, Sat 9.30–1.*
ITA Brescia: Corso Zanardelli 34, near the central Piazza del Duomo, **t** 030 43418, *www.bresciaholiday.com*.

Where to Stay

Brescia caters mainly to business clients, and its best hotels are comfortable though not inspiring.

*****Vittoria**, Via X Giornate 20, **t** 030 280 061, *www.hotelvittoria.com* (*very expensive*). The city's premier hotel has everything it should – large, sumptuous rooms, palatial bathrooms of French Rosa marble, banqueting suites, and liberal use of marble and chandeliers throughout. The severe Fascist-era architecture is rather soulless, however.

****Ambasciatori**, Via Crocifissa di Rosa 92, **t** 030 399 114, *www.ambasciatori.net* (*expensive–moderate*). A bit outside of the centre, very modern, with a garage; it also has very good, air-conditioned rooms, all with private bathroom and TV. A warm welcome; family-run.

***Master**, Best Western, Via L. Apollonio 72, **t** 030 399 037, *www.hotelmaster.net* (*expensive–moderate*). Near the centre by the castle, with a new family-run management team. Parking, a nice gazebo in the garden, with a restaurant **La Corte** (*inexpensive*) and spacious if simple rooms.

***Cristallo**, Viale Stazione 12A, **t** 030 377 2468, *www.hotelcristallobrescia.com* (*moderate*). An adequate albeit nondescript place that is convenient, but near the train station. *Always open.*

***Antica Villa**, Via San Rocchino 90, **t** 030 303 186, *www.hotelanticavilla.it* (*moderate–inexpensive*). Outside the city centre. Offers warm hospitality in a secluded 18th-century villa at the foot of the Ronchi hills. Soundproofed and air-conditioned rooms; car park. Also restaurant offering local recipes.

***Astron**, Via Togni 14, **t** 030 48220 (*moderate–inexpensive*). Clean, simple rooms with windows overlooking the station. Conveniently located for the city centre but near the train station.

Trento, Piazzale Cesare Battisti 31, off Porta Trento, **t** 030 380 768 (*moderate– inexpensive*). Conveniently located within walking distance of the city centre and castle. Rooms have all modern comforts including air conditioning, with a good-value restaurant.

Eating Out

Brescians are rather stolid conservatives at table: kid, stews, *risotti*, meat on a skewer and polenta have been in vogue since the Renaissance. A typical dish is made of the *casonsei*, huge, home-made ravioli filled with eggs, hard cheese or ricotta cheese, spinach or meat, and served with sage and melted butter.

Castello Malvezzi, Via Colle San Giuseppe 1, t 030 200 4224, *www.castellomalvezzi.it*. (*very expensive*). A lovely medieval place just north of the centre. Serves delicious food, cooked by a French and an Italian chef, to go with a superb selection of wines. *Closed Mon and Tues, 15 days Aug and Jan.*

I Templari, Via Matteotti 19, t 030 375 2234, (*very expensive*). The freshest of seafood with a Tuscan touch. Try the 'Catalana', a great mix of seafood. *Closed Sat lunch, Sun and Aug.*

La Sosta, Via San Martino della Battaglia 20, t 030 295 603, *www.lasosta.it* (*very expensive*). This elegant restaurant is set in a 17th-century stable (of the Palace Martinengo delle Palle) which has been stripped and completely overhauled; a *secondi* menu features prestige fish and Italian classics. *Closed Mon, Sun eve, Aug and first week of Jan.*

L'Artigliere, Via Forcella 6, at Gussago, 5km west of Brescia, t 030 277 0373, *davidebotta@libero.it* (*expensive*). Emerging chef Davide Botta and his wife Silvana offer gourmet local cuisine in an old country *osteria*, refurbished with care, with a nice portico for open-air dining in the summer and a cellar to visit. *Closed Mon–Tues.*

Vasco de Gama, Via dei Musei 4/C, under the Torre di Porta Bruciata, t 030 375 4039 (*expensive*). Another cellar setting, offering dishes such as octopus with courgettes and cream, little Andalusian soup with crayfish tails, *pastellaccio del pescatore* and cream pudding. *Closed Tue.*

Locanda dei Guasconi, Via Beccaria 11, t 030 377 1605 (*expensive–moderate*). In the city centre. A medieval setting for traditional dishes such as polenta and lamb, but also more unusual fare such as ostrich meat. Very popular with young people. *Closed Mon.*

Duomo Vecchio, Via Trieste 3, t 030 40088 (*moderate*). An intimate place near the Duomo Vecchio. The restaurant serves an excellent range of southern Italian dishes; try the reasonably priced lunch menu. *Closed Sun.*

Hostaria Porta Bruciata, Via Beccaria 11/D, t 030 49591 (*moderate*). A popular place serving home-made traditional cuisine; near the Duomo. *Closed Sun.*

Giovita, Via San Faustino 63, t 030 290 6513 (*moderate*). Serves a selection of soups, risottos, boiled meats, vegetarian dishes and other local specialities in an informal environment. Cheap and hearty single-dish menus at lunch time for hungry university students. *Closed Sun.*

Al Granaio, Piazzale Arnaldo 15, t 030 375 9345 (*moderate*). This *piazzale* is very lively on summer evenings, and is a popular meeting place, specializing in meat, and including Fiorentina steak and salami. *Open until 2am. Closed Mon.*

Osteria Vecchio Botticino, Piazzale Arnaldo 6, t 030 48103 (*moderate*). A good-value, unpretentious restaurant. *Closed Sun and Aug.*

Bersagliera, Corso Magenta 38, t 030 375 0569 (*inexpensive*). A good, popular pizzeria. *Closed Mon.*

La Vineria, Via X Giornate 4, t 030 280 477 (*moderate*). Here you can feast on excellent cured meats and salami, herby risotto, *casoncelli* and home-made tarts. *Closed Tues and 2 weeks in Aug.*

Due Stelle, Via San Faustino 48, t 030 42370 (*inexpensive*). One of Brescia's oldest *osterias*, situated in the city centre, with a nice cellar to taste wine and an inner courtyard with fountain for dining in the summer. Local versions of tripe, *casoncelli* and old peasant dishes revisited, such as chicken and bread dumplings in broth. Dried cod from Thurs to Sun; good *antipasti*. *Closed Mon, Sun eves.*

Osteria Al Bianchi, Via Gasparo da Salò 32, t 030 292328, *www.osteriaalbianchi.it* (*inexpensive*). A noisy, typical *osteria* with hearty local dishes. *Closed Wed, Tue eves, Sun lunch.*

Osteria dell'Elfo, Piazza Vescovado 1/B, t 030 377 4858 (*inexpensive*). A popular place for an *aperitivo* and snack, with a good selection of wines. *Open until late. Closed Mon.*

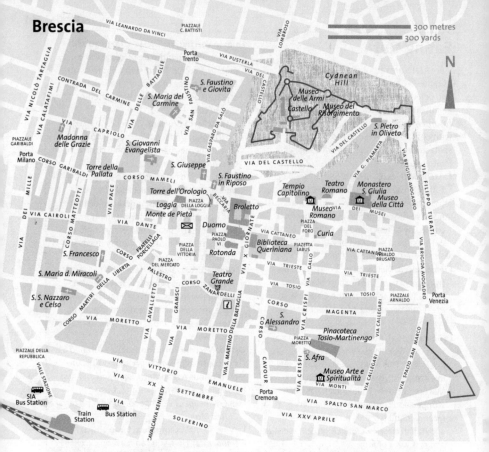

Brescia

300 metres
300 yards

N

chief manufacturer of arms for the last 400 years. Perhaps it's because the local Fascists saw fit to punch out the heart of the old city and replace it with a piazza as frosty and heavy as an iceberg. The Brescians seem to detest it, but it's hard to avoid. The rest of their historic centre has been spared, however, with the Brescia Due, a mini-version of Paris's La Défense, to quarantine all its gangly new office buildings.

History

Brescia was founded by the Gauls, an origin remembered in its name Brixia, from the Celtic *brik* (hill). Brixia saw the inevitability of Rome early on, became a willing ally, and in 26 BC achieved the favoured status of a *Colonia Civica Augusta*, when it was embellished with splendid monuments. By the 8th century Brescia had recovered enough from the barbarian invasions to become the seat of a Lombard duchy under King Desiderius, whose daughter Ermengarda was wed by Charlemagne – the condition imposed by the Italians before they crowned him emperor. He later repudiated her, and the forlorn Ermengarda returned to Brescia to die in the Abbey of San Salvatore. When Brescia joined the Lombard League against Frederick Barbarossa, its opposition had a voice: that of a Benedictine monk, Arnold of Brescia, who studied under Peter Abelard in Paris and went to Rome, preaching eloquently against the tyranny of the emperor and the corrupt, worldly materialism of the Church. In 1155, Barbarossa, with Adrian IV, arrested the troublesome monk and handed him over to the pope, who burned Arnold alive at the stake in front of Castel Sant'Angelo.

Brescia itself was too tempting a prize to be left in peace. Firmly in the Guelph camp, for the freedom of cities against imperial pretensions, it held tight when Frederick II besieged it for 68 days, then suffered under his lieutenant, the unspeakable Ezzelino da Romano, in 1258. In 1421, when the detested Visconti horned in, the weary Brescians turned to Venice for relief and asked to be adopted. The Venetians didn't have to be asked twice; Brescia meant access to the unusually pure iron deposits in the valleys to the north. By the 16th century Brescia had become Italy's major producer of firearms, and the Republic imposed severe emigration restrictions to keep skilled workers from wandering.

Venice not only brought peace and prosperity, but initiated an artistic flowering as well. The Brescian Vincenzo Foppa (1485–1566) was a key figure in the Lombard Renaissance; his monumental paintings were among the first to depict a single, coherent atmosphere. The individualistic linear style of Girolamo Romanino (1485–1566) may stand somewhat apart, but Romanino's contemporary Alessandro Bonvincino (better known as 'the little Moor' or *Moretto*; 1498–1554), an ardent student of Titian, contributed the first Italian full-length portrait and taught Giovanni Battista Moroni of Bergamo. His contemporary Giovanni Girolamo Savoldo, a Brescian who later worked in Venice, was neglected in his day but is now recognized for his lyricism, especially in his use of light. Recently Giacomo Antonio Ceruti (1698–1767) has been the centre of interest for his realist, un-romanticized genre paintings of Brescia's humble, demented and down-and-out – a unique subject for the time. His nickname was *Il Pitocchetto* ('The Little Skinflint').

The Central Squares

Hurry, as the Brescians do, through the deathly pale **Piazza della Vittoria**, designed in 1932 by Marcello Piacentini; that frigid, Fascist square that melts each May, when it acts as the starting gate for the famous *Mille Miglia* vintage car race across Italy. Duck behind the post office to enter into a far more elegant display of power: the closed, Venetian-style **Piazza della Loggia**, named for the **Palazzo della Loggia**, Brescia's town hall, a neo-Roman confection begun in 1492 and designed in part by Venice's top architects, Sansovino and Palladio. Its great white roof swells over the old city like Moby Dick on the prowl. The public areas can be visited during office hours. Opposite the Palazzo della Loggia, the **Torre dell'Orologio** is a copy of the clock tower in St Mark's Square, complete with two bell-ringing figures on top. The Brescians must have been hopeless spendthrifts: the other chief buildings on the square are the old and new municipal pawn shops, the **Monte di Pietà Vecchia** (1489) and the **Monte di Pietà Nuova** (1590s); the Roman inscriptions embedded in the façade of the former constitute Italy's very first lapidary collection.

Looming up behind the clock tower rises the third-highest dome in Italy, the green-lead-roofed crown of the **Duomo**, built in 1602 by Gianbattista Lantana (*open Mon–Sat 7.30–12 and 4–7.30, Sun 8–1 and 4–7.30*). From the **Piazza Paolo VI** itself, however, the dome is hidden by a high marble front – a Lombard 'wind-breaker' façade. Over the door a bust of Brescia's great Cardinal Querini 'winks mischievously, as if inviting the faithful to enter'. You should take him up on it, not so much for the few paintings by Romanino and Moretto that try to warm the cold interior, as to visit the adjacent **Duomo Vecchio** or La Rotonda (*open April–Oct Tues–Sun 9–12 and 3–7, Nov–Mar Tues–Sun 10–12 and 3–5*). Built in the 11th century over the ruins of the Basilica of San Filastrio and the ancient Roman baths, this singular old cathedral is the only one in Italy designed in the shape of a top hat, low and rotund, with a massive cylindrical tower rising from its centre, supported by eight pillars, the light diffused through its upper windows. Inside, its simple form is broken only by a 15th-century raised choir; the altarpiece, an *Assumption* by Moretto, is one his greatest works. The crypt of San Filastrio, a survival of the ancient basilica, contains a mixed bag of Roman and early medieval columns, and mosaics from the Roman baths. Several medieval bishops are entombed around the walls, most impressively Bishop Mernardo Maggi in his sarcophagus of 1308; the treasury holds two precious relics – the 16th-century *Stauroteca* containing a bit of the True Cross, and the 11th-century banner once borne on the *carroccio* (sacred ox cart) of the Brescian armies.

Opposite the new Duomo, the 12th-century **Broletto** was the civic centre of Brescia prior to the construction of the Palazzo della Loggia, which later became the seat of the Venetian governor; its formidable tower, the **Pegol**, predates it by a century. Just behind the new cathedral, on Via Mazzini 1, the 18th-century **Biblioteca Queriniana** (*t 030 297 8200; open Tues–Fri 8.45–12 and 2–6, Sat 8.30–12.30*) contains 300,000 rare books and manuscripts, including the 6th-century 'Purple Evangeliary' with silver letters, from San Salvatore, and Eusebius' 11th-century *Concordances of the Gospels*.

Roman and Lombard Brixia

Flanking the Broletto is the ancient *Decumanus Maximus*, now the **Via dei Musei**, along which stands some historic buildings such as Palazzo Maggi and Martinengo, where temporary exhibitions are held (*info on t 030 297 551*). This leads to the heart of Roman Brixia. Its forum, now the narrow **Piazza del Foro**, lies under the mighty columns of the **Capitolium Temple**, erected by the Emperor Vespasian in AD 73 and preserved for posterity by a medieval mud-slide that covered it until its rediscovery in 1823. In 1955 an earlier, Republican-era Capitoline temple was discovered beneath Vespasian's, with unusual mosaics of natural stone. The Temple is divided into three *cellae*, which were dedicated to the three principal Roman deities – Jupiter, Juno and Minerva. The *cellae* contain the lapidarium, tablets, altars and architectural fragments of the Roman age. The central *cella* has displayed inscriptions, including reproductions of walled tables from public and private buildings in Brescia and its province, mounted there in 1830. The Roman remains formerly shown at the Civico Museo Romano (*closed, see below*), within the archeological area of the temple, now constitute the Roman section of the Museo della Città (*see p.269*). Next to the temple is the unexcavated *cavea* of the **Roman Theatre**, while down Via Carlo Cattaneo, in Piazza Labus, you can make out the columns and lintels of the third building of the forum: the **Curia**, or senate, imprinted like a fossil in a house wall.

From Piazza del Foro, Via dei Musei continues to the **Monastero San Salvatore-Santa Giulia** (*t 030 297 7833 for booking, www.bresciamusei.com; open end Oct–May Tues–Sun 9.30–5.30; June–Sept Tues–Sun 10–6; adm*), founded in the 700s by the wife of the Lombard King Desiderius, disbanded at the end of the 18th century and now the **Museo della Città**. At the entrance are the remains of a large Roman *domus*, uncovered during the recent rearrangement works, with original mosaics and frescoes. The museum documents the various layers of Brescian history, from the prehistoric period to the Venetian age through the Roman, the Lombard, the Carolingian and the medieval age of the *comuni* and *signorie*, with over 11,000 finds on display. The heart of the complex, the 8th-century **Basilica of San Salvatore**, was modelled on the 6th-century churches of Ravenna. In the nave, the capitals are either ancient Roman or made of stucco, an art at which the Lombards excelled. Some Carolingian frescoes remain under the arcades; others were painted by Girolamo Romanino in 1530. The semicircular crypt, where the relics of St Giulia were laid in 762, was enlarged in the 12th century, with vigorous capitals sculpted by the school of Antelami; the one on the life of Giulia is a serene masterpiece. The same century saw the addition of another church, sturdy **Santa Maria in Solario**, crowned with an octagonal dome or tiburium, its lower vaults supported on an ancient Roman altar, its upper level frescoed by Floriano Ferramola (1480–1528). In the 16th century a third church, **Santa Giulia**, was built; the nuns' choir has more bright frescoes by Ferramola (*the church may be closed to the public for special events*).

The **Civico Museo Romano** (*closed for refurbishment; info on t 030 46031*) contains a considerable collection of Roman remains, formerly kept in the Civico Museo, and preserved thanks to the foresight of the 1485 municipal council which forbade the sale of antiquities outside Brescia. Treasures include: six gilded bronze busts of emperors and a 6ft bronze *Winged Victory*, all found in the temple; the *Victory*, bereft of the object she once held, seems to be snapping her fingers in a dance. There's a gilt bronze figurine of a Gaulish prisoner, believed to be Vercingetorix, a beautiful Greek amphora from the 6th century BC and a facsimile of the 25ft-long Peutringer Map of Vienna, itself a 12th-century copy of a Roman road map. The other sections of the museum contain at least two other exceptional pieces. One is the 8th-century golden Lombard *Cross of Desiderius*, studded with 212 gems and cameos, including one from the 4th century of a Roman woman with her two children, peering warily into the approaching Dark Ages; the Brescians like to believe it is the great Galla Placidia of Ravenna. The other is a 4th-century ivory coffer called the *Lipsanoteca*, adorned with beautiful bas-reliefs of scriptural scenes. One of the superb 5th-century ivory diptychs originally belonged to the father of the philosopher Boethius. Lombard jewellery, medieval art and Renaissance medals round out the collection.

The Cydnean Hill

The poet Catullus, who considered Brixia the mother of his native Verona, was the first to mention the Cydnean hill that rises behind the Via dei Musei. Named after the Ligurian king Cidno, the legendary founder of Brixia, the site has been inhabited since the Bronze Age. It was the core of Gaulish and early Roman Brixia – on Via Piamarta are the ruins of the city's last surviving **Roman gate**, as well as the attractive 1510 **San Pietro in Oliveto** (*open Sun 8.30–12 and 3–6 except during Mass; other days ring Padri Carmelitani, t 030 41531*), named after the olive grove that surrounds the church.

Up on top of an imposing Venetian gate in Istrian marble, still guarded by the Lion of St Mark, is the entrance to the **Castello** with its round 14th-century Mirabella Tower, sitting on a Roman foundation and providing a lovely view of the town. Built in 1443, during the brief reign of the Visconti, the donjon houses the **Museo Civico delle Armi Antiche Luigi Marzoli** (*t 030 297 7830 for booking groups; open Oct–May 9–1 and 2–30–5; summer till 6; adm*), one of Italy's most extensive collections of Brescia's bread-and-butter industry, with a special collection of 15th–18th-century firearms. The castle's Venetian granary now houses the **Museo del Risorgimento** (*same hours*) with paintings, uniforms, decrees and weapons, with special honours going to Brescia's Ten Day revolt in 1849, bloodily suppressed by Austria. The gardens around the castle are a favourite refuge from the car-filled city below.

The Pinacoteca and Around

From the Capitolium Temple, Via Crispi descends to Piazza Moretto, site of the **Pinacoteca Civica Tosio-Martinengo** (*t 030 2977883, www.bresciamusei.it; open June–Sept Tues–Sun 10–1 and 2.30–6; May 9–7; adm*), housed in a 16th-century patrician palace. It showcases Brescia's talent, including Foppa (*Madonna and Saints*), Savoldo, Moretto (his *Salome* is a portrait of the Roman courtesan-poetess Tullia d'Aragona), Romanino, Moroni and Ceruti; there's also a lovely *Adoration of the Magi* by Lorenzo Lotto, a *Senator* by Tintoretto, a *Portrait of Henri III* by Clouet and two early works by Raphael – a not altogether wholesome, beardless *Redeemer* and a lovely *Angel*, and an anonymous golden fairytale picture of *St George and the Princess*, which was painted around 1460. The Pinacoteca also houses paintings due to be exhibited in the Galleria d'Arte Moderna e Contemporanea, which is still awaiting a permanent location.

South on Via Crispi, there's more art in little 16th-century **Santa Angela Merici**, by Tintoretto and Francesco Bassano (*t 030 295 675; open Mon–Sat 7.30am–9.30pm, Sun 3–5.30, or ring Compagnia S. Angela Merici*), and at Via Monti 9, in the Istituto Paolo VI's **Museo Arte e Spiritualità** (*open Sat–Sun 4–7; other days upon request and by previous appointment on t 030 375 3002*), devoted to contemporary religious art. **Sant'Alessandro** (*Via Moretto; open Mon–Sun 6.30–11 and 5.30–7.30; no visits during Mass 5.30–7.30pm*), contains a pretty *Annunciation* by Jacopo Bellini; further north, in elegant, porticoed Corso Zanardelli, the **Teatro Grande** (*info t 030 297 9311, call if you want to book a visit*) with its luscious foyer and five tiers of boxes is one of the most lavish theatres in Lombardy; here in 1904 Puccini's *Madame Butterfly* was wholeheartedly vindicated by the public after its disastrous premiere.

West Side Churches

The piquant quarters west of the Piazza della Loggia are rich in interesting old churches. Just west of Via S. Faustino (off Piazza della Loggia) there are two strikingly unusual ones – **San Faustino e Giovita** (*t 030 291 195; open Mon–Fri 7.30–11 and 3–7,*

Thurs 7.30–10 only, Sun 7.30–12 and 3.30–7), a cylindrical, steep-roofed drum of a church from the 12th century (near the intersection with Via dei Musei) and, further up, on Contrada Carmine, the 15th-century **Santa Maria del Carmine** *(open June Tues–Sun 10.30–7; July–Sept Tues–Sun 10.30–12 and 4–7)*, crowned with a set of Mongol-like brick pinnacles; it contains frescoes by Foppa, among his finest work, and a 15th-century terracotta *Deposition* by Mazzoni.

Just off Corso G. Mameli, Renaissance **San Giovanni Evangelista** *(t 030 375 5146; open daily 7–11 and 4–6.30)* has good works by Moretto, Romanino and the Bolognese painter Francia. Further along the Corso stands the giant **Torre della Pallata**, a survivor from the rough-and-tumble 13th century, with a travesty of a 16th-century fountain like a bunion on its foot. From here Via della Pace heads south to the venerable 1265 **San Francesco** *(t 030 292 6701; church open Mon–Sun 7–11.30 and 3–6; cloister Mon–Sat 8–12 and 2.30–6.30)* with its cloister in red Verona marble and frescoes (a few by Romanino and Moretto), and the nearby **Santa Maria dei Miracoli** *(open Mon–Sat 6–12 and 3–6; no visits during Mass 8–10am)*, with a lovely 15th-century Lombard Renaissance marble façade that survived even though the interior was blown to smithereens in the last war. Inside, there is a picture of the Madonna believed to have miraculous powers. Further south, on Corso Matteotti, the 18th-century **Santi Nazaro e Celso** *(open Mon–Sun 2–4; to get in otherwise ring t 030 375 4387)* houses the Averoldi polyptych (1522), considered the masterpiece of Titian's youth, with a gravity-defying, virtuoso *Risen Christ* in the centre that soars overboard into the numbing bathos of spiritual banality. The chapels hold works by Moretto.

North of Brescia: Lake Idro

Although Iseo and the Valle Camonica attract most of the visitors, two green valleys north of Brescia have their quiet virtues. Due north of Brescia, the **Val Trompia** is named for the ancient Ligurian tribe, the Triumplini. Pope Paul VI's birthplace at **Concesio**, 9km from Brescia, is marked with a plaque, and there's a painting by Palma Giovane in the parish church. But what the lower valley is really known for is guns: **Lumezzane** makes excellent reproductions of ancient firearms, while the handguns produced since the 1500s by **Gardone Val Trompia** were so valuable that the town enjoyed the special protection of Venice; it still makes hand-crafted sports rifles. North of Gardone the road climbs to two popular summer and winter resorts,

Eating Out

Miramonti L'Altro, Via Corsette 34, Costorio hamlet, t 030 275 1063, www.*miramonti laltro.it* (*very expensive*). When Brescians have a hankering for something special, they drive up to Concesio's celebrated restaurant set in a neoclassical villa. You'll be hard pushed to find better traditional Brescian *maccheroni, risotti*, kid, duck, game and

rabbit dishes anywhere, especially when wild mushrooms are in season. In addition, every year French chef Philippe Leveillé conjures up some new tempting delicacies. For afters, there's a fine array of cheeses, or one of Miramonti's great desserts. Try ravioli with rabbit and butter, or the lamb. The enormous cellar features French and Italian wines. *Closed Mon and 5–20 Aug. Booking advised.*

Bovegno and **Collio**. Beyond Collio a new road continues up to the scenic **Passo del Maniva** (5,453ft/1,662m) and over to the Passo di Croce Domini (*see* p.262); in summer, you can also drive east to Lake Idro.

In the next valley east, the Val Sabbia, the River Chiese widens to form a fjord in the mountains known as **Lake Idro** (the ancient *Eeidio*). Long, narrow, surrounded by a corniche of steep dark mountains, it is the highest of the larger Lombard lakes (1,214ft/370m), and one of the best for trout fishing. A scattered collection of hamlets form **Idro**, at the south tip of the lake; in one, Castel Antinco, you can visit the ruins of a 1st-century BC village. **Anfo**, on the west bank, has a 15th-century castle built by the Venetians, where Garibaldi set up his headquarters briefly in 1866 during the battle of Monte Suello, just to the north. Although 8km up the Val Sabbia from the lake on the trout-filled River Caffaro, picturesque Bagolino with its medieval streets is Idro's most important town, where the most traditional carnival in Lombardy takes place, with the bizarre dances of the *ballerini*. The 18th-century parish church that dominates **Bagolino** has minor paintings attributed to Titian and Tintoretto; 15th-century **San Rocco**, on the village edge, was frescoed in 1486 by Giovan Pietro Da Cemmo.

Lake Garda

The Italian lakes culminate in Garda, the largest (51.5km long, 17km across at its widest point) and most dramatic, its 'Madonna blue' waters, as Winston Churchill described them, lapping at the feet of the Dolomites. Shaped like the profile of a tall-hatted witch, its Latin name *Benacus* is of Celtic origin, a word similar to the Irish *bennach*, 'horned one', for its many headlands. If memories of the two Plinys mingle in the waters of Lake Como, Garda's shores recall two of Italy's greatest poets of pure passion: ancient, tragic, lovelorn Catullus and that 20th-century Italian fire hazard, Gabriele D'Annunzio. The other lakes are warm but Garda, Venice's 'little sea', has a genuine Mediterranean climate. Open to the south and blocked off from the cold winds of the north by the Dolomites, Garda's great volume (its average depth is 445ft/136m) make it a giant solar battery, heating the surrounding hills throughout the winter and keeping deadly frosts and clammy mists at bay. For Goethe and generations of chilblained travellers from Middle Europe, its olives, vines, citrus groves and palm trees have long signalled the beginning of their dream Italy. No tourist office could concoct a more scintillating oasis to stimulate what the Icelanders call 'a longing for figs', that urge to go south.

Perhaps it's because Lake Garda seems more 'Italian' that it has traditionally been less stuffy and status-conscious than its sister lakes. It attracts more families (thanks to Gardaland), partygoers (at Desenzano), beach bums (the water's very clean) and older package tourists (especially German and Austrian). Sailors and windsurfers come to test their mettle on the winds, first mentioned by Virgil: the *sover* which blows from the north from midnight and through the morning, and the *ora*, which puffs from the south in the afternoon and evening. White caps and storms are not uncommon, but on the other hand the breezes are delightfully cool in the summer.

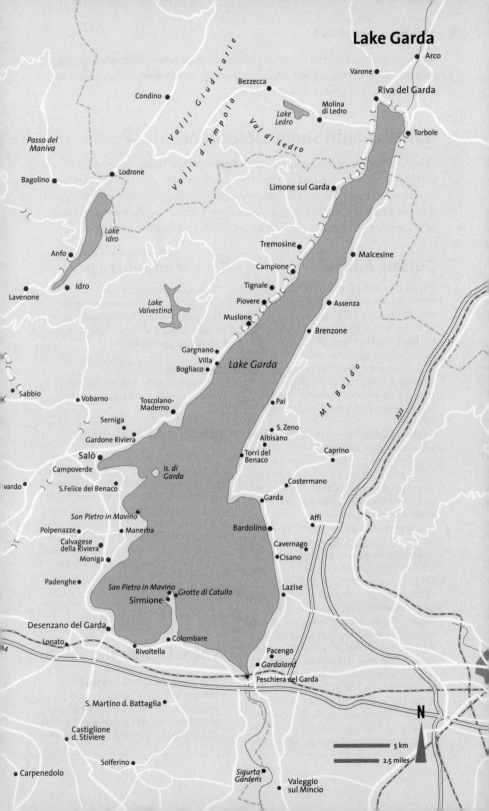

Lake Garda

Arco
Varone
Riva del Garda
Torbole
Bezzecca
Molina di Ledro
Lake Ledro
Condino
Valli Giudicarie
Valli d'Ampola
Val di Ledro
Passo del Maniva
Lodrone
Limone sul Garda
Bagolino
Lake Idro
Tremosine
Malcesine
Anfo
Campione
Idro
Tignale
Piovere
Assenza
Lavenone
Lake Valvestino
Muslone
Brenzone
Gargnano
Villa
Bogliaco
Lake Garda
Sabbio
Vobarno
Toscolano-Maderno
Pai
Serniga
S. Zeno
Gardone Riviera
Albisano
Salò
Torri del Benaco
Caprino
Campoverde
Is. di Garda
vardo
S. Felice del Benaco
Costermano
Garda
San Pietro in Mavino
Affi
Polpenazze
Manerba
Bardolino
Calvagese della Riviera
Cavernago
Moniga
Cisano
Padenghe
San Pietro in Mavino
Lazise
Sirmione
Grotte di Catullo
Desenzano del Garda
Lonato
Colombare
Rivoltella
Pacengo
Gardaland
Peschiera del Garda
S. Martino d. Battaglia
Castiglione d. Stiviere
Solferino
Carpenedolo
Sigurta Gardens
Valeggio sul Mincio
Mt Baldo
A22

N

5 km
2.5 miles

Although services drop to a minimum, winter is a good time to visit, when the jagged peaks shimmer with snow and you can better take in the voluptuous charms that brought visitors to Garda in the first place.

Garda's South Shore: Desenzano

Lively, colourful and thoroughly pleasant **Desenzano del Garda**, on a wide gulf dotted with beaches, is Garda's largest town, built up in the 15th and 16th centuries (if you arrive by train, a bus will take you to the centre). Life centres around its busy portside cafés, presided over by a statue of Sant'Angela, foundress of the Ursuline Order, who seems appalled at all the carryings-on; another statue on the lake front, the

Getting Around

There are two **train** stations (from Italy), t 892 021, www.trenitalia.it at the southern end of Lake Garda, at Desenzano and Peschiera, both of which are also landings for the lake's **hydrofoils** (aliscafi) and **steamers**. **Buses** from Brescia, Trento and Verona go to their respective shores; Desenzano, the gateway to Lake Garda, is served by buses from Brescia, Verona and Mantua. Frequent buses connect Sirmione to Desenzano and Peschiera.

Other local bus lines run along the road that winds around the lake shores – a marvel of Italian engineering, called La Gardesana, Occidentale (SS45) on the west and Orientale (SS249) on the east. In summer, however, their scenic splendour sometimes pales before the sheer volume of holiday traffic.

All **boat services** on the lake are operated by Navigazione sul Lago di Garda, Piazza Matteotti 2, Desenzano, t 030 9141 9511, toll-free (from Italy) t 800 551 801, where you can pick up a timetable. There are two **car ferries**; one crosses from Maderno to Torri, the other between Limone and Malcesine; between Desenzano and Riva there are several hydrofoils a day, calling at various ports (2 hours for the full trip), as well as the more frequent and leisurely steamers (4½ hours). Services are reduced from November to April. Full fare on the 4-hour sail from Desenzano to Riva on the steamer is €10.30, on the hydrofoil €14.50. Children travel free (up to 4 years) or at reduced rates (4–12 years). There's 20% discount for EU over-60s (ID must be shown).

Tourist Information

Desenzano del Garda: Via del Porto Vecchio 34, t 030 914 1510, www.desenzano. net. Also some tourist information on www.gardalake.it, www.hotelspromotion.com, and www.gardainforma.com.

Market Days

Desenzano: Lakeside, near the Municipio, Tues. **Rivoltella hamlet**, Sun morning April–Dec.

Sports and Activities

You can rent a **bike** at Girelli, t 030 991 2200, a **scooter** at Easy Motor Bike, t 030 911 0504, and a **charter boat** at Co Vetro, Viale Cavour 45, t 030 991 2419, or in Limone at Peroni, t 0365 954 210, or Limone Jet, t 0365 954 702. To **dive** in the lake's cleanest area contact Coltri, t 030 991 0297, Mydive, t 030 999 1541, Dian Sub, t 030 914 4821, or Tritone, t 030 912 0809. To **sail**, contact Fraglia Vela, t 030 914 3343. **Horseriding** is at Spia d'Italia, t 030 913 0235. **Karting** is in Lonato at South Garda Karting, t 030 991 9958. If you need a mountain guide, ring Davide Brighenti, t 338 545 9922.

Where to Stay and Eat

Desenzano del Garda ✉ 25015
******Piccola Vela**, Via T. dal Molin 36, t 030 991 4666, www.gardalake.it/piccola-vela (expensive). Only a short walk from the city pier. Has its own olive grove, and views

whooshing **High Speed Monument**, celebrates an air speed record (709km per hour) set here in 1934 by Francesco Agello. On the lower end of the technological scale, Desenzano's Bronze Age (2200–1200 BC) inhabitants lived in pile dwellings, recently discovered in the peat bogs southwest of town and yielding the contents of the new **Museo Archeologico Rambotti** in the cloister of Santa Maria de Senioribus (*Via Del Molim 7/C, t 030 314 4529; open Tues, Fri, Sat, Sun and hols 3–7*). There are models of houses and, amongst the ornaments, little 'pearls' of amber: Desenzano was on the ancient trade route between the amber-rich Baltic and the Mediterranean, which endured until the end of the Roman period.

Desenzano, also on the Bergamo–Verona Via Gallica, became a popular resort (read refuge) of the Romans towards the end of the empire, when the rich and powerful retreated from the growing anarchy to their country estates. Incorporating vast

over the lake from the balconies. All modern comforts are provided, including air conditioning, safe, minibar, laundry, garage, swimming pool. Has flats with kitchen in the back garden suitable for families or those with pets.

★★★**Tripoli**, Piazza Matteotti 18, **t** 030 914 1305, *www.hotel-tripoli.it* (*moderate*). Small, white lake-front hotel; has renovated, well-equipped-rooms in the centre of the action and a garage.

★★★**Hotel Piroscafo**, Via Porto Vecchio 11, **t** 030 914 1128, *www.hotelpiroscafo.it* (*moderate–inexpensive*). Family-run hotel in the centre of the town, right on the old quay. Rooms are simple, without air conditioning, but some have nice balconies overlooking the quay, with a restaurant. *Closed Jan–Feb.*

★★**Alessi**, Via Castello 3, **t** 030 914 3341, *www.hotelalessi.com* (*moderate–inexpensive*). Up in the old city centre and no views, but plenty of family atmosphere – there's even an ironing table for the hotel guests in the breakfast room!

★★★**Mayer e Splendid**, Via U. Papa 10, **t** 030 914 2253 (*inexpensive*). A venerable hotel situated by the quay, allowing you to tumble out of bed and on to a steamer. Not all rooms have bathrooms. *Open Mar–Nov.*

Desenzano has a larger selection of good restaurants than any town on the lake:

Cavallino, *Via Murachette 29*, **t** 030 912 0217, *www.ristorantecavallino.it* (*very expensive*). An unforgettable feast; the chef creates imaginative, seasonal dishes based on lake fish and seafood, duck, pigeon (the pigeon

stuffed with *foie gras* is superb) and offal, followed by an excellent cheeseboard and desserts. In the city centre. *Closed Mon. Booking advised.*

Esplanade, Via Lario 10, **t** 030 914 3361 (*very expensive*). Equally delightful if rather formal, with a lovely lakeside terrace, where clients tuck into the likes of a delicate lasagne with seafood fused with wine, or zucchini flowers stuffed with goat's cheese; excellent wine list and desserts. Over 800 Italian and foreign wines. *Closed Wed.*

Vineria La Lepre alla Lepre, Via Bagatta 33, **t** 030 914 2313 (*very expensive–expensive*). Classy restaurant with a table full of truffles and delicacies (also for sale), serving creative Mediterranean cuisine. **Bagatta Alla Lepre Wine Bar** offers cheaper fare in a more informal, if trendy, ambiance. *Closed Tues.*

Ristorante Al Portico, Via Anelli 44, **t** 030 914 1319, *www.info-desenzano.it* (*very expensive–expensive*). Traditional cuisine: lake and sea fish, home-made pasta.

Trattoria Bicocca, squeezed in a tight corner at Vic. Molini 6, **t** 030 914 3658 (*expensive*). Good home cooking is the draw at this picturesque *trattoria*, offering a wide variety of lake fish – salmon trout, *coregone*, perch, sole, pike and gilt head, prepared with fresh herbs. *Closed Thurs, 1 week near Christmas.*

Il Molino, Piazza Matteotti 16, **t** 030 914 340 (*expensive*). Same owners as the Caffè Italia. Specializes in fish, including raw fish. *Closed Mon and Tues lunch time.*

Caffè Italia, Piazza Malvezzi 19, **t** 030 914 1243, *www.ristorantecaffeitalia.it* (*expensive–*

agricultural lands, maintained by hundreds of slaves and retainers, these estates were the origins of feudalism. One of the most important was Desenzano's **Villa Romana** (*just in from the Lunglago at Via Crocifisso 2, t 030 914 3547; open Mar–mid-Oct Tues–Sun 8.30–7.30, Nov–Feb Tues–Sun 8.30–5; adm*). Although begun in the 1st century BC, the villa was not given its present form until the 4th century, when it was fitted with such luxuries as sumptuous heated baths, a *triclinium* (dining hall) with three apses, and a series of other rooms covered with the most extensive mosaic floors in northern Italy. Visitors can pick up a free archaeological itinerary pamphlet in English.

Nearby, along Via Roma, **Santa Maria Maddalena**, built between 1586 and 1611, has 27 huge canvases by a transplanted Venetian, Andrea Celesti (d. 1712), and a strikingly different *Last Supper* by Gian Battista Tiepolo.

moderate). Wine bar and restaurant offering a good selection of hot and cold dishes, including very selected Chianina beef, under the porticoes near the Duomo square. There's a good selection of wines also by the glass; ideal for breakfast, brunch and late-night snacks. *Closed Mon (in winter) and Jan–Feb.*

Calvagese della Riviera ✉ 25080

★★★★★**Palazzo Arzaga**, at Carzago della Riviera, about 10km from Desenzano, t 030 680 600, *www.palazzoarzaga.com* (*luxury*). On the hills overlooking Lake Garda, this luxury hotel offers accommodation in a 15th-century villa set in its own grounds and comprising 2 golf courses (18 and 9 holes), tennis courts, indoor and outdoor swimming pools, cycling and jogging paths, horse-riding and even hunting. Also spa treatments, gym, sauna, health trail and a baby-sitting service. There are several restaurants and bars scattered around the villa and its park. There are 84 elegant rooms and suites, and two frescoed rooms. *Closed Dec–Feb.*

Lonato ✉ 25017

Da Oscar, Via Barcuzzi 16, t 030 913 0409, *www.daoscar.it* (*expensive*). This stylish restaurant serves ambitious dishes that score high on the palate and sometimes come up trumps: folks drive from far and wide for fresh potato, asparagus and pea soup, but the speciality is lake fish, for example in the *bigoli alla carbonara*. Some

delicious meats too, such as the lamb *carré* cooked in the oven. *Closed Mon and Tues lunch, two weeks in Jan.*

Entertainment and Nightlife

On summer nights, Desenzano becomes the vortex of one of the hottest scenes in north Italy:

Sesto Senso Club, Via Dal Molin 99, t 347 258 1875, *www.sestosenso.it.* A Liberty villa where posing with Italian TV celebs is part of the fun. *Restaurant also open Wed–Sun 8.30–2.*

Genux, south of the A4 in Lonato, t 030 391 9948. Bop the night away at the 'Greatest Disco in the World,' on four dance floors, with a million watts of light and sound and 150 computer-controlled fountains. *Closed Mon and Wed.*

Rising Sun Pub, opposite the Genux, t 030 991 9919. Czech beer, spaghetti and live music. *Open 8pm–3am; closed Mon.*

Less than 1km from the A4's Casello di Sirmione exit, two other discos attract punters from as far away as Milan and Venice:

Mazoom, t 030 991 0319, *www.mazoom.com*. For experimental and progressive music (*Fri and Sat*).

Le Plaisir 'Sound Sitting Room', same phone number as Mazoon, above. For underground and garage sounds (*Sat*).

Other hot night spots include:

Art Club, t 030 999 1004, with gay nights. **Baraonda**, in Rivoltella, t 030 911 9734.

Wine, Wine, and More Wine

One secret of Desenzano's success through the ages lies in a bottle, or rather bottles: a bewildering number of wines are grown on all sides of town. The south shore of Garda is the restricted growing area of a prestigious white wine, dry, fresh, straw-coloured Lugana DOC, both still and spumante, produced from Trebbiano di Lugana grapes. When they weren't guzzling out of fresh skulls, Lugana was a favourite tipple of the Lombards; today it goes better perhaps with *antipasti* and delicate fish dishes, and is reputed for its joyous quality: '*Ubi Lugana ibi gaudium magnum*' or so they say. A second white, San Martino della Battaglia, is made exclusively from tocai grapes from Friuli, grown on the hills south of Desenzano, and has a distinctive bitter almond aftertaste; golden San Martino della Battaglia liquoroso is a floral, fruity 16 per cent wine, best drunk with desserts or blue cheeses.

Desenzano also forms part of the Garda Bresciano area, which extends west and north into the Valtenesi behind Manerba, although the vines here have a hard time competing with the shore's new-found interest in olive oil. You won't see any Garda Brescianos back home, but they go down well enough on the spot. A mix of gropello, sangiovese, barbera and marzemino (the same grape lauded by Don Giovanni in the opera) goes into ruby Garda Bresciano Rosso and into Chiaretto, a young claret-type wine invented by Venetian Senator Pompeo Molenti in Moniga in 1896. Gentle, savoury Gropello is made of 85 per cent you guess what; Garda Bresciano Bianco is a fresh white made from a mix of Rhine and Italian rieslings.

Near Desenzano: the Risorgimento Hills and the Red Cross

Desenzano is the base for visiting not only Lake Garda but the low, morainic amphitheatre of hills to the south. Although famous for battles, perhaps more important for western civilization was the combat averted in 425 at the twilight of the Roman empire. Attila the Hun, having devastated northeast Italy, was marching to annihilate Rome when he met Pope Leo I south of Desenzano. The pope, with Saints Peter and Paul as his translators, informed Attila that if he should continue to Rome he would be stricken by a fatal nosebleed, upon which the terrible but superstitious Hun turned aside, sparing central Italy.

Move the clock ahead 1,400 years, when Italy, fragmented for all that time, was beginning to reunite in the Risorgimento. In a single day, 24 June 1859, the Italians and their French allies pounded the Austrian occupier twice, when King Vittorio Emanuele II and his Sardinian army crushed the Austrian right wing at San Martino, while Napoleon III defeated Emperor Franz Joseph at Solferino, 11km to the southwest. At **San Martino della Battaglia** (*Via Ossario,* **t** *030 331 0370; open daily throughout the year 9–12.30 and 2.30–7, closed on Mon; adm*) the victory is commemorated by a monumental complex. An **ossuary** in a 13th-century chapel contains the bones of 2,619 dead from both sides. At the highest point of the hill the round 213ft (65m) **Torre Monumentale** was inaugurated in 1893; a winding ramp inside leads up to the panoramic terrace, passing rooms with frescoes and statues on the events and heroes of the Risorgimento. A **museum** behind the tower contains photos, weapons, letters and other mementoes from the campaign.

Solferino saw the single bloodiest battle in the whole war; the **Cappella Ossuaria** behind the church of S. Pietro (*same hours/periods as San Martino; adm*) contains the remains of 7,000 mostly French and Austrian troops. The **museum** (*same hours as S. Martino; adm*) traces the history of Italy from 1796 to 1870, and contains weapons, arms and documents from the battle: other memorabilia is housed in Solferino's mighty tower, the **Spia d'Italia** (Italy's Spy) first built in 1022 by the Scaligers of Verona and restored in the 17th century. Nearby stands a simple **Memorial to the Red Cross**, erected in 1959 to commemorate not only the centenary of the battle, but Henry Dunant's founding of what was first known as the Committee to Aid the Wounded in War. You can learn more about it in the **Museo della Croce Rossa** in **Castiglione delle Stiviere** (*Via Garibaldi 50, t 0376 638 505, www.micr.it; open Nov–Mar 9–12 and 2–5; April–Oct 9–12 and 3–6; closed Mon; donation*).

Before inspiring the creation of the Red Cross, Castiglione delle Stiviere witnessed the birth of St Luigi Gonzaga (every great Italian family managed to churn out a saint or two) and built a big Baroque basilica in his honour. His life is chronicled in the **Museo Storico Aloisiano** (*Via Perati 6; t 0376 638 062; open Sat–Sun 3–5, 4–6; booking is neccessary in summer; donations*), in the early 17th-convent of the Vergini di Gesù. The museum also holds a ripe bounty of mostly religious Baroque paintings (by F. Bassano, Barocci, Piazza and Guardi), a beautiful, functioning clock of 1567 called the Orologio di San Luigi and an important pewterware collection.

Lastly, if it's a weekend, stop in **Lonato**, north of Castiglione and only 4km from Desenzano, to visit the **Fondazione Ugo Da Como** (*Via Rocca 3; open Sat, Sun and hols 10–12 and 2.30–6.30, winter until sunset; other times by appt on t 030 913 0060; adm*).

Organizing Compassion: the Invention of the Red Cross

Henry Dunant of Geneva was trying to get to Napoleon III to present a petition requesting concessions in Algeria when he heard of the battles and stopped to spend the night of 24 June 1859 in Castiglione, 8km west of Solferino. Over the next few days, some 6,000 wounded from both sides were brought into temporary hospitals thrown up overnight in Castiglione's churches, convents, homes, streets and squares. The villagers – outnumbered by the wounded – pitched in to help and supply what food, blankets and clothing they could, while Dunant worked at their sides, deeply impressed not only by the horrors wrought by war but by Castiglione's selfless dedication, although few of the inhabitants could even understand French or German. Inevitably, in spite of the good intentions, confusion reigned.

A week later, as he returned to Geneva, Dunant formed the idea of setting up a permanent, trained committee of partial volunteers to succour the battle-wounded. In 1862 he published the *Souvenir de Solferino* at his own expense, a book that brought many across Europe over to his point of view. In 1863, what became the International Committee of the Red Cross was founded by Dunant in Geneva. The museum, founded in 1959, contains early ambulances, medical kits and portable field hospital beds as well as photos and videos on current Red Cross work around the world and the first Nobel peace prize, awarded to the tireless Dunant in 1901, as well as the three others presented to the Red Cross over the years.

Ugo Da Como was a Brescian scholar and humanist who, when he died in 1941, left his house, furnishings and priceless library of parchments, codices and manuscripts to a foundation for scholars; the house-museum, with its rich, eclectic collection of ancient sculpture, antiques, detached frescoes, Renaissance and Mannerist paintings, ceramics, antique pewter and more, is impressive to stroll through. It becomes even more so when you learn that Da Como bought the house, the 15th-century residence of the Venetian Podestà, in a public auction in 1906 for L1,000 (or 50 cents).

South Lake Garda: Sirmione and Around

Sweet Sirmio! thou, the very eye
Of all peninsulas and isles,
That in our lakes of silver lie,
Or sleep enwreathed by Neptune's smiles
Catullus

Few towns enjoy the dramatic position of Sirmione, strung out along the narrow 4km-long peninsula that pierces Lake Garda's broad bottom like a pin. Lake views and a lush growth of palms, cypresses and parasol pines keep the medieval core from ever feeling claustrophic, even when it's heaving with people in the summer. To find fewer daytrippers and more of the atmosphere that inspired Catullus, Dante, Goethe, Byron, and later Pound and Joyce, who met here, come before June or after September.

The Rocca Scaligera to the Grotte di Catullo

Large car parks signal the entrance into the historic centre of Sirmione; only the vehicles of residents and hotel guests are permitted into town over the bridge of the fairy-tale castle, the **Rocca Scaligera** (*t 030 916 468; open Oct–May Tues–Sun 8.30–4.30; June–Sept Tues–Sun 9–7; adm*). Built by Mastino I della Scala, *signore* of Verona in the 13th century, it is entirely surrounded by a moat where mallards and swans bob and float. Palms fill the courtyard; Dante slept here, but there's not much to see inside, though the views of lake and town from its swallowtail battlements and lofty tower are lovely. A second set of battlements protect the 15th-century church of **Santa Maria Maggiore**, overlooking a slender beach; note the reused Roman capital on the porticoed façade and the unusual pastel brick ceiling. Nearby begins the *passeggiata panoramica* that skirts the peninsula's east shore.

Rome's greatest lyric poet, Catullus, was born in Verona in 84 BC, only to die some 30 years later in the fever of a broken heart. In between passionate bouts in the Palatine home of his fickle mistress, 'Lesbia', he would cool his heels at the family villa at Sirmione. But chances are the great late 1st-century BC villa at the very tip of the rocky promontory known as the **Grotte di Catullo** wasn't it – only a millionaire could have afforded such an opulent pleasure dome. The Grotte can only be reached by foot (1km from the Rocca Scalipera) or, from April to October, by taking an electric train leaving from the town. The superb site (*t 030 916 157; open April–Sept Tues–Sun*

Tourist Information

Sirmione, Viale Marconi 2, **t** 030 916 114. The tourist office website, *www.sirmione.net*, has a comprehensive list of hotels and restaurants as well as details of nightlife and other activities. There is also a sub-site for Sirmione, at *www.gardainforma.com* with details of local excursions, shopping and other activities. Guided tours of the city leave from Viale Marconi 26 (*summer: Sat, Sun and hols at 10, 11.15, 3.15 and 4.45, lasting about 2 hours; adm; free for under-14s; t 0220 404 175*).

Peschiera del Garda, Piazzale Betteloni 15, **t** 045 755 1673.

Festivals

Open-Air Concerts, *June–Sept*. In the piazzas of Sirmione's city centre.

Markets

Sirmione: At the end of Via XXV Aprile, approaching the peninsula. *Mar–Sept Fri, and June–Aug Mon.*

Valeggio sul Mincio: In Piazza Carlo Alberto. Hobby and antiques market. *Every 4th Sun of the month – open late.*

Sports and Activities

Anyone who wishes to go **windsurfing** should contact Martini, **t** 030 916 208, and Lana, 338 624 3650, to rent a board. Bar Chocolat, **t** 030 990 5297, to rent **bikes**; Adventure Sprint, **t** 030 919 000, rents **car-scooters** for cautious bikers.

Where to Stay and Eat

Sirmione ✉ 25019

If driving, have your reservation confirmation on hand for the castle guards.

*****Villa Cortine, Via Grotte 12, **t** 030 990 5890, *www.hotelvillacortine.com* (*luxury*). A neoclassical villa built by an Austrian general and converted into a hotel in 1954. It offers an immersion in romance, and perhaps the rarest amenity in the town – tranquillity. Its century-old garden occupies almost a third of the entire peninsula, with exotic flora, venerable trees, statues and fountains running down to the water's edge. Inside, all is plush and elegant under frescoed ceilings and perhaps a bit too exclusive, but it's ideal for a break from the real world, with private beach and dock, pool and tennis court. *Half-board compulsory during high season (Easter and mid-June–Sept). Dogs admitted at €30 per day. Open April–Oct.*

*****Grand Hotel Terme, Viale Marconi 7, **t** 030 916 261, *www.termedisirmione.com* (*very expensive–expensive*). A top choice, with a private beach, pool, gym and a full health and beauty programme, as well as a lovely lakeside restaurant. *Special discounts if combined with spa treatments. Open Mar–Dec.*

***Catullo, Piazza Flaminia 7, **t** 030 990 5811, *www.hotelcatullo.it* (*expensive*). In the heart of the old town, with good-sized rooms, beautiful views and all modern amenities. Panoramic terrace and solarium. *Open Mar–mid-Oct.*

8.30–7; Oct–Mar Tues–Sun 8.30–4.30; adm, but free for under-18s and over-60s) is romantic with a capital R, set among ancient olives and rosemary hedges. Rigidly rectangular, symmetrical and vast (550ft/167m by 310ft/94m), the villa was flanked by porticoes on the east and west (as well as a long underground cryptoporticus on the west), while a belvedere on the north end overlooked the lake. Of this only the supporting hall called the Aula dei Giganti survives, strewn with enormous chunks; some of the ceilings here once stood over 55ft (17m) high. Olive trees trace the villa's main residential section which collapsed in the 4th century. A huge cistern, 141ft (43m) long, fed the large bath complex and heated pool.

A small **museum** (*open same hours as the grotte*), was expanded and reopened in 1999. It contains a comprehensive exhibition that includes fragments of vases, lamps,

★★★★**Eden**, Piazza Carducci 18, **t** 030 916 481, *www.hoteledenonline.it* (*expensive*). Also in the centre, in a medieval building. It has been remodelled with fine marbles, and co-ordinated bedrooms with princely bathrooms, TV and air conditioning. Unusually, it does not have a restaurant. *Open Mar–Oct.*

★★★**Pace**, Vicolo Carpentini 17, **t** 030 990 5877, *www.pacesirmione.it* (*expensive*). The family that runs the Catullo also manages this smaller hotel, in the old city centre, where the veranda overlooking the lake and the nice early 20th-century decor compensate for the lack of air conditioning in the rooms. Restaurant too. *Open Feb–Dec.*

★★★**Corte Regina**, Via Antiche Mura 11, **t** 030 916 147 (*moderate*). In the city centre and recently refurbished, this hotel has all modern amenities and welcomes children (convenient family rooms) and small pets. *Open April–Oct.*

★★**Speranza**, Via Casello 2, **t** 030 916 116, *hsperanza@jumpy.it* (*moderate*). No lake views, but all the fittings of a three-star hotel, including air conditioning and marble bathrooms, but at significantly lower prices. *Open Mar–Nov.*

★★**Grifone**, Via Bocchio 4, **t** 030 916 014 (*inexpensive*). More attractive on the outside than in the rooms, but has a great location overlooking the Rocca Scaligera. *Open Mar–Oct.*

Trattoria al Pozzo, Via Brescia 36, **t** 030 919 138, *www.ristoranteilpozzo.it* (*moderate*).This atmospheric restaurant at Colombare di Sirmione (1km south of Sirmione) has a tempting menu of local and Italian recipes. Try the lake fish or the vegetarian soups. There is seating for 70 people, with a large, non-smoking room; all credit cards accepted; reserved parking. *Closed Wed and Thurs lunch.*

La Rucola, Via Strentelle 3, **t** 030 916 326 (*very expensive*). An intimate and classy atmosphere to go with its gourmet fish and meat specialities, changing seasonally and according to the genius of young chef and patron Gionata Bignotti, who creatively mixes aromatic herbs and fruit flavours with traditional Mediterranean cuisine. Excellent selection of wines (over 700 labels), whiskies, cognac and grappas. Near the Scaliger castle. *Reservation necessary. Closed Thurs and Jan.*

Ristorante Risorgimento, Piazza Carducci 5–6, **t** 030 916 325 (*very expensive*). Very popular place managed by four young partners, two in the kitchen and two serving at the tables. Dishes range from fish (try the spaghetti with lobster) to meat (flambé fillet with porcini mushrooms). Cheaper dishes at lunch times. *Closed Tues except in summer.*

Al Progresso, Via Vittorio Emanuele 18, **t** 030 916 108 (*moderate–inexpensive*). Family atmosphere and dishes; also in the city centre. *Closed Thurs, and Dec–Jan.*

Osteria al Torcol, Via San Salvatore 30, **t** 030 990 4605 (*moderate*). For a late cold or hot snack or meal and excellent wines – and oils – to taste. Try local cheeses and *affettati*, or be treated to home-made pasta or *ravioli al bagoz* close to the old wine press inside or outside, with your table in the *osteria's* kitchen garden. *Open 6pm–2am; closed Wed.*

spearheads along with other items that were salvaged from the villa's ruins, as well as prehistoric and medieval remains discovered around the peninsula and Lake Garda.

Near the Grotte di Catullo, standing alone on the peninsula's highest point, the Romanesque **San Pietro in Mavino** was built of scavenged Roman bricks; inside are frescoes from the 13th–16th centuries by the school of Verona. Also near here is the thermal **Stablimento Termale Catullo** (*t 800 802 125, www.termedisirmione.com; open mid-Mar–Oct Mon–Sun 7–6.30*), where a pipe brings up steaming sulphuric water from the bottom of the lake – just the thing for respiratory ailments. The medieval lanes in the very centre have been given over to boutiques, bars and pizzerias; for an escape, you can swim off the rocks along the west shore.

Peschiera del Garda, Gardaland and the Sigurtà Gardens

East of Sirmione, Peschiera is an old military town near the mouth of the River Mincio that drains Lake Garda. It has been fortified since Roman times, though the imposing walls that you see today are actually 16th-century Venetian, reinforced by the Austrians when Peschiera was one of the corners of the empire's 'Quadrilateral'. Today Peschiera is mainly a transit point to the lake from the Veneto but its massive purifying plant, the ultimate destination of what goes down every drain in every lakeside town (thanks to an underwater pipeline) still helps it to fulfil its ancient role as a defender, this time of the lake's status as the cleanest in all Europe.

Here, too, you can give your children a treat – at **Gardaland**, Italy's largest and most popular Disney-clone theme park (*on the SS149 between Peschiera and Lazise, t 045 644 9777, www.gardaland.it; open mid-Mar–mid-June and second half of Sept 10–6; mid-June–mid-Sept 8.30–12pm; Oct Sat–Sun 8.30–6.60; Dec–Jan open holidays 10–6.30; closed Feb and Nov; adm, children under a metre high free, as well as disabled visitors with a carer; also, reduced ticket for under-10s and over-60s*). Attractions include the Magic Mountain roller coaster, an African safari and some fairly scary rides. Recent additions include an orbiting space station that offers a panorama of the lake and surroundings. There are free toddler pushchairs at the Information Office.

The region south of Peschiera is known for its flavourful dry white wine, Bianco di Custoza, and for the pretty gardens and groves that line the Mincio all the way to the lakes of Mantua. The most amazing of these, the **Sigurtà Gardens**, 8km from Peschiera and considered to be one of the five most beautiful gardens in the world (*t 045 637 1033, www.sigurta.it; open Mar–Nov daily 9–7; last entrance 6pm; adm, under 5s free*), were the 40-year project of Dr Count Carlo Sigurtà, 'Italy's Capability Brown' – who, granted water rights from the Mincio, used them to transform a barren waste of hills into 500,000 square metres of Anglo-Italian gardens along 7km of lanes. Thirteen parking areas have been provided on the route so you can get out and walk as much as you like. The Sigurtà Gardens are near **Valeggio sul Mincio**, an attractive town in its own right, with a castle and a bridge built by the Visconti, and a pair of competing water fun parks that stay open until midnight.

Lake Garda: Up the West Shore

The west or Lombard shore of Garda is its most prestigious, with the oldest villas (one belonging to Gabriele d'Annunzio) and grandest hotels. The climate is especially benign between Gardone Riviera and Limone.

The Valtenesi and Salò

Six kilometres north of Desenzano, **Padenghe** marks the beginning of a peaceful olive- and wine-growing and white-truffle-finding corner of gently rolling hills called the Valtenesi. The old Valtenesi villages – Padenghe, but especially **Moniga** – preserve tracts of their walls going back to the 10th century. The Valtenesi's fortress, the **Rocca di Manerba**, sits high on the headland that extends into the lake like a great wolf's

Tourist Information

Salò: Lungolago Zanardelli 39, t 0365 21423, *iat@comune.salo.bs.it.*

Festivals
Estate Musicale Gasparo da Salò, *July–Sept.* Open-air concerts in Salò's Duomo square.
Classical Music Conerts, *May and June.* In Palazzo Fantoni in Salò.
International Classical Music Festival, *Aug.* Held in Manerba.

Market Days
Salò: Piazza dei Martiri. *Sat.*
Manerba: *Tues.*

Sports and Activities

Ciclimata, t 0365 41492, rent out **bikes** and **scooters** in Salò; or try Podavini in Manerba, t 0365 551480. **Golf** at Gardagolf (27 holes) *www.gardagolf.it,* in Soiano del Lago, t 0365 674 707, and at Palazzo Arzaga at Calvagese, t 030 680 600, *www.palazzoarzaga.it.* **Horse-riding** at West Garda, in Padenghe, t 030 990 7293, and Ranch Tex, t 0365 552 110, in Manerba. For **trekking** in the hills contact Alpinando, in Salò, t 0365 52 1945. Manerbo has **archery** at Arcieri della Valtenesi, t 0365 551 335.

In Manerba, Arcangeli, t 0365 43443, do **boat charters**; Garda Yachting Centre, t 0365 520 733, hire out sailing boats; Centro Nautico Velico, t 0365 43245, give sailing lessons in Salò. To **sail** in Padenghe contact West Garda Yacht Club, t 030 990 7295; in Manerba, Circolo Nautico, t 030 990 7217. Diving Centre Taras, Salò, t 0365 20225, lets you go **underwater.**

Where to Stay and Eat

Padenghe sul Garda ✉ 25080
★★★★★**Relais Sant' Emiliano**, on Lungolago Marconi (*very expensive*). An 18th-century *cascina* set in its own grounds, with 80 suites on the lake, private beach and mooring, covered and open-air swimming pools, fitness trail and centre, and even a library and church. *Open Mar–Dec.*
The family who run the locanda (*opposite*) have also opened an exclusive retreat residence and hotel, in Le Corti Del Lago.
★★★★**Locanda Santa Giulia**, Lungolago Marconi, 78, t 030 99950 (restaurant), *www.visconti.info* (*expensive*). Just ouside the city centre, on the lake. All modern amenities including a private beach and a pool. With a renowned restaurant featuring fish and local specialities. *Closed Mon.*
Il Ghetto, Via Ghetto 3/A, in Soiano del Lago, a medieval farm town overlooking the lake, t 0365 502 986, *www.ilghetto.it* (*inexpensive*). In a farmhouse; country hospitality and food with all the amenities, including a swimming pool.

Manerba ✉ 25080
Capriccio, Piazza S Bernardo 6, Montintelle hamlet, t 0365 551 124, *www.ristorante capriccio.it* (*expensive*). A beautiful family-run restaurant with a pretty terrace looking out on to soft rolling hills and the lake, where you can tuck into a novel variety of dishes that include fresh tagliolini with prawns, scallops and slated vegetables, or prawn and crab pincers glazed in bread-crumbs with courgettes and aubergines tempura, or *parfait glacé* of bourbon with Szechuan berries and pears marinated in vanilla. *Open for lunch by appointment only; closed Tues and Jan–Feb.*

Salò ✉ 25087
★★★★**Duomo**, Lungolago Zanardelli 63, t 0365 21026, *www.hotelduomosalo.it* (*very expensive–expensive*). The first-floor rooms are the ones to request here – all lead out to a geranium-laden balcony overlooking the lake; rooms with no lake view are less expensive. Rooms are big and modern, and there's a fine restaurant. Additional

muzzle; under the big rock the shore, with Mediterranean flora and beaches, is now a natural park. The Rocca looks out over the **Isola di Garda**, the lake's largest island. When its monastery, visited by St Francis in his peregrinations, fell into ruins in the 19th century, it provided the foundations for a white confectionery neo-Venetian-

amenities include a sauna, solarium, whirlpool and fitness hall.

★★★★**Laurin**, Viale Landi 9, t 0365 22022, www.laurinsalo.com (*expensive*). One of the loveliest places to stay on the lakes: an enchanting Liberty-style villa converted into a hotel in the 1960s, retaining the elegant period decor in the public rooms. The charming grounds include a swimming pool and beach access. For stylish dining amid frescoes, Art Nouveau windows and beautifully presented gourmet dishes, indulge at the hotel's restaurant. *Open Mar–Nov.*

★★★**Benaco**, Lungolago Zanardelli 44, t 0365 20308, www.hotelbenacosalo.it (*expensive*). Also boasts a good roof terrace restaurant. All rooms have a lake view. *Closed Dec–Jan.*

★★★**Vigna**, Lungolango Zanardelli 62, t 0365 520144, www.hotelvigna.it (*expensive–moderate*). Comfortable and modern rooms, with scene-stealing views. Its more expensive junior suites are larger, with whirlpool bath or shower. *Closed mid-Dec–mid-Jan.*

Il Bagnolo, in Bagnolo di Serniga hamlet, in the hills above Salò and Gardone di Riviera, halfway between the two, t 0365 20290, www.ilbagnolo.it (*moderate*). In an old, restored, 18th-century *cascina* and a newer farmhouse. The restaurant offers milk and meat produced in house, and local wine, oil and cheeses. The farmhouse is convenient for trekking: ask for maps to reach nearby peaks Pizzoccolo and Spino (2½ hour walk) to enjoy an unparelled view over the lake and the pre-alpine chain. *Open daily May–Sept, and Oct–April weekends only. Restaurant closed Tues.*

★★**Lepanto**, on the lake at Lungolago Zanardelli 67, t 0365 20428 (*inexpensive*). This is Salò's best kept secret. The signpost advertises the restaurant (*moderate*), on a nice garden terrace, but there are also six rooms to stay in, all overlooking the lake. *Restaurant closed Thurs. Hotel closed mid-Jan–Feb. Booking advised.*

Antica Trattoria delle Rose, Via Gasparo da Salò 33, t 0365 43220 (*expensive*). Run by the same family as the Osteria dell'Orologio (*see* below). Go for *pasta e fagioli*, or lake fish with fresh pasta. *Closed Wed, and Nov.*

Il Melograno, Via del Panorama 5, in Campoverde hamlet, south of Salò, t 0365 520 421 (*expensive*). A hidden jewel. The young chef experiments with home-made *foie gras* dishes with excellent results – try the *scaloppa* filled with *foie gras* – as well as mouthwatering risottos and lake fish soups. Good selection of wines. *Closed Mon eve, Tues and Nov.*

Osteria dell'Orologio, Via Butturini 26, t 0365 290 158 (*expensive*). In an old, beautifully restored inn where you can indulge in local dishes such as *tonno del Garda* (pork cooked in wine and spices), lake fish and skewered wild birds. A very popular place, so book in advance and be prepared to wait to be served. *Closed Wed, 2 weeks between July and Aug.*

Trattoria alla Campagnola, Via Brunati 11, t 0365 22153 (*expensive*). Despite its rustic name, the restaurant is classy and service and food refined. Garden-fresh vegetables are served with every dish, the pasta is home-made, and they make great use of wild mushrooms in season. *Booking advised. Closed Mon, Tues lunch, and 15 Dec–10 Feb.*

Cantina Santa Giustina, Salita S. Giustina 6, t 0305 20300, www.cantinasanta giustina.com (*inexpensive*). The place for a cold snack of cheeses and local *affettati*, salted *coregone* or readily made grilled vegetables, and an excellent selection of local wines. The vaulted *cantina* features books, wines, cheeses and a beautiful old slicing machine. Mario Felter is a charming host and guide through local delicacies. *Open until 5am. Closed Mon. Open only eves. Booking advised.*

Pasticceria Vassalli, Via San Carlo 84–86, t 0365 20752, www.pasticceria-vassalli.it. A must for chocoholics.

Gothic-style palace, owned by the Borghese; one scion of the family, Scipione, won the famous race from Peking to Paris in the early days of the automobile. With its green trees trailing over the water, the island is as tantalizing as it is off limits, unless you can wheedle an invite from the Count.

On the north edge of the Valtenesi, **Salò** (the Roman *Salodium*) is traditionally Garda's 'capital', the seat of the Venetian magistrates. It enjoys a privileged location, set on a deep bay with a grand promenade. In 1901 an earthquake shook it hard; when Salò was rebuilt however, it was with a Liberty-style flourish. Some fine older buildings survived the quake, including a late Gothic **cathedral** with a Renaissance portal of 1509 stuck in its unfinished façade.

The Venetian-style **Loggia della Magnifica Patria** at Lungolago Zanardelli 55 contains the tourist office. The small Museo Civico Archeologico, also housed here, with items found in Salodium's necropolis, is closed prior to relocation (*for information ring **t** 030 43418*). **L'Ateneo**, in the Renaissance Palazzo Fantoni, has a collection of 13th-century manuscripts and early printed books. The nearby **Museo del Nastro Azzuro** (*Via Fantoni 49, **t** 0365 20804; open Thurs, Sat, Sun 10–12 and 3–5; adm*) is dedicated to 'blue-ribboned' Italian military figures from 1797 to 1945 and includes a collection of uniforms, weapons and portraits, and a room on Italy's Fascist period.

Gardone Riviera and D'Annunzio's Folly

North of Salò, sumptuous old villas, gardens and hotels line the lovely promenade at **Gardone Riviera**. Gardone became the most fashionable resort on Lake Garda in 1880, when a German scientist noted the almost uncanny consistency of its climate. One place that profits most from this mildness is the **Giardino Botanico Hruska** (*t 0336 410 877; open Mar–Oct daily 9–6; adm*), a botanical garden with 8,000 exotic blooms and plants growing between imported tufa cliffs and artificial streams.

Above the garden waits **Il Vittoriale degli Italiani** (*t 0365 296 511, www.vittoriale.it*), the home of Gabriele D'Annunzio (1863–1938). This luxurious Liberty-style villa in an incomparable setting, designed for a German family by Giancarlo Maroni, was presented to the extravagant writer by Mussolini in 1925, ostensibly as a reward from a grateful nation for his patriotism and heroism during the First World War, but also as a sop to keep the volatile, unpredictable poet out of politics. D'Annunzio immediately dubbed his new home 'Il Vittoriale' after Italy's victory over Austria in 1918; with Maroni's help he recreated it in his own image, leaving posterity a remarkable mix of eccentric beauty and self-aggrandizing kitsch.

The Tour

Runs Oct–Mar daily 9–5; April–Sept daily 8.30–8. D'Annunzio house (the Prioria) open Oct–Mar Tues–Sun 9–1 and 2–5; April–Sept Tues–Sun 9.30–7; Museo della Guerra (war museum) open Oct–Mar Thurs–Tues 9–1 and 2–5; April–Sept Thurs–Tues 9.30–7; ticket office closes one hour earlier; adm exp but you can buy a cheaper ticket for the museum and grounds only (Vittoriale); expect queues; children under 7 free.

D'Annunzio made the Vittoriale his personal monument, suspecting (correctly) that one day crowds would tramp through the estate to marvel at his cleverness and

Tourist Information

Gardone Riviera: Corso Repubblica 35,
t 0365 20347, *iat.gardoneriviera@tiscali.it*.
Gargnano: Piazza Feltrinelli 2, t 0365 71222,
*www.prolocogargnano.it. Open Wed–Sat
9–12 and Mon also 3.30–6.30.*
A good website is:*www.gardaworld.com*.

Festivals

Jazz Summer Season, *June–Sept*. Held in
Gardone Riviera.
Estate Musicale Gasparo da Salò, *July–Sept*. A
recurring season of open-air concerts played
in Salò's Duomo square, in Gardone di
Riviera, Desenzano and Gargnano.
Guitarists' Festival, *Sept*. Held in Gargnano.

Markets

Gardone Riviera: Antiques. *Evenings, July–Sept*.

Sports and Activities

To **sail** in Gargnano contact the local Circolo
Nautico, t 0365 71433, or 43° Parallelo,
t 0365 790035, *www.parallelo43.it* (rental), in
Bogliaco. At Parco Fontanelle, in Gargnano,
t 0365 579 0012, you may rent **windsurfers**,
canoes, **pedalos**, **bikes** and **mountain bikes**, or
play **volleyball**. **Archery** and **clay-pigeon**
shooting at G.S. Arcieri di Gargnano, t 0365
72222, **horse-riding** at La Genzianella, t 0365
71133, **golf** (9 holes) at Golf Club Bogliaco,
t 0365 643 006. The local Comunità Montana,
t 0365 71449, organizes **trekking** in inland.
Gargnano is also the starting and arrival point
of the historic **Garda Marathon**, run in
Gargnano's hinterland (last weekend of Sept).

Where to Stay and Eat

Gardone Riviera ✉ 25083
*****Villa del Sogno**, Corso Zanardelli 107,
Fasano, t 0365 290 181, *www.villadelsogno.it*
(*luxury*). Another excellent choice, this
upmarket hotel was its creator's neoclassical
'Dream Villa', built in 1904. Immersed in
trees, there's a private beach 5 minutes' walk
away and a pool in its flower-filled garden.
Also tennis, sauna, two restaurants and bars.
Open April–Oct.
****Villa Fiordaliso**, Corso Zanardelli 132,
t 0365 20158, *www.villafiordaliso.it*
(*luxury–very expensive*). A Liberty-style
palace set in luxuriant gardens directly on
the lake. It has only seven rooms, all finely
equipped. You can request (for a price) the
suite where Mussolini and his mistress Clara
Petacci spent their last few weeks. Located in
a serene park, with a private beach and pier,
it also boasts an elegant restaurant, the best
in Gardone, featuring classic Lombard
dishes. *Restaurant closed Mon and Tues
lunch; hotel closed end Nov–mid-Feb*.
****Grand Hotel**, Corso Zanardelli 84,
Gardone, t 0365 20261, *www.grangardone.it*
(*very expensive*). With its 180 rooms this was
one of the largest resort hotels in Europe
when built in 1881. It is still recognized as a
landmark, and its countless chandeliers
glitter as brightly as when Churchill stayed
there in the late 1940s. Almost all the
palatial air-conditioned rooms look on to the
lake, where guests can luxuriate on the
garden terraces, or swim in the heated
outdoor pool or off the private sandy beach.
The dining room and delicious food match
the quality of the rooms. *Open Mar–Oct*.
*****Fasano Grand Hotel**, Corso Zanardelli
190, in the suburb of Fasano Riviera,
t 0365 290 220, *www.grand-hotel-fasano.it*
(*very expensive–expensive*). Built in the early
19th century as a Habsburg hunting palace
and converted into a hotel around 1900.
Surrounded by a large park, it's furnished
with belle époque fittings; there are tennis
courts, a heated pool and private beach. The
restaurant is excellent. *Open May–Oct*.
****Villa Principe**, also on the lake, the
refurbished annexe lodge in the hotel park,
offers more of a country-style stay, with all
amenities and a beach.

taste, if not sheer acquisitiveness: the villa is a pack rat's paradise, its every nook and
cranny filled with quirky, desirable and hilarious junk, more or less all left as it was in
1938 when a sudden brain haemorrhage put an abrupt end to the poet's hoarding.

★★★**Bellevue**, Corso Zanardelli 81, t 0365 290 088, *hotelbellevuegardone.com* (*moderate*). Above the main road overlooking the lake, with a garden sheltering it from the traffic. The Bellevue offers comfortable, modernized rooms, all of which have private bathrooms. The hotel has its own swimming pool. *Open April–Oct.*

★★★**Monte Baldo**, Via Zanardelli 110, t 0365 20951, *www.hotelmontebaldo.com* (*inexpensive*). A good-value lakeside hotel where a well-aged outer appearance conceals a fully refurbished and modern stylish interior. The hotel also has its own swimming pool. Breakfast, meals, snacks and drinks are served on tables placed along a terrace by the lake. Nestled in the lakeshore garden is the refurbished annexe Villa Acquarone, which, at a slightly higher price, offers more rooms, all of which have lake views and plenty of atmosphere. *Open Mar–Oct. Easter, mid-July–mid-Sept, either half-board or full-board only.*

★★**Touring**, Corso Zanardelli 143, t 0365 290 660 (*inexpensive*). A modern, solid year-round budget choice in Fasano, all rooms have their own bathroom.

Ristorante Casinò, Corso Zanardelli 42, t 0365 20387, *www.ristorantecasino.com* (*expensive*). Old-style atmosphere and service, where you can enjoy the lake views from under the portico or eat right on the lake on the front mooring. Lake and sea fish and meat dishes. Try the truffle tortelli. *Closed Mon and Jan–Feb.*

Locanda Agli Angeli, Piazza Garibaldi 2, in Gardone Sopra hamlet, t 0365 20832, *www.agliangeli.com* (*moderate*). A very good family-run restaurant where you can eat home-smoked *magatello di manzo* (beef) with local capers, delicious gnocchi in a *parmigiano* wrap, meat and fish, and local cheeses with red onion sauce and bread with nuts. The locanda's 9 rooms (*moderate*) are simple but comfortable. Swimming pool. *Restaurant closed Mon; Locanda closed Dec–mid-Feb. Booking advised.*

Gargnano ✉ 25084

★★★**Baia d'Oro**, Via Gamberera 13, in Villa, just outside Gargnano, t 0365 71171, *www.hotel baiadoro.it* (*expensive*). This is a small but charming old place on the lake front with an artistic inn atmosphere (owner Giovanbattista Terzi is a painter; his works of art are on display in the hotel). It has a private beach and picturesque terrace; all rooms have bathrooms. *Open mid-Mar–Oct.*

★★★**Du Lac**, Via Colletta 21 in Villa, t 0365 71107, *www.hotel-dulac.it* (*moderate*). A salmon-tinted charmer smack on the water; all the rooms have bathrooms and satellite TV, and are furnished with turn-of-the-last-century pieces. The restaurant, with panoramic terrace, features local cuisine. There's also a bar, and a piano in the small sitting room. *Open mid-Mar–Nov.*

★★★**Gardenia al Lago**, Via Colletta 53, t 0365 71195, *www.hotel-gardenia.it* (*inexpensive*). A few hundred yards from the Du Lac, owned by the same family, offers a slightly less charming stay. Between the two hotels is the private Villa Igea, where D. H. Lawrence stayed (look out for the inscription on the wall). *Open mid-April–Oct.*

La Tortuga, Via XXIV Maggio 5, t 0365 71251 (*very expensive*). A celebrated gourmet haven near the port, specializing in delicate dishes based on seasonal ingredients and lake fish. There are also delicious vegetable soufflés, innovative meat courses, mouth-watering desserts and fresh fruit sherbets, and an excellent wine and spirits cellar; only 7 tables, so book ahead. *Closed Mon except summer, Tues, 1 week in Dec, mid-Jan–Feb.*

Lo Scoglio, Via Barbacane 3, in Bogliaco di Gargnano, t 0365 71030 (*moderate*). Highly recommended restaurant featuring chef Agnese Bertolini. Specialities include all kinds of lake fish, home-made pastas and cakes. *Closed Mon, and Jan–Feb.*

Osteria del Restauro, on the main square, Piazza Villa 19, t 0365 72643 (*inexpensive*). Overlooks the small harbour; good for hot and cold dishes. *Closed Wed.*

Once past the entrance gate to the Vittoriale, note the double arch, a copy of the bridge pier on the Piave, where the Italians held the line against the Central Powers in 1917–18. Like many a jerk, D'Annunzio loved fast cars and two of his favourites are parked near the courtyard – one is the the 1913 Fiat he drove in triumph to Fiume. The tour begins with the 'cool reception' room for guests D'Annunzio disliked – it's austere and formal, compared to the comfy one reserved for favourites. When Mussolini came to call he was entertained in the former; D'Annunzio escorted the dictator over to the mirror and made him read the inscription he had placed above: 'Remember that you are of glass and I of steel'. Perhaps you can make it out if your eyes have had time to adjust to the gloom. Like Aubrey Beardsley and movie characters usually played by Vincent Price, D'Annunzio hated the daylight and had the windows painted over, preferring low-watt electric lamps.

The ornate organs in the music room and library were played by his young American wife, who gave up a promising musical career to play for his ears alone. His bathroom, in spite of 2,000 pieces of bric-a-brac, somehow manages to find space for the tub. In his bedroom, the Stanza della Leda, he kept a cast of Michelangelo's slave, the

More Italian than Any Other Italian

Born Gaetano Rapagnetta into a very modest family in the Abruzzo, the self-styled angel Gabriel of the Annunciation (one wonders what he would have thought of Madonna!) went on to become the greatest Italian poet of his generation, a leading figure in the fin-de-siècle Decadent school who managed to have nearly all of his works placed on the pope's Index. But Gabriele D'Annunzio scoffed at the idea that the pen is mightier than the sword. A fervent right-wing nationalist, he clamoured for Italy to enter the First World War, and when it was over he was so furious that Fiume (Rijeka), a town promised as a prize to Italy, was actually to be ceded by the Allies to Yugoslavia that he took matters into his own hands and invaded Fiume with a band of volunteers (September 1919). In Italy D'Annunzio was proclaimed a hero, stirring up a diplomatic furore before being forced to withdraw in January 1921.

Luigi Barzini has described D'Annunzio as 'perhaps more Italian than any other Italian' for his love of gesture, spectacle, and theatre – what can you say about a man who would boast that he had once dined on roast baby? Yet for the Italians of his generation, no matter what their politics, he exerted a powerful influence in thought and fashion; he seemed a breath of fresh air, a new kind of 'superman', hard and passionate yet capable of writing exquisite, intoxicating verse; the spiritual father of the technology-infatuated Futurists, ready to destroy the old bourgeois *Italia vile* of museum curators and parish priests and create in its stead a great modern power, the 'New Italy'.

He lived a life of total exhibitionism – extravagantly, decadently and beyond his means, at every moment the trend-setting, aristocratic aesthete, with his borzois and melodramatic affairs, with the actress 'the Divine' Eleanora Duse and innumerable other loves (preferably duchesses). Apparently he thought the New Italians should all be as flamboyant and clever, and he disdained the corporate state of the Fascists. For Mussolini, the still-popular old nationalist was a loose cannon and an acute embarrassment, and he decided to pension him off into gilded retirement on Lake Garda, calculating correctly that the gift of the villa would appeal to his delusions of grandeur.

naughty bits veiled by a skirt. In his spare bedroom, adorned with leopard skins, there's a coffin he liked to lie in to think cosmic thoughts. He designed the entrance to his study low so that visitors would have to bow as they entered; here he kept a bust of Duse, but covered, to prevent her memory from distracting his genius. The dining room, with its bright movie-palace sheen, is one of the more delightful rooms; but D'Annunzio didn't care much for it and left his guests here to dine on their own with his pet tortoise, which he had had embalmed in bronze after it expired from indigestion, to remind his visitors of the dangers of overeating.

In the **museum**, located in the Art Deco Casa Schifamondo ('escape the world') that D'Annunzio built but never moved into, you can ponder his death bed and death mask, more casts of Michelangelo's sculptures, paintings and biographical memorabilia. In the adjacent auditorium hangs the biplane our hero used to fly over Vienna to drop propaganda leaflets in the War. The recently opened **private garden** occupies an 18th-century lemon terrace, where a magnolia grove contains D'Annunzio's war memorial, with a throne and stone benches for nationalist legionary ceremonies, which must have been a hoot. The open-air theatre, designed by Maroni after the ancient Greek theatre in Taormina, has a magnificent view from the top seats, stretching from Monte Baldo to Sirmione; in July and August it hosts D'Annunzio's plays. There's a nice surreal touch nearby: the prow of the battleship *Puglia* from the Fiume adventure, jutting out mast and all through a copse of cypresses. Walk above this to the **mausoleum**, the poet's last ego trip, a perverse wedding cake in glaring white travertine. Within three concentric stone circles, the sarcophagi of the Fiume legionnaires pay court to the plain tomb of D'A himself, raised up on columns high above the others like a pagan sun-king, closer to his dark star than anyone else, the whole in hellish contrast to the mausoleum's enchanting setting.

Toscolano-Maderno and Gargnano

The double-barrelled *comune* of Toscolano-Maderno has one of the finest beaches on Lake Garda, a 9-hole golf course and the car ferry to Torri. Toscolano traces its origins to the Etruscans, and Maderno was the site of *Benacum*, the main Roman town on the lake. In the 12th century, many of Maderno's Roman bits were incorporated into the extremely elegant **Sant'Andrea**, a Romanesque beauty benignly restored in the 16th century by St Charles Borromeo; inside, the capitals, some retaining their original paint, are sculpted with fighting animals. The 18th-century parish church has a *Sant'Ercolano* by Paolo Veronese and a *Martyrdom of St Andrew* by Palma Giovane. Toscolano was the chief manufacturer of nails for Venice's galleys and had a famous printing press in the 15th century; to this day the Cartiera di Toscolano paper mill is Garda's largest industry. The cool, green **Valle delle Cartiere** – the valley of the paper mills – is a favourite excursion.

To the north, **Gargnano**, the last town before the towering cliffs, means sailing. Since 1950 it has hosted the colourful Centomiglia regatta the second week of September, attracting yachts from as far away as the US, New Zealand and Australia. The Franciscans were among the first to live here in the 13th century; their church has been baroqued inside and the cloister's capitals have carvings of lemons and oranges, a reminder of the tradition that the Franciscans were the first to cultivate citrus in Europe. The church's beautiful portal is dedicated to San Francesco. In the 14th century Gargnano was the capital of the villages in the hinterland proudly known as the Magnifica Patria, and in 1866 an Austrian flotilla sailed up and fired cannons at the port; if you look closely you can see the scars.

After the Borghese ranch on Isola di Garda, the largest villa on the lake is just south of Gargnano: the enormous 18th-century **Villa Bettoni** in Bogliaco (*check at villa for opening hours*), used as a set in a dozen films. In another villa, built for the publisher Feltrinelli (whose chain of bookstores is a blessing to the English-speaking traveller in Italy), the University of Milan runs summer courses for foreign students; a second Villa Feltrinelli, designed by Milanese architect Belgiojoso in 1854, was Mussolini's home during the Republic of Salò. D. H. Lawrence stayed in Gargnano in 1912–13 and wrote *Twilight in Italy* here.

Two kilometres from Gargnano in **Calino** the church of **San Giacomo**, the *comune*'s oldest, has an interesting fresco on the lake-front façade, representing San Cristoforo, patron saint of travellers. In antique times big effigies of the saint were painted at each crossroads, visible from afar. Ask the local tourist office for itineraries in Gargnano's hinterland – especially spectacular is the one across fjord-like lake Valvestino, the plateau of Rest, beech-wooded Mt Tombea and Lake Idro through the Valsabbia – or stroll through the neighbouring picturesque hamlets of Villa and Bogliaco or panoramic Muslone and Piovere.

Northern Lake Garda: Limone, Riva and Malcesine

The highest mountains embrace northern Lake Garda, and the consistent gusts of wind and air currents make the triangle between Limone, Torbola and Malcesine the stuff that windsurfing dreams are made of. World Championship meets take place here on a regular basis, and the shores are well supplied with rentals and schools if you're inspired to give it a whirl – nearly every hotel is equipped to give customers the option of windsurfing. Expect to hear a lot of German as sun-starved Austrians, Swiss and Germans pour down here for ersatz Mediterranean weekends among the bougainvillaea and olives.

Limone sul Garda

North of Gargnano the lake narrows, the cliffs plunge sheer into the water and the Gardesana road pierces tunnel after tunnel like a needle. In the morning, when the wind's up, windsurfers flit across the waves like a swarm of crazed one-winged butterflies. On weekends their cars are parked all along the road around **Campione**, a tiny hamlet huddled under the cliffs. For tremendous views, take one of the several turnings inland that wind precipitously up to the cliffs: to peaceful **Tignale**, with its church perched on the edge of a spectacular viewpoint, and **Tremosine**, atop a 1,000ft (305m) precipice that dives down sheer into the blue waters below, looking across the lake to mighty Monte Baldo.

Tourist Information

The local tourist offices organize free **guided tours** to the Trentino castles, or the biotope of the Marocche of Dro or the historical centres of Riva and Arco. Ask the tourist office also for a list of cellars where you can taste and buy wines from Trentino.

Arco, Viale delle Palme 1, **t** 0464 532 255.

Limone sul Garda, Via Comboni 15, **t** 0365 954 070; there is also a seasonal tourist office at Piazzale A. De Gasperi, **t** 0365 954 265.

Riva del Garda, Giardini di Porta Orientale 8, **t** 0464 554 444, *www.gardatrentino.it*.

Torbole/Nago, Via Lungolago Verona 19, **t** 0464 505 177.

There are plenty of other websites for a virtual visit: *www.garda.com*, *www.limone. com*, *www.cittadiarco.com*, *www.gardare sort.it*, *www.gardaworld.com*.

Festivals

Young Musicians Festival, *end July*, in Riva.

Rustico Medioevo, *first half Aug*. Medieval dance and folklore shows in Canale di Tenno.

Traubenkur (cure of the grapes), *mid-Sept– Oct*. Commemorating the autumn sojourn of the Middle European elite at Alto Garda to rest from the fatigue of the summer; an opportunity to taste local wine and grappa.

Markets

Torbole: *2nd and 4th Tues of the month, April–Sept*.

Riva: *2nd and 4th Wed of the month, June–Sept*.

Arco: *1st and 3rd Wed of the month, June–Sept*.

Sports and Activities

There are plenty of water and mountain sports to practise in the area. Ask the tourist office for the list of companies providing **windsurfing** and **sailing** courses and rental, and for a description of local winds, sailing areas and hydrofoil routes (to avoid). You can **dive** and see the underwater Christ with Gruppo Sommozzatori Fips in Porto San Nicolò, Riva, **t** 0464 555 120. **Fishing** is allowed in Lake Garda (guided excursions €2pp): you need a fishing licence – €1, unlimited validity all over Italy – you can buy the stamps (*Marche da Bollo*) for the licence, equal to the amount, at the tobacconist, but the licence must be requested at the Ispet Torato Distrettuale Forestale, Via San Nazzaro 2/D, Riva del Garda, **t** 0464 552 338 (*open Mon–Fri 8.15–12.30 and 2–5*); or Amici della Trilindana, Via Ballino 3/B, Riva, **t** 0464 556 379. Daily local permits are available at several fishing clubs and shops. On Lake Bagatol (nearby) fishing is permitted without licence or special permits; the cost instead is €12 (for 6 trout) or €7.80 (for 3 trout).

Also available is the list of companies organizing canyoning, climbing and excursions in the surrounding area. **Ufficio delle Guide Alpine**, Via Santa Caterina 40, Arco, **t** 0464 507 075, *www.guidealpinearco.com*, organizes most of them: **guided excursions**, **climbing**, **canyoning**, **mountain biking**, **riding** and **paragliding**. For **trekking**, the tourist offices provide maps of the surrounding areas. There are many places to hire **bikes** and mountain bikes, but Coast to Coast, in Torbole, **t** 0464 506 115, also provides a shuttle bike service for downhill biking (*daily 9.30am, 11.30am and 2pm*).

Club Ippico San Giorgio, San Giorgio hamlet near Arco, **t** 0464 556 942, provides **horse- riding** lessons and excursions. **Archery** is at Virtus, in Riva, **t** 0464 552 759; for **clay-pigeon shooting** (in Marocche hamlet on the main road), call **t** 0464 504 279. **Bowling**, **table tennis** and **billiards** can be played at Clem's Bowling, Viale Damiano Chiesa 4, **t** 0464 553 596, in Riva, which is also an Internet cafè.

For kids the Riva Sport Centre, Viale dei Tigli 40 in Riva, is an **acquapark**, with water slides, 'wondercastle' and children's playground, **t** 0464 552 072. Parco Busatte, Torbole, has **rollerskating**, **tennis** and **table tennis**, **volley- ball**, five-a-side **football** and free **climbing** for kids, **t** 0464 506 112 (open Mar–Nov).

Where to Stay and Eat

Limone ✉ 25010

★★★★Le Palme, Via Porto 36, **t** 0365 954 681, *www.sunhotels.it* (*moderate*). Housed in a pretty Venetian villa in the historic city centre, preserving much of its original charm alongside modern amenities.

Named after its two ancient palm trees, it has a fine terrace and a good fish restaurant. *Open mid-Mar–Oct.*

***Hotel Coste**, Via Tamas 11, 10 minutes from the city centre, t 0365 954 042, *www.hotelcoste.com* (*moderate*). In an olive grove, this family-friendly hotel has its own outside pool, *boules* area and children's playground. Minimum stay of three days. *Open Mar–Oct.*

***La Limonaia**, Via Sopino Alto 3, t 0365 954 221 (*moderate*). Enjoys a superb position above the centre, and has both an adult and a children's pool and playground. Needs refurbishing. *Open April–Oct.*

***Sogno del Benaco**, Lungolago Marconi 3, just outside the city centre, t 0365 954 026, *www.hghotels.com* (*moderate*). Fairly standard, modern rooms.

****Villa Margherita**, Via Luigi Einaudi 3, t 0365 954 149 (*moderate*). Further out and up from the city centre. Staying here is like entering Ms Margherita's private house, spotless and carefully decorated and furnished. In the olive groves, it is a peaceful retreat with a stunning view of the olive tree slopes and the lake. Rooms each have a different colour and flowery decor; the corner ones are particularly nice with windows on two sides and a private terrace. *Open Mar–Oct.*

****Mercedes**, Via Nanzello 12, t 0365 954 073, *www.mercedeshotel.com* (*inexpensive*). Above the lake in an olive grove, outside the city centre; has a pool and lovely views. Some apartments too. *Open Mar–Dec.*

Riva del Garda ✉ 38066

For cheaper accommodation there are plenty of rooms to rent in private houses in the area. Ask the local tourist office for the list.

*****Hotel du Lac et du Parc**, Viale Rovereto 44, t 0464 566 600, *www.hoteldulac-riva.it* (*very expensive*). When German intellectuals from Nietzsche to Günter Grass have needed a little rest and relaxation in Italy they have for many decades flocked to Riva del Garda to check in here: a modernized, spacious, airy and tranquil hotel, set in a large lakeside garden. Facilities include indoor and outdoor pools, a beach and tennis courts. *Open April–Oct.*

*****Grand Hotel Liberty**, Viale Carducci 3/5, t 0464 553 581, *www.grandhotelliberty.it* (*very expensive–expensive*). Provides a stylish stay in a Liberty villa set in its own grounds at the back of the city centre. It has an indoor pool and whirlpool baths.

*****Grand Hotel Riva**, Piazza Garibaldi 10, t 0464 521 800, *www.gardaresort.it* (*very expensive–expensive*). A turn-of-the-last-century hotel majestically positioned on the main square. 87 modern rooms look out over the lake; there's air conditioning in lake-front ones only. The restaurant combines fine food with incomparable views.

*****Sole**, Piazza III Novembre 35, t 0464 552 686, *www.hotelsole.net* (*expensive*). Right on the port in Riva's main square. Plenty of atmosphere and a beautiful terrace. All the rooms have private bathrooms; plenty of atmosphere from outside but modern refurbishments inside have caused some of the character to be lost. *Closed 2 weeks between Dec and Jan.*

****Centrale**, Piazza III Novembre 27, t 0464 552 344, *www.welcometogardalake.com* (*moderate*). Fully equipped, spacious rooms and bathrooms; beside the harbour.

****Portici**, Piazza III Novembre 19, t 0464 555 400, *www.hotelportici.it* (*moderate*). Competely refurbished and with modern rooms, all with bathrooms. *Open April–Nov.*

Restel de Fer, Via Restel de Fer 10, t 0464 553 481, *www.resteldefer.com* (*moderate*). Built in 1400; only five rooms and a good restaurant, with summer dining in the cloister.

****Villa Moretti**, Via Mazzono 7, 3km up in Varone, t 0464 521 127, *www.rivadelgarda.com/villamoretti* (*inexpensive*). If you want peace and quiet, a garden and pool in a panoramic spot, this family-run hotel will fit the bill.

Ostello Benacus, Piazza Cavour 10, t 0464 554 911, *www.ostelloriva.com*. Riva's hostel, with cheap meals and packed lunches. Some rooms have bathrooms. *Open mid-Mar–Oct.*

Villa Negri ai Germandri, Via Bastione 31/35, t 0464 555 061, *www.villanegri.it* (*very expensive*). Overlooking the lake and the city centre, and set in the historical villa of architect Maroni (of D'Annunzio's Vittoriale), just below the castle (a shuttle service in golf carts is provided for restaurant guests from Riva's car park). The villa hides an exclusive restaurant, with silver cutlery and silk tablecloths, napkins and wall covers, and two round terraces perched over the lake. Four chefs look after the cooking, serving a 9-dish daily menu (no surprise it's called an itinerary) of local cuisine creatively revisited (€80, there's also a smaller menu for €50). Try the risotto with potatoes or the *fonduta* (an Italian take on cheese fondue) with truffles. In the back, the terrace bistro, less formal and expensive, has an outdoor chef overseeing the grill (fish, meat, vegetables) and holds Mozart evenings on Friday nights in the summer. Take some time to visit the cellar, with over 1,800 labels kept in a former First World War shelter excavated in the rocks. *Closed Tues (but not in the summer), and Nov. Open eves only. Booking advised.*

Al Volt, Via Fiume 73, t 0464 552 570, (*expensive*). Located in an old 17th-century palace. The specialities here include onion soup, *salmerino* (stream fish), and pork fillet with gorgonzola cheese sauce. *Menu degustazione* (changed twice a week) is €38 for 5 courses. Try fish *luccio* with polenta. *Closed Mon except Aug, and closed mid-Feb–mid-Mar.*

Arco ✉ 38062

****Palace Hotel Città, Viale Roma 10, t 0464 531 100, *www.welcometogarda lake.com* (*expensive*). A modern hotel with a balcony for every comfortable, fully equipped room (satellite TV, air conditioning). There's a pool, a gym, a sauna and a slimming programme, and an optional vegetarian menu in the restaurant.

***Al Sole, Via Foro Boario 5, t 0464 516 676, *www.soleholiday.com* (*moderate*). A popular place to stay, with a wine bar. Its restaurant also has a good wine list and features local produce – try gnocchi with local prunes. *Restaurant closed on Sat.*

Alla Lega, Via Vergolano 8, t 0464 516 205 (*expensive*). Offers local cuisine. *Closed Wed and mid-Jan–mid-Mar.*

Belvedere, Via Serafini 2, in Varignano, t 0464 516 144 (*inexpensive*). Probably the best place to eat. The specialities are delicious and include salted meat and Trentine dishes such as *canederli* (meat and bread dumplings in broth), also home-

grown vegetables, local salami and fresh pasta. *Closed Wed and July–Sept.*

Torbole ✉ 38069

****Lido Blu, Via Foci del Sarca 1, t 0464 505 180, *www.lidoblu.com* (*expensive*). Beautifully located on a spit of land with water on either side, this modern hotel is excellent for families, with a private beach, a gym, covered pool, windsurfing school and more.

****Piccolo Mondo, Via Matteotti 7, t 0464 505 271, *www.hotelpiccolomondotorbole.it* (*expensive*). This upmarket hotel has as a very good restaurant with specialities from Trentino. *Closed Tues except summer, and Oct–Mar.*

Le Terrazze della Luna, t 0464 505 301 (*moderate*). You can dine well and romantically in a 19th-century Austrian fort in nearby Coe. *Closed Mon except in summer, and Nov.*

Entertainment and Nightlife

Riva enjoys a hectic nightlife in season, much of it geared towards the hordes of Brits and Germans who invade the town:

Disco Bar Cafè Latino, Via Monte Oro 14, Riva, t 0464 557 380, *www.cafelatino.it*. For disco music. *Open Thurs–Sun until 4am.*

Bellavista, Via Lungolago Verona, Riva, t 0464 505 174. For a more sedate evening this piano bar is fairly calm except when karaoke takes over (on request).

Tiffany, Giardini di Porta Orientale, Riva, t 0464 552 512. This is the main place in town to get down on the dance floor; in a lovely position in the gardens leading down to the lake with music of the 1970s–1990s. *Open daily 10pm–4am.*

Disco Pub Conca D'Oro, Lungolago Verona, Torbole, t 0464 553 457, *www.puballoca.com*. *Open Thurs–Sun 10–4.*

La Capannina, Via Santa Caterina 91, in Arco, t 0464 521 247. This club has a mixed crowd and caters for the elderly, with '*liscio*' dancing, and for the youngsters, under the name Kaos, in the afternoons. *Open Fri, Sat and in winter.*

The inland route from Tremosine rejoins the lake and La Gardesana shore road at **Limone sul Garda**, a popular resort town with a teeny tiny port and a beach over 3km long. Its name comes from the Latin *limen* (border), although by happy coincidence Limone was one of the main citrus-producing towns on Lake Garda, and to this day its lemon terraces with their white square pillars are a striking feature of the landscape: D.H. Lawrence, who lived south of Limone for a spell, liked to see them as the ruins of ancient temples.

Riva del Garda and Around

North of Limone the lake enters into the Trentino region, where the charming town of Riva sits snug beneath an amphitheatre formed by Monte Brione. An important commercial port for the bishops of Trento beginning in 1027, it was much sought and fought after through the centuries, ruled at various times by Verona, Milan and Venice before it was handed back to the bishop-princes of Trento in 1521. In 1703, during the War of the Spanish Succession, the French General Vendôme sacked it and all the surroundings, leaving only a ghost of the former town to be inherited by Napoleon in 1796.

With its long beaches and refreshing summer breezes, Riva revived as a resort during the days of Austrian rule (1813–1918) as the 'Southern Pearl on the Austro-Hungarian Riviera', a pearl especially prized by writers: Stendhal, Thomas Mann, D. H. Lawrence and Kafka were among its habitués. The centre of town, Piazza III Novembre, has a plain **Torre Apponale** (1220) where salt and grain were stored (*closed at the time of writing, ring t 0464 554 444 for info*), and the **Palazzo Pretorio**, built by Verona's Cansignorio della Scala in 1376, while the lake front was defended by the sombre grey bulk of the 12th-century castle, the **Rocca**, surrounded by a swan-filled moat. This now houses Riva's **Museo Civico** (*Piazza Cesare Battisti 3, t 0464 573 869; open mid-Mar–mid-June Tues–Sun 10–6; mid-June–mid-Sept daily 10–6; guided tours: Wed 4.30 and Sun 10.30, only by booking – guide costs €1 (+ ticket); adm*) with finds from the Bronze Age settlement at Lake Ledro, and six statue-stelae with human features from the 4th–3rd millennia BC, recently discovered; and from Roman Riva, as well as paintings, detached frescoes and sculpture gleaned from the surroundings. Riva's best church, the **Inviolata** (1603), was commissioned by the princely Madruzzo family of Trento from an unknown but imaginative Portuguese architect, who was given a free hand with the gilt and stucco inside; it also has paintings by Palma II Giovane.

Only 3km north, a dramatic 287ft (87.5m) waterfall, the **Cascata del Varone** (*open Mar and Oct 10–12.30 and 2–5; April and Sept 9–6; May–Aug 9–7; Nov–Feb Sun and hols only 10–12.30 and 2–5; adm*), crashes down a tight grotto-like gorge by the village of Varone; walkways allow visitors to become mistily intimate with thundering water. From the west side of Riva the exciting Ponale road, a walking path since the recent opening of a gallery, rises to **Lake Ledro** (a 5km walk, but you can also drive), noted not only for its scenery but also for the remains of a Bronze Age settlement of pile dwellings (*c.* 2000 BC), discovered in 1929. One has been reconstructed near the ancient piles around **Molina di Ledro**, where the **Museo delle Palafitte** (*t 0464 508*

*182; open mid-June–mid-Sept Tues–Sun 10–1 and 2–6; end Sept–mid-June Tues–Sun 9–1
and 2–5; adm free for children 12 and under)* houses the pottery, axes, daggers and
amber jewellery recovered from the site; the visit includes the new prehistoric
botanical garden, dedicated to the plants cultivated by northern Italian farmers in
the Bronze Age. From here you can continue to Lake Idro, through the shadowy gorge
of the **Valle d'Ampola**.

One of the most dramatic sights on Garda is just behind Riva, in a natural balcony
of hills overlooking the lake: the jagged crag and **Castello di Arco** (*t 0464 510 156; open
April–Sept 10–7; Oct–Mar 10–4; adm free for children 12 and under)*, dramatically
crowned with ancient, dagger-sharp cypresses and the swallowtail crenellations.
Built to defend the Valle di Sarca, the main funnel of northern armies into Italy, it was
controlled from the 12th century by the cultured Counts of Arco, who tugged their
forelocks at various stages to Verona, Milan and Trento. The path up (20 mins) is lovely
if a bit tiring on a hot day and, despite the damage wrought by Vêndome's troops,
there are a few frescoes left, including one of a courtly game of chess.

Arco itself, once heavily fortified and moated (the surviving gate has a drawbridge)
became, like Riva, a popular Austro-Hungarian resort in the 1800s, prized for its
climate. In the centre, a Baroque fountain dedicated to Moses splashes before the
Palladian-inspired **Collegiata dell'Assunta** (1613): another Madruzzo project, this time
by Trentino architect Giovanni Maria Filippi, who went on to become court architect
of Emperor Rudolph II in Prague. There's a pretty public garden full of Mediterranean
plants, near the equally pretty 19th-century **Casino**, while on the edge of town, off Via
Lomego, the park laid out at the end of the 19th century by the Habsburg Archduke
Albert is now an **Arboretum** (*t 0464 517 111; open winter daily 9–4; summer daily 9–7)*.

Dro, up the Sarca valley, is near the small lakes of Cavedine and Toblino, and **Sarche**,
where an ancient glacier deposited the *marocche*, a remarkable field of enormous
boulders. Olive trees as well as enormous chestnuts grow around **Drena**, at the
bottom of Val Cavedine. The landmark here is the stark **Castello** (*t 0464 541 220; open
Nov–Feb, Sat and Sun only 10–6; Mar–Oct Tues–Sun 10–6; adm free for children 12 or
under)*, its keep rising up like a finger accusing heaven. Built by the Counts of Arco in
1175 and ruined by Vêndome in 1703, the lists, where knightly tournaments once took
place, have been restored to host congresses and theatrical performances; the keep
has splendid views, taking in the mighty *marocche*, and contains a museum of local
artefacts, dating from the 18th century BC to the Renaissance as well as some
archeological findings.

Torbole

Back on Garda's northeast shore, **Monte Baldo** looms over **Torbole** and the mouth of
the Sarca, the most important river feeding the lake. An old fishing village and a
pleasant resort, Torbole is famous in the annals of naval history. In 1439, during a war
with the Visconti, the Venetians were faced with the difficulty of getting supplies to
Brescia past the southern reaches of Lake Garda, then controlled by Milan. A Greek
sailor made the suggestion that the Venetians sail a fleet of provision-packed
warships up the Adige to its furthest navigable point, then transport the vessels

over Monte Baldo on to Lake Garda. Anyone who has seen Herzog's film *Fitzcarraldo* will appreciate the difficulties involved, and the amazing fact that, with the aid of 2,000 oxen, the 26 ships were launched at Torbole only 15 days after leaving the Adige. But after all that trouble, the supplies never reached Brescia. The same trick, however, perhaps even suggested by the same Greek, enabled Mohammed II to bring the Ottoman fleet into the upper harbour of Constantinople the following year and capture the city.

The East Shore: Malcesine to Bardolino

Garda's east shore belongs to the province of Verona. The silvery groves that grace the hills gave it its name, the Riviera degli Olivi, but its most outstanding feature is Monte Baldo, a massive ridge of limestone stretching 35km between Lake Garda and the Adige valley, cresting at 6,989ft (2,130m). Baldo is anything but bald: known as 'the botanical garden of Italy', it supports an astonishing variety of flora from Mediterranean palms to Arctic tundra; some 20 different flowers first discovered on Monte Baldo bear its name and it contains a 150-hectare protected area known as the Bes Corna Piana Botanical Park. The southern third of the Riviera degli Olivi is more grapey than olivey, the land of Bardolino.

Malcesine

South of Torbole, the forbidding cliffs of Monte di Nago hang perilously over the lake (but nevertheless attract scores of Lycra-bright human flies) before Malcesine, the loveliest town on the east shore. The Veronese lords always took care to protect this coast and in the 13th century, over the old Lombard castle, they built their magnificent **Rocca Scaligera** (*t 0457 400 837; open mid-Mar–Dec 9.30–7.30; adm*) rising up on a sheer rock over the water; inside are natural history exhibits, prehistoric rock etchings and a room dedicated to Goethe, who was accused of spying while sketching the castle. As well as the Scaliger castle, note the 16th-century **Palazzo dei Capitani del Lago** in the centre of Malcesine's medieval web of streets.

A pair of cable cars run vertiginously up **Monte Baldo** (*every ½hour; journeys from 4pm; about 10min; t 045 740 0206 for information; adm*); they have rotating cabins to further enjoy the ravishing views, and the ski slopes at the top are very popular with the Veronese. Malcesine also has pretty walks through the olives, and the shore has lovely places to swim and sunbathe, especially around the cove called the Val di Sogno. To the south, the hamlet of **Cassone** straddles the Aril, said to be the shortest river in the world – although the Fiumelatte on Lake Como begs to differ.

Torri del Benaco and Garda

Further south, past a steep, sparsely populated stretch of shore, there are two pretty towns, one on either side of Punta di San Vigilio, that played minor roles in the 10th century. The first, laid-back **Torri del Benaco**, owes its name to a rugged old tower in the centre that served as the headquarters of Berengario, the first king of

Getting There and Around

APT **buses** run up the east coast from Verona and Peschiera as far as Riva, **t** 045 800 4129, *www.aptv.it*; another company offering a bus service around the lake is Societè Italiana Autoservizi, **t** 030 377 4237, *www.sia-autoservizi.it*. The **car ferry** crosses year-round from Torri del Benaco to Maderno.

Tourist Information

Malcesine, Via Capitanato 6/8, **t** 045 740 0044, *malcesine@aptgardaveneto.com*.
Torri del Benaco, Viale F.lli. Lavanda, **t** 045 722 5120, *tourist@libero.it*. Open in the summer.
Garda, Lungolago Regina Adelaide 13, **t** 045 627 0384, *www.aptgardaveneto.com*.
Bardolino, at Piazzale Aldo Moro, **t** 045 721 0078, *bardolino@aptgardaveneto.com*.

Other useful websites include: *www.torbole.com*, *www.malcesine.com*. Also there's *www.torridelbenaco.com*, and *www.bardolino.net*.

Market Days

Bardolino. *Thurs and Mon.*
Garda. *Fri.*
Malcesine. *Sat.*
Torri del Benaco. *Mon.*

Sports and Activities

The northern part of Lake Garda is buffeted by strong winds, challenging both beginner and expert sailors and windsurfers. In Malcesine, for **windsurfing** contact WWWind Square, in Sottodossi hamlet, **t** 045 740 0413, *www.wwwind.com*; Nany, in Navene, **t** 045 740 0407, Sunrise in Molini hamlet, **t** 045 7401104, Stickl Sport Camps in Val di Sogno, **t** 045 740 1697 (also boat sailing), International Sailing Centre, c/o Sailing Center Hotel, Via Molini 3, Campagnola hamlet, **t** 045 740 0055, *sailing@malcesine.com*, and Fraglia Vela Malcesine, **t** 045 740 0274, *www.fragliavela.org*, (sailing only). In Bardolino contact Centro Nautico Bardolino, Lungolago Preite 10, **t** 045 721 0816; Yachting Club Torri, Via Marconi 1, **t** 045 722 5124, in Torri del Benaco.

The neighbouring mountains offer **trekking**, **mountain bike** excursions and **winter sports**. For the latter contact Furioli, Piazza Matteotti, Malcesine, **t** 0457 400 089; while Mirosso, Campagnola hamlet, **t** 045 740 1104, caters for hikers. You can fly down Monte Baldo with **Paragliding** Club Malcesine, **t** 045 740 1657.

To relax, Villa dei Cedri, Piazza di Sopra 4, in Colà, on the inland of Lazise, has a warm thermal lake equipped with fountains for **hydromassage** in a century-old cedar park; it's also open in the evening, (€19 adults, €13 children). For info call **t** 045 759 0988, or *www.villadeicedri.com*.

Where to Stay and Eat

Hotels on the east shore tend to be cheaper than their competitors across the lake.

Malcesine ✉ 37018

***Sailing Centre, Molini Campagnola 3, **t** 045 740 0055, *www.hotelsailing.com* (*very expensive*). A hotel with accommodation in low houses, in a lake-front garden, each room with private balcony or access to garden. North of the centre with a beach, sailing and windsurf schools, sauna, pool and satellite TV. Free mountain biking and tennis for longer stay. *Open mid-April–mid-Oct. Half-board only; min 3-day stay.*
****Val di Sogno, Val di Sogno hamlet, about 3mins out of town, **t** 045 740 0108, *www.hotelvaldisogno.com* (*very expensive–expensive*). In a beautiful setting

Italy, in his 905 campaign against the Magyars. Later, it was defended by another **Scaliger castle** (1383), now a museum (**t** 045 629 6111, *www.berengario.com*; *open Tues–Sun, Jan–May and Oct 9.30–12.30 and 2.30–6; Jun–Sept 9.30–1 and 4.30–7.30; adm*) with displays on olive oil, citrus, fishing, and rock engravings found in the area from *c.* 2000 BC, similar to those in the Valle Camonica. The church of **Santa Trinità**

in its own grounds on the lake shore; with pool, sauna, gym, tennis, beach for guests' use, a lakeside restaurant, and modern rooms with balconies. *Min 3-day stay. Half-board, though B&B only during low–med season. Closed mid-Oct–mid-Mar.*

****Park Hotel Querceto**, Campiano hamlet, **t** 045 740 0344, *www.parkhotel querceto.com* (*expensive*). South of the centre, this is a romantic place to stay, with lovely views, a pool, garden, and one of the best restaurants in the area, where the cuisine is light and tasty and adapted to the season. There is a large terrace. *Closed Nov–Mar.*

***Vega**, Viale Roma 10, **t** 045 657 0355, (*expensive*). An inviting lake-front hotel in the city centre with big, modern rooms, all with satellite TV, minibar, safe and air conditioning, and a private beach. *Half-board only; min 3-day stay. Open April–Oct.*

***Malcesine**, Piazza Pallone, **t** 045 740 00333, *www.chincherini.com* (*expensive–moderate*). Beautifully positioned on the lake in the city centre; has a garden with swimming terrace, average rooms, and an excellent-value if average restaurant. *Half-board only. Open Mar–Oct.*

****Erika**, Via Campogrande 8, **t** 045 740 0451 (*moderate*). Just behind the city centre; offers family-run, cosy hospitality. Own garage and bike garage. *Open mid-Mar–Oct.*

***Stella Alpina**, In Dos de Feri hamlet, 0.5km from the city centre, **t** 045 740 0078 (*moderate*). From the same management as San Marco's. Swimming pool, and parking in a shady garden. *Open Mar–mid-Oct.*

***San Marco**, Via Capitanato, **t** 045 740 0115, (*inexpensive*). In the centre, you can sleep where Goethe snoozed in 1786; all simple rooms have bathrooms. *Open Mar–Oct.*

The town of Malcesine has only 35,000 inhabitants but 17,000 hotel beds. Once a playground for the elite, it is now a typical tourist destination with the obvious consequence that restaurant food is generally dreadful and terribly touristy – expect overcooked spaghetti with meat sauce.

Trattoria Vecchia Malcesine, Via Pisort 6, **t** 045 740 0469, *www.vecchiamalcesine. com* (*expensive*). An exception to the above: a charming escape from the hurly-burly, on a panoramic terrace, with high quality food cooked by young chef Leandro Lippi and served by his wife Lidia. Try the *canederli di speck* (ham-flecked dumplings), seasoned with Monteveronese cheese from Veneto, or butterfly pasta with porcini mushrooms and ricotta. Lake recipes include sardines with tagliolini mint and pine nuts, or poached pike with a caper-based sauce; but there is also seafood, such as warm lobster salad with pineapple and curry, or meat, such as duck legs with caramelized oranges or rack of lamb and mushroom-stuffed quail. For the desserts there is strudel, warm poppy seed pies with date cream centres, and fruit tarts. Over 400 wines to select. *Booking advised. Closed lunchtime, Wed, Feb.*

Trattoria la Pace, Via Casella 1, **t** 045 740 0057 (*moderate*). By the Porto Vecchio; a popular place with outdoor tables for seafood by the lake.

Hippopotamus, Piazza Covour 19, **t** 0456 570 069. A small wine bar open until late where you can taste and buy a vast array of local wines. *Closed Wed.*

Kambusa Boat, Via Parrocchia (*inexpensive*). At the centre of the action, this rather touristy pirate-look restaurant-pub-pizzeria has live music to cater for all tastes. *Open until late.*

Torri del Benaco ✉ 37010

***Gardesana**, Piazza Calderini 20, **t** 045 722 5411, *www.hotel-gardesana.com* (*expensive*). A comfortable hotel right on the harbour with splendid views of the lake, old harbour and castle. All rooms have bathrooms, and

has good 14th-century Giottoesque frescoes. One of the many lovely walks in the region is up to the old village of **Albisano**, with beautiful views, then on to Crer and Brancolino, where the largest of Torri's prehistoric etchings can be seen, especially near Crer's church. The first recorded pleasure tourist in Torri was the great Medicean poet Poliziano in the 15th century; more recent fans have included André Gide and Stephen Spender.

breakfast and meals are served on the harbour patio when the weather is good. The hotel is housed in a 1442 building, the former seat of the Gardesana dell'Acqua Council. The owners have carefully refurbished it to provide all modern amenities and decorated it in old Venetian style. King Juan Carlos, Vivien Leigh and Laurence Olivier, Kim Novak, Maria Callas and French writer André Gide all sojourned there. The fame of the hotel is also due to its restaurant, the best on the Veronese shore according to many, which serves lake specialities revisited with a creative touch: the soup of Garda lake fish is worth the journey alone, but also the fillets of lake sardine marinated in cider, the trout carpaccio or the pike with polenta. *Min 3-days stay. Restaurant open eves only; closed Tues out of season. Hotel and restaurant closed end Nov–end Feb.*

★★★**Al Caval**, Via Gardesana 186, **t** 045 722 5666, *www.alcaval.com* (*moderate*). Near the lake, this plain and simple hotel has a park and windsurfer rentals. It has a very good restaurant (*moderate, but expensive à la carte*), but with a vegetarian menu and a *menu degustazione. Restaurant open Sat and Sun lunch time only; hotel and restaurant closed Jan–Feb. Closed Wed, Sat and Sun lunch time only, except in the summer.*

Garda ✉ 37016

★★★★**Locanda San Vigilio**, Punta San Vigilio, **t** 045 725 6688, *www.locanda-sanvigilio.it* (*luxury*). This little inn, hidden out by Sammichele's villa by a little private harbour, has seven romantic rooms and a beach. Delicious food. *Open Mar–Nov.*

★★★★**Hotel Regina Adelaide**, Via Francesco D'Assisi 23, **t** 045 725 5977, *www.regina-adelaide.it* (*very expensive–expensive*). In Garda's centre, with all modern amenities, carefully styled rooms and a fully equipped health and fitness centre: personal trainer; personalized health and fitness programmes and indoor and outdoor pools. The annexe has been restored with a nice old touch.

★★**Du Parc**, Via Marconi 3, **t** 045 725 5343 (*expensive*). A lakeside villa set in its own grounds, which has been entirely refurbished and upgraded. The rooms are basic for the price category.

★★★**Flora**, Via Giorgione 22 and 27, **t** 045 725 5348, *www.hotelflora.net* (*inexpensive*). An exceptionally well-priced hotel above the town in its own grounds, slick and modern with pine fittings, spacious rooms, all with balcony, and fantastic amenities – tennis, mini-golf and two pools. No restaurant. *Open Easter–Sept.*

★★★**Continental**, Via Giorgione 14, **t** 045 725 5100, *www.hotelcontinentalgarda.it* (*moderate*). Next door to the Flora, this hotel is in its own grounds, but not quite as modern or comfortable – and with only one swimming pool. *Open Easter–Oct.*

★★**Ancora**, Via Manzoni 7, **t** 045 725 5202, *www.allancora.com* (*moderate*). In the centre of the action, and a good-value lake-front option. Clean and comfortable rooms. *Closed end Oct–end Mar.*

★★**Hotel degli Olivi**, Via Olivai 2, **t** 045 7255 637 (*moderate*). Cosy place behind the city centre, although rooms are less pleasant than the ground floor public areas. *Closed mid-Mar–Oct.*

Stafolet, Via Poiano 9, on the landward side of Garda, **t** 045 725 5427 (*moderate*). This is worth asking directions to for its tagliolini with truffles and grilled meat and dish. Pizza also available. *Closed Mon, and Jan.*

Al Pontesel, Via Monte Baldo 71, **t** 045 725 5419 (*inexpensive*). Less distinguished, but good restaurant, featuring stout local cooking. There are also also four rooms with bathrooms. *Open all year.*

Laurence Olivier, for his part, preferred enchanting **Punta di San Vigilio** with its Sirens' rocks, occupied by the beautiful **Villa Guarienti** (*not open to the public*) by the great Venetian Renaissance architect Sammicheli, the old church of San Vigilio, and a 16th-century tavern, now an inn. In Punta San Vigilio, the Mermaid bay, a private beach accessible by walking through a large park shaded with olive trees, has play-grounds for children and two refreshment bars. On the other side of a green soufflé of a headland, the Rocca del Garda, lies **Garda** itself, a fine old town with Renaissance *palazzi* and villas. It gave the lake its modern name, from the Lombard *Warthe*, 'The Watch'. After Charlemagne defeated the Lombards, Garda became a county, and in its long-gone castle the wicked Count Berenguer secretly held Queen Adelaide of Italy prisoner in 960, after he murdered her husband Lotario and she refused to marry his son. After a year she was discovered by a monk, who spent another year plotting her escape. She then received the protection of Otto I of Germany, who defeated Berenguer, married the widowed queen, and became Holy Roman Emperor.

Bardolino

To the south, Bardolino is synonymous with its lively red wine with a bitter cherry fragrance that goes so well with fishy *antipasti*. You can learn all you want to know about it at the Cantine Zeni's **Museo del Vino** (*Via Costabella 9, t 045 721 0022, www.museodelvino.it; open mid-Mar–Oct daily 9–1 and 2–6*) or by following the wine route through the soft rolling hills, dotted with 19th-century villas. There are two important churches in Bardolino itself: the 8th-century **San Zeno** and the 12th-century **San Severo**, with frescoes and a landmark campanile. **Cisano**, south of Bardolino, has a museum dedicated to the Riviera degli Olivi's other cash crop, the **Museo dell'Olio d'Oliva** (*Via Peschiera 54, t 045 622 9047, www.museodellolio.com; open daily 9–12.30 and 3–7, closed Sun pm; Jan–Feb closed on Sun*).

The next town, **Lazise**, was the main Venetian port and near the harbour retains an ensemble of Venetian buildings, as well as another castle, this one built in the 9th century by the Magyars and taken over and rebuilt by the Scaligers. Just inland from Lazise, at Bussolengo, the **Parco Natura Viva** (*t 045 717 0052*) is a private foundation devoted to the protection of endangered species, and is divided into a zoo, with a tropical aviary and dinosaur models (*open year round 9–6*) and a drive-through safari park with animals from the African savannah (*open Mar–Oct daily 9–6; Nov closed on Wed, Feb Sat–Sun; adm*). Near here too is Gardaland – *see p.282*.

Glossary

atrium: entrance court of a Roman house or early church.

badia: *abbazia*, an abbey or abbey church.

baldacchino: baldachin, a columned stone canopy above the altar of a church.

basilica: a rectangular building, usually divided into three aisles by rows of columns. In Rome this was the common form for law courts and other public buildings, and Roman Christians adapted it for their early churches.

Calvary chapels: a series of outdoor chapels, usually on a hillside, that commemorate the stages of the Passion of Christ.

campanile: a bell tower.

campanilismo: local patriotism; the Italians' own word for their historic tendency to be more faithful to their home towns than to the abstract idea of 'Italy'.

camposanto: a cemetery.

cardo: transverse street of a Roman *castrum*-shaped city.

carroccio: a wagon carrying the banners of a medieval city and an altar; it served as the rallying point in battles.

cartoon: the preliminary sketch for a fresco or tapestry.

caryatid: supporting pillar or column carved into a standing female form; male versions are called telamones.

castrum: a Roman military camp, always neatly rectangular, with straight streets and gates at the cardinal points. Later the Romans founded or refounded cities in this form, hundreds of which survive today (Pavia, Como, Brescia are clear examples).

cavea: the semicircle of seats in a classical theatre.

Cenacolo: fresco of *The Last Supper*, often on the wall of a monastery refectory.

ciborium: a tabernacle; the word is often used for large free-standing tabernacles, or in the sense of a *baldacchino* (q.v.).

comune: commune, or commonwealth, referring to the governments of the free cities of the Middle Ages. Today it denotes any local government, from the Comune di Roma down to the smallest village.

condottiere: the leader of a band of mercenaries in late medieval and Renaissance times.

confraternity: a religious lay brotherhood, often serving as a neighbourhood mutual aid and burial society, or following some specific charitable work (Michelangelo, for example, belonged to one that cared for condemned prisoners in Rome).

cupola: a dome.

decumanus: street of a Roman *castrum*-shaped city parallel to the longer axis, the central, main avenue called the Decumanus Major.

duomo: cathedral.

forum: the central square of a Roman town, with its most important temples and public buildings. The word means 'outside', as the original Roman Forum was outside the first city walls.

fresco: wall painting, the most important Italian medium of art since Etruscan times. It isn't an easy method; first the artist draws the *sinopia* (q.v.) on the wall. This is covered with plaster, but only a little at a time, as the paint must be on the plaster before it dries. Leonardo da Vinci's endless attempts to find clever short cuts ensured that little of his work would survive.

Ghibellines: one of the two great medieval parties, the supporters of the Holy Roman Emperors.

gonfalon: the banner of a medieval free city; the *gonfaloniere*, or flag bearer, was often the most important public official.

Guelphs: (*see* Ghibellines). One of the two great political factions of medieval Italy; supporters of the Pope.

intarsia: work in inlaid wood or marble.

narthex: the enclosed porch of a church.

palazzo: not just a palace, but any large, important building (though the word comes from the imperial *palatium* on Rome's Palatine Hill).

Pantocrator: Christ 'ruler of all', a common subject for apse paintings and mosaics in areas influenced by Byzantine art.

pietra dura: rich inlay work using semi-precious stones, perfected in post-Renaissance Florence.

pieve: a parish church, especially in the north.

predella: smaller paintings on panels below the main subject of a painted altarpiece.

presepio: a Christmas crib.

putti: flocks of plaster cherubs with rosy cheeks and bums that infested much of Italy in the Baroque era.

quadriga: chariot pulled by four horses.

Quattrocento: the 1400s – the Italian way of referring to centuries (eg. *Duecento, Trecento, Quattrocento, Cinquecento*).

sinopia: the layout of a *fresco* (q.v.), etched by the artist on the wall before the plaster is applied. Often these are works of art in their own right.

stigmata: a miraculous simulation of the bleeding wounds of Christ, appearing in holy men like St Francis in the 12th century, and Padre Pio of Puglia in our own time.

telamon: *see* caryatid.

thermae: Roman baths.

tondo: round relief, painting or terracotta.

transenna: marble screen separating the altar area from the rest of an Early Christian church.

travertine: hard, light-coloured stone, sometimes flecked or pitted with black, sometimes perfect. The most widely used material in ancient and modern Rome.

triptych: a painting, especially an altarpiece, in three sections.

trompe l'œil: art that uses perspective effects to deceive the eye – for example, to create the illusion of depth on a flat surface, or to make columns and arches painted on a wall seem real.

tympanum: the semicircular space, often bearing a painting or relief, located above the portal of a church.

Language

The fathers of modern Italian were Dante, Manzoni, and television. Each did their part in creating a national language from an infinity of regional and local dialects; the Florentine Dante, the first 'immortal' to write in the vernacular, did much to put the Tuscan dialect in the foreground of Italian literature. Manzoni's revolutionary novel, *I Promessi Sposi* ('The Betrothed'), heightened national consciousness by using an everyday language all could understand in the 19th century. Television in the last few decades is performing an even more spectacular linguistic unification; although the majority of Italians still speak a dialect at home, school and at work, their TV idols still insist on proper Italian.

Perhaps because they are so busy learning their own beautiful but grammatically complex language, Italians are not especially adept at learning others. English lessons, however, have been the rage for years, and at most hotels and restaurants there will be someone who speaks some English. In small towns and out of the way places, finding an Anglophone may prove more difficult. The words and phrases below should help you out in most situations, but the ideal way to come to Italy is with some Italian under your belt; your visit will be richer, and you're much more likely to make some Italian friends.

Pronunciation

Italian words are pronounced phonetically. Every vowel and consonant (except 'h') is sounded. Consonants are the same as in English, except the 'c' which, when followed by an 'e' or 'i', is pronounced like the English 'ch' (*cinque* thus becomes 'cheenquay'). Italian 'g' is also soft before 'i' or 'e' as in *gira*, pronounced 'jee-ra'. 'H' is never sounded; 'z' is pronounced like 'ts'.

The consonants 'sc' before the vowels 'i' or 'e' become like the English 'sh' as in 'sci', pronounced 'shee'; 'ch' is pronouced like a 'k' as in Chianti, 'kee-an-tee'; 'gn' as 'ny' in English (*bagno*, pronounced 'ban-yo'); while 'gli' is pronounced like the middle of the word 'million' (Castiglione, for example, is pronounced 'Ca-steely-oh-nay').

Vowel pronunciation is: 'a' as in English 'father'; 'e' when unstressed is pronounced like 'a' in 'fate' as in *mele*, when stressed can be the same or like the 'e' in 'pet' (*bello*); 'i' is like the 'i' in 'machine'; 'o' like 'e', has two sounds, 'o' as in 'hope' when unstressed (*tacchino*), and usually 'o' as in 'rock' when stressed (*morte*); 'u' is pronounced like the 'u' in 'June'.

The accent usually (but not always) falls on the penultimate syllable. Also note that, in the big northern cities, the informal way of addressing someone as you, *tu*, is widely used; the more formal *lei* or *voi* is commonly used in provincial districts.

Useful Words and Phrases

yes/no/maybe *sì/no/forse*
I don't know *Non lo so*
I don't understand (Italian) *Non capisco (l'italiano)*
Does someone here speak English? *C'è qualcuno qui che parla inglese?*
Speak slowly *Parla lentamente*
Could you assist me? *Potrebbe aiutarmi?*
Help! *Aiuto!*
Please/Thank you (very much) *Per favore/(Molte) grazie*
You're welcome *Prego*
It doesn't matter *Non importa*
All right *Va bene*
Excuse me *Mi scusi*
Be careful! *Attenzione!*
Nothing *Niente*

It is urgent! *È urgente!*
How are you? *Come sta?*
Well, and you? *Bene, e Lei?*
What is your name? *Come si chiama?*
Hello *Salve or ciao (both informal)*
Good morning *Buongiorno (formal hello)*
Good afternoon, evening *Buonasera (also formal hello)*
Goodnight *Buonanotte*
Goodbye *Arrivederla (formal), arrivederci, ciao (informal)*
What do you call this in Italian? *Come si chiama questo in italiano?*
What?/Who?/Where? *Che?/Chi?/Dove?*
When?/Why? *Quando?/Perché?*
How? *Come?*
How much? *Quanto?*
I am lost *Mi sono smarrito*
I am hungry/thirsty/sleepy *Ho fame/sete/sonno*
I am sorry *Mi dispiace*
I am tired *Sono stanco*
I am ill *Mi sento male*
Leave me alone *Lasciami in pace*
good/bad *buono, bravo/male, cattivo*
hot/cold *caldo/freddo*
slow/fast *lento/rapido*
up/down *su/giù*
big/small *grande/piccolo*
here/there *qui/lì*

Travel Directions

One (two) ticket(s) to Naples, please *Un biglietto (due biglietti) per Napoli, per favore*
one way *semplice/andata*
return *andata e ritorno*
first/second class *Prima/seconda classe*
I want to go to... *Desidero andare a...*
How can I get to...? *Come posso andare a...?*
Do you stop at...? *Ferma a...?*
Where is...? *Dov'è...?*
How far is it to...? *Quanto siamo lontani da...?*
What is the name of this station? *Come si chiama questa stazione?*
When does the next ... leave? *Quando parte il prossimo...?*
From where does it leave? *Da dove parte?*
How long does the trip take...? *Quanto tempo dura il viaggio?*
How much is the fare? *Quant'è il biglietto?*
Have a good trip *Buon viaggio!*

Shopping, Services, Sightseeing

I would like... *Vorrei...*
Where is/are... *Dov'è/Dove sono...*
How much is it? *Quanto costa questo?*
open/closed *aperto/chiuso*
cheap/expensive *a buon prezzo/caro*
bank *banca*
beach *spiaggia*
bed *letto*
church *chiesa*
entrance/exit *entrata/uscita*
hospital *ospedale*
money *soldi*
newspaper (foreign) *giornale (straniero)*
pharmacy *farmacia*
police station *commissariato*
policeman *poliziotto*
post office *ufficio postale*
sea *mare*
shop *negozio*
room *camera*
tobacco shop *tabaccaio*
WC *toilette/bagno*
men *Signori/Uomini*
women *Signore/Donne*

Days

Monday *lunedì*
Tuesday *martedì*
Wednesday *mercoledì*
Thursday *giovedì*
Friday *venerdì*
Saturday *sabato*
Sunday *domenica*

Transport

airport *aeroporto*
bus stop *fermata*
bus/coach *autobus/pullman*
railway station *stazione ferroviaria*
train *treno*
platform *binario*
taxi *tassì*
ticket *biglietto*
customs *dogana*
seat (reserved) *posto (prenotato)*

Numbers

one *uno/una*
two/three/four *due/tre/quattro*
five/six/seven *cinque/sei/sette*
eight/nine/ten *otto/nove/dieci*
eleven/twelve *undici/dodici*
thirteen/fourteen *tredici/quattordici*
fifteen/sixteen *quindici/sedici*
seventeen/eighteen *diciassette/diciotto*
nineteen *diciannove*
twenty *venti*
twenty-one *ventuno*
thirty *trenta*
forty *quaranta*
fifty *cinquanta*
sixty *sessanta*
seventy *settanta*
eighty *ottanta*
ninety *novanta*
hundred *cento*
one hundred and one *centouno*
two hundred *duecento*
one thousand *mille*
two thousand *duemila*
million *milione*

Time

What time is it? *Che ore sono?*
day/week *giorno/settimana*
month *mese*
morning/afternoon *mattina/pomeriggio*
evening *sera*
yesterday *ieri*
today *oggi*
tomorrow *domani*
soon *fra poco*
later *dopo/più tardi*
It is too early *È troppo presto*
It is too late *È troppo tardi*

Driving

near/far *vicino/lontano*
left/right *sinistra/destra*
straight ahead *sempre diritto*
forward/backwards *avanti/indietro*
north/south *nord/sud*
east *est/oriente*
west *ovest/occidente*
round the corner *dietro l'angolo*

crossroads *bivio*
street/road *strada/via*
square *piazza*
car hire *noleggio macchina*
motorbike/scooter *motocicletta/Vespa*
bicycle *bicicletta*
petrol/diesel *benzina/gasolio*
garage *garage*
This doesn't work *Questo non funziona*
mechanic *meccanico*
map/town plan *carta/pianta*
Where is the road to...? *Dov'è la strada per...?*
breakdown *guasto/panne*
driving licence *patente di guida*
driver *guidatore*
speed *velocità*
danger *pericolo*
parking *parcheggio*
no parking *sosta vietata*
narrow *stretto*
bridge *ponte*
toll *pedaggio*
slow down *rallentare*

Useful Hotel Vocabulary

I'd like a double room please *Vorrei una camera doppia, per favore*
I'd like a single room please *Vorrei una camera singola, per favore*
with bath, without bath *con bagno, senza bagno*
for two nights *per due notti*
May I see the room, please? *Posso vedere la camera?*
Is there a room with a balcony? *C'è una camera con balcone?*
There isn't (aren't) any hot water, soap, *Manca/Mancano acqua calda, sapone,* light, toilet paper, towels *luce, carta igienica, asciugamani*
May I pay by credit card? *Posso pagare con carta di credito?*
May I see another room please? *Per favore potrei vedere un'altra camera?*
Fine, I'll take it *Bene, la prendo*
Is breakfast included? *E' compresa la prima colazione?*
What time do you serve breakfast? *A che ora è la colazione?*
How do I get to the town centre? *Come posso raggiungere il centro città?*

Chronology

80,000 BC Give or take a couple of 10,000 years: Palaeolithic settlements along the Riviera

8000 BC First rock incisions in the Val Camonica

236–22 BC Romans conquer Po Valley from Gauls

222 BC Celtic Mediolanum (Milan) comes under Roman rule; Roman colony of Ticinum (Pavia) founded

219 BC Hannibal and his elephants cross the Alps

87 BC Catullus born at Sirmione

70 BC Virgil born at Mantua

AD 23–79 Pliny the Elder, of Como

62–120 Pliny the Younger, of Como

284–305 Diocletian divides Roman Empire in two; Milan becomes most important city in West, pop. 100,000

313 Edict of Milan: Constantine makes Christianity religion of the empire

374–97 St Ambrose, bishop of Milan

387 St Ambrose converts and baptises St Augustine in Milan

539 Goths slaughter most of male Milanese

567 Lombards overrun most of Italy, and make Pavia their capital

590s Pope Gregory the Great converts Queen Theodolinda and the Lombards to orthodox Christianity

c. 730 Desiderius, King of the Lombards, born near Brescia

778 Charlemagne defeats Desiderius, repudiates wife, Desiderius' daughter; crowned King of Italy at Pavia

888 Berengar crowned King of Italy at Pavia

1109–55 Arnold of Brescia, monk and preacher against worldly Church, only to be hanged by Pope

1127 Como destroyed by Milanese, rebuilt by Barbarossa

1154 Milan sacked by Barbarossa

1155 Barbarossa crowned king of Italy at Pavia

1156 Barbarossa does it again

1158 Milan obliterates rival Lodi; Lodi rebuilt by Barbarossa

1176 Lombard League defeats Barbarossa at Legnano

1183 Treaty of Constance recognizes independence of Lombard cities

1252 Inquisitor St Peter Martyr axed in the head by Lake Como

1277 The Visconti overthrow the Torriani to become signori of Milan

1334 Azzone Visconti captures Cremona

1335 Como becomes fief of Milan

1348–9 The Black Death wipes out a third of the Italians

1386 Gian Galeazzo Visconti begins Milan cathedral

1396 Gian Galeazzo Visconti founds the Certosa of Pavia

1402 Gian Galeazzo Visconti, conqueror of northern Italy, plans to capture Florence but dies of plague

1421–35 Genoa under Filippo Maria Visconti; the Genoese fleet crushes Aragon

1428–1797 Bergamo and Brescia ruled by Venice

1441 Bianca Visconti weds Francesco Sforza, with Cremona as her dowry

1447–50 Ambrosian republic – Milan's attempt at democracy

1450 Francesco Sforza made Duke of Milan

1494 Wars of Italy begin with French invasion of Charles VIII

1495 Battle of Fornovo; Leonardo begins his *Last Supper*

1500 Duke of Milan, Lodovico il Moro, captured by French at Novara

1509 Defeat of Venice at Agnadello by Louis XII of France, Pope Julius II, Emperor Maximilian and the League of Cambrai; Venice loses new acquisition of Cremona, but soon regains Brescia and Bergamo and other terra firma real estate

1525 Battle of Pavia; Spaniards capture French King Francis I

1527–93 Giuseppe Arcimboldo, first surrealist, of Milan

1533 Federico Gonzaga of Mantua picks up Monferrato by marriage

1538–84 St Charles Borromeo, Archbishop of Milan

1559 Château-Cambrésis Treaty confirms Spanish control of Italy and returns Turin to the House of Savoy

1567–1643 Claudio Monteverdi, opera composer, of Cremona

1573–1610 Michelangelo da Caravaggio

1596–1684 Nicolò Amati, violin maker, of Cremona

1620 Spanish governor of Milan orders 'Day of Holy Butchery' in the Valtellina; Catholics massacre Protestants, initiating 20 years of war

1630 Plague in Milan (described by Manzoni in *I Promessi Sposi*)

1644–1737 Stradivarius, violin-maker, of Cremona

1665 Carlo Emanuele II and Louis XIV persecute Waldensians in Piedmont; Cromwell and Milton protest

1683–1745 Giuseppe Guarneri, violin-maker, of Cremona

1700–13 War of the Spanish Succession

1713 Austrians pick up Milan

1745 Alessandro Volta, the physicist, born in Como

1778 La Scala inaugurated

1785 Alessandro Manzoni, author of *I Promessi Sposi*, born in Lecco

1790 Wordsworth lives by Lake Como

1796 Napoleon first enters Italy, defeats Austrians at Lodi, makes Milan capital of his Cisalpine Republic

1798–1848 Gaetano Donizetti, of Bergamo

1800 Napoleon defeats the Austrians at Marengo

1805 Napoleon crowns himself with Iron Crown of Italy in Milan Cathedral

1813 Rossini composes *Tancredi* on shores of Lake Como

1814 Overthrow of French rule

1816–17 Queen Caroline of England at Lake Como

1831 Mazzini founds Giovane Italia; Bellini composes *Norma* on the shores of Lake Como

1848 Revolutions across Italy; Austrians defeat Piedmont at war

1849 Restoration of autocratic rule

1852 Cavour becomes Prime Minister of Piedmont

1853 Verdi composes *La Traviata* in a villa on Lake Como

1854 Piedmont enters Crimean War

1859–60 Piedmont, with the help of Napoleon III, annexes Lombardy at battle of Solferino; in return gives France Nice and Savoy; while Garibaldi's 'Thousand' conquer Sicily and Naples

1860–65 Turin is capital of Italy; in 1865 moved to Florence

1870 Italian troops enter Rome; unification completed and Rome becomes capital

1871 Mont Cenis (Frejus) railway tunnel, first great transalpine tunnel, opened between France and Italy

1879 Queen Victoria takes a holiday by Lake Maggiore

1881 Angelo Roncalli (Pope John XXIII) born at Sotto il Monte, near Bergamo

1900 King Umberto I assassinated by anarchist

1901 Verdi dies in his hotel room in Milan

1902–7 Period of industrial strikes

1905 Simplon Tunnel, the longest rail tunnel in the world, completed

1910 Peruvian Georges Chavez makes the first flight over the Alps, and is killed in a crash near Domodossola

1915 Italy enters First World War

1925 Mussolini makes Italy a fascist dictatorship

1925–7 D. H. Lawrence at Lake Como

1938 Gabriele D'Annunzio dies at Il Vittoriale, by Lake Garda

1940 Italy enters Second World War

1943 Mussolini deposed; rescued by Germans to found puppet government of Salò; Milan burns for days in air raids

1944 Vittorio Emanuele III abdicates

1945 Mussolini tries to flee to Switzerland but is executed near Como with mistress Clara Petacci.

1946 National referendum makes Italy a republic; King Umberto II exiled in Portugal; new Italian constitution grants the Alto Adige a special autonomy

1949 The church excommunicates communists; strikes by farmers in the Paduan Valley are bloodily repressed.

1956 Italy becomes a charter member in the Common Market

1965 Completion of Mont Blanc motorway tunnel

1970 Divorce is introduced in Italy and confirmed by national referendum (1974)

1978 Prime Minister Aldo Moro is kidnapped and killed by communist terrorist group Brigate Rosse. Abortion becomes legal. Karol Wojtila, first non-Italian Pope since 1523, is elected as Pope Giovanni Paolo II

1980 Completion of Mont Cenis (Frejus) motorway tunnel

1983 Major landslides wreak havoc in the Valtellina

1988 More landslides and floods in the Valtellina

1990 Emergence of Umberto Bossi's Lombard League

1992 The arrest of Mario Chiesa starts the Bribe City investigation: Socialist Bettino Craxi investigated, entrepreneurs Gardini (Montedison) and Cagliari (ENI), involved in the scandal, commit suicide. The church rehabilitates Galileo Galilei

1994 The Christian Democrat party dissolves. In one year media magnate Silvio Berlusconi creates a new party, Forza Italia, wins the elections, becomes Prime Minister and sees his government fall

1996 After a 'technical' interim, Italy's first ever government guided by the (former) Communist party, Democratici della Sinistra (DS), gains power headed by Romano Prodi

2000 Italy is flooded with pilgrims for the Catholic Jubilee year. Bettino Craxi dies in exile in Tunisia. Floods in the Bassa Padana and Lake Maggiore area

2001 Silvio Berlusconi, leader of Forza Italia party, becomes Italian Prime Minister once again, in a coalition with right wing parties Lega Nord and Alianza Nazionale

2002 Controversy deepens over Berlusconi's business dealings as he faces trial on charges of corruption

2003 Berlusconi appears in court on corruption charges. Multi-billion euro fraud uncovered at the food-manufacturing giant Parmalat.

2004 Berlusconi is cleared of corruption.

2005 Regional administrative elections result in major defeat for right-wing coalition parties supporting Berlusconi. Pope John Paul II dies (April 2). Joseph Alois Ratzinger is elected as Pope Benedict XVI (April 19).

Index

Main page references are in **bold**. Page references to maps are in *italics*.

Lombardy &
the Italian Lakes
touring atlas

Rovigo

Adige

TRENTINO ALTO

Stelvio

National

Park

Verona

Mantua

④

Riva del Garda

Malcésine

Lake Garda

Garda

Bórmio

Ponte di Legno

Edolo

Parco Nazionale Incisioni Rupestri

Paspardo

Gardone Riviera

Sirmione

Desenzano del Garda

Lake Idro

Saló

Brescia

Sabbionéta

Po

Mincio

Valtellina

Boário Terme

EMILIA ROMAGNA

Clusone

Lóvere

Lake Iséo

Iséo

Chiari

Cremona

Sóncino

Sondrio

Alpi Orobie

S. Pellegrino Terme

Bergamo

LOMBARDY

Crema

Piacenza

Morbegno

Val Brembana

Lodi

Madésimo

Chiavenna

Mandello del Lário

Lecco

③

L. Mezzola

Gravedona

Bellágio

Menággio

Tremezzo

Lake Como

Como

Sarónno

Monza

Milan

Pavia

SWITZERLAND

Locarno

Lugano

Varese

Chiasso

Legnano

Novari

Abbiategrasso

Vigévano

Alessándria

Luino

Gavirate

Cánnobio

S. Maria Maggiore

Lake Maggiore

Verbánia

Strésa

Aróna

Malpensa International Busto Airport Arsizio

Novari

Vercelli

Asti

Omegna

Lake Orta

② 20 km / 10 miles

N

Domodóssola

Macugnaga

Biella

PIEMONTE

Val d'Ossola

10 km
5 miles
SWITZERLAND
N
Formazza
Val Antigorio
Simplon Pass
Premia
Baceno
Crodo
Val d'Ossola
Parco Nazionale
della Val Grande
Val Divedro
Val Vigezzo
Ascona
Ronco
Brissago
Marone
Druogno
Craveggia
S. Maria Maggiore
Malesco
Domodossola
Finero
Beura
Gurro
Falmenta
Pino
Cannobio
Cardezza
Val Cannobina
Maccagno
Val d'Antrona
Vogogna
Cannero Riviera
Toce
A26
Intragna
Aurano
Luino
Germignaga
Macugnaga
Campello Monti
Valle Anzasca
Candoglia
Miazzina
Premeno
L. Miazzina
S233
Lake Maggiore
Mt Orfano
Forno
Mergozzo
Intra
Grantola
Feriolo
S. Antonio
Gravellona Toce
Verbania
Valstrona
Baveno
Borromean Is.
Laveno-Mombello
Omegna
Mt Mottarone
Stresa
Santa Caterina
Mt Campo dei Fiori
Vezzo
Belgirate
A8
Lake Orta
Gavirate
Isola S. Giulio
Pettenasco
Lesa
Biandronno
Pella
Orta San Giulio
Ranco
Calcinate
Meina
S394
Ameno
L. Varese
Lagna
Angera
Comabbio
Pogno
Gozzano
Arona
Oleggio
L. Comabbio
Sesto Calende
Vergiate
Golasecca
Borgo Ticino
Somma Lombardo
Arsago

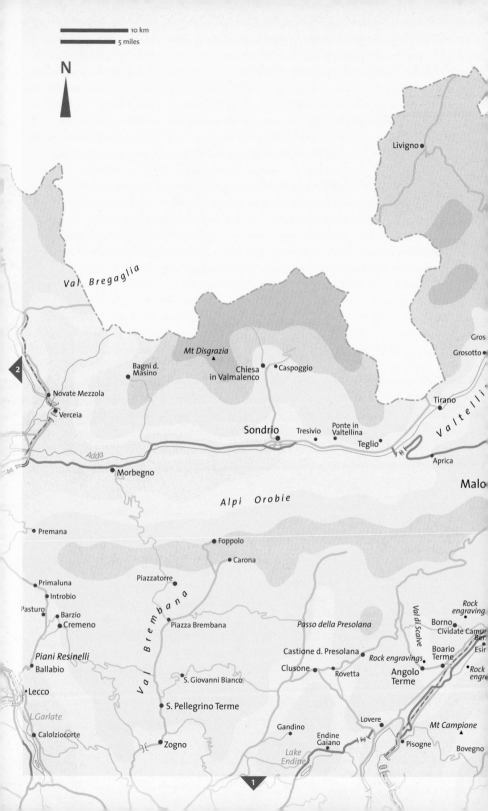

TRENTINO- ALTO

ADIGE

Stelvio

National

Park

Bormio

S.Caterina
Valfurva

V a l   d i   S o l e

Sóndalo

io

na

Ponte di Legno

*Passo del
Tonale*

Edolo

Adamello Mts

nna

Cedegolo

*Rock
engravings*

*Parco Nazionale
Incisioni Rupestri*

Paspardo

Sarche

Capo di Ponte
Rock engravings
Cerveno

Breguzzo

Ceto

V a l l e   C a m o n i c a

Niardo

Drena

Dro

s

Breno

Daone

V a l l i   G i u d i c a r i e

Varone

Arco

zo

Bienno

ne

Bezzecca

*Lake
Ledro*

Riva del Garda

ravings

Condino

Molina
di Ledro

*Passo de
Maniva*

Val di Ledro

Torbole

Bagolino

Lodrone

Collio

Limone sul Garda

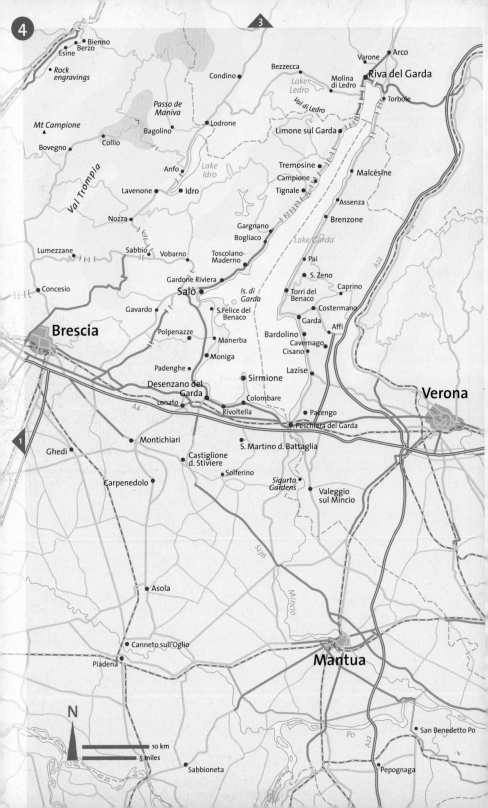